# THE
# ETHICS
# OF
# FREEDOM

by Jacques Ellul

translated and edited
by Geoffrey W. Bromiley

William B. Eerdmans Publishing Company

*Copyright © 1976 by Wm. B. Eerdmans Publishing Company*
*255 Jefferson Ave. S.E., Grand Rapids, Michigan 49502*
*All rights reserved*
*Printed in the United States of America*

**Library of Congress Cataloging in Publication Data**
Ellul, Jacques.
  The ethics of freedom.
  Translation of Éthique de la liberté.
  Includes bibliographical references.
  1. Liberty.  2. Free will and determinism.
3. Freedom (Theology)  I. Title.
BJ1462.E4413  241  75-31592
ISBN 0-8028-3472-8

Translated from the French *Éthique de la Liberté*, Labor et Fides, Geneva.

# Editor's Preface

This translation of Ellul's *Ethics of Freedom* has a complicated background which the reader might find helpful to understand.

Ellul's volume forms part of a comprehensive ethics which he planned in four volumes: *Introduction, Ethics of Freedom, Ethics of Holiness,* and *Ethics of Relationship.* He published the first part of the *Introduction* many years ago, but due to various interruptions could never complete the second part and decided instead to move on to material questions in *The Ethics of Freedom.* The scattered references to an earlier work or to the first part of the *Introduction* in the present text are to the uncompleted ethical prolegomena.

In order to expedite matters the present translation was made from the typescript of the French with some manuscript additions and corrections. Before it could be published, however, Ellul brought out the first half of it in French as Book I (Parts I-III of the English version) under the title "The Flame of Freedom." Changes made in the printed text have been incorporated in the translation, but Ellul's Book II (Part IV) makes its debut in the English, and readers should be prepared for some slight differences when the French finally appears. (Experts in literary analysis might exercise their skills by disentangling Ellul 1, Ellul 2, Ellul 3, Translator, and Publisher's Editor, with possibilities of cross-checking that the books of Scripture no longer afford.)

A further point to notice is that Ellul writes an idiomatic French and at many points has specific situations in mind which are peculiar to his own land. This means that a certain freedom in translation is essential both to avoid bondage to alien turns of expression and to eliminate references which only elaborate footnotes could elucidate. Yet accuracy in presenting Ellul's thought has been consistently sought and it is hoped that a readable and reliable version is the result.

It might be added that if Ellul's work is to achieve its proper effect it should not be read as a definitive statement which one can appropriate only if assent is given but rather as a spur or stimulus which provokes new and exciting effort. Ellul may often be wrong but he is never platitudinous or dull. Much can obviously be gained from his acute and informed expositions. Even more can be gained, however, from critical interaction with his original and brilliant discussions.

*Pasadena, Michaelmas, 1975*                                     G. W. Bromiley

# Author's Preface

This volume, written over a period of years, is premature inasmuch as the second part of the *Introduction to Ethics* has not yet been published. The first part contained a discussion of the problem of the good and of the relation between the Christian faith, Christian ethics, and other moral systems. The aim in the second part was to sketch the conditions which a Christian ethics should fulfil and to outline the problem of social ethics. A good deal of material has been put together on this, but it now seems that priority should be given to the publication of the first main volume.

I had announced that I would not follow the common plan of dealing with general ethics first and only then with special ethics. In view of the unity of life which is constituted by the relationship with Jesus Christ and the conduct which ought to result from this, it seems to me to be theologically and rationally untenable to regard ethics as a series of concrete questions posed by institutions like marriage and the state, by civilization, by nature, or by whatever else demands a response. To the contrary, ethics ought to flow out of the relationship with Christ.

Some mediation, however, is needed, and I think I have found it, as I shall try to show in the Introduction, in the theological virtues which are presented by Paul. To each of these a sector of Christian life seems to correspond, and every question needs to be seen from the standpoint of these three virtues. But each expresses a specific type of behavior. Thus it seems to me that hope corresponds to an ethics of freedom, faith to an ethics of holiness, and love to an ethics of relationship. I resolved in 1960 to write the ethics of freedom, even though hope does not come first, because I was becoming increasingly convinced that freedom is the location and condition and arena of all Christian ethics and that holiness and relationship are possible only on the basis and in terms of the functioning of freedom. The two other parts of ethics would then be closely linked to one another. Thus holiness as separation, service, and witness for God, or as the conflict of faith, expresses the distinctiveness of incarnate Christianity, but separation has a place only for the sake of mission. The break has to come first, but it implies rediscovery of the world, society, and one's neighbor in a new type of relationship. Holiness in isolation is inadequate. It demands relationship. This, then, is the plan of the present ethics which I shall have to justify at greater length in the Introduction.

Obviously the way in which I am tackling the problems is not the traditional one. On the other hand, my way of expounding scripture will be traditional for the most part. I am well enough aware of the extensive work being done in theology, exegesis, and hermeneutics at the present time. But after listening seriously to the questions posed and examining carefully some of the investigations, I am convinced that there is no real future for them. Most of the problems raised give an appearance of exacting and rigorous enquiry but in reality they are false questions. The methods used simply produce juggling with words. There is more faddism than serious research, possibly because there is a sense that something different has to be done in the post-Barthian era. Hence, without disparaging them, I shall take these orientations into account only in a way which is incidental and supplementary. From some angles, therefore, the present ethics (or essay) might well seem to be in the classical tradition. It has to some extent been inspired by the theology of Karl Barth. I do not deny this, although I have never been an unconditional "Barthian." My point is that most of the questions put by the new theology are implied, outlined, and even at times fully discussed in the *Church Dogmatics,* which modern theologians and hermeneutical experts, especially those in the Bultmannian tradition, seem to ignore in a way that is very odd. As to my own ideological and philosophical presuppositions, I have tried incessantly for the last thirty years to clarify and criticize them in the light of revelation rather than using them to offer my own version of revelation. This is the orientation of the present study.

Jacques Ellul

# Contents

# Introduction

## I

We are plunged at once into the contradiction which ethics as such involves for Christians. What we have gained in Christ is freedom. But if so, how can one speak of ethics? Free man is free. What need is there of more than this? Why does one have to propose to him rules of conduct or values by which to live? Will not these be a threat to his liberty? The linguistic contradiction here is obvious. It is the inexplicable and insoluble paradox of the Christian life. It is the tension between the Already and the Not Yet, between the new life which has already been given and the resurrection which we await with sure and certain hope, between salvation by grace and working out our salvation with fear and trembling. We can, of course, explain and coordinate and systematize. But this is lost labor. For the contradictions are in our logic and not in our life when we have begun to live out things on the basis of grace. Explanation stifles life. This is true here. Free man is free. Discussion of freedom can only attenuate freedom. Free man is free because he has been freed by God. In virtue of this fact he stands under the authority of God. Theological discussion is an interloper when it tries to play the part of a mediator in this direct relation. Free man is summoned to act as free man. He has thus to choose himself. Ethical discussion severs his freedom either from itself or from its responsibility. I am aware of this even as I write. Yet I have so frequently and over so long a period noted a lack of freedom even in very serious Christians that I feel I must try to remind us of what we are.

Is it necessary to begin, however, with a philosophical concept of freedom? It is our view that this will emerge as the work proceeds. Yet one may accept the classical distinction[1] between freedom defined as freedom of choice, which rests on a static conception, on the existence of a clearly established nature, or good and evil, in which freedom is to choose (the good), and freedom viewed as the coming of something new into the world with a creative adherence to an inexhaustible good. Incidentally, it is doing Descartes too much honor to see in him the originator of this new

---

1 Cf. P. Remy, "Théologie de la liberté, son Evolution," in Mazerat, *La liberté évangélique.*

understanding, since one may see it plainly in the Old Testament and it is the heart and center of ancient Jewish thought.[2]

Is there any point either in remembering to what degree the church has been an opponent of freedom?[3] That it should be this might seem incredible and yet there is nothing more alien to theology and ecclesiastical organization than freedom, whether it be that which is acquired in Christ, or that which Christians bear on behalf of all, or that which Christians should ask for others. In fact, whenever the church has been in a position of power, it has regarded freedom as an enemy. This raises incidentally one of the themes which will crop up again and again, namely, the incompatibility between freedom and power.

## II

Freedom is the ethical aspect of hope.[4] An ethics of freedom can be founded only on hope and can only try to express hope. Now it is easy enough to write or to find an ethics of love, but an ethics of hope is rare. Usually we find only vague statements about the need not to despair, about the trust we should put in providence, and good advice about not committing suicide. The gap which is to be seen here is due to common forgetfulness of the link between hope and freedom, obliteration of the fact that freedom expresses hope, and a failure to note that the man who hopes is acting as a free man. It must be remembered, of course, that hope is more than a vague hope that things will be better tomorrow, or a stupid obstinacy that it will work out successfully next time, or confidence in

---

2 In this study I have not made much use of the fine book by A. Manaranche, *Un chemin de liberté* (1971), since it seems to be rather too lofty for me. This is a remarkable book of an almost mystical spirituality. The way of freedom proposed is an imitation of Jesus Christ for the modern age. If there is too little analysis of specific problems, I am in basic sympathy with many of the points made: the dialectic in man between fear and yearning for God, the affirmation of the uniqueness of Christianity, the link between prayer and freedom, liberty as a break with the world, the critical transition, freedom received by the loss of self, and modeling on the relation to the cross (the cross as more than a test or setback), contemplation of the cross, and the freedom of the companion of the Crucified. Yet there are points of disagreement too. I cannot believe that man's desire will always lead in some way to the critical point which is Jesus Christ. Nor can I accept the commonplaces of natural theology that a point of contact is needed if the appeal of Christ is to be heard or that this appeal will be missed unless there is already present a certain grandeur of soul. Apart from this, however, the book is an excellent meditative introduction to enquiry into an ethics of freedom.

3 Cf. the historical and critical survey of R. Coste, *Théologie de la liberté religieuse* (1970).

4 This passage, which was written in 1960, is in a moving way very close to Moltmann's *Theology of Hope* (1967) and to the articles of Ricoeur which followed in *Herméneutique de la liberté* (1968) and *La Liberté selon l'espérance dans le conflit des interprétations* (1969). I do not want to modify what I wrote, but Ricoeur's philosophical interpretation, which he calls a philosophical approximation of freedom according to hope, certainly goes beyond this study in a way that I could never have done.

human nature that it will survive the next test too after getting through so many, or the assurance which is based on a philosophy of history. Hope is none of these things. It does not rest on man or on objective mechanisms. It is a response of man to God's work for him. Only at this level and to this extent is it expressed by freedom.

Again, however, freedom does not spring out of hope *ipso facto* or by a kind of necessity. The Christian does not become a free man because he becomes a man who hopes. God produces in us both the willing and the doing. Freedom is created by God for man and in man. If hope is the response of man to God's love and grace, freedom is the response of God to man's hope, giving man the possibility of living out hope concretely and effectively in daily life after a fashion which is not just hypothetical or sentimental. There is thus a strict reciprocity between hope and freedom. God loves, man hopes, and God makes free. Or, to put it in another way, God is the liberator and on this ground man is authorized to hope and to live out hope. Because he has experienced the act of liberation this man knows that hope is not vain. Only the free man can hope, since the breaking of his bondage guarantees all the rest. While man is still a slave, there is no real hope for him. An external force has to intervene, and there is nothing to suggest that it will. Reciprocally, however, hope is the virtue from which freedom can draw meaning and which it is charged to express. If there were no hope in the heart there could be no freedom.

One may thus see the difference between the freedom which is in Christ and the movement of a freedom which derives from a mere (if necessary) act of awareness and which taken alone can only be a despairing freedom. Because this freedom is given by God, it is not tied to the past nor linked to objective conditions, not even to those which are imposed by God. For God gives real freedom, and this is why he permits us to hope in more than figures, signs, or symbols.

Our first glimpse of the link between hope and freedom is in the struggle between man and God, i.e., the wrestling of Jacob, Job, or Abraham. If man lays hold of God to get something from him, it is because he has been freed even to this point by God, who allows himself to be seized and challenged and fought. At the same time the struggle makes sense only if a great hope has been so strongly planted in the heart of man that he may believe that in this unequal contest he can overcome God, make him yield, and bring him over to his own view. A very strong hope is needed for the audacity to push freedom to this extreme which is far more extreme than that of Nietzsche.

We shall have to show that one axis of freedom is God's glory. The force which drives us on is hope of God's glory. Christ dwelling in us is this hope of glory in us. This leads us on to freedom. "We rejoice in hope of the glory of God" (Romans 5:2). There is no question here of glorification in the ordinary or human sense. We are to affirm in our freedom the truth of the glory of God which will be fully manifested. Our freedom makes sense only as it feeds on this hope. And to the degree that Paul speaks of Christ in us as the hope of glory, he is recalling that we are free. This is how Christ can be revealed in us. When the liberator acts to set us free, we know that he is Christ in us, and he also introduces us at the same time into the kingdom of hope, of that hope which is not uncertain or without object, of the hope which can be only that of glory. It is because we have the solid hope of glory that our freedom can be oriented functionally thereto.

This glory, however, is manifested only in the resurrection. It is a fact that our hope rests on the victory of Jesus Christ. In the measure that he conquered death it is hope for us (Romans 5:4). This victory enables us to put our hope in the living God (1 Timothy 4:10). If this hope is more than a passing emotion or an invention of man, it is because in God hope relates to a life which can never pass away, to a life which has triumphed in Christ (1 Peter 1:21). This hope is connected with freedom, however, because it shows that the victory of Jesus Christ does not just place us in a situation of what has already been done. This victory makes freedom possible. Three things call for consideration.

First, destiny has been lifted by the act of Jesus Christ. There is no more ineluctable necessity. What science calls determination still holds good. But it is not fate. It is a concatenation of conditions. We have determinations and no more. By destroying the power of the powers, Jesus Christ restores the world to the status of things, as by God's creation. By vanquishing death, Jesus removes the most decisive form of fate. From now on, freedom can inscribe itself on acts which express the presence of Jesus Christ. When we refer to ineluctable necessity or destiny, we have in view situations without a future. In the working out of an algebraic equation there is neither history nor future. But when fate is set aside, even though pure freedom is not yet achieved, there is some play in destiny. The situation becomes more fluid. It acquires the possibility of a future. In this situation man has some room for maneuver and can thus construct a history. Hence he can have a hope. Hope relates to what is not yet closed. In Jesus Christ, then, unity is revealed at the level of hope and freedom.

Secondly, even if the God of the Old Testament really is the God of omniscience, omnipotence, etc. that some theologians describe,[5] Jesus Christ as Lord makes it clear that what is established is not divine authoritarianism but freedom. In Jesus Christ, who is fully obedient and also fully free, the will of God is freedom. The Father grants perfect freedom to the Son. And since there is no other God than God in Jesus Christ, since lordship is granted by the Father to the Son, what controls the world is not the oppressive will of a dictator God who directs all things, but the total freedom of the one who says: "My yoke is easy, and my burden is light" (Matthew 11:30). God's will still exists for us, but it is a will not to coerce or determine. Now in Jesus this freedom is for us. This makes sense,

---

5  In our view this presentation is incorrect; cf. J. Ellul, *Politique de Dieu, politiques de l'homme,* ET *The Politics of God and the Politics of Man* (Eerdmans, 1972).

however, only if we hope in him, only if God is the hope of man (Jeremiah 14:8), only if our hope is in the Lord, i.e., if we hope that he will give us the future which is now possible (Psalm 27:14; Isaish 8:17). Through the freedom of Jesus our hope is born and our freedom is assured.

Thirdly, we must not bring back authoritarianism by ascribing to the victory of Jesus Christ the value of an *opus operatum.* An ontological restoration of the world is not brought about by the incarnation and crucifixion of Christ and the redemption thereby effected. A rebellious world does not become objectively obedient in this way. The beauty of a shattered world is not objectively restored. An evil world does not become objectively good. An enslaved world does not become free. There is no objective restitution in the sense that everything that man now does is acceptable to God. The demons and sin are not objectively eliminated.

Such a theology of glory would be a negation of freedom. What would be the point of doing our own work if everything were already done? The Jews are right: If this is what is expected of the Messiah, then Jesus was not the Messiah. We are not dealing, however, with an *opus operatum* because, in saving men, Jesus sought to introduce them to the kingdom of freedom, i.e., to enable them to participate authentically in the will of his Father, to set them in a situation in which they could exercise true freedom, which presupposes that his work is not yet over. All that he has done is adequate and complete. Everything is finished. Yet the work is not over. A perfect building has not been erected whose doors are closed. The kingdom of heaven is now committed to our freedom. From now on it is this freedom that comes into play. The miracle is not that of control from above. It is the miracle which is mediated by our free hands. We have to remember that if our freedom ceases to operate, if we stop acting and living (we Christians and only Christians) as free men, then necessity and fate will take over again, the world will again become the place of revolt and evil and sin, and there will be nothing else. The power will come back into play. The victory of Jesus Christ is not just a past achievement. It is a victory for our freedom. Hence my lack of freedom renders this victory inoperative today (although it does not negate it). The action of Christ takes effect in daily life through the mediation of our freedom.

This means that we can sterilize it. We can prevent Christ's victory from manifesting itself as such. Does this suppress his lordship? Not at all, but it prevents its being lived out by men. Does it negate the victory won? No, it has still been won, but it is not being exploited or utilized, so that it is as though it did not exist. Because it does exist, there is always a new possibility of freedom. But when we are freed in Christ, we can always restore force and power to the powers and dominions that have been defeated. This is why hope exists. We are saved in hope. We are really saved. Salvation is a reality. But the fact that we are saved in hope means that our freedom has to live out this salvation. If we go back in our life we can sterilize this life. It is in hope that we have passed from death to life. It is in hope that the world is transformed. If we simply say that everything *is* changed because Jesus Christ is Lord of the world, we wipe out at a stroke both freedom and hope.

Let us not say that if the world were not changed Jesus would not be the Messiah. It is changed in the sense that what was destined to destruction is now bound for the heavenly Jerusalem by way of destruction. What was enslaved to fate is now invested with hope. What could not be a history but only a succession of events can now be a history by hope in the play of freedom. What could not be a work but only an accumulation of inventions, philosophies, and so forth can now be a work by the hope of our freedom. It has often been said that Christian action ought to consist in the setting up of signs of the kingdom of God in the world, and this is quite true. But it does not go far enough. The exercise of the freedom which we are given should involve more than putting up signs. It should involve the actualization by the world of the hope which is given. For this hope is not just the hope of our personal salvation and resurrection, although this is vital and is not to be minimized. It is the hope implanted in the world that the world can have a true history, that it can have the possibility of a future instead of a mathematical or dialectical nexus of effects. It is the hope that the world will lead to the heavenly Jerusalem. Now I do not say that this hope will actualize itself, since it can be actualized only by the gracious decision of God. But it can actually be present only in the acts of the freedom which is given to Christians and not strictly to anybody else. We can open or shut the hope of a history for the world. This is the force of freedom.

Now hope is not just an emotion. It is not an evanescent impression. It is not the vague hope of a better future. It is linked to freedom. It finds expression in freedom lived out here and now. Hence it is a present reality. It is actual and active. Hope is entry into the kingdom of heaven which is already here and which manifests itself through our freedom. It is actual participation in anticipated life and glory. We are already heirs. The mode of our participation in the inheritance is hope (Titus 3:7). The meaning of this in the Bible is very different, of course, from what is meant when we talk in human style of our "expectations" with regard to an inheritance. Things are the direct opposite here. A human heir cannot say that the inheritance is actually his until the one from whom he inherits dies. Jesus Christ, in contrast, has already given it all to us. The way in which we live out the inheritance, however, is hope. Hope is a way of living and not a dream of paradise. The existence of hope in us is a reality which modifies already our conduct and company. Why should love be the only thing to change our relations with others? Hope, too, is a transformation of being with and with reference to others. Actual man needs a share of hope as well as love. He needs to live with men who live in hope. For this hope changes us. It is a link with the last things. The last things move towards us (the kingdom of God has drawn near). They thus have a true and significant effect on us now. To live in hope is to give to life an eschatological dimension. It is to make each of our acts a function of the coming kingdom, an anticipatory act which will be explained by what comes. At the same time each of our acts helps to actualize and make present the coming kingdom in our midst. We cannot try to set up this kingdom on earth. We cannot establish a Christian factory or a Christian philosophy. What we are to do is rather to manifest the reality in which our hope incarnates the kingdom of God. What is required, then, is hope, or active expectation of what is announced. For hope is strictly a mark of the distance between us and the kingdom, and yet as such it is also the guarantee of proximity.

The manifestation will take different forms. Thus Paul in Titus 2:13 and John in 1 John 3:3 tell us that hope means a self-purifying life in wisdom, righteousness, and piety. This is in keeping with our hope of the coming of the heavenly Jerusalem. The desire for purity is a material sign of the realization of our hope. It is because we know that we are going forward to life and resurrection that we must purify ourselves in order that we may be presented holy and faultless. This purification, of course, is not just ritual or moral. It is purification from the stains of the world. It will manifest itself in our freedom with regard to the things of the world. This is why hope and freedom are so often related in the texts. The hope which binds us to the risen Christ by a full and actual bond is precisely that which allows us to reject the validity of all secular powers. It takes concrete shape in the freedom which we live out in relation to these powers. For it is evident that if our hope is in Christ it cannot be in other things. There is radical incompatibility between two hopes. We can no longer hope in riches (1 Timothy 6:17), just as we cannot serve two masters. What is at issue is liberation and not the fear one might have in relation to the things of the world. Similarly Paul shows in 2 Corinthians 3:12 that hope introduces us into the ministry of the Spirit and already gives us a share in glory, so that we are freed from tradition or the law. We are now in the sphere of that which is lasting. "For if that which was done away was glorious, much more that which remaineth is glorious. Seeing then that we have such hope, we use. . . ." A notable feature of this text is that it expressly links the three elements of permanence, hope, and freedom. The point is that the revelation in Christ and the ministry of the Spirit are far superior to the revelation given to Moses and the ministry of the law. Now contrary to what one might suppose—and this explains what we said above—it is the revelation to which the ministry of the Spirit relates that is endowed with permanence. This revelation remains the same throughout events. And hope is linked to this permanence, so that having hope of this permanence we can act in freedom. In other words, the more full and complete the revelation of God is, the more free we are. This freedom is a freedom from the law and the human means of revelation, as the text plainly shows. We no longer need to inscribe the revelation on tablets of stone nor do we need to veil it. In the direct and personal relation in Christ, as hearts are converted to the Lord (v. 16), the human veil which hides the revelation of God (and which Moses could not escape putting on) is now taken away (v. 14). This conversion to the Lord sets us free. Thus permanence ceases to be formal and petrified; it is not an intangible. At the same time hope is actualized by the exercise of this freedom. The main point of the text is to remind us of the inseparable character of these modes of living.

Hope bears witness to us that there is a future. We can escape destiny. We have scope for life. Life has triumphed over death. The worst man, the most lost, is not lost. Nothing has been definitively settled. This is what opens up for us the path of freedom. Because hope enables us to live by a possible future, freedom commits us to the fashioning of a real history which is chosen and willed and shaped. We are no longer subject to sociological conditioning or individual influences or a simple and incoherent succession of things that just happen. Nothing is definitively settled. That is to say, nothing that shapes us is so decisive that the game is over. Even if we can say that "the game is over" with reference to the death and resurrection of Jesus Christ, what is settled is the possibility of living rather than the impossibility. What has been achieved for us is our freedom. This means that nothing is lost. Nothing and no one. Hope obliges me to believe that the last of men is in Christ, and by last I do not just mean the harlot or the savage or the idiot, which would be too obvious, but also the Nazi fanatic, the American millionaire, the killer, the dope merchant. These men are prisoners but they were not made to be prisoners. They are not yet finally lost. Hence I can be free in relation to them and on their behalf. I am not conditioned by their past. My conduct can be a new approach to them. If they did not have this hope, I could not have this freedom in relation to them. My freedom in relation to them means that hope begins to appear in their lives. Hell is not theirs, for hope is given for them, and I can be free in relation to them. I can be free to give a new meaning to our relation.

Freedom, as we shall see, must translate itself into the attributing of meaning. This is possible, however, only if there is hope, if what I do and see, and the situation I am in, have an ultimate meaning. I cannot impose this meaning gratuitously and theoretically from without. My freedom would be completely fallacious if it were expressed in a magical act of this kind. It would certainly be incommunicable. It takes on strength when it obeys the hope which indicates to me the meaning which God has given and which is thus possessed already by institutions, things, men, and events. This is why hope consists precisely in hoping against hope and against all the evidence. Hope is believing in the beatitudes in spite of appearances. Happy are those who weep—how foolish that is, for those who weep are unhappy and promising them consolation is a sorry jest. In any case Jesus says that they are happy now, already, at the present time. The one who weeps is happy now. This beatitude is true only because it is a word which

God himself pronounces over the one who weeps. Hope teaches us to accept as true what God says and to regard as untrue what the evidence of the senses affirms. It is the direct opposite of what Eve does when she accepts the evidence of the fruit which she is offered. It rejects appearances. It rejects the reality which impresses man when he regards it as a mandatory totality. Hope interposes as another and equally present and actual and far more effective reality the assurance of those things which are known by faith. Hope takes into account the solid and powerful reality of invisible things which faith can descry. It deciphers the signs which God has placed in man and the world but which are visible only for and by hope. It creates open situations and shatters every closed situation. It breaks restrictions. It uncovers the meaning both of immediate things and of those that are still to come. It fashions thereby a specific life-style in the present. In sum, hope is the true and only hermeneutics whether in relation to the world or to scripture. The rest is mere algebra and theory. But if hope authorizes a present style of life, this can be only the style of freedom, for hope, because it sees, produces a dimension which puts all forces and powers in their relative place. It breaks into the best regulated life. It can accept neither evidence nor the realism of appearances. It thus forces us to be free in relation to them. In particular, it brings freedom with regard to the means of power. The attitude of power, of control, of rigidity (including the rigid economic planning of totalitarianism), is a negation of hope. Where hope lives the instruments of power are devalued, whether they be political, scientific, ecclesiastical, economic, or psychological, and scope is given for freedom, which is itself opposed, negated, and constricted as the means of power develop. In the unity of revelation, then, the gift of hope corresponds to life in freedom. The ethics of freedom takes shape accordingly with all its uncertainty and paradoxicality.[6]

---

6 Ricoeur stresses the fact that freedom according to hope is the meaning of my existence in the light of the resurrection, i.e., as it is set in the movement which we have called "the future of the resurrection of Christ." In this sense a hermeneutics of religious freedom is an interpretation of freedom in conformity with the interpretation of the resurrection in terms of promise and hope.

# General Bibliography

D. Bonhoeffer, *The Cost of Discipleship* (1948) and *Ethics* (1955).
P. Bonnard, *L'Épître de St. Paul aux Galates* (1953).
Castelli *et al.*, *L'herméneutique de la liberté religieuse* (1968).
V. Eller, *The Promise, Ethics in the Kingdom of God* (1970).
H. Gollwitzer, *Forderungen der Freiheit* (1964).
G. Gusdorf, *Signification humaine de la liberté* (1962).
H. U. Jager, *Ethik und Eschatologie bei Leonhard Ragaz* (1971).
E. Käsemann, *Der Ruf der Freiheit* (1968).
E. Levinas, *Difficile liberté, Essais sur le Judaïsme* (1963).
*La Liberté et l'ordre social* (International Conferences at Geneva, 1969).
Mazerat *et al.*, *La liberté évangélique. Principes et pratiques* (1965).
R. Niebuhr, *An Interpretation of Christian Ethics.*
K. Niederwimmer, *Der Begriff der Freiheit in Neuen Testament* (1966).
M. Schlier, Art. "Eleutheros" in *TDNT*, II, pp. 487ff.
R. Schnackenburg, *Christian Existence in the New Testament* (1968).
C. Spicq, *Théologie morale du Nouveau Testament* (1965).

For more detailed literature the reader is referred to the works cited at individual points in the text and notes.

# Part I

# Alienated Man and Liberation in Christ

# Chapter 1

# Alienation and Necessity

## § 1. Alienation

The Bible often talks about the bondage of man. Israel is enslaved in Egypt and Babylon. There is bondage to men. We read of the institution of slavery. We also find bondage to corruption, to the *stoicheia* of this world. The Bible reminds us that we are born in servitude.

These terms do not mean much to man today. We have a vague idea of what it means to be a slave. But slavery, we think, has been abolished. In any case the word does not affect our heart or strike our imagination. It is only a figure of speech to talk about slavery to sin. This was not so, however, in biblical times. Slavery was an obvious if variable social situation in the Mediterranean world, and when the authors of scripture used this social and legal word to describe the situation of man as regards sin or the basic corruption of the world, this was no innocent, rhetorical, or exaggerated comparison. They were referring to the hardest and cruelest human condition. The term was not chosen merely to give us an idea of what was at issue but to denote as accurately as possible the profound truth of man and of his situation before God.

The ending of formal slavery has softened the term. But the situation described remains the same. In our own age the equivalent of slavery is alienation. This is not just a matter of modernizing our vocabulary and changing a word to give better understanding. The reference is to a concrete condition of man today just as the reference in the prophets and Paul is to a concrete situation in their day. For the slavery they had in mind was not social slavery on the one hand and spiritual slavery on the other. There was no separation between the two. We have to remember that the slave belonged body and soul to the master who had bought him. Being a slave, he was no longer a true man. The charge against Babylon is that it traffics in the souls of men. When we speak of bondage to sin, this is again a possession of the whole being. To the degree that the whole man is concerned, it is also, or in the first instance, man who is the slave of a master. For Israel's slavery in Egypt or Babylon has finally a wholly spiritual sense and is part of the history of Israel's relation with God. The object of biblical proclamation is the whole man who is the slave of sin. The socially determined slave is the type, model, figure, and meaning of man. The slave is man. Nowadays it is more usual to talk about alienated man. This is what we shall try to do.

Our starting-point must be the description of alienation which was given, if not first, at any rate most forcefully by Marx. Now it should not be forgotten that for Marx alienation is not a localized fact. It is not just a mark of the proletariat in a capitalistic world. It is not just an economic condition nor does it arise merely at one period in history. It is the total condition of man and of every man the moment he steps out of the primitive commune and falls victim to division of labor and to exploitation. Alienation is not the mere fact of subjection to others and exploitation by them. It goes much further. Play can constantly be made on the two orientations of the term. Alienation means being possessed externally by another and belonging to him. It also means being self-alienated, other than oneself, transformed into another. The problem has both these dimensions for Marx. This is why he speaks of alienation in work, in the worker's lack of time to live. Man has no control of time. His whole life is taken over by work. He is thus less than a beast. He is physically broken and spiritually bestialized. The man who is no more than a mobile working force is lost; he is alienated. Furthermore capitalism integrates this force which is the whole life of man into an object which is mere merchandise. This merchandise which is sold is not just a product. It contains part of the life of the man who has worked on it. He has been robbed of this by the capitalist process and its organization of work. The man himself is put at the mercy of the winds of commerce. He himself is sold, not merely in terms of the force which he has contributed and which is assessed commercially, but also in terms of the product of his work. He is alienated because he cannot get himself back. He cannot escape this condition which depends on a global system. This is the situation of every worker.

The alienation in money is even more serious. Marx finely shows that this applies both to those who have money and also to those who do not. This alienation is the other aspect of economic alienation. We know how Marx shows that money is finally the only real need in the capitalist world. The amount of money becomes the only essential quality of man. But by the play of the economic system the power of a given amount of money constantly diminishes and man is reduced to a machine for amassing money in order to try unceasingly to cover this mortal wound. Money reduces man to an abstraction. It reduces man himself to something quantitative. Man is taken into consideration only to the extent that he has money. The man who has nothing is nothing nowadays. The problem is that of man's possession by the fact of non-possession. To the extent that money has become the only active agent in the world, the only mediator or intermediary between all secular realities, the only common measure, and finally the only link between man and the world, the man who has no money is literally separated from the reality of the world and from existence in general. In other words, he is reduced to his own unreality. What is real is what is not man. Lack of money means that man is possessed by anti-nature and the anti-human. The situation of the man who has money and is dedicated to gaining it is no better. The possession of money is the mark of a lesser existence according to the celebrated dictum: The less you spend the less you exist, and the less you exist the more you have. For economical spending augments one's fortune. The greater the renunciation of life the greater the alienated essence of man. What man can no longer do, money can do in his place. It becomes the real power, nourished by man's own substance. The man who has money is completely alienated even in its possession. The capitalist is simply capital made man. He has no existence of his own.

The alienation, however, is more than an economic phenomenon. It includes ideological and especially religious alienation. Man is alienated because, once launched on the venture of exploitation in which he no longer acts justly, he is obliged to view everything with a corrupt conscience and to create an ideology which will conceal the true situation. His religion is the most complete and misleading ideology. It is here that he is most completely divested of himself. This is partly because, as in Feuerbach, he dreams up an illusory supreme being out of all that is best in himself, out of his own worth and righteousness and goodness. He transfers these to the Absolute. He thus robs himself by the projection. Partly, however, it is also because man expects liberation from someone else instead of himself. Religion is the "opium of the people" because it impedes action by causing man to transfer his own possibilities to another being. It thus gives him false hopes and deters him from taking his destiny into his own hands. Religion is undoubtedly man's highest achievement. It is a general theory of the world, its logic in popular form, its spiritual point of honor, its enthusiasm, its moral sanction, its solemn complement, its general ground of consolation and justification. It is the fantastic realization of human energy. Religious misery is on the one hand an expression of real misery and on the other hand it is protest against this misery. Religion is the sighing of the crushed creature, the heart of a world without heart, the spirit of an age without spirit. These fine words of Marx should not deceive us. Just because it is these things religion is the worst of all things. It is man's profound alienation. When Marx describes it along these lines, he is writing critically, not appreciatively. Religion is the solemn complement, the justification, and the moral sanction of *this* world, i.e., of this alienating structure of the world, of the organization of man's exploitation by man. It is a fantastic realization of human energy, not in the sense of the extraordinary or prodigious, but in the basic sense of the phantasmagorical. Humanity makes a tremendous effort to respond to itself and it lands up in the fantastic world of religion. Again, religion is the heart of a world without heart and the spirit of an age without spirit, but this means that it is the final and most total deception, for in this world without heart or spirit it gives to man the illusion of heart and spirit, preventing him from perceiving the truth, i.e., the inhumanity of the world, and thus substituting an illusory consolation for a real examination of the situation.

This whole cumulative set of alienations reaches its climax in the person of the worker. For if the point of departure, the origin of the alienation, is to be found in the objective economic situation of the worker, the alienated condition of the worker goes far beyond his economic state. He is a man who is completely shut off from himself. He has become an appendix of the machine. He is born in the anonymity of a city. He has no access at all to culture. He is stripped of family and country. He is unrestrictedly dependent. He does not depend at all on himself. His only wealth is his power as a worker, and this is not dependent on himself, but on the one who buys it. He has to have a purchaser. The purchaser will come forward only if it is in his own interests. This will be so only if conditions are favorable in the world markets. Marx comes here to one of the most important aspects of the alienation of modern man. His fate depends completely—and in a way which rules out any intervention on his part—on objective global phenomena which man is impotent to control no matter what his place may be.

Now what Marx tells us about human alienation can be contested in part, e.g., in respect of the economic analysis. One might argue that the worker in the western world is no longer in this position of radical dependence, of complete deprivation. One might point out that the causes of alienation are not those suggested by Marx, that some of the things which he indicates are no longer true. This does not alter in the least, however, the accuracy of Marx's analysis of modern man. We have to accept his description as perspicacious and even prophetic. We have not only to accept it; we have also to add to it and to develop it.

In our own time many of the traditional aspects of alienation such as poverty or inequality have largely disappeared. Alienation today is not that of misery or social inferiority. It has taken on a more profound and total sense. It extends to more than the economic sphere. It is a psychological or moral problem. Nor is it limited to individuals. It embraces social categories. It is political in the larger sense. Elimination of exploitation does not banish alienation. One can see this in Yugoslavia, China, Cuba, or Algeria.[1] If we say that the life of a worker in the twentieth century has few interests, that he has no social life, that his union life is insignificant, that his family life and status are the driving forces in his existence, this is simply to transfer to the proletariat problems which were previously those of the leisured classes. This is not accepted without a struggle. Workers and most militants refuse to go beyond the concept of exploitation. Yet surely the ideal of continually increasing production in lands where there is neither cold nor hunger makes no sense whether one is exploited or not. Making second-rate goods which are not really needed makes no sense

---

1  Cf. Mothé's remarkable book *Militant chez Renault* (1965).

*Alienated Man and Liberation in Christ*

whether one is exploited or not. Working one's whole life like an automaton with no individual initiative makes no sense whether one is exploited
or not. Not having any power over what is around us makes no sense
whether one is exploited or not. Being subject to autonomous forces which
one cannot control makes no sense whether one is exploited or not. This is
Mothé's fine description of alienation and it shows us that alienation, on
the Marxist basis, has now taken on a new dimension and depth which
justifies us in speaking of modern man as alienated man. This testimony
agrees with the more general reflections of Ricoeur, which will form a
fitting conclusion to our next consideration.

In the most advanced modern societies man is essentially alienated.
Adoption of socialism in no way changes this. The alienation has now taken
on new dimensions. It is alienation in the multiplicity, the complexity, the
crushing rigor, the non-criticizable rationality of social systems. Man is
self-dispossessed because he has come under the possession of phenomena
which have an increasingly abstract character and over which he has less
and less control. The important fact in alienation is no longer the exploitation of man by man. This still exists in the third world and even in part in
the west. But it is not the decisive or determinative force. Man's enemy is
no longer another class of men, nor is it a relatively simple system set up in
the interests of a special class. It is a collection of mechanisms of inde-
scribable complexity—technics, propaganda, state, administration, planning,
ideology, urbanization, social technology. Man is set in these complexes
which no one can control but whose functioning strictly governs the state,
the future, the sphere of liberty, conformity, and adaptation. Man is less
and less the master of his own life. It is easy to say, of course, that he never
has been, that he has always been in authoritarian groups, that he has been
subject to the traditional family, etc., that he has never been free. I reply,
as I have done so often before, that my concern is not with alienation in
other civilizations. It is with alienation today. I do not have to say whether
man is more free or less free now than he once was. I also reply that
alienation is more difficult today because it is the product of abstract and
calculated systems. There is less chance about them and more mathematics.
A scientific attempt is being made to get to the inner forum of man and to
change it. Hence I firmly believe that it is in terms of the tradition which
goes back to Marx that we must consider man's present condition and that
we are dealing with alienated man. The period between 1900 and our own
time shows us that man is more deeply alienated than he was at the
beginning of the industrial age. It is in relation to alienated man that the
problem of freedom arises and that we need to reflect on an ethics of
freedom. This society is the present context of discussion just as a slave
society was the context of discussion in the days of the prophets and
apostles. The term alienation cannot just be substituted for the term
slavery. The two words are not completely identical in orientation or
content. Hence we have to think out what Christian freedom means in

relation to alienation. We have to think out what it implies for conduct.

Ricoeur adds to all this[2] an analysis of alienation under three heads.

(1) Man takes note of his means and hence of the autonomy which he has thanks to the possibilities of action. He does not see this as progress or freedom but as a charge or burden, as a kind of condemnation.

(2) Man has the means to assure his well-being. These are not regulated, however, by true well-being, by consumption and distribution, but by a desire for maximum well-being, an inauthentic increase of needs, an infinite and indefinite desire, an ability to destroy the fruits of accrued creativity, with not the least response to his situation.

(3) Man has the means of power which enable him to exercise almost absolute control and this makes him want to manipulate everything. We wish to alter the human condition, to annihilate distance in space and time, to prolong human life indefinitely, to control both birth and death. We impose on every aspect of life a type of existence borrowed from the technical model and we place all beings in a relation which brings them within the sphere of what can be manipulated and utilized.

Under all three heads the result is an accumulated alienation, not intrinsically, but because the central problem which is nowhere solved is that of meaning. This brings us to a favorite theme of Ricoeur, the essential one, as we shall find, of meaning or lack of meaning. As he sees it, it is a serious mistake to assess our age in terms of increasing rationality. Instead we should assess it in terms of increasing absurdity.

The testimony of technical progress should not be separated from that of revolt and absurdity as this is manifested in contemporary literature and art. The same man in us executes the double movement of technical or economic rationality on the one side and of breaking meaning in pieces on the other. The basic reason for this "nonsense" is discovery of the insignificance of the collective project of maximal consumption, whether in a project of domination like the moon flights or in a project which is purely instrumental. In the technical and economic domain we develop an intelligence of means. In this sense one might talk of progress. At the same time, however, we see a kind of dissolution of ends. Our problem is that the more we find means to control the industrial and technical world the less we see the reason for it. The increasing absence of ends in a society which is augmenting the rationality of its means is the profound source of discontent. To the degree that the elementary needs of food and shelter and leisure are met, we enter into a world of the capricious and the arbitrary, into a world of aimless gestures. We come to see the insignificance of work and leisure and sex. We thus reach the point where what we do has lost all meaning. The very grandeur of means produces the situation of alienation

---

2 Ricoeur, "Notre responsabilité dans la société moderne," *Bulletin du C.P.O.* (July 1965).

in our society when the meaning we can attach to life and action is no longer commensurate with these means. At this point man is effectively alienated in his own means and his own power.

Now one may certainly object against the thought of Marx and the descriptions of alienation which he influenced that they are both imprecise (in spite of their objectivity) and merely objectivizing (in spite of their precision). One may argue that it is too abstract to say that the situations which alienate are global. Such a description is not realistic. It has an imaginary reality, a reality which is interpreted by a prior ideology. The idea of a globally alienated society is suspect. In effect man cannot recognize general phenomena or mechanisms of alienation. Things and institutions do not alienate. Whole groups are not in a situation of alienation in relation to others. This kind of approach does not alone enable us to lay hold of alienation with any exactitude. To get a clear analysis one has to begin with the experience of alienation by man. Four aspects of experience may be distinguished:[3] (1) the experience of the powerlessness of each of us in face of the world, of the society in which we are but which we can neither modify nor escape; (2) the experience of the absurd, of seeing that the events we have to live through have no meaning or value, so that we cannot find our way in them; (3) the experience of abandonment, of knowing that no help is to be expected, that neither others nor society will grant any support, the idea of dereliction which is so dear to existentialism; and finally (4) the culminating experience of indifference to oneself, in which man is so outside himself that his destiny is no longer of interest to him and he has neither desire nor zest for life.

This experience of the alienated situation, lived out at the subjective level, enables us to isolate the factors in alienation. Three elements may be discerned: first, a loss of control, whether of the situation in which we are set or of our responses to it; then a lack of motivation in which man no longer knows why things are as they are but simply does what he does without knowing what it is all about; and finally a lack of information in which an individual feels isolated because the flow of information between his environment and himself (and *vice versa*) has been stopped. In sum, the adaptive function of the individual has been put out of joint in relation to the physical world, society, a group of individuals, or his partner. In consequence one cannot speak of absolute alienation or the reverse. We simply have degrees of alienation.

But if conditions do not strictly alienate, some conditions do with a degree of probability expose the individual to alienation, i.e., to a loss of control which is more or less serious, e.g., a society in which the level of information is very small or is perhaps so great that the individual cannot get proper information because of the excess, or membership in a group

---

3   Cf. Bourricaud's *L'aliénation* (Conference of the Faculty of Law at Bordeaux, 1966).

which global society may or may not regard as valuable, and if it does not the individual who is strongly attached to his primary group has the impression of being himself in a world without meaning. The individual may find himself in a situation of minimal participation in society (perhaps by reason of the group to which he belongs), or in contradiction between his ambition to do something and the absence of means to do it, or in the presence of a field of action which greatly limits his possibilities. In other words, alienation is a malfunction in the controlling mechanism which the individual suffers in relation to his sphere of action. To understand it, one has to get a precise picture of social control and examine the variables which modify it. Thus the role of sociology is to know what are the social groups, in a given context, which come up against this loss of control or which possess to an excessive degree the power of control.

This analysis seems to me to be a matter of importance and it adds a remarkably precise dimension to the general interpretation of Marx. It helps us to grasp the subjective side of alienation which is so decisive. Alienation cannot be reduced to a sociological or psychological concept without amputating some of its richness. To be sure, one may try to discern in it a working concept which is indispensable if one is to achieve a correct sociological analysis. But alienation has also an emotional signification deriving from the general analysis of Marx and playing a dominant role at the present time. Now I do not believe that one can abstract away from this emotional qualification, which is an integral part of the very idea of alienation. A precise picture of alienation might be given, but it would of necessity be impoverished and bloodless. It would be clear but would finally lack any warmth and hence it would not really be exact. For if one deprives the concept of alienation of its emotional potential, one takes away part of its reality.

Along such lines one might arrive at a form which can be manipulated and utilized but which does not correspond to what alienation is for the man who is alienated. I believe that in truth alienation is a moral category rather than a sociological or psychological category. But as a moral category does it take a certain reality of man into account or not? This is the question. For this situation may present itself as a way of living it rather than a situation as such. From this standpoint there is no alienating situation in itself. A man may live out his condition as one that alienates whereas another in exactly the same position may not have this experience. Mass production offers a good example. Some workers are well adapted to this and do not feel truncated or alienated by their job.[4] We have here a matter of subjective interpretation. Different people have different experiences in the same condition, even if by and large the situation of workers today, which is far better than it was a hundred years ago, is in fact one of alienation.

---

4  Friedmann, *Problèmes humains du machinisme industriel.*

Alienation has to be seen, then, as a situation which can be considered from the external standpoint. Ultimately, however, it can be viewed as alienation only in terms of a given model of man. This is why we say that it is a moral category. Only as we project a given type of man into the situation can we say that this man is alienated.

Now we live in a certain society which has a certain positive concept of man that we share and in terms of which we can speak of alienated man if he cannot measure up to the model for reasons external to himself. If this permits us to describe a given objective situation as alienating no matter what people are set in it and no matter what their reactions may be, this is because we have a concept of what these people or the life of these people ought to be. Marx takes this line, and to some extent we all do. The most precise analysis that we can give will have to begin with a concept of man as one who has control, motivation, and information. Hence it is not "scientific." At the same time this obviously brings us back to the problem of the way of living out a situation, for it is in terms of our concept of man that a situation is found to be alienating or not. We have thus to begin with the moral category of alienation if we are to interpret both what has been said above and also the relation between this (effective) alienation of man and God's decision for him in Jesus Christ.

The thinking of Marx, which is polemical, as is its extension, is not scientific to non-Marxists. It cannot be included among the sciences. It has a global view of man's being and situation, but correctly to evaluate the situation of man we have to take other orientations into account, especially those of modern sociology and social psychology. These deal with something very different, namely, facts which are as scientific as possible, which relate to points of detail rather than a global view, and which are not polemical. But what are these facts? I venture to say that scientific works in these areas, written by authors of very different philosophical and religious persuasions, nearly all give the same impression, namely, that man is determined. Note that we are not referring to a metaphysical option or argument. We have in mind detailed investigations, as scientific as they possibly can be, into the conduct, the situation, the attitudes, and the opinions of man. Furthermore, these works do not reach any general conclusion that man is under total determination. Being specialists, the writers do not enter this field. They do not try to offer global conclusions that would pass as metaphysics. This is why I spoke only of an impression which is given. Indeed, many of these scientific writers are liberals who believe in the particularity, uniqueness, and freedom of man. This is why there often seems to be a kind of contradiction between the body of the work and the conclusion.

Gurvitch has shown this clearly in his moral sociology. He makes it plain to what extent the content and structure depend on external factors so that in practice everything is determined by social organization or levels of "sociability," and morals are extremely variable and uncertain. To safeguard a hierarchy of values and human freedom, however, Gurvitch later tells us that this work is that of a sociologist and ought not to be confused with the work of a metaphysician, whose task it is to decide what values are right and good and to choose between them. Sociological relativism, he says, has nothing whatever to do with philosophical relativism. The philosopher ought to find ways of integrating the multiplicity into a whole which will have universal validity. How he can do so is not shown. For the philosopher, too, belongs to a given setting and culture. He, too, is precisely determined by these, as the sociologist has demonstrated. He is not an independent demiurge. Ethical thought is dependent on the social structures in which it is formulated. The philosopher is not free to choose, so that the sociological analysis is of no value to anyone. There is no real possibility of synthesis, since every moral system is dependent on the sociological setting and cannot be detached from it. Synthesis presupposes absence of setting.

Another example of the attempt to save freedom is to be found in the noteworthy work of Stoetzel on public opinion. Stoetzel shows convincingly to what extent public opinion is determined by the social structure and a concatenation of external factors. These indicate the true situation in which the individual is placed. Analysis of the correlations between the different factors and opinions makes it clear that the whole thinking of the individual is determined and not just his action. But Stoetzel cannot accept what seems to be the conclusion of his own analysis, namely, that we are psychological robots. Cannot opinions become the work of the individual? We thus have a reversal of the process. If the individual can achieve a certain personal maturity, if he is endowed with a minimum of freedom, then explanations of the relation between him and his opinions become inadequate. They are not wrong or useless. . . . If they take into account the personal history of the individual and his opinions, and if they enable us in part to predict these, they have their place in a theory of opinions. But they leave a vacant spot in the total picture. This brings us up against the impenetrable mystery of personality.[5] Personality is a phenomenon at the heart of man's being which cannot be localized, analyzed, or explained. It has to be said, of course, that there is nothing in the actual study of the formation of opinions to prepare us for this conclusion. The rigorous scientific analysis seems to set before us a group of exact mechanisms which explain pretty well everything that is accessible to it. One can understand the scruples of the authors which lead them to make the final transition, but one has also to recognize that we have here two totally

---

5 While I reject completely the definition of freedom which is given in *La liberté et l'homme du XXe siècle* (1966), namely, that it is being able to become what we ought to be—which is a false solution of the problem of liberty and necessity and which also introduces a moral criterion—I like the central thought of the authors when they insist on the contradiction between the desire or sense of freedom and scientific proof of non-freedom.

different procedures. On the one hand we have scientific analysis of all the available material, while on the other hand we have a leap into metaphysics. Now if we follow what the social sciences teach us today, we have to agree that as experience and knowledge increase the list of the spheres of human determinism increases also.

This area is a very different one from that of alienation. We do not have here man's dispossession by forces or by other men but simply the documenting of the many determinative elements which condition all man's psycho-sociological activities. To give a summary of some of the more important points, we may refer to man's conditioning by culture (in the sense of American sociologists). A man's cultural setting not only furnishes him with a certain life-style, mode of behavior, and morality. It also furnishes him with the instruments of his intellectual life and the structures of his emotional life. It gives him his language and consequently the images, stereotypes, and interpretations by which he apprehends the totality of phenomena. He has no direct contact with facts. He has contact with them only via the intellectual apparatus which is given him in advance by his culture. There is thus no freedom in this sphere, for what is called freedom can be exercised only in the area circumscribed by a man's culture and with the mediation of the various instruments with which the individual finds himself endowed and which he cannot escape. Recognition of this conditioning by language and the desire to escape from it can lead to desperate enterprises such as we are witnessing today, e.g., the destructuring of language, or the establishment of a meta-language. But if these give the sense of a recovery of freedom, it is at the expense of any possibility of communication, which for its part entails a radical loss of freedom. Nor do we find determinism merely at the level of intellectual apparatus. It is to be found in the field of the affections too. The cultural variations of emotional expressions and situations are becoming increasingly known. What we think is a completely spontaneous expression of sorrow in bereavement or of love is in fact fully enframed and determined by given cultural factors. There is an institutionalization of the emotions, as there is also of memory and so forth. These determinations are the result of a social apprenticeship of which we are not at all aware and which we can in no way escape. This, as culture, quite literally forms our "nature."

In addition to culture, we need only mention here the other determinations which are best known, which are the most profound, and which are also the most external. Thus we have determination by motivation. The reference here is to motives which, quite apart from our pretentious claims to act as free and independent persons, really control our conduct, decisions, and choices. Analysis of motivations increasingly shows that our voluntary acts, on which we base our freedom, are performed for reasons which are indeed within us, which have their roots in our innermost being, but which are completely outside our control. Our conscious motives are just a lying screen for acts which are dictated by impulses over which we have no mastery but which we are either unable or unwilling to recognize. To put it in paradoxical form, the very thing here which seems to be most free is in fact the most determined (cf. Friedmann, *7 études sur l'homme et la technique*, 1967; Lefebvre, *Langage et société*, p. 374).

I might also refer to determination by membership in a group. This is a different problem from that of culture. Our conduct here is the result of the totality of individual interactions within the group and of the pressure which the group exerts on us. Techniques of group dynamics enable us increasingly to grasp the way in which conduct is fashioned in the group. Here again, then, we are not as free and independent as we imagine. We find in the group the satisfaction of strongly felt needs, e.g., the need for security or control. For the satisfaction of these needs we are prepared to adopt the behavior which permits us to live in the group.

Finally, we should not forget the works which show how man is conditioned by his urban environment, by the development of organizational techniques, by the application of individual or mass psychological techniques, by the growth of the apparatus of state, by the expansion of global and unitary ideologies. In actual society man is at the mercy of a multiplicity of forces which act upon him, no doubt to the raising of his standard of living but also to the augmenting of the growing complexity of determinations. These determinations are different in kind from those which may be seen in the earlier relation with nature. They are technical, planned, and calculated, except that their effects cannot be foreseen. This seems to suggest that man can know and master them. Experience shows, however, that man cannot do this and that while actual technical determinations can be exercised by men on other men, they can be mastered only at the level of the operation and not at that of the determinative factor itself.

To sum up, we find three aspects of conditioning: (1) the alienation brought to light by Marx, which is still true; (2) the determinations by culture which the social sciences have discovered; and (3) the resultant growth of artificial techniques of determination. In these conditions it is absolutely impossible to say that man is free.

We thus come up against a remarkable fact. At the very time when the concrete discovery of man's lack of freedom is being effected with the greatest rigor and precision, philosophies of freedom are obviously flourishing. Throughout the centuries the freedom of the will has been debated metaphysically. No solution has ever been found for the problem. From about 1850, however, scientific knowledge of man and society has enabled us to conclude with some degree of certainty that man is not free at all. This has not taken place at the metaphysical level. In the older debates already some champions of the bondage of the will—I do not refer to Luther—insisted on the material determination of man, e.g., in relation to bodily needs. Since this could not be denied, a strict differentiation was made between body and soul. There is scope for a far deeper examination than is possible here of the role of the dichotomy of body and soul in the whole conflict between the bondage of man and the freedom of man. The body is patently enslaved but in compensation the soul is free. Now what modern psychological analysis makes clear is that with a profundity we cannot yet assess or limit the soul is also in bondage. Determinism applies to man with respect to all the things that we can lay hold of by our instruments of measurement and analysis. One may go even further and state categorically—for it is more than an affirmation—that man is not so enamored of freedom as some have supposed. Freedom is not an inherent personal need. The needs of security, conformity, adaptation, happiness, economy of effort, and so forth are far more constant and profound. Man is completely prepared to sacrifice his freedom in order to satisfy these needs.

The word "freedom" is very evocative. Freedom is a good subject in propaganda, in which individual freedom and national independence are often confused. The remarkable thing is that man cannot tolerate direct oppression or subjection to a superior. He cannot tolerate material constraint which reduces him to the brutish level, e.g., confinement in prison or being chained. He has a biological need for autonomy of movement. This is the instinct of freedom which Pavlov found to be a kind of reflex. As concerns revolt against the domination of a superior, however, this is less a matter of liberty than of the will for power, of self-affirmation, of the instinct of superiority. To be governed arbitrarily, to be ordered about, is intolerable, not because I am a free man, but because I myself want to do the ordering; which is why what normally happens is politics is that a more dictatorial government than ever is set up by the movement which has staged a revolution in the name of freedom. Hence when we speak of man's impulses towards liberty, we are not at an inferior level but we are confronted by a wholly different phenomenon. And when it is a matter of exercising individual, personal freedom, it may be noted that in practice man gives priority to many other needs and longings and that he fears freedom more than he desires it.

In all spheres, then, scientific experience brings to light more and more determinations and fewer and fewer possibilities of freedom. The astonishing thing today is the disagreement between this finding and the philosophy of human freedom.[6] Marxist philosophy has become less inflexible and more voluntaristic. Existentialism thinks that the human condition can be annulled and it defines man as free. One might also refer to phenomenology and even the "theology" of Teilhard. There is not a single movement in modern philosophy which takes into account the findings of a more scientific study of man.

---

6 Cf. in this regard Ricoeur, Cardonnel, Cotta, Bultmann, Moltmann, and Tillich.

We may quote in this connection the pertinent studies of Stéphane Lupasco.[7] Lupasco speaks very generally of the serene, confused, and facile way in which contemporary philosophy uses certain key-terms to build up theories and doctrines without bothering about the modifications their ideas might have to undergo in the light of scientific investigation. Only in the later decades of the twentieth century has philosophy found the hope and will to work outside if not contrary to the work of science. Every philosophy and metaphysics prior to this century has always tried to build on what passed for the scientific experience of the age, i.e., on the exercise of mental functions as they grapple with the world and as knowledge is thus made possible. One is reminded of how J. P. Sartre told a physicist to be quiet when he was speaking about the composition of matter since philosophers have a far better idea of what matter is than physicists do. The phenomenon of freedom characterizes this conflict. Philosophers deliberately ignore what sociology, political science, economics, and social psychology teach about man. A reading of the literature of philosophy conducts us into a world of imagination, inconsistency, and gratuitousness. Everything is, of course, verbally possible. But we do not get beyond the verbal. Nor does the mere affirmation of the freedom of man in modern books of philosophy and ethics dispose us to set aside the evidence that socially he is not free or to resist the continual nibbling away at this supposed freedom by the social sciences. In philosophy we find an affirmation of faith, taking up of a position, a choice, which enjoys a certain respectability as a decision (I am wagering that man is free). Nothing will convince me, however, that this is a correct choice. I will simply refer to the disparity between scientific findings and the philosophical affirmation and say that for my part I side with the former even though I am aware that philosophers can argue that science itself is merely a systematic interpretation of the world and man which is just as arbitrary as any other. I cannot accept this facile evasion, for when in the writings of the same philosophers I come across examples taken from spheres of science with which I am not entirely unfamiliar (e.g., sections of history and sociology), I find such ignorance and glaring errors that it is difficult to treat seriously their evaluation of scientific matters.[8] One can hardly help concluding that this desire to reject the findings of science is due to the constricting, hampering, and limiting effect of science on thought and also to the fact that the tremendous expansion of knowledge is destroying the possibility of constructing a single, all-embracing system or interpretation.

Nevertheless, a deeper analysis is probably demanded. Why is it that at the very time when science is showing that man is determined by a

---

7 "Qu'est-ce qu'une structure?" *Médecine de France* (1963-1964).

8 Thus almost everything that Mme de Beauvoir writes about the historical condition of women in her *Seconde Sexe* is a tissue of errors and contradictions.

multiplicity of mechanisms philosophy is proclaiming freedom? Is there an element of compensation here, a kind of escape, an unconscious rejection? The prospect is too frightening if science is right. We must avoid its iron yoke. The interesting thing is that modern philosophy inclines specifically to the absurd, to anguish and ambiguity. It would rather affirm an absurd and tragic existence than accede to a rational universe of determination. Absurdity, even if terrifying, is a consolation face to face with the rigor of necessity. Eroticism, political involvement, ambiguity, and nonsense can be accepted as a justification of presupposed freedom. Anything is better than the pure and simple evidence of determination. The more terrible this becomes, the more man has the sense of freedom. In this regard we are on the plane of what Marx called ideology. Modern philosophers, in their refusal to face up to the realities of life, are undoubtedly a product of this erroneous feeling. They refuse to see themselves in their reality as men. This is why I shall ignore them here and simply consider the situation described by Marxism and sociology.

### §2. Necessity

When we refer to the determinations which affect man, their totality forces us to consider that man lives in a universe of necessity. At the very outset, however, a distinction must be made between necessity and fate. Fate in the sense of an ineluctable destiny which will come to man in spite of all man's attempts to escape it and which finally determines each of his thoughts and actions is a metaphysical problem on which I shall not attempt to make any pronouncement. There is no evidence for fate. It can be a construct of the mind, but only in the same sense as freedom is in modern philosophy. Furthermore, when I speak of determinations I do not have in mind a general concept of determinism. If many determinations affect and evoke human opinions and acts, I cannot infer from this that man is totally determined. I certainly cannot have in mind a simplistic determinism, i.e., the phenomenon of direct, unavoidable, and all-powerful causality. In relation to determinism we know how complex is the phenomenon of chance and what modifications the theory of chance may impose. I will not enter into this debate, which far exceeds my own sphere of competence. There is value, however, in establishing the boundary between necessity and fate.

The one is a theory of life and nature which involves an ineluctable structure. The other means that several forces act on man but we cannot say that they represent the totality of his universe or that they condition directly and immediately his whole life and work. Thus I can accept neither the formula of Dupree: "Nothing is determined and everything is indefinitely determinable," nor the commmentary of Mehl: "No established determination can be regarded as adequate but each will finally be seen as a mode of indetermination."[9] It is true that there are no total, absolute, or exclusive determinations. But to say that established determinations are simply a mode of indetermination seems to me to be paradoxical. If the point is that nothing is determined, that there is in the life of man and society an element of indetermination, then I agree wholeheartedly. I do not view either man or society mechanistically. But I have to accept the fact that there are necessities which we cannot escape. Apart from those which we have already discussed in section 1 we may now quote as examples some internal necessities, as I call them. When we consider the structures of a society and the constituent elements of our world, when we try to understand development, fulfilment, and decline, we note that everything happens as though in obedience to imperious necessities which in practice are unavoidable, since the same developments take place, the same trends come finally to expression, and there are regularities which at the very least we have to describe as tendencies.

Thus we may consider political power. No matter what may be its form or level, it inevitably tends to enhance itself and to initiate a movement towards centralization. No political power will ever reduce itself or accomplish decentralization. There is a law that power will grow without limit. The only recognized limit is fact. Power will always go as far as it possibly can geographically or judicially. It ceases to expand only when it comes up against an obstacle that is more powerful than itself. Power is under the necessity of becoming absolute and totalitarian. This depends neither on the men who wield it nor on the ideology nor on the circumstances. Political power would not be power if this were not so.

We might also consider money. Wherever money exists we find trade. This is self-evident. But once trade is generalized by money it tends to become the normal mode of relation between individuals and to impose itself on everything. Money is under the internal necessity of extending to everything and universalizing itself. When a society develops a financial organization there is within it nothing that can finally avoid being bought and sold, whether it be love, religion, work, or country. All these become matters of finance. Money thus becomes a necessary intermediary. Relations are not only calculated in terms of money; they are impossible without it. The analysis of Marx is perfectly correct. Here again, however, we are not to think merely in terms of those who have money or of circumstances. We are confronted by a rule which extends to all life and by the profound reality of money itself.

I might also adduce the internal necessities of the phenomenon of technology, but since I have dealt with this in *The Technological Society* (1964) I need only say here that this phenomenon, too, obeys its own law of development and that there is no real possibility of modifying its course. At a level where analysis is more difficult we might examine the necessity

---

9  Mehl, *De l'autorité des valeurs*, p. 191.

expressed in and by the city. Once the city comes into existence it carries with it its own laws and implications. Here, however, we leave the sociological sphere and enter another dimension. In the Bible the city is depicted as the world which man makes for himself in rejection of what God has created for man andconsequently in rejection of God himself. The city is the world in which man wants to be without God. It expresses the attempt to exclude God, to shut oneself off from him, to fabricate a world which is purely and exclusively human. I realize that in this summary form these statements might seem to be abrupt and even shocking and I therefore refer to my work *The Meaning of the City* (1970) for a fuller treatment of the question. My point here is simply that these necessities do not have to be merely rational or sociological. They have also a spiritual and theological dimension. The city tries to be man's exclusive world. It actually becomes this with all that it implies even from the intellectual and religious standpoint. It obeys a kind of imperative whereby man curves in upon himself while trying to find a compensating outlet in abstract idealism.

Finally, in the same order of ideas even religion obeys intrinsic necessities. No matter what may be its origin or content, we always see an attempt on man's part to lay hold of the event. Religion becomes a department of man's activity. It is a means to meet certain needs and to compensate for certain deficiencies. Religion always develops in two directions. On the one side it undergoes an intellectual elaboration which tends to become dogmatic and desiccated as it provides a theoretical framework for all thought in a given area. On the other hand it undergoes a moral elaboration in which it becomes a system of attitudes and duties. No religion can escape this twofold movement. We can thus speak quite aptly of necessity here too. We can do so even in relation to what ought to be the very opposite of religion, namely, the revelation of God in Jesus Christ. This is constantly reduced and degraded to the level of religion, of formulas, of dogmas, of morality. It is so even when Christians are aware of it, even when they fight against it, even when they want to preserve for revelation its youth and freshness as an event. The iron circle of religious necessities always closes in on it in the long run.

Now it is true that in each instance given, extensive development would be needed to prove the point which I am making. The very range of the examples, however, can give the reader an idea of what I have in mind when I speak of the inner necessity of things as well as the alienation and determination of man. Two aspects of this necessity should again be emphasized. First, all the forces and structures of the social order have an unavoidable tendency to expand until they become as total as possible. Each element in the order has a kind of call to universalize itself, whether we think of law, economic production, religion, or anything else. Only to the degree that it comes up against another factor which is also aiming at totality is it arrested. We have here a phenomenon of expansion which forces itself on man and which he cannot control even though it is he who makes laws and writes newspapers and constructs factories and so forth. This man is alienated in the work of his own hands, which assumes autonomy in relation to him.

This leads on to the second aspect of necessity. Since all social forces make a bid for totality and try to become totalitarian, they all necessarily take on a spiritual meaning and value. The thing does not remain a thing. It has to have a value. It has to be invested with justice and authority. It has to represent meaning in a world without meaning. It cannot in effect be universal unless it ceases to be itself in order to be more than itself by taking on spiritual significance. The state has to be more than an administrative and political mechanism. It has to represent God on earth. Technology has to be more than an assembly of means to achieve utilitarian results. It has to be the privileged expression of man's demiurgic vocation. Money has to be more than a useful instrument for measuring value. It has to be mammon—an idol which satisfies all human needs. We have here a development which is by no means accidental or accessory. It can be observed as a general rule, so that we are justified in speaking of a kind of internal necessity.

In this brief analysis of necessities we must also show that they do not all have the same force and rigor. This completes what we have been trying to demonstrate in our attempt to avoid the simplistic problem whether there is determination or not, whether there is necessity or freedom. It seems to me that this is a purely theoretical way of putting the question. My own aim will be to try to grasp the situation at the level of experience and fact. At this level constraints and necessities undoubtedly differ in force and weight. The constraint imposed by the Gestapo was more severe than that imposed by the police of Louis XIV. The psychological constraint imposed by the family group differs in degree from that exercised in a totalitarian party. The same phenomenon can also have a different force in different ages. Thus the family had far more influence in the thirteenth and fourteenth centuries than it has in our own age. Primary groups such as the clan, tribe, or village have been gradually losing their power over the individual. In contrast global society had only a vague and fluid relation to individuals prior to the eighteenth century, but it has now become an increasing constraint and it represents one of the most complex necessities that man will encounter. What we can show in a general way, however, is that no matter what the phenomenon its character as necessity will increase to the degree that it achieves its full scope and reaches its object. Thus a social factor like religion, political power, technology, or propaganda will still be the work of man in its earliest forms, so that at its commencement it can still be modified by man. Man is its master and the arbiter of its destiny. But as this factor solidifies in its means and methods, as it extends its sphere of application, as it invests itself with spiritual meaning, man progressively loses his possibilities of intervention and modification. A reversal takes place. Man no longer organizes the object. The object has its own life and it develops like a true organism according to its own necessity. The more it obeys this law of its own development the more it forces itself on man and becomes a necessity for him. Technology makes this especially clear. Up to the eighteenth century man was obviously in control of his technical life. But once technology reached a certain perfection and dimension and the technical phenomenon arose, technology threw off completely the control of man and became in some sense the destiny or even the fate of man. It should be noted, however, that this could happen only because there was not merely an inner mechanism but because man consented to go along with it. Man is not stripped of his mastery apart from or contrary to himself. The movement of reversal always has two aspects, first, the expansion of the phenomenon by its own inner dynamic, and secondly the psycho-spiritual attitude of man, which can take such different forms as total unawareness, simple passivity, rational assent, mythical hope, and delirious passion. When man is caught up in a system of sociological expansion he himself gives his support to the system. He wants it to be realized. He hopes that it will come into being. This adaptation always takes place. Hence it is easy to reverse the order of events and to say that if the development takes place it is because man wants it to do so.

Now it is quite possible to analyze closely the order and succession of events if we take such precise realities as the growth of the state, the expansion of technology, or the application of psycho-sociological methods. At first the vast majority of people are hostile. But a minority organizes the system and gives it its form and structure. Then the system obeys its own logic of expansion and most people are prepared to give it their admiring and passionate support. The necessity becomes rigorous only as this support is given. This might give us courage to believe that in this regard at least man is free. Unfortunately experience teaches that this support is never the result of a deliberate choice or of reflection. It has its origin in a passionate feeling that according to all the evidence we have here something that is good for man. For example, leisure, popular culture, health, raising the standard of living, and economic growth provide justification for the technological process and hence stir up support for it. But when man gives his support, he cannot expect much from his freedom, for he ties the bond of necessity around himself. He is assenting to necessity itself, as may be seen on almost any interpretation.

Now as I have tried to show in *The Political Illusion* (1967), the more complex and refined civilization becomes the greater is the "interiorizing" of determinations. These become less and less visible, external, constricting, and offensive. They are instead invisible, interior, benevolent, and insidious. They make an appeal to the reason. They ask for cooperation. They step forth as the champions of well-being and happiness. They are less and less resented as necessity and more and more accepted as self-evident. They are no longer a burden imposed on us. They are now a quiet internal channel.

They can be justified rationally. Our alienation takes on an increasingly acceptable form, since it seems to be more and more justifiable. Thus the metaphysical problem of lack of freedom undoubtedly begins to overlap the concrete situation of determinations, thanks to the growth of technological complexity, and a man becomes a creature of external determination.[10]

Obviously to claim that thought is free within this complex of determinations is completely illusory. It involves a simplistic level of belief according to which the only obstacles to freedom of thought are a religious system or the imperatives of the law. A more serious look will quickly show to what extent our thinking is not free. It is determined by our education and background, our culture, and the voluntary means of persuasion (publicity, information, and propaganda). Thus so-called freedom of thought is a tissue of conditionings which are more rigorous than is often perceived. In contesting a (religious) system it does not fight these radical determinations but surrenders unwittingly to them, and innocently accepts a system of thought which is narrow precisely because it is so thoroughly constructed as an antithesis to the religious system.

All the same, even in these conditions one can still argue that it is possible to escape necessity. As I see it, one has to recognize necessity where it exists. To begin with, a distinction must be made between the collective level and the individual level. At the former, it does not seem to me that it is possible to escape necessity. Can one really act in such a way as to change the broad development of society? It seems not. One can act. But collective action always develops in accordance with the most profound and rigorous necessities. There may be at the level of necessities different types which affect and determine conduct in different ways. This leaves man a measure of choice between them. Thus one may oppose an actual, relatively superficial, visible, and experienced determination to a deep-seated one which is already in effect. After a certain period of pressure institutions and sociological phenomena do in fact lose their vigor, fall into decay, and thus cease to constitute necessities. Thus successive forms of morality or capitalism or socialism may be studied from this angle. At different periods they will be seen to obey a certain number of necessary forces which operate by right of survival and which retain their appearance of necessity for a time even when they have weakened and are simply the residue of an earlier necessity of great depth. Thus in face of the traditional structure of bourgeois capitalism, which has imposed itself as a necessity, a new economy has emerged which is based on growth and which derives its force from technical development. Those who advocate the new forms have the impression that they are expressing their freedom when in effect they have simply chosen the most profound and expressive form of actual

---

10 Cf. Riesman, *La foule solitaire* (1964), whose analysis is much more useful than that of Marcuse.

*Alienated Man and Liberation in Christ*

necessity. They simply feel the burden of this necessity more keenly than others.[11]

The transition from colonization to decolonization offers a parallel example. It is no use describing this as a good. There is nothing good about choosing a necessity. Marx is quite right when he poses the problem of choosing the most probable historical determination. This is the precise problem of modern man.[12] At this point, however, Marx is self-consistent (unlike many of his successors) when he excludes completely such notions as goodness, justice, truth, or other values from the decision. On the other hand he does regard as a conscious operation the choice of the most probable meaning when experience shows that in reality man acts more or less unconsciously and involuntarily, following the line of least resistance. The point is that man cannot tolerate being led only by necessity, and so when he does have to yield to necessity he vauntingly justifies himself by claiming that in letting himself be impelled thus he is achieving what is right and good.

Face to face with the complex determinations which pressure man in today's society one of the most dangerous illusions is to confuse freedom with the fight against dictatorship. To be sure, dictatorship is alienation and ought to be resisted. But the real dictatorship today is that which has its origin in the labyrinthine web of psychological, sociological, and technological conditionings. Fighting dictatorship does not rescue us from deeper bondage. But it kindles enthusiasm because of known cruelties and the secret police, whereas the fight against determinations arouses little interest, since these are not clearly visible and those who bring them to light are dismissed as intellectuals. Furthermore, for most people the only dictatorships to be denounced are those of the right. They see a distinction between an authoritarian government of the left and a dictatorship. The former is justified on the ground that it expresses the will of the people and is leading to a higher standard of living. It is forgotten that all dictatorships have tried to find positive solutions for the problems of collectivity. Hitler did much to improve the collective situation of the German people. As for representing the people, I need only refer to the criticism raised by Trotsky against party dictatorship as far back as the days of Lenin. In reality dictatorship of the left is identical with that of the right, as Lenin himself perceived. Taking away freedom has no more justification in the one case than in the other. The mechanism of our economico-political complex suggests that in certain conditions dictatorship is the only way to solve the

11  Cf. in analysis J. Baechler, *Trois définitions de la liberté* (1971). With great acuity Baechler shows that freedom of the will leads normally to a negation of freedom. Freedom is beautiful and distils a philter we cannot refuse, but it is a fatal one.
12  Naturally any element in society which in fact brings more alienation can be viewed ideally and theoretically as a means of freedom, as many writers have shown, e.g., de la Rochefoucauld, *L'homme dans la ville à la conquête de sa liberté* (1971). Ironically, however, what is achieved is not freedom, but the very reverse.

problems which arise and therefore fighting one dictatorship can lead only to the setting up of another. Thus military dictatorships can be defended as good and useful in black Africa, as was stated at the ecumenical Conference on the Church and Society.

Nevertheless, the problem can also be put at the purely individual level, and here one cannot say that all individuals are equally subject to the burden of this necessity. Certainly they all adopt more or less completely the collective attitude that we have just described in summary form. They all have a part in it. But there are differentiations between individuals just as we have seen that there are differentiations between determinations. To the extent that determinations are not abstract, theoretical, or philosophical for me, but can be analyzed in terms of *this* society and *this* epoch, it is not by a theoretical operation like that of negation that one can be free in relation to them. Mehl is quite right when he asks how a conscience which is simply a projection of negation can ever fulfil ethical tasks, or how a freedom which is null and without foundation can without caprice pose such tasks. But he is over-optimistic when he argues that the subject can disengage itself from the world which besets and determines it (*L'autorité*, p. 90), this separation from determinations being effected by a choice which brings the world before me as a task to perform, as an opportunity of asserting my presence in the world, as a field for the imposing of values. In reality there is no such separation from determinations if we consider the matter concretely. We simply have the process already described. For to view the world as a task to be performed is to measure the limits of possible achievement. But these limits are set exactly by the determinations. The only area of choice and value is in the adoption of what is most probable in the field of necessary accomplishment. One might say that the first step which is seen to be necessary—leaving open the possibility of a second step—is that of recognizing and evaluating necessity. But this means that there is no concrete possibility at all of disengagement from social, political, and economic determinations. The only freedom man has is to recognize these and to recognize that he is determined by them. The first act of freedom is a recognition of necessity, not theoretically, but with a personal reference, and an attempt to put this recognition to work by trying to assess necessity, to discover its meaning and significance. To face up to the necessity that is seen at work in oneself, to perceive that I myself obey necessity, and to consider the implications of this—this act of recognition is an act of freedom. But precisely because we have here a phenomenon of cognition, only an individual decision is entailed.

As we shall see later, this recognition of alienation, the way of liberty for Marx and Sartre, is the first act of the man who is seeking to be man. But it is only a beginning and may become extreme alienation. It entails disarray in man. Besieged by history and society, he finds he is nothing and has no power to change his situation. It can thus be supremely destructive. Man finds he cannot be free. Even his movement toward freedom is conditioned. This may work out at both the material level, the discovery of determination, and also the spiritual level, the inability to extract value from myth. It thus leads to insoluble anguish (Kierkegaard), that of finding oneself in the world and of the final submission to necessity which comes when man discovers that he is not just mortal but dying (Heidegger), so that he is subject to the ineluctable development of a destiny which no recognition of any kind can change.

To recognize necessity, to accept the fact that one is determined, does not have to mean endorsing the inescapable determination as one that is right and good. I perceive that I am acting under the constraint of a powerful social mechanism but I do not have to say that it is good. The spiritual problem arises only when I face the necessity which makes me act and pass judgment on it. In judging the necessity, however, I judge myself, since the one who obeys it, and has to do so, is myself. I am not a divine court which can see determinations from outside. I myself am implicated in their operation. I follow their movement. But I can also see it. Only as I do can I go further.

Now it should be noted that the constraints, of which we shall give some examples, are not necessarily those of the concentration camp or the proclivity to evil. They may well orient us to what society (and we ourselves) would regard as good and just and beautiful. It is not at all true to think that the good and the just are the product or expression of freedom. The striving after freedom will often bring incoherence, destruction, weakness, hatred, eroticism, and sterility. Social necessity will often constrain me to do what is regarded as good. Social necessity raises the standard of living, prolongs life, fights hunger, leads to the use of psychoanalysis, etc. These things are not the result of freedom. Furthermore, necessity cannot be rejected from the standpoint of the good. This would make no sense. The good is what expresses necessity. We have here the basic trap which prevents man from seeing necessity and knowing that he himself is determined. If the product of necessity can be called good, man focuses on the good and ignores necessity. In infantile pride he is convinced that he himself produces the good. He necessarily ascribes the good to his freedom, since he himself has produced it. Technologists take this view, and so, too, do the liberators of oppressed peoples.[13] When a social determination is perceived, we must beware of justifying it, of assimilating it to the good (because it may in fact produce what society calls good). For if we do so, we justify ourselves in obeying it and thus negate the first step of freedom.

Spiritually the most destructive and deceptive act is that of making a virtue of necessity. Obeying determinations is never a virtue even if it leads

_____

13 Naturally I am not against the liberation of oppressed peoples. My only point is that it is the product of historical necessities and not of human decisions, so that we cannot ascribe it to human liberty.

to success (choosing the best chance of historical realization) or the good (as our particular group defines it). This does not mean that we ought to resist all necessity (as if we could). What it does mean is that we cannot have and accumulate everything: independence and happiness, liberty and a sense of history, autonomy and efficiency, etc. On the contrary, we have to admit that it is perfectly normal to obey necessity. The man or group or state which obeys necessity is not to be condemned for this reason alone. A state has to have a police force and an army. A society such as ours has to explore for oil or create a television culture. We have simply to recognize that there is nothing sublime about what we do nor exceptional about our leaders. All this is normal. But this is not to say that it is good or that it is freedom. Once we have tried to consider the determinations and to recognize the necessity which to the same degree fix the orientation both of the society in which I live and also of my own life, I may try to reject what I see either by negation—obeying necessity is freedom—or by justification—to follow the movement of history is good. But I may also—and this is my only freedom as a natural man—try to assess the necessity, to isolate it, to analyze it, to pick out its significance and implications.

What does this mean for a society which has to obey the necessity? When I say that the state has no alternative, e.g., that it has to go to war, that it is under constraint in this regard, what judgment can I pass on the necessities which are at work in society and which have brought the state to this sorry situation? The necessity is not metaphysical but sociological. When I say that revolutionaries commit acts of violence and then blame the other side for starting it, I ought to consider the validity of this revolution from the standpoint of freedom even though I do not deny its character as necessity, as obedience to necessity. The existence of such determinations is not neutral, meaningless, objective, or scientific. On the contrary, it is charged with significance on and for the man of this society. And the deepest judgment one can pass on a society consists precisely in asking what necessity it is obeying, since it has placed itself in it. In this context and regard, from the standpoint of aloofness towards the determinations which are both collective and individual (even though I cannot detach myself from them thereby), from the standpoint of the view that to obey them is normal, how can I find and proclaim a good which is not to be equated with the necessity? The question is an open one, and Marxist analysis of this affirmation of value is always valid as an introductory criticism. If, however, I persist in spite of the criticism, this implies that I am questioning the necessities of this society which is also my own, including the determinations which I think to be good as well as those that might be considered bad. If I question the necessity of an increase in the power of the state, I am challenging social security as well as war. If I question the necessity of technological acceleration, I am challenging productivity as well as the hydrogen bomb. The one is just as much a product of necessity as the other, and once the necessity is accepted and justified, I have to accept both, for within a system of determinations man has no freedom to choose one item and reject the rest, to decide for this and not that, to make a selection. The worst illusion in actual society is not to see the global nature of phenomena, their close imbrication, and the impossibility of separating the good effects and the bad effects of the determinations to which we are subject. Man thinks that he is protecting his freedom in this way when in fact it does not exist at any level, and his pretension, and the apparent evidence that he can choose the one thing and leave the other, bears clearest witness to the way he is conditioned by his environment. Thus the man who thinks that he can choose between the good and the bad effects of technology proves by this very idea that he is totally set within technical determination and that he has not even taken the first step of freedom, i.e., that of seeing that he is wedded to technology for good or ill and that he must accept the fact, since not to accept it is pure idealism and can only give rise to illusions.

### § 3. Alienation and Necessity as an Expression of Sin

We have stated that we are writing an ethics for Christians. Hence in introducing the term sin at this point we make no claim to be offering an explanation or key. Nevertheless, if philosophy, neglecting the findings of the humane sciences, can affirm the freedom of man, why should it not be acceptable for the Christian to affirm man's sinful character? We are confronted here by choice and decision. If the decision of faith in Christ implies a reference to scripture, then I do not see how else real man can be described but as a sinner, born in corruption, and unable to do the good that he wants to do. Nor is this merely a kind of external condition which is added to a good nature. It applies to the totality of man's being and existence. We may not be prepared to talk of a sinful nature, but scripture certainly tells us that man is rigorously determined by his sinful condition. We may not want to think in terms of an original sin which is transmitted from generation to generation as it were by heredity, but scripture undoubtedly teaches us that from the very outset and once and for all Adam represents the whole of mankind before God, so that for God the sin which brings separation from him does not just take place once but is indissolubly present in everyone; there is no other situation or attitude.

Now our concern here is only with one aspect. Man's condition as sinner is described as one of bondage.[14] Man is the slave of sin and

---

14 According to Bonhoeffer the fall is refusal to live out freedom within the limit of the relation to others. It entails obscuring the structural relation of freedom and destructurizing the reality given by God (A. Dumas, *Bonhoeffer*, 1968).

ultimately of nothing else.[15] Nor is this a mere comparison, as we saw earlier. It is the simple reality. It affects all aspects of man. If the word "slave" has been used to describe man's situation, it is designed to show that sin not only has an inner form but also takes every possible outward form. It concerns the social and professional life as well as the spiritual life. The concept of bondage implies a refusal to divide man into a spiritual entity where sin is found and a material entity where other forces and realities are manifested.

We do have to distinguish, of course, between the domain of man's finitude and that of his sin. Finitude means that man has a body, that he is limited by space, that he is conditioned by such functions as having to eat. That he is set in nature to work there is also part of his creatureliness. The point is, however, that the body becomes a passion and eating an all-consuming concern. The appetite for material things becomes insatiable. Man comes to be possessed by his body and by what can satisfy it. Thus the simple mark of legitimate creaturely finitude becomes a slavery that results in separation from God. Similarly work becomes a law, a constraint, a way of dominating others, a mortal duty in virtue of its own domination, or the fabricator of idols and hence a delirious passion whereby what ought to be a joyous exercise is a bondage resulting from separation from God.

It undoubtedly results from this separation, for when man is in fellowship with his Lord he cannot set up any other god nor become the victim of any other passion or of mortal care. Hence sin perverts what ought to be the normal realm of finitude. Separation from God means that man is always seeking another god on whom he prefers to depend. He is always subject to the forces and constraints which are unleashed by virtue of the fact that all creation is plunged into the same separation by man, so that a reversal takes place and the king of creation is always and in all circumstances the dependent and slave. Ordered creation has become a battleground of powers that compete for supremacy. Now only God can exercise total supremacy. But the currents of power, the levels of its exercise, the options of conflict, can be so numerous and complex that it may finally be said that in a kind of circle man is always both dominated and dominating.

One of the merits of Marx is to have brought to light the universal character of alienation. In this world which wants to be separate from God, the condition of sin and mark of alienation is that each autonomous desire for freedom leads man into greater servitude.[16] Adam seeks to

---

15 This is why the new theology which wants to rehabilitate man and establish the validity of his works tends to reject as outmoded the conception of man as a sinner. But it contradicts itself in its insistence on the political need to liberate man. For what is the source of the evil will and the wicked systems that reduce men to slavery? Are they mere accidents of history?

16 Cf. the fine analysis of Bovon in his "Vivre dans la liberté." Pagans think they are free but they are slaves because they are strangers to the life of God and are deprived of

liberate himself from the limits which God has set for him and in so doing he enters into rivalry with other forces and becomes subject to sin. The whole of the Old Testament describes Israel's unceasing search for freedom and its constant fall into ever deeper bondage. It wants a king in order to be equal with other nations and it comes into subjection to political power. It makes alliances with Egypt and Syria to safeguard its security—being sinful it cannot accept the security which comes only from trust in God—and it is ravaged by Assyria. Separation from God and the law of sin entail this regular turning of man's desire and work into its opposite. Ecclesiastes has something similar in view when it says that "he that increaseth knowledge increaseth sorrow" (1:18). This sorrow is finally connected with distance from God, with powerlessness, and with servitude.[17]

If we say, then, that man's condition affects his whole life and that this is what is denoted by the social and legal term "bondage," this conception of man as a sinner has at least the merit of corresponding with the findings of psycho-sociology, i.e., with man's alienation and determinations. This is why alienation is to be regarded as the best modern equivalent of slavery as a description of man under the determination of sin. Thus the ethics of freedom has to take into account all aspects of this alienation. It cannot restrict itself to the purely inward side. One aspect must not be lifted out at the expense of others. For too long the church has concentrated on the inner, spiritual world. Sin has been made an individual matter expressed in conduct at the purely personal level. The matter has been dealt with at the individual level without reference to the global context. Bondage has also been made into an inner matter, into enslavement of the soul by the devil and spiritual isolation from God.

Today, of course, the temptation is to go to the opposite extreme. What counts is the material and social sphere, the political and economic attitude. The individual spiritual adventure has neither value nor import. The idea of bondage to sin raises a mild laugh and preoccupation with sexual purity or honesty in individual financial dealings is ridiculous in face of global problems such as contraception or capitalism and socialism. The collective dimension and social expression are where the problems of life are posed. What counts is not inner freedom from sin but, e.g., political liberty, the fight against colonialism, exploitation, and segregation. As usual,

---

his reality. They are thus alienated when they think themselves free, and this alienation finds expression in their desire to possess and in their despondency and depression.

17  In some Roman Catholic circles and in Liberal Protestantism the break with God is regarded as a myth, reintegration by grace is viewed as universal and total, and hence revolt against oppression (or an oppressor) is seen as an expression of human dignity. The man who seeks to fulfil his will and hopes is free. The man who fights is free. The man who accepts constructive responsibility in the world is free. Man in search of himself is called upon to achieve freedom. The universal affirmation of freedom is a good thing. For a list of such platitudes cf. L. Fèvre, *La liberté des chrétiens* (1969), who with great honesty, and many good intentions and sentiments, adopts all the truisms of the day on this matter.

there is a swing of the pendulum. It seems to me, however, that we should cling firmly to both aspects and remember that the two extremes are indissolubly connected with one another.

We must accept the fact that alienation and the determinations are expressions of the attitude of man before God, i.e., of his condition as a sinner. Oppression is the same whether at the level of an individual act or at that of global participation in an oppressing society. No matter what may be the form or structure of society, oppression constantly appears in it by virtue of man's inward condition. Conversely, it must be realized that man's sinful condition before God is not just an inward and personal affair. It necessarily finds expression in collective action, in participation in all the structures and forces of social, economic, and political life. No inward sin is without outward repercussions. No global phenomenon arises apart from man's sin. Thus the problem of an ethics of freedom concerns at one and the same time what should not be called two aspects of the reality of man, but this reality as a whole. Publication of the gospel of freedom will necessarily lead to the adoption of a position in relation to common problems. When we said earlier that alienation constantly appears and man unceasingly comes into bondage, we did not mean that this alienation should not be fought here and now or that freedom should not be attempted. Inwardly, too, I know that sin will return, but I cannot give up in discouragement. Liberated by Christ, I have also to liberate myself. I have to take up the fight unceasingly both for myself and for others, well aware of its relativity, yet attaching supreme importance to this relativity as the total sphere of life that is assigned to me, and thanking God for this relativity. For what would life and society be if our acts were not relative? The limit which constantly reminds us that we are in a world that is not hell is surely a happy one!

That alienation expresses what is traditionally called sin should not surprise us. Sin is alienation from God (Cheik Kahne, *L'aventure ambiguë*). The man who is alienated from God by his own, not God's, decision is also self-alienated. He finds his source in himself, imposes on himself the law of his own autonomy, makes himself the measure of all things, chooses his own good and becomes his own meaning. Behold the man!—real if not authentic.

Finally, in faith we can accept the witness of Jesus to man's bondage in John 8:37. We shall have to show that freedom has its source in the Word. If it is not in us, we are fundamentally unfree. This is seen in our desire to kill Jesus, who defines precisely our lack of freedom. Captive man takes God captive. He wants to use God. His bondage becomes the bondage and death of God. This took place. Jesus was put to death. Our responsibility for this expresses our inability to receive freedom. Jesus explains the act. It bears witness to an old situation perceived by history and sociology. There can now be no illusions. We can talk of freedom only in the light of the cross.

*Alienated Man and Liberation in Christ*

# Chapter 2

# The Freedom of Christ
# and the Emancipation of Man[1]

## § 1. The Freedom of Christ

We shall not attempt a theological meditation on the freedom of God, since it is impossible for us to talk about this. We cannot even say that God is freedom, since this would be pure speculation. God tells us that he is love; he has not told us that he is freedom. Certainly we can see no obstacle to his will and hence we cannot say that God is not free, but this again is inference. God reveals himself constantly as the liberator, which is something very different to which we shall come back later.

We know God fully only in Jesus Christ. Now Jesus Christ is free, and this—but only this—enables us to speak with complete assurance of the freedom of God. The Gospels clearly show that Christ is the only free man. Free, he chose to keep the law. Free, he chose to live out the will of God. Free, he chose incarnation. Free, he chose to die. Note the emphasis on choice. Choice is the most tangible expression of freedom. To speak of choice is to show that Christ is not in the same situation as Adam. In the divine fellowship of an as yet unshattered creation Adam did not have to choose. All that counted was the relation to God and its expression in action. Adam could break the fellowship, but strictly even in doing this he did not have to make a choice between alternatives. He was not asked to decide between good and evil. He had fellowship with God. That was all. He was then tempted to break this fellowship. He did not have to make a choice between two possible issues. In contrast Jesus Christ has been made like us in all things (apart from sin). He is thus confronted incessantly by choices. He comes up against the alternatives which characterize human life. Jesus does not have the sovereign freedom of God. Precisely because he is in a condition of finitude and even alienation his freedom is of radical significance. Naturally, when we speak of his condition of alienation we do not mean subjection to sin itself but subjection to the structure of a sinful

---

1 On Christian freedom in general cf. W. Brandt, *Freiheit im Neuen Testament* (1932); H. Schlier, *Von Freiheit der Kinder Gottes* (1947); L. Lochet, *L'Evangile de la liberté* (1968); H. Küng, *Liberté du Chrétien* (1967). I flatly oppose the thesis of van Buren (*The Secular Meaning of the Gospel,* 1963) that Jesus is the incarnation or personification of freedom.

world and subjection to sinful men. The situation and the decision of Christ may be seen in all their tragedy and triumph in the temptation.

At the very beginning of his ministry we have a vivid account of the temptation which was actually to be with him each day and which is reflected in every decision of the Son of Man. It is to the degree that he was tempted like us in all points (Hebrews 4:15) that Jesus is free man. It is also by considering the specific nature of the temptations that we can discern already the liberty of the one who is liberated by Christ. This is why we shall be bold to say a few things about the temptation of Jesus in spite of all that has been said already by scores of commentators.

Jesus is in the wilderness. This is the place where we do not find the social and cultural supports of life. He cannot be protected by environment or tradition. He is involved in a face-to-face encounter, which may be with God, but which may also be with the devil. For traditionally the desert was for the Hebrews the abode of spirits. Jesus stays there forty days—a familiar number which represents the period of total testing. He is repeating exactly the adventure of Noah. He is advancing towards the master of destruction and annihilation in order to bring about a new creation. It is the flood again in the sense that if Jesus goes down in this total test man will be at the end of his possibilities. Jesus is led to this test by the Spirit. The Spirit decides on it. To say that God puts his Son to the test is to say far too little. We are not to think in terms of testing for purification. God accepts the risk of losing everything. If Jesus is not tempted, nothing can be won for man, for in this case the test is not serious and Satan remains the lord of this world. Man is definitively alienated to Satan. God is ready to hazard his Son, not merely in death, but in temptation, in which the Son might usurp the glory of the Father and thus play the role of Adam all over again with an infinity which represents the fact that God betrays God. The temptation also comes after the baptism. Jesus has been acclaimed as the well-beloved. This surely does not mean that he is declared to be the Eternal Son, begotten not created. It means rather that God acknowledges him as man, as very man, as the authentic Adam whom God loves with the fulness of his love as he loved Adam. If a hint of deity is given, it is to be found perhaps in the phrase "on whom I have set all my love." God is love, and the totality of his love is placed by God himself in this man. Hence he, too, is God. As the Son, however, he is also the fulness of man. It is this human fulness which is to be subjected to temptation. He is going to meet the deceiver, the divider, and the accuser.

The three temptations are the sum of the temptations that man can encounter. In them Jesus faces all the possibilities of temptation. His later temptations, as he is well aware, are simply variations on those that he undergoes here. The first temptation is that of need at the most lowly, concrete, immediate, and pressing level, i.e., the need of food. After forty days Jesus is hungry. Satan suggests that he make the stones into bread. The whole sphere of physiological or bodily need is covered here, the sphere of instincts and elemental necessities. The problem is that of knowing whether primacy is to be given to hunger, to economic need. Is everything else subordinate to this? If man's first concern is to eat, the rest is surplus. We must be careful here. It is not a question of the harmony and continuity of needs. The problem is that of an either-or. Does the hungry man have absolute rights because he is hungry, so that he may do anything? Are we to say that worshipping God and obeying his commandments are all very fine but they apply only to those whose stomachs are full. Hence, as some say, we are not to spend our energies in preaching the gospel so long as Indians are dying of hunger, or, as others say, moral problems arise only when essential needs are met.[2] Now the point of this temptation is to warn us that the moral problem becomes truly serious only when the individual is subjected to cruel need; apart from this it is an intellectual diversion and a middle-class pastime. The temptation shows us that the word of God ought to have priority. This is the first true food. It is the decisive thing. Material nourishment is the additional thing that follows. This temptation, which covers all human needs including the sexual, teaches us a good deal about Satan's approach. Natural things are used, things which are good to eat, or which are valuable and reasonable in themselves. Let us begin by

---

2 This is why the first temptation is of particular importance for young Christians today. And we can relate it directly to freedom. A sincerely and deeply Christian girl, whose testimony is significant for this reason, said to me once that if dictatorships are needed to overcome hunger and bring economic progress to underdeveloped countries, then let us have dictatorships. This is a single instance of the widespread conviction that the most important question is that of food and raising the standard of living. Freedom is of little interest.

I can accept this in the young. But I take it amiss that adult Christians should yield to the shallow thinking that there is freedom only where there is food (La Fontaine had a better view of the problem), that freedom is only for the wealthy, that the only freedom of the rest, according to a phrase which is as stupid as it is striking, is to die of hunger, that the human race has never known freedom prior to our own day, and that Christians have no right to preach the gospel to those who are dying for lack of food.

These platitudes, which tend to justify our productive society and its focus on trade, fly in the face of the historical evidence and ethnological experience. The North American Indians and the Berbers of Africa, although poorly nourished, knew quite a bit more about freedom than our productivity experts, and as for preaching the gospel to those with empty bellies, our Lord himself seems to be a good enough example.

Naturally, we are to be concerned about human misery. The question, however, is that of correlating freedom and full stomachs, or of attributing freedom to a high standard of living. This is where the error lies with its implication that, if we have to choose, freedom must be sacrificed for a full stomach. It is on this basis that we could observe earlier that man is not all that concerned about freedom. He is ready to let it go. Ideologically freedom is a western term. But even western man has seldom known what to do with it. He is ready to give up anything for peace and plenty. If dictatorships can raise the standard of living, then let us have dictatorships. This brings us to the heart of the first temptation. The freedom of Jesus is that he prefers to go hungry rather than to follow the prompting of Satan and the demand of his stomach.

*The Freedom of Christ and the Emancipation of Man*

finding food. Then we can obey the word of God. Naturally if we accept the fact that the satisfaction of material needs is secondary as compared with obeying the word of God, we must always remember, and state with vigor, (1) that this is not a judgment on those who, not knowing Christ, try to meet their needs first, but on Christians who do this, and (2) that this is not a commandment that we can apply to others, so that the employer sees an excuse to neglect the material well-being of his employees or the developed nations a pretext for turning aside from underdeveloped countries since their primary need is spiritual. The temptation comes to each of us and each of us has to make his own response to it. What Christ undergoes is my temptation. The freedom to which he bears witness is the freedom to which he calls me. I have no right to put someone else in my place. When Christian employers or developed nations adopt the attitude described above, their attitude to men is in reality the same as that of Satan. What the temptation tells each Christian is that the primary response to needs does not lie in technical or economic development *at all costs*. This is a constant temptation, for mammon is not just money. It is all economic power under the symbol of money. A choice of priorities has to be made. Each Christian has to make it. There is, of course, no question of denying or rejecting the need of bread. Jesus, who is hungry, does not deny that he is hungry. He does not say: "Man does not live by bread." He adds: "alone." The temptation is to concentrate all man's life upon, and dedicate it to, technological and economic development. The temptation is to say, not that man does not live by bread alone, but that he lives primarily or essentially by bread. It is to harness the power of God to the meeting of our needs. That the baker should bake bread and that Jesus should eat it is fair enough. But one is not to try to bring the omnipotence of God into the circuit. It is lawful for man to work and to produce. But he must remember that this is a secondary and relative matter. The greatness and the glory of God are not implicated. This is not as such a fulfilment of the vocation of Adam. In my view the application of Psalm 8 to technology is a precise example of falling into the first temptation. What matters is that we realize that seeking God's kingdom comes first, and the rest (the response to every need, material, sexual, and so forth) is added to us. What matters is that we realize that man's attitude before God is one of waiting, of prayer, of hope, of supplication that a word of God will be granted, and with it all else. Man must not adopt the attitude of conquest, of seizure, of self-realization.[3] He must not repeat the act of Adam and lay his hands on the forbidden fruit. He must not create himself, as Marx put it, without bothering about God or

3 The active prototype of the complete aberration of the young Christian girl under the influence of sociological conformity is provided by Harvey Cox, whose sociological analysis is as superficial as his theology is vague. The important thing for Cox is that man should pull himself together and take his fate in his own hands, as though this were not precisely what he has always been trying to do. Surely we do not have to listen to Cox to become the captain of our fate and all that!

even considering whether he is up to the job. In our own society pan-technicism and the complementary pan-sexualism are an expression of the changing of stones into bread. What we have here is admittedly the normal view of man in his situation of autonomy over against God. But to the extent that Jesus exemplifies another attitude, which is that of freedom, we are forced to conclude that what man has chosen is his own alienation and that the result of his choice will be the exact opposite of the hopes of Marxism.

The second temptation in Luke—the third in Matthew—is that of power. At issue here is the conquering and ruling of all the kingdoms of the world. Once again it seems to me that rule is to be taken in the broadest sense. What is envisaged is not just military conquest or political domination but every kind of secular domination, including that of masters ("Do not call me master"), employers, ecclesiastics, institutions, parents, and so on. Every kind of power which men exert, or try to establish, over other men, is in view. Whatever may be the means of power, whether money, personal authority, social status, economic structure, military force, politics, artifice, sentimental or material extortion, seduction, spiritual influence, what is proposed by Satan is power in any or every form. When Satan promises Jesus that he will give him these kingdoms, he is not lying. He can do so. He is the prince of this world. While it is true that all authority comes from God, it is also true that every manifestation of power is an expression of the might of Satan. "You know that the princes of the Gentiles exercise dominion over them, and they that are great exercise authority over them" (Matthew 20:25). This is how things are. Jesus is not attacking or criticizing here. He is simply describing the situation in the world realistically. His description corresponds to the description of monarchy which God gives to Samuel when the people of Israel asks for a king. In the separation of man from God, this is how it has to be. There is no such thing as a good ruler (not even the sovereign people or the proletariat!). There is no such thing as a good master. This should neither horrify us nor surprise us. Satan controls this power and he grants it in order that men should subjugate one another. The granting of this power entails either explicit or, more often, implicit worship of Baal Zebub. In contrast, Jesus reminds us that he has not come to exercise power but to serve. In the Bible authority is always the authority of service. As Calvin puts it, this is an authority of fellowship rather than kingship. Thus the husband cannot be head of the wife in the sense of oppressing her or not considering her. He has to realize that the authority which he enjoys places him under the greater obligation (Sermon XXXIX on Ephesians). The same applies to all authorities. In this devaluation of force and government, Jesus shows very clearly that he attributes both their orientation and also their exercise to him who is always the prince of this world. "It shall not be so among you" (Matthew 20:20). "You see your calling, brethren, that not many wise men . . . , not many mighty, not many noble, are called" (1 Corinthians 1:26).

*The Freedom of Christ and the Emancipation of Man*

This stands in sad contrast to the church today in which there are many very intelligent people and not a few powerful ones too. But even if some Christians do wield power in society (and this ought to cause problems), Jesus strictly reminds us that it must not be so "among you" (and the temptation shows how this applies to Christians), but that "whosoever will be great among you, let him be your minister." Faith means that there is no more power to exercise. Nevertheless scripture constantly brings before us servants and masters, children and parents. It criticizes neither the hierarchy nor the rule. The essential point is, however, that the texts themselves base power on obedience and (social) superiority on an attitude of service to the other. In other words, any human superiority can be accepted in Christ only if it expresses the will to serve of him who serves, who is under rule, who is subordinate. In faith the subordinate, whether employee, child, or citizen, should accept this situation of service as part of his condition as a Christian. He must transform the obligation imposed on him into service for Christ.

I realize that this will give offense to many people today. The only course that they regard as acceptable is that of abolishing subordination. But how can Christians let themselves fall into this trap of independence when the whole of historical, social, and political experience shows that in all circumstances and at all levels movements of independence have always, without exception, replaced one form of subordination with another that is far more strict? I am also aware of the fact that the superior will try to force or pressure the subordinate into accepting his position for spiritual reasons. In the case of a non-Christian superior this is normal. It is what Jesus was talking about when he said that the great exercise authority. The scandal is when the superior is one who claims to be a Christian and he is using God's word to get himself obeyed. This happened in the case of the middle class in the nineteenth century and it gave Marx good cause to denounce religion as the opium of the people, for, biblically, it is both satanic to use God's word in this way and also wrong that a superior should ever manifest himself in any other way than as one who serves. Whether he be husband, parent, teacher, statesman, employer, or pastor, he is to put himself in the service of those over whom he has authority. He can never use a means of external authority. He is not to use his authority to his own advantage nor as something self-justified. In Christ the relation between superior and subordinate rests on a twofold foundation of service. No other relation is legitimate. It is an illusion to think that we can get out of this situation of service. Service is always at issue. The problem is that of knowing whom to serve, and in this regard the temptation is clear. He who uses the means of domination, power, and authority, he who crushes and exploits others (whether it be the one who crushes or the one who is crushed, for a rebellious people that crushes its former masters is simply a new master which uses power in worldly fashion)—such a one is in the service of Satan.

Now it is true that we come up against the same problem in the church. Here, too, we find dominating powers. But now it is purely man's fault. The legitimate authority which ought to hold sway in the church is of a different order. It can change its character, however, because man is still a sinner and he brings back his false freedom and will for power into the church. He thus uses the word and the truth to crush and subjugate others. But this is man's doing. It is not integral to the church even as an institution.

To attain to power in any manifestation man has to bow down to Satan and worship him. There is no legitimate power as such. Acquisition of power in this world is linked to service of the prince of this world. Appearances to the contrary, there can be no question here of either service of men or service of God.

When Peter uses his sword at the moment of the arrest of Jesus he is not defending the cause of God. He is serving Satan. Jesus himself has power (the twelve legions of angels). But he does not use its weapons. In other words, the exercise of power, the employment of the means of force and domination, is a sign of lack of freedom. To serve Satan, who is himself bound, is lack of freedom *par excellence.* To renounce the means of power, to serve by willing to obey God, and thus to worship God alone, is a mark of the freedom that Jesus Christ gives. It is by renouncing the manifestation of his power that Jesus Christ is fully free (cf. Kierkegaard on this).

The third temptation is spiritual. Although it is not so easily perceived, this temptation is just as common today as the temptation of materialism or that of power. Satan wants to get Jesus to give a demonstration or proof that he is the Son of God. The site chosen for the demonstration is the temple itself. Figuratively one might say that Satan puts Jesus above his Father when he leads him to the pinnacle of the temple which is God's abode. This is the temptation of all those who want to assert themselves, who want to be independent of God, who reject their situation as creatures, who think that alone and by themselves they can fulfil man's vocation and find the key to life, or the meaning of their history within it, either in a universe of their own fabrication or gods of their own invention, in sum, in anything but the God of Jesus Christ. This is especially the temptation of the intellectual, the scholar, the religious man, the artist. Man as a creator in some way takes himself to be the Creator and tries to replace him—an act which is in part applauded or justified by the new theology in what is obviously a justification of Adam too. For it is the act of Adam when he takes it upon himself to decide between good and evil. Religion is undoubtedly the most enticing form of this temptation. It seems to be obedience to God when it is really an invention of man and a means to satisfy his religious needs. The same is true of morality. In all this we have the temptation: "Prove on your own that you are the Son of God." As creatures, we too are God's sons and we are constantly tempted to demonstrate it. Note that the more true the sonship the greater the temptation.

For Jesus himself it was total. It is less for man, and for modern man less than for Adam, since its reference now is to a less authentic object.

Of the forms of this temptation for modern man those of science and art are less severe than that of religion, and that of religion is less severe than that of Christianity. For we have to realize that Satan can use God's truth itself to tempt man. He even uses holy scripture. He tries to trap Jesus in a biblical text, in a prophecy which Jesus would in fact fulfil. Thus obedience to the letter of scripture can be obedience to Satan if the text serves to bring about isolation and independence in relation to the one who has inspired it. It can be a means of self-affirmation over against God in repression of his truth and his will. The biblical text, and obedience to it, do not guarantee anything. They may be the best means of not hearing God speak. This statement is perhaps a bewildering one. But we should never forget the problem of the Pharisees, who were authentic believers, faithful adherents of scripture, and rich in good works and piety. In reality everything depends on our attitude to the text of scripture. If I seize it, use it, and exploit it to my own ends, whatever these may be, then I am obeying Satan under the cover of what the Bible says. Perhaps I want to prove my theology, or acquire merit before God, or show that I am right, or find evidence that I am fulfilling my divinely given vocation, but in each case I am manipulating Jesus Christ and his death and resurrection and trying to demonstrate that my own attitude, even if it is that of a publican, is in itself sufficient before God. It is thus that all of us use scripture far too often. It is thus that Christians justify themselves when they refuse to admit that the fall is radical and that separation from God is total. For they try to show on a scriptural basis that they still have worth and are still in a relation to God quite apart from the relation in Jesus Christ. In addition to the fellowship with God in Christ there is also a fellowship with God by means of the situation of unseparated creaturehood. The worst feature here is that Jesus Christ is himself used to restore worth to ourselves, to validate what we do, not as believers, but simply as men. For when by means of a christocentric theology we confer on mankind restoration to man's first estate, we confer it on ourselves. We do this when we allege that in Christ religions of man's own invention are an approximation to revelation, a mediation, an inclination of man towards the God of Jesus Christ, or when we allege that (in Christ) technology is simply a fulfilment of man's God-given vocation to exploit the earth, to till Eden, and to deplenish the riches of creation in so doing. All these are Christian ways of yielding to the temptation of Satan and of thus becoming representatives of Satan on earth.

Now the divider's use of the text from Psalm 91 is worth noting. He asks for a proof of the sonship of Jesus. This seems to be quite legitimate. He does not deny the sonship. He simply asks for prophetic verification as he allows that Jesus is the Son of God. To this end he takes a fragment from the psalm and mockingly breaks it off from the continuation which

*Alienated Man and Liberation in Christ*

characterizes the Son of God who is protected by the Father in terms of his love, his obedience, his gratitude, and his refraining from any pretensions to be the Almighty (Psalm 91:14–16). The extraordinary thing is that the fulfilment of the prophecy of this psalm lies in the fact that between verses 10–13, to which Satan appeals, and verses 14–16, there lies the temptation. It is at this point that the obedience of Jesus to his Father and his lack of any pretension to be the Almighty fulfil the saying in the psalm. It is not fulfilled by an attempt on the part of Jesus, relying on verses 10–13, to realize for himself what is a promise that God will fulfil when he chooses to do so and not when man, even though he be the Son of God, decides to bring it into effect. At the point when Jesus refuses to make God's decision for him, he takes a very great risk. Under his Father's protection he would not have risked anything physically if he had in fact jumped down from the pinnacle of the temple. The angels would have intervened to save him. But if he had done this he would no longer have been the Son of God. Under the protection of his Father he would not have been taking any intrinsic risk. He risks himself, however, when he decides not to give any demonstration in this regard. He risks himself when he rejects public investiture with the power of God. The temptation is the same as that put to him by those at the cross who, acting for Satan, told him to save himself and then they would believe in him (Matthew 27:40–42).[4] They would believe in the Savior if they saw a miracle demonstrating unambiguous and incontestable power to save. The risk that Jesus takes by refusing is that everything remains ambivalent, contestable, and unproved. For Jesus this meant taking a very great risk.

If we can assimilate all human temptations to these three temptations of Jesus, we certainly have to realize that our temptations are infinitely less total, complete, and radical. They correspond far less to what Jesus is than to what we are. Jesus can in fact effect the miracle of changing stones into bread. For us there is no question of miracles. Only by a circuitous route can we accomplish similar changes. Jesus can also prove that he is the Son of God, since he is this in fact. For us, however, there is need of lengthy groping and a constant effort to discover in what we do a meaning that is not immediately obvious. Jesus has in fact come to be the Lord of the world and to establish the reign of God among men. Our power, however, is always fragile and unstable, and if we were sure that we existed for this we would not put so much toil and trouble into ensuring it. Furthermore, when Satan addresses Jesus, what he proposes is precisely what God has charged him to be and do, namely, to rule creation, to be the Son of God,

---

4  This reminds us that the three temptations sum up and symbolize all the temptations that Jesus encountered as we see them. Thus the first corresponds to the temptation of fear of death in Gethsemane, to the temptation to heal for healing's sake, and to that put by Peter, while the temptation to enter Jerusalem as a king, or to use force to resist arrest, corresponds to the second.

to come as the Lord. This is God's will, but, used by Satan, it becomes temptation. When the tempter comes to us, it is also under the cover of God, but with a radical difference that is based on the ambiguity of our condition as creatures. The temptation is weaker and less total, as is in keeping with our own strength. It is also more ambiguous. Nevertheless, it is fundamentally the same.

In the first case Jesus is tempted to grasp for himself, by the miracle that he can perform, that which he should await from God. In the event God does in fact feed him after the temptation. In the second case Jesus is tempted to establish rule over the world by force instead of by service and sacrifice. He is tempted to take what is his rather than waiting for God's sovereign exaltation in virtue of his own self-abasement. In the third case Jesus is tempted to demonstrate and prove what God wills that we should simply believe.

Now if Jesus had yielded to temptation,[5] he would apparently have done exactly what he had come to do and yet at the same time the totality of the work of God for the salvation of men would have been negated. Hence in the temptation, which prefigures the dereliction on the cross, God actually risked everything, his Son, his creation, and in the last resort himself. Now in the face of temptation what Jesus has is infinitely fragile. He simply has the revealed word. This is why he does not make up his own replies to the three temptations. He does not search for an adequate rebuttal. He does not try to concoct his own defense. He refers on each occasion to what is written, to the prophecy of the Old Testament, which is so obviously sufficient, so perfectly in accord with the will of God, that Jesus can efface himself behind it.[6]

In the temptation Jesus does not use his own power to overcome Satan. He does not make the affair a contest of force or wit. The only conflict is between obedience and self-affirmation. In the attitude of obedience Jesus does not even ask for a miraculous intervention by God which would rid him of Satan but which would also mean that the temptation was ended by the power of God.

On the contrary, Jesus knows that the word recorded in scripture is truth as such. He does not dissociate himself from what is written or from the revelation of God which is truth. No doubt it is because he uses the written text that this text becomes the undeniable fulness of the will of God. But the fact that he uses this alone, that this is enough for him, shows that for him only the written text, apart from and along with the incarnation, is the only event—not a past or dead or ossified event—in which God has revealed himself and is accessible to man. Jesus knows that the word

---

5 We need not enter here into the question whether Jesus might have yielded. This theological problem is beyond our present scope. I will simply say that as the death of Jesus was a real death, so his temptation was real temptation.

6 It might be noted incidentally, and polemically, that the attitude of Jesus here is not very Bultmannian.

recorded in the Bible is fully adequate to repel Satan and to nail his lies, since this word relates always to him who spoke it, to the eternal Father. In all the temptations the biblical text offers the reply, blunts the edge of the temptation, and offers full satisfaction to that which in man serves as a point of entry for the temptation, to that which in man makes Satan's temptation seem to be legitimate, self-evident, and normal. The word which comes from God is the response to all the necessities to which man is subject. Jesus renews it when he says that he has another source of nourishment, i.e., that his nourishment is to do the will of his Father (even though he still needs physical food). Man is called upon to feed on the word of God and this is the reply to the necessity which oppresses him.

So too in face of the temptation of power the only reply is the adoration of God alone which puts the powers in their places and at the same time sets a limit to the power of man by recognition that he is a creature and no more. In face of spiritual pretension the final answer is that this is tempting God himself. Jesus does not seem to be saying here that he is God and that in tempting him Satan is tempting God. On the contrary, his point would appear to be that man's desire to demonstrate his own spiritual supremacy is a temptation for God—the temptation to destroy man, to reject him, not to love him any more, to turn from him. Thus Jesus turns to God alone to learn what he has come to do. He is perfectly obedient.

This is where we see his freedom. He is authentically and completely free in the fact that he accepts his relation to God. He allows that he has come only to do what the prophets foretold. He has no pretensions of his own nor independent will. This true and total freedom is disclosed with regard to the physical necessity that is laid on human life, with regard to power, with regard to human pretension, and with regard to temptation itself. Jesus is not the slave of sin.

This freedom is also disclosed in the choice which he makes with such free sovereignty in his locating of the debate. His replies are fully adequate, as we have noted. But they are in a sense "off the point." They put the battle on a different plane from that which Satan selected. Jesus manifests his autonomy and independence over against the necessities, the world, and Satan by refusing to accept the perspectives of Satan or to be caught by his dilemmas.

This freedom is manifested too in the choice or decision of Jesus not to use forces that he might legitimately have used. No one could take his life from him. He himself gives it. He might have refused. He might have kept his life. But he gives it. This is his sovereign freedom. We need to remember this, for if Jesus is fully man, if he is free as man, then his freedom is not the exercise of superior power. It is not an unrestricted use of all his capabilities. On the contrary, it is a renunciation of possibilities, a refraining from use, a controlled mastery of force.

Again, the freedom of Jesus is manifested in his choice or free decision not to shelter in the power of God nor to hide behind God. For the freedom of Jesus is not a renouncing of being himself. He exists as Jesus. He is not an amorphous shadow of a sovereign God who works automatically. It is as a free person that he chooses to obey God. In so doing he assumes full responsibility. He does not throw the problem and the solution back on God. He takes the very opposite stance from that of Adam, who blamed the woman that God had given him.

This is something that we must remember in relation to Christian obedience. Freedom is not sitting back and letting God work. Freedom is knowing God's will and doing it. God is not a *tertium movens* or a *Deus ex machina*. Jesus respects God's own freedom. He shows his love and obedience by not referring Satan's question to God. Hence he is truly free, both in relation to Satan and also in relation to God. For if obedience to sin, the flesh, and the world is bondage and alienation, obedience to the will of God is freedom, and cannot be anything else.

The tragic mistake has always been that of changing God's will into religion or law, i.e., into something which binds man and effectively alienates him afresh. The tragic mistake has been that of regarding obedience to God as servitude. This has been Satan's supreme achievement in the spirit of men. If God himself is free, however, he surely cannot bear to be obeyed by slaves. He surely wants obedience to be free and voluntary. If God is love, surely he cannot tolerate being loved in return, not freely, but out of fear and debasement. Love presupposes freedom. God can hardly subjugate without being confused with Satan. This is why obedience to God's will is itself freedom. Jesus exercises the freedom of God himself when he obeys. We, too, are invested with the freedom of God himself. It is thus by fulfilling scripture as the will of God that Jesus bears witness to his freedom in the temptation. For us as well being free men means discerning this will in scripture and obeying it.

If, then, we too can live as free men in Christ, this is because of the word of God. The only true, complete, absolute, and intrinsic freedom is that of the word of God. For this word is the basis and ground of our freedom, as it was of the freedom of Jesus himself. It is necessary, then, that we should consider what the freedom of the word is. To this end we shall follow the remarkable analysis of Karl Barth.[7]

Our task is to find out what is the specific power of this freedom which differs from all other freedoms. Barth at one point makes a sharp differentiation between the power of the word of God and man's own religious forces. He recalls that the freedom of this word is a power and that this coincides with what we say about the power which is demanded of the Christian as a free man. The freedom of the word of God implies a questioning of the intrinsic abilities of all subjects.[8] But the power or

---

7  *Church Dogmatics*, I, 2, pp. 673ff.

8  The work of Jesus may well be described, with Cardonnel, as anti-fate, but only so

might repay the ransom and regain his freedom thereby. Or the redeemer who paid the ransom might remit the debt and he would immediately become free, having the status of a full citizen and not of the freedman, who still had some obligations to his former master. The man restored to citizenship in this way was an *ingenuus*. He was regarded as "born free." He had no obligations to anyone. He was again in the fullest possible sense a citizen.

Now this was the redemption that the fathers had in view when they adopted the metaphor. It was not changed under the Empire until the fifth century, and even then the significance and content remained the same. In our view the use of this concept by theologians is perfectly adequate and even today it gives point and meaning to the work of Christ. It is important that the fathers chose redemption rather than the manumission of an ordinary slave. Redemption implies that man was originally free. He was a citizen of the kingdom of heaven. He became the prisoner of an alien and hostile power. He came into bondage to this stranger and completely lost his humanity. His redeemer paid the ransom and then freely and graciously remitted the debt which ought to have been paid back. In consequence of this, man not only regains his freedom but also becomes a full citizen again of the kingdom of heaven. He is fully reintegrated into his former position, unlike the manumitted slave who is never completely free. This comparison is a good one, since there is exact correspondence to the reality of the work of Christ for man.

Theologians adopted this terminology because it was familiar in the Roman world, especially in the third and fourth centuries A.D. It had a place in the vocabulary of the time. It evoked images which everyone could understand. It made possible a transposition of the spiritual work of Jesus Christ into the socio-political experience of the age. It made this work generally intelligible.

To insist on the term today, however, is to produce obscurity and incomprehension. Our task, then, is to retain the content but to find a modern institution or socio-economic reality to which we can relate it in the same way. It seems to me that the term liberation is too vague and weak to serve in this capacity. It does not have the rich connotations that redemption formerly had. Another possibility is "de-alienation," but this is not a popular or simple word, nor does it have adequate force. It is easy enough to replace slavery by alienation but the new system of imagery does not seem to offer a similar replacement for redemption. We certainly have to begin with alienation, and this can hardly lead us on to the thought of ransom (which has no modern reference) nor to that of reimbursement or free remission, nor to comparisons between a freed prisoner and a manumitted slave. In other words, the juridical mechanism cannot be retained. Nevertheless, we have to take into account the fact that alienation means possession by "another" with complete despoilment of the self. It also implies the gracious character of the work of God in Jesus Christ and the

*The Freedom of Christ and the Emancipation of Man*

inability of the prisoner or the slave to liberate himself or to have any part in the transactions which might take place between the one who frees him and the one who holds him. Finally, it implies total reintegration into freedom.

To do justice to these elements we have to use a different socio-economic context and refer to a different mechanism. It seems to me that the familiar analysis of Marx, according to which a revolution consonant with the meaning of history brings liberation to the alienated, offers some points of similarity but cannot be used because it insists on self-liberation. Lenin's doctrine is better in this regard, since it gives the party a media-torial role on behalf of the proletariat. The work of the party with reference to the alienation of the proletariat corresponds figuratively to that of Jesus Christ with regard to the alienation of man. Since the proletariat cannot liberate itself with its feelings of revolt and spontaneous reactions, the work has to be done from above. The proletariat comes into the act when it recognizes the reality and is thus in effect de-alienated already. Along these lines the work of Jesus Christ is a revolutionary action in the sense that it is a revolt against alienating forces. This action is consonant with the meaning of history, except that this is not the meaning seen by Marx but that established by God. The liberation effected by Jesus Christ means that man is transported from Eden to the earthly Jerusalem in a recapitulation of all human history. This is perhaps the best way that we can make the work of Jesus Christ intelligible to many westerners today who have come so greatly under the influence of Marx.

We should not entertain any false hopes. If we say that the true revolution is that effected by Jesus Christ, not by Communists, that Jesus Christ is the true liberator from alienation and not the communist party, that this de-alienation leads to the kingdom of heaven and not to a communist world, which is no less alienated and alienating than a middle-class world, then we may well get a hearing but the battle with Commu-nism, far from being ended, will be all the more open and vigorous. For after all, to the degree that Communism represents the true power of the actual world, the conflict is simply a reproduction of that which raged in the earliest days of Christianity when it was asserted that the only Lord is Jesus Christ and not the emperor. We have to realize that if we do in fact update both our Christian vocabulary and our way of explaining the work of Christ the battle with the forces of the world will regain its fierceness. For the movement will always be that of a basic theology using current concepts. What man tries to do socially, politically, and so forth is illusory. The one redeemed is not truly free. The only true redeemer is Jesus Christ. Only the act of God is true. When the concepts are put to this use, accusation is leveled against the world's work and its meaning is confiscated in the interests of the lordship of Jesus Christ.

What we are proposing is obviously the direct opposite of what Bultmann has been sponsoring. Bultmann begins by affirming the given realities of the world, e.g., science or history, and then proceeds to criticize, not just the modes of explanation, but the very core of what is passed on to us by the Bible. When the Bible has been stripped in this way, all that finally remains is myself in relation to a God to whom I have given existence. The same applies to the attempt of Tillich to find common ground between culture and revelation. What is clearly needed here is the either-or which is more consonant, I think, with scripture, not the synthesis or reconciliation which each age attempts with new methods and which gives no help to those who famish through appeasement and toleration.

If the work of Christ which has traditionally been called redemption is in full reality the transforming of a prisoner-slave into a free man who participates in the freedom of Jesus Christ himself, it is evident—and this will be one of the constant themes of this study—that we are not dealing merely with matters of behavior, with "ethics," but with a change in man himself. More than the external situation is at issue. If we were to retain the metaphor of the prisoner today, we might conclude that no more than the situation is involved. He was behind bars and now the door has been opened. But whether inside or out, he is the same man. This is another reason why the metaphor is no longer adequate.

In Roman law the prisoner-slave was not the same man. His whole being had been changed. He no longer had any family. His marriage was declared to be dissolved. His wife could remarry. He was regarded as dead. His goods were distributed among his heirs. He no longer had any civil rights. He was removed from the list of citizens. This is why redemption was a real return to life.

Today the idea of alienation is more adequate. It, too, suggests an attack on man's being. Alienated man is not just exploited. His very being is changed. His relations with others are disrupted. His relations with nature are falsified. He is inwardly lacerated. He is stripped of all that we think makes a man a man. De-alienation is more than being released from jail. It is the full, inward reintegration of man.[11] Similarly the freedom which we have in Christ is a way of becoming new. Jesus Christ gives us a possibility of being which is quite different from any that we have in ourselves or can acquire by our own work.

It seems to me that this change gives us the most profound and total view of man that we can have. For man can no longer be defined now as a being booked to die. Reduced to his own dimension and alienated, he is indeed booked to die. He is subject to all the determinations and can move only from the one to the other. He knows himself only in his flight and vanishing. He sees himself only as a "has been." He lives out his life only as

---

11 Ricoeur (*Philosophie de la volonté*) puts this well when he says that freedom in hope is not just freedom for the possible but more fundamentally it is freedom for the denial of death, freedom to decipher the signs of resurrection under the contrary appearance of death.

it slips away. He may prefer illusions and contemplate his activities and a future which he can imagine but never grasp. But this is only another form of dissolution. From determination to determination he advances in a constantly narrowing circle. As life goes on necessities become more numerous and take on a fatal aspect. The number of possibilities decreases daily. What he could do yesterday he can no longer do today. The number of his liberties is restrained, not by the fiat of a tyrant, but by the force of things, and perhaps it should be added that this force affects not only individuals but also collectives and groups, which are also progressively pressed into narrower and less numerous paths. This reduction of possibilities continues until he reaches the final necessity which is the climax of the long process of restriction, hardening, restraint, and deprivation. Death is not just a cutting off of life. Nor is it its opposite. It is the ordinary conclusion of the increase of determinations in every life. Its rigidity simply symbolizes what we have long since become.

To define man as a being booked to die is to say in effect that there is in him no fount of freedom nor possibility of passing into a state of freedom. To say that man is booked to die and yet to attribute intrinsic freedom to him or the possibility of acquiring it, is self-contradictory and gratuitous. It is not possible for the man who is booked for death to attain to self-liberation, or to do anything which will survive death, or to nullify his own situation and secure freedom. He has no choice here. "Liberty or death" is not an option. Nor is there any triumphant way to "liberty and death." Death without freedom is the only reality. The idea that man can elevate himself, especially in Sartre, is in the last resort only a concession to death.

If man is really booked to die (as he is), and this is more than a pleasant philosophical formula for intellectuals with which we can take all kinds of liberties because it is not taken seriously, this means that man, bearing even in life this mark of destiny, can never at any point escape its rigor. Changing political or economic conditions makes little difference. Going to the moon confers no greater freedom. Collectivization of mankind does not mean that in a group man can be what he is not as an individual. As for the common talk of freedom through violence, violence may destroy one political order but it simply replaces it by another that is equally restrictive. To be sure, individual violence can be an outlet for pent-up feelings and can soothe the nerves, but apart from this the idea of its liberative value is infantile and pathetic. Other means of release at this level exist in plenty. Alcohol and drugs are the most common. But human experience teaches us that the pretended freedom which man thinks he finds for himself in one way or another never pays off. It simply leads to greater restriction and narrower determination. The tyranny of Louis XVI yields to the dictatorship of the Convention. The exploitation of Russian capitalism under the Tsars yields to the vampirization of the communist state. It is when man proclaims his own freedom that he is most firmly riveted to his beloved chains. The ways to freedom are the more surely ways to slavery, as may be seen today in our vast technological enterprise. If we consider facts and not hypotheses, if we break free from our dreams and desires, we shall have to accept the common experience that man cannot free himself from his determinations. The best he can do is to change them, to break away from one and submit to another. The great temptation—and philosophers offer many examples—is to close one's eyes to this sombre reality, to put reason to sleep, and to let dreams of freedom flourish, not even daring to admit plainly: "I am only a poor and fallen king, but the kingdom of illusion is mine."

As in the case of the prisoner, freedom has to come from outside. [12] There has to be an invasion from without. There has to be someone who decides to free this man, who sees to the necessary legal formalities, who opens the door, who intervenes, i.e., who places himself between the prison and the prisoner, between the machine and the material it uses, between the master and the slave, between the need and its satisfaction, between death and mortal man. No freedom is conceivable for the one who is booked to die unless a liberator comes from beyond death. There is no freedom without mediation.

This is true even in the natural order. In all areas mediation is the condition of the concrete possibilities of secondary freedom that man has actualized. The mediation of the hand brings liberation from the mouth in speech. The mediation of the tool liberates primitive man. The mediation of culture means liberation from nature. Liberation from tyranny comes by the mediation of law. I have never contended that these liberations, these approximations to the liberty to which man feels called, are not possible. But each carries with it a new alienation. In the new situation set up by the mediation, intervention is always needed.

For true freedom there has to be a mediator who is not circumscribed by the context of what is merely human, since the point at issue is that man should be liberated from his condition. This mediation cannot be the work even of the man who is to be liberated from his specific reality and to cease to be man. Nor can this mediation be the work of an abstract force, e.g., the movement of history in Marx. History knows only the play of necessities, and necessary mechanisms never lead to freedom. Furthermore, events since Marx have shown that the communist world has not expanded simply by the play of dialectical necessity. Man's willed interventions have

---

12 We are at odds here with the view of most Roman Catholic theologians, and also some modern Protestants, as this is naively expressed by L. Fèvre (La liberté des chrétiens) when he states that God has confidence in man and that the church right up to Vatican II also has confidence in him, in his creativity, experiences, and freedom, so that it has been led to recognize and to strengthen his liberties; Christian freedom simply adds fulness of meaning to ordinary human freedom, since freedom can come only from the human person, gushing up from within. This romanticism may be very comforting but it bears no very evident relation to biblical thinking.

*The Freedom of Christ and the Emancipation of Man*

also had a hand. History in the abstract did not bring Central Europe into the communist camp. What did it was occupation by the Soviet army. Nor was the victory over Hitler the product of dialectic or an imperious law. It was due to a concatenation of fortuitous events and a grouping of military, industrial, and social forces. An accumulation of necessities will never create a new and different condition. It will simply produce more necessities.

What is required if freedom is to be possible is the intervention of the Wholly Other, of that which has nothing in common with the human condition, of that which is not subject to any necessity. Reciprocally, if man is introduced into a new mode of being which is that of freedom, then he ceases to be a creature that is booked for death and becomes a creature that is destined for life, since the two specifications are strictly interrelated. This does not mean, of course, that there is an automatic transition. We shall see later that a serious question arises whether our affirmation is valid for the totality of men.

The mediator who comes from beyond death, who is not shut up in the human condition, who assumes it, who comes into the determinations and the condition—this liberator by whom and in whom is freedom, is given to us by God in his Son Jesus Christ. It has to be so. If it were not, there could be no hope of freedom of any kind for man. It is Jesus Christ who existentially makes the creature that is booked for death into a creature that is destined for life. Here is the basis.

In Christ we can no longer see man as natural perception, biological examination, and philosophical analysis show him to be. We are forced to admit that at a level that neither our senses nor reason can penetrate man has become different. This transformation is the work of God by the insertion of the Wholly Other into our condition and history. From this moment our history and condition are changed as water is changed into vapor by the action of fire; they are the same and yet they are quite different.

The creature which is destined for life can now be free.[13] Our reference is to a man who is and remains freed but is not free by nature and origin. He is placed in a new situation. This situation does not imply the negation of God's will for him, of the commandment. On the contrary, it is because he is free that the commandment now takes on its true meaning.

By analogy this reminds us that the change in situation does not modify the will of God which is revealed for us in scripture. In other words, the modifications in values brought about by the transition from traditional national societies to a global industrial society give the impression that morals are changing fundamentally and that the commandments correspond to various types of society which are now outmoded, e.g., patriarchal

13 Bovon ("Vivre dans la liberté") has admirably described this freedom as christological, eschatological, and pneumatological. We need only refer to his analysis here.

*Alienated Man and Liberation in Christ*

(as in the Bible), feudal, or bourgeois, so that the only thing of abiding worth in our society is an invitation to unconditional love with varying applications to different situations. The New Testament itself relates to different personal cases and sociological situations the one mystery of the offering up of Jesus Christ through unconditional love. But in offering himself up Jesus claims that he is fulfilling the law and the prophets. The commandments are not set aside; they are actualized. Situation does not replace norm. It allows its incarnation. Marxist and Freudian criticisms may well assume that the commandment is in the interests of the dominant class and represses the instincts, but we still find in the law the content which love can fulfil rather than deny.[14] This is a connected development of the relation between the freedom acquired in Jesus Christ and the ethics of this freedom. Not only is man freed by the intervention of the liberator. Implied in this change is his initiative in the way of freedom. For what would be the point of being free if there were no responsibility for this freedom? We thus move on from being to behavior, from the new situation to its expression, or, in other words, from liberation as Christ's act on and for man to the life in liberty which involves more than a direction, even though this comes from Christ himself, and more than a commandment. This is why we should begin with the ethics of freedom. The rest will then be written on the heart and will flow from it.

We must be more precise. When redeemed and freed, the Christian is not put in a state of freedom. Liberation is not a point of departure or cause or principle from which a free existence follows. What the Bible describes is infinitely more complex. Throughout the Christian life there are renewals, new interventions and commitments, each expressing both freedom and eschatological irruption. This redemption does not introduce us into a new situation of freedom. It is an act, not a virtue. We agree with Kierkegaard, Bultmann, and Malet that freedom is not a quality but may at each moment become an event. Malet's distinction here between the Stoic view of freedom and the Christian affirmation seems very convincing to me (*Mythos et Logos,* 1962, pp. 26f., 221).

A being in freedom is given in Christ. This reality has then to be lived out. If freedom can be gained only as the fruit of intervention and mediation, if it results from the act of the mediator, once it is achieved it is impossible that the liberator should establish a tutelage or direct and dictate the acts of liberated man. On the human level this would be like ex-colonial powers which have granted liberty to African peoples claiming that they must still watch over these peoples so that they will use their freedom well. From the human standpoint this is easy to understand. It accords with human logic. But the result is not true liberty. The problem of the ethics of freedom, which begins with the liberation granted by Christ, is to discover what can be the choices and orientation of this man who has

---

14  Cf. the 1965 Conference on the Church and the World.

been freed, and yet to do so without enforcing a fixed model, a body of doctrine, or stereotyped conduct, and thus making ethics a negation of freedom.

A final remark is in order. When we referred earlier to the condition of alienated man and the strictness of the determinations, I realize that the reader might be tempted to reject what scientific knowledge has increasingly forced us to admit. But I was writing here for the Christian. What shows us even more radically the depth of servitude, the pressure of necessity, and almost, one might say, the fate of man in his present situation, is the fact that no less than the death of God himself was demanded for his liberation. The Father had to tear himself away from the Son. The Son had to humble himself, become a man and a slave, and die. This abnegation of the Father and the Son was needed. Gethsemane was needed. No less could free man. The greatness of the work of the liberator is an exact measure of the depth of the bondage. If this had only been an accessory of man's life and situation, if there had been another way to freedom, if there had been even a feeble will and determination whereby man might have raised himself up, if there had been an intrinsic mechanism in mankind making for liberation, then there would have been no point in God's sovereign sacrifice and self-abasement. There would have been no point in the anguish and agony of the impassible God. There would have been no point in the death of the living Lord. It is when we start at the cross of Jesus Christ, and at the strict chain of circumstances which in the depictions of the Gospels show how the machine rolls on which leads Jesus implacably, if also voluntarily, to his death, that we can begin to appreciate the greatness of the necessity which pressures man and which we can never minimize. Furthermore, this point of departure teaches us that the one who was sovereignly free did not live out this freedom in the clouds or permanently as the one who walks on the water. He lived it out in a world of necessities which he accepted as such. He knew hunger and weariness. He felt the pressure of forces. At Gethsemane he experienced even his Father's will as a kind of constraint. He submitted to the restrictions that his social environment imposed.

So then, if we start with the freedom of Christ as those who are freed by him, this liberation does not entail an objective suppression of necessities and determinations. We know very well, and we often feel, that it is a burdensome limitation, a defect in the work of Christ or in our law, that we are still subject to sickness and death. Moreover, even as Jesus declares our freedom, he warns his disciples that they will be the target of the most virulent persecution on the part of the world. ("If ye were of the world, the world would love his own; but because ye are not of the world . . . the world hateth you. . . . If they have persecuted me, they will also persecute you" [John 15:19f.].) Now this means the exertion of tremendous pressure and an actual increase in necessities and determinations, as though they necessarily became more extreme the moment liberation came through Christ. Precisely because death has been vanquished in Christ and resurrection is a fact, we can have no illusions about death. We cannot regard it as the natural end of life. We cannot depict it as a friend, a solution, sleep. It is the king of terrors. It is a threat to creation. And it becomes the more rigorous precisely because of the resurrection and the victory. The cross of Jesus Christ tears away all illusions about it. Our freedom to live is not, then, a suppression of necessities. It is freedom lived out within and by means of the determinations.

Freedom is introduced by grace into a world of necessities. It does not form a free zone or privileged status for certain people. It produces the interplay of tensions and reciprocal challenges. Appearances seem to suggest that determination is incompatible with freedom. Nothing is more false. Freedom has meaning only in relation to an authentic necessity. Freedom is fate overcome, an obstacle surmounted, a limit passed, a sacred sphere secularized, a burden on man lifted (cf. Ricoeur, *L'herméneutique de la liberté religieuse*, 1968). Freedom loosens up a tightly regulated mechanism. It is a little space where man can breathe in the midst of constraints. It is the recoil from political restriction. It is the transcending of an imposed suffering or end. But this Christian freedom is concrete freedom. It is lived out in man's reality. It is not just mystical or spiritual. It is a recognition rather than an evasion of reality. It is not a taking refuge in miracle or the bosom of the church. It is an apprehension of the totality of man and its setting in a new dimension of his being. This is what redemption leads us to, at least on the ethical plane.[15]

---

15 Bultmann, e.g., in his *Primitive Christianity* (1956), constantly confuses freedom with autonomy or independence. Thus he says that freedom is part of the Greek and Hellenistic legacy and argues that it is a concept alien to the Old Testament. He finds a striking analogy between the freedom of the Stoic and Christian freedom as Paul understood it (pp. 142ff., 185ff.). To my mind, there is in fact a radical difference between the two: Stoicism traces back freedom to man. Bultmann is misled by his strange idea that Christian freedom means being resolutely open to the future, although he recognizes that this involves a distinction from Stoicism, since Christian freedom is open to all encounters as man commits himself to grace, whereas freedom for the Stoic means that he is closed to all encounters and lives in a non-temporal dwelling. In spite of this, Bultmann takes his view of freedom from Greek philosophy, makes of it a matter of ideas, and is thus unable to appreciate the Jewish reality of liberation. This leads to significant aberrations. While freedom comes by the gift of the Spirit, it is still man's own power. As openness to the future it means accepting as occasion arises the desire that God has to act. It is because Bultmann is so confused that I cannot accept his interpretation.

# Chapter 3

# The Universality of Freedom

We are now confronted by an introductory question of supreme importance. If the freedom of man is the result of the sacrificial death and resurrection of Jesus Christ, if Jesus Christ came for all men on the earth, if freedom is connected with the fact that Jesus Christ has become the Lord, and if the Lord is the Lord of history and of the human race as a whole, can we refuse to allow that this freedom is the freedom of all and is to the profit of all? Man was a slave and he has now become free. Vigny has a fine description of this in his *Les Destinées* when he first presents man as pale and withered and bowed down, but then the cry goes forth and all stand up straight again. The condition of man has thus undergone an ontic change. In Chapter 1, however, we wrote about the alienation which exists and the determinations which seem to be both better known and also more numerous than ever. Surely there is a contradiction here. On the other hand, can we really say that freedom belongs to Christians alone? Would not this be an inadmissible privilege? Does not experience in any case prove the contrary?

## § 1. Metaphysical Freedom or Ethics of Freedom

To ask whether all men have access to freedom in Christ is necessarily to consider the matter from the standpoint of what I pejoratively call metaphysics.[1] It is also to bring it into connection with fate. We have been at some pains not to describe alienation as fate, that is, as a universal and irremediable power which man can do nothing about, in which he does not participate, and which strictly conditions the totality of human life without any possibility of resistance or rejection. This is not our point. We are not suggesting that man is just a well-regulated machine made up of wheels and cogs and obeying a detailed and implacable law. If we confronted this kind of fate, we should have to speak in absolutes.

---

1 Naturally we shall not enter here into the debate between the bondage and the freedom of the will or into the problem of predestination. These questions are discussed today in philosophical terms which are very different from the terms used in the sixteenth century. In my view, however, Luther's works on *The Freedom of a Christian Man* and on *The Bondage of the Will* are still pertinent today, although one has to demur when he fails to distinguish between the freedom of life which is given by grace,

On the one hand we might say that Jesus Christ has done his work for all by overcoming fate. But fate is no longer fate if it can be even partly broken, if the mechanism is loosened a little, if it will no longer ineluctably attain its objective, if man can escape it. In such circumstances it is simply an inconstant and uncertain force. It can no longer dominate some and not others. A kind of cosmic miracle has taken place. That which even the gods obeyed according to antiquity has now been reduced to nothing and all men escape fate and become free if the problem of their freedom is raised at this level.

On the other hand we might say that the work of Jesus Christ avails only for those who believe in him But what does this mean? It means that fate remains the same for men. It has not changed. But there is now one possibility of vanquishing and surmounting, or rather escaping, fate. This is by giving oneself to Jesus Christ in faith. To do this is to break free from the circle of fate.[2]

Now it seems to me that both answers are wrong. The unacceptable element in the first solution is the magical nature of the operation. Man is a purely passive object and the work of Jesus Christ is a kind of *opus operatum*. Everything is done outside man. He has no knowledge of it nor

---

the need of freedom to exercise Christian faith, the civil right of religious freedom, and the freedom of the Christian in the church. He had to be within Christendom to write as he did in *The Babylonian Captivity* that "neither pope nor bishop nor any other man has the right to impose a single syllable of law upon a Christian man without his consent . . . no law, whether of men or of angels, may rightfully be imposed upon Christians without their consent, for we are free of all laws" (*Three Treatises* [1960], pp. 193ff.). This presupposes that all men in the social structure are Christians, and that authority recognizes the freedom which is given in Christ. Now it is not just that circumstances have changed. We have here a wrong interpretation of the relation between man and society and a wrong understanding of freedom in Christ. One has to remember that Luther's interpretation of freedom is marked by a certain dualism and overemphasis on the spirit according to which the freedom of the body does not serve the soul, since this is not a slave when the body is, so that the only problem is that of spiritual freedom. "All things are yours" means spiritual sovereignty; the attribution is spiritual. The Christian's freedom is to love God, to obey his commandments, to be his priest. The works of freedom are fasting, watching, and working for God. Spiritual freedom derives from faith and its work from love. This leads Luther to the conclusion that Christian freedom is not independence in relation to others but service; its main concern should be to meet their needs. Nevertheless, for Luther the real question regarding Christian freedom lies elsewhere: " 'You will see heaven opened, and the angels of God ascending and descending upon the Son of man'. . . . It is a spiritual and true freedom and makes our hearts free from all sins, laws and commands. . . . It is more excellent than all other liberty . . . as heaven is more excellent than earth" (*ibid.*, p. 309).

2 As I see it, the question of fate has been raised in a new way by Leopold Szondi, *Introduction à l'analyse du destin*, I, 1 (1971). Setting aside metaphysics, he approaches the matter from the standpoint of concrete determinations, eagerly assembling the findings of genetics and depth psychology. The concept of destiny is thus viewed from such varied angles as the structural, the functional, and the impulsive.

does he take part in any way. He is changed by a stroke of the wand, by an act that remains strange and secret to him. The drama is enacted in heaven, or hell, or at any rate a region to which man has no access. The victory of Jesus Christ is a purely divine affair except insofar as it might involve shady transactions between God and Satan about the price of man's liberation, as in certain fathers. Man was a slave. He becomes free. But he knows nothing about it. Whether Christ has been preached to him or not, whether he has received baptism or not, he becomes free and acts (unwittingly) as a man who has been liberated from fate by God's act. There are thus two categories of men, those who for hundreds of years lived under fate, and those who since the incarnation live in freedom. If, on the other hand, the work of Christ is retroactive, there never was any fate, and what is the point of the whole masquerade? All this seems quite unacceptable to me, nor does it agree with what scripture teaches about the work of Jesus Christ. Christ became flesh and his work was done on earth even if it did have cosmic dimensions. This fact alone shows that God did not want to push man aside and act on him from without. The incarnation would not have been needed if he worked in this way. He could simply have decided to abolish fate; it would have been as easy as that. The incarnation at a specific time and place means that Jesus did a localized work, a fragmentary work, a work of which we see only the commencement and the signs. Furthermore, the Bible shows everywhere that from creation onwards God never acts without man. God loves man. Hence he never regards him as a mere object. He respects man. Hence he never acts on him from outside. God is no magician. He does not rule out man's love and commitment and cooperation. When Jesus heals he asks for this cooperation in the form of prayer and confession of faith. God does not do unknown and incomprehensible works. If he reveals himself, then even in his incomprehensibility this is in order that man may know him as his partner. All this shows how impossible it is to talk of the work of Jesus Christ as an *opus operatum* which changes everything, including the very essence of man, independently of man himself.

It is equally unacceptable, however, to say that the victory over fate depends on the faith of man. This is to magnify unduly both man and his faith. The work of Christ is merely passive and virtual, not actual, on this view. Man has to grasp it and make it active and actual by his faith and decision. This is to make everything individual, since it all depends on faith. But to regard Christ's work as a kind of box of pills in a drawer which is inert until I open the drawer and take one of the pills and swallow it is just as contrary to revelation as the first hypothesis. Faith alone is not what frees man. The work of Christ does not have validity and power only for him who declares his faith. In this domain of freedom we do not have two classes of men, first, those who remain subject to fate because they do not believe, and secondly, those who have become free through faith.

To my mind, if the problem seems to be insoluble, this is because it is seen from a metaphysical angle. The great debate between the bondage of the will and the freedom of the will is equally badly put. Biblically, freedom is not situated on this plane.

To ask whether man is free apart from grace is not to talk of freedom in the way that scripture does. To ask whether, at the moment when God reveals himself, man is free to respond or not, whether acceptance of revelation thus depends on human choice, is to raise a false problem. No fate determines man, whether it be mortal fate on the one hand or divine fate on the other. What separates man from God is not fate; it is sin. Sin is not fate even if it does bring man into a world of necessities and determinations. The problem of freedom must not be connected only with the moment when man has to choose his spiritual destiny, when he has to make a decision in the presence of the grace of God. The Bible does not tell us whether he himself chooses or not to believe or not. It does not even ask this question. The question does not arise. For even if we grant, as I do, that sin is an impassable and insurmountable barrier, that man cannot of himself gain access to God, and that Christ's work has not changed the situation globally, even so, when God reveals himself to man, when the distance between them is removed and every barrier is broken down, no choice has to be made, since what is at issue is not a solution but a fellowship which is set up in the possibility of reciprocal decision. God's word, when it is addressed to man, places man by virtue of the address itself in a position in which he can hear it (it opens his eyes and ears), so that he can enter into this work of God and be in fellowship with him (cf. Castelli, *L'herméneutique de la liberté religieuse*, 1968).

The work of Satan has been unhappily confused with fate and that of sin with the bondage of the will. This forces us to turn again to the Already and the Not Yet, which seem to me to be incontestable. Thus the kingdom of heaven is already among us and yet it will come at the end of the age. Again, we ourselves are already saved but have still to work out our salvation with fear and trembling. In fact this movement cannot be given a full logical explanation. One cannot say that what is virtual now has to be made actual later. Not at all, for all Christ's work is already fully sufficient. It is not just virtual. It has already been finished. Nevertheless, one cannot see it or grasp it yet. Again, one cannot speak in terms of given principles from which conclusions will later be drawn. Nor can one speak of an inner reality of salvation which is yet to be seen externally. No logical or chronological explanation is adequate.

It seems, then, that we must hold together two contradictory truths. As concerns sin, which is separation from God and not just the individual acts of wrongdoing that result from this, one might say that it is suppressed in Christ, since in him God and man are identified, there is no more separation, and reconciliation between God and man has been fully made. In terms of the perfect reconciliation made in Christ, all humanity is reconciled to God, or, better, God has reconciled all men to himself. It is

God who does the reconciling of the world. Nor is anyone left out. Nevertheless, one cannot say at all that this accomplished revelation is lived out by all men, nor that all behave as reconciled men, nor that the movement of reconciliation is now from man to God. The movement is always a unilateral one from God to man. The gulf between the two has been filled in. Separation no longer exists. But more than ever man acts as though God were infinitely and incommensurably far away, as though the separation from him were more radical than ever. It even seems as though man's attitude is wanting to accentuate the distance. Oddly enough, when the separation was decisive, man tried to get back to the absent God by every possible means, religions, vows, sacrifices, ziggurats, prayers, and magic. But now that God is present, now that he has made reconciliation, man has radically renounced any possibility of rejoining him or hearing him. He has assigned God to his heaven, or his nothingness. He has absolutized the separation at the very moment when it no longer exists. In the presence of such a fact, which is seen to be repeated wherever Christianity goes, one can say only that the truth provokes in man a supreme outbreak of revolt in its most radical and aggressive form.

This is to say at one and the same time both that the work of Christ is universal and also that it is arrested, rejected, and undermined by the very one in whose favor it has been done. We are obviously tempted to see here, not so much another manifestation of sin, but rather the work of the very power of the revolt and accusation, namely, of Satan. For we have to say the very same thing about Satan. We have undoubtedly come to see that Satan, and with him all the powers or *exousiai,* was vanquished on the cross by the death of Jesus Christ. Satan has been stripped of his power as an accuser before God. He has been hurled down from heaven. Whereas he used to stand incessantly before God, denouncing man and trying to obtain a sentence of final condemnation, there is now seated at the right hand of God the one who unceasingly pleads for man, who intercedes for him, who tries to obtain a sentence of grace, and who can do this because he took the place of the one who ought to be condemned. This traditional image, which is naturally to be construed as such and not stupidly confused with a material reality, is an admirable one and offers a good reading of the situation. Satan has in effect been totally deprived of his ultimate power. He who is the master of falsehood and the worker of death has been decisively robbed of any possible victory because the absolute truth has been made flesh and has lived among us. Because death had to let its victim go, the resurrection has taken place effectively. The man who was dead has risen from the dead, not just spiritually, or in the faith of the disciples, but in the most concrete way, as John's Gospel rightly insists, although not in any sense as a concession to man's spontaneous materialism.

This victory over Satan is not just a virtual one. We do not have to await the progressive unfolding of its consequences. It will not become effectual later. It is a present situation. It can neither be negated nor reversed. Satan is denounced as such. There can be no mistake about it. The recommencement of the history of Eden is possible. If Satan has been bound by Christ for a thousand years, i.e., an infinite span, he has also been let loose for a short time (Revelation 20). I think the distinction here, however, is one of degree as well as time. Not only is Satan able to act only for a brief period (the last days). His absolute power has been broken and only a relative and (for God) minimal power remains. The difference is similar to that between the thousand generations and the three or four generations of the second commandment. Satan is still as such the prince of this world. It belongs to him, as we have already said. Its power, riches, progress, and history are under his control. It is he who institutes capitalisms and imperialisms. It is he who establishes states and triggers revolutions. It is he who formulates moral systems and provokes transgressions of such systems. It is he who formulates morality and provokes its transgression. It is he who structures progress and makes it so fatal. World events are the product of his actions as they constitute the history which God uses to set up his kingdom.

We cannot say, of course, that after Jesus Christ history is simply the history of God united with man, and so there is no longer any difference between sacred history and secular.[3] This is both true and false. For even after Jesus Christ the components of history are still the same as we find them in Revelation, namely, war (and political power), famine (and economic power), and sickness (with the whole demographic context). But there is now a fourth component, which is the true conqueror. This is the word of God. History is still made by the liar, who attaches unexpected consequences to all human hopes and actions, and the deceiver, who continually cheats man of his legitimate expectations. Attained unity is continually disrupted by the divider, both at the individual and ontic level and at the national level. Satan can no longer hope to win. He cannot destroy man. But he can constantly upset the course of history. He can foil God's work in detail. He can set man against man. He can impose the crushing weight of necessity on man. He can plunge him into an ambiguity of life from which there is no exit. This characterizes the last times (Matthew 24).

It is childish to try to deny the concrete and visible reality of history as we live it, and also the biblical text, by talking disdainfully of little Jewish apocalypses and rejecting all apocalyptic in the name of a dogmatic construction on the basis of what is supposed to be the essential kerygma (e.g., that where sin abounds grace superabounds). Man has undoubtedly entered upon the last days. The times changed with the historical coming of

---

3 In place of the dialectic of Already and Not Yet one might refer here to the noteworthy formula of Kierkegaard, namely, that as Paul, when he says: "I am a Roman citizen," can be put under house arrest but not imprisoned, so, when a man cay say: "I am a citizen of eternity," he can only be put under house arrest by necessity, but not held captive.

Jesus. After his birth history is no longer the same. There is a qualitative distinction of the times and a break in their order. The historian may regard it as irrational, inconceivable, and unacceptable. Nevertheless, the Christian centuries are quite different from all those which preceded. Nor is this only a spiritual or divine break. It is a real change in the significance and the actual content of history.

Theologians agree, however, that this does not imply entry upon a new aeon. The new creation has not yet come. It has not even begun at the level of civilization, of human works. It is hidden, enclosed, shut away, invisible, and incommensurable. It is the kingdom of heaven which is like leaven, differing from the dough, yet incorporated in it, and finally changing it. It is the grain of wheat, which differs from the earth and produces a product different both from the earth and from itself. It is the treasure hidden in a field, mysterious and useless, but present and finally put to use by man. Everything is changed by this presence even though nothing is changed. Historians can describe the history of the last two millennia in exactly the same way and according to exactly the same methods as in the case of preceding centuries. This shows that unless we want to spiritualize the work of Christ—and this is a great temptation to those for whom the Already takes precedence—we cannot claim at all that the realized and actual lordship of Jesus Christ modifies in expression and nature either man or his work, society, and history. The fact that we are in the last days and under the lordship of Jesus Christ does not mean that the kingdom of God is being set up by our hands. Scientific or technological progress does not in itself prepare the way for the coming of the kingdom. We are still wholly on this side, i.e., of the barrier which still radically exists even though it has been crossed by Christ. Man has in no sense become the new Adam. The fact that he is under the lordship of Jesus Christ does not change the perverse character of what he does.

Nevertheless, this is to be carefully distinguished from the problem of salvation. Even though I could hardly teach it as dogmatic truth, I might accept the fact that all men are saved by Christ. It seems to me that the universality of salvation is implied by the fact that the totality of condemnation fell on Christ. Since Christ was God, he did not assume a mere part of our condemnation, or the condemnation of a section of men. The measure of his deity means that he bore the condemnation of all men. Hence there is no condemnation in Christ. Even while I admit the theological and biblical difficulties which this opinion involves, it might still seem that this is a gracious gift to all men and all ages by the God who is love.

This belief in the universality of salvation, however, does not mean that I have to equate this salvation with the work of man. The lordship of Jesus Christ is not displayed in any validated work of man. Man is saved in spite of his works. His works are not automatically validated by the universality of salvation. Man is under the lordship of Jesus Christ in spite of his history, and his history (which he himself makes) is not automatically sanctified or validated by this lordship. The universality of the salvation and lordship of Christ does not mean that the freedom universally acquired by man comes to light. Man is not clothed with the freedom which is attributed to him whether he knows and wills it or not. He is not restored to the original freedom of Adam. He is not invested with a kind of freedom of nature in the sense that all that is said about the man whom God willed and created, and about the works of this man, may be applied without further ado to all men.

Outside faith, man is always the one who rejects the reconciliation with God that has been won for him. Outside faith, he is always the one who yields regularly to the three temptations put to Jesus Christ. If by these temptations we can measure the true freedom of Jesus Christ, then to the degree that these temptations portray the actual way taken by actual man we have to recognize that this man is in no sense free. Although saved, he is nevertheless in bondage. Although saved, he is not by necessary consequence free. What he has in virtue of the work of Christ does not find expression in liberty even if he does belong to the kingdom of heaven. This is surely what the Bible teaches very plainly. We have stressed it only because there is a powerful tendency today to confuse the actual and universal sovereignty of the lordship of Jesus with a specific characterization of history and of the works of man, as in the culturalization and the resultant relativization of scripture and ultimately the death of God teaching and the whole movement of secularization and humanization.

We must now try to say more precisely what is the value of the freedom acquired for man by Jesus Christ. This raises again the problem of the universality of Christ's lordship. It has been said that this lordship is universal but hidden. It is radical yet not expressed. Instituted, it is not institutional. Royal, it is also mediate.[4] Total, it is "suspended."

As I see it, this is easily explained. Our reference is to the lordship of him who is servant. He does not cease to be servant because he has been exalted by the Father above every name or power. We do not have three stages, the first when the word was God, the second when the word humbled himself and became a servant, and the third when Jesus was lifted up with sovereign power. As the servant, he is the Lord crowned with thorns. When he is the glorified Christ, he is the suffering servant, the lamb always slain before God. Hence his lordship is not the control established by a king.

Opposition arises between this lordship and secular states, i.e., the political power exercised by man. This is the lordship of love. Hence it does not use force. It can be exercised only in a mutuality of love. It is in no sense authoritarian. The Lord is he who constantly stands at the door and knocks, waiting until the door is opened, not because he could not force his way in, but because, being love, he does not want to exercise his authority

---

4  Cf. Kierkegaard's emphasis on the individual.

without the assent of the one upon whom he exercises it. Because the only face of this lordship is one of love, its only authority is that which is based on reciprocal love. The love with which God loves man can be rejected or flouted by man. If it is, no authority or lordship is exercised. Everything depends on reciprocity.

We may now take a further step. In these circumstances the lordship of Jesus Christ cannot be an immediate lordship.[5] Jesus Christ does not manifest himself as the Lord who directs man and history. If God is self-revealed as the eternal Lord in the Old Testament and the Apocalypse, this is only on man's behalf and in address to him. Man's response is needed by this lordship. One might say that it is in order not to assume authoritarian control of the world that God manifests himself as the "I am."

In spite of separation and the fall, God decides to continue the mediateness which he set up in Adam's favor in Eden. God does not himself supervise his creation. He leaves this job to Adam. As a result of the fall, Adam is no longer God's vice-gerent. He aimed to be the lord of creation. He is. But he exploits it in very different conditions from those set up by God. Like the husbandman of Jesus' parable, he wants both the produce and the property. He denaturalizes creation. He exploits it to death. He leaves it no rest. He subjugates it to his own ferocious appetite. In return, nature is no longer friendly to him. It brings forth thorns and thistles. It represents danger, resistance, and hostility. Relations between man and creation are no longer reciprocal in the way that God intended.

Nevertheless, in his patience and out of respect for man, God lets things be. He is still the Lord. But he is not ready to exercise direct lordship outside the participation of man which he willed for Adam. The only problem is that the power of mediation between God and creation cannot be restored to all men. Strictly, it can relate only to those who acknowledge God's lordship. Apart from this any such restoration of power would be meaningless. Or rather it would imply, not God's patience and love, but his abdication and abolition, as we see it in the death of God theology with its desire to give man absolute independence and autonomous responsibility (cf. also Harvey Cox). If man were reinvested with his mediatorship without recognizing expressly that Jesus Christ is Lord, this would mean on the one side that God gives man ownership rather than stewardship of creation and on the other side that the design of Satan in Eden finally succeeds. Now if God gives man this mediatorship, it is in order that man confess him as God and use his power for God. When the power of God takes on the form and aspect of the lordship of Jesus Christ, which is in truth the only form and aspect of God's sovereign power that we can know, this means that the lordship can be exercised only through the mediator-

---

5 As unbelievers and some Christians constantly suppose, substituting man's idea of God for the God hidden in Jesus Christ (cf. S. Cotta, *L'herméneutique de la liberté religieuse,* 1968).

ship of man, but obviously not of all men. To allege that the man who does not know or acknowledge Jesus Christ can be the mediator of his lordship means identification of man and Jesus Christ and severing of the relation between the servant Lord and God. Only he who confesses the lordship of Jesus Christ can be made a representative of this lordship by God.

To be such a representative man has to be free. It is in the form of free man that creation can mediate God's power. It is to the extent that man is restored to freedom that he can exercise the lordship of Christ. We thus have two theses. First, this lordship is exercised only through the mediation of man, and secondly, man has to be free man to be the intermediary. Man becomes a vicar, king, and priest in this freedom (1 Peter). This is the only rationale and significance of his freedom.[6] All freedom's orientations and decisions derive from this mediatorial function. So, too, do its limits. And so do the persons who are called to this freedom.

This freedom is not a gap which is to be filled, an indeterminate force which is to be used, a field of open possibilities which is to be exploited no matter how. This freedom indicates man's vicariate and *vice versa*.

We have said that the lordship of Jesus Christ is both actual and secret, both total and suspended. This is simply to say that it is mediated. Jesus Christ is the Lord. As several parables show, however, he is the Lord who is not present. The recollection and the promise of his power are present. He himself is undoubtedly with us to the end of the age. He is in and with his church as Saviour, Comforter, and Lamb of God. But he has committed his power to his servants. As concerns the actualization of his lordship and its exercise, it is exercised by the man who is freed for his service.

Now if it is true that freedom is the condition of the man who is called to exercise and express the lordship of Christ, it is plain that the real problem of freedom is not metaphysical. The problem of freedom is ethical.[7] For the lordship exercised by men is not the lordship of glory or omnipotence. It is not the lordship of Christ Pantocrator. In this intermediate period it is a secret lordship which does not manifest itself in miracles or authority but in love, word, and freedom. As Jesus Christ is Lord when he refuses to be so at Satan's behest, so it is with the man who exercises this authority for Christ. As we learn from the parable, he must not begin to beat his fellow-servants or to exploit them. He cannot exercise

---

6  Cf. Tillich on justification and freedom and Bonhoeffer on freedom and relation.

7  Moltmann, followed by Ricoeur, has formulated the ethics of hope as an ethics of mission (the promise, *promissio*, means mission, *missio*). In mission the present obligation is based on the promise and opens up the future. This ethics of mission has social and political implications. It does not center on subjectivity or personal authenticity. It invokes a reconciliation which has to find expression in the recapitulation of all things (Ricoeur). This is all very interesting and true, but it seems to me that mission does not exhaust all the ethical implications of hope. The true ethical question is that of freedom; mission is only part of this.

his authority after the manner of the world. This is no more and no less than the authority of the Lamb which was slain.

On the other hand, this lordship has to be expressed in society, among men, and ultimately in the world. In other words, a specific manner of life is required of the man to whom Jesus Christ commits this lordship. He is called upon to express this lordship by his conduct, life-style, decisions, and choices. The lordship begins in him but is also to be manifested through him. Plainly, then, only he who knows that Jesus Christ is Lord can live out this lordship. Only he who believes and confesses that Jesus Christ is true God and true man, that he was crucified to save men, that he died and was raised again, can be summoned by God to denote and signify the lordship of Jesus Christ.

In this regard the work of the word differs from that of sociological, economic, and political forces, which are by nature blind and necessary. The action of the word is always election (*eligere,* "to choose from"). It is never a generalization or globalization. As God is not yet all in all, so the word is not a general law and its field of action is not *ipso facto* the whole world. The freedom of the word, which calls forth the freedom of the Christian, is the act of choosing a specific man or area which is not designated as an order of creation but which is designated and circumscribed by the word itself. "The kingdom of God is really the kingdom of God, and therefore its establishment is not surrendered to the power and control of man. Not even the most passionate missionary spirit, not even the deepest sensitiveness to the need and longing of the world, can alter in the very slightest the dividing line between belief and unbelief, obedience and disobedience, which in this world separates the sphere of God's lordship from a world which is not yet reconciled with Him. Nor can it alter the fact that for our human eyes this boundary is determined by the distinction between the service and contempt of the Gospel . . . so that it is defined by the boundaries of the Church" (K. Barth, *Church Dogmatics,* I, 2, pp. 686f.). This means that freedom exists only for the man who confesses Jesus Christ as Lord and Saviour both with his heart and with his lips. If man is to be sanctified, and, as we have seen, this is related to his freedom; if he is really to belong to God, then he has to recognize that the commandment of God judges him. In this judgment he has to accept his condemnation and execution. It is by recognizing this that he becomes free. There is no other way. There is no other possibility.

I realize that this runs contrary to the strong modern movement of authentic Christian humility which has it that Christians do not differ from other men and that the work of Christ avails totally for all men. Assent has already been given to this insight, but not as regards the vicarious and mediate exercise of Christ's lordship. It seems to me that we do have to distinguish between the man who knows and the man who does not. This knowledge is not just virtual. It is more than theoretical and intellectual knowledge. The fact of knowledge, as the Bible everywhere teaches, is a

*Alienated Man and Liberation in Christ*

fact which concerns the whole person and engages the whole life. It is often said that the only difference between Christians and other men is that the former know who Jesus Christ is. This is true so long as one restores to "knowing" its full biblical significance as a commitment of the whole life, wisdom in the practice of life, and a realignment and reorientation of life. From this standpoint knowing is decisive and not just supplementary.

We have said that in order to be the vicar and intermediary of the lordship of Jesus Christ man has to be free, and that these two things are tightly linked. The only freedom that God gives is for service. Conversely, one cannot mediate lordship unless he is free. Furthermore, he who knows Jesus Christ as his Lord is free (cf. Vahanian in *L'herméneutique* . . . ). He is freed for service. He is also free because he is associated with the victory which Jesus Christ won against temptation and in obedience to God. When Jesus Christ resists Satan he does not do so unconsciously in a kind of natural reaction. When he obeys the Father, and chooses to obey him, we do not have here a simple and charming spontaneity. Jesus knows the scriptures and he obeys the scriptures. In the same way, it seems to me that freedom in Christ is not given out wholesale. It is not an automatic transformation of all men who are freed. It is a condition of the new life of those who have to render service. For these alone freedom in Christ is not just a theory but a reality.

It implies more than knowing who Jesus Christ is. It also implies knowing the scriptures. It implies a voluntary course of action (self-mastery, as Paul calls it in Galatians). It implies choice between options which are not always simple and obvious. Only the man who confesses Jesus Christ as his Lord is a free man. The rest are still in their "normal" ethical condition—the condition which has been the same for millennia. Their life and works are the product of necessities. Their behavior is dictated by the totality of conditionings and rationalizings to which man is subject and which he imposes on himself. They may know the freedom of Christ in the kingdom of God but they do not have it now.

Can it be said that Christians have become free men by nature? Do they have a different nature from other men? This would imply a metaphysical transformation and we do not contend for this. The real point at issue when we speak of Christian freedom is ethics. Christians, like all other men, are still subject to pressures, temptations, determinations, and necessities. The Christian, like everyone else, obviously knows what it is to be hungry; he can be tempted when he is hungry. His distinctive gift, however, is that of participation in the secret lordship which enables him to give a different reply from that of all others in the same conditions, and which allows him to introduce a lever of freedom into the dense mass of constraints. We believe that this is possible for him alone because necessities have been overcome only once in Christ, and therefore this is a possibility only in express association with the work of Christ. This does not mean that the Christian has this possibility automatically on every occasion. He is not a free man making his own free way. He is not himself Jesus Christ. Yet he does have the possibility and he is destined to realize it. He does not have to make his own way. He has only to express in his own way the presence and the lordship of Jesus Christ. All this boils down to a style of life, a mode of conduct, a concrete decision which may be just as humble and hidden as the lordship itself. This is why I believe that freedom in Christ is the core of ethics for Christians but has no meaning for anyone else.[8]

### § 2. Privilege or Responsibility

This brings us up against the well-known problem of the superiority of Christians. How can the privilege of freedom be conferred on them alone? In addition to all their other privileges, truth, salvation, the good, are they also, in spite of every appearance to the contrary, to enjoy a monopoly of freedom?

In spite of every appearance to the contrary! In the last resort the lives of Christians do not seem to show at any point that they are more free than other men. If one turns to history, it is surely apparent that Christians have more often imposed restraints than championed liberty. Once they achieved recognition in the Roman Empire they quickly set up a dictatorial state and eliminated the liberties that Romans had previously enjoyed. As Christianity expanded, the church itself adopted an authoritarian stance both in things temporal and in things spiritual. It assumed extensive powers both by setting up imperial dogmatic rule and by trying to dominate the imperial power. When movements of freedom appeared in the Christian world, whether in the economic realm or in the sense of social revolution, the church was hostile to these movements and tried to suppress them. In the sixteenth century the reformers were far from being liberators, as may be seen from Luther's attitude to the peasants, or from that of Calvin in Geneva, or from that of both to the Anabaptists. Hence, in spite of Protestant propaganda, the Reformation did not represent a victory for freedom or its establishment. In the seventeenth century the church supported materially and justified doctrinally the authoritarian powers of monarchies. If European monarchies were able to become what they did, it was due to the presence of the church and to its authoritarian view of truth, the state, and spiritual things. It was also due to the church's monopoly on justice and truth. The church as the depository and dispenser of grace identified itself with monarchy and became the place of salvation.

It has to be recognized that during this long period of the church freedom finds little place within the church's history. Christian freedom is

---

8 Käsemann notes that the determinative factor in the personal life of the disciple, the dogmatic force behind the church, and that which produces its birth and possibility, is the liberty of the children of God which is received in knowledge of the cross of Jesus Christ.

at the heart of neither its teaching nor its activity. After the age of the fathers, redemption lost its significantly human and social character and became a doctrine. The debate about freedom became a theological *locus*. Freedom could be discussed, and a correct theological understanding reached, at the very time when the church was most authoritarian. Preaching often centered on fear of hell and conversions were won by spiritual force. The act of faith could coincide with the stake for heretics (*auto-da-fe*) with a view to ensuring their salvation. The metaphysical doctrine of freedom could go hand in hand with force exerted on both the body and the soul. "We will force men to be free" is a motto which characterizes only too well the attitude of the church. Finally, in the nineteenth century we have in France and elsewhere the alliance of throne and altar which confirms the negation of liberty by the church.

Now I realize that this is a very general sketch. I know that Christianity did in fact support movements of emancipation. Slavery was gradually suppressed under its influence (in spite of opposing doctrines which were simply rationalizations of the situation). A spirit of freedom constantly surged up in non-official church circles. Heretics in every age protested on behalf of freedom even when they were really heretical theologically. The Reformation meant liberation from a host of superstitions and idolatries. Many libertarian movements came to birth in the fifteenth and sixteenth centuries. The world was desacralized and man achieved freedom in the spheres of science, technology, and economic power. One might also cite the principle of free enquiry, the protest of the church against authoritarianism, its opposition to colonialism from as early as the sixteenth century, its concern in the nineteenth century for the welfare of the working classes, its work in investigation, its social achievements, its legal reforms, its protective legislation in the field of industry, in which the church was at work before the socialists and Marx in spite of popular opinion to the contrary. Nor should one forget its part in revolutionary movements from the very earliest times, not to speak of the work it has done in the missionary sphere to liberate primitive peoples from sorcery, fear of demons, and the despotism of tribal chiefs.

When we speak of the church's liberating work on the mission fields, however, we are brought right back up against our problem. Was not this liberation achieved only at the expense of the imposition of a crushing and meaningless moralism, of an association with colonialism in a continent like Africa, of a destruction of social structures, and of the entry of, e.g., Christianized black peoples into a new spiritual universe which was no less oppressive, although for different reasons, than that which it replaced? Thus it is easy enough to argue that Christians have also been promoters of freedom in the world. It is easy enough to write a history of the church as an agent of liberation among men, as some authors have done. But one cannot say that its work in this regard has been completely unambivalent.

It also seems to me that the dominant note of the church has been incontestably that of authority and the negation of liberty. The efforts at emancipation have been secondary and often clandestine. Furthermore, one has to admit that efforts at human liberation, whether they be intellectual, political, or social, have often been initiated outside the church. Many movements of revolt, modern republicanism and socialism, the Enlightenment, and much scientific development might be cited as examples which are certainly secular and in some cases definitely anti-Christian. In this context one need not point out that the result of such efforts has often been the very reverse of that intended. The important point is that in so many instances the starting-point, initiation, and inspiration were non-Christian.

How can it be said, then, that freedom exists only in Christ and only for those who confess Jesus Christ as Lord and Saviour? In spite of the experience of history, however, I do say this. Only in Christ and through Christians can authentic and undeviating freedom arise, take form, and spread in the world. Nevertheless, the history of Christianity and the church is also marked by terrible failures. As I have often said, I do not like to accuse our forefathers in the faith of having been wrong, as though we were better and more enlightened than they. The church is a unity in time. We cannot dissociate ourselves from the church in the middle ages, at the time of the Reformation, or in the nineteenth century. At these periods, too, the church was the church of Jesus Christ. It was his authentic witness. It carried the truth to men. But in relation to its ethical task, and its function of representing the lordship of Jesus Christ on earth, we can only say that it has been a serious failure and indeed a veritable catastrophe for man in general. This enables us to measure the degree to which grace alone has made it the church of Jesus Christ and always sustained it as such.

The error of the church has been to try to represent the lordship of Jesus Christ along the lines of authority. Since all honor must be given to the Lord, it has been inferred that all honor must also be given to the church. Because the Lord is truly Lord of the world, it has been thought that the vicar of Christ (a mere man) should be invested with an authority exercised in human style. The opposite mistake has been to think of the church as merely the servant of men, for this is no new discovery.[9] From the very first, and throughout the church's history, love for men has led Christians and the church to dedicate themselves to the service of the poor, the lowly, and the disinherited. But this has only too often been the counterpart of authority, i.e., a service which bears witness to the love of Christ, but not a manifestation of the most important thing of all—we shall justify the surprising superlative later—namely, freedom. The church's mistake from the time of Constantine to our own age has been a failure to see

---

9 In spite of the close tie between freedom and love, which we shall examine later, freedom is not to be construed merely as service, as is done far too facilely today (cf. Bovon, "Vivre dans la liberté").

that every Christian in effect represents the lordship of Christ but that in the last resort the only expression of this is freedom.

The proper reply to this error is not to reject the church, to condemn it as ineffectual and unfaithful in its work, to ascribe freedom to man in general, to make all men (wittingly or unwittingly) the carriers of the freedom of Christ. As I have shown above, I believe that this is a theological impossibility and that it forgets completely the teaching of scripture.

Let us return to the question of Christian privilege. Are we to regard it as advantageous and a mark of superiority that some are free in contrast to the rest who are still under the pressure of necessity? If what we have said above about the radical failure of the church in the exercise of this freedom is true, can one see in it a privilege? Has the fact that the church can carry the freedom of Christ actually taken on the aspect of a privilege concretely in history? On the one hand the church has never fully assumed its freedom. It has betrayed its role. One may thus conclude that the matter is not as simple as it seems. Living in freedom is not a particularly felicitous gift. On the other hand failure to fulfil the task has turned the majority of men against the church. They savagely accuse Christians, as is so apparent today. The accusation covers many other areas as well as that of freedom, but in effect all the other charges stem from the fact that the church has failed to represent the freedom which it ought to represent among men and for them. Whether the accusation is that the church has lacked respect for men, that it has exercised authoritarian power, that it has heaped up riches, that it has supported the strong and forsaken the poor, the real charge is that it has not demonstrated its freedom. For even if men have not realized it theologically, ontologically they are well aware that what they should expect of the church is witness to freedom and conduct which leads to freedom.

To say, then, that the Christian is liberated is not to say that he is superior or that he enjoys an advantage. There is no worse present than freedom. To view freedom as a privilege is to surrender to the absurd ideology that man is free by nature, that he is made for freedom, and that only minor obstacles like economic or political constraint prevent him from being fully free. This fails to take into account that whenever man has made a beginning of liberty he has taken fright, retreated, renounced his freedom, and sighed with relief at being able to put his destiny finally in the hands of someone else. Freedom is the most crushing burden that one can lay on man. In his vanity and boasting man pretends that he wants to be free. He also has a visceral fear of confinement, conditioning, and servitude. What he calls his love of freedom, however, is really his rejection of imprisonment. It is a revolt against slavery, which he cannot tolerate. Once a little freedom is offered him, however, he starts back at the sight of the void which he must now fill, the meaning he must now provide, and the responsibility he must now carry. He prefers the happy state of belonging to a group. He wants a mediocre happiness which brings no risks.

This is the basic experience which is described in Exodus. The people has been delivered from hard, blatant, and crushing bondage in Egypt. It has come into the desert of freedom. Behind it is the heroism of faith at the crossing of the Red Sea, which had all the thrill of revolution and the first step into freedom. It must now advance in this dangerous land in which is no guarantee and neither past nor prospect. At once the people begins to protest. It regrets having left Egypt, where "we sat by the flesh pots, and we did eat bread to the full" (which was, of course, far from the truth; Exodus 16:3). It wants to go back to the land of servitude and security.

This story is an illustration which has validity for us and for all men. For man is deceiving himself when he pretends that he wants freedom and loves it. In fact he does not really know what it is. As Cortazar says so well in *Les Rois*, "He knows nothing about the conflict between love of freedom and fear of what is different, of what is not immediate, possible, and permissible."

In effect we have to enter into what is different, and man is afraid of what is different. In freedom we have to enter into what is not immediate or assured in advance. We have to pioneer impossible and impermissible ways. This is freedom. But man is afraid of leaving the ways of what is possible, immediate, and reasonable. Are we to say, then, that freedom means superiority? As we consider man, we should have to say that it would be his severest punishment if we did not know that freedom is God's will for man. But it is God's will and therefore we have to go forward in those new ways.

Freedom not only implies what we have said at the human level. In addition it also entails responsibility. From the very outset the man who is liberated is given responsibility for all his decisions in the presence of God. The man who is not free, who is crushed by necessities and determinations, is not responsible. But God, who is not a harsh and severe master, does not hold him responsible when he is oppressed by sin. He comes to him, bears the penalty, and saves him. He does not demand an account in respect of what he is not. In contrast, the man who is freed by God knows now what is really at issue.

Among all the many interpretations given, it seems to me that this is the real reason for the difference in Jesus' attitude to Pharisees on the one side and sinners on the other. The scribes and Pharisees, as believers, know the work of God for them and are thus free men. Jesus summons them to account with respect to their freedom. And once again the result is not too good. In contrast, Jesus brings only healing and pardon to the poor, the sick, the Galileans, the ignorant collaborators, and the rich who are corrupt in their lack of understanding. To be responsible for the use of our freedom, to have to give answer to the Lord, we have to know. We have to know the work of the Lord for us.

Now if the freedom which creates our responsibility is primarily a use, a practice, a mode of conduct, a style of life, we may once again be sure that the only free man is he who knows who Jesus Christ is, for he alone can be held responsible. This fact that only he who confesses the Lord with heart and lips is free explains the apparently odd fact that the last judgment which is intimated to us begins with the church, which goes through the fire first.

We are not dealing, then, with a privilege, superiority, or dignity that has been conferred on Christians. The situation of Christians is, on the contrary, very dangerous, uncomfortable, harassing, and ambivalent. Christians are set very definitely in a situation which is "against nature." This is often forgotten. In Jesus Christ they are called upon to overcome and to shatter the nexus of determinations to which we referred earlier and which according to modern science constitutes the true nature of man. They are to do this at the level of the most elemental determinations, as Jesus showed when he overcame hunger, or when he mastered pain in the freedom of prayer, interceding on the cross for those who put him to death. This is against nature.

Freedom, in fact, demands unceasingly that we set aside what seems natural to man, that we break free from our conformism and cultural setting, that we rise above our tendencies and inclinations (not loving father or mother more than the Lord), that we break our beloved chains and even at times our self-consistency, as in the case of Jesus, who on the one hand attacks riches and yet on the other hand does not hesitate to visit the homes of wealthy toll-collectors when they invite him to feasts as Levi did.

To say that liberation in Christ introduces us into a situation against nature runs contrary to two traditional positions: (1) that the work of Christ completes, extends, and perfects nature, and (2) that it simply restores us to the state of nature which was corrupted by sin. If Christ introduces man to a truth which is infinitely superior to anything that Adam could know (for do not the angels themselves wish to look into these things? [1 Peter 1:12]); if Christ introduces man to a fellowship with the Father which, established by the sacrifice of the Son, infinitely surpasses the fellowship that Adam could have; if Christ promises man a dignity (you will sit on thrones alongside the Son of Man [Matthew 19:28], and you shall judge angels [1 Corinthians 6:3]) which is infinitely greater than that of Adam, it is surely obvious that nature is not just restored or improved. The condition of freedom is not in conformity with nature; it is against it.

Now the nature of man as alienated man still continues, as we have seen. It is perhaps more tragic than ever today. There is no total restitution of man to freedom. Natural freedom has not been achieved for all. Faith alone permits our actual association with the work of Christ. Faith alone enables man to have the freedom which Christ won for him. Even for the man who believes, who confesses Jesus Christ with heart and lip, there is no more any *opus operatum* than there is for pagans. The Christian is not in himself a free man. He is not a free man irrespective of what he does. He is not a free man in the sense that we can speak of two categories, pagans who are slaves on the one side and Christians who are free on the other. As in the case of the church, so in that of the individual Christian, freedom which is not practiced as such does not exist. Freedom is nothing unless it is translated into specific forms of life, specific decisions. If freedom is not ethics, then the Christian, in spite of his claims, is not free at any level.

The Christian can always lose his freedom, as we shall see, although it must be recalled that freedom is not the equivalent of salvation by grace. If he does, he is tragically responsible (1) to himself for not having been what he was summoned by grace to be, and (2) to others for not having represented freedom to them and therefore for having aggravated their bondage and alienation. For the introduction of freedom into the world by Christ means that freedom which is not assumed and lived out is not just a lack. It is a fatal poison for men, as we shall see later. It can sterilize and render inoperative the lordship of Jesus Christ.

If what we have been saying is true, namely, that this lordship is always mediated, that it is exercised through men and not otherwise, that it can manifest itself only by way of free men, then only freedom which is lived out in the world is a sign of the presence, work, and efficacy of the lordship of Jesus Christ. Hence to lose this freedom, to fail to practice it, is to render impossible the efficacious work of the lordship of Jesus Christ. It is to hand the world over again to a life as though Jesus Christ were not the Lord. This is the ultimate responsibility of every Christian. This is the responsibility one should have in view when he talks of the Christian as a servant.

### § 3. Freedom as a Primary Factor or as a Superstructure of Revelation[10]

In developing our theme we shall often refer to Paul and to quotations or examples from his letters. In the generation which followed the death of Jesus Christ, Paul in his exposition of the gospel seems to have been the first to describe Christ's work as a liberation or *redemptio ab hostibus* (a redemption from enemies). He can present the Christian life to us as that of a freed captive, suggesting at times that we have now become slaves of Christ rather than slaves of sin, and thus adopting the metaphor described earlier, namely, that as ransomed prisoners we are in a sense the slaves of him who ransomed us. More often, however, Paul depicts the Christian life as that of a man who has now become free. In so doing, Paul is not just using a figure of speech or an illustration to make his

---

10  As Bovon (*op. cit.*) points out, it is of no great significance that the word group "free, freedom" is rare in the Synoptic Gospels; the person of Jesus of Nazareth is the source of Christian freedom.

meaning clear. He is not merely adopting a mythical or culturally conditioned expression. His aim is to convey to the church the very reality of the act of God for man in Jesus Christ. He is not offering a parable which needs demythologization. He is concerned with man's condition, and his transformation by Christ, as lived out constantly and unambiguously in his reality.

For Paul there is no remove between the work of Christ and the vocabulary he uses to disclose it to us. Hence we must be careful not to introduce a distance and ambiguity that allow us not to feel any radical commitment to what is written.

The fact that Paul above all others in the New Testament presents the doctrine of freedom is easily proved statistically. Terms which describe man's situation as slavery, Christ's work as liberation, and the Christian life as a life of freedom occur about sixty times in Paul as compared with only twenty-five times in the rest of the New Testament.

This raises the question whether we have here an invention of Paul, or, better, a personal interpretation, a theological superstructure relating to Jesus Christ. Certainly, development of the doctrine of freedom is almost entirely dependent on Paul's teaching. If one adopts a Johannine rather than a Pauline view, for example, one might describe the work of God in Christ along very different lines and with hardly any appeal to this doctrine. Freedom would have its place in theological interpretation but it would not be essential or central, and this individual perspective of Paul might well be ignored altogether.

On the other hand, this makes no sense for those who take the Bible as a whole in which each part has its place with all the rest, none being self-sufficient but each indispensable. On this view it is not a question of Pauline and Johannine presentations as the fruit of different cultures and temperaments. It is rather a matter of convergent and complementary expressions which in combination make possible a more exact approach to the totality of revelation. No text can stand alone. We achieve a more authentic understanding if we accept all the texts, recognizing their individuality, not playing off one against the other as more true, but allowing each to play its significant and irreplaceable instrumental role. We should not insist on this so strongly if there did not exist today a theological style which tends to sunder the biblical texts from each other and which especially tries to push Paul aside as an unreliable theologian. We shall constantly find this ancient and ongoing attempt at evasion, e.g., in the form of exalting the Gospels as the sole vehicle of revelation at the expense of all the other writings which have come down to us.

Now the present issue is whether Paul is presenting a purely personal opinion and system or whether we may rightly put his doctrine of freedom at the center of the Christian life. In fact, it is easily shown that Paul is not just presenting ideas peculiar to himself. He is building on the traditional thinking of the Jewish people, and especially on the acts of God in relation to this people as they are recounted in holy scripture.[11] For after all, what are the books of Moses and the prophets and the historical writings really talking about? In reality they are talking about one thing, namely, that the people which carries the promise, and which has been chosen to represent the freedom of God among men, falls back constantly into bondage and God constantly liberates it afresh. The history of Israel is marked by deliverances. Israel is constituted a people at its liberation. The exodus is a threefold phenomenon. God reveals himself to his people as its God and brings it into his mystery. God liberates his people from various forms of bondage, including idolatry as well as oppression. God institutes his people a people by giving it his law, which is the charter of its liberty rather than its servitude.

From the very first, then, it seems that freedom is the necessary condition and situation if man is to be the carrier of revelation among other men. It seems that God's revelation produces, evokes, and entails liberation from the powers and structures of the world. It seems that it is in and in virtue of its freedom that this people bears the majesty, revelation, and law of God in the midst of other peoples. This people is the only one to carry God's lordship because it is the only one to have been freed by God himself. The intertwining of these two themes sets freedom at the very heart of this history. As Pury emphasizes (*Le libérateur,* p. 38), "God does not want to be the God of a people of slaves. He is either the liberator of this people or he is not its God."

This is well put. God is our God as our liberator. He is our liberator and hence we know that he is our God. This implies that our freedom is in fact God's own presence. God has to be ours, and sovereign, if we are to be truly free. Israel is free only to the extent that its God is absolutely

---

11  It is odd that Bultmann in his *Primitive Christianity* (1956) can speak of a striking analogy between the freedom of the Stoic sage and that of the Christian (cf. pp. 142ff.). In effect he brings out a decisive difference only a few pages later. The Stoic is free because he is master of himself through rational thought; for Paul man's will is corrupt and in himself he is totally incapable of freedom. The Stoic finds certainty of existence by self-restriction, and this is freedom; for Paul responsibility to self drives man to despair and he can achieve freedom only as he is freed from himself. The Stoic can separate himself from time and deny the future, thus achieving freedom by abstraction; for Paul temporality is inherent in man's nature, so that, even though conditioned by his past, he continually has to make new decisions for the future, and he cannot do so, since he is his past and can have freedom only as a gift of grace. Finally, it is by reason that the Stoic has freedom as he concentrates on himself, shuns all contacts and demands, and thus escapes the temporality of existence, living in the non-temporal logos; for Paul, however, the Christian is freed by God's grace when he surrenders to this grace, finds pardon for the past, is liberated from the demands of the present, and is thus free for the future, open to all encounters and living in terms of the concrete future. This is an exact account of what Bultmann himself says and yet on two occasions he can also make the general claim that there is a considerable relationship between Paul and the Stoics on this matter. He says in addition that Jewish thought is completely destitute of any concept of freedom. These are strange contradictions.

sovereign. "Any questioning of the sovereignty of God is a questioning of the freedom of Israel" (or the church or ourselves). This is the point at which Israel's troubles begin. Because it continually doubts whether God is the Lord, the eternal God, the Almighty who has revealed himself as such, it falls constantly into slavery. There is a close tie between its faith and freedom on the one hand, its unbelief and bondage on the other.

This confirms what we have said about Christian freedom. Israel must worship Yahweh alone, and if it does so it is free. But again and again it falls into different forms of slavery. It comes under political bondage at the exile, and this is the occasion of a magnificent proclamation of God as the liberator. It also knows bondage to false gods, to the idols which bring it back under spiritual determinations. God reveals himself as the liberator in relation to these too (as in the problem of Baal). Then it is enslaved by the state, by the power of the king, and God, having warned it about this, brings liberation by transposing the monarchy into another key, making it prophetic of the Saviour with David. Israel even comes finally into bondage to the Torah, and this leads on to the final liberation by Jesus. Thus Israel loses its freedom in every possible way, and Yahweh does not cease to liberate it by different means.

Now one should remember that if God is the liberator of Israel the terms used in this regard are most important. On the one hand we find *go'el,* which is often translated "surety," with the implication not merely of a liberator but also of one who steps in to take upon himself the weight of debt and condemnation. The *go'el* is the one who buys back, who pays the slave's price, who ransoms the prisoner, always with a view to liberation. He can also be the kinsman who has to avenge blood or free his relative from bondage. The same term can apply either to social liberation or to deliverance from evil. The *go'el* has both a right to ransom and a duty to avenge.

The other common word, i.e., *miphelath,* carries with it the idea of protecting or making safe, but always again with a link to freedom, so that Israel will see that being liberated is the same thing as being made safe. Thus the Psalms can speak of God as a rock, a fortress, and a liberator. This complex of ideas shows that Israel can find no true security or protection except in God. God is its liberator. Accepting freedom is recognizing that one is under the protection of God alone. Conversely, to put oneself under the protective authority of God is to be free. To seek any other protection, whether it be in the army, in fortresses, in alliances, or in the state, is to fall into slavery again. If there is freedom only because God frees Israel, an exclusive relation between Israel and God is implied, and the liberator is thus the only security that this people can find.

We have here a situation which will shed light on the rest of our study. The freedom which is given in Christ is radical insecurity from the human standpoint or from that of social structures and technical and political forces. For our only security is Christ. If, however, we seek and even accept some other protection or security, e.g., that of the state, or wealth, or social security, or socialism, or violence, or revolution, or justice, this will be a repudiation of our security in Christ and consequently it will be an alienation of our freedom. There can be no compromise here. As noted above, an express confession of faith is demanded if we are to be free in Christ. Freedom is both supreme insecurity and yet, as the whole of the Old Testament reminds us, it is the only true security.

Now the Jews themselves, when they considered God's deliverances, were well aware that the grand sweep of their history could not be reduced to historical events alone. The individual incidents, since they happen to the elect people, have an all-embracing spiritual and prophetic sense. The Jews themselves saw that the first liberation from Egypt is the guarantee and promise of all the others. It is because God frees them there that he is the liberator and henceforth there can be no other. The covenant made then means that he will always be the *go'el*. The deliverance from Egypt has also a spiritual meaning for the Jews. It is not just political. It is also liberation from the kingdom of evil. It is a liberation which symbolizes all liberation. Finally, for Israel, too, this first liberation guarantees the final and definitive liberation which will complete world history and which the people awaits.

When, therefore, Paul says that Jesus Christ is the liberator, and when he sets up his doctrine of liberty, he is not acting merely in his own name. He is taking up the whole thought of scripture. One might almost say that he is aligning himself with the whole of the Old Testament. He is showing that the constant prophecies of liberation have been fulfilled in Jesus Christ. He does not invent anything. He simply points to the complete and radical fulfilment of these successive liberations.

Two questions remain. The first is this: If freedom plays so constant a role, if it is so important in biblical thought, why is Paul almost the only writer in the New Testament to have this emphasis? Why is freedom a secondary theme in the other works? One answer seems to me to be clear enough. (We shall find others in Part II of the present work.) This is that Paul is the apostle to the Gentiles. The work of liberation whose prediction is fulfilled in Jesus Christ is already familiar to Jewish Christians. The converted Jews who make up the original church know very well what scripture says about God as Liberator, Redeemer, Guarantor, and Protector. They thus realize that his work as such has been fulfilled in Christ. They do not have to be taught this. Many of the New Testament writings are addressed in the first instance to them, and therefore these works do not have to stress the fact that Christ is the liberator. To remind them of what they know only a single word is needed, which will evoke all the teaching of scripture about freedom.

Paul, however, is speaking to Gentiles who know nothing of all this, who do not know God as Liberator, who cannot refer to this whole history which is not their own, and whose contacts with the gods have been the exact opposite. He thus has to teach them these things. He has to reveal to them, not merely that God is love, but also that he liberates. He has to bring out for them the meaning of the freedom that God gives and its implications for their lives. At the same time, adopting the Gentile standpoint and beginning with the fact that now there can be only one people and not two, the same Paul, as an apostle to the Gentiles, has also to turn to the Jews and set before them a new dimension of the freedom which God has granted them, namely, freedom from the law. This was the one point that the Jews had still to learn, and it was necessarily the apostle to the Gentiles who had to be their teacher in this regard. This seems to me to be an adequate reason why the thinking of Paul has this focus on freedom.

The second question is as follows. In the Old Testament it is very plain that there is no differentiation of freedom. We do not find any distinction between spiritual or religious and internal freedom on the one side and socio-political or external freedom on the other. Political liberation from Egypt symbolizes and guarantees spiritual liberation. In the prophets of the exile spiritual liberation announces and implies liberation from Babylon. Actual liberation from Babylon finds fulfilment in the rediscovery of the law. The slave who wants to stay among the people of Israel becomes free and at the same time he is associated with the election. As is well known, this characterizes the whole thought of Israel. We do not find two realities, the one spiritual and the other material. On the contrary, the latter is simply a guarantee, attestation, and expression of the former. Now the question is whether Paul has spiritualized the matter in his teaching on freedom. He does not combat social slavery. He does not speak out in favor of the emancipation of women. Is the freedom of which he speaks a purely inner freedom?

In my view one does not find in Paul the slightest dualism of body and soul, of the outer situation and the inner situation. He does not plead for an internal freedom no matter what may be the social or physical condition. In this regard he is no Stoic. He is solidly in the tradition of the Old Testament revelation, and, as we shall see, he constantly applies the freedom gained in Christ to the various departments and responsibilities of concrete life. We may thus say that Paul is not an innovator in his teaching on freedom. He follows the lines laid down by the God of Abraham. If we refer continually to him, this is merely because he lays such emphasis on the ethics of freedom.

Do we have to recall that the theme of freedom is just as strong, if not so developed, in John? If Paul says that where the Spirit is, there is liberty, John says that the Spirit moves where and as he wills and gives liberty to man. He also says that the truth will free you. When the Jews answer that they are not in bondage, Jesus says that whoever sins is the slave of sin (John 8:30, 35). Sin and bondage to it are the equivalent of ignorance of the truth. Truth is what finally delivers from sin. But John also says that the Spirit leads us into the truth. Hence the Spirit reveals

Christ's mystery. The free Spirit creates freedom by communicating this truth. Freedom is thus objectively tied to Christ's redeeming work. If we are alienated and bound to a false conscience, Christ's work makes this point positively. Alienated man cannot know the truth. But there is a way of de-alienation toward knowledge of the real. This is the way of the truth.

The act of God's Word addressed to man, calling him in his alienation, triggers the process, and gives a mind which can know and receive the truth, at the same time putting man in a new situation, that of freedom. Thus Paul continues the thought of Israel and prepares the way for that of John. He has not invented the notion of freedom. It is just as central both before him and after him.

This phenomenon of freedom is precisely what prevents Christianity from becoming what Kierkegaard calls a handful of axioms. Without freedom it does become this. And when it becomes doctrine and principles there is no freedom. Christianity could easily become axioms were it not for freedom, i.e., when it is lived out as though there were no freedom.

The constancy of man's liberation reconciles the approaches of decision in Bultmann and salvation history in Cullmann. On one side we are in the presence of a historical intervention by God which is constant and which represents a history when we talk of freedom. Liberation is indeed associated with salvation history. On the other side liberation is the act of God by which man is unceasingly confronted by decision here and now with no antecedents or conditions; free man has to decide and he can decide only as free man. He is free, however, only because he is freed. (No analysis of existentially free man will hold, as we have seen.) This freeing or liberation is a divine pre-decision which refers to God's history with man. Decision should be stressed when freedom manifests itself, but the act of Jesus is not just a call for decision. In the actual conditions of life man could never make the decision. The act of Jesus is the liberation of man which makes it possible. Thus the theme of freedom is a primary factor in revelation, as Ricoeur rightly observes, although we prefer to put it in direct rather than symbolical terms.

# Part II

# The Object of Freedom and the Will of Man

# Chapter 1

# What Freedom?

## § 1. Virtues and Freedom

We have seen that freedom is a situation which is made for us. We are placed in this relation because we are first freed and set in fellowship with Christ. Hence freedom is not something won by our own will. It is not an expression of our own being nor a constitutive element in human nature. Nor is freedom a virtue. Among the fruits of the Spirit mentioned by Paul as an expression of the work of God in us, we never find freedom. Freedom is not a result of the divine work that we have to live out by a more or less voluntary act. We are to be clothed with mercy or to be pure; the gift of grace has been made and we have now to live it out in some way, since it has ethical orientations which are given and which formulate an ethics. Freedom, however, is not one ethics nor is it one virtue among others. Again, when Paul refers to the highest gifts, faith, hope, and charity, he does not mention freedom. It seems strange that freedom should have an important place and should finally express the totality of God's work for us, and yet that it should not be listed among the commandments nor be one of the imperatives of conduct. The explanation, as I see it, is that freedom is not a partial expression of the Christian life. It is not a fragment like joy or patience or faithfulness of temperance. Freedom, the freedom which God gives, is to be understood from the very first as a power or possibility. It is a power to act and to obey. It is a possibility of life and strength for combat. In this connection, although the terms are the same, there can be no confusion with other powers which do not derive from freedom nor work in its favor. It we adopt the usual words—everyone agrees that freedom is a power—it is only in order to bring out the more forcefully the inversion which these words imply in this context.

In Christ there is no autonomous power nor is there any might which is not service. From this angle one might say that freedom is a personal and spontaneous activity which is not conditioned in a world of objects. Yet in the case of Christian freedom the meanings differ again from the usual ones. If this activity characterizes man's responsible conduct, the spontaneity at issue here is given and acquired rather than innate. It is linked to the spontaneity of the Spirit of God. Non-conditioning implies obedience to the will of God. My relation to objects does not mean that I can rule creation as God does. On the contrary it is in recognition of my proper place in relation to this creation that my freedom becomes true freedom. This recognition, however, implies that I do not think of myself as an independent subject nor do I regard this creation as delivered up to my arbitrary and autonomous will for power. The very opposite is true. My freedom exists only as I cease to think of God as an object. For me he is the liberating subject. In the same way the freedom resulting from this liberation means that the world around me can no longer be an object which I use. It is the place of my freedom, obedience, and service.

Freedom is not one element in the Christian life. It is not one of its forms. It does not express itself accidentally, or according to circumstances, or through encounters. In some circumstances temperance is the work of faith, in others faithfulness, in others strict justice, in others extreme clemency. Freedom, however, is not like this. It is not a part or a fragmentary expression of the Christian life. It *is* the Christian life.[1]

Freedom lies outside the list of virtues. It is not one of the fruits of the Spirit. It is the pedestal on which all the rest can be set. It is the climate in which all things develop and grow. It is the signification of all acts. It is their orientation. It is the condition of the rest of the Christian life. Freedom is not, then, one of the elements in Christian ethics or morals. Without it there would be no ethics. The Christian life is set within it.

Again freedom is not an attitude that we can put on or put off as we please. We are so accustomed not to bring freedom into our Christian thinking that it does not occur to us that it is the situation on which everything depends. We are ready to accuse ourselves of not being just or loving. But we hardly ever dream of questioning our lack of freedom or asking whether we are expressing it in the totality of our lives. If we are theologians, we may well argue that this situation is made for us. We are free because we have been freed. Freedom has been acquired. It has been given. We have become free. There can be no altering this. It has become more or less a constitutive element in my life and nature. Why, then, should I worry? It is part of the new nature with which I have been invested. I cannot lose it since it is secured to me by grace.

We thus equate freedom with, e.g., justification. It is a matter between the self and God. It is secret in this sense. It is sure. As we are always sinners and always righteous, so we are always slaves and always freed. Now it is true that justification is a spiritual matter. The gift of God sets me before God, and in relation to him I am a new being beginning a new history which is the history of God with man. The only point is, however, that in classical theology justification has to find expression in sanctification. The transmutation of the being has to manifest itself in a style of being, in the virtues which Paul enumerates. Sanctification sets up a new relation be-

---

1 In this regard I am in full agreement with Käsemann, who seems to me to be the only modern theologian to give freedom the central place which is its due.

*The Object of Freedom and the Will of Man*

tween God and us which proceeds from us as the knowledge and acknowledgment of the work of God in us. It sets up a new relation with our neighbors as a manifestation of the grace which is given us.

Freedom, however, is not set by us in a similar relation. Nothing results from freedom. We do not know where to list it. We know that we are now in this new situation, but how are we to express it? We are free and not slaves, but how is this manifested? In this regard we are completely dumb. This transformation of the being has no consequences in our lives. At the most we say that we are liberated from the law. But even in this regard we are oddly inconsistent. What may be implied is that part of the law, e.g., the ceremonial part, no longer has any meaning or interest for us. Or it may be that the Jewish law expressed in the Old Testament is peripheral and irrelevant for us. Or it may be that if we are free no moral teaching is necessary; we are guided by the Spirit and need no other direction. But none of this has anything to do with freedom. Liquidation of the law of Israel is not what Paul means when he says that we are no longer under the law or that we are set free from it. (We shall have to go into this later.) Again, being free does not mean the suppression of ethics in Paul. We shall soon see that it means the direct opposite. And in any case the dimension of freedom goes far beyond the problem of the law. We are freed, not merely from the law, but from all alienation.

Now this message finds so little place in the teaching of the church that we never find even the slightest reference to it in our catechisms, nor is there any investigation of Christian life on the basis of freedom. Manuals of ethics either ignore freedom, or tentatively place it among the virtues, as Paul does not do, or find a place for it in the description of human nature. Freedom is nowhere presented as a global situation which ought to find expression in each of our acts. Perhaps this is something which is taken for granted. But the question of the visible and concrete manifestation of freedom is never taken as a starting-point.

Barth, of course, has a great deal to say about freedom in his *Church Dogmatics.* In most cases, however, the reference is to God. Freedom is a freedom for God manifested in the cultus, the holy day, and so forth. Now all this is very true. But it is far too restricted. In these circumstances it is not surprising that for ordinary people in the church freedom has neither meaning nor content and poses no questions. It is a theme which has vanished from the Christian horizon. The believer is not concerned about knowing whether he is free nor is he worried in the least about ways of manifesting his freedom. In my view this is the very thing that explains the insipidity of the Christian life, its lack of meaning, its failure to make much impact on society. Works of love and service may be multiplied, justice may be demonstrated, and faith may be expressed, but none of this is worth anything without freedom. All it amounts to is the pious activity expected of Christians. Christians are there to do such things. Such virtues surprise nobody. After all Christians are amiable and useful people and possibly rather stupid. What is missing in all these works, in all these expressions of the Christian life, is the vital spring, the incontestable point, the incomprehensible quality, namely, freedom. This alone is what makes the work significant and surprising.

The real need today is not to secularize Christianity nor to plunge into political action. This can accomplish nothing unless it is an expression of freedom. It is through freedom that the non-Christian can be struck by the surprising and unexpected. It is in freedom that he can have the sense of a new beginning. It is in freedom that the Christian can find joy—joy even in the sense of fun—in the living out of virtues. Freedom is not itself one of the virtues. It is the climate of all virtues. As the power which is essentially obedience, and recognition of the freedom of God, it is the climate in which the rest of our life can develop in God and for God. It informs the whole of the believer's life and not just this or that aspect in haphazard fashion.

This freedom, however, is freedom under the word of God. This is why it holds a central place. By this freedom we can understand how the word of God in holy scripture comes to us natural men. As Barth puts it (Church Dogmatics, I, 2, p. 666), this "happens through free obedience." We are here in the presence of a phenomenon which is decisive and global and which imparts meaning to the Christian life. It is this that gives color, orientation, and distinctiveness to obedience and works. Without this freedom, there is no Christian life at all.

We see this at the decisive points of Christian ethics. One can achieve righteousness, humility, perseverance, and purity; one can engage in revolution and fight for the poor, but even all this is of little worth if it is outside freedom, i.e., if it is outside grace, outside generosity, outside the condition of life that Jesus came to set up for Christians. The works may be precisely those that are described in the Old Testament or Paul, but in spite of the external resemblance they add up only to secular morality if they are not done and lived out in freedom. They are then no more than an expression of kindly feelings which may approve of what Paul says and find it good and helpful. This is how Christian morality can become the morality of society, whether capitalist or not. Once Christian conduct is isolated from freedom, it falls back into necessity, i.e., into the organization of a workable moral life in abstraction from grace.

The freedom of man's obedience is the response that should be made to the freedom of God's grace. Without this twofold movement the life lived by the so-called Christian has about it nothing distinctive or unique. Faith is no doubt apprehension of the salvation given. But it cannot express itself in the works of God in the world. The works are still those of the law. They are external works of constraint. They also express very forcefully the past.

Naturally there is continuity between the Old Testament and the New if, as we have seen, freedom is not an innovation and God is from the very

The Object of Freedom and the Will of Man

first the Liberator. It is important to remember this. Nevertheless a break also comes in Jesus Christ. The situation is no longer the same.

The reference under the old covenant is to the past. God delivered out of Egypt. This guarantees the other liberation. But while man waits for this his works have only a past reference. They are not the works of a freedom which is lived out today. They merely bear witness that there has been liberation at a point in history and for a specific generation. God revealed himself as the Liberator. But man has not yet been liberated. He simply knows that God did once liberate out of bondage. He knows that his God is he who liberates. In his own life, however, he is not liberated in such a way that he can choose to live according to his liberty. This is how it has to be under the law. The will of God, although it is a liberating will, finds expression in a law which is inevitably constraint and obligation, being oriented to the past.

In Jesus Christ, however, the liberation is total. It is new and present every moment. This means that, while it refers to the historical moments of the incarnation, crucifixion, and resurrection, it is not limited to a historical period or to a single generation. It is not tied to any specific instance of slavery. It is constantly actualized afresh. Hence our freedom is not oriented to the past; it is oriented to the future. Again, our faith cannot express itself in works of the law, only in those of liberty. This projection towards the future, this straining forward in life to what is ahead (while things behind are forgotten, Philippians 3:13), is characteristic of freedom, and the presence of freedom for its part now implies transformation of life. For what is ahead is not just a future. It is not just an extended span of life which may be long or not but which has no real meaning since it is merely an addition of successive moments. When man is freed in Christ, when this freedom projects him forward, this means that he has a real future and not just a wall which blocks any further view. His life is no longer an absurdity. A breach has been made in absurdity and meaninglessnes. We do not have here an automatic orientation. We have a restoration of all possibilities. A way has been opened up which leads to a goal. This is not a closed or necessary way. It is not a single way. It does not have tracks like a railway. This way is as diversified as human life itself. For all human life is assumed in Christ and Christ is himself the way.

When we say, then, that in virtue of the freedom given by grace man again has a future, this does not mean a set future. This would be the future of meaninglessness or fate. The possibilities which are now open for man presuppose man's own intervention in freedom. He himself has to decide on his works, orient his life, take up his responsibilities, and therefore work out his own future. The freedom which gives man a future implies that he should make this future. The freedom which abolishes absurdity implies that man himself should give his future meaning.[2]

---

2 Naturally we do not mean mankind, or all men, but liberated man. I am not advancing a global view of history.

This freedom, however, begins and ends in the freedom of God. The future which man freely fashions serves God in the doing of his own work, the fashioning of the heavenly Jerusalem. We thus see how it may be said that freedom gives to works and virtues their meaning, climate, and color.[3]

One might ask why, if freedom is so important for Paul, he does not himself make the connection that we have just made, or state more clearly what we have been trying to expound. Our answer is that once Paul focuses his preaching on the freedom that is given by grace then the Christian life is naturally included with all its different forms and works. This is in itself an adequate reply. Yet one might also add that the texts do in our view offer a more precise relation. If all the epistles are studied, it will be seen that Paul has two ways of showing that freedom is the climate of all ethics, or that justification issues in sanctification.

In one group of letters he has a brief affirmation of freedom between theological instruction and moral exhortation. Thus in Romans the point of juncture is at the beginning of chapter 12, where we find the words: "Be not conformed to this world" (v. 3)—this is, as we shall see, one of the most important marks of freedom. In Ephesians the transition comes at the end of chapter 3 and the beginning of chapter 4; here two aspects of freedom come to light, namely, freedom of access to God and freedom from the world in captivity to Christ. There is an even clearer transition in Colossians, for the song of triumph celebrating the overthrow of powers at the cross is followed by a declaration of freedom (2:16–23) and then comes the ethical teaching.

In a second group of letters, however, Paul spreads his affirmation of freedom through the whole development of his message, returning to it with each new point. 1 and 2 Corinthians and Galatians are instances of this. Thus in 1 Corinthians freedom underlies all that the apostle says, whether it be God's freedom in calling into the church (1:27–28) or freedom in our own conduct (6:12; 9:1; 10:23; 12:4). The same is true in Galatians where we read of freedom from the law in 3:25, freedom by adoption in 4:7, and freedom in the context of exhortation in 5:1, 13.

This rapid sketch is enough to show that even if Paul does not have any systematic teaching of his own on freedom this is because his whole theology expresses it as the possibility of the Christian life.

We maintain that freedom is the climate of ethics and the coloring of

---

3 Although freedom is so important in revelation, thinking on the Christian life at the present time almost completely ignores and rejects it. At a conference in May, 1972, a brilliant intellectual told me that we have had enough twaddle about freedom. This is interesting because so few people in the church talk about it any more. The general feeling seems to be that we already know all we need to know about this subject. There is little reference to it in our imposing official statements. The volumes of the Conference on the Church and Society say nothing at all about it except in an allusion on the subject of the theology of revolution. The Uppsala Assembly of the World Council says nothing about it. This says something about the orientation of thought in official church circles.

*The Object of Freedom and the Will of Man*

virtues. But we must go further. It is the very condition of the Christian life if this is to be defined with Barth[4] as the obedience of free man to the free God. If there is no freedom there is no Christian life at all. Freedom is preliminary and antecedent to every ethical expression of freedom. We cannot move on directly from the grace that is appropriated in faith to action. If action is to be possible, freedom is necessary. It is both the setting in which virtues can develop and also the condition which allows them to exist.

I think this is adequately enough expressed in the idea of fruit. The law produces works. It forces itself on us by a kind of coercion. It leads us like a pedagogue. It pre-forms our actions. It is needed if actions that well up from a heart possessed by the devil are to be brought under external constraint, broken, pressed, molded, and objectively expressed. The law is a help to our will in the fight against evil. Unhappily the fight is feeble and futile. In reality all that the law accomplishes is to make it clear to ourselves and to God that our will is ineffectual and that our actions, no matter how we try to control them, derive from a heart that is corrupt (Matthew 15:19).

Once the heart is changed by grace, however, the new fount of life finds expression in acts and words and thoughts that are no longer works of the law and cannot be so, since if they were, this would prove that the heart had not really changed. Once the root of the tree has changed, the fruit it bears changes also. We cannot gather figs from brambles. No matter how we force and train them, brambles will produce only berries. A change of root is needed. But once the root is changed (and obviously we cannot change our own root ourselves), then the fruit changes too.

We refer thus to the teaching of scripture in both the Gospels and the Epistles simply to show where freedom is grounded, i.e., in a change of heart. This basic transformation of man is the transition from bondage to freedom. So long as we are in bondage to the world and Satan, God's will can be translated into our lives only by the constraint of the law. Once we are freed from this bondage, God's will is expressed in our freedom. Freedom is thus a condition of the authenticity of works.

In effect we now have fruits rather than works. The commonly used term "fruit" expresses spontaneity. The idea of work suggests an effort of will directed to a goal and building bit by bit. Fruit, however, suggests the rise of sap, the freedom of nature, the generosity of gift, effortless expression on the part of the fruit-bearing tree. Fruits have to be borne freely as a spontaneous expression of the effected inner mutation without which there would be no fruits.

---

4 *Church Dogmatics*, III, 4, p. 13. Luther in his *Freedom of a Christian Man* rightly perceives that freedom is the condition and climate of the whole Christian life. Works of service for others make sense only if done in freedom. Obedience to the powers that be make sense only as a free decision. There is no reality of love except in service that is free.

Here again we must be more precise. Fruit does not have to be concretely and objectively different from work. As Paul reminds us when he says that the law is not an enemy, the same word or act or commitment or abnegation can be either work or fruit. We came up against this problem in the *Introduction* when we referred to the similarity between Christian ethics and, e.g., Stoic ethics. The virtues can be similar and the acts can seem to be identical. On the one side, however, we have the work of constraint, while on the other we have the fruit of freedom. For an objective spectator, e.g., for the sociologist who measures attitudes, these are the same thing. For the recipient of a gift it makes no difference whether the gift has its source in the law or in faith, whether it expresses a bitter fight against avarice or cheerful generosity. The recipient has the money which will help him to live. Nevertheless there is a decisive difference, not merely before God, nor in the inner life alone. The origin and meaning of the act are not the same. Hence there is a qualitative difference in the act itself. This certainly cannot be measured psychologically or sociologically. What is qualitative cannot even be measured indirectly. Nevertheless the qualitative rather than the quantitative is what constitutes the human relation.

This freedom can be felt by those who are associated with a free man. A certain manner of being bears witness to it. It can light up relations as lightning does the night. But it cannot be measured statistically, nor categorized and schematized, without ceasing to be freedom. There is thus, as one might put it, a total attitude of life which is that of freedom. We find explosive signs and much patience but we cannot say that some acts come under a free category and others under a servile category. We cannot say that certain acts are fruit and others work. A list of free acts cannot be given. Freedom has no incontestable signs. It is folly to look at a man externally and to judge an act or a writing as servile or free. Even psycho-sociological analysis cannot do this. Only the personal relation can perceive this secret quality. Hence we may never say that a people is free or, unfortunately, that Christians are free men. In this ethical study we shall not show how one may become a free man nor shall we indicate the distinctive marks of such a man.

As regards freedom of action, conformity to the will of God expressed in scripture is no guarantee. Good deeds can be done automatically and, as it were, by remote control. Education, social pressures, and cultural assimilation can produce acts that conform to what is regarded as good. Certain highly developed and refined forms of Christian instruction can have the same result in relation to what God reveals as the good. We need only refer to the serious Pharisaic development of the law, the exercises of Ignatius Loyola, and the pastoral use of psychological techniques such as non-directive pedagogy or group dynamics. All these aim at good conduct, but unfortunately the result is not Christian since it is not evoked by freedom and does not express it.[5] This truth is particularly important in relation to psychological techniques, since these claim to be respecting the freedom of the subject and to be aiming at free action, whereas in fact they do far more to determine and condition the subjects than the pressures previously mentioned.

The importance of freedom as a condition of Christian ethics is so great that its presence or absence decides whether there is any Christian ethics or not. This alone constitutes the particularity of this ethics. The existence of the freedom of the Christian man is what makes it ethics rather than morality. If freedom is suppressed, then what is manifested as exhortation, the fruit of the Spirit, the free expression of grace, identity between the inner heart and the word that issues from it, the coherence of work and faith, the discovery of joy, is all turned back again into morality, into dull virtue, into a list, a decalogue, constraint, and the computation of merits. It is freedom that makes the commandment what it is, i.e., the word of him who is free, addressed to a free and responsible person. Spoken in freedom, the order is both possibility and permission. Received in freedom, the order is the living word of God to the here and now. Received in freedom, it is the presence of the gospel itself. Take away the freedom of him who receives the commandment, however, and it can be only law, an eternal and pre-existent determination towards an ineluctable and foreordained goal.[6]

This is why freedom makes Christian ethics into something which, as we have seen, both exists and yet does not exist. This is why it makes Christian ethics into something that cannot be compared with any moral system. Freedom means that we must reject all moralism, asceticism, and mortification. There are, of course, moral systems that dispense with obligations and sanctions. One need only refer to anarchists, or theorists, or all those who base morals on naive idealism, on the blind belief that human nature is good, on the wager that evil is provoked by obligation, so that to abolish the police will solve the problem of theft. We have to resist such a belief. But we do not lay emphasis on this rejection when we differentiate between a morality without obligations or sanctions and Christian ethics. The point of difference is that such a morality presupposes a consonance of morality, freedom, and human nature, whereas Christian ethics sees a basic dissonance. There is a dissonance between morality and freedom, for, as we have said, the existence of freedom is what prevents the commandment from becoming a moral system. There is also dissonance between freedom and nature, for, as we have seen, the situation of freedom is against nature. Hence a life in freedom has nothing in common with a morality destitute of

---

5  As Kierkegaard points out, only he who wills the good in truth is free, i.e., free through the good; hence he who wills the good through fear of punishment does not will it in truth, and the good merely makes of him a slave.

6  The link with freedom means that the commandment is always specific (cf. Bonhoeffer's *Ethics*, p. 251).

obligation or sanction, especially when we consider the theme of this life (which we are merely indicating here and will have to develop at length later), namely, that it constitutes a veritable dialectic of freedom and love.

There is no love without freedom. On the other hand, as we shall see, there can be no freedom, according to Christ, without love. The two mutually imply one another even though they are contradictory. Freedom in itself excludes love. Ministering love excludes freedom. But the whole of the Christian life can advance and unfold only in the dialectical development of the two. This is the mark and expression of freedom in life.

Here, then, is the explanation of something we said earlier. No specific act can be clearly called a sign or irrefutable manifestation of freedom. Nevertheless, our reference is not just to an inward and spiritual freedom. A total orientation of life, the entire movement of this life, is the witness to this freedom. This means, however, that we have to know this life. We cannot cut off a single slice from it, take a photograph of it, or extract a saying. Slice, photograph, saying—these do not bear witness to anything. They do not allow us to say that this act is free or that this man is free, just as a single shot from a film does not tell us who is the hero or what is the meaning of the story. If freedom is movement (and what else can it be?), then it finds expression in the movement of the life of a man, but as it cannot be grasped in its totality by any observer, so no final judgment can be passed on this freedom, nor can any irrefutable sign of it be given. Every sign will necessarily be ambiguous.

Witness may be borne to Jesus Christ by faith or hope or love. It cannot be borne by freedom. This gift is the one that permits the others to expand. One may infer freedom from love. But one can never grasp it directly. Freedom does not have significative force. It is not a designation of the man who is free. It is not the light that illumines his acts; if it were, it would usurp the place of the word. It is not witness to itself. It is like the light that has value only because it is reflected on objects. Even though the light gives these their form and solidity and color, the objects are the important things. We look at these, not at the light. The light is taken for granted. We fail to realize that the details which attract our attention would not exist without this light that we ignore. So it is with freedom.

### § 2. Freedom and Choice

Traditionally all ethical situations are reduced to that of choice. Moral problems arise when the individual has to choose. We have already stated in the Introduction that this does not seem to be correct and we have thus dealt with the argument that Adam before the fall was already in a moral situation since God himself put him in a situation in which he had to choose. Nevertheless, we must return to this question of choice as we begin to portray freedom as the climate and condition of the whole of the Christian life. For here again we come up against the notion that freedom consists in making choices. We are free when several orientations or objects are before us and we can choose one of them without constraint. This is the most formal and simplistic concept of freedom. We are free in a democracy because we can elect one of several politicians (manifesting this freedom in the ballot) or opt for one of many policies (manifesting this freedom in our opinions). We think that information is free if various sources are available, if we can choose between various newspapers representing different points of view.

In reality this concept of freedom is very superficial. For our choice is never free. We are conditioned by a number of factors that cause us to elect this or that representative, to sign this or that manifesto, to buy this or that newspaper. The man who chooses is always alienated man, man subject to many necessities. Hence his choice is not an exercise of freedom.[7] For it is not he who chooses. The choice is made by his cultural setting, his upbringing, his environment, and the various psychological manipulations to which he is subject. In this regard we need to probe much deeper than Marx did in his criticism of formal democracy. It is not just a matter of the capitalist context of class conflict. It is not just that bourgeois democracy offers only a freedom to choose exploitation of the people. We are not dealing merely with external and authoritarian determination. The determination is inward. Publicity, propaganda, psychotechnics, and human relations determine our choices with increasing rigor. Even the multiplicity of sources of information, although it is a fact, is an illusion, for it has to be multiplicity for someone, and who of us has sufficient freedom of mind or detachment to read newspapers of all hues and to believe that each is right up to a point and that their contradictory reports are of equal worth? Indeed, if we did find a man who would be so little committed as to be able to do this, we should at once say that such a man is not free, since an attitude of pure indifference is not freedom. Yet we are so invincibly convinced that if the possibility of choice (however unreal) does not exist in politics and information, then we are slaves and freedom has vanished from the earth.

Serious evaluation of such a view is needed if we are to see that an artificial choice is not freedom. Is, then, the absence of such a possibility of choice freedom? Not at all. But to admit this absence is at least honest. It faces reality. It does not allow man to live in a dream of freedom and an illusion of power. The reader should not infer, of course, that I am

---

7 Naturally I accept Kierkegaard's analysis of decision as an expression of freedom, but only in its strict form and not in terms of the theory of decision of post-Heideggerians or Bultmann. [For a good criticism cf. O. Cullmann, *Salvation in History*.] Absence of choice may very well go hand in hand with freedom, this combination being the essence of prophetism as it is magnificently described by Neher. The prophet cannot express his freedom by choice, since his only option would be to refuse his vocation. The man to whom God speaks comes under a "burden" which rules out choice. But this is the very thing that makes him a prophet and hence makes him as free as the Spirit of God.

advocating a totalitarian rather than a democratic form of government, or a single source of information. This is not in the least my intention. All that I want to do is to show (1) that even if all the objective conditions of freedom were present man would not exercise this freedom and (2) that the situation of choice is not the ethical situation *par excellence* because, concretely, choices are illusory and the dice are loaded.

All the same, one might say, freedom is restored in Christ and therefore the Christian, having become the free man whom we described earlier, can now make a valid choice. But things are not quite so simple. The Christian has not become a superman. As noted, he has not been freed from the constraints and necessities of the world. He has not been restored to the situation of Adam. He is not Jesus Christ.[8] This means that in face of the conditions of life he does indeed have to make choices. What characterizes the situation of Adam or of Jesus Christ is, in contrast, that this is not a situation of choice like ours. Theirs is a situation of choice in fellowship.

Adam in Eden does not have to choose between obeying God's command and listening to the voice of the serpent. He has only one possibility. This is the divinely given possibility of being Adam and living as such. This is the only possibility; he does not have to choose between two. This situation means in effect that Adam does not have to say or to determine what is good. Nor is he confronted by two mutually exclusive objects. In the unity of creation these mysteries do not arise. There is no either-or. There is unity. Everything truly belongs to a well-ordered whole whose parts are not separated and which allows of no contradictory possibilities. Even in the fallen world, when the prophets and psalmists invite us to look at creation, e.g., the movement of the stars, and to see there the work of the Lord, their reference is to this unity and order. In its purity the movement of the stars suggests the harmonious totality of the original creation. But it also suggests absence of choice. There is no incoherence in this harmony; only incoherence introduces choice. Nevertheless the impression made by the stars can be fallacious since to us their order suggests mechanism and implacable rigor. In fact, the original creation expresses the freedom of God and it lives in and by this freedom. If there is no choice, this is not as in a machine in which calculation rules out choice. It is in the harmony of fellowship. Adam, living in fellowship with God, is free. But his freedom is not choice between this life and life outside fellowship with God. For it is not a present reality, a known object, a disclosed possibility. Fellowship does not involve choice. Freedom is living in God's own freedom through this fellowship and in the unbroken unity of all creation in which there are no separate and incoherent bits and pieces between which to choose.

Nevertheless, might it not be said with some plausibility that there was a clearly expressed will of God and hence a possibility of disobeying

---

8 Cf. Bonhoeffer, *Ethics*, p. 250.

this? Was there not the actual situation on the one side and the offer of the serpent on the other? Does not this imply two choices? But this is to see things from the standpoint of our situation after the fall. Things are like this now. In Adam's fellowship with God, however, there was no situation of choice. Life was without a break. The will of God was not the right thing and disobedience the opposing wrong. It was life, and there was no death to choose. What the serpent offered did not differ from the existing situation of Adam. It was itself a promise of life (here we see the serpent's guile). Hence it seemed to maintain unity. Indeed, it promised greater unity, communion, and even identity with God. But once Adam's freedom leads him into a situation different from that which God had chosen, everything is shattered. The mirror no longer reflects the image of God, for it is broken. Fellowship no longer exists. The unity of creation is divided in pieces. Freedom has become independence of God, and independence expresses itself in choices between opposing things which are hostile to one another and mutually exclusive.

Now even if Jesus lived in communion with his Father, creation has not yet recovered its unity. It has not regained its fulness. It is still broken. It still waits. Hence we too, being set in this creation, are still in the situation of independence and consequently of choice. But to claim that choice is an expression of freedom is simply to show that we are still in the fallen state, i.e., in that of division and non-communication. Choice implies fracture in the elements of creation and in our own lives. Choice is made between contradictory truths or attitudes. If we describe freedom as the possibility of choice, it is because in our present situation we can think of freedom only as independence, as not being subject to anybody, as not being responsible to anybody for our decisions. Unfortunately, in the situation of division and non-communication, we are subject to the necessity which is bound up with separation from God, and therefore, in spite of our vaunting claims to independence, we are in the grip of predetermined choices. The more we claim to be independent, the stricter is the determination of our choices, for the greater is our separation from him who is the only Liberator. By way of this theological excursus we thus see once again that the sociological reality of determinations finally conditions our choices.

We have said that faith in Christ and his lordship over us do not restore us to the integrity of Adam. Our nature is still subject to vanity. What is certainly shattered, however, is our pretended independence, and since we now know where true freedom lies, what it is, and who gives it, we cannot confuse independence with it. From another angle, because in this world we are still subject to the necessity of having to choose, choice does not have to imply independence. It implies division in the world, so that I have to select one thing and reject another. This is not an expression of my freedom. On the contrary, it is an expression of my determination, of my inclusion within this world, of my finitude at least. I am not reintegrated into the one world. Although reconciliation has been achieved, the unity of creation with the Creator is not that of the Father and the Son. But the freedom which is in Christ intervenes. The choice which was subject to all the determinations of the world and its powers becomes a possibility of exercising the new freedom of the one who used to be a slave and is now called a son. As choices have to be made in life we can show our freedom by not following the inclinations of sociology, nature, passion, law, and the state, or rather, by following them consciously and as a new decision.

Merely making a choice, however, is in no way akin to freedom. It is not the privileged situation of freedom. It does not exhaust by a long way the sphere of freedom. Choice will always find expression in a decision, a commitment, or taking sides, for we are not always deciding between two hypotheses. But this will be a closed decision. The decision of freedom, in contrast, will be creative. It does not have to begin with a given situation. It is not enclosed by solutions. It does not mean choice between pre-established facts. It will manifest openness to something different, a third way, a reading at a different level, a rephrasing of the question, a situation which allows of some other path than that of constraint by necessity. Choice remains. For we cannot do all things in a new way. We cannot begin afresh. We are in solidarity with all men. To that degree we are also caught in the same dilemmas as they are.

When the ethical situation is assimilated to one of choice, this always means more or less, even if in different words, a choice between good and evil. Now precisely what we want to stress here is that the difference for the Christian is not one of power in making the choice which is freedom. For the Christian the choice itself is different. We need only recall what was said in the *Introduction* about the relativity of what men call good and evil. Relativity does not mean unimportance. But relativity within disobedience is enough in itself to show that choice in this area is not definitive or total. Nor is it choice between "doing" or "not doing" a will of God which has been objectified and brought within the orbit of our knowledge and comprehension, so that it is determined and fixed by our reason. In reality the choice which the Christian may be called upon to make is characterized already by its immediacy. It is not a choice through an intermediary or through the mediation of an interval of time. When there is choice it is in God's today. Hence this is not choice through reference to a continuity or in terms of a supreme end. The choice is not a calculation of values nor a reference to some good which can be determined intrinsically and abstractly, as we would like God's will to be. This choice is made in immediacy through commitment rather than deliberation. Even when revealed truth is at issue, choice as an ethical attitude and an ultimate expression of freedom is in effect a kind of art of the possible as our life in Christ comes into confrontation with the reality of our presence in the world. Ethical choice is not choice between a good and an evil. In the first instance it is choice between what is possible and what is not. I realize that

*The Object of Freedom and the Will of Man*

this statement may cause confusion and may in particular support the anti-Christian slogan that what is not possible is not binding. This is not at all what we have in mind. If we speak of the choice of the possible it is because this seems to be the first area of freedom open to us. We have already insisted on the fact that Christian ethics is essentially an ethics of means. The importance of means, of actualization, is basic for the Christian. It is much more decisive than that of ends. For it is in the sphere of means, of the transition from what is given to what is lived out, that freedom is effective, as I have tried to show in my *Politics of God and Politics of Man* (1972).

At a deeper level, however, the choice is not merely that of the means whereby the truth is expressed. It is also the choice of what God has done. We have to choose what has already been accomplished in us and for us. I cannot put this better than H. Roux has already done in his *Épitres pastorales* (p. 102): "You know in whom you have believed; seek faith. You have been loved; seek love and its corollaries patience and gentleness. For the Christian the choice is not between sins and virtues but between perdition and salvation, between death and life. Now salvation and life are Jesus Christ. To be for him and to live in him is to receive from him the order and meaning of life and hence to search and find in him the impulses of action and the determinant values of existence. It is because righteousness, piety, faith, and love are the very reality of the new life of the new man in his relation with God through Jesus Christ that they can and should be the object of seeking, the decisive goal towards which the heart, the will, and the mind of the man of God are oriented. There can be no question here of taking the list of terms as an enumeration of Christian virtues or spiritual values to which material values may be opposed and which the Christian is invited to cultivate or seek on the basis of some decision of good will." This passage brings out the true meaning of choice. In Christ this is not an expression of our free will. It is based on what is already given to us, on what has already been done for us and in us. In this regard, but only in this regard, we have a duplication of the situation of Adam.

Righteousness has already been given to us. Our task is to choose it, to incarnate it, to live it out. This gives choice both its signification and its limit. It is a matter of great profundity: a choice between death and life which involves a choice between good and evil. We cannot merely say that the good as such is in our lives, nor is it to be equated with what we regard as righteousness, piety, patience, and longsuffering. A distinction has also to be made in this regard between the situation in the Old Testament and the situation in the New Testament.

We may begin by quoting Deuteronomy 30:15-19: "See, I have set before thee this day life and good, and death and evil . . . therefore choose life, that both thou and thy seed may live." Here the people of Israel seems to be precisely in the earthly situation of choice between two given things, although these are not just objective and distant, since the passage also says: "This commandment . . . is not in heaven . . . the word . . . is in thy heart . . . " (vv. 11–14). While not totally objective, it is, however, presented to man so that he may choose. Naturally the commandment is addressed to the people of Israel and yet it does not refer to something which is already realized and achieved and written on the heart. The present mark of God's love and patience and help is the exhortation: "Choose life. . . ." This is a sufficient reason why Israel should choose life and good. For this word of God which is addressed to man creates within him both love and power. Nevertheless, a choice has to be made along the lines indicated, i.e., in disrupted nature.

After Jesus Christ, however, the commandment of God is not the same. Man's situation before God has changed. The statement which best brings out the difference is that of Paul in Romans 12:21: "Be not overcome of evil, but overcome (or surpass) evil with good." The symbolism here is not so much that of battle as of leaving behind. The situation of man is not that of a choice that has to be made between two objects. It is that of a march or movement. Neither good nor evil is an object to be grasped. There is a situation in evil which has to be left behind. We have to go beyond evil. This "going beyond" is good. An active force, that of the prince of this world, chooses us. Another active force, which is Jesus Christ, also chooses us. The choice is not ours. The life is ours, and it consists of going beyond evil. Hence the good which is a surpassing of the situation of evil is expressed, not in a choice, but in a fundamental transformation, an excelling of what we are. Being truthful is not in this sense the opposite of being a liar, as though we could be either the one or the other by choice. Being a liar is the condition of him who is subject to the prince of falsehood, and we are unable by our own efforts or choices to introduce a little truth into it here and there. What we have to do is to get beyond this situation and to enter into one ahead which is that of the truth, in which the power of lying is reduced to that of the past, the surpassed, the defeated, and the impotent. This is the singularity of life in Christ and it shows us both what choice is and where it is located. For choice is not at issue when all ethics may be summed up in "putting off the old man with his deeds, and putting on the new man, which is renewed . . . " (Colossians 3:9). Freedom is precisely the transition from a past of bondage to a present of liberty.

But this attitude of choice combined with hope as the basis of freedom means for the Christian projection to the future. Return to the past and seeking refuge in it are incompatible with freedom, whether at the individual level or at the social level of clinging to past customs and ideas. I am not here subscribing to psychoanalysis or to an ideology of progress. There can be no hope of promoting progress. But in Christian realism we must not hope either for a return to the past. We must go forward in the hope of meeting the Saviour who comes. We do not put the future above the past. We live by tradition and recollection. Our whole life rests on events of the past (the call of Abraham, the incarnation, the cross, the resurrection). This past is essential. But we must express our freedom, not in relation to the past but in relation to the future which must be changed into a history and to which we must give meaning. Our freedom is freedom to advance, not in a progress which is the product of historical forces and which is thus more or less automatic (cf. both Marx and Teilhard), but in a voluntary and deliberate advance effected by choices.

Our choices must be constantly criticized when they merely conform to the trend of the age. This is important in relation to technology, which has no theological basis but toward which we must adopt some position, since we cannot get back behind it. There is no point, in my view, in preaching the natural life (Lanza del Vasto), which provokes sympathy but makes no more collective sense than freeing instinctive forces, as Bataille advocates when he suggests that only eroticism can bring freedom in our over-organized world. The technological society leaves no real room for this hope in nature. We are forced to participate but in so doing should exercise every possible choice and decision. Only the man liberated by Jesus Christ (if he is bold enough) can do this. Man is so possessed that liberation has to come from outside. A man is needed who relies on a more decisive power than reason or nature and who is both individual and collective. Only on this condition can our future choices express freedom. But just because freedom is at issue, there can be no guarantees that these choices will be this, or what they will be.

In freeing us from the past, freedom includes us in a history. It permits us to be creators of history. Only as free men can we be this. In this regard we must insist on Cullmann's distinction between salvation history and history (in his *Salvation in History*). I do not believe that general history rests on freedom, though this is a common view. To me it is the fruit of mechanisms and the combination of forces, wills, groups, and systems. It exists as interrelated circumstances unfold with increasing complexity. It makes no sense either for those who live it or for those who analyze it. Only the philosopher who detaches himself from it, and finally does not really know it, can give it meaning. For participants it is no use being free. It is made by millions of alienated men in succession or collaboration. Liberation sets us in the series of God's liberating acts and makes us bearers of the future, but of this future, a continuation of salvation history. This is why the advance that rejects the past and moves toward things to come is so important. But this advance is not progress. It is not the history of men. It is the pursuit of new things. This pursuit alone is the meaning of the freedom given by Christ. The two histories should not be confounded, not should the possibilities of a future of man be confounded with social progress.

## § 3. *Freedom for God*[9]

Freedom as thus defined is acquired in the first instance for service of God. It is freedom for God. We shall not discuss at length this vital, decisive, and primary aspect for two reasons. First, it belongs essentially to the domain of theology and we cannot enter into all the related problems here. Secondly, Karl Barth has dealt very thoroughly with the matter at various points in the *Church Dogmatics,* and since, as indicated above, I am in full accord with his presentation, there seems to be no point in repeating it. We shall thus restrict ourselves to a brief summary.

It should be understood, however, that brevity does not signify lack of interest in the subject. In fact this expression of freedom is central. Freedom finds its first expression here. This is the starting-point for its further expression in life and society. It is also because freedom is in the first instance freedom for God and the service of God that it cannot be synonymous with emancipation, arbitrariness, or autonomy. What is given to man is in the first instance a freedom to recognize both the freedom and

---

9 We shall not discuss in detail the problem of religious freedom. Since Vatican II many studies have appeared on the subject, especially the texts issued by the World Council and the articles by Carillo de Albornoz. It does not seem to me that any useful purpose will be served by listing or summarizing these. I will simply pick out at random two works which are of larger interest.

For a comprehensive survey one may consult R. Coste, *Théologie de la liberté religieuse.* This is a vast work with an almost exhaustive bibliography. It is well argued theologically and there is a minute investigation of the implications. The historical facts are studied as well as the theological aspects, and there is a good analysis of the arguments for and against prohibiting and enforcing belief, especially in relation to the record of the Roman Catholic Church.

My own criticism is that we have here a specifically Roman Catholic mode of reasoning, analysis, and construction. The author wishes to show that religious freedom is based both on rational, natural, and social factors, and yet also on a biblical foundation, the two being consonant with each other. In typically Roman Catholic fashion he thus tries to establish a general and universal doctrine of religious freedom which will be acceptable to everyone. For all that, this is a fine presentation of the many problems involved and the concepts which may be utilized.

The work ends with an interesting proposal for what Coste calls a "code of professional ethics" for the churches. He thinks that the churches should adopt ten principles which embody full religious liberty. These may be summed up as follows: (1) granting to others full liberty of thought, conscience, and religion, (2) respecting the conscience, ethical values, and religious traditions of those who belong to another faith, (3) holding conversations with other religious confessions and with unbelievers, (4) examining the positive witness to the truth which is to be found in all confessions and among unbelievers, (5) stressing that which unites more than that which divides, although without obliterating all distinctions, (6) avoiding indoctrination and pressure in Christian witness, (7) respecting the right of parents to choose what religious instruction should be given to their children, (8) cooperating with other religious confessions in work for peace, etc., (9) showing loyalty to the political community, and (10) learning to see all human beings as brothers with no distinction or discrimination.

A good summary of the labors of the Council, of the various stages of Schema XIII, and of the discussions, may also be found in Louis Fèvre, *La Liberté des chrétiens.*

*The Object of Freedom and the Will of Man*

the authority of God. This freedom is first oriented to God because it does not exist except as man sees who it is that has freed him. Hence it can never be a freedom which turns its back on God.

To the degree that it is freedom for God, however, we cannot escape the problem of determination. Have we escaped necessity (that of the world) only to fall into a far tighter constraint? Have we been de-alienated by Christ only to be alienated afresh in God? If God's will is almighty, if his decision concerning us was made in eternity, this seems to be the case. As we see it, however, this is to pose the problem in metaphysical terms and not in terms of the reality of what God reveals about himself in relation to us.

Karl Barth tells us that "the sovereignty of the divine decision to which the command bears witness does not really affect the freedom of our own decisions. It is our own free decisions whose character God decides even as we ourselves make them. It is they which are claimed and measured by His command. It is the use of our freedom which is subjected to the prior divine decision—the decision of the question whether it is right or not, whether it consists or not in the witness required of us. It is in the use of our freedom that we give an account how we stand in the sight of God" (*Church Dogmatics*, II, 2, pp. 633f.). And later: "Between the arrogance of those who regard themselves as judges of what they will and do, and the false humility of those who take no notice of God's judgment because they cannot change it, there is the third possibility—the sense of responsibility of those who know that God alone is their Judge and not they themselves, and that because God is their Judge they have every reason to remember Him in all their willing and doing" (*ibid.*, p. 636).

Even in these passages, however, does not one detect in spite of everything the rigor of the absolute? The reference is always to submission. It is always to a judgment of God under which we place ourselves in our freedom but in relation to which we finally have no option. As I see it, scripture goes much further and shows us to what extent God in his love limits his own decision, judgment, and influence.

Even in the Old Testament, as I have tried to show in my *Politics of God and Politics of Man*, we are in the presence of a God who accompanies man on his earthly paths. This God is at man's side on the roads which man himself chooses. He did not act thus only during the brief span of the life of Christ on earth. At every moment he has committed himself, and does commit himself, to the enterprises which we choose. He does not do so, of course, as a passive witness, a mute spectator, or a reflection in which we see ourselves. He takes part. He plays his own role. He modifies the system or our own hearts. But he does this at our level and with the humility which his love imposes on his power. He does not crush. He acts in concert with man's action. He takes part in the most hazardous or ridiculous situations that man can invent. He makes history with us. From this standpoint, to say that freedom is in the first instance freedom for God is not to speak of freedom as though it were a needle which always points to the pole, or which is fixed in advance. This freedom is an effective freedom even though it finds expression in obedience and is subject to the judgment of God. When seen in this light, the passages quoted from Barth take on what is for me their true, if more restricted, significance.

Freedom for God means that man becomes responsible before God. At a later point we shall have to examine responsibility as an expression of freedom. The first element in responsibility, however, is this responsibility towards God. God, the Creator, wills that man should be responsible before him because this responsibility itself is an expression of dialogue and communication. God speaks and we have to respond. Man finds himself questioned—although he is not, of course, responsible before being freed by God. This is a point which is often made in the New Testament epistles: If you had not known the law, you would not have committed sin (cf. Romans 7:7). Knowing the law surely means more than being set in a moral system, and committing sin means more than disobeying such a system.

The deeper meaning is that the law is the word of God. It is thus liberation. The aim of the commandment is to free, not to enslave. It is when I have the freedom to receive God's word, and to see in it a commandment which concerns me, that I know what it is to obey and I become responsible for my act. For it is then that I am free to reply to God's question. To be responsible is not to be crushed by an indefinite culpability. It is not having to bear the burden of all that takes place or is produced in the world. It is not having to accept the penalty of an inevitable fault which is the result of original sin. On the contrary, it is being questioned by the God who frees us so that we can freely respond to his question. This question is both the question: "What hast thou done?" (Genesis 4:10; cf. v. 9) and the question: "What wilt thou that I should do unto thee?" (Mark 10:51), or: "Wilt thou be made whole?" The two questions belong together. We become responsible the moment we hear at one and the same time this double question of God. At this moment what we traditionally call the law is transformed, for it ceases to be a pressing duty and becomes permission. Freedom for God is the permission which man is given to obey God and to serve him.

I realize that these statements sound paradoxical. We find it so hard to believe that God is truly the Father and that he is totally in Jesus Christ giving his life for us. Because of this lack of faith we continue to regard the law as morality, duty, constraint, and obligation. To read it thus is always the result of unbelief. If we have even a little understanding of the fact that God did seriously undertake to live with and for man in Jesus Christ, if we truly think of him as radically different, so that finally we cannot say anything about him at all but can only bow down and worship him in silence, as his undertaking demands if it is really taken seriously, then we can see that this unlikely and unheard of event represents a summons to the service of God, that it is in effect a permission that has been given us and not a constraint, an authorization and not a duty. For in this service we do

*The Object of Freedom and the Will of Man*

something with God and even for God even though God does not finally need it and could get on quite well without it. In this service we have a part in the work that God does even though this is complete in itself and we have no right to have a part in it. In this service we discover a hidden and secret dimension which gives meaning to our lives. We lift the lid, and we are allowed to do it ourselves. Without us, as Baudelaire rightly says, the lid cannot be lifted. The authorization which God grants is for us a fulfilment and an accomplishment. The commandment of God which begins with this service of God is never a personal restriction and diminution.

When we speak of an authorization that God gives us to serve him, this has two extraordinary implications. (1) When we remember to what extent everything in us is marked by evil, we see that God is calling into his service the forces of sin, disobedience, and death. This should cause us the same astonishment as the prophets felt when God called them to serve him. Authorization to serve God means that we, as the people we are, with our nature and using our own powers or powerlessness, are given the possibility of achieving God's purpose in history even though the disparity between this purpose and our condition is so great that *a priori* their association is inconceivable. (2) The authorization also has perhaps—I speak cautiously here—a second aspect. Man is religious by nature. He has religious feelings which he works off on idols, powers, and works, and which constantly force him to invent new gods. He has confused aspirations towards a wholly other. But he can never attain to this wholly other. He does not want to in view of the risks it presents. The origin of all religions lies here. Now it might be that in the authorization that he gives us for service God shows us that he is letting us express our confused aspirations and our natural religious instincts in a true service of the true God. (If this is so, it means that the distinction between religion and God's revelation in Christ is not as clear-cut as one would like to think.) For ultimately God calls us to this service as we are and even with all that we are. He thus allows the religious element in us to be transformed into authentic service, changing it because he authorizes us to be before him and to have a part in his work.

What characterizes this authorization, this permission to serve, is the union of two attitudes which are generally regarded as mutually exclusive, namely, obedience and freedom. If God authorizes us to serve him, this undoubtedly implies obedience. But this obedience is in no sense servile obedience to a tyrant. As Barth puts it (*Church Dogmatics*, I, 2, p. 661), "obedience to God is genuine precisely in that it is both spontaneous and receptive, that it not only is unconditional obedience but even as such is obedience from the heart. God's authority is truly recognised only within the sphere of freedom: only where conscience exists, where there exists a sympathetic understanding of its lofty righteousness and a wholehearted assent to its demands. . . . If we refuse to see the equally necessary subjective side of obedience as freedom . . . we have to consider whether we are not involved in a philosophico-political systematisation. . . ." It is here that we discern the great difference from all secular forces, for, as we have seen, these tend to enslave man, to make him obey, so that obedience is subjection to authority, the impossibility of escaping alienation. In contrast, God's decision frees man in order that he may obey, so that obedience through freedom is the meaning of all his work in man.

It is thus apparent why everything is to be set in the light of the service of God. Self-fulfilment is to be found here. For by setting our powers and nature in his service, God fulfils that which we truly expected, in a dimension which men ignore, and vaguely hoped but at the same time were afraid to be. This is our full stature. It is the climax of the dialogue with God and consequently the beginning of the dialogue with other men. For here finally obedience ceases to be oppression and is freedom instead. Freedom is expressed first in the service of God because this is what makes possible all the rest.

Naturally this service does not exhaust freedom. It is inseparable from the service of men. But the two are not the same thing. As I cannot confuse the church and the world, so there is a distinctive service of God which is the chief expression of freedom, which is freedom itself, outside which there is no freedom, and which makes the service of men possible as a result. The sequence cannot be reversed. The service of men is not in itself freedom, nor is it necessarily the service of God.

We have said that our freedom comes from the word which God addresses to us and which makes liberation in Christ actual.

The word of God is the source, guarantee, and thrust of the freedom of its witness. It is also the limit, for it puts an obligation on him who bears it. Jesus in his freedom also fulfils the law in all strictness. He does word for word what is intimated. He who awaits his time has come. Neher (*L'essence du prophétisme*, 1955) shows that God's hand constrains the prophet. Once committed, the prophet has to follow a straight line, bearing a burden he cannot put down. He is in bondage, just as Paul calls himself the slave of Christ. The false prophets, as Neher points out, are the independent ones, proclaiming their own ideas and imaginings in words and images of their own choosing. True prophets carry a burden laid on them from without. They neither seek nor desire it. They cannot free themselves from it. Their prophecy is true because it entails a dialectic of freedom and necessity. The prophet wants to regain his independence or autonomy but can never do so. As I am bound to the word and therefore freed from all else, I am truly free. There is no contradiction between this freedom received from God and a vocation which involves total constraint. To share in God's freedom is to lose individual autonomy but to gain autonomy in relation to the world.

This is not easy. A radical choice must be made. The (glorious) liberty of the children of God is not the happy fluttering of a butterfly from one attractive flower to another. It is joyous, but it is also radical, hard, and absolute. Anarchists who reject God in the name of freedom have a point. They do not see, however, that in rejecting God's freedom they subject themselves to their own fatalities. Man becomes truly man by putting off the illusions of human freedom, autonomy, and eternity (Neher). Giving us our burden, God launches us into an unsuspected adventure, a conflict, which is finally that of freedom. The prophets, crushed under their burden and bound, are always for all of us the real protagonists of freedom. Only he who is radically tied to the freedom of God's word and squeezed and crushed and bruised by it can carry authentic freedom in the world for all men. This is a self-effacing struggle for a freedom which is not for personal profit.

Being itself free, the word of God keeps us free. This means concretely that the word constantly turns on us and questions us. As noted already, the fact that we have been liberated does not mean that we are in a state of liberation. We shall see later that we can always lose our freedom. This is evident when we consider the service of God or freedom for God. For we are always leaving this service. We are always ceasing to be free for God. We are always trying to be free first for ourselves, or for others, for society, etc., which is exactly the same thing. Our freedom is upheld only by conflict or tension with scripture, which reveals God's word to us. "The continued life of the church depends . . . on whether Scripture remains open to it, whether all its conceptions, even the best, remain transparent to its content—so that it can itself confirm and legitimate, or qualify, or even completely set them aside. But Scripture cannot be the breath of life to the Church apart from this freedom. If the Church is true to itself, it will allow this sovereign freedom to Scripture . . . " (Barth, *Church Dogmatics*, I, 2, p. 691). Similarly our freedom has no chance to express and renew itself unless we constantly accept scripture as an open book. This means on the one side that we shall not use this freedom in such a way as to rid ourselves of it. It means on the other side that we shall not take possession of this book on the ground that it belongs to us in virtue of our freedom. We remain free only to the extent that we are continually questioned afresh by scripture and know the constant surprise of the transition from scripture to the living word. This transition, which is the sovereign work of the Holy Spirit, will not take place, however, unless we let ourselves be reached and criticized and denounced and called in question in this way. To allow this is not just to submit to an unforeseeable event. It is to want our living out of freedom to be criticized, and to be so first of all by ourselves on the basis of scripture, which permits us to exercise permanent control as a proper response and condition of liberation.

This, too, depends on us. It is part of our responsibility as free men. We are responsible not merely for using our freedom for God but also for using scripture, in which God grants us his revelation, as a means whereby we may criticize our own use of freedom through the word of God. This seems to be part of what James has in view when he speaks of the law of liberty which judges us (James 1:25). Similarly Paul says: "I judge not mine own self. For I know nothing by myself . . . but he that judgeth me is the Lord" (1 Corinthians 4:3f.). The service of God presupposes that our lives will be constantly open to the renewed scrutiny of the word which gives force and meaning to our freedom. In other words, as Barth shows, this freedom is freedom under the word. "The testimony of Scripture cannot be received unless those who accept it are willing and ready themselves to assume the responsibility for its interpretation and application. This readiness and willingness to make one's own the responsibility for understanding of the Word of God is freedom under the Word" (*Church Dogmatics*, I, 2, p. 696). Now all freedom should be freedom under the word as expressed in this readiness. But the primary expression lies in the service of God. And Barth continues by showing to what degree liberation transposes our being and our abilities into another key, noting that one may "define this freedom as the freedom of conscience" so long as conscience is understood as the divinely given ability to "know with" God and not as a universal and autonomous faculty. Along these lines conscience has its place in ethics on the ground of freedom and through freedom. It is not the innate ability of man to distinguish between good and evil, which we brought under criticism earlier. Conscience, then, is one of the possibilities of serving God with freedom as a starting-point.

As a form of freedom the service of God, specifically in the church and as distinct from service of our fellow-men, finds expression, as Barth tells us, in prayer, confession, the holy day, and reading scripture. Barth studies these forms of freedom for God in *Church Dogmatics*, I, 2 and III, 4. "To pray is clearly a free act of man. Certainly the Holy Spirit intercedes for us in prayer with groanings which cannot be uttered, because we do not know how to pray as we ought (Romans 8:26f.). But this does not alter the fact . . . that *we* pray when we pray. But prayer is the one free act of man in which he confesses that the initiative lies with the freedom of God. . . . He knows that he cannot do this of himself, but is disposed and empowered to do it by God Himself. When we pray we turn to God with the confession that we are not really capable of doing it, because we are not capable of God, but also with the faith that we are invited and authorised to do it. For these reasons, prayer is literally the archetypal form of all human acts of freedom in the Church" (I, 2, p. 698). No doubt one can easily get the impression that when man prays he is impelled by a need or a fear or some inner motivation. In reality, however, this facile view of the matter does not do justice to the movement of prayer. It is not true that need teaches a man to pray, especially today, when man in general relies on himself or society. In reality true prayer is an expression of the freedom of man, i.e., of the relation which God in full freedom sets up with man, and which is a relation of prayer. The will of God is that man should talk to him and address him, but that he should do so as a free man. The problem, then, is that of man's obedience, which can be only that of a free man, but which is obedience within the framework and orientation of a permission. Prayer, whether as petition or praise, is an act by which man accepts a life by grace

*The Object of Freedom and the Will of Man*

have left the written record of revelation were invested with authority precisely because they had to bear witness to God's word. But they were also men and had to bear witness as such, being granted freedom for this purpose. It is in the same freedom as theirs that we are to receive their witness. This rules out the biblical literalism that would make the Bible a paper pope or a law. We have to read it and understand it as free men, i.e., as those whom God has freed for their responsibilities and also for the risks involved. It is thus that freedom can be service of God and freedom for him. For if we had to read the Bible as law and duty, there would be no freedom. We should be bound to the letter and we should have to transmit it. This would rule out service of God. In this field freedom for God means reading scripture in such a way as to receive its actuality and to hear it as a summons (which makes me both free and responsible), not at the level of my secret, hidden, inward, and spiritual life, but in a movement into the totality of my life, social, political, professional, and so forth. This actuality implies on my part a certain freedom towards the text, but not contempt for it. I myself have to read it. I feel an obligation to do so. But as I do so I have also to actualize it. If we have here authentic freedom, there can be no question of reading the text fancifully, or of independence in relation to it, or of controlling it. On the contrary, actualizing the text (and keeping a proper distance from it) is real freedom for God. It is on my part the act whereby I confirm that the text is a word that grasps me. If I do not take up this (given) freedom I might just as well relegate scripture to a museum of antiquities.

At the same time freedom as service of God presupposes in this area that I will pass on the text to others; this is part of the confession of faith. Here again we come up against the same problem. We are not to pass on a closed, historical, and outmoded letter. We are to bear witness to scripture as word. We cannot simply transmit it. We again have to take the risk of freedom. Transposition is needed so that through my freedom scripture will again be word, a living and actual summons to others which is relevant to them too. If true service is to be rendered to God, we must commit ourselves—and we can do so now that we are de-alienated—to this enterprise of the word that issues forth from scripture.

Hence the two implications of freedom presuppose a certain procedure in reading scripture. There has to be sound understanding of the text. For if as God's word it needs no explication, since it is always perfectly clear in itself, as scripture it requires elucidation both objectively and subjectively. The methods of exegesis have to be used. We have then to press on into the realm of hermeneutics. This is part of freedom for God; it is indeed an essential aspect. Nor is it merely a matter for experts. Disturbing as this might sound, it is a matter for every believer to the degree that he is liberated, and it is also a matter for the whole church, which is not without responsibility in this matter. Experts are auxiliaries who lend objective support by providing the materials whereby this freedom may be exercised. But they cannot replace believers, who may not commit their own freedom to them. Nor should they become necessary mediators between scripture and people. We are thus faced by an imperative that might frighten the humble Christian. But every exercise of freedom carries with it both this fear and an initial sense of weakness and incompetence. We shall have to work out the implication of our principles.

*The Object of Freedom and the Will of Man*

# Chapter 2

# Freedom from What?

It seems that each of the biblical authors develops a specific aspect of freedom. Paul shows us in detail what it means to be freed from the law. John stresses the fact that there is liberation from the world. Isaiah and Deuteronomy speak of freedom in relation to the work of our hands. Exodus with its account of deliverance out of Egypt proclaims emancipation from the powers. Finally, freedom from the flesh is also part of the message of Paul. Hence we are not to speak exclusively of the freedom of the Christian from the law as a pedagogue, as we so easily do.

## § 1. Freedom in Relation to Self

The first step of liberation on the way of freedom is that of being set at a distance from ourselves. This could lead to a detailed psychological study, but that is not our present concern. It could also lead to pious exhortation or mystical flights, but these too we shall avoid, restricting ourselves to the teaching of scripture.

The self to which the Bible refers is called in the first instance the flesh. Now it is perhaps worth recalling the well-known fact that in scripture the word "flesh" can have many different senses. We thus come up at once against a problem of interpretation which we shall run into again later when we come to speak of the world. It is perfectly legitimate to stress the different meanings of flesh as the term is found in the various layers of the Old Testament and then in the writings of John and Paul. Even in a single work the word can have different senses according to a given context. The basic question, however, is that of knowing whether the different meanings are to be sharply differentiated from one another. Can one say that in a specific verse the word flesh may mean only the body (flesh and bones) in a strict sense and to the exclusion of any other implication? Or on the basis of the unity of the inspiration of scripture by the Holy Spirit is there a fundamental unity of sense underlying all the different meanings?

If the latter view is correct, this does not rule out differences in sense, which would be absurd. It simply excludes the idea that a biblical term can be carved up into mutually exclusive meanings. When a word has a dominant sense in a passage, we are to take it and understand it in correspondence with all the other meanings as these throw light on it, evoke connotations, and set up a continuity of usage when no one sense can be laid down specifically.[1]

Having said this, we may note that "flesh" has three dominant meanings. Very generally in the Old Testament it denotes, not the body, but that which distinguishes man from God, that which makes him a creature, that which prevents him from being God's equal. This sense is both positive and negative. It is positive inasmuch as the flesh is man's way of existing before God. Created, Adam was flesh in Eden. This marked his finitude without being a mark of evil, sin, or the fall. If, however, we consider man in his separation from God, the negative aspect comes to the fore. The flesh is not just finitude. It is a boundary that cannot be crossed. It encloses man like a prison. God and Adam differed from one another in Eden, but they did so within communion. Chased out of Eden, man sees the boundary marked by the cherubim with the flaming swords. The flesh thus becomes an expression of weakness and of fear of nothingness. "My spirit shall not always strive with man, for he is only flesh" (Genesis 6:3). "All flesh is grass" (Isaiah 40:6). In contrast to this weakness is the power and eternity of the word of God. When God shows his pity, it is a sign of the recollection that man is only flesh (Psalm 78:39). He is only flesh because this is now the negative boundary. In obvious compensation and opposition the fear of nothingness becomes the source of covetousness, i.e., of man's desire to take what belongs to others, to master others, to destroy them both in what they have and in what they are. It is the source of the desire above all things to take possession of God. "We had our conversation in the lusts of our flesh" (Ephesians 2:3). This certainly does not refer merely to physical impulses and carnal desires. Far more profoundly it is parallel to "the lust of the flesh" of 1 John 2:16, where the flesh is the seat of covetousness, i.e., of that which drove Adam to lay his hands on what was reserved for God in a rejection of his finitude, i.e., his flesh. It seems to me that these two different senses both explain one another and are implied in one another.

When, however, the flesh is a provocation to covetousness, this leads on to a third sense. The flesh is the power of man in his opposition to God. It is not in the strict sense man himself. If man is flesh, the flesh is not man. It has taken possession of man in the sense that man has been invaded and dominated by this "impotence-covetousness," as James stresses so well when he says: "Ye lust, and have not" (4:2). The flesh becomes a power within man which governs him, provokes all his actions, and determines his conduct—all in opposition to God and in solidarity with sin. In my view one can hardly separate this sense from the others, nor can one differentiate the sayings of John from those of Paul. "The flesh (as distinct from

---

1 This principle finds little support in modern theology but is regarded as the most scientific by Benveniste, one of our greatest linguists.

the spirit) profiteth nothing" (John 6:63) and "Ye judge after the flesh" (8:15) correspond exactly to the Pauline antithesis between the works of the flesh and the fruit of the Spirit (Galatians 5; cf. also Romans 8:1: walking after the Spirit and not the flesh).

Now this opposition to God, which is present in germ in the first sense, can lead only to death: "To be carnally minded is death" (Romans 8:6); "the carnal mind is enmity against God" (8:7); "they that are in the flesh cannot please God" (8:8). Nor is it merely man in his limited person who is invaded by the flesh and brought under its sign. The invasion applies to the whole sphere of the human, to everything that bears the stamp of man, to all that he invents and "creates," to all his works and self-expression. Nothing that man does escapes the invasion of the flesh. There are even "wise men after the flesh" (1 Corinthians 1:26). Now the freedom that Christ gives is first of all liberation from the flesh (Romans 6:6). The invasion of the flesh means submission to what has become an alien power even though it is ours. Man is now occupied by the flesh, by covetousness-impotence. This is different from himself. The flesh is no longer the being of man in Eden. It is a being which is against man as well as against God. The flesh holds man subject, the desires of the spirit being contrary to those of the flesh. The freedom that we are given encompasses the whole complex of the flesh: the power which is against God, covetousness-impotence, the spirit of might and conquest, and the simple boundary and finitude which is a reminder of man's distinction from God.

Today it is no longer possible to differentiate the order of finitude and the order of sin. For in separation from God the two orders are closely intertwined and indissolubly linked. Death was a mark of finitude and it is also the wages of sin. In the resurrection Christ both overcomes the last enemy and pushes beyond the frontier set for Adam. What is promised to us is incomparably superior to what was accomplished in Adam. This victory, however, is actual as well as yet to come. Already we can live according to the Spirit who is given to us, for the Spirit now dwells in us, not the flesh. Our body is the temple of the Holy Spirit. We are possessed, not by the flesh, but by the grace of God. The only point is that as yet the fruits are limited and contested. They are never definitive. Nor can we pretend that the limit crossed by Christ has so far been removed for us. We cannot pretend that the unity of our being has as yet been reconstituted in the sole and exclusive presence of the Spirit. God is not yet all in all in us. We are brought into discord and division within ourselves. This is the experience of the actuality of death. "Who shall deliver me from this body of death?" (Romans 7:24). We are indwelt by the Spirit of life, but the flesh is always there in power, and covetousness can flare up again at any time. There is no simple and definitive replacement of one power by an identical one. The power which has now come is that of freedom. "Where the Spirit is, there is liberty" (2 Corinthians 3:17). We have not passed over from bondage to the flesh to bondage to God. We have passed over to the freedom of the children of God. Hence we are in the threatening and threatened situation of freedom. This is a far more difficult situation. The Spirit can certainly produce fruits in us and by us. But our freedom can constantly lead us to want to relive our experience of power and conquest, i.e., to go back to the flesh. Paul says expressly to the Galatians: "Having begun in the Spirit, are you going to finish by the flesh?" (Galatians 3:3). God has made reconciliation with us for our freedom, but are we reconciled to God in our freedom? This alienation will find expression in conduct. This is why Paul sets forth the contrast between the fruit of the Spirit and the works of the flesh. But we need not return to that here.

There is, however, one aspect of the flesh on which we do need to insist. This is man's anxious self-centeredness.[2] We can consider various dimensions of this. We may think of self-awareness, which so soon becomes obsessive and takes on giant proportions. The moment I am aware of myself I become the unique, central, and essential person who lies behind everything. Only my own destiny concerns me. For me I am the central thing in the world. We thus see the dawn of pride, of egoism, and also of worry and anxiety. For if the self is the center of all things, if everything begins with me, then how can I avoid the anguished realization that everything also ends with me? Crushed by anxiety, man unceasingly tries to find an answer to the question of his future. He wants to possess it. He wants to safeguard it against insecurity. The mechanisms he sets up to this end manifest the same anxiety as the consultation of diviners, sorcerers, and prophets. The methods have changed, but the situation of man has remained constant. Insurance and planning are simply an expression of the care, fear, and preoccupation that arise out of the conviction that I am the center of the world and that ultimately I see only myself. My horizon and future are dominated by the enormous balloon that I have become for myself, that I have placed before myself, and that constitutes my whole perspective.

Self-importance, however, is confronted by its opposite, namely, the insignificance which is also implied in self-centeredness (we have here once again the covetousness-impotence which is a mark of the flesh). I live in fear because I anticipate what seems to be certain defeat. There is no happy ending for me. Modern society bears strange testimony to the contradiction we see here. On the one side it carries with it an unparalleled growth of devices to ensure the future concretely, institutionally, and objectively. On the other side there is a corresponding growth of fear which for many psychologists is the dominant characteristic of western man. At the natural level this contradiction is hard to explain. If we view it in terms of the flesh, however, we shall find light at least, if not a solution. Now Barth stresses the fact that "anxiety and fear . . . are obviously the direct opposite of

---

2 In this regard Christ's liberation differs sharply from the existentialism of Sartre and the excessive focus on self in modern intellectuals.

*The Object of Freedom and the Will of Man*

what the New Testament describes as freedom. . . . When we see ourselves threatened by the possibility of a coming catastrophe in such a way that we postpone the continuance of our course until better days in order first to deal with this catastrophe . . . we are not free. . . . What we see in the future means for us that we are not free in the present" (*Church Dogmatics*, II, 2, p. 598). In reality liberation from the flesh means liberation from self-centeredness. This does not imply the end of self-awareness. Quite the contrary! It means that God grants us freedom by lifting the increasing burden of self-centeredness from us. I no longer have to be myself the one master, guarantor, and captain of all that I am and of the whole course of my life. In Jesus Christ God has truly taken upon himself what I am. From this moment onwards God, not self, is the center; I live for him, not for myself. This is a real deliverance. A permission is given which opens up for me the possibility of living. I am freed hereby from myself, not in the sense that the self—and the same would apply to others—is now without interest, value, responsibility, or work, nor in the sense that I can now be indifferent to myself and to others, but in the sense that I am no longer a self-encumbrance which paralyzes me or tangles all my paths, so that I live in anxiety or self-exaltation and either have no horizon at all or chase a mirage (cf. Heb. 2:14).

To be freed from the self is true freedom. It is the first step in the life of freedom. It will be seen, then, that we are leaving altogether the sphere of traditional morality for which egoism, pride, disdain, envy, and jealousy are faults or sins or tendencies which have to be suppressed. No morality or education can prevent me being egotistical so long as I am self-centered, i.e., encumbered with the self, obsessed with the self, and enclosed in the self. We need to make it plain, however, that when we speak of this freedom its aim is not that man may cease to be egotistical, vain, and so forth. Morality or the practice of virtues is not the goal. There is no ulterior aim. When man is a slave to himself, he just is. When he receives permission to be different, when he is liberated by this divine permission, the fact that he learns patience and takes an interest in others and learns to love is a fruit of this. It is not the main aim but a secondary consequence. It is a possible but not a necessary implication. It is an unexpected bonus.

This is why we find so often that an order is given not to be concerned about the future, not to fear it, nor to be anxious about it. "Take no thought for your life" (Matthew 6:25). "Take no thought for the morrow" (Matthew 6:34). "Take no thought how or what ye shall speak" (Matthew 10:19). "Fear not"—a saying addressed to Elijah, Isaiah, Zacharias, Mary, Simon Peter, the women at the empty tomb, and John when he had his vision on Patmos. The link between bondage and fear on the one side, freedom and confidence on the other, is noted by Paul when he says in Romans 8:15: "Ye have not received the spirit of bondage again to fear. . . ." John teaches the same lesson when he reminds us that "perfect love casteth out fear" (1 John 4:18). To be unburdened of the self is to be free, to be without anxiety or fear. Paul states this in an outburst of joy when he claims: "I know both how to be abased, and I know how to abound" (Philippians 4:12), and again: "I live, yet not I, but Christ liveth in me" (Galatians 2:20).

This, then, is freedom in relation to self, and this is its result. It should be emphasized, however, that the texts quoted are commands as well as promises. When Jesus tells us not to be anxious in the Sermon on the Mount, or when he strengthens the disciples by telling them not to be afraid, we are not to see in his statements mere counsel or exhortation. God is issuing an order here through his Son. A commandment is truly given, as may be seen from the fact that the context in the Sermon on the Mount is an explanation and confirmation of the law. That a commandment is given is especially important to the degree that the basis of the whole law is exhibited here. For this is a liberating commandment. There is nothing in it to increase our burdens or to establish new obligations. When Jesus sums up his sermon in the exhortation: "Take no thought for your life," this means that the sermon is not meant to add additional anxiety or burden to our natural disquietude. The order not to be worried or not to fear is not meant to set up new worry or new fear. Intrinsically and for us this command is a liberating command. The real aim is to free us from anxiety about ourselves or fear as to our life and future. In its totality, then, the commandment of God is on the side of freedom.

It is a terrible thought that the church has often used fear and constraint in all their different forms, that it has crushed man with anxiety, when the key to the whole law is the freedom which God himself gives us to live without fear or worry.

It is also true, however, that to the degree that this is a commandment we cannot take it lightly. We cannot regard it as no more than a pious recommendation.

This liberation from self is the only possible answer to the inclination or temptation to suicide. I will not deal with this as an ethical problem. Barth and Bonhoeffer have fine passages on it. But these are irrelevant, for to deal with suicide as an ethical problem is not to deal with suicide. For before suicide looms as the only possible response to life, there is no question of it. Hence it cannot be dealt with as an abstract exercise in theology or ethics. But when the demand for suicide arises, theological and ethical arguments are pointless. They contain truth but have no objective reality. They show that suicide is not God's will but suicide is not a matter of theological debate. In face of it the only answer is the birth of hope and liberation from self. What counts is witness to the potential suicide that there is hope for him, that freedom is possible, that the self can be freed for the self. No discourse can show this but only freedom received and lived out (cf. Barth in *Church Dogmatics*, III, 4; N. Tétaz, *Le suicide*, 1970; G. Ras, *Ce soir je me suicide*, 1971).

If suicide is not a sin it is not an act of freedom either. It shows that there is no freedom from self. It makes one's own destiny the most important thing, whether as witness to a cause, to escape suffering, to free friends, as an act of despair, under the impulse of self-importance, to escape the devil and the world, or to set a fine example. All these noble or tragic reasons for suicide always demonstrate lack of freedom, since they involve an act that sets self at the center of the universe. Why condemn this? How can a man who has not been freed in Jesus Christ fail to think that he is the lord of his death? Does he not always think he is the lord of his life, which is the same thing? And both attitudes are taken up in the cross of Christ and set in the love of God.

The matter is different for believers. In face of God's grace suicide is a revolt that nothing can excuse or justify. Freedom before God is not freedom for suicide, as Barth says. But again suicide is not an isolated act. It is set in a clear and conscious relationship with the God of Jesus Christ. It shows my lack of freedom, but do not all my acts do the same? Suicide is surely possible in faith too. It can be to God's glory and express love of neighbor, although this is hard, for detachment from self, which is true freedom, does not let me be self-important. Humility and love of others show me that I am nothing before God but that God loves this nothing, as others can also love me.

The true issue in suicide does not concern the one who commits it but the Christians who know him. A suicide close to me simply teaches me that a person has gone into absolute despair, or into idolatry, or into solitude, or into the abyss of evil, and I have not been able to bear to him convincing witness of God's love, or teach him that he has been blessed and freed and saved and given the promise of resurrection, or give him hope and set him on the path of freedom. How, then, can I judge this person? There can be here only total obedience or total disobedience. The freedom to live without fear or anxiety has to be lived out, and there is no middle ground between freedom and servitude to self.

From the standpoint of liberation from the flesh, we may set freedom in relation to the future. As noted earlier, the man who is liberated by Christ has an authentic future and not just the kind of future which is a mere passing of unlimited time. We may also set freedom in relation to the past. By the intervention of Christ we are freed from the past. This is simple enough if we cling to the familiar and simple theological truth that my past is the past of transgression and sin, that by the cross I am pardoned and redeemed, that God does not impute my sin or hold my faults against me, that these, and with them my past, are blotted out. In our formulation of the theological proposition, however, we should also take note of the ethical implications.

In the first instance one might refer to various psychological aspects, e.g., the sense of guilt, the burden of a guilty past, and the complexes that can result from this. These do not belong strictly to the ethical sphere, however, and since they have been fully dealt with elsewhere I will simply mention them in passing.

It seems to me, however, that the declaration of pardon demands fuller attention. This does not mean that my life should be divided up into a pardoned past under the sign of sin and a future under the sign of grace. We must go further even than Luther's "always a sinner and always righteous." The declaration of pardon does not mean that my past is cancelled out and annulled because it was wholly sinful and that sin has been obliterated. This would mean in the long run that I myself have been annulled and that in the last analysis the whole of my life would count for nothing and would fall into nothingness, I myself being raised up again at the end of the age. But surely the love of God in this pardon cannot mean the reduction of what I am to nothingness. The blotting out of sin is not the blotting out of my past.

If I am freed and delivered from my past, this is not because it has disappeared. Quite the reverse! Nothing has disappeared. The past is not a finished past. It is a regathered past. God has regathered it. He grasps it, assumes it, takes charge of it, keeps it, and recapitulates it in Christ. My past, fortunately, is no longer my own. But it has not been obliterated. It has come into the hands of God where the totality of my life is accumulating bit by bit and being built up in truth. Thus the past lives, not in the hell of my unconscious, but in the holiness of God.

Human wisdom tells us that our deeds follow us. Now this is true in the sense that we ourselves can never amend what we have done. But the saying is completely false in God and according to his revelation. At each step and stage of life my deeds are taken by the hand of God, assumed by him, saved, and passed through the fire by him. God reconstructs my life without sin as I myself construct it in sin. Hence I need not torture myself about the past which I cannot undo. I need not repent forever about what I was at a given moment. This does not mean, of course, that I can treat it lightly or forget my sin or the evil that I did to my neighbor. If I were to take it lightly, forgetting what it cost God, this would show that I have no understanding of God's work for me, that I do not put my trust in it, that I am nullifying God's grace and pardon, and that as a result what has been said here is not true for me.

Only by grace am I liberated from the crushing weight of the past and its spiritual and psychological implications. Nevertheless I am authentically liberated from it. I am constantly being refashioned by God as a new creature, as a man who can begin again. This means that more is demanded than pious contemplation and the work of grace. There is a vital ethical implication. Paul sums up all that we have been saying in his well-known phrase: "Forgetting those things which are behind, and reaching forth unto those things which are before, I press on. . . " (Philippians 3:13f.). His point is that liberation from the past carries with it projection towards the future.

Because I am freed from the evil that I did yesterday, because what I was yesterday has been gathered up in the Lord's hand, I can press on towards what is ahead.

The Christian cannot be a man of the past. He can only hurry on to meet his coming Lord. This should be taken very concretely, and it seems to me that the story of Jethro is highly significant in this regard (Exodus 18). Jethro, a Midianite and a stranger, realizes that Yahweh is the only true God. He sees his work and blesses the Lord. He is also able to give advice to Moses and helps him to organize the people. He teaches both Israel and Moses. But he refuses to take part in the march that the people would make. "He went his way into his own land" (v. 27). He returned to his own country, to the gods of his fathers, and in the last resort to his past. He goes back even though he has been convinced by what God has done, and by what has been done through him. He is too deeply rooted. He will not march towards the promised land. He does not appropriate the promise. He remains the man of his past. Similarly we too, attached to our collective past, whether it be national or religious, are constantly going back and avoiding the risk of pressing on with God.

We may repeat that it is in no sense our purpose to suggest that the past is not important. It is so important that God himself assumes it. Our point is simply that the past is no longer our affair. We are no longer subject to its determinations and conditionings. Its necessity has been lifted. We have been liberated. We have to take it into account. We ought to learn its lessons. We should remember it, as Israel is frequently summoned to do. We should remember it as our point of insertion. But we should then leave it at once. Freed from Egypt, Israel did not remain on the shore of the Red Sea and look backward. It had constantly to remember the past which had been its own but which had been transformed by God—and it had to march on to the promised land.

Again we must be more precise. When we speak of the future we are not referring to progress. We are not suggesting that yesterday was worse than tomorrow will be. To be a man of the future does not have to mean believing in progress and confusing the historical future of human society (or my own life) with this real future. When Paul says that he presses on, it is towards the mark, i.e., the heavenly calling of God in Jesus Christ. When Israel sets off on its march, its aim is not to make history but to get to the promised land. I am not saying that there is a division between the spiritual goal and the human activities, political, economic, and so forth, which make up the historical future, and which are without importance. This would be the direct opposite of all that I have ever thought or written. It should be noted, however, that contrary to what many philosophers think, history is the past, and only the past. For me as a Christian, history is made by the way in which I live out the grace and freedom of God in my cultural context. This produces a complete mixture between grace and faith on the one side and my biological and psychological being on the other side. Grace and faith are inscribed on this being to produce my work. It is from this personal or collective past, or history, that I am liberated—being no longer conditioned or determined—so that I can undertake afresh to inscribe, insert, and infuse grace and freedom into the world where I am, attempting thereby to change its future into an authentic future. This is possible, however, only if I build strictly on the fact that this authentic future is the kingdom of God and not a specific social organization. This future is my salvation and not the practice of my profession or my elevation to a higher standard of living. History exists only for the past, and as Christians we are freed from this by grace. We have to press on into the future, not to make history (it will make itself), but to set freedom in contest with the necessities which have their origin in the past and which are the logicians of the future. Projected thus into the authentic future, pressing on ahead, the Christian is not simply moving toward socio-political fulfilment nor is he engaged merely in man-made progress. He is pressing on to the kingdom of God which, even as he advances towards it, he has to manifest in the cultural and socio-political context, as he has also to manifest the grace of liberation from self in personal commitment to the ever new vocation which he has from God.

The final aspect of liberation from self is liberation with regard to "the work of my hands." Now obviously when the Bible speaks of the work of man's hands this is to be taken very concretely. We are not to spiritualize it. We are not to think in terms of moral and spiritual works. In my view, when the Bible speaks of works without specifying them in detail the reference is to a total reality of life and not just to moral works, as we so often think. The same applies even where there is express mention of the "works of the law."

No matter what the work of man's hands may be in detail, it is always an aspect of work. As we shall see later, in the Bible work has positive meaning and value for God. But this is not all, for the work of my hands may also be negative. There can be no guarantee. We find no necessary movement from sinful man with his sinful works to saved and pardoned man whose works become good. In reality the works of man's hands in their social context and their concrete signification may have positive value but they may also be destructive. They are this when man submerges himself completely in his work, when he exalts it above himself, when he falls down before it and worships it.

The Old Testament uses these very phrases. Isaiah 2:8 says: "They worship the work of their own hands, that which their own fingers have made"—the fact that the reference is to an idol makes no difference, for it is the work of man's hands that is fashioned into an idol. Habakkuk also, with a precision that throws light on the other passages, says in 1:14–16: "Men catch them in their net ... therefore they rejoice and are glad. Therefore they sacrifice unto their net, and burn incense unto their drag, because by them their portion is fat, and their meat plenteous." Again

Deuteronomy 8:17 says: "My power and the might of mine hand hath gotten me this wealth." This attitude of man towards the work of his hands explains the common complaint of God that men have angered him by the work of their hands. The wrath of God is provoked, not by the work in its material reality or objectivity, but by the posture which man adopts towards it.

Naturally the important thing is the meaning of the attitude rather than the external posture as such. We no longer bow down physically to our works today. We do not kneel to an airplane nor address a prayer to it—although as regards the latter point I am not so sure that passengers might not do some praying, for one person at least has had the courage to tell me that he does. Again, we do not offer incense to television sets and other gadgets. On the other hand, the basic attitude denoted by these external forms has not changed. On the one side we transform the work of our hands into a value. On the other we ascribe saving significance to it.

As regards the first point the phenomenon is a familiar one. Work which is purely material and which has results that are purely material, although by no means negligible, since there can be no contesting the value of technical progress in its own sphere, this work is triumphantly transformed by man into a value, i.e., into a criterion of good and evil, into a significant aim in life, into an irreplaceable factor without which life would not be worth living. The work of our hands is what justifies life and gives it meaning. Instead of being a purely useful and utilitarian affair which is modestly kept in its own place, it takes on the significance of truth or justice or freedom. It is itself truth, justice, or freedom. We ascribe to it that which really belongs to God. In exchange for the material blessings it confers on us, we attribute a spiritual value to it.

This leads on to the second point, namely, the belief that man's salvation will come through technical progress, or the uncontested idealization of productivity and a higher standard of living, or the view that feeding mankind is our most urgent priority, or the assumption that goodness, justice, and so forth can be achieved by political means. The real significance of such beliefs derives from two related convictions. The first is that morality is not possible below a certain standard of living. Up to our own time man has been living only in pre-history. He has just now come of age through technical development. He will grow spiritually thanks to the amelioration of his material life. The second is that any attack on the (purely material) work of the hands of modern man is sacrilegious, scandalous, and destructive of values. The exasperation of those who cannot tolerate any such challenge shows that their attitude is a religious one and that they are in fact worshipping the work of their hands. Saving value is ascribed to it. Through it mankind will finally save itself, whether the work leads to man's reconciliation with himself, with others, and with nature, as in Marxism, or whether it leads to a mutation of humanity and its projection through synthesis to point Omega, as in Teilhardism.

The work of our hands is thus the continual trap into which we fall in trying to avoid worshipping the Lord and him alone. This work is an emanation from ourselves. It is ourselves objectified and detached from us. We may apply to it the analysis which Feuerbach applied to God. We are worshipping ourselves when we worship the work of our hands. We divert worship to ourselves because we regard ourselves as God. We repeat the act of Adam. The demiurge, the technical creator, is the true object of our love and hope and truth. This is the point of the denunciations of Isaiah and Habakkuk.

It is from this that freedom in Christ liberates us. Without this liberation we should be completely and perpetually imprisoned in the worship of our own work. We cannot break free from it by any criticism or any philosophy. We constantly maintain a religious attitude to what we have made with our own hands. This is the climax of alienation. On the basis of liberation by Christ, however, it can all be reversed. Things, however beautiful, useful, pleasant, or clever, can again be things that are to be treated as such and that do not merit our adoration or our love. Only liberation by Christ, however, can bring us back to this realism which is not at all destructive but simply honest, to this relativism which is not at all negative but simply respects proper proportions, to this scepticism which is not at all unbelieving but stands in correlation with faith in Christ.

Liberation in Christ is able to do this. I do not say that it has been done. Our attitude to the work of our hands is not changed by a sudden shift in position. The liberation introduces us to true freedom. This means that we have to make a choice or decision about our attitude to the work of our hands. We may start to worship it again. We may live very differently. Liberation by Christ opens up the possibility of being different from that which is purely determined and determinative. This possibility, however, means that we have to stand at a distance from ourselves in a kind of duplication. We have to be prepared for the critical scrutiny which Christ himself evoked in his debates with the Pharisees.

### § 2. Freedom in Relation to the Powers[3]

Liberation in Christ frees us not only from the flesh but also from the powers. Here again some explanation is necessary. The Bible speaks of forces which subjugate man. These are distinct from the flesh, which in some sense assimilates itself to man. They are not just evil and rebellious powers. They are not just powers which scripture has rightly or wrongly, realistically or mythically, personalized. We have to take the term "power"

---

3  Cf. the fine phrase of Cardonnel: "Faith in Christ makes us atheists in relation to the gods."

*The Object of Freedom and the Will of Man*

in its broadest sense, for the law and religion can also be described as powers.

Liberation from the law is liberation from a power. We find ourselves in the common movement whereby man loses his freedom when he uses it against God and receives it when God re-establishes dialogue with him. God imposes a commandment on man. The decisive and constantly repeated act of man is to separate this word from the one who speaks it and to try to make it his own.

Adam did this. Faced by the one commandment of God, he isolated it under the serpent's influence. He set God aside and controlled the commandment by giving it another point and meaning. Finally he made the commandment into a word of his own by himself saying what is good and evil. The relationship with God was thus broken and Adam's finitude became his alienation.

Now the Old Testament shows that this process was constantly repeated by man. It was especially repeated by the chosen people; Paul brings out the implications of the changing of God's commandment into law. We must not think, however, that the process was peculiar to Israel. At issue here is the relation of all men to God, and particularly of Christians.

As is shown by Jesus in the Sermon on the Mount, and also in the exhortations in the New Testament epistles, we constantly separate the commandment from him who speaks it. This means that it ceases to be a living word. It is a living commandment only because he who formulates it is the living God. Apart from him this word becomes a dead word comparable to any quotation from any author. It no longer draws its value, force, and authority from the one who has spoken it. The commandment is not seen to be true for man because God is the true God. It now derives its authority from itself and its content. Man can thus evaluate its content according to his own criteria, e.g., reason. It is no longer invested with what God reveals himself to be for us, namely, love. Once we isolate the commandment from him who speaks it, it is no longer the commandment of love. It necessarily becomes word alone, and as such constraint, duty, and obligation.

Above all, when man separates the commandment from God in this way and sees it only as commandment, it becomes man's own word. He can then go on to treat it as his own word. He may still view it as the supreme and perfect word, but it is still the word of man. We should note this well, for it is still true even though, like the Jews, we continue to maintain explicitly that we regard it as the word of God.

What we are describing is not a philosophical or theological attitude. It is our natural and unconscious inclination. It is our innermost tendency even though in good faith we believe that we are defending the word of God. This always happens when we legalize the commandment, when we isolate it, when we try to obey it to the letter, or conversely when we dismiss it easily by saying that it is outmoded, when we make a summary of it (an ethics), when we bring it into our own circuit of good and evil, when we use it in our own lives to justify ourselves (before God) or to condemn ourselves (in God's place), when we harden it into a reality that has been declared once and for all, when we measure it by our own standards, or when we take possession of it in exposition, discussion, or dissection. In all these common and familiar attitudes we seize the commandment of God and make it our own word.

This brings dialogue with God to an end. When we make the word of God our own word we simply talk to ourselves. Our dialogue is with our own reflection in a mirror.

Why do we unconsciously separate the commandment from him who speaks it? It is because the latter makes us uncomfortable. He disturbs us by his incalculability, by his actuality, by the weight that he gives to his words. We prefer to deal with mere words, with a formula which is stable, which does not budge, which we can count on, which enables us to estimate our chances.

A strange thing happens, however, when we make this separation, when we seize the commandment and make it into our own law, so that the living word is only past scripture. We believe that in so doing we shall establish our power over this law and to some degree make it a chattel of ours. Instead, we invest this law itself with power.

The power that we have denied to God (the power of love) is transferred to what we have made an emanation of our own, namely, the law. But now it is legal, moral power. It is an implacable power of judgment that hangs over us. We have made the law into a law of death. We wanted to make it into something else, but we are caught, for the law is a much weightier matter than we supposed. It was given by God. It was invested with power by God. It cannot be changed into a mere object in our own hands. It cannot be something mediocre and neutral. It was the word of life and it is not going to become a mere phrase in fiction. It becomes the cause of death (Romans 7:7–13).

The law itself becomes a power over us[4] which constrains and binds us and pushes us further and further away from God. This is what the Bible is showing us when it describes the exaltation of the Torah, the adoration of the word and the letter, and the fanatical obedience that will lead to conflict with the Son of God and ultimately to his death. For we should not forget that when we deaden the commandment so that it is no longer the place of dialogue with the Father, when we make of it our own word and thus break off the relation with the love of the living God, this does not simply mean that we quarantine ourselves and shut ourselves up in a

---

4  Malet, *Mythos et Logos* (1962), 208 points out that the law is a power, not because it incites to sin, but because fulfilling it leads to the supreme sin of denying grace.

*The Object of Freedom and the Will of Man*

ghetto. It means that we do violence to God himself. God willed to be love, and in refusing this love we bring about the death of God.

In the form of word or law or morality, the law invades our lives. It becomes a crushing and oppressive power that drives us away from God. It brings us under the attraction of evil and makes the good sterile and desiccated. It becomes demanding and mingles with the moral systems of the world except that it is infinitely more rigorous, being a power in a sense that moral systems can never be. It takes possession of our lives. Thus man comes to be made for the sabbath. Man himself brings this about, but only because the law comes from a higher place than man. This is why the law becomes a source of bondage. And this is why Crespy[5] is right when he says that "the law corresponds to the 'nature' of man. . . . This is why it exists and also why it is a burden. When Jesus attacks the Jewish commandments . . . he acts as a liberator who deals with everything that enslaves man. The law was made for man, but man has been made for the law in the hope that he can be saved and freed by subjection to it. In reality a new bondage has been set up, a gilded bondage in some regards, for the moment man was brought under the law he was given the hope, in spite of all the evidence, that a means was given him whereby he could please God and escape his wrath." This was possible only because the law itself not merely had power but had itself become a power with its own intrinsic authority. This is why it can enslave and why its threat continues even to our own day. Crespy is also right when he says that "we are always in danger of being satisfied once more with a purely external law, alienating our freedom, through sloth or false comfort, by complying with the order outlined by the law. We are constantly tempted to reinvest our freedom in unimaginative obedience to commandments. Hence the commandment replaces our freedom and takes charge of our moral existence."

Precisely to the extent that the law is a power over us,[6] its authority infinitely surpasses our own possibilities of action. We are absolutely unable to gain freedom from it ourselves. A negative attitude in no way brings release from it. To deny that the law is God's word is precisely to transform it into a subjugating power. To deny that its content has any value at all is precisely to imprison oneself in the movement of good and evil that we described in the Introduction. Finally, by a curious coincidence, those who think they have freed themselves from the law are the very ones who have constructed far more oppressive moral (or immoral) systems incorporating

---

5 "Une morale pour les chrétiens," *Christ. social* (1957), 833ff.

6 For confirmation of this understanding cf. Colossians 2:14f.: "Blotting out the handwriting of ordinances that was against us, which was contrary to us, he took it out of the way, nailing it to his cross, and having spoiled principalities and powers, he made a shew of them openly, triumphing over them in it." Here and elsewhere Paul equates the law and the principalities and powers.

essential features of the law itself (as may be seen in the bourgeois morality of Voltaire or the neo-bourgeois morality of the Soviet Union). In an odd and mysterious way man can never free himself from this power that subjugates him.

As Bonhoeffer points out in his *Ethics*, the attitude of Jesus to the law is the direct opposite of that of the Pharisees. He rejects their casuistry and will not solve their hard cases (Matthew 22). His freedom will not let him be drawn into their debates. Freedom in relation to the law means freedom in relation to the good as well. The good is not a value or achievement. Liberated man need not worry about it or even try to know it. To do this is to fall back into the debates from which Jesus frees us.

Only to the degree that we become free men are we liberated from the power of the law. Note that I do not say that the power of the law is broken and we become free men as a result. The movement is the reverse of this. The Liberator frees us, and when we become free we are freed from the power. Why this nuance? It is because the issue in our liberation is not the annulment of the law. Being freed we enter into dialogue with God again. We reply to him. The exchange recommences. God is again the living God for us, for we are now alive again, i.e., free, in Christ and through Christ. The word can again become for us the word of *God,* and our own word takes on a new seriousness when our freedom for God makes it into prayer, which is the source of every authentic human word. To the degree that the dialogue recommences, however, God retrieves the word that he gave. He makes it his own word again. He takes it away from us. He transforms it into a living commandment. It is a living commandment because it has been lived out and fulfilled by Jesus.

Since the law is now the law of the life of the Liberator, it is not and cannot be any longer constraint, bondage, or necessity. The commandment of the life of the Liberator is living and actual as the Liberator himself rose again. Hence the law cannot be suppressed or left behind or pushed aside. It is the law of God. It has been transformed, however, for it is now the law of liberty. (We shall discuss this later.) Here again we may quote Crespy: "If it remains the law for Christians, this is because it is not a means of salvation but a guide to obedience within the salvation which has already been acquired. . . . Freedom alone recognizes and validates the law. This is why Christian obedience, which is guided and directed by the law, can have its source only in freedom, as Luther firmly established." It is because we are liberated that the law has the full value of law, and that it is absolutely valid and true and serious for us in all its details, with no cultural or spiritual attenuations.

This is true, however, not because the law is anything in itself, but because it is God's law, and if God has appropriated a cultural form it is not for us to argue with him. It is true because we are now absolutely free and we neither hope nor expect anything from the law nor do we attribute to it any higher meaning than it actually has. This is how the familiar transformation takes place that the law becomes law for us.

The law ceases now to be the act that accuses us. It is not even a restrictive schoolmaster. The law is now made for man. It is set in the service of freedom; it does not judge this freedom. It no longer has any direct power over our lives. Because our freedom sees and hears the word of God in it, we take it very seriously. But even as we do so, we note a change in key. As the law of liberty, the law is never negative. It no longer diminishes or weakens. It is not a barrier or constraint. Its "No" exists only for alienated man who is under the powers. Only as a power is it negative and alienating. This is what Paul says in Romans 7:7–13: "I had not known lust, except the law had said, Thou shalt not covet. But sin, taking occasion by the law, wrought in me all manner of concupiscence. . . . Sin, that it might appear sin, worked death in me by that which was good." It is in the situation of bondage that the law is negative. The "No" of the law brings the work of sin to light. It is the "No" that God pronounces on the work of the natural man, but it is such because this word has been seized by enslaved man.

On the basis of liberation, the law becomes positive. It becomes a source and spring of action, an incentive to discovery, invention, and expression. As the life of the Living One, it promotes life.

Yet do we not have to say that its formulation remains the same? Do not the innumerable negative commandments remain unchanged? When we read the Ten Commandments, whether we be slave or free, we shall still read: "Thou shalt not kill," and this is obviously negative. But another transformation of the law now takes place to which Barth, Cullmann, and others have drawn attention. Two senses are now possible. The commandment may certainly be read as a prohibition. This is all that it is for the sinner. For alienated man it is only negative. For the man who has been liberated in and by Christ, however, it has another meaning. It is still, of course, a limit. It is the boundary of his obedience. It delimits the circle of his freedom. But it is much more than a limit. It is also a promise. It sets before man that which God promises he shall be as free man, as the man who has entered into dialogue with God again. The negation becomes an opening.

The Lord himself bears witness to this. The Liberator promises that man will be set free from the law of murder, theft, and adultery. What is opened up for him is no mere possibility (that it is now possible not to kill any more, etc.). It goes much further. He is not just enabled to make a choice. The promise of God is that he will in effect become this free man.

For this is free man. A mark of alienation is the strange perversion according to which being free means being able to do wrong. To kill is the one thing that gives a sense of being free, says Wright in *Native Son*. Similarly the *Journal d'un Voleur* shows that stealing means freedom.

Innumerable works say the same about adultery or taking drugs. It is remarkable that modern man has this feeling of freedom when he is alienating himself from his most profound human inclinations or habits and is sliding down this slope. Opposition to social stability or middle-class morality is understandable, but this is a superficial explanation, for sodomy and alcoholism have always existed and are by no means peculiar to a moralizing age. What we really have here is obedience to determinations, and this is called freedom.

In contrast, the promise is that we will be emancipated from these alienations, not because they incline us to do wrong, but because they are alienations, and mortal ones at that. Thus the prohibition that is placed in front of us becomes a permission which we can now take advantage of in the perspective of the promise which bears witness to us that the permission is not given in vain. In God's intention the commandment is the source of life. It does not prohibit; it permits. It does not limit; it designates. It does not weaken; it supports. It constitutes the basis of freedom by giving a task. Thus the commandment not to eat of the tree in the garden permits, designates, and underlies man's presence before God without the distance represented by the anguished knowledge of good and evil. God commands in order that man may use.[7]

The imperative in this law has the same character as the prohibition. The one will of God is to free man, to place the promise before him, and to open finally the gates that are closed. But this is so only if we read the words in their proper relation, i.e., their relation to the Lord who speaks them. This is why, according to Crespy, "Christ in his preaching offers us a broken law which we cannot obey, which certainly cannot save us, and which thus forces us to go back to the Saviour. The absoluteness of the moral demands of Christ and their impracticality attract our attention to the fact that Christ is our Saviour." Hence this law becomes the charter of our freedom because it has ceased to be a power.

Note should be taken here of the seriously mistaken view that according to Paul we are simply freed from the kingdom and pedagogy of the law when we live in faith, that we have passed from the state of law to that of grace. But things are not quite that simple. Can we be certain of living in faith and expressing grace in our lives? Once we diverge from the love of God we fall back into the law, not as pagans, but still under the law in all its rigor. For when the word of God has come it will not go away again. We cannot live as if we had not heard it. It sets us either in the freedom of faith or under the rigor of the law.

How do we know that we are living in the freedom of faith? Not by uneasy introspection which will finally lead to the question whether we have faith, but by seeing that the law is indeed a thing of the past. The "I say unto you" of Jesus does not make the law harder; it expresses freedom.

---

7  Cf. the report of *Church and World*, May 1965.

As law, saying "Thou fool" or "looking on a woman" means impossible and absurd rigorism, but the point is that we are freed from ourselves, from lust or hatred. Yet if hatred and lust are still there, this means that we are not free; we are not living by Christian freedom. But happily the law is still present to welcome and guide us. Freedom does not take us outside law. Hence, even though we are not free, we are still trying to do what is stated in the law. This is an act of the humility of faith and the first step of freedom.

Freedom says: Sell all you have and give to the poor. You cannot do it? Then the merciful law tells you to give at least a dime. This will be a little act of freedom, of recognition of inability to do more, and hence of appeal to God's grace.

In the Christian life there is continual coming and going between law and faith, an advance in freedom and falling back on the law. We are not yet in the absolute and beatific state of being free.

If we think we are, our condemnation is the more severe. For we then make a pretext of grace and freedom to neglect the law and live on a lower level than the commandments. In freedom from the law my wicked mind tells me I need only give a nickel instead of a dime, since the dime is shocking legalism unworthy of my spirituality. Freedom from the law opens the door to cupidity and hardness of heart, so that I can ignore the poor and cheat my employees and have no scruples about murder or divorce. What is unleashed here is animal freedom, the autonomy of sin.

This common view is simply a mark of blindness, hypocrisy, delusion, stupidity, and vanity. I would rather see Christians use phylacteries and keep the Sabbath in Jewish style than see them as they are, abusing grace and freedom, not even going beyond minimal demands, living as they like. This is the height of imposture. Puritans and literalists were far more serious than we who make a comedy of freedom, a pretext of grace, a mere emotion of faith, and the crassest social conformity of the Christian life. We are fornicators in relation to the love of God, appealing to our freedom to transgress his commandments a hundred times a day.

There are, of course, other powers apart from the law. I do not propose to enter into the theological debate about these powers.[8] Are they demons in the most elemental and traditional sense? Are they less precise powers (thrones and dominions) which still have an existence, reality, and, as one might say, objectivity of their own? Or do we simply have a disposition of man which constitutes this or that human factor a power by exalting it as such (cf. what was said about the work of our hands)? "Shadows and illusions are the fruit of the sinful free decision of man which has made the world into a power that dominates and subjects him."[9] In this case the powers are not objective realities which influence man from

---

8  There will be a fuller discussion in our ethics of holiness.
9  Malet, *La théologie de Bultmann*, p. 55.

without. They exist only by the determination of man which allows them to exist in their subjugating otherness and transcendence.[10] Or finally, at the far end of the scale, are the powers simply a figure of speech common to the Jewish-Hellenistic world, so that they merely represent cultural beliefs and have no true validity?

I cannot go into these four possibilities here. I can only state my own view, which lies somewhere between the second and third interpretations. On the one side, I am fully convinced with Barth and Cullmann that the New Testament *exousiai* and the power of money personified as Mammon correspond to authentic, if spiritual, realities which are independent of man's decision and inclination and whose force does not reside in the man who constitutes them. Nothing that I have read to the contrary has had any great cogency for me. Neither the appeal to Gnosticism nor reference to the cultural background seems to me to explain the force and emphasis of the New Testament writers in this area. In particular the opposite view has to follow the common practice of ignoring certain essential passages where Paul cannot be adequately demythologized.

On the other side, however, the powers do not act simply from outside after the manner of Gnostic destiny or a *deus ex machina*. They are characterized by their relation to the concrete world of man. According to the biblical references they find expression in human, social realities, in the enterprises of man. In this sense the occasion of their intervention is human decision and action.[11] To this extent, then, man does constitute them. But he does so only because they exist in their singularity and personality. It is the fact that they act on the level of the concrete reality of human life, and not just in the spiritual or moral sphere, which leads me to believe that the world of which the New Testament speaks is not just a spiritual and abstract reality but one which is identical with what man in general calls the world, i.e., society.

I shall have occasion to speak about this later. For the moment I will simply say that to me the powers seem to be able to transform a natural, social, intellectual, or economic reality into a force which man has no

---

10  *Ibid.,* p. 211.

11  From a nonbiblical angle K. Jaspers also discovers the reality of the powers, which he calls anonymous forces that attack the very being of man, who is under threat of loss by dispersion as non-being seems to want to annex the whole sphere of existence. Jaspers shows that one aspect of these anonymous forces is the perversion of freedom, which finds expression in confusion, in the revolt of alleged truth, and in a false search for peace and justice, and which produces hatred and freedom when man finds escape from himself in a generally recognizable action under the pretext of the common good. In the organization of existence everything seems designed to free man from the necessity of being himself which is intrinsic of him. . . . Being oneself is a summons to be free. Man's striving towards his freedom, which is in reality independence, consists in freeing himself from the necessity of being himself. It is the work of the anonymous forces, which negate freedom while pretending to achieve it. Cf. *Die geistige Situation der Welt* (1932).

ability either to resist or to control. This force ejects man from his divinely given position as governor of creation. It gives life and autonomy to institutions and structures. It attacks man both inwardly and outwardly by playing on the whole setting of human life. It finally alienates man by bringing him into the possession of objects which would not normally possess him.

All this seems to me to correspond both to the situations which cause us to speak about the powers and to the description of them which is given in the different biblical passages, as, for example, when Paul says that we do not wrestle with flesh and blood but with principalities and powers (Ephesians 6:12). A text like this is not distinguishing between spiritual and material factors, between the powerful tendencies of our corporeal being and the disincarnate powers that reside only in heavenly places. Such a dichotomy, although traditional in commentaries on Ephesians, seems to run counter to Paul's whole teaching both about the relation of soul and body and about the powers. The real point, it seems to me, is that flesh and blood are redoubtable, not as such, not when they are considered alone or left to themselves, but when they are seized, used, and modified by the powers.

This is certainly true of what from a naturalistic angle we consider to be institutions, structures, or social forces. The Bible mentions two of these explicitly, the state and money. We have here political and economic structures or factors about which there is common agreement as regards one point, namely, that if they are viewed simply in their concrete reality and natural dimension, and at the level of their function, it is impossible to understand their power, to measure their zone of action, or to grasp their true reality. No one has ever yet been able to find the basis of political power or the reason why men always irresistibly and irremediably obey it.[12] On the face of it this obedience is completely irrational and absurd. It is out of all proportion to the reality of the power. There is no logical explanation why this power should be able to seduce men. Political power has many dimensions, e.g., social, economic, psychological, ethical, psychoanalytical, and legal. But when we have scrutinized them all, we have still not apprehended its reality. I am not speaking hastily or lightly here but as one who has passed most of his life in confrontation with this question and in this power. We cannot say with Marx that the power is an ideological superstructure, for it is always there. The disproportion noted above leads me to the unavoidable conclusion that another power intervenes and indwells and uses political power, thus giving it a range and force that it does not have in itself.

The same is true of money.[13] The question is identical. An examination of money and its functions from the naturalistic standpoint does not

---

12  Cf. J. Ellul, "La théologie de l'état" in *Les Chrétiens et l'état* (1967).
13  J. Ellul, *L'homme et l'argent* (1949).

explain its power. If one tackles the matter from a psychological or ethical angle rather than the economic angle it is still impossible to show why all civilizations have attributed to this measure of value a dimension, force, and attraction that we do not attribute to measures of length or volume. Nor is it easy to establish the relation between the economic function and the psychological aspect. To talk of avarice is to explain nothing, for it is simply not true that the individual thirst for gold causes whole societies to be structured in terms of money and its function. Marx was right when he stripped this question of its moral character and brought to light the mechanism of naked power, just as he was right when he brought to light the mechanism whereby man is alienated in money, whether he has it or whether he does not. On the other hand, Marx fails to offer any explanation of the complexity of the problem. His historical analysis is not a solution. As I see it, money is what it is only because Mammon indwells it. We are not in the presence of a mere economic phenomenon. We are in the presence of an economic phenomenon which is quickened by a power that destroys man, that man himself does not create, and that does not issue from the heart of man.

These two examples suggest others. Thus one might ask whether technology is not also one of these powers. The answer seems to be simple enough.

More difficult is the question whether the various elements in society which come under a sign of power (in the mathematical sense) correspond to the *stoicheia* of the world to which Paul refers in Galatians. I hesitate to say this. There is obvious uncertainty as to the correct understanding of these *stoicheia*. They have to be "constitutive elements"—and it seems most unlikely that Paul would have fallen into the Gnostic error of thinking in terms of the material elements of the cosmos, the stars, and so forth. They are also elements of the "world," which can hardly be separated from society even if it is more than this. "Bondage" to these elements is also at issue, and in the context they can hardly be the body. It should also be noted that the phrase comes between the end of chapter 3, which deals with the distinctions between Jew and Greek, bond and free, male and female, and 5:4f., which speaks of the law under which man is set when he is yet to be redeemed. In my view this suggests that the *stoicheia* are in part the social structures which imprison us (as at the end of c. 3) and in part the law, whose power we studied earlier. This link with the law seems to be clearly indicated by the parallel verse, Colossians 2:20, while Colossians 2:8, which refers to the tradition of men, might very well be referring to what we have called the social structures.

If this interpretation is sound, the *stoicheia* are the elements of society, or of the world in general, which are transposed into force, activity, and seduction by the intervention of a power which is superior to man but which man accepts and to which he attributes force and authority even to the point of subjection to it. In Colossians Paul tells us that philosophy is based on these elements and assigns value to them.

Among the powers from which we are freed the system must be mentioned, not in the sense of the normal tendency to systematize, but in the extended sense we find in Marx and modern structuralism (cf. Foucault, "Les mots et les choses" and Lefebvre, "Le Nouvel Eléatisme," *L'Homme et la Société*, I and II). This dangerous manifestation of man leads to man's negation and proclamation of the triumph of death. It aims at a total, mechanical, and exclusive definition and explanation of the world. It pretends to offer a mechanism of history and society which is both blind and implacable. It is pure form and also final cause. We are all oriented to its realization. In modern thought it replaces the clock-maker God. It rules out all that is living: human projects, the idea of freedom, and the shaping of history. Man's only value in it is to serve economic and social development. Things exist for it alone. They do not count in themselves. The system is a nexus of relations which exist and change apart from them. Men as well as objects merely have their functions in relation to other men or objects.

The totality obeys a kind of code. Social organization, like scientific research, follows a secret plan that it cannot escape from. Since it is anonymous, man cannot change it. It negates human possibility and initiative. What man can do has no importance. He cannot affirm himself, or find himself, or even find reality (Levi-Strauss). His transitory and contingent experience has significance only for superficial observers who accept wrong explanations and are content not to know. The system is the basic and abstract organization on which is played out the charade of actions and decisions. The impersonal structures everything, including the personal.

My task here is not to criticize the system philosophically, which I could not do, but to show that it confronts us with a general, objective, and constant code. Possibly those who elaborate it are right. Perhaps things are like this. Perhaps it offers a better explanation than the nuances and fluctuations and pluralities of personalism. Perhaps it is more in keeping with our concrete situation. But if so, it is from this that Christ frees us: not just from the determinations but from the system which explains them.

Man's being caught in a web of coordinated necessities is one thing; his making of them into an implacable system is another. In doing this he attaches his own view of fate to the determinations. He makes it impossible to change them. Hence when freedom in Christ frees us from the system, this is not the same as liberation from the forces themselves. It is liberation from man's bent to create the system, to adjust himself to reality by bolting the prison door. It is liberation from the seductive power that inclines us this way, for man does not take this direction simply on his own. He feels he has to explain necessities by making them completely necessary. Christ frees us from this power. For, when we are freed in Christ, we see that the system is a human theory which leaves us with the possibility of choice. We do not have to accept the system. We have to make a judgment, not of coherence with reality, but of truth. Even if the system is coherent with reality, is it the last word on the truth of man and the truth about man?

Freedom in Christ forces us to reject it. But this entails rejection of all systems, including specifically a Christian system. There can be no accepting a Christian philosophy or a dogmatics. These are not forbidden. Nothing is forbidden. But we must proceed with caution. Even though Barth prudently sets dogmatics in the service of the church, he finds it hard to avoid a system in which principles and their consequences are organized and questions achieve their own totalism, so that Christian freedom is menaced. The reaction against Barth's system is in my view wrong theologically but right as an expression of freedom. Barth's work and results may be used, but the system should be rejected. Dogmatics in spite of every precaution cannot avoid becoming a system, but we should not let the powers use dogmatics to imprison the church. The church has constantly to engage in debate to keep the tension between individualism and ecclesiastical dogmatism. Each of these must protect the other against its peculiar dangers. The danger here is that of dogmatics becoming a system.

Another power which merits special attention is religion (cf. Ellul, *Les nouveaux possédés*, 1973). For religion is one of the constant forces in man's alienation. As noted earlier, I fully accept the analyses of Feuerbach and Marx in this regard. This seems to me to be the point in the Old Testament struggle against (false) gods, which scripture, as I see it, distinguishes from idols, since idols are a creation of man which he invests with a value and authority they do not have in themselves. On the subject of idols Bultmann's analysis seems to me to be correct. The authors of the Old Testament, however, were not deceived. They describe idols in this way. But alongside them—and this is no mere question of their age—they also see gods who have a kind of reality of their own quite apart from human concepts. If on the one hand the eyes of men have to be opened so that they can see the alienation they themselves have brought about, on the other hand external forces have to be destroyed, and the chosen people is God's instrument in this conflict, for its liberation from Egypt means its emancipation from the powers; Egypt is a symbol of these and not just a political power.

Now if in this conflict it is stressed that God is the only God and that the gods are falsehood and vanity—although this does not mean at all that they are non-existent or powerless—we are hardly justified in speaking of the struggle between a true religion and a false religion. For what we have on the one side is not religion at all. It is revelation and fellowship, which does not have to find incarnation in any religious form invented or elaborated by man. On the other side we simply have religion in its etymological and sociological sense, namely, as the bond which man has

*The Object of Freedom and the Will of Man*

created between the gods and himself with a view to binding the gods, as a bond which society needs if it is to survive, as an expression of the natural religious feeling of man, of the need which he has to draw near to a god which he himself makes, which is designed to satisfy him, and which is made according to his own measure.

Now religion shows itself to be a power to the extent that it can lay hold of its opposite, namely, the revelation of God in Christ, and constantly make it fulfil the double function of a social bond and a psychological satisfaction. Religion in this sense is injurious to the very reality of God, for it incites man to refute, reject, and revolt against the bond, so that when he can negate religion he thinks he may also proclaim that God is dead.

No matter whether religion takes a positive form or provokes negation, either way it offers man a fine method of avoiding true encounter with God. In this regard it is a power because the result is not at all what man consciously or intentionally has in view. Man may be acting in good faith when he assimilates the revelation in Christ to religion. He simply wants to put something that eludes him in its accustomed and traditional place. He does not want to destroy the work of God. This makes it all the worse. One might say that man is the victim of unconscious hypocrisy. A better way to put it, however, is that he is the victim of the religious power which possesses and dominates him.

Set among the powers, and to some extent their prisoner, man is ultimately unable to break free from them himself. The reintegration of the object by which Hegel thinks he can give man the power to escape the objects that determine him is a mere illusion. A mark of the powers is that they give these objects a quality which far exceeds all the resources of man. What shows us yet again that a power is at work is that all man's efforts to free himself lead ineluctably to new bondage. This rule holds good whenever we see man trying to work his way out of a situation. A good example is his struggle against religion.

The nineteenth century had the grandiose idea, or came under the great illusion, that the age of religion was over. History could be described in terms of a religious period, as in Comte and Marx. But now purely rational man would break out of the fogs of the spiritual and substitute science for religion. Since Christianity had been assimilated to religion—and with good reason, for Christians had succeeded in making a religion out of it—all that was needed for man's emancipation was to get rid of Christianity.

The religious spirit, however, is both tenacious and subtle. New religious forms soon began to appear. If we grant that a religion is present when we have a group of beliefs and of practices related to the objects of these beliefs; if we note that the religious phenomenon as thus defined is accompanied by great feeling and intransigence and that the beliefs take concrete shape in symbols which are rallying points for believers; if finally the religious spirit is characterized by strong opposition to all other beliefs, then we find a whole crop of religions at the end of the nineteenth century and especially in the twentieth century.

There is the religion of science, and here we see the power of religion bringing about the same reversal as in the case of revelation, i.e., the transformation into religion of something that was intended to destroy it. There is also the religion of the state, especially in the three great religious forms of communism, nationalism, and national socialism, which are not by any means exhausted. Any rigorous sociologist is forced to conclude that these movements are in the first instance religious movements. They are also worldwide, so that the age of reason is in fact the most religious age that man has known since the sixteenth century.

The same mechanism may be seen at other levels. Thus one might refer to political alienation. It is an odd fact that every time man tries to free himself from dictatorship or from the exploitation of man by man, this leads at once to the setting up of a tyranny just as great. Louis XVI is overthrown only to be followed by Robespierre and Napoleon; this is the implacable pattern of history. Nicholas II gives place to Stalin, Batista to Castro, and Farouk to Nasser. It is pretended that things are now different, that the structures of power have changed, that institutions or intentions or aims are no longer the same. But this is simply a partisan way of hiding the truth, of concentrating on the trees so that the wood will not be seen. It is an imposture, especially when the well-known distinction is made between reactionary dictatorships which are simply trying to perpetuate the past, like that of Franco, and progressive dictatorships which are preparing the ground for the future, such as that of Castro. The important thing is not progress; it is the fact of dictatorship itself. This is always an end, never a means. It always manifests the same forms. It produces an extraordinary mixture of archaic and retrogressive brutality on the one side and geometric and progressive benignity on the other, two indissoluble elements, as may be very well seen in the supreme example of Stalin. The main point, however, is that liberation carries with it a reproduction of the power that has been destroyed. The power of the state may be seen in this.

Naturally this type of sociological determinism does not mean that it is not worth fighting for freedom or trying to topple dictatorships. This is always well worth the effort, as will be shown later. Nevertheless, we are given concrete warning that in such movements of liberation or revolution we are not fighting against flesh and blood but against principalities and powers. Hence to the degree that man uses human methods and acts only on the socio-political plane he will always be finally vanquished by his own victory. Caught in the snare of victory, he will himself refashion the very thing he was trying to eliminate.

The powers are certainly stronger than man. How can even a man of goodwill escape the power of money which holds him at every level of

*The Object of Freedom and the Will of Man*

existence? He can be saved from the powers only by an external intervention which has then necessarily to become internal. He can be saved only as the objective intervention of Christ against the powers overcomes them. Neither individually nor collectively can man break free from them himself.

The powers have in fact been defeated in the crucifixion of Christ. What has beaten them is that on the cross, as in the temptation and in the self-abnegation of deity (the *kenosis*), Christ did not meet force with force. He did not engage in the type of combat described by medieval authors. The armies of heaven were not mobilized as on the canvas of Breughel.[14] God did not deploy his absolute power. He stripped himself of power. The principalities and powers were themselves stripped of power because they encountered the one who did not compete with them but let himself be stripped. They did not meet a victor. They met a prisoner who gave himself up to them. The powers were thus stripped of the one thing they have, namely, their power to vanquish. They had nothing here to vanquish. They were robbed of any possible victory. The worst tyrant wins no triumph when his enemy voluntarily yields to him, neither in supplication nor fear, neither in combat nor negation, but simply in love. The tyrant who can kill this enemy kills himself, for he loses at a stroke both purpose and meaning. The powers have been defeated because Jesus could say that no one could take away his life; he gave it himself.

Greater precision is needed, however, regarding the meaning and scope of the victory of Jesus. We are told in Colossians 2:14 that the powers have been despoiled. These alien forces no longer have any authority or attraction or means of operation. They are still powers but they have lost their demiurgic ability to make a different world from that of God and man—a world of temptation and habit, a world of passion and worship, in which, as we have seen, things are invested with value and glory and man is subjugated and despoiled in the name and to the benefit of these realities which appear to be different from what they are.

I am not relapsing into Gnosticism. I am not thinking in terms of intermediary worlds that are inhabited by the powers. This is beside the point altogether. What I said earlier about the astonishing character of the state and money, which are man's creation but which slip out of his control, ought to be enough to show that we have here a demiurgic force. The powers, however, have been despoiled. Things have become things again. We are thus called upon to live in a desacralized world. But the process constantly begins all over again. The woods and springs and grottoes used to be peopled with gods. It is too facile to say that this was only poetic or childish fancy. Man alone did not create the powers. They existed

---

14  One should not forget, of course, the campaign of Revelation 12:7. But the result of this campaign was to hurl Satan and his angels down to earth, where he deceives the world (v. 9). That is to say, the powers were set among the things of this world and were thus placed in the situation that we have just described.

in a sacral universe. They were destroyed. The wood became a mere wood again and the spring water. The powers have found a new habitation, however, in the universe of man. Desacralization has not been accomplished once and for all. It has to be done again and again.

Nature was desacralized through the preaching of revelation in the second and third centuries. But the powers are tenacious. They were able to find a way into Christianity itself. Many saints are simply canonized gods. Sacralization by the powers found its way especially into another sector of the human background.

The Reformation brought about a second desacralization,[15] and we have now moved on to a third. This shows that even though the powers have been despoiled and cannot possibly win, even though they have no true reality or legitimacy, even though they are denounced as falsehood and illusion, nevertheless they enjoy an extraordinary vigor and to all appearances are the same as they ever were. They still have to be fought, and we shall have to speak of this fight later. They have no power, however, for the believer. The decisive matter is the distinction between the man who believes in Jesus Christ and the man who does not. The powers have not been destroyed in themselves. They have no hope of winning but in their objective reality they keep the power of action that we have described. They lose this power only in relation to the man who attaches himself in faith to the victory of Jesus Christ, who bears his cross, who lives in the strength of his grace and resurrection. This man can be freed from the powers and he can also fight them on behalf of men, the world, and of course himself.

Only with the weapons of the Lord, however, is victory possible (Ephesians 6:13ff.). The man who does not have this faith and knowledge remains vulnerable to the powers and will in fact be seduced by them.

My position, then, is the very opposite of what is often found today. For the "demythologizers" the powers have no objective reality but exist only for those who freely constitute them themselves. For the "socializers" (not in the sense of socialism) the victory of Christ over the powers in this world is an objective victory and liberation for the world and for all men with no distinction between those who believe and those who do not. As distinct from the first group I maintain that the powers have objective reality and that they act for themselves apart from the force that man gives them. As distinct from the second group I am convinced that the victory of Jesus Christ can be grasped and lived out only by those who believe and who are thereby put in the position of fighting for other men and for their liberation. It is thus that man, living in a world in which the powers have been despoiled, finds himself free in a validated world and his free action has no other meaning than that which it bears in itself to God's glory.

---

15  Cf. my article "Signification actuelle de la Réforme," *Foi et Vie* (1959).

## § 3. *Freedom in Relation to Revelation*

We now come up against a crucial question. What freedom can we have in face of God's revelation? This question has two aspects. The first is theological or, from another angle, metaphysical. When God reveals himself to a man here and now, does this man retain his freedom? Or does God's act in speaking rule out all human liberty? The second aspect is that, since revelation is an objectified fact (in history and the Bible), does this leave any place for freedom in relation to it? In the present context we shall ignore the first aspect and deal with the second, since this alone is ethical in nature.

Revelation is an objective fact. At a given moment God revealed himself to a man in his singularity. This man then passed on the fact and content of revelation to others. This transmission is witness. It can leave traces. A second generation of witnesses may arise who bear witness to the same revelation—they have received the content of the first revelation and want to pass it on. Or the first witness who has been the direct recipient of revelation may put in writing what has happened and what has been said to him. Either way there is objectification. It is through a secondary medium that the revelation can be passed on and its fact and content can be grasped, weighed, and interpreted like any message. To the degree that this message has its source and origin in a revelation, however, one cannot make of it something abstract. One has to say that it is a revealed datum, unless the first witness who received it is viewed as a liar or a fool and the message is thus dismissed without examination as irrelevant. The point is, however, that the revealed content of the datum cannot be received directly as such. We also have an objectification which claims to be a continuation of the revelation of God.

This in turn is not directly perceptible or comprehensible or receivable as such unless we can reproduce the original situation in which God reveals himself here and now to me as he did to Paul and the rest. The Bible constantly describes the movement whereby God accomplishes this. What he imparts to those to whom he reveals himself is not something new but the same revelation as he made to the original witness. Hence the witness of the Bible is the objectified datum both of what has been revealed and of what is potentially revealed. If what is potential is to become actual, however, there is needed not only God's decision here and now but also study of the original datum of revelation and the attempt both to understand it and to grasp it by human means. Only as we make the effort to lay hold of it through the traces left by the witnesses do we have any chance of seeing it transformed into revelation for us.

Without waiting for God's act, then, we have to lay hold of the witness concerning his past acts. To some degree, however, the objectification by witnesses will not coincide exactly with the impact of revelation, which is a subjective act. There is distance and difference between the dialogue of revealer and witness and that of witness and hearer. Hence we still have some freedom in relation to the revealed datum.

It must be stressed, of course, that this is Christian freedom. It is the freedom of the man who has been converted by God and who is trying to get at the meaning of scripture because it is in fact a revealed datum for him. If we had in mind purely intellectual research which regards the given text merely as a literary or historical writing this would be independence over against the Creator. In this light one may say that freedom in relation to the revealed deposit is to be found on three levels.

First (1) it is freedom of interpretation of hermeneutics. Then (2) it is freedom of deviation. Finally (3) it is freedom of research.

(1) Freedom of interpretation. This is obviously not the place to go into the question of interpretation or to try to establish good hermeneutical methodology. Our sole concern is with freedom. To what extent is there hermeneutical freedom, and what does it mean?

We may begin by noting that hermeneutics is usually justified today by a reference to cultural background. The existing text which bears witness to God's revelation was written in a specific cultural context. The men who wrote it lived under a specific political regime, shared the religious, intellectual, and social beliefs of their age, and were conditioned by their language and the concepts formulated in it.

The background has now changed. We no longer think in the same way today; rational thinking has replaced mythical thinking. Our language does not follow the same rules nor carry the same concepts. We have changed our beliefs with the transition to a scientific age. Hence we cannot preserve the biblical text as it is. Interpretation is needed if it is to have any meaning.

This line of argument, which is endlessly repeated, is much too simplistic. It presents innumerable difficulties in spite of its obvious strength; I have tried to draw attention to these elsewhere, and will not go into them again here. Naturally I do not reject the thesis as such. My main point in this context is that it has nothing whatever to do with hermeneutical freedom. What it proves is that interpretation belongs to the order of necessity rather than freedom. We have to engage in successive reinterpretations with successive cultural changes. If we refuse to do this we shall never be able to understand the text or to make contact with the original witness. We are not free in this regard. To engage in interpretation for cultural reasons is simply to submit to a necessary movement of the history of civilizations. There is nothing here at any level to guarantee even the least freedom in interpretation.

Indeed, one of the things that disturbs me about modern hermeneutics is its complete subjection to the modern cultural background with its fashions and fads and scientific façade and ideology. I find not the slightest sign of freedom here nor even the most modest approach to truth. Applying a structural method to the text of the Bible is not in any sense an act of freedom.

The very basis of hermeneutics is thus to be sought elsewhere, and in my view it lies in the act which God performs to liberate us. If God really frees us, it is not in order to subject us at once to automatic conditioning or to plunge us into endless repetition. Biblical literalism is what transforms the freedom of faith into an arrested system that cannot avoid being scholastic in intellectual form and repetitive in the ethical domain.

Now the automatic and repetitive, as we have often said, are the direct opposite of freedom. The God who frees us undoubtedly does so in order that, loving his will, we may do it, but not in the sense of the infinite reiteration of a word spoken once. The very freedom that God himself gives us means that we have to act as free men in relation to the text that objectifies God's word. We have to stand at a distance from this text. We are under obligation—and I use the term advisedly, for once we are freed we are under constraint to be free—to act as interpreting subjects of the revealed datum.[16] Interpretation of the expression of revelation becomes an act of our freedom and not the automatic result of cultural change.

It is because the one who reveals himself is love, i.e., liberty, and because he reveals himself in freeing us, and in order to free us, that his liberating word cannot be tied to a definitive interpretation nor condemned to redundancy.

On the other hand, because it is always the word of him who is the Lord, this word cannot be handled arbitrarily, and because it is the word of our freedom it cannot be set aside. In other words our hermeneutical freedom is bound to and by the word which creates this freedom.[17] The fact of freedom of interpretation can never lead us outside this word. We cannot act as though it did not exist. We cannot toy with it as though dealing with idle words. Nor am I alluding to purely imaginary perils.

Above all, we must not do hermeneutics for the mere pleasure of doing it, as often seems to be the case in modern works.

At the same time, hermeneutical freedom is impossible without a serious study of the sense. If this is more than a mere application of method to texts whose sense is immaterial, as often in structuralism, it is also more than a mere study of meanings. We have to bear in mind that there is a great difference and sometimes even opposition between sense and meanings. Hermeneutical freedom is thus the work to which we are committed to the utmost of our power in order that there may be the unveiling of sense which can come only by the act of the Holy Spirit.

---

16  For excellent examples cf. Xavier Léon-Dufour, *La Résurrection de Jésus* (1971), who shows how Paul treats his encounter with the risen Lord with great variety, and therefore with great freedom.

17  One needs to be on guard here against an Idealist view (cf. R. Schaeffler in *L'herméneutique de la liberté religieuse*, 1968).

We do not have to wait beatifically until the Spirit comes. We must plead constantly for this coming. The purest form of this plea is hermeneutical labor. Our freedom of interpretation is our surest guarantee that at the proper time the freedom of the Holy Spirit will manifest itself.

Is there then a correct hermeneutical method? Not at all; there are many methods. Once we think we can work out a closed method of interpretation, we lose hermeneutical freedom. If we think we have found a key to every lock, this inevitably leads to error. The examples of Gnosticism, allegorical interpretation, and the Cabbalists may be recalled. One cannot say that Gnostic interpretation was completely false. Nor is one to reject absolutely the allegorical method. The jokes made about it today are far too facile, and similar jokes might easily be made about the hermeneutical and structuralist nonsense that passes for scientific interpretation in our own times. Scripture itself gives examples of both Gnostic and allegorical interpretation. The error is to make a closed, universal, and exclusive system out of a given method. When we say that we have found the correct method of interpretation we rob ourselves of hermeneutical freedom and fall into error.

If in contrast we study the relation between the culture of the time and the expression of revelation, we find a complex interplay of adoption and adaptation. In a given cultural and historical setting, the intervention of revelation takes the following course. First we have appropriation; the message of God uses the cultural modes of a specific time and place and enters into them. Then there is contradiction; the difference between the content of revelation and that of the particular culture becomes apparent, perfect adaptation is seen to be impossible, and the greater the appropriation, the more glaring is the contradiction. Then there is expropriation; the cultural schema or concept is absorbed by the content of revelation and the cultural sense is expropriated in favor of the revealed sense, as, e.g., in such words as resurrection or even God.

Now freedom of interpretation consists in applying the same procedure to our own cultural concepts and intellectual environment. A twofold detachment is required, first, detachment from the biblical text, and then from modern culture itself. We have to reproduce in relation to our own world and its schemas that which we see the Bible doing with the Near Eastern and Hellenistic world. The main point of risk lies between appropriation and contradiction. The decisive and basic thing—the foundation of everything—is that freedom of interpretation should be freedom in relation to our own cultural context as well as the biblical text.

What vitiates the hermeneutical enterprise today is the ideology of science. We mean by this the belief that modern science is the truth and that the scientific method enables us to get at the sense or forces us to choose between the myths and (false) ideologies of the biblical past on the one side and the exactitude that we have now finally achieved on the other. All this is pure ideology. We act towards science in just the same way as the

*The Object of Freedom and the Will of Man*

Canaanites did towards their Baals and their deities of fecundity. But why should interpretation have to have only one approach and orientation? Why should the text of the Bible have to be interpreted in terms of a collection of intangible truths which are called scientific? If the revealed datum can be challenged, so too can the cultural datum, which in our own case is especially science. Freedom of interpretation applies just as well to the one as to the other. If we do not exercise it in relation to the cultural datum, we cannot do so in relation to the revealed datum, for we can no longer follow the procedure of appropriation, contradiction, and expropriation which was outlined above. We can no longer do today what the first witnesses did. Hence we can no longer apprehend the sense of revelation in their witness.

Hermeneutical freedom cannot just be an investigation of the sense of the biblical text by an inner deciphering of the text. It has to be a discovery of the sense in the context of a questioning of our own cultural milieu. This means that our own world has to be read as well as the text of scripture. Our own culture has to be appropriated for exposition of the revealed datum.

Hermeneutical freedom demands, then, that we reverse what has been going on during the last few decades. If we do not, our scientific method will harden quickly and become the equivalent of cabbalism.

What we are proposing, of course, is no novelty. In the long run it is what has been constantly attempted. The first generation of Christians was not the only one to adopt the procedure of appropriation, contradiction, and expropriation. Auerbach in his *Mimesis* (ET 1953) gives an extraordinary depiction of the same thing in the period that followed. I know of no profounder analysis of the irruption of Jewish and Christian freedom into the intellectual and spiritual world. This book, which is central for an understanding of the western world, shows strikingly how Christianity (and Judaism before it) radically transformed the cultural setting by fusing categories that the ancient world had tried to keep apart and by thus giving a new (genetic) dimension to the whole description of reality. Genetic thought is thus a product of Christian freedom. This is also expressed in an unfamiliar form, the witness to reality in becoming. For the first time in history this freedom is freedom to transcend cultural categories and to overturn the whole representation of reality.

*Mimesis* clearly stands in contrast with the study of the history of form and composition. My own view is that even scientifically Auerbach gives a better account of the texts and achieves a depth that the methods of scientific criticism can never do. For he shows the unity of the flow of thought about reality from the Old Testament by way of the New Testament to Christian thinking in relation to the various cultures which are called in question. Realism, the insertion of verticality, the interplay of figure and fulfilment (as phenomena and events) are new features in the world of Christian culture which do not derive from any other and which cannot be compared with anything in any other. There thus arises a specific style which Auerbach calls a mixed style, since it knows no aesthetic restriction. This too is an expression of Christian freedom towards culture. Finally Auerbach brings out the distinctive element in the Christian affirmation of the individual, of the indestructibility of historical and particular being which is formed even contrary to the divine order. Here again we have an expression of freedom. We see historical becoming in the bosom of intemporal being.

Here, then, we have testimony to hermeneutical freedom throughout the church's history. Again, however, this is freedom in relation to both the revealed datum and the cultural datum. It is not the supposedly scientific subjection to the cultural datum which sits in judgment on the biblical text. The analytical method is what really ought to be judged. It can offer only approximations and not a true biblical science. Hidden motivations always stand in the way of real objectivity.

What is really needed is the greatest possible freedom of interpretation. This freedom, however, carries with it the freedom of deviation. It implies that we may make mistakes, and recognition of the right to make mistakes is recognition of the freedom of others. It also implies the freedom of research.

We recall that God does not tie us to the text. He does not want the text to be dead. He does not want the Christian life to be automatic: inspiration by the Spirit and illumination by the Spirit. Man has his part. He has to work at the text. He has to study it in freedom. If the text is true only by the Spirit's illumination, this illumination comes only to the free man, who in freedom does not view scripture as a set of taboos or magical recipes. There is a strict relation between man's freedom and the Spirit's illumination, for the Spirit gives man freedom, and only in this freedom can the Spirit bring illumination. If the man freed by the Spirit cannot profit by the first act of the Spirit, i.e., freedom, how can he profit by the second, i.e., illumination?

This freedom in relation to the text means wrestling with it to get at its contents by every human method possible: exegesis, criticism, analysis. Yet freedom is oriented to the glory of God and love of neighbor. If not, it is meaningless and illusory.

In criticism and exegesis, then, freedom must be to God's glory. This is an orientation, not a limit. If I finally use my scientific methods against God, to seize him or to put him to death, they show not just that I am in freedom but also that I am outside truth. My exegesis and so forth are to bring out the splendor of God, his work, and the meaning he has put in the text which feebly and palely transmits his revelation. If criticism becomes a weapon of war with a pseudo-liberalism which mounts an independent attack on the text and leads to a denial of God's existence, all that is expressed is man's autonomy and his situation outside freedom. Freedom

*The Object of Freedom and the Will of Man*

toward the text aims at better knowledge of the God who reveals himself in it, the Father whose love is manifested in Christ. On the other hand, criticism is not to become an apologetic machine, which brings no true glory to God, but simply presents an uninteresting theory of God and shows no freedom. Criticism in true freedom in Christ leads to a better exposition of God's revelation, i.e., his glory, and to more fitting worship of the Lord. (This may come about even through what seems to be a blasphemous theology, cf. Castelli, *L'herméneutique de la liberté religieuse*, 1968).

The second main thrust of freedom is love. Critical freedom regarding the text can never crush others. When those with the intellectual ability to do so help those who have not to read the Bible as they desire, their work should lead the latter to see in this document of revelation a new depth of God's love and so communicate it as to bring them to the truth. It should never violate brotherly love by causing a scandal or destroying genuine faith (as distinct from sociological belief). The man who feels free in relation to the Bible must never take the view: I must say what I have to say, and so much the worse for others. It will be objected, of course, that this overthrows freedom and involves false criticism. We shall have to deal later with the relation between love and freedom. What I want to stress here is that this freedom is in Christ. The text brings the love of God to others and I am not to make it a weapon against those whom God loves as he loves me. I study the text with all the resources of exegesis to learn that God loves these others. How then, in so doing, can I cast them into doubt and despair? If my criticism does this, it cannot be true. My motives are wrong.

This is the crux. Why do I study the biblical text? If it is because I am free in Christ and freedom relates to the text too, then I know what is God's glory and the love of others, and my exegesis can be only a better comprehension and adoration of revelation and a positive ministry which builds up others. But my reasons may be very different. I may view the text simply as a historical one. I may be so enamored of science that I am ready to use its resources without control or reflection. But all this has nothing to do with freedom in Christ. Only for the autonomous man who is in revolt against God can exegesis testify to the absence of revelation and cause less intelligent little ones to stumble. As for science, it is only a tool with which one can do different things, for in spite of its devotees it is not objective. It is used by sinful man. Even when its fruits seem to be rational and accurate, they are the product of sinful man. When exegesis leads to negation of God and harm to others, it is not because of science but because its presuppositions are those of sinful man. We know its motif and purpose, not by the standard of the scientific method used, but by the results in the heart of men.

By the standards of the glory of God and love of others I can see finally whether I have obeyed the freedom God has given me by affirming myself thus in relation to the biblical text and applying myself to it, or whether I have obeyed the impulse of my own heart, the savagery of my own autonomy, and the wheedling and scientific hatred I have for God.

(2) Freedom of deviation. Towards the end of the last century and the beginning of our own, with the crisis of Roman Catholic modernism and Protestant liberalism, the traditional positions of the church were questioned. People in the church began to refer to other values, first, to love of neighbor, then to Christian humility, not in life, where it had always been lived out, but in thought, then again to respect for personality, and finally to respect for scientific truth. Theologians, playing their usual role, were able to find in revelation legitimate foundations for this new attitude on the part of the church and this refocusing on the truth about man. The church, then, progressively came to admit that man does in fact have the right to make mistakes and that in the darkness he may sometimes find a few specks of light. It was conceded that other Christians might enjoy some part of the truth and that we ought, then, to listen to those whom we regard as being in error. For even revealed truth is never completely plain.

By a strange paradox, the church was discovering this at the very time when there was in the world a reaction against liberalism and against the recognition of the right of deviation. This was the time when strict orthodoxies began to appear, when secularism became the aggressive secularism that claims to incarnate truth to the exclusion of all others, when National Socialism plainly presented itself as absolute truth, when Communism, after a relatively more liberal period, became totalitarian, in brief, when ideologies could tolerate neither doubt nor error. At this very time the church took a more liberal stance.

Furthermore, at the very moment when the church began to recognize the validity of scientific truths, science itself entered upon an era of greater scepticism. From 1920 onwards all the sciences have been going through crises which have left them in doubt whether they will ever establish anything solid or certain. What passes for history, for example, has been defined as no more than a tracing of the frontiers of our ignorance. Now it is just at this time that the church recognizes that science has discovered some very true and important things. Thus Robinson and Bultmann begin with the idea that there is a scientific man with scientific reasoning who gets at the truth. They do this at the very time when all scientists are admitting: We do not really know where we are going.

In face of these authoritarian systems and this scepticism the church by a curious twist feels led to defend humanism, liberalism (democracy!), and the right of error. Is this just another instance of the church being out of date? Has it not always been a step or two behind? When the world was liberal the church was orthodox, and now that the world is orthodox the church discovers liberalism? Is it as simple as that? Christians, to advance, must surely be ready first of all to question every question.

We concede much too easily that this new position of the church is the true and Christian one and that it represents spiritual progress. But is this so certain? Has the church really taken this new attitude out of spiritual motives, in obedience to God? Is it not rather (or also) for factual, historical reasons that the church has become a sociological body? Is it not, for example, because the church no longer dominates what has become a liberal society, because the Constantinian period is over, because Christendom has broken up, because the state is no longer the servant of the church, because Christian ideology no longer inspires the acts of individuals and institutions? In such a day the church's recognition of the right of error seems to be simply the banality of making the best of a bad job.

We must look a little deeper. Today, as is well known, Christianity itself is under attack. It is a minority view. It is no longer the victorious Christianity which embraced the world and which added catechumens every year. It is on the defensive and is retreating, e.g., before Islam. To defend the right of error against Communism or Islam is to ask that they recognize the right to be Christian. To defend personal freedom is to defend the possibility of conversion. In fact one has to admit that the church's liberal stance is all the stronger in countries where the church has lost its power and where Christianity is being effectively combatted.

At the same time—and this, I think, brings us to the heart of the matter—we have to realize that this position, which is popularly known as jettisoning the ballast, has some consequences which are not at all Christian. Secular ideas are adopted and confusion ensues. Thus a Christian attitude is confused with philosophical liberalism or a type of agnosticism. It is no longer recognized that there is one truth and one alone. But if one is a serious Christian, he is forced to admit that this metaphysical liberalism of uncertainty and indifference is incompatible with revelation. This liberalism is not Christian humility when it recognizes that others have a part of the truth and of revelation and that I do not have it all. When the world speaks of liberalism, the reference is always to this metaphysical liberalism. For a Christian, however, there can be neither uncertainty nor indifference.

Similarly intolerable confusion arises when the Christian speaks of toleration. Toleration is not a Christian virtue since it is a negative and passive attitude. As the word shows, it consists of tolerating someone else without engaging in true and authentic dialogue. Toleration implies always contempt, ignorance, and aloofness. It is closing one's eyes to error and sin. This is not at all in keeping with the attitude demanded in Scripture when it calls upon us to bear one another's burdens. Christians must carry one another and support one another. If they think another is in error they must come to his aid and support, for they are following the same road. If, however, we proclaim the right of error for sociological reasons, we are adopting either liberal agnosticism or mere toleration.

Finally, there is another sociological trap. This is the trap of love. The primacy of love is being rediscovered in Christianity. Love leads us to take our neighbors seriously as persons. But they are taken so seriously as persons along with their sin and error that any wounding of them, even with the wounds of truth, is unacceptable. Neighbors have such value and importance in our eyes that at no point can we engage in total dialogue with them. They are given, as it were, an unconditional right to err, since they must be accorded absolute respect. Thus the truth must be hidden so as not to offend them.

We have here one of two extremes in the history of the church. The first extreme is to affirm with rigor the truth which the neighbor has missed. He must be forced to admit it, and all means to this end, including threats and penalties, are good. The other extreme is that of a sentimental love for the neighbor which dare not affirm the truth at all. The difficult thing is to profess the truth in love. This is the real problem of the right of error. If we speak of this as Christians, we have to be clear what we mean. Error is always error. The right of error implies a reference to the truth. It is not man's unconditional right to say anything. We must not fall into the attitude of hearing and allowing and accepting everything that the other says. Recognizing the right of error means neither liberalism, toleration, nor equation of a minor error and a truth. Some philosophies are seriously in error and others less so. Even the slightest error, however, is an error. We have to be absolutely rigorous at this point.

Recognizing heresy and its importance and necessity is an ancient attitude. "For there must be also heresies among you," says Paul in 1 Corinthians 11:19. Augustine agrees. Yet even though heretics necessarily arise, heresy is still heresy. We can tolerate no relativization of revealed truth.

Finally the right of error does not imply that we should attempt syntheses or try to integrate what man calls truth into Christianity. We should not attempt to make Christianity into a system which embraces all human thought nor should we admit that errors can make us change the truth when they put the human person above all else.

We have thus been led to question the question. We have criticized the present attitude of openness, liberalism, and acceptance of the right of error. This means that the Christian basis of the right of error is to be sought outside temporary, historical, and sociological reasoning. It is to be sought outside the adaptations of the church to intellectual fashions.

Two elements are decisive. The first seems to be the indissolubility of truth and love in revelation. Love is the content of truth. Truth leads to love. The Gospel and Epistles of John show this with extraordinary clarity. Hence there can be no question of imposing Christian truth by force. Even intellectual force is ruled out; apologetics is an example of intellectual terrorism. The only way by which the other can see and receive the truth is by the birth of love. We have in effect to accept the other as he is along with his errors. We have to realize that errors cannot be removed by external knowledge or assent, not even by a conviction which arises more or less purely and clearly. They can be removed only by revelation, and the

*The Object of Freedom and the Will of Man*

power of revelation does not depend on him or me, or, as Paul puts it, on him that wills and runs. It can encounter us effectively only when God shows what love is at the same time as he shows what truth is.

When we say that love is the content of truth, however, we do not refer to any kind of love. This love is not human sentimentality. It is not eros in any of its actual manifestations. It can exist only as love-truth, i.e., love as it is exclusively revealed by God in Jesus Christ. Man's love for God and his brethren is, then, neither weakness nor sentimentality. It is not the same as the collection of feelings that are popularly called love. It is man's response in fulness to the love of God. This response is the response of love-truth. It is not the response of abasement and bondage. It is the kind of homage that, according to Peguy, St. Louis paid as a French baron with all that that meant by way of power and strength and pride, even the pride of error.

This love towards man has to be a demanding love, i.e., the love that demands the truth. This is the point when the Bible speaks of the jealous God. God loves so totally that he cannot let the creature whom he loves deceive itself. Because he is love, he cannot let it remain in error, falsehood, and sin. But if our relation to others is to be that of love-truth, there can also be no question of superiority or domination. We cannot pretend to be in any way their guide or light or mentor.

The second biblical basis of the right of error is the attitude of God himself to man as we find it revealed in the Bible. God constantly accepts human error. He enters human history to participate in it. God is almighty but he respects man's independence and does not force him to accept either his love or his truth. We see this in relation to Adam. It would have been easy for God to stop Adam's defection. But he lets Adam choose. He lets him make his own mistake. Another example of the same thing may be found at the institution of the monarchy in Israel. The people, whom God has hitherto ruled directly, want a king like other nations. Samuel tries to dissuade them, but when he fails God says: "They have not rejected thee, but they have rejected me" (1 Samuel 8:7). God describes the calamities that will follow: conscription, taxes, requisitions, oppression, imprisonment, etc. But God lets the people make its mistake. The first king is Saul, and things turn out badly as foreseen. But the second king is David, and this shows us that God uses the error and disobedience of his people, and integrates it into his plan, so that David is not just the ancestor of Jesus Christ, but also the one who intimates his kingship.

We may also recall how Jesus accepted to the very last the error of Judas, the very Judas who was among the twelve whose feet the Lord washed. We see here the extent to which God accepts the right of error and betrayal. And how does Revelation present the Lord? "Behold, I stand at the door, and knock." The Lord does not break down doors. He stands at our door as a suppliant. He waits until we open it. He accepts the situation if we do not.

Thus God still accepts Israel's right to err. He makes it part of his incomprehensible design of love. This people is mistaken about Jesus Christ. It ceases to be God's people in order that we Gentiles, as Paul puts it in Romans, may receive revelation. Nevertheless this closed and obstinate people is still the elect people which will enter first into the kingdom of God. For it is still the true olive, the true root, into which we pagans are merely grafted. We come second, and what is second is not necessarily better. If, as Paul puts it, their death has been the occasion of our conversion, what will their conversion be but resurrection from the dead? This people will enter first into the kingdom and then the church. Having first refused, having blundered, and having profited by the right of error, this people will still be the one that is dearest to God's heart.

If, then, God grants man this right of error, if he so respects man's independence in regard to the truth, if he exercises so great patience to each of us, how can we fail to grant man the same right in his pride or his misery? How can we be more intransigent? How can we be more impatient than God? Let us remember that Jesus in the parable warned against rooting out the tares lest the grain be rooted out too.

Does this mean that we must not combat error? Are we to be merely passive? Not at all! God enters into human errors and makes them part of his plan, but recognizing the right of error and not getting impatient is not the same thing as inertia. For God's revelation cannot be put under a bushel. We thus return to the formula mentioned above; we are to profess the truth in love. Without merely playing on words I think one might say that the *pro-fari* means speaking for as well as before. When we profess the truth, we are uttering truth for man and not against him. This truth is good news, even when it speaks of God's demand, of the law enclosed in the gospel. The law and the gospel are one. Nowhere in scripture is there pure condemnation with no gospel, with no good news, even though the unheard of good news be simply that it is God who speaks. For even though God speaks to condemn me, it is the God of love who speaks. The only bad news would be that God ceases to speak to me. Throughout the Bible we find the recurrent phrase that God turns aside his face, and if he were indeed to turn away from man this would be real disaster. So long as he speaks, however, even though it be in condemnation, reproof, or demand, this is good news.

Face to face with the one we believe to be in error, we have to be those who bring the good news of love. We have to be for him and not against him. Thus our great weapon is prayer, intercessory prayer, which gives the other the full right of enquiry and error, but which is the source of the truth in him and which is for us our commitment to him, our way of going with him on the path to God. We do not have to drive the other into our own path. On the path where we believe he is in error we must be those who go with him as God goes with us. We must be moving together towards the Lord, knowing, according to the promise that is given to the church,

*The Object of Freedom and the Will of Man*

that when we walk with someone the Lord is with us. It is thus that we can respect the errors of others and yet be with them on the march to this unique truth, revealed truth.

(3) Freedom of research. As R. Coste has rightly observed, the attitude of research is basic to the Christian life. Free personal investigation of truth has its own dynamic. This must be free and personal even as it stands in relation to others. The Christian has to be a *homo viator* who knows that the truth is not the property of any one system and that nothing can ever cease to be called in question, whether by God's intervention, the development of social conditions, or the interrogation of Satan. Whatever may be the cause, this implies recognition of the fact that we are never installed in a truth or the proprietors of a doctrine.

But is it so certain that we have taken a decisive step as Ricoeur thinks when he says that we have entered a new phase of Christianity and a new kind of freedom in interpreting the word? Is this a new phase or a passing crisis? Ricoeur is right to think that we are in a situation close to that of the earliest days of Christianity. He appeals to the four gospels and their primary witness that there are different ways to the same result. But I am less sure that hermeneutics leads us to our present response. Does not the passion for hermeneutics reflect a crisis, that of the discord between the traditional message of the gospel and the evolution of our society? We must be certain that the gospel was at first received and understood "normally." We must be certain that the signs of transformation in our society are good. If we are wrong here—and it seems to me that hermeneutical research is in fact wrong—then the presuppositions of hermeneutics are vitiated at the outset. This is why I have doubts about this orientation of the freedom of research.

Now if we compare dogmatic research to scientific research, this freedom seems to be self-evident, for research is negated by a program or by advance restriction or definition. Again, progress in the biblical sciences of exegesis, history, language, etc. has shown how important freedom is in theological matters if there is to be any profit from this progress. Finally, if doubts are cast on this freedom, the argument is raised, quite rightly, that Christians should not refuse to let the faith be questioned. All obstacles to theological research are put there for bad reasons, e.g., fear that faith will perish (what kind of faith is it that cannot face exposure?), or acceptance of dogmatism, which is the very opposite of explication of the faith.

These considerations all have an appearance of reason and solidity. But only the appearance! For it is not too hard to see that theological research has its own distinctiveness due in part to its object and in part to its aim. The arguments used to establish its freedom often take no account of this and thus skirt the true problem. In contrast, we may point to a series of much more serious arguments.[18] When this freedom is related to

---

18   Cf. G. Delteil, *Les conditions de la recherche théologique* (1968–1971).

the freedom of the gospel, research expresses the life and movement of the faith, "for the faith cannot be reduced to closed definitions nor made into something that can never be questioned. It cannot be just the repetition of a language which conserves knowledge. It is constantly summoned to take the vocabulary of apostolic witness and to risk translating it, i.e., fashioning a new terminology for the man of today." This is a serious matter, and so is the relation between thought and life which must find expression in freedom of thought if the Christian life is a life in freedom.

The question arises, however, whether freedom of theological research implies then a complete independence, i.e., the possibility of saying anything at all or moving off in any direction. It seems that certain steps are needed here: (1) Does the method adequately specify the research? (2) Is there the necessary study of preceding researches? (3) Is there an objective? (4) Are there prior requirements? (5) Are there limits? These are the questions which must be successively asked.

As regards method, it is often said that science is characterized by the scientific method. It is then argued that if theology wants to be called a science it has only to apply a rigorous method. It can move off in any direction and engage in any project. The theological world is a void. Advance will be made so long as the rigor and exactitude of the method guarantees the scientific quality of the work. But this seems to me to be completely fallacious, for in fact a method in the humane sciences cannot possibly be compared with that used in the physical sciences. It has rightly been shown that history is not a science in this sense,[19] and even less so is theology. There can never be true rigor of method in these areas since there is such a great element of contingency even though structuralism gives a false air of exactitude. Nor can there be achieved in such existential fields the necessary abstraction from the person of the investigator with his interests and opinions. All theological research necessarily expresses the prior views and positions of the student. It is hypocrisy to disguise this under the guise of exactitude in research. Furthermore one has again to recall in this connection the reversals that take place in interpretation. If it is right to criticize methods and the results obtained twenty years ago by one method, it is also right to bring the new method and its finality under scrutiny. Exactitude is not the whole story. A method indisputably stands in relation to the object to which it is applied. There is no universal scientific method. We merely have certain criteria which enable us to judge whether the method used is scientific or not. But the method has to be appropriate to the object. If as regards the first point we must begin with inner methodological criticism, in relation to the second we must begin with the object. The thing to be determined, then, is what this theology which is being investigated is. In what field does it lie? Only when we have settled this can it be said whether what is being attempted is scientific or

---

19  Cf. the remarkable essay by J. Vayne, *Comment on écrit l'histoire.* (1971).

not. If there is freedom of research, there has also to be, as we shall show later, freedom in relation to research. In other words, the scientific character of the method used is necessary to validate the research but it is not in itself sufficient for this purpose. One may say that if theological research does not apply a scientific method it has no right to freedom. But the exactitude of the method does not confer the right to do or to say anything at all in the name of freedom. This is not by a long way a condition of science. Already, then, the criterion of method enables us to set aside innumerable theological pronouncements which have been made in the name of the freedom of research and which arise by the rule of numbers or the need for individual catharsis or sheer fantasy.

The question of preceding researches will not detain us long. All that needs to be said is that in this field as in many others research is directly conditioned by the prior stage of reflection. Little more is done than the adoption of a position. When the pressure of Barth's theology became intolerable, it was set aside at a stroke and there was a rush in other directions for reasons that have nothing to do with research but are simply psychological and sociological. In matters of exegesis and history too, previous results have a conditioning effect as one adds to them or pursues them. Much of what is called theological research is thus determined by the prior stage of reflection, and one can hardly talk about freedom. Freedom is claimed on the ground that tutelage to prior reflection is renounced, but this is in fact only a matter of fashion. The Barthian fashion is succeeded by the Bultmannian or Moltmannian fashion, the historicist by the structuralist, etc. There is no freedom here. We simply have vagrancy for reasons that have no obvious connection with concern for the explication of theological truth. The opposite is no less a fact, i.e., conditioning by assured results which have become sacrosanct. The work of exegetes is familiar enough—it reminds us of that of exegetes and historians in other fields except that they have now abandoned it. Recalling these different positive and negative conditionings by what has gone before is not meant as a criticism of theological work. It is a simple reminder not to exalt too highly the theme of theological research, its scientific character, and the freedom that ought to reign in it.

The third question goes much deeper. Ought this research to have a predetermined objective? Should it define what is sought in advance? Now we are not asking here a theoretical question which it is fairly easy to answer in general. This is a very practical question. The question of the freedom of theological investigation is not posed in any society or against any background. It is posed in western society in an intellectualizing milieu and as a result of many motivations. To say at the metaphysical level that one should respect the pure freedom of research, that this is indeed a necessary condition of research, is to say nothing at all. For this freedom is not pure. The investigator is not a free spirit. The question arises in relation to existing political, sociological, and other factors. The vindication or rejection of the freedom of research is in effect an expression of these factors and motivations. A serious reference to science is the most common justification. But a century and its historians who are resolutely and aggressively against Christianity at the outset will demand the pure freedom of historical science in order to combat Christianity. If we look at the matter factually we are forced to say that on the one side theological research manifests the greatest incoherence—anything can be done, even bad sociology and poor political science, and it can be done in any way, with no particular meaning, and irrespective of the place or object of search—while on the other hand the themes of research and its centers of interest are assigned far more by society than by science (whatever sicence may be in view). I realize, of course, that the answer will be given that this is how it has always been, that theological research has always been defined by the dominant class, but if I understand this argument the implication is that we may approach the matter realistically, that it is a matter of ideological rather than theological research, and that what is at stake is not the freedom of science but the freedom to attack class enemies in the church, which is a very different matter. Hence I do not feel that one can accept purely free research, i.e., the research which in fact is done incoherently and under politico-sociological determinations.

The freedom of theological research implies determination by its objective. I cannot better define this than G. Delteil does when he says that research has to do with the witness and proclamation of the church. What is at stake in theological research is the ability of believers to live out and to confess their faith in the midst of their human responsibilities. This witness has been challenged by the pressures of the movement of contemporary culture on the one side and the traditional expression of the faith on the other. This means that the church must examine its preaching critically in the light of the confession of faith. Research is not gratuitous curiosity or a purely intellectual exercise. It is an establishment in perspective of the task of confessing the faith. The movement is thus from faith to faith, from faith badly informed and badly confessed to faith better informed and better communicated to men. This marks it off from pretended scientific research. The result is that research never comes first. It is not an end in itself. It is secondary. It is in the service of the witness of the gospel to the world. Hence there can be no independence of research. Its true freedom is inscribed in the freedom which is given by Christ.

Now research is not characterized by finality. It is oriented to a question that is put to us. Most writers, however, even including Delteil, seem to see the question as coming from the world. The progress of science, cultural change, and the mental climate put the question. As those who are freed by Christ, however, we should not forget that in the first instance we are placed under a question that is set by God. (We may ignore here the usual evasion that it is through events, politics, etc. that God speaks to us.) But what is this question which research should answer? Not just: "Where art thou?" (Genesis 3), nor simply: "Where is thy brother?" (Genesis 4), but also: "Whom say ye that I am?" (Matthew 16:15), and: "Will ye also go away?" (John 16:67). That is to say, the question is that of fidelity to the revelation which has been made in Jesus Christ.

Now if to some degree we may admit that being questioned by society and modern man means seeking an answer, we can claim even more so that being questioned by God carries with it the same requirement. God's question, however, is formulated in and throughout the Bible. This implies that the question must be taken from the Bible. But we have here a reversal of the attitude of many actual investigators. Basically the questions posed in a good deal of modern research are in general questions about the Bible. (Putting questions to the Bible, and regarding the Bible itself as a manual of answers, has long since been censured, but the procedure of posing questions about the Bible is perhaps equally invalid.) We put the Bible itself to the question. Are we so certain, however, that our aim in so doing is not in effect to avoid the Bible's own question? Are we so certain that the proper method of research is in fact to center it on the Bible with a view to finding out what degree of reality it has or what word of God it contains? Should we not take the Bible as a point of departure for research that bears on the world, on our society, on modern man? Since research always has a certain number of postulates, why cannot the Bible itself be one of them? Because it has not been adequately explicated? But what postulates have?

In any case we have to realize that we destroy our own freedom if we begin to doubt or question what is our only witness to this freedom. To take what I regard as my freedom and to use it to rob scripture of its significance, which is what a good deal of modern theological research seems to be doing, is to undermine the foundation of this freedom, so that it ceases to exist. Our only possibility of research is to accept the biblical data as a postulate and hence to move on from the Bible to a criticism of our other postulates and methods. A choice has to be made here, and it goes far beyond the problem which is often raised, and which is not nearly so serious or decisive as believed, namely, the problem how the Bible is to be understood in view of the differences in language, metalanguage, culture, and epistemology. We shall take up this question at a later stage.

We now come to the question of prior requirements, where again we follow Delteil. Three may be discerned. Research must be rooted in the Word. Its thrust, then, will be to reduce the distance between the cultural milieu of revelation and our own cultural milieu, at the same time bringing to light the authority of scripture, not as a theological principle, but as an accepted reality. Then research must be located in the fellowship of the church. It implies confrontation within the community. There should be no question of mutually exclusive trends which have no knowledge of one another and which try to startle the church. Research of this nature is false research, although the problem of the relation of freedom of research to the institutional church naturally arises at this point. Finally research must be ordered to the confession of faith. Its aim is to purify the faith that we confess, since we are always tempted to put the Word into images or idols. The mission of research is to denounce our false interpretations of God and to clear away that which serves as the envelope of our preaching and theology. This is why we have to ask unceasingly whether this specific critical examination of the text of scripture, whether this interpretation which the church offers, whether this new formulation, does in fact serve the church's confession of faith.

The question of requirements leads on at once to that of limits. Are there limits to theological research? The very question horrifies the champions of research. Scientific work cannot tolerate any limits. No frontier can be traced in advance. No object can be placed off limits. No affirmation or basic fact can be said in advance to be beyond criticism. All this is familiar enough. Even so balanced and perspicacious a thinker as Delteil is forced to conclude that research in effect has no limits, its freedom being based upon the freedom of the gospel. Nevertheless, the matter is not that simple. What was pointed out above must be recalled. Theological research cannot be assimilated to scientific research. If the latter has no limits—and this is not so evident as it once was, for many scientists today are beginning to raise the question of limits (which is, of course, another story)—the same does not necessarily apply to the former. Again, one has to realize that there is a difference between the ideal of research and the actual practice. Even if I accept the utility, importance, and necessity of theological research as an expression of freedom, I must still say that the practice, as I see it, expresses more of an absence of freedom that bears bitter fruits from the standpoint of spiritual and intellectual life. The problem is always the same, i.e., that of the inability of the one to whom this freedom is given to use it for edification and in love. Naturally this reservation does not in itself entail the establishment of a teaching office or of inviolable dogmas. The scholar has to be reminded, however, that he must be just as free in relation to secular data as he claims to be in relation to revealed data. In particular, theological research, according to the familiar causal mechanisms of science and technology, depends on prior scientific results. What is regarded as inviolable is now something different, not dogma, but what the investigator thinks has been scientifically established. Thus few scholars today call in question the documentary theory in relation to the Pentateuch. For many people this is far more solidly grounded than the existence of God. What is sacred is now understood differently. Thus anyone who attacks the results of historico-critical exegesis will cause the kind of horror (mingled with pity and disdain) that an attack on the Trinity would have caused in the sixteenth century. This is in itself a limit to the freedom of research, although in my view it is just as illegitimate as any other.

Finally, we should surely be ready to admit that limits are set once requirements are laid down. If research does not satisfy the requirements, can it still be called research? If it is not subject to the question of God's Word, but begins with: "Yea, hath God said. . ."; if it does not take place within the fellowship of the church but is instead an instrument to destroy it; if it does not aim at the confession of faith but is an arrogant attempt at understanding, can one really speak of freedom? But does not all this mean that limits are set, not limits that can be stated in advance, but limits which in conformity with the play of freedom disclose themselves in the exercise of that freedom?

Now it must be said that, as I see it, a major part of actual theological research does not in fact meet these criteria. Many modern historians and exegetes are concerned only to show how the text is constituted. Their concern is to explain the fact of revelation as this was lived out by the prophets and apostles. They try to trace the processes of elaboration. They want to classify genre and style, to bring to light the dependence on background, to piece out the various fragments, to nail down the authors and the strata and literary forms within the writings of a single author. Now all this is, intellectually, very exciting. It seems to be bringing light into the dark forest of scripture. Nevertheless the intellectual satisfaction offered has no bearing on the better understanding of the matter of the text. The sense is not made apparent by an explanation of the manner or origin. Quite the contrary! We have here a choice in our approach to scripture which cannot be avoided. It is the choice between "recovery" of the Bible and intellectualization. My own belief is that these avid researches help but little in the actual reading of scripture. They correct some crude errors but they bring with them others that are even worse.[20] Or, more commonly, the sense is reduced to a few grains of dust or to nothing at all. There is a shift from the Word of God that is spoken in a passage to elaboration on, e.g., the mechanisms of the tradition.[21]

A declaration that there are no limits to the freedom of research may be accepted, then, on the condition (1) that research is subject to the criteria mentioned, (2) that the possibility is granted that there is a research which may not respect them—any expression of man's independence is possible, since man is in fact independent—(3) that such research is seen not to be theological, nor an expression of faith, and (4) that the fruits and consequences of research are submitted to the criticism of the very freedom which research itself claims to monopolize.[22]

---

20  In making this criticism I am not discounting the solid and useful work done by scholars such as Conzelmann, Campenhausen, von Rad, and others.

21  Again I do not refer to the greater scholars who can use these methods with great power but to men of second rank in whose hands they are disastrous.

22  Thus it seems to me that the works of Ennio Floris, whom one dare not criticize for fear of appearing to be an inquisitor and the champion of a dead and arid orthodoxy, are indeed the fruit of a lively imagination, great sensibility, and a strong desire to conform to the thought of the left, but are not in any sense the product of a true freedom of theological research.

May we recommend at this point that research not be too public but be essentially discreet and secret. Obviously a Christian intellectual should be aware of developments in his field, face up to the encounter between science and his faith, accept questions both linguistic and material, accept the risk of dialogue, and do all this openly if he is truly scientific and authentically Christian. He must be ready to submit to severe criticism of his faith and move on from this to true study of revelation. If he is not, he cannot be serious before God. His freedom, however, is not that of taking the path of science but of achieving the mastery in which he need not do all this publicly. His freedom is that of knowing the relative character of his discipline, of taking his own slow and painful course with all its doubts and difficulties, for why publish non-existent results or alarm humble Christians who can neither understand what he is doing nor follow his path but will get a wrong impression of what he is up to. His freedom is that of keeping quiet except for sharing his work with other intellectuals in the church. Taking any other course means vanity, passion, or idolatry.

The question of doubt arises here. This cannot be a good source of theological research, for it is visceral, not scientific. Christians do doubt. The final word of faith is: "Help thou mine unbelief." Faith involves doubt. The history of the Christian life brings crises. But none of this is theological research. The latter does not systematically justify existential doubt. There is no need of a scientific comedy to give us reason to doubt. Doubt is a living matter between man and God. Theological verities do not have to be proclaimed as its outcome nor should others be involved in it by intellectual attacks. If Cartesian doubt is easy to grasp and works well in a scientific operation, the situation is confused when revelation is at issue. For here doubt cannot be purely intellectual. Mostly it is not. This is why I can say *a priori* and incontestably that doubt is never a good starting-point for theological research.

It should also be said that if theological research wants to be scientific it must conform to the canons of ordinary scientific research. It has no right to cash in on its independence.

For research too has undoubtedly to be submitted to the criticism of freedom. One must begin by freeing himself no less from relativization than from dogmatism. As regards the latter, the task has been rightly and vigorously pursued. In contrast, there reigns in research a relativism which is nothing more than conformity to current ideas in intellectual circles. It is true that we are subject to and are in part influenced by language, culture, and so forth, but can we be sure that this is the last word? If it were, we should be condemned to complete incommunicability, and this is manifestly not true. We have some idea of what others say to us. This is especially so in our own linguistic and intellectual circle, although our assurance decreases the more what is said is abstract and the less it is experimental. We have to remember, however, that the content of the Bible is not abstract and theoretical. It is concrete and experimental, as the

*The Object of Freedom and the Will of Man*

process of witness itself shows. A first error in research is to treat as theoretical texts the concrete expressions of a witness.

On the concrete plane there is understanding. It may be crass, as in the saying about not giving our children stones for bread, if we take it in all literalness. But at least we know what it is about. If all biblical statements were construed on the level of bread and stones we should not have to go through so many hermeneutical crises. It is certainly not true that within a single language and culture, or even between the twentieth-century west and the Semitic world, there is a ditch that some cannot get across. Only partially can this be said. Whether we like it or not, our cultural origin is also Greek and Hebrew. Our cultural basis is closely related to that of antiquity. There have not been only errors and misunderstandings during the last two thousand years, in spite of what our modern conceit would lead us to believe. We have a derived if not a common language. There are many stable factors in the flow of culture. It is an illusion to think that science has changed everything or that Descartes has modified all western thought. I have often emphasized the radical novelty of the technical world, its incommensurability with what went before. I can thus say without fear that there is also cultural continuity. I admire those who state unhesitatingly that one can enter into the thought of Mao Tse Tung or the spirituality of Zen Buddhism or who contrive in so many ways to communicate the thought of Jeremiah or Ecclesiastes. In reality it is inexact to write off as impossible any comprehension of the thought of a different language or culture, or to argue that the transition can be made only by a tremendous effort. Naturally some knowledge of the cultural background is needed to give a better grasp of what is being said, but even without this, meaning and truth can be transmitted with far fewer gross misunderstandings than modern theological scholarship is prepared to admit. Elucidation is required, but transcultural problems are not to be exaggerated.

In particular, we have to realize that the idea of total relativity, of the impossibility of communication, of entrapment in language and culture, is itself a cultural notion peculiar to our own age and setting. It is no more valid than the medieval idea of the universality of cultures or of exact comprehension across linguistic barriers by simple translation. Our conflicting modern view is itself a prejudice, a means of self-assurance, a guarantee. The challenge to the literal sense is bound up with the failure of evangelization. The relativity of cultures goes hand in hand with the impact of technical society and our situation as a sociological group. Entrapment in language expresses our fear of reality—it is a nominalistic refuge. We do not have here impregnable scientific facts. We have the three main ideological foundations of actual theological research.

No less to be questioned is the supposed preeminence of research. Often in the church and in research centers freedom is claimed for it just because it is scientific and is and has to be free within its stated limits. But when this principle is set up, are we not simply obeying the current ideology of science which grants it superior rights to all else? Other civilizations which deserve some attention (the Greek and Indian) did not see it this way, but now the freedom of research is enunciated as a veritable law of nature. I do not question the value and validity of science but I do question its final value and the unquestionable rights of research. We have here a sociological obedience to the irresistible flow of modern western beliefs, and the passion for investigation simply expresses the state of mind of a society that has lost its certainties and is trying to latch on to the only certainty left, namely, science.

Science thus replaces all things. It replaces morality (J. Monod). When faith goes, science becomes an object of faith and a means of dealing with revelation. This approach is not one of strength but one of weak and servile obedience to the sociological context. There is a place for research in theology and exegesis. But it is not the final word. It is subject to reflection. It does not have absolute rights. It, too, must serve. Its value depends on the service it renders and the references it receives. If this is not accepted, the result is a pride of research which is understandable on the human level but does not measure up to a Christian profession.

The problem here is the same, namely, that the non-Christian can do as he likes in this area, so long as he checks that it is scientific, but he should make it clear that he is not a Christian. The Christian, however, must ask whether his research and its methods are consonant with the fact that truth is revealed. He cannot evade this by saying that we have here two different worlds. This solution is too simplistic to be of any value.

Every scientist knows that his methods must be in keeping with the object of study. What he works on here, however, if he is a Christian, is revealed truth. He cannot put his faith in brackets or forget that this truth is revealed so as to be able to go ahead as he wishes. This would be like a surgeon forgetting that the patient he is operating on is a live person and acting as though he were dissecting a corpse or conducting an autopsy. Many Christians act this way, adopting the scientific method without worrying about the consequences or calculating the risks—for others.

Surely it is reasonable to accept only those methods which are in accord with the fact of revelation. Nor can one escape by leaving the matter of revelation and concentrating on the human, visible, tangible element, e.g., scripture as a historical text. This distinction between form and content is a poor excuse and not very scientific. One cannot speak of the form without referring to the meaning, content, and message, and the question now is whether one receives it as revelation or not. Even the argument that one must read off the true message from the cultural expression will not do.

If, however, I take the classical position that the hypothesis of revelation has no place in scientific research, how can I criticize Christians who make the same distinction in other areas? I am simply giving another example of dichotomy as we find it between the spiritual and temporal,

Christianity and politics, Christianity and business, and so forth: a Christian on Sunday and a pagan the rest of the week. Research can claim no privileges here because it is supposedly so lofty.

If, on the other hand, I admit as a Christian that I am working on revelation, on a text that potentially contains the Lord's self-disclosure, then I must take many other elements into account and adopt a different attitude than a non-Christian would. Non-Christians may indeed deal with the biblical text as they will and use the methods they believe to be scientific, but the Christian will probably not use the same methods nor attain the same results, for he must take into account an element which is both fundamental and secret.

A final aspect of research must also be considered. This is the demonic aspect. When a modern reader sees this word he will probably think of medieval obscurantism or a desire to impugn free research, which, as I have been trying to show, is not really so free as all that. Now within a Christian outlook one can hardly avoid raising the question of the demonic as Castelli understands it. Are we really sure that our automatic questioning and challenging of the testimony of the witnesses and of scripture is merely an expression of our desire to love better the God of Jesus Christ and his revelation? Might there not be also the mere desire for an academic exercise, or, better, the desire to make things "intelligible"? "Now everything is intelligible if it is circumscribed" (this might have been written to describe the modern method of research) but "the demonic disruption is that if everything is intelligible nothing is comprehensible, for comprehension comprehends, that is, it grasps more, more than the detail which alone is intelligible. It grasps more because it leads the individual to the intelligence of something (a phenomenon) even to the point of being able to infer what is beyond understanding. If there is no beyond there is no comprehension." Now it seems to me that in effect all modern theological work is oriented to what is intelligible by the dissecting of revelation (the revealed data) and that it rules out the comprehensible because it rejects in advance what is beyond (the very word being objectionable because it is so grossly anthropocentric, localizing what cannot be localized). With this orientation, does not research belong to the domain of the demonic? And what then becomes of its freedom? Furthermore, the play of the occult and its unveiling are also demonic, as Castelli shows clearly when he says: "The powers of evil exploit the fraud that the desire to know promotes. The satanic formula is to make us see so that we do not see" (does not this again seem to apply to a good deal of modern research?). "Everything is there to make us believe in an occult world which merits discovery, to make us accept the necessity of a voyage (research) which will lead to such discovery . . . and yet at the same time it is all a fraud, an invitation to futility, although this is not seen until later." "The unknown is not desirable just because it is unknown and yet there is an unknown that is desirable. The reference, however, is to the unknown whose existence is known, to the world of the unknown. An unknown exists—the serpent has indicated it. The promise of the serpent is the promise of the unknown. . . . Indeed? Why? Again and always: Why? The unknown of the why . . . the power of darkness is illuminating but its light has no reflection. The temptation is to ask unceasingly since the unknown is the only thing that is truly desirable now that the Lord has succeeded by temptation in raising the suspicion that there is really something hidden. . . . There are thus two questions, the why of the unknown and the why of the unknown of the why. . . . The unknown is the mystery of the desire to question in order to know, the mystery of the concupiscence of the intelligible." The demonic sign is made "in order to hide and not to disclose. Hiding is the positive side of nothingness. Hiding existence from the existent is a form of damnation." One may see from all this in what sense this research is the opposite of revelation. Nor can one avoid this preliminary question about theological research in face of the claim of this research to complete freedom from all questioning.

It might be said, of course, that all this is mere obscurantism, a refusal to understand, the attempt of faith to avoid the risks of scientific clarity. In relation to these and similar objections, one can easily reverse the criticism which is so often made against the Christian position. These objections simply bring to light the fear that the scientist may have of seeing scientific ideology challenged. Now it is science that is seeking refuge and trying to safeguard its treasures. Why is it that the criticism which is so easily adopted in relation to faith and theology is supposed to lose its validity in relation to scientific belief and science itself? These are the questions that the freedom which is in Christ asks about theological research. As Castelli finely puts it, "Only the holiness which opposes the seduction of the occult (i.e., that science will reveal and give comprehension), only this symbolical pillar of resistance to the deceitful sign, can give us an intuition how terrible is the weapon of the fraud of nature denaturalized."[23] There can be no theological research without holiness. This is the measure of its freedom.

---

23 All the quotations in this final passage are from Castelli, *Le démoniaque dans l'art* (1958); the phrases in parentheses are my own.

*The Object of Freedom and the Will of Man*

# Chapter 3

# All Things Are Lawful

The constant problem of freedom is the problem of its limits. This finds expression both in the simple formula that liberty is not license and in the more elaborate discussions of the philosophers of freedom or the thinkers of democracy. Freedom is legitimate so long as it does not harm others. The only limit of freedom is the freedom of others. Freedom knows how to limit itself or else it is not freedom. Freedom exists only in virtue. Or, politically, freedom exists only in law. Freedom expresses itself in obedience freely conceded. All these limping or absurd formulae show what a labyrinth of difficulty, incoherence, and impossibility we enter when we begin with the notion that man is intrinsically free, that freedom is a political reality, that it is man's normal situation. Given the actuality of man, one can easily foresee that he will use his freedom badly. Hence the limits have to be traced. Freedom has to be given a framework. Freedom can be conferred on man only when he has been brought into line, so that there is no fear that he will cause trouble or scandal, but is well adjusted. After all, this is the way we handle our children when we free them progressively from our tutelage to the degree that we find them more "reasonable," i.e., ready to behave like everyone else. Is not the terrible hypocrisy in all this obvious? A free animal is not an animal in a cage or one that has been trained. We need to begin with something very simple and with a primary insight.

Now we know that absolute freedom is intolerable for man. It is truly impossible. Only utopian anarchists have for a brief period been persuaded of its possibility, e.g., that the presence of the policeman is what makes a thief. On the other hand, it is also to be affirmed that freedom encaged in the regulations of law or morality or education, or in some kind of hierarchy, is no freedom at all. The formulae cited above make of freedom a permission that is granted to man, a possibility of maneuver within narrow limits, an evasion when reference is made to inner freedom, and a serious trap when it is explained that freedom increases with the standard of living.

A word must be said about the last hypocrisy. Technology makes it possible for man to consume more goods and to have a wider choice. He can free himself spatially by various forms of transport. He is freed in principle from work for leisure. On the other hand technology molds and manipulates man totally. He is brought under increasing constraints. He has in fact to work more than ever. His leisure cannot be free loafing. It has to be organized like everything else. It bears no obvious relation to freedom.

If modern philosophers cling so firmly to the link between freedom and consumption, it is only because they cannot abandon the metaphysical presupposition that man is free, and hence there has to be a parallel between material movement and spiritual reality. They are thus thrown back on the constant problem of freedom, i.e., freedom which is more and more confined and regulated. The basic error is to view freedom as a situation, as a datum, as a definable ontological quality, as something that can be presupposed, as a static phenomenon. But no matter to what reality freedom may correspond, it cannot be presupposed. It is actualized in the filling out of act or thought, without which it is no more than a theorem. Furthermore, it cannot be static, for it has to have its being in the invention of the new, without which it evaporates into the immobility which is necessity. The trouble today is that freedom is no longer understood. It is reduced to the principle of freedom. "All men are born free," we read in the Rights of Man. This is why we have to form a police force. For there is no alternative on this view of freedom. Nor has this kind of freedom, and the restrictions it imposes, anything that is authentically Christian about it except perhaps for the term and at a deeper level a touch of nostalgia.

### § 1. All Things Are Lawful

The freedom won in Christ is alive, unlimited, without restrictions or obligations. It enables us to throw off all constraints and admonitions. It is true freedom: freedom to choose, to decide, to go where I want to go, to break that which dominates, to transgress prohibitions, to profane what man holds sacred, to conform if conformity is chosen and yet not to conform, to enter into and to break free from commitments, to give and to take back again.

Four times Paul says that all things are lawful. He does not mention any limits or barriers. And why should we not set this freedom under the sign of that fine passage in Ecclesiastes (3:1—8): "There is a time to every purpose under heaven: a time to be born, and a time to die; a time to plant, and a time to pluck up that which is planted; a time to kill, and a time to heal; a time to break down, and a time to build up; a time to weep, and a time to laugh; a time to mourn, and a time to dance; a time to cast away stones, and a time to gather stones together; a time to embrace, and a time to be far from; a time to seek, and a time to lose; a time to keep, and a time to cast away; a time to rend, and a time to sew; a time to keep silence, and a time to speak; a time to love, and a time to hate; a time of war, and a time of peace"?

Naturally this passage from Ecclesiastes is not to be regarded as a list of things that man has to do at times that he cannot control, so that he is

*The Object of Freedom and the Will of Man*

completely helpless and passive. Nor is it to be seen as a statement of indifference, as though one thing were as good as another, since neither of them has meaning. The final verse teaches the exact opposite: "God hath made everything beautiful in his time" (v. 11). If these things are all as good as one another, it is not because they are indifferent or without meaning but because God has made them beautiful. At every point we have acts and decisions of men which may be contradictory but which have been made beautiful and hence accepted and approved by God. That is to say, in these very contradictions we are in the presence of the freedom of man who in a given time chooses his actions.

I want to affirm as strongly as I can that the freedom given by Christ is in effect this: "All things are lawful"—absolutely all things.[1] There is no specifically Christian way of life which imposes this or that conduct or forces us not to choose certain things, or not to take this or that attitude. There is no discrimination between acts, things, professions, commitments, manners, systems, ideas, or philosophies which are Christian and those which are not. Any attitude, opinion, or choice, if it proceeds from freedom in Christ, if it expresses this freedom here and now, if it is a manifestation at the chosen time of the tension experienced by this free man between the God who frees him and the world which oppresses him, is legitimate. It is so to the point where Christians may take up contradictory attitudes. Thus Paul says that we may or may not eat sacrificial meats, or that we may or may not marry. A uniformity of Christian opinion and attitude would be the strange thing in the conditions of this freedom. It would be strange and disconcerting, for such uniformity would be a mark of orthopraxy and a fruit of propaganda.

Hence a Christian may be a monarchist or he may be a Communist, so long as being either the one or the other is an expression of his freedom in Christ. He may be a militarist or a conscientious objector on the same condition. In relation to scripture he may be a literalist or a demythologizer. It is right and good and customary to dress up for Sunday services; in the parable of the wedding-garment does not Jesus tell us that the man who was not suitably dressed for the feast was thrown out? But wait! This is the freedom of divine worship and not of the middle-class conformity which prompts us to dress up in our best for others. It is equally right and good and customary not to dress up for worship, to go in everyday clothes so as to show that worship is part of daily life, that we come before God as before our Father, and that we should bring the reality of life and not a sham. But wait again! This must be the freedom to be oneself before God and not an affront or a challenge to the wretched middle-class people who put on their best for divine service. The same rule applies in relation to many differences between Roman Catholics and Protestants. It is good and

---

1 Thus one can say with Tillich that revelation or faith has no specific ethical content, although obviously the problem of the specific arises, since revelation relates to the whole man.

legitimate to have a concern to give God the best, to build beautiful cathedrals to his glory and honor, to sacrifice gold to God, to offer as a pure offering what is most precious for the adornment of the altar, but only so long as this is an expression of the liberty of faith and not of the church's constraint, and only so long as this does not merely heap up riches for the church. Conversely, it is good and legitimate to build very simple structures for worship, naked and unadorned, with no refinement or elegance, in order to manifest the rejection of this world's goods, the scorn of riches, and concern for worship in spirit and in truth, but again only so long as this is an expression of the stripping of our lives in freedom for God's sake, and is not just a matter of middle-class economy, of content with mediocrity, of a failure to give lavishly to God.

Any life-style, then, can be an expression of freedom. All things are lawful, even those that might seem to be the most audacious and unacceptable. One may even wrestle with God. Abraham offers an example of discussing and even bargaining with him which is as admirable as it is sordid. Job flings questions at him (3:20ff., etc.). We even get downright refusals. Jonah will not go to Nineveh, Moses will not go to Pharaoh, and Isaiah and Jeremiah are both reluctant to accept their commissions. Indeed, there are those who fight against God either in resistance or in an attempt to force God to change his mind. Jonah says fiercely: "I do well to be angry" (Jonah 4:9). Jacob wrestles at Peniel. Ecclesiastes engages in bold confrontation. Man can even accuse God. Job complains that he is unjust, that he is a tyrant and persecutor, and that he is a kind of demon (Job 24:1, 12; 9:22, 24; 16:6, 14). Elijah asks that he may be allowed to die since God has forsaken him. Although all this may be very surprising, it is an expression of the freedom that God gives to the man who believes in him. When we see that this freedom extends even to accusing God, why can we not give the "All things are lawful" its fullest and most extended sense?

At the same time, we recognize that any of these attitudes which are a possible expression of freedom may also be an expression of conformity—this is the ambiguity always implied in freedom itself. An act which begins in freedom may degenerate into habit, or repetition. It may through continuity become something trite and banal that no longer has anything at all to do with freedom, which is always demanding and innovative. The act expresses freedom only in its first freshness and in terms of a specific setting, character, or culture. All things are lawful. All, then, are to be dared. But daring is not imitating and repeating. Daring involves the courage to live one's own life in one's own style. This is what freedom in Christ means. "Do as you like" is the second part of the celebrated formula of Augustine. The death of Christ has snatched us from the fatal grip of sin. It has liberated us from the powers. It has ended the inner ownership of evil which made all our acts and thoughts unable to stand up to encounter with God. The Holy Spirit dwells within us. I live, yet not I, but Christ lives in me. There has thus been a tremendous reversal which has changed the very root of our being and made us free. Hence, when we act, we no longer express the evil one; we express the Holy Spirit. We can thus choose our own acts. We can ourselves decide what we should do. The change of root carries with it a change of fruit. When the tree is bad the fruit is bad. Now, thanks to the benevolence of God, the fruit is good. We must persuade ourselves, then, that there is no limit to our freedom. This does not mean rejection of the law or revolt against God's order. On the contrary, the law is written in our hearts of flesh, as was prophesied along with the re-establishment of the divine order. The law is no longer external to us. Our acts do not overturn God's order; they are in harmony with it.

Nevertheless, in spite of all the theological explanations, we accept the "All things are lawful" only with great difficulty. We are constantly tempted to restore limits to this freedom. To be set in unlimited freedom seems to be incompatible with the fact that we remain sinners (as we do) and with the keeping of the law (which is certainly to be kept). Yet Paul puts it as clearly as anyone could in Colossians 2:20: "Wherefore if ye be dead with Christ from the rudiments of the world, why, as though living in the world, are ye subject to ordinances, (Touch not; taste not; handle not; precepts which become pernicious with use;) after the commandments and doctrines of men?" The negative aspects, the prohibitions which man invents as limits to freedom, are all rejected here. For these limits set up by man are always negative. They cannot become permission and promise as the law does.

A second aspect of this great latitude is: "All things are yours." You may not only decide, essay, and venture all things. You may also use all things. This teaching is first found in the symbolical form of Peter's dream when what the law forbade him to eat was allowed and authorized: "What God hath cleansed, that call not thou common" (Acts 10:15). Now it had been called common or unclean by God's own law. Here, then, we have the change in the meaning of the law which comes about in Christ. Even more remarkably, the offering of unclean meats in Peter's vision intimates the coming of the pagan, of the unclean man. Hence we have not only the removal of the barrier between the things in the dream but the removal of the barrier between men. We are summoned to cross this barrier.

A freedom is thus given to transgress. This is one of the essential signs of freedom, as we shall see later. For the moment, however, our point is: "All things are yours." There is no further distinction between things. Realities do not have intrinsic value. They are not right or wrong *per se*. Only for the man outside grace and faith is this so. This man has to live in an ordered world—a world where objects have specific stability in the ordering of good and evil by man. For him objects have to have their place in the hierarchy of values and judgments. He cannot do without the attributing of ethical quality to things. He has to see things as intrinsically good and evil. It would be terribly dangerous to try to do anything else, for in this case man would have to view himself as intrinsically responsible for what is right and wrong. He would live in a world of uncertainty and permanent responsibility, which would be quite intolerable. He tries to avoid this, obeying the post-Adamic impulse to set up an objective good and evil.

Grace, however, when received in faith, shatters this ordered universe, this scale of values, this classification. Things are no longer good and evil. Jesus himself says: "Not that which goeth into the mouth defileth a man, but that which cometh out of the mouth, that defileth a man" (Matthew 15:11), for "those things which proceed out of the mouth come forth from the heart; and they defile the man" (v. 18). Hence one cannot be defiled by an object that is intrinsically bad. The defilement is in man himself; this is what provokes the evil around him. Grace confers freedom in relation to all things. All things can be used without restriction. We do not have to have respect to the specific nature of an object, act, or profession, as though it had its own being and had individual qualities which were as such pleasing or displeasing to God.[2] God does not accept the sacrifice of Abel rather than that of Cain because he prefers lambs to fruits. This principle must be extended to the things around us and especially to the products of technology and art. Notwithstanding the impression abroad in some circles, I have never said that technology and its products are evil and that man ought to shun them. On the other hand, I have certainly not said that they are good. "I know, and am persuaded by the Lord Jesus, that there is nothing unclean of itself" (Romans 14:14). I realize that this attitude will find ready acceptance, especially among those who say that everything depends on the use that we make of things, i.e., that things are neutral and we may utilize them as we will. But this seems to me to be a serious error. It is not at all an implication of our freedom towards things and the universe in spite of appearances to the contrary. Paul says: "For every creature of God is good, and nothing to be refused, if it be received with thanksgiving, for it is sanctified by the word of God and prayer" (1 Timothy 4:4f.). Everything, then, is good, and yet Paul makes the strange addition: "It is sanctified by the word of God and prayer." We are not dealing, therefore, with things which are already sanctified and holy, so that they are good and can be used at once. But surely, one might think, there is no need for anything more if God has created them good. The

---

2  The Old Testament laws of the clean and unclean seem to contradict this statement. These apparently involve the classification of acts and things *per se*. Now I do not wish to bring the Old Testament into opposition to the New. The reader may consult von Rad's *Theology of the Old Testament* and Ricoeur's *Finitude et Culpabilité* on the matter. The views of these authors are different but complementary. They bring out the real point of the classification. I may simply note here that what we have in the Old Testament is a law of holiness or separation, and hence of indications which are relative in themselves, since they are never to be considered in themselves but only with reference to and in the service of the One who pronounces them and who is the Holy One. Within these limits the classification is not contrary to freedom in Christ.

*The Object of Freedom and the Will of Man*

explanation is that in Paul's thinking, in spite of those who discount the accident of the fall, there is a difference between what God has created and the world which is around us. The latter has to be sanctified if it is to be of value before God. Creation did not need this, since it was already perfect. But now only that which is sanctified by the word of God and prayer is pure and good. We may use all things if we do so in prayer, if we do so in the action of grace, if we bring these things into the world of the grace that God confers on us. It is we who bring them in. They are not there in advance. Nor is the right use of these things the issue. The work which has to be done in relation to them is much deeper. We have to sanctify them. The grace with which God clothes us has to fall on the things that we eat and use and possess. One might almost say that the things have to be "abused," for, as in the Old Testament there was a pollution by unclean-ness (unclean things make unclean), so the grace which is given us, the holiness of Jesus Christ, "contaminates" the things which are around us, spilling out over this universe which is ours. Naturally, we are not to take the terms used here too literally, for there is nothing magical or automatic about what happens. I am simply employing the comparison to try to get at the meaning. Yet there is a danger of misunderstanding the meaning too, for the cleanness and holiness are not intrinsic to us nor are they incorpo-rated into us. They transform us, and we have to live them out. Nor do the things which we are free to use become pure automatically by a kind of contract. They do so by a deliberate, voluntary, and definite act—that of prayer and blessing. This act is possible, however, only because we ourselves are the recipients of grace.

This brings us to the decisive verse: "Unto the pure all things are pure: but unto them that are defiled and unbelieving is nothing pure; but even their mind and conscience is defiled" (Titus 1:15). What is stated here is that the world is not transformed in itself by the lordship of Jesus Christ. It has not become good. Nor is the freedom which is gained in Jesus Christ a freedom for all men. Not all men are enabled and permitted to use all things. When Paul says: "All things are yours," the "yours" does not embrace the totality of men. It refers restrictively to those who have been pardoned and blessed, who have grasped by faith the grace which has been given them, and who have recognized that Jesus is the Christ.

Things can be good, then, only for those who have been sanctified in this way. "You are clean," says Jesus to his disciples, "but not all" (John 13:10), even though he had also washed the feet of Judas. Not all—Paul rigorously confirms this. For unbelievers nothing is pure. The choice is not now between good and bad or clean and unclean things. On the one side everything is possible and on the other side nothing is possible. On the one side all things are yours and on the other side you do not possess any-thing—for it is a blunder of the first magnitude to say tranquilly that, no matter who a man is, he is still the vice-gerent of creation and comes under the order which was given to Adam to exploit the earth. On the one side you can use all things and on the other nothing is finally legitimate but everything becomes an occasion of falling and sin.

Once again, the issue is not the quality of the world and of things but the relation of man to God. The problem is that of man. Man has to ask himself: Who is pure? Who *is* pure, not who thinks or makes himself pure? This is an ontic question. It is a question of the relation to Christ. It is not a question of personal evaluation or of morality. We pass on to the second part of the saying far too quickly, as though the ontic aspect could be taken for granted. In reality, however, the freedom to use all things is granted only to the man for whom Christ is the Son of the living God and whose feet Christ washes, i.e., to the man who is in communion with Christ, not just an inner communion, but one which finds expression in the Lord's Supper, whose expression in this form is desired, and which is lived out without our having to calculate whether our deeds are pure (this would always entail the fault of mere externality) and without our having to examine whether the state of our soul is pure (for God alone knows this). In this field we have simply to go forward as those who live on the promise and who believe that God has blessed them. Whether or not things are pure and good for use, whether or not we can use all things, does not depend on what we think of them or how we evaluate them, but on what we ourselves are.[3]

There has never been found anything better in the eyes of men than the fruit of the tree in Genesis 3. As verse 6 puts it so well, "She saw that the tree was good for food, and that it was pleasant to the eyes, and a tree to be desired to make one wise." What more could be wanted? Good, pleasant, and useful, offering food, aesthetic pleasure, and intellectual profit, serving both the economy and culture. What better?—and yet we know the outcome. The moment Eve listens to the serpent and is ready to hearken to what he says, all is lost. From this moment she has a defiled mind and conscience. She can no longer see things straight. She has lost everything. Nothing is pure for her any longer. Things are impure for the impure. But man cannot accept this and so he imposes his own classifica-

---

3 At first glance Romans 14:14 might seem to be saying that everything depends on our opinion. Something is unclean only for the man who thinks it is. It is a mistake, however, to think that we have here no more than a matter of human appraisal, as though a thing were pure merely because I thought it so. For the only opinion at issue is that of the believer, of the man who is purified: For the pure all things are pure. If the man in Christ, however, thinks that some things are bad, impure, and dangerous, then they are so for him. How is this? The passage explains it. There are brothers who are weaker in faith. They do not have full freedom. They do not live full lives. They come up against moral obstacles. They are wrong, but we must respect them. For the things they think bad become a temptation to them, a trap, an occasion of falling away from God. Hence they are in effect bad. We are not to apply this rule generally, however, to those who are not express believers in Christ. What Paul says is to be taken in context.

tions on the world. He says that one thing is good and another bad. He speaks of noble professions and base professions, of valid acts and invalid acts. In his decree he obeys what we define as the knowledge of good and evil. From now on he lives in this divided universe and even when he says that all things are neutral and everything depends on their use, he is simply extending the division to the use, which changes nothing. Man is still not free and the world has not been made one again.

On the other hand, to say, in Christ, that all things are lawful and all things are yours is to say that you may use all things as you wish without distinction. This is not at all an affirmation of the indifferent neutrality of things, which simply brings us back to differentiation in act and usage. The only question is the question of man. Is he in relation to Christ or not? We have here the antithesis between a static world and a world of movement. To classify things and actions, to set up lists of what is pure and permissible, is to belong to a static, arrested, and defined world in which freedom can never be anything more than a frail appearance, since if it were real it would challenge that which is ordered and codified. On the other hand, to affirm the full freedom in Christ in which all things are lawful and all things are yours is to belong to a world in the making, to a world of movement and development which is a free field for man's initiative and which leads to the kingdom of God.

All this, however, is in Christ. It has to be in Christ. It is for the man who is pure. Left to himself in unbelief, man can only want to order and stabilize and immobilize the world in which he finds himself. He has to classify it. He could not live otherwise. He would be in an intolerable situation if he had no point on which to fix his conduct. Perhaps what I am saying seems extravagant to some. The evidence clearly seems to be against it. What seems to arrest, immobilize, paralyze, divide, and ossify the world and society is the church and its morality. In contrast, what seems to promote and change things, to open up the world, is the science, technology, politics, and unionism of non-Christians. Christianity seems to be patently a reactionary and retrogressive force, while its opposite is the driving force of progress.

If, however, Christianity and the church are in fact reactionary and static, it is because they have lost the basic meaning of the Christian life, which is freedom. They have transformed revelation into a religion. Religion is indeed a conservative, retarding, and restrictive force. In this transformation fellowship with Christ is lost and with it the purity for which everything is pure and everything is possible. This is why it seems to me that the most urgent and decisive task for Christians today, on the basis of fellowship with Christ, is to recover the full meaning of freedom.

As regards the other side of the coin, I maintain that it is an illusion. As it is an illusion to think that modern man is adult and reasonable, so it is an illusion to think that we are in a world of authentic movement. True qualitative and spiritual transformation, the expansion of personal liberty, development from seed to plant, plant to flower and flower to fruit, the opening up of free fields, are all being confused with the manipulation of things by increasingly complex processes—an increasingly narrow and systematic regulation, an increasingly detailed organization, an increasing rigor of mechanisms of change. To be sure, many things and even all things are changing. But nothing decisive is being modified in spite of our prophets. Certainly nothing is being transformed. The world in which we live is as static as it could ever be so long as one perceives that a wheel which turns 3000 times is still static in relation to its axle, or that the static element in society consists in the rigor of its structures and options rather than in events. In fact we live in a society whose structures are more rigid and whose options are more restricted than ever. With all humility I would plead with the reader to ponder for a moment this judgment which seems to be erroneous but which is passed by a historian who is passionately concerned about the problem of technical progress and who neither denies progress nor resists it. The only thing that can set the world going is the entry of Christian freedom. Without this it is absolutely useless to expect anything from the atom or the cosmos. Man cannot want anything but full stability, dichotomy, a clear path, a plain knowledge of what is permitted and what is prohibited. The more complex society becomes and the more it changes and moves, the more it has need of rules of conduct and of immobilization, e.g., in planning or the authoritarian state. The more, then, it needs the exact opposite of the freedom to which Christ calls us.

Let us return for a moment to technology. We have said that the problem is not that of use (good use). It is that of the man who uses. Is he pure? This limits considerably the free and legitimate use of technology. But some aspects of technology itself also call for study. Technology entails the close association of parts in such a way that they cannot be dissociated again.[4] The individual technical object cannot be isolated and accorded independent worth or meaning. Each technical object is in reality a piece in the technical system and is just as closely tied to it as the cell is to the living body. A man cannot say that he as an individual makes use of his car or television set and that is all there is to it. He is part of a global phenomenon just as a member of the middle class is part of that class no matter what he may be in his own life and conduct, or just as a policeman cannot dissociate himself from the police no matter how mild a man he himself may be or how opposed to police brutality. There is an individual use of each technical object, but by that very fact there is also participation in a collective system which has its own distinctiveness and signification, which cannot be influenced, and apart from which one cannot truly proceed to discriminations, since one is swept away by the current.

Indeed, the two solidarities mentioned as illustrations, i.e., that of the member of the middle class and that of the policeman, are far less complete

---

4  Cf. J. Ellul, *The Technological Society* (1964).

*The Object of Freedom and the Will of Man*

than that produced by technology. A characteristic of our society is the creation of a web of abstract integrations. Money is an example. In the middle ages the use of money was still an individual matter. One could break solidarity by acting individually. Today this is no longer possible. I may refuse to worship Mammon but I am still part of the capitalist society. The system of technical objects is more integrated than ever.

When we say, then, that to the pure all things are pure, this is stated from an individualistic angle. The reference is to individual actions (e.g., eating) which are not integrated into a collective system, or which, as Paul shows, are part of such a system but in such a way that individual action can break the coordination. Thus when Paul speaks about idol meats, these are integrated into a system, namely, that of sacrifices, idol worship, paganism, etc. But the attitude of the Christian who eats these meats as mere food and who thus desacralizes and profanes them shatters the socio-ideological system of which they are a part. The free individual act of the man who is purified in Christ is enough to give them back a different quality which is natural and individualized.

In contrast, the technical object belongs to a double system. It belongs to a system of ideology and belief which the individual act of freedom can still break and profane. But it also belongs to the material system of correlation and integration which it is practically impossible to break by an individual act, since the characteristic of technology is precisely that it functions by general coordination and in bulk, whether in production, consumption, or organization. This throws a different light on the saying: "To the pure all things are pure."

For if the technical object in its individuality has nothing impure about it as such, we have to realize that in making use of it we take part in a system with which we are brought into absolute solidarity. Hence the slogan: "To the pure all things are pure," does not solve anything. We do not purify the system, for in the main it is used by unbelievers, by men who do not give thanks to God for his blessings, who do not sanctify his gifts by the word of God and prayer. In other words, the fact of use by a Christian does not in the case of a global phenomenon like technology alter the fact of use by unbelievers too, so that the impurity remains. We cannot strictly isolate ourselves, for no individual act modifies the integrated system. Yet this is precisely what we needed to find, namely, individual conduct which expresses in this sphere God's grace and love. We are thus in a serious predicament, and the principle: "To the pure all things are pure," does not seem to be an adequate solution.

One might, of course, evade the question by working out a theological doctrine which bypasses it. This is what Teilhard does, and he certainly owes much of his success to the ease with which he can present technology as a factor in the fulfilment of the divine plan. One might also recall a doctrine to which we have often referred, namely, that of the actualized lordship of Jesus Christ over the present world. But if we cannot accept these fallacious inventions, we are up against the wall. The difficulty seems to be insoluble. It is undoubtedly true that the saying: "To the pure all things are pure," applies to the technical object too. But in our actual use of it, we are also undoubtedly plunged into solidarity with what is impure, so much so that we are acutely conscious of the dichotomy and we cannot use the thing with a good conscience as we could do in a universe which was justified and holy.

At this point, however, a twofold question arises. First, are we so certain that the sayings: "All things are lawful"; "All things are yours"; "To the pure all things are pure," were meant to give us a good conscience? Is it the point of these sayings that we should not worry at all, that we can do anything, and that the moment we are pure everything we do is good? Are we just being told that we can go ahead confidently and will always have an easy conscience? We know the kind of Christian for whom nothing is ever in doubt. And if the abuse of a bad conscience is wrong for faith, if it expresses a lack of freedom, a fixed (and rather simple?) good conscience is not Christian either and expresses a lack of responsibility. We have often underlined the fact that there is no freedom without responsibility and *vice versa*. Hence I do not believe that this freedom can mean conduct which is always right and which leads then to self-admiration and a permanently good conscience.

On the one hand we are certainly not to be scrupulous over trifles. We do not have to ask on grounds of conscience whether meats were or were not sacrificed to idols, as Paul says. On the other hand, we cannot be wholly indifferent, since we are told to give thanks for all things and to invoke over them the word of God. Hence we may well use technical goods, but we must always remember what is implied by participation in technological civilization, which is far more negative and destructive than it is positive and constructive. We cannot endow this civilization with supplementary holiness on the imagined ground that it is fulfilling a supposed purpose of God.

The second point relates to results. Using anything has consequences for me; the saying: "To the pure all things are pure," takes care of that. But it also has collective or global consequences. It has repercussions on others. It has sociological and psychological effects. This is especially true of technology, whose collective results, whether positive or negative, are deep, unavoidable, and interrelated. We have to realize that when we use a technical product we have a part in these results. We accentuate them either one way or the other. Now the texts relating to freedom constantly evoke this problem of the effects of our acts. We must be careful to weigh our decisions. This is what calls now for examination.

We must see to it, of course, that the principle: "All things are lawful," is not weakened in any way. It invites us to live a full life. All moralism, asceticism, and mortification must be rejected. There can be no casuistry of what is permitted and what is prohibited. Replies to choices are not to be fixed in advance. Freedom consists in advancing freely in the field which God has opened up to us.

Just because all things are lawful we must not try to classify freedom as L. Fèvre does in his *La liberté des chrétiens* when he tries to differentiate between a freedom of refusal and a freedom of gift. The former, being characterized by a thirst for autonomy, a will to be oneself, a rejection of commitment, and a desire to remain intact, is for him obviously bad. The latter, which is shown by scholars and militants—I am not sure why the military are not also included—is naturally good. This distinction is completely meaningless. The free man in Christ can be at times a man who refuses and at other times a man who gives. Freedom may take either form. Outside Christ, the one may indeed have its source in egoism and anguish, but the other is symbolized by activism and a deficiency in good will.

### § 2. But . . .

If we insist only on the formula: "All things are lawful," are we faithful to scripture? Paul says of himself: "I keep under my body, and bring it into subjection" (1 Corinthians 9:27). We also remember his cry of despair when he does the evil that he does not want to do and does not do the good that he wants to do. Again, how can we escape the law, which still persists? Are we not driven back against the wall when Jesus addresses the rich young ruler? Is not this a rebuke and a challenge to the very core of our lives? Can we really interpret the saying: "To the pure all things are pure," as a possibility of using our money, for example, for our own selfish pleasure and enjoyment? Does the principle: "All things are lawful," mean that adultery, eroticism, exploitation of the poor, and murder are things we may now do and God will not mind? If so, why are there so many moral exhortations in the epistles? Why are there lists of virtues?

I can imagine what the reader may be saying at this point, for my own reaction is similar. Christians are always the same (and so is God, some would add). They affirm a general principle only to demolish it again. Thus the theologian says that God is unknowable. But then, as Jeanson points out, having made this essential declaration he writes whole volumes about God and analyzes him as though he knew him very well.

We are indeed tempted to think that this applies to God too. He gives and he at once takes away again. He gives a promise to poor Abraham which the latter never enjoys. He gives a salvation which is only virtual. Similarly he gives a freedom which is put in a yoke of obligations. Are we not wrong, then, to speak of escaping the traditional problem of limits to freedom? What we have just been talking about, are these not limits? Are we not forced back into the common framework?

I think not. The great difference seems to me to hinge on the following point. In the one case freedom is viewed as a datum to be organized, as a situation which brings with it its own statute and limitation. In the other case we have a movement, a creation which is continually renewed, the surprising and the unexpected, which like all movement is aiming at something.

Hence the "But" is not a limit or yoke. It is not the negation of a statute. It has the orientation of a movement, of the "what" to which it leads. For the freedom which is won for us in Christ is not a freedom of pure indifference in which doing one thing is the same as doing another, in which we may drive on the right side or the left, since it makes no essential difference. As we have seen, the fact that all things are lawful does not mean that all things are neutral and have no value or import. To say that all things are lawful does not mean that north and south are identical. On the contrary, Christ's coming into the world introduces us to a universe which is charged with meaning, value, and import. We do not enter an incoherent universe. The freedom which is given us is not the simple possibility of doing anything since nothing matters anyway. It is not an expression of the arbitrary and incoherent. As I tried to show earlier, God's free decision, which is the good, is never fantasy or incoherent or absurdity. Our own freedom, which derives only from God's, is like God's. It is not just foolishness. (Cf. Castelli on Christian and non-Christian freedom in *Le démoniaque*.)

But . . . Paul's "but" is not just a way of taking back what has been given. When he says that "all things are yours but you are Christ's," he undoubtedly has in view, as Tillich says, the Christ whose cross is weakness and foolishness to the world, not the Christ Pantocrator, but the Christ whose cross represents all his power and lordship over us, since its weakness and foolishness are ultimate wisdom. This wisdom does not make Christ the representative of the wisdom and power of the world but the representative of God. The folly which gives us wisdom enables us to use all things that are ours, even the wisdom and philosophy of the world. When not broken, this dominates us. When broken, it is ours. Broken does not mean reduced, impoverished, or mastered, but freed from its tendency to idolatry. In this fine passage in his *Courage to Be* Tillich offers the exact sense of the "but." It is not a restriction of our freedom but the way that makes it possible.

Thus the freedom which is given to us is not without direction or signification. It is given with a meaning for us and with signification for the men around us. On the one side it is completely gratuitous. We are truly free. All things are truly lawful. We must make our own choices. On the other side our decisions have a bearing on others. They affect the common life, for in Christ no one lives to himself, and it is not true that we are always alone, as the convenient formula of existentialism would have it. Our freedom bears witness to something. It is not achieved alone. One is not free simply to be free. Freedom leads somewhere. Every act of freedom has meaning or not. It is a force or not. It can give rise to freedom in others or bring about their enslavement. In this regard we always have movement, orientation, advance. Freedom is "in order that . . ." or "with a view to. . . ." Freedom is truly freedom when it commits us to an action which we choose, when it aims at certain objectives and marks. These may be well known and obvious, like dazzling lighthouses. Or they may be hard to descry and sometimes covered over by the waves. But they are present for him who has eyes to see. God does not leave us without signs in the navigation of our freedom.

Paul has at the very outset two specifications in the very same passage in which he says that all things are lawful: "But all things are not expedient . . . but all things edify not" (1 Corinthians 10:23ff.). We must now try to see what he means by "expedient" and "edifying."

As regards the former, he is not using the term in the concrete, material, or, as we might say, ecclesiastical sense. He does not mean what is good for the development of Christianity or the strength of the church. As regards the second, he does not have in mind the current spiritual sense or the moralizing sense, as when we speak of an edifying discourse or edifying conduct, which is virtuous in the sense of insipid conformity. The first word means useful in the sense of serious or important. The second has the strong sense of constructive.

Paul brings out the meaning of the words in the rest of the passage. The issue is meat sacrificed to idols. Paul has shown that all things are lawful; hence I may eat this meat. Yet he also emphasizes that some brothers will be shocked at this and so I must be careful. He concludes with two theses. On the one side, everything must be done to God's glory. On the other, scandal must be avoided.

The meaning of the two orientations of freedom is now plain. It is not expedient that I should eat this meat which is sacrificed to idols if my doing so offends, wounds, and shocks my brothers. I can equally well not eat (am I not free?). But I have to take the other into account. I must not hurt him needlessly. On the contrary, I have to build him up, or help him to build himself up. Giving offense is unlikely to do this. But doing something to God's glory can help to build him up and hence it has meaning; it is both useful (expedient) and edifying. Our actions must be chosen in such a way that they will be useful to love and to God's glory. They must be chosen in the freedom according to which they build up our brothers and the church of God. Paul thus gives us the two specifications of freedom.

We quoted earlier one part of Augustine's famous dictum. The dictum as a whole connects two things: "Love (God) and do as you like." Freedom thus finds both its orientation and its possibility in the love of God. When we speak of freedom for God we are saying the same thing. Love for God charges freedom with force and assigns it signification. We are in the presence, not of incoherence, but of coherence and certitude.

Yet we must also find a place for love of neighbor.[5] For the love which gives direction to freedom is that which responds to the two commandments. Paul refers to the different aspects of love in his discussion of freedom in 1 Corinthians. "All things are lawful for me, but all things are not expedient. . . . Let no man seek his own, but every man another's interest." This seeking is love for one's neighbor. Love wants what is useful for others, what is in their interests. This demands extraordinary freedom and availability. It demands freedom to despoil oneself, to do what is almost impossible, i.e., to efface oneself, or to put oneself so radically in the place and situation and "skin" of the other that one knows what is good for him, what is in his true interests, because one is the other. This is, of course, an abnormal action. Modern existentialism says that it is impossible. The odd thing here is that a philosophy of freedom is the very one that asserts also our solitude and incommunicability, i.e., the absence of love. Scripture, however, maintains that there is no freedom where there is no love. The two realities are tied together so closely that to destroy the one is necessarily to destroy the other. This is decreed already in Eden. It is also illustrated continually in the history of Israel. Israel loses its freedom the moment it ceases to love.

Freedom finds its possibility in love because outside love it is nonsense. On the other hand, love presupposes freedom. To have regard to the other is to be completely open. When Jesus says: "If any man . . . take away thy coat, let him have thy cloak also. And whosoever shall compel thee to go a mile, go with him twain" (Matthew 5:40f.), he is showing us concretely what is meant by freedom in love. The first step in human relations is always one of constraint. Each man in society wants to assert his rights and to impose something on others, to bring them under obligation. But if you love the one who forces you, the enemy, then you remove the relation of power and set yourself in the relation of love. At the same time, you take from the relation the element of constraint and you act in freedom. Something is taken; give. You are forced; choose to do more. This is not "virtue" nor is it weakness. It is a complete changing of the relation. By the act of love you set both yourself and the other in freedom.

For love can take concrete shape only in freedom.[6] It takes a free man to love, for love is both the unexpected discovery of the other and a readiness to do anything for him. It is the imagination which responds to his need and suffering and mediocrity. But you can have this imagination

---

5. Bovon, "Vivre dans la liberté," makes the interesting observation that the only place where the adjective "free" occurs in the Gospel narrative (Matthew 17:26) is in the discussion of the temple tax: "The children are free and do not have to pay, but to avoid scandalizing others they choose to pay the tax as free men." In other words, the one Synoptic use of "free" relates freedom to love in exactly the same way as Paul does in 1 Corinthians.

6. A. Dumas in his *D. Bonhoeffer* (1968) contrasts eros, which shuns the reality of one's neighbor, with agape, which serves it. Eros is independent; agape is free.

*The Object of Freedom and the Will of Man*

only if your freedom allows you on the one side to put yourself in the place of the other and on the other side to do something innovative and imaginative to meet the situation. There can be no imagination if there is no freedom—no freedom to use all things. Love cannot express itself in a framework of laws, constraints, and obligations. It is never the point-by-point realization of a program. It is never the execution of a law, however perfect this may be, nor the fulfilment of obligations. When law and morality come into play, love takes flight. Planning excludes love. In society law and morality uphold the social organism. They function between beings who do not love each other but have to live together. Where love is, however, all that is left behind and is not to be taken into account. Love implies the richness of instant free presence. A total person, in the fulness of his strength, is totally with you. For this person is free, has left all else on one side, and has no ulterior motives or constraints or attachments which might cause division or restriction or pressure.

Love by its very nature finds expression in the freedom to see and to choose what is good for others, what fits them best, what is in their interests. Love also means that nothing will be done to cause others to be grieved. In this regard Paul has in mind the apparent conflict between freedom and love. "If thy brother be grieved with thy meat, now walkest thou not charitably. Destroy not him with thy meat, for whom Christ died" (Romans 14:15). The teaching here is the same as in 1 Corinthians. All food is pure and may be used. We are free in relation to idols and need not be troubled if meat was sacrificed to them. This is of no importance. The meat is still only meat, for idols no longer have any power over us. We may thus eat it. But in exercising our freedom we must always consider the result of our free acts on others. This is what we had in mind in relation to technology. If we love others, we must ask whether the act of our freedom might not be harmful to them. As Paul says, we may be among those who are not yet liberated from the power of idols. Those who fear idols and are convinced of their reality warn us: "Be careful; this meat was sacrificed." They think the food is full of power and evil. Hence we should refrain from eating it, not because the food is impure, but because if we did it would give offense to these others, whether they be Jews or Christians. Their view of the Christian life may be quite wrong. They may even think that I eat the meat because I still believe in idols and am adopting the pagan rite. A wrong expression might thus be given to Christian freedom. Hence I abstain from eating, for freedom offers the possibility both of doing and of abstaining. Everything depends on those around me. I have to love them and to live out my freedom among them.[7]

---

7  Cf. the excellent study of 1 Corinthians 8 by J. F. Collange in *Foi et Vie*, 1965. Collange brings out very well the fact that there is an attack on Gnosticism here and a conflict between *agape* and *gnosis*. In the situation of freedom knowledge does not help. Love, not speculation, is our guide. Collange offers a rather different interpretation of verse 10. But he recalls forcefully that in the relation to others there must be constant

Paul confirms all this in a famous passage: "For though I be free from all men, yet have I made myself servant unto all [we have already seen the relation between freedom and service] . . . . To the weak became I as weak [he does not say: To the strong became I as strong!] . . . . I am made all things to all men . . ." (1 Corinthians 9:19–23). Freedom permits all things. The law and traditional morality may be observed and they may not be observed. I may know how to be rich and also how to be poor. I may work strenuously and unceasingly or I may be idle with a good conscience. I may squander money or economize. But I do all things, not because I want to do them, but because the other is there and he demands of me a particular style of life. I must adapt myself to him and accept him for what he is and how he is. As no object is unclean in itself, so no man is unclean in himself. As a Christian I can thus associate with all men no matter what may be their occupation or social status or race. I can accompany them in their struggles and problems and doubts and precepts and moralities and attitudes and habits without attaching any decisive importance to such things.

I realize that all this might be called hypocrisy. Freedom in Christ will always be regarded thus by those outside, for it implies an absence of ultimate and total commitment in any human situation. We accompany the other to show our love and so as not to hurt him, but we cannot regard his political and philosophical convictions, in which we go forward with him, as having any final or decisive seriousness. We respect them because they are his.

It is to be noted that the love of which scripture speaks is love for man, not for ideas, doctrines, social status, political conduct, etc. What counts is man, not revolutions, principles, or ideals. No matter what contemporary thought may suggest, principles are less important than people. The freedom and love which are in Christ do not allow us to adopt a slogan like: "Let humanity perish rather than justice (or truth, or country, or church)." A man is worth more than all the doctrines of justice. We cannot agree to the sacrifice of one or more generations if only the revolution is achieved. Our devaluation of ideologies, works, and commitments in favor of the reality of man is precisely what causes Christian freedom to be taxed with hypocrisy by those who think principles and doctrines are worth more than men.

Nor can we agree that the totality of a man consists merely in his activities and habits and culture and opinions. To love there is something more in man than this. This something more, however, can be perceived and grasped and reached only by love. Objective scientific observation permits us to see only that which is objectifiable, i.e., with regard to which we can adopt any attitude or opinion we like. But that in relation to which

---

recollection of the "for whom Christ died." This is what gives worth and importance to the weaker brother. If in our freedom we neglect the weaker brother we act as if Christ did not die or as if his death had no real significance.

*The Object of Freedom and the Will of Man*

we are not free is what love discerns in the other or what this other is for love.

The objection need not be raised that this involves an intolerable dichotomy, i.e., that one cannot set man on one side and his ideas, works, commitments, and profession, in a word his condition, on the other. This objection is prompted by a narrow sociologism and has no real cogency. It is simply a sign that the true relation of freedom and love has not been grasped.

For if I go an extra mile with someone, if I can be a leftist with leftists, if I can be a Teilhardian with Teilhardians, this is precisely because I take people seriously *with* their works, commitments, and occupations, not questioning these because I know that my doing so would cause hurt.

To the degree, however, that these things are objectifiable, i.e., detachable from the man (for after all they are only a role and I radically reject any identifying of a man and his role), I cannot regard them as having any decisive importance. To this degree then, because I am free in relation to them, I can be very close to this man whom love discovers for me, not being deflected by his opinions and functions, which, spontaneously and in my non-freedom, I might well dislike.

Thus I have constantly to choose and decide my attitudes, actions, and commitments in terms of the other whom love makes my neighbor and not in virtue of the worth of this or that doctrine, orientation, or occupation. This does not have to mean, of course, that I can never disagree with him or oppose him in any way. Love can also consist in opposition. Choice always arises and balance has to be maintained.

Sometimes we have to adopt the attitudes and opinions of the other. We are not to cause offense about secondary matters. We have to go with him even in his opposition to what he thinks is the revelation of Christ. We have to be with him in his sin, and this might sometimes lead the church to adopt the structures of the world. When I stressed the conformity of the church to sociological currents in my work *Fausse Présence,* I was commonly criticized for accusing the church unjustly. But if what I wrote is read properly it will be seen that what we have here is a question rather than an accusation. Freedom forces us to raise this question. Do we have simple, blind, sociological obedience to the *stoicheia* of the world or do we have a free decision to go along with men and the society in which we live? This demands in each case a very serious and strict examination,[8] and the

8  Naturally the examination has to be up to date. There is no point in denouncing the conformity of the church of yesterday. Research will show that some secular structure has always affected and influenced the church in its choices and decisions. Even what are regarded as incontestable free innovations on the part of the church will always be shown on closer analysis to have prior models. The Reformation offers some good examples. Thus presbyterianism is often said to be a specifically reformed creation which shows great inventiveness. But recent studies, e.g., those of Ourliac, have made it clear that elements in this order were formulated at the Council of Basel, and that the

dilemma cannot be avoided that it is hard to distinguish between mere swimming with the tide and temporarily adopting things which are not really taken seriously in order to be close to men, to be understood by them, and to meet them on their own ground.

On other occasions we have to oppose the men around us, repulsing their ideas, rejecting their commitments, and criticizing their occupations. We can adopt an attitude of resolute nonconformity with the world. We shall have to come back to this. For the moment, however, we again have to face the question whether in so doing we are in the last resort only maintaining our own ideas, to which we attribute major importance and which we regard as intrinsically better than those of others (in which case we are not liberated in relation to our ideas); whether we are only confirming our own social and political commitments, which we think are of greater worth than those of our neighbors (in which case we are not liberated in relation to our commitments); whether we are only following our own aggressive and contradictory temperament (in which case we are not free in relation to ourselves); whether we are only practicing conformity with our own age and background (in which case we are not free in relation to these).

This is a vital question for a Christian whether he is engaged in doctrinal debate, in theology, in apologetics, or in proselytizing (in the wrong sense). For a lack of love here means once again a lack of freedom. And this is what normally causes the Christian to change revelation into religion. This is what leads the church to act like a power structure. On the other hand, if I offer disagreement and opposition in freedom and love, what does this mean? It may mean that my nonconformity puts a question to the other and causes him to think about his life, or that it induces him to put a question to me about the meaning of what I am doing, so that there is a chance to bear witness to Jesus Christ. At the same time my attitude may just be a cause of offense, and at this point we must be careful. Offense is a serious matter and the violent nonconformity allowed by Christian freedom can cause it. Christ condemned offenses. We may also remember, however, that Christ himself gave offense. He scandalized the priests and Pharisees, the scribes and the temple merchants, the patriots (by associating with toll-collectors) and the left-wingers (by associating with the rich, whose banquets he attended, for we recall that the toll-collectors were far wealthier than the Pharisees). The condemnation of offenses is clearly a condemnation of offenses against one of these little ones (Matthew 18:6), and Paul's attitude in relation to idol meats is exactly the same. We are not to shock the weaker brothers, i.e., those who are weaker because they are

---

presbyterian structure was probably inspired by the canons of this council, which the Roman Church did not adopt. Similarly French academies are often regarded as a Protestant innovation, but recent research shows that in pedagogy, curriculum, and structure they had already been sketched and in part put into practice by the Humanists as early as 1525.

full of doubts and scruples on the issue, or those who are weaker in faith and have not yet grasped in all its fulness the freedom which Christ gives.

As noted above, Paul speaks about being weak with the weak but not about being strong with the strong. This is the real point. Jesus, too, says that he has not come to the healthy but to the sick. The respect which is demanded in love is respect for the weak, whether their weakness be corporal, mental, intellectual, social, moral, or spiritual. It is respect for the sick and the ugly, the lonely and the despised, the poor and the foolish, the exploited and the colonized, the overscrupulous and the confused.[9]

In contrast the gospel is always hard on the rich, for their wealth, whatever it may be, is power. For them Christian freedom may legitimately be an offense. If, then, our freedom shocks the mighty, the moral, the bigoted and violent capitalist or communist establishment, the ruling class, the absolutists, the men of intransigent principle, those who are sure of their principles or their authority, we can only rejoice in this. Offense is of profit for them. When we shake human certainty with our freedom, we are seeking the interest of these others. To introduce doubt and questioning where an equal conscience and tranquil self-righteousness reign, to shatter social, intellectual, and spiritual conformity, to jolt those who live by conventions and platitudes, to arouse uncertainty where security holds sway, is not this an extension of the saying of our Lord: "Go and sell that thou hast, and give to the poor . . . and come and follow me" (Matthew 19:21)?

Now normally only Christian freedom, since it is total independence, can be so disengaged from conformities that it can challenge these attitudes, riches, and powers. Only Christian freedom! We must see that all other challenges will lead man to new conformities, powers, and justifications. This is why the situation is so serious when the Christian does not take up his freedom.

The relation between love and freedom is finely stressed by Bultmann (*Glauben und Verstehen*, I, 235) when he points out that love does not give us the content of action but its manner. (We see here the basic importance of means, on which I have insisted for many years, since ours is a technological society.) In doing this Bultmann is simply repeating in modern terms what Paul says in 1 Corinthians 13:1ff. The act is not indifferent, but it is love alone that qualifies it. Love makes it impossible for us to draw up a list of virtues. This is freedom. The free man in Christ chooses in the act of his freedom. He chooses in love and acts in love. This prevents the freedom from being merely negative. Love demands action without saying what action. It does not allow avoidance of the other. For it does not give me a concept of the neighbor but shows him to me each time in encounter, and shows me each time what I must do, as Bultmann excellently puts it.

---

9 Naturally the colonized, when he becomes a proud and spiteful nationalist, is a man of power, whereas the despised and universally hated American or whatever is one of the poor.

For the free man the situation is always new. Stirred by the novelty of his discovery of the neighbor, the free man expresses his freedom in the act of specific love for the one who is thrown in his path and who seems at a first glance to be an obstacle or impediment to freedom.

Valette (*Au milieu de vous, il y a quelqu'un*, 1966) sums this up well when he speaks of freedom as a meeting with Christ and neighbor. Christ is free and the neighbor should be. Where one of these two freedoms inspires and awaits the other, I am in an unforeseeable situation which is an opening for love. Valette then shows how disconcerting Jesus was. What he says to one does not help us to see how he will deal with another. His varied and contradictory freedom still surprises us. Where others observe a moral code which they regard as universally valid, Jesus looks at the man and in love finds the word which is valid for this one man in this one situation. He replaces a morality of abstract rules by a free word which delivers man by setting up a relation that means life. The law, being itself enslaved, enslaves. Love, being free to find its own reply, frees.

We see, then, that according to an analysis of the texts thus far, love is not a restriction of freedom. It gives it its meaning and orientation. At the level of human behavior one might say that the totality of the Christian life amounts to a dialectic of freedom and love. Everything leads up to the movement in which freedom is incarnated in love and love stimulates freedom. The whole of ethics consists in this dialectical movement, constantly renewed, from love to freedom and from freedom to love. Each time a new situation is set up by the one and called in question by the other. Each rests on the reality created, which is then lived out and surpassed in a new freedom and then again in a new love. We find here a situation which is the very opposite of what we naturally think and of what actually goes on in the world in the relation with men. For in the world love is always in one sense or another alienation. "Where your love is, there is your heart, i.e., your total life." Whatever the love may be, however sublime it may be, no matter what its object may be (another human being, money, the poor, mankind, science, or country), it always involves self-dispossession (usually described positively as self-giving) and enslavement. This exclusive relation to the other or to an object, this attachment which detaches from all else, this rooting in a place or person, excludes freedom.

It is not just the family that ties us down. Love itself does so. This is why "free love" has been advocated as a chance to change partners whenever desired. The only question here is whether there is any real love. For this advocacy carries with it indifference to the other, the partner. "I" cease to love the other and hence I change, I disengage myself, I go towards another. It is evident that the possibility of change is linked to the end of love. It is also evident that there is no concern about the sufferings, expectations, hopes, or needs of the other. I gain freedom by rejecting the other. Hence I do not love the other. This was the kind of liberty proposed in the eighteenth and nineteenth centuries: Each for himself, whether in economic liberalism in which the strong crushes the weak, or in licentiousness in which instinct and intelligence are assuaged and self-realization is achieved by using the other as an object or the means to an end.

Normally the freedom that man wins for himself rules out commitment. Hence revolutionaries have good reason to suppress religious vows and the indissolubility of marriage in the name of freedom. Normally, from the human standpoint, liberty cannot allow love for God or man to produce this kind of enslavement. Love, which presupposes reciprocity and which implies that the one who is loved can count on the other and knows that the other will not pull out on a whim, will be found to be a limitation. It excludes freedom. In nature and man, love and freedom are antithetical modes of life.

Not the least peculiar feature of Christianity, which is contrary to nature, is that in it love and freedom are indissolubly united, not by a halting conciliation, not by an attempt to hold together two ill-matched horses, but by the essential implication of the one in the other.

To be noted at this point is the fine saying in 1 John 2:11, which closes the rigorous theological demonstration with the old and new commandment of the Word which is love: "But he that hateth his brother is in darkness, and walketh in darkness, and knoweth not whither he goeth." In an ethics of freedom a basic matter is to know that freedom without love resembles a blind man without a guide. In an open space a blind man is free. So is a man who is autonomous in relation to God's command. But so too—and this is even worse—is the Christian who thinks he is living out freedom in Christ but does not have the light which is exclusively that of love, and not just of any love but of the love of God which is manifested in him, which is first addressed to him, and which is then addressed to the brethren. For John speaks first of love of God and then of love of the brethren. As regards freedom, of course, the love which gives orientation is love of the brethren. Without this our freedom is that of the blind leading the blind. The blind are those who are without love; they do not see the other.

If we are freed, it is because Christ loves us. If Jesus is free, even in temptation, it is because he loves his Father. If we live out the freedom which is given us, we are led to love the one who frees us. If we love our brother, it is because we are fully free in relation to every alienation. If we are free with this freedom that is given by Christ, we see in the other the neighbor who himself is also called to be free, and this can be so only in and by love. In Christ there is no freedom without love, for without love freedom would be incoherent and a turning back upon itself. How can we believe that self-admiration or self-centeredness is freedom when all that we have is enslavement to what is most immediate and alienating, our body, our opinions, our needs, and our passions?

At this point a strict distinction has to be made between freedom and independence. What man claims as freedom is no more than independence, and confusion of the two is the atrocious illusion on which we have lived for the last two centuries. We shall return to this problem in the third part.

In Christ there is no love without freedom. But this freedom is not independence in regard to the one who is loved. It is not the simple possibility of breaking off and beginning again (although it is this too, as the story of Adam shows). When freedom is used to break off love and to begin again, then the astonishing teaching of scripture is that man becomes independent in his own eyes—illusorily autonomous—but in reality he becomes alienated, lost, and deprived of his freedom. It is when freedom has been used to deny love that it has disappeared. This freedom is an expression of the love that abides, for love cannot abide except in and by and for freedom.

We refer, of course, to true freedom both with regard to our sociological context and with regard to ourselves (our needs and passions and transitory emotions). Real freedom is lived out in love. It does not break it off. It presupposes this basic relation with the other in which (alone) I can be fully myself because I can give myself as I am to the other, in whom I have the full confidence, which love gives, that he will not possess or alienate me, because the other can receive me as I am in freedom, because in love the other knows and yet accepts and supports me, giving to me and giving himself. Hence I am fully myself and fully free only when I love and am loved. This truth, which is first lived out by Christ for us, is accessible to us only in this love and freedom in Christ. For the other to whom we have been referring is not just the woman I love; it is my neighbor and even my enemy. In this regard the biblical affirmation is completely at odds with anything that man might say.

We are led at this point to a theme which Buber has admirably set in focus, for his meditation on the encounter between the I and the Thou is an accurate description of what Christian love can be. For one thing we should note the intensity and immediacy of the relation—the fact that there is authenticity of the one for the other without the interposition of any means or ends. As Buber puts it, there is neither aim, appetite, nor anticipation between the I and the Thou. Encounter takes place only when means are abolished. The one cannot serve the other. There can be no seizing or using, whether concrete or spiritual. Again, the mutuality or reciprocity of the relation is to be noted. Each summons the other, becomes a Thou for him, and makes him an I. In a sense each creates the other. We are reminded of the truth of love in Christ. The neighbor, the one who approaches, who thus becomes a Thou, stirs the other to become an I. In order that this may be so, and when it is so, freedom holds sway. Buber condenses this in his famous statement to the effect that when the sky of the Thou opens above me the winds of causality come to heel and the tornado of fatality settles. Love shatters fatality and brings in liberty. Love does not obey the law of causality. Love is freedom. There can be no freedom, no breaking of causality and fatality, apart from encounter with the Thou who awakens me and makes me an I.

Buber also realized that man can act toward the world as an It, i.e., as an assemblage of objects, instruments, and mechanisms. When he does so he chills the world and men around him and in so doing makes himself a thing. This is a relation without freedom. Only when he accepts the dialogue which puts himself in question is he real man. But this is not finally possible unless he is first addressed by God, for whom he is Thou. It is not possible except in the face-to-face encounter which God sets up and which gives him freedom for other relations too.

Love of neighbor apart from freedom is dust and ashes. It is no more than a calculation of what I have done and of what the other owes me. It can never be more than a rule and ultimately a chain. Love of neighbor means nothing unless it releases us from the fatal circle of calculation, unless it is a constantly renewed flame, unless it is an act of freedom. For it is the combination of love and freedom which relativizes all else.

When we have this combination, then duties, claims, moral and psychological considerations, and sociological conditionings all seem to be infinitely relative. Naturally, they still exist. One can accept them and play a part in them, knowing that it is only a part. Politics, philosophy, social action, and art all become a possibility which is undoubtedly always open, but they are always called in question too. Love restores all things to their true dimensions. They are mere things compared with the neighbor, who alone counts. Freedom gives to acts and commitments their temporary character. For freedom, nothing is more durable than love. For love, nothing is more significant than freedom. This relativization, however, does not imply any rejection of what may offer itself. In virtue of freedom all openings for social or individual action are acceptable. In virtue of love for my neighbor I am unceasingly impelled to recommence whatever can serve him.

Thus the man who is freed by Christ is called upon to choose his acts in terms of the neighbor whom he loves, of the enemy, and of his situation and condition. He may be summoned sometimes to support him and sometimes to scandalize him according to the diversity of the neighbor. An objection might arise here. This line of conduct can surely produce contradictory attitudes. They will certainly be different according to the different backgrounds and people. Is not this very shocking? Is it not a simple adaptation to context?

Now there may very well be contradictions. We may be led to say white in one situation and black in another. We may go with the right in one case and with the left in another. Something of the same may be seen in the life of Paul. On one occasion he may flee when death threatens while on another he may go to meet it voluntarily. Again, it is sometimes good to eat or to marry and sometimes it is right not to eat, to follow an ascetic rule, and not to marry. Similar contradictions may be found especially in the prophetic writings. Indeed, for the past half-century it has been a rule of interpretation that this or that passage cannot belong to a given prophet because it is in contradiction with the general message of the work. An argument of this type implies rejection of the freedom of the prophet (and of the Holy Spirit). It is normal enough that within his lifetime a prophet should speak truths which are both true and yet contradictory as he speaks according to love in freedom. Everything depends on the circumstances, on the men concerned, on their reality and needs and misery and pride.

If there is, of course, a revealed truth in Christ which is unique, total, unchangeable, complete, and sure, this revelation leads us into infinitely varied modes of thought and conduct. In other words, we cannot speak of a Christian morality which establishes a particular line of behavior (apart from that of love in freedom). Again, we cannot speak of a fixed Christian doctrine or form of government or economic model or church structure or relation to science. Various doctrines are possible, and we must not be offended at this adaptability or (secular) presence or actuality. What we are forbidden to do is to settle down, whether in the past by adoption of a permanent attitude which is thought to be Christian, or in the future by rejecting present economic or political realities in favor of an ideology that has yet to be put into practice. The Christian life cannot be ossified in a particular conception of the good. It must be a waiting and watching and praying and advancing. It must decide each moment what is to be done. It must be ready to see who is the poorest and most deprived for whom everything must be done. It must also be ready to leave this one at once to go to someone else when there has been some relieving at least of his plight. In all this, of course, the rule of conduct is not to be our own imagination or desire or conformity or adaptation to changing society. It is to be only our assessment of the best possible expression of our love for the poor and the stranger and the enemy, i.e., for the neighbor.

This leads us to another implication for conduct which is much debated and is also shocking (although not for the same category of Christians). The fact that freedom is choice of acts in terms of love for others means that we are faced with a purely individualistic ethics. This freedom can be demonstrated only by individual acts in individual cases. Intrinsically and primarily it does not have any social or political dimension in the traditional sense.[10]

We shall have to discuss later the connection between Christian

---

10 I.e., in the sense of commitment to a collective movement, a part, a union, etc. The personal act of freedom at the individual level, if it is truly an expression of freedom, naturally and necessarily has a general dimension. It is not a private act. But I think we have to make a distinction between individual and private. What is individual, even though done by only one individual, can have a far wider bearing. I do not think that the Christian life can ever be a private life, i.e., a life enclosed within the confines of our home and the group of our choice.

*The Object of Freedom and the Will of Man*

freedom and what is called political freedom. We already see a wide distinction, however, in virtue of the unbreakable relation between freedom and love. For this love which informs our freedom cannot be general and abstract. It does not concern mankind as a whole. It does not concern a class or people. It concerns a specific man. Why do I have to say this? Not because of a general theory of love which already justifies it, but because the New Testament itself impels me. When I am asked to have a care for the interests of another, to see to his personal needs, to put myself in his place, to seek what is good for him, generalization is impossible. For each man has his own needs and interests which apply to him alone. The problem is a very serious one and yet also a very simple one. Today we are all accustomed to thinking collectively. This is our modern mind-set. It may be traced to the influence of the humanities, of political science, and of socialism. We find it easy to speak of the needs of the working class or of underdeveloped peoples. This is right enough in the political and sociological domain. But it has nothing at all to do with love.

A closer analysis will help us to make the distinction. It may be true, for example, that the working class has general (very general) characteristics. Nevertheless, it is increasingly perceived that no two members of this class are really alike. Love addresses itself to this singularity. The man we are called upon to love is the particular, unique man, viewed according to his ultimate worth. To consider him thus is to give him precisely what he does not have—he himself and not this or that member of his class or nation. Love does not take account of average needs or collective interests but of the unique need of this man, the specific interest of the real man. The man has to be known fairly well (and not just in terms of averages or generalizations) if what is suitable for him is really to be known. When we begin to love in this way, we see that the real need of man is not the realization of collective interests. This naturally has its place, but let us not confuse love or freedom with it. These have first to consider each man in his particularity. Only thus can it be seen what hurts him and what must be avoided on the one side and what supports and edifies and serves him, so that we must go after it, on the other. I think that in these areas the passages in Paul which show us concretely what is meant by love in freedom are not at all accidental or occasional but convey basic teaching.

I must repeat that in spite of enthusiasm for the theory of love that can express itself in "long relations" and in spite of criticisms of my rejection of it, I have not yet found any philosophical or anthropological proof or argument to convince me how love can exist apart from knowing others and by a mere network of communications.[11] Only God can love the totality. The theory simply expresses an idealism and sentimentalism out of accord with scripture or else it tries to modify the reality of love in terms of a collectivization of being. But to me this seems to vitiate the

---

11  For "long relations" cf. the instructive work of J. Lohisse, *La communication anonyme* (1970).

truth by conformity. I also refuse to admit that love as a lasting and full personal relationship is merely the cultural result of a certain epoch. For we find it in both the Old Testament and the New. We find it in the Roman period and the Middle Ages. These did not have an individualistic and middle-class view of love. Precisely in these collectivist societies love was an essential phenomenon of individuation.

A final aspect of the freedom which is oriented to love concerns once more the variability in our attitudes. If we agree that each, according to what he sees in his neighbor, must decide what to do in order to show him the truth of love in Christ, then the judging of others is forbidden. For we have here free acts, and I have no authority to constitute myself the judge of another's freedom. When I see an act which expresses this unique relation of love, I, who am not in this relation, who do not know the exact motives, who do not know the neighbor for whom my brother has been led to make this decision, how can I make any judgment on this act and decision? This is all part of the individual character of such expressions of love in freedom. If one Christian thinks he should accompany a Communist on his political adventure, what can I say against him? If another thinks that he should refrain from wine or tobacco to help rehabilitate a neighbor, why should I charge him with legalism? If another thinks that he should be a literalist to help the humble folk in his parish rather than giving offense, or if yet another thinks that he should demythologize scripture to reach the critical intellectual, why should I take issue with them so long as in each case we have a true expression of love in freedom and not the application of a dogmatic attitude which is felt to be universally applicable? If, however, the demythologizer does his work in such a way that he gives offense to the most lowly sheep in the flock, then he is not obeying love but the intellectual pride and carnal vanity to which he is enslaved.

Here especially we again meet with suspicion. We have been in an era of suspicion since Marx, Nietzsche, and Freud. Behind the man who speaks and acts, who is the real I? A bad conscience? Class membership? The subconscious? Events and complexes? Man is never what he seems to be, or thinks he is, or would like to be. Suspicion rules. I cannot believe in him or accept his word or his good faith. There are always other motives for what he does. This is the current attitude, and in my view it destroys freedom.

I know that man is not free, no matter what his pretensions, but my suspicion crushes even the little seeds of freedom. If he has a chance of becoming free, it sterilizes him. It encloses him in the bondage of his sociological or psychological determinations. It rules out freedom. For it ruins the freedom that is possible, supposed, hoped for, or affirmed. It shuts me up in a definite absence of it. It cuts the root of freedom by stopping me from moving out to the other in a clear witness to freedom.

Freedom excludes suspicion. A choice must be made here with no compromise or half measures. If I think I am free in Christ, I can have no suspicion of others and must break with Freud, Marx, and Nietzsche. If there is freedom only in the reciprocity of love, I must lay down all weapons. This is the act of freedom. A choice has to be made. I can advance with all my equipment and analyze the other sociologically and psychologically. I can pin him down and dissect him like a butterfly. But if I do I lose my own freedom and shut myself in the circle of his determinations. I can do this or I can advance in freedom. A choice which is both intellectual and vital must be made here.

Paul says that love believes, hopes, and endures all things. It suspects no evil (1 Corinthians 13:5,7). If it is not lived out thus, freedom is mere talk and self-perversion. This is not naivety. A choice must be made. Suspicion is known, and it is rejected by the free man in a deliberate act. Freud and Marx and their analyses are known. It is known that the other is a hypocrite, a liar, a slave of desire and class. Yet the free man chooses to destroy suspicion, to have confidence, to re-establish simplicity. He chooses freedom, which is not the slave of obvious suspicion and scandal and judgment and determination.

This attitude is not an absence of realism. It is not the stupidity of Don Quixote. Love believes all things, not because it is ignorant or foolish, but because it wills to be ignorant, to go beyond suspicion. It bears all things, not because it is weak and inadequate, but because it is strong. Simplicity of heart is on the far side of knowledge. Love is associated with freedom because it is not the mediocre opposite of evil but the power which breaks out of the vicious circle. Thus it rejects the rules of Marx, Freud, and Nietzsche. It stands outside the suspicion which stigmatizes a man as tied to a class, or race, or interests, or taboos. It does so after the diagnosis and not before it. I see and know and am disillusioned—and I forget all that, for freedom consists in my relation to the other. Perhaps I can free the other in performing this act of freedom which makes me welcome him without suspicion.

We have now sketched the first specification of freedom. Paul shows us that there is a second. At issue is the glory of God. The two essential texts on freedom in 1 Corinthians both have this orientation. Thus we are first told in 4:12–20 that all things are lawful but we are then shown that this does not imply the possibility of using one's body in any way at all, e.g., lying with a prostitute, for: "Glorify God in your body, and in your spirit, which are God's" (v. 20). Again, 10:23–33 begins by saying that all things are lawful, then shows that this must be oriented to love, and finally says: "Whether therefore ye eat, or drink, or whatsoever ye do, do all to the glory of God" (v. 31). The very same relation between freedom and the glory of God is to be found in Romans, too, when Paul speaks of the "glorious liberty of the children of God" (8:21). As regards this verse, it is to be noted that the liberty itself is not glorious; it is only a reflection. Again, the reference is not to the glory of the children of God, for the only glory is that of God himself. But rightly the words do tie freedom and glory very closely together.

Now we should remember that the glory of God is no mere comparison or formula. Today we are vague in our understanding of the word "glory." It conjures up images of military or political triumph. In effect our ideas of glory do not help us to understand at all what is at issue. Fame? Honor? Praise? Glorious exploits? Splendor? Honors? None of these really applies to God. They are all in the sphere of human reality—a great man, a ruler clothed in the symbols of government and renown and exalted by public opinion above the ordinary level of a man. Voltaire is right when he says in his *Dictionnaire philosophique* (*s.v.* "Gloire"): "It is not that the supreme being can have glory but that men, having no suitable term, employ in relation to him the words which most gratify them." He is right to the extent that glory is this human dimension. Indeed, expositors are just as vague when it is a matter of God's glory. To glorify God, they say, is to render him homage. But what does this mean for modern man?

Littré offers a strange explanation: " 'For the greater glory of God' is a kind of pious phrase which is used to express the fact that the glory of something is related to God." Old Testament commentators argue that glory is assimilated to the splendor by which God surrounds himself, etc. This means precisely nothing. For it is impossible to see how such vague and uncertain ideas could be used in any way to affect and direct our choices and acts.

If, however, we pay a little more attention to the texts of the Bible, we shall soon see that the word "glory" has in fact a very strict and precise sense. This sense seems to be the same in the Old Testament, John, and Paul. The glory of God is not a quality, appearance, luster, or added supplement which in sum makes God more than God. God is glory in his total manifestation or revelation. When God reveals himself, he is such that man in his frailty can find only the word "glory." The important thing here, however, is obviously "when God reveals himself." In other words, God's glory is his revelation, both general and particular, to the eyes of men. It is the revelation of God as he is, or as he gives himself to be known.

Glory is the reality of the hidden God that we can grasp. We do not say that it is God himself nor an intrinsic quality of God, for of this we know nothing. But when Jesus is manifested as the one he is by his Father, he is transfigured, to employ the usual term. He has an appearance that we can effectively render only by "glory" (dazzling light, etc.).

We also find that biblically God never glorifies man nor can man glorify himself except in Jesus Christ. For in itself the appearance of man is never glorious. It becomes this only when man is viewed in him who is glorified and who is glory, i.e., the Almighty. We can be in the Almighty, however, only in Christ.

The reciprocity of glory is the glory of God by Christ and the glory of Christ by God. That is to say, God is not plainly revealed except in Christ. Christ glorifies his Father when he reveals him as the one as whom he gives himself to be known. Similarly God glorifies the Son when he reveals him as the one he truly is. Hence glory is closely related to revelation.

When, therefore, the texts speak of glorifying God and rendering him glory, they really mean bearing witness to God. It is not a matter of uttering words of praise or chanting canticles but of displaying God in his truth and reality as the one as whom he has given himself to be known. It is a matter of showing him to those around us. It is a matter of acknowledging what God has done for us, of repenting and turning back to the life that God wills. It is a matter of discerning God's work everywhere and publicly declaring it.

This is best done by a manner of being rather than by words. Glorifying God is testifying, especially by our lives, to the way in which he appears to man. It is also very definitely to carry and to live out the gospel. When Paul says that he does everything for the sake of the gospel, he glorifies God. Here again, however, we come up against an obstacle that might change completely the expression of freedom.

We have already quoted 1 Corinthians 9:19: "But though I be free from all men, yet have I made myself servant unto all, that I might gain the more." Now there is no need on the one side to go into the worth of freedom as such (we have seen this already). Nor is the dynamic conduct that we have described—the fluctuation of being rightists with rightists and leftists with leftists, etc.—to be considered on the other side as a simple method of winning converts. When Paul speaks of gaining men, we are not to take it in that sense but solely in the sense of glorifying God among men by passing on the gospel to them. This witness to the gospel is the real glorifying of God. Serving men cannot, then, be separated from it. We can neither regard it as having intrinsic value (it has value only as it makes God known as he has given himself to be known and only as it thus leads men to glorify him), nor can glorifying God be an inner reality with no expression in service.

If, then, freedom takes on significance in love it does so also in the glorifying of God. For love and the glory of God are inseparable. Calculated proselytizing is thus ruled out, for everything is located in freedom (naturally the freedom of the other too). Nor is glory rendered to God by even a little Machiavellianism, which does not take into account who God is. Man is not to be confiscated to God's profit. He is to be told of the covenant that God has made, of reconciliation. This work consists more in the presence of life than in words and declarations. Yet everything can and should be oriented to God's glory. "Whether therefore ye eat, or drink, or whatsoever ye do, do all to the glory of God" (1 Corinthians 10:31).

Here again we first see that no acts are indifferent. We then see that all our acts are to be to God's glory. That is, they are to be in the service of witness to God. It is not that some acts have the special privilege of glorifying God (worship, or singing), while others are base or useless. The

*All Things Are Lawful*

glory of God may well shine through most concretely for man in trivial everyday acts. Everything can be turned by faith to this glory.

The whole domain of freedom is thus covered. As we have seen, freedom concerns the whole realm of existence and not just the spiritual sphere. It is not for nothing, then, that the above text comes in a passage on freedom. Freedom is oriented to a concern to give glory to God. It is thus at each moment the choice that we can make of an attitude that glorifies God. We have to choose our acts in such a way that those who see them can find there a reflection of God and can therefore learn to love God. We see, then, that this freedom is far removed from one which is indeterminate, absurd, and permissive.

We are also to perceive a deeper sense in this significance that is given to freedom by glory. For after all the freedom thus received through Jesus Christ is God's own freedom towards his creation. It is God's own freedom to the degree that we are the children of God, i.e., to the degree that we are in fellowship with him, and hence to the degree that this freedom expresses the will of God. This being so, one can see how this freedom can be to God's glory.

In effect the true use of this freedom, the life in freedom which we have received and which is both independence and availability, manifests to men what is God's own action. Our freedom in itself redounds to God's freedom. It bears witness to others that God is free, and that he has put himself at our disposal. Thus the freedom, not merely of our acts but of our whole life, is a reflection of revelation.

This naturally carries with it considerable responsibility. For if our freedom is linked thus to God's glory, this glory is at stake in its acts. If, because our life has been made free, it is by this life that we render glory to God, we must realize that this glory is not rendered by an exceptional act. God is not glorified merely on the day that we preach a fine sermon or achieve true love or engage in politics but on all days with all their acts. We thus present a false image of God and give him the wrong kind of glory if we act as he does not act.

This is why in another passage in 1 Corinthians (6:12–20) Paul offers as an illustration the particular problem of sex relations with a harlot. All things are lawful. Can I then take a prostitute? This is not just a moral question. By grace I am a member of the body of Christ. This is my freedom. "Shall I then take the members of Christ, and make them the members of an harlot?" (v. 15). To the degree that we are united with Christ, we commit Christ himself to our acts, our decisions, and our sins. "Know ye not that your body is the temple of the Holy Ghost?" (v. 16). This is not a guarantee that I will always do the right or follow God's will or make a good use of freedom. On the contrary, since our freedom is true freedom, we can take God with us—he has willed it thus—on our own crooked paths. At issue are not just disdain for the prostitute or for the immorality of the act. At issue is what the prostitute represents biblically.

*The Object of Freedom and the Will of Man*

The relation between a man and a prostitute is the exact opposite of what God is for man, of the man-woman relation that God has established, and finally of the authenticity of love. This is what is at issue in this problem. This is why making use of a prostitute cannot be an act to God's glory. For the glory of God is again the final theme in the passage (v. 20). All our freedom is oriented to this.

But the fact that freedom can exist only to God's glory leads us on to another question. For those with eyes to see it God's glory is visible in creation, as Job and the Psalms (cf. Psalm 19) bear witness. God gives us a likeness of his glory in the grandeur and beauty of the earth. Hence our freedom cannot consist in effacing God's glory in creation by effacing creation itself, by tormenting and deforming and destroying it. If our freedom is to God's glory this means total respect for that which God has chosen to manifest his glory. We cannot do with creation as we like.

A curious theological perversion, which is so common as to be hardly contested, argues on the basis of Genesis 1:28 that man fulfils his vocation by laying violent hands on creation through technology. But this verse relates to man before the fall and at most it makes man God's vice-gerent. He cannot seize and use creation as he chooses.

Ignorance of facts accompanies the theological error. Only a superficial view of science and technology can speak in this way, namely, the view that science unfolds the secrets of creation and thereby helps us the better to worship God. This bears no relation to reality. The reality is the rape of the earth, the exploitation and depletion of its resources. Secrets are pierced not to the better worship of God but to the greater wealth of man.

Have we any right to disintegrate matter? Have we any right to find the origin of life in order to reproduce it? Can we pay the price of penetrating all the mysteries of God? These are not metaphysical questions. They have to do with the results of our autonomous conquest that God allows: death, the extermination of animal species, the pollution of air and water, the transformation of the simple things of creation into a universe of things, into a giant sophistication. The key to this is not at all obedience to a vocation but the expression of a mad lust for power, for unlimited consumption, for rapacious seizure.

These things are not accidents accompanying the adventure of technology. There would have been no adventure without the lust for power and possession. Even if it be said that the scientific mind is not like this at all, which I accept, this is irrelevant, for what counts is the mentality of the millions who profit by scientific discoveries, and without these consumers there would be no credit or prestige for scientific research. Indeed, there would be no scientific research. If it is further said that the discoveries themselves are to God's glory, is this true? Is there much concern for God's glory among scientists? Is there even any unconscious promotion of God's glory? How does contemplating a cyclotron speak to me of God's glory? As for the content of scientific work, if I am one of the vast majority who do not understand it, how does this bring glory to God? Does the incomprehensible ever promote God's glory? In the Bible, when man comes up against an incomprehensible fact, it is only when God explains it to him that glory appears.

I think there is no more dangerous illusion today than the justifying of science and technology by Christians. I am not interdicting or condemning scientific work. I am simply saying that it is open to question, that it does not express a divinely given vocation, that it does not set forth God's glory but effaces his creation. Man views himself as an owner, not a steward. He thinks everything is his.

This may be seen in the parable of the wicked husbandmen, which may apply in the first instance to Israel, but which also has a wider application to man and creation. If we reject this, then the parable can hardly be extended to the church and it is no concern of ours. It is purely local and temporary and teaches us nothing. But is not the heart of the parable man's attitude to God? Is not the real meaning this: God gives what he has made to man so that man may use it to God's glory? But man will not accept God's lordship. He seizes it even to the point of killing God's Son in order to do so. Do we not have here the heart of the problem, the Jews serving only as one illustration? If so the passage says something about the attitude of man to nature.

A second passage with something to say on the matter is Philippians 2:1ff. Jesus does not regard it as his prey to be equal to God. . . . Do we have to take this only in a spiritual sense? The Bible does not differentiate between the spiritual and the temporal. The passage relates to man's total attitude. The approach of Jesus is the exact opposite of that of Adam. Adam wanted to be equal to God. It was not enough to be his image, to be the steward in charge of all his goods, to talk to God face to face. He wanted to be an absolute master and he snatched creation out of God's hands. This is the attitude of all of us. The passage is not just teaching us to serve one another. It has a larger reference to our relation to God. We must not take from God what belongs to him. But we do this with our mad exploitation of the planet. Inasmuch as our freedom is to God's glory, it does not authorize us to despoil creation which is also God's glory. It does not let us use things as we like. It gives us no right to kill the Son in attainment of this mastery.

Since, then, God's glory may be seen in his creation, the scientific and technological enterprise is not validated by our freedom, for it is not to God's glory. It manifests man's glory and power and dominion. No more. Freedom presupposes respect in relation to that of which God makes us free. Technology means absolute disrespect for that to which it applies. Hence the glory of God as the meaning of freedom questions and, I believe, condemns our science and technology.

The two "functions" of freedom, love and the glory of God, lead us to the ethical question. All things are lawful. But in the presence of others our freedom consists in specific choices. A new decision has to be made continually. New invention is demanded. We have to consider what will be profitable for them, what will be useful, what will edify or build them up in Christ. In the presence of each of our acts, desires, inclinations, and words, what we need to know is what will be the sign of true freedom. If acts are this, they cannot be ridiculous or absurd even though they are full of whimsy, humor, or spontaneity. For what they represent is not the crushing weight of duty. If it were, they would not be freedom. Even whimsy, humor, spontaneity, indolence, and loss of time can be infinitely profitable, can be signs of true freedom, can edify the neighbor in Christ, far better than moral discourses. In any case, the main characteristic will be concern for one's neighbor.

Paul often gives lists of virtues. He can do this even within his teaching on freedom. But in so doing he is not giving us rigorous codes but examples of what such a use of freedom can be. For the virtues in which freedom is manifested relate to what is normal or current in the society at issue. These examples cannot be made into a law again. They are not absolutely binding. They serve to warn us. They are a remedy for our sloth and weakness.

The other aspect ethically is God's glory. We have to choose acts in which those who see them can find a reflection of God and learn thereby to love him. Freedom helps to achieve this. Without freedom it would not be possible. Again, it is obvious that freedom can never be absurd. All things are lawful, but before undertaking anything, in recognition of our unworthiness and need for pardon, and also of the fact that we shall be pardoned, we have to put the question: Is this to God's glory? Can I honestly believe that this act that I am about to do will bring glory to God? These are the specifications of the freedom that is effectively given to us.

# Part III

# The Assumption of Freedom

FREED IN CHRIST AND LIVING TO GOD'S GLORY, WE HAVE TO LIVE THIS out visibly. When we say this we are not expressing what most people think of first, or what is stated in the classic formula that the freedom which is won for us is a potentiality. We are not saying: You now have the power to be free; you may grasp this power and be free indeed; if you do not, however, nothing will happen; everything will be as it was; you have a possibility, a freedom which is as yet virtual and which you yourself have to make actual.

In my view this is not at all the meaning of the very definite passages that we have been studying. The liberty at issue is one that has been won and is already actual. Man is not able to make it effectual or not by his own act. This act does not move on from the sphere of the virtual to that of the actual. For this would mean that man's own decision is easily the most important thing in this matter and that God's work is merely preparatory.

On the other hand we are also to avoid taking it in a sense which seems to be more scriptural but is still debatable: You are free (this is accomplished and acquired) in him (in heaven) and so you are to live as free men, since you have the possibility of doing this. The difference between this view and the first one is as follows. In the first one freedom in Christ is virtual; here it is real. In the first one freedom itself is only a possibility; here it is its application which remains only a possibility.[1] My essential objection to this second interpretation has to do with the chronological break. First comes the work of God that frees us (internally and spiritually). Then comes the work of man which works out the inferences.

I realize that this seems to be in accord with many theological notions, e.g., about the relation between faith and works or justification and sanctification. But it seems to me that although these divisions are academically useful in explanation, they are not really exact. There are no such categorical distinctions in the Bible itself. One need only consider the well-known injunction of Paul: "Work out your own salvation with fear and trembling, for it is God which worketh in you both to do and to will" (Philippians 2:12f.), or his formula: "you are saints . . . be saints" (Ephesians 1:1; Romans 6:19). In other words, man's act is not separated from

---

1  Bonhoeffer in his *Ethics* rightly stresses the importance of action.

the work of God in us. And God's work, I would venture to say, exists only in the work that is done by man in fellowship with God. If there is foreknowledge and predestination, if there is prevenience and primary love, on God's part, there is no actual accomplishment apart from us or outside us.

We are not speaking of an open-ended virtuality. Salvation has been won and achieved. It is a gift of grace. Nevertheless we have also to work it out. This is not because Christ's work is in any way deficient. We cannot add to his "It is finished." Yet without our life being offered up and lived out in Christ, nothing has been accomplished. We are not speaking of anything added or complementary. It is simply that God's love cannot bear to be or to do without man. Man is elected from all eternity in Jesus Christ to work out his salvation, to be a saint, etc.[2]

In the same way it would be absurd to say that during the course of history man adds anything of any kind to the creation which God effected and which was complete. It would be foolish to represent creation as a virtuality that is put in man's hands and that he may exploit as he chooses. This again involves chronological disruption. In fact, however, God's whole thought was for this work of man. Creation was for man. Man does not add anything; God gathers up what he invents, however absurd or foolish it may be.

We cannot say, then, that freedom is first given in Christ and then it is applied. In reality, freedom does not exist at all if the Christian does not live it out. Conversely, the Christian life can be only that of the free man. Hence we have to assume this freedom, to take it to ourselves, to incorporate it into our decisions. We have to accept its responsibility and bear it. We have to do this knowing that only Christians can live it out and that if they fail there will be no freedom of any kind on earth. We have to assume it as the life which is accomplished for us. You are free and therefore be free; dare to be what basically and essentially you are.

God's work of liberation is not abstract. If the people of Israel does not live out its freedom, there is no liberation from Egypt. To be sure, liberation was achieved for man by the cross. Yet the freedom of man has still to be lived out and expressed. God will not act alone for man and on man. This would make man a thing. Man must also act with or by means of what God puts in his hand. By God's grace we have a conjunction, a tight interweaving, in which God refuses to distinguish between his part and ours. God does his work through man, and man's work can be done only through God.

All this is simply an expression in our own lives of the incarnation of Jesus Christ. It means, however, that we have the terrible power of destroying God's work, not because this is virtual, but because it takes place only when it is incarnate in men. This is the responsibility of the man

2 Cf. on this whole issue Vahanian's fine study *La condition de Dieu* (1970).

to whom the revelation of this work is granted. Now destroying God's work—be it noted—is not just rubbing out something that is written by crayon on a slate, so that the slate is clean again. For the work of God *is*. Jesus Christ is the Son of God. He died and rose again. This does not depend on us. It does not exist because our faith believes it. It is an object that has been set in the world. Hence destroying God's work is not returning to zero. It is not beginning again. It is falling into nothingness. For annulling God's work is nothingness. To adjust our metaphor, it is like a canvas that is freshly painted in fine strong colors and a sponge is rubbed over this to produce a terrible blur, an unrecognizable smudge, a filthy confusion of color in which there is neither meaning, relation, nor purity.

This is what destroying God's work means. If this work is not positive, it shows itself to be negative. Salvation destroyed is not just man left to himself. It is hell. The cancelled love of God means the absurdity, not the independence, of man. It means this, not just for the man who has made this decision, but for all men. Every Christian who fails to be a saint is responsible for all the daubings of the world. The same is to be said about freedom. If it were only virtual we could easily say: "Well, we have failed; we are still prisoners . . . that is all." Unfortunately this is not all. For freedom has already been lived out by Jesus Christ on earth. It has been planted. It is part of our history. If the world does not have it because the Christian does not know what it is to be free, the result is monstrous perversion and incoherence. There happens to all mankind what took place for the people of Israel after its liberation from Egypt. Liberated by God, it did not live out its liberty. It was continually protesting because it was short of water or food or because the manna was tasteless. Because it did not live out the freedom of God, it had to wander for forty years in the wilderness. Its freedom was broken in this senseless march, in this incoherence, in this proneness to fall into pits of every kind, in this fear of involvement, in the fate which tied it to the wilderness.

When freedom is not positively assumed it becomes a negative power. It does not merely cease to be. Now that Christ has brought freedom into the world, we either live it out, assuming it because this is God's own work, or we do not get off unscathed but transform it into a type of fate or fury which perverts everything, which detaches what is from what was ordained to be, and which brings about incoherence, ideology, and a break between the spiritual and the temporal. If the cross is made into an empty symbol, this means that it remains planted there for the world's damnation.

It is thus basic and decisive that we should take up the freedom which has been won for us. When we do, we must not yield to the foolish notion that we are doing something very remarkable, important, or meritorious. When we live out the freedom of Christ, we are not to think that this deserves a reward or that we are adding something to the work of God. To live out the work of God is its own reward. Paul tells us this most forcefully in a passage which has a bearing on freedom: "Though I preach the gospel,

I have nothing to glory of: for necessity is laid upon me; yea, woe is unto me, if I preach not the gospel. For if I do this thing willingly, I have a reward: but if against my will, a dispensation of the gospel is committed unto me. What is my reward then? Verily that, when I preach the gospel, I may make the gospel of Christ without charge, that I do not use my right as a preacher of the gospel. For though I be free ..." (1 Corinthians 9:16–19). The reward is contained already in the fact that Paul preaches the gospel freely. It is the preaching itself. It *is* the freedom which is given to Paul to be a witness. It *is* the freedom to be "all things to all men." It *is* the freedom not to use his prerogatives. The reward is to do joyfully and wholeheartedly this work of God which in the long run—happily for us—cannot fail to be done. Hence we are not to think that by living as free men we acquire merit before God or add something to his grace. To obey God's will carries its own reward in the fact that this man is a free man and knows that he is, although this does not offer any basis for boasting or superiority.

Freedom, then, lays a tremendous responsibility on us. Yet it does not cause us to profit by any reward. For there is nothing greater than this participation in the freedom of God himself.

# Chapter 1

# Recognition

Now that God's work has been done in Christ in behalf of man's freedom, the first step to be taken by man is that of recognition. We do not refer to the simple theoretical and abstract knowledge that might be learned from the catechism. At this level nothing has been done and nothing makes any sense. For freedom, like love, is a matter of life rather than definition. Definition alone, while possible, is futile. The act cannot be reduced to a mere knowledge, for it cannot be detached or dissociated from the one who knows. Nothing relating to freedom takes place on the plane of a separate operation, whether in respect of will, action, or knowledge. Freedom is an implication of the entire person or it is nothing. Recognition obviously has its intellectual aspects, as we shall see. It presupposes a conceptual and analytical movement. But the relation between the one who recognizes and that which he recognizes cannot be merely that of subject and object. There is no difference between the two, for finally he recognizes himself and he cannot project himself beyond himself. He cannot objectify himself. There are two reasons for this.

The first is that he cannot comprehend himself by introspection, by depth analysis, by external psychological investment. For it is himself that he has to comprehend—himself in his singularity which cannot be reduced to human similarities. What is at issue is freedom. Now the objectifying methods of psychological knowledge can deal only with identities, similarities, and determinations. It is from these, however, that man is freed. As we shall see, this is the very thing which he must accept in his recognizing—in recognizing and not in reification. It is in his uniqueness and distinctiveness that man is called upon to comprehend himself and this is a lived reality, although clearly surrounded on all sides by that which can only undermine and reduce and deny it. Only the vital movement of self-consideration can cause the "self" to be truly known in its remoteness and fragility.

The second reason is that we are dealing here with the global situation of the self and the setting in which it finds itself. Recognition cannot be fragmented. Successive bits of knowledge are possible but not successive recognition. It does not refer to this or that specific point. At issue is apprehension of the total condition of the one engaged in it. There is thus a double movement of recognition, the one from without inwards, which presupposes a knowledge of the being in its profoundest ordination, and the other from within outwards, which presupposes attack upon or involvement with this outer side. Naturally the distinction between within and without is purely expository and pedagogic. It does not presuppose a break, as though the skin denoted qualitative distinction between inside and outside. The key term in what we are saying is movement—movement with a twofold orientation. Hence, although the outside and the inside are differentiated, they can never be severed.

Having recalled these generalities, which are in no sense original, we must now ask about the content of recognition. To the degree that this is that of a Christian, the act has two orientations. It is recognition of the work of Christ for him and in him, of his liberation, the fact of the appropriation of this freedom. This might seem to be enough. For basically, after this knowledge is gained, what more is there to hope for or expect? Transition from the work done to the work done *for me* always seems to be enough for Christians. But I believe that it is precisely this conviction which produces the feebleness of manifestations of the incarnation of faith and the lack of ethical imagination. This is the essential and decisive thing in the relation with God without which there is nothing, but if it becomes exclusive and not just privileged it can finally sterilize the Christian life. This brings us to the very heart of one of the most serious problems for Christians. Naturally the work of the Holy Spirit in leading us into all truth, in enabling us to participate in Christ's work and in making salvation personal, is decisive. But after that? Here we come up against three general attitudes.

The first is that of traditional ethics. Strictly, a model for this might be found in the famous "Wherefore" of Paul in Romans 12:1. Here we are shown the implications of the work of Christ for our lives as if there were a continuous line between God's eternal and spiritual act on the one side and our own acts on the other, the incarnation and our own incarnations. This necessarily leads on to the elaboration of a closed ethics, a domain of order and necessity. If, however, we view ethics as an ethics of freedom, it cannot be of this kind. There cannot be unbroken continuity between Christ's work and ours.

The second attitude, which preserves freedom, manifests itself in exclusive confidence in the Holy Spirit as the guide of our lives. In extreme form this entails an individualism which enables us to detach ourselves both from the precision of God's revelation in holy scripture (the only possible link with God's Word) and from concrete daily reality. Action under the inspiration of the Holy Spirit can produce individual holiness which is very detached and which often bears no reference to the practical situation of man.

Finally, the third attitude consists in resolute orientation to the world and involvement in it on the view that the work done in Jesus Christ concerns both our own lives and the life of the world, that a certain unity is established between these by this work, and that only along these lines can we live the Christian life in modern society, in the involvements of politics, and in the ethical options of our groups. In other words, unity is again the temptation. This time, however, it is not a biblically based unity producing a strict, theologically inferred ethics, but a secular unity which presupposes the renewal of the world by God's love, so that the incarnation of faith can be found in its works.

It is hard to estimate the evil that has been done in Christian thought and ethical research by the obsession with unity. This obsession led to Gnosticism, and we find it again in Teilhard de Chardin. We cannot accept the fact that we are divided, as is natural enough. We cannot accept the fact that even as Christians who are reconciled to God and to others in Jesus Christ we are still divided, that we are still in the situation of the man who cries: "Who shall deliver me from the body of this death"? (Romans 7:24), and that we can never escape this.

In the field of ethics this means that our ethics must be an ethics for the man who is at one and the same time both a Christian and a non-Christian, both free and enslaved, both reconciled and in revolt, both saved and judged. This supports those who are always repeating *simul peccator et justus*. Yet this does not mean the superseding or annulment of the one term by the other. It means their co-existence and hence the division of man. The saying that "where sin abounded, grace did much more abound" (Romans 5:20) does not mean that grace suppresses sin. If this were so, it would hardly be worth noting. The situation is not one of grace alone. It is a state of laceration in which sin does in fact abound. Grace abounds even more, but it does not set sin aside. We can grasp the superabounding of grace only in promise. It is real, but it does not actually bring us into the kingdom of God now. On the contrary, it enables us to see properly to what degree sin abounds and to what degree we have to live our lives in this situation which is both that of the world and our own. Hence the whole of the Christian life presupposes this break, this encounter, this twofold movement from grace received to life lived and from life known to the promise believed. These reverse movements are both indispensable to the existence of the Christian life and it is at the point where they intersect and meet that the incarnation takes place.

The point of all this is that recognition has to relate to the concrete situation of what I am in the world in which I live. This aspect of recognition is no less important than the other. It is the very condition of the possibility of freedom. Again, the problem is not that of drawing the logical consequences of liberation in Christ which will be our freedom. Just because freedom is at issue, this is impossible. The act of our freedom is purely human at the level of this recognition of my human condition.

As regards the first act of recognition there is not much to say. We are faced with an act of faith which in one movement seizes, actualizes, comprehends, lives out, personalizes, and universalizes the work of God in Jesus Christ. Recognizing my freedom, as we have tried to define it, is not different from recognizing my salvation. We find the same association of knowledge and self-forsaking, of confidence and dialogue, of rigor and mystery, of commitment to what has never entered the heart of man and of simple clarity about my life. Recognition that I have effectively become a free man, that everything is open before me, that all things are lawful, that I am given a surprising orientation, obeying attractions and determinations which are quite different from those that man can know naturally—recognition of all this sets me in a new world.

My task is on the one side to live out this unexpected and unsettling grace which has broken former bonds and set me in a sphere in which in spite of all the evidence I have to believe that all ways are open so long as it is I myself who trace them. On the other side my task is to know and understand and scrutinize all that scripture has to say about this freedom which is now mine. I have to believe on the one side that the work of Christ has been done for me, for me alone and for me primarily, in spite of all the evidence to the contrary, while on the other side I have to put the question of the certainty of faith in order to prove its authenticity. I have to believe both that the work of Christ is universal, that the world is subject to the Lord of its freedom, and I have to believe that this is meaningless if faith, the fragile faith of man, does not carry, incorporate, and affirm it.

Jesus, infant, saviour and already lord of the world, adored by angels and kings, is still nourished and swaddled and carried by the hands of men without whom he could not have survived. This is why I prefer to speak of recognition rather than faith to the degree that the former embraces the latter and presupposes my total participation in all dimensions and with all my activities, participations, choices, singularity, and similarity to others.

The precise question is that of knowing whether what we have described as freedom in Christ is fully received into our lives, whether it is a mere affair of doctrine, or whether we are to go forward in this newness of life. This is what recognition consists of as an explosion of my being in the fulness opened up for me by Christ.

The second act or aspect of recognition is the one that calls for elucidation. In brief I may say that the first step of freedom, the first testimony to the concrete assumption of the freedom that God effects, rests in the recognition of alienation and unfreedom. We have here, then, the opposite of the preceding act. As we had to recognize our effective liberation in Christ, so we have to recognize our effective alienation.

Now we must be very clear on this point: We do not have here a necessary first step. The movement is not at all that I know that I am alienated—a negative discovery in some sort but filled out as I desire alienation—and then I come to know that I am freed in Christ—a positive discovery and antithesis. Recognizing that I am alienated can only come later as a result or implication. Any preliminary recognition of this kind is false, illusory, and partial.

Only as I know my true freedom can I discover to what degree I am really alienated. Only as I have the measure which is the freedom of Christ himself can I discover the depth of human bondage. Moreover, this discovery is not just negative. This recognition is not just a discovery of the fact of my alienation which convinces me of my unfreedom. It is the first act of my new freedom acquired in Christ.

If I do not proceed to this recognition, all my efforts to live out my freedom and all my attempts to incarnate it are empty and devoid of truth. But we must make it clear once again that this recognition is not a philosophical and theoretical act. It does not merely consist in reasoning or in a general consideration of man as such. It is a personal act which considers not just my deeper being (the metaphysical issue of determinism) but also all that besets and seizes and determines and constrains me from outside.

I do not know my bondage by plumbing the depths of my heart nor by reasoning about existence. Recognition depends on a concrete grasping of my particular situation. I am part of a world which is increasingly precise, rigorous, and constraining. Apprehended on all sides by administrations that condition each of my acts, controlled by the police and by patrons, involved in a collective enterprise which I cannot escape even though it does not in any way concern me—I do not depend any more on myself, on my own choices and decisions, but on the technical laws and unforeseeable decisions of the powers that surround me. I am overwhelmed by crushing duties which represent all the enterprises of my life but do not correspond to my own taste or will or personal life. Finally, in the secret recesses of my inner life, I am assailed by information and conditioned by propaganda which I can see no way to escape.

I do not have to ask whether the actual alienation which I find in my life has always been the condition of man or whether it is better or worse than in the eighteenth or nineteenth centuries. Asking such questions would be intellectual research which could give knowledge but would not be recognition and hence could have no bearing on my freedom. What I have to grasp and to live out as well is my own alienation. This has two disquieting aspects.

The first is the inner aspect. I am not just under external constraint. My freedom is not merely threatened by the police or by torture. The real threat is the work which is slowly done within. It is the progressive modeling of my inner self which begins in the kindergarten, continues at school by means of the special materials prepared for students, and is finally pursued in propaganda, information, and public relations.

The other aspect is that of the freedom which society offers me. The more minutely society constrains man, the more he has a horror of being determined. But instead of recognizing this by a strict look at the situation, he prefers not to see or know. He rejects determination. He is resolved to see himself as free in spite of everything. We thus have the freedom of ideology, escape, or fantasy.

Now society itself offers the means whereby to imagine this freedom. All kinds of compensations are at hand. On the one side we have leisure, vacations, sports, and television. On the other side we have the mystique of politics and economics—grandiose objectives such as national greatness or independence, individual happiness, anti-colonialism, or the fight against imperialism. It may be that a reasonable attempt is made to show that I am a free man in virtue of democracy or the raising of my standard of living or possibilities of travel or the universality of my culture and information.

These are some of the ways in which society tries to spare me the suffering of discovering my alienation. Society does not want its members to suffer. It offers them remedies. The individual for his part does not want to know the real situation. He is ready for anything rather than this. Hence he joyfully accepts these possibilities and demonstrations. In so doing, substituting illusion for reality and a fake for real life, he brings about his ultimate alienation.

Obviously the rejected recognition of the actual and effective condition not merely of eternal and intrinsic man but of the actuality of my being is both destructive and cruel. It destroys all the evasions and compensations that are offered us by the theoreticians of society, by the psychologists and political sociologists, by the politicians and philosophers, by the artists and novelists, by the technicians of the cinema and television, by the mystics, whether of Communism or Christianity. All the lies which combine to prevent the act of recognition have to be dispelled in order that we may understand our effective situation. We have to do the same work as that of Marx, but now in relation to ideology, democracy, and idealistic Christianity and socialism.

In fact the confusion is far greater, and criticism, being harder, has to be much deeper. Since it destroys our consolations, recognition is a bitter business. It is cruel to see one's alienation just as it is cruel to see one's sin. The two things are not the same, but they both enable us to grasp ourselves in the reality of the self which escapes us if we do not pin it down by beginning with the condition of our existence.

The difference between alienation and sin shows that in recognition a decision is involved, a new, different, and autonomous act. Recognizing my determinations is not conditioned by recognizing the liberty that is given me in Christ. It is not the natural result of this, even though only freedom in Christ enables me to have a full and decisive knowledge of alienation. It starts elsewhere and is possible for a non-Christian. When a Christian attempts it, this sets him among other men. He is like them in his alienation and in bearing the cost of the fight for liberation. Any man can take this course, and the Christian is not exempt therefrom because he has carried through the first act of recognition. If he tries to avoid it he falls prey to all the alienating illusions and his freedom in Christ dissipates.

Now recognizing my real bondage in society does not in itself bring freedom. Recognizing alienation does not magically rid me of alienation and make me a free man. It is no automatic remedy or panacea. It may well be an excuse. The man who attempts recognition, and who thinks that he has escaped conditioning and is a free man thereby, may be simply avoiding any living out of freedom. For by simply making a declaration he evades the great venture of freedom itself.

Hence recognition may well be the excuse offered by a bad conscience. If so, lucidity does not create liberty. On the contrary, it becomes a new alienation which thinks it has escaped the common lot, which leaves the feeling that one is cleverer than others for having seen the pits into which they have fallen, and which thus offers the satisfaction of having mastered the situation. But this is all an evasion and therefore an illusion. The man who achieves recognition in this way is alienated in his paralyzing lucidity and action is ruled out, since he always sees it to be both futile and alienating. This man can never be himself. He can never get beyond his understanding of the determinations. His freedom becomes individualism and idealism. It is thus as false as the pretended freedom of the activist, of the political, idealistic, or religious partisan.

If our recognition is authentic, it does not produce the complacency which interdicts us from going further. As we have said, it is (necessarily) destructive and bitter. It does not cease to be this by being repeated or renewed or deepened. It sets us in an intolerable situation which we have to get away from. One might get out of it by flight, refusal, consolation, or obfuscation. But one might also get out of it by pressing ahead, by accepting the incarnation which means action. Here, however, we are confronted by a dilemma.

If our recognition is serious, it shows us the immensity of the task, the complexity of the determinations, the quasi-impossibility of changing the course of this kind of society, the vanity of our means. This kind of recognition discourages endeavor. Actual lucidity makes nonsense of involvement. When we look at activists, we see that some of them have no idea of the reality of the world and of their own conditioning, as in the case of most politicians and economists, while others expressly renounce lucidity in favor of action on the basis of a mechanically applied interpretation, as in the case of Communists and Nazis, and others again trust in a past lucidity, in the act of recognition they performed perhaps twenty-five years ago, but on which they still rely, although changed conditions make it too late to live and act in the new society on this basis—intellectual activists like Mounier, Sartre, and Rougemont are examples of this.

Our dilemma, then, is as follows. If recognition does not lead to action, it is not freedom. But in actual society, lucidity seems to rule out action. Hence recognition does not in itself create freedom.

Even though this be so, however, recognition is the condition and the first step of freedom. The decisive thing, it seems to me, is that we understand that liberation in Christ does not have magical effects. The man who is totally free in Christ is nothing and does nothing if he does not follow the path of freedom which goes by way of the act of recognition and not by any other way. On the other hand, the man who recognizes his lack of freedom, his alienation, the determinations, can never find the fulness of freedom if he has not been freed by Christ and received the gift of freedom by faith in the Saviour.

The act of recognition is an act of freedom by which I get outside myself and achieve objectivity in seeing the object which alienates me. When I am able to hold at arm's length these powers which condition and crush me, when I can view them with an objective eye that freezes and externalizes and measures them, when I can see that what has become most intimate to me by the processes of acculturation or psychological intervention is an object without life or color, I have the same freedom as in relation to the avalanche which may destroy me but whose nature and threat I know. This projection outside myself (in contrast to the Hegelian or Marxist process) is what creates freedom, since that which alienates me and is outside me wants to invade me and finally become more myself than I am myself.

The act of recognition along these lines has several consequences. As recognition of my alienation, it dismisses all ideologies or philosophies which assume that man *is* free by nature or attribute. This type of freedom always falls into confusion with the sphere of the empty and imprecise and the ideal of the indifferent. We see this in economic and political liberalism. The state sets aside empty zones that the individual is to fill. Freedom, however, is not exercised in the void. When there is nothing there, there can be no freedom, for there is no activity. Such ideologies and philosophies do not let man see his real condition. Hence they are a powerful agent of unfreedom. For a pretense of freedom when everything determines us is the childish position of defeat, of refuge in an imaginary paradise. To shatter these philosophies by recognizing determination is to see that freedom is exercised in given realities and a hostile environment. If there is no resistance, freedom is an illusion. Freedom is exercised in relation to a determination. The yachtsman has to take account of wind and tide. His freedom is freedom to use determinations. With them he can do almost anything. Without them he can do nothing. Nothing is worse than a calm. The sailor is useless in this. He is not free.

Now we have said already that freedom is not a simple choice between indifferent and equal factors or lifeless things according to our own disposition. Such a situation never arises. The relation between ourselves, the things that constitute the framework of our lives, the institutions and the men around us, and the backgrounds to which we belong, is such that we can view ourselves only as one part of a web or system. It is foolish to look upon ourselves as free agents in an empty universe.

Now evidently the freedom which in these conditions results from the act of recognition is subjective and relative. Nevertheless, it affects the totality of man. It is the affirmation and act of the man who on the basis of recognition adopts a decision and position in concrete situations. This man has seen a truth of his life even though it is not necessarily "the truth," objective and total. His freedom can be expressed only in this affirmation. It is a choice that he must make in terms of this affirmation and not of the determinations which he has perceived and measured. It is a decision.

To be sure, this decision cannot claim immunity from necessities and influences. Man is not freed from these by the act of recognition. All the same, by this act he is called upon to venture a decision which will be his own. It will be this all the more, the more precise and profound the recognition. For obviously recognition is not just an initial or initiatory act which is done once and can then be set aside as we go on from the point of departure. Recognizing our alienations is something that we have continually to begin again, to repeat, and to deepen. Hence freedom is always engagement. To pretend to be disengaged is childish. We do not engage ourselves. The current slogan that the intellectual ought to be involved is ridiculous. It rests on the myth of a free and disengaged man. We are all involved whether we like it or not. But the engagement of freedom is the act in which man knows that he is menaced on every hand, that he is questioned and invaded and despoiled of self. It is the act in which he sees that the threat to himself is so total that a total effort must be made to meet it. The freedom we have here is not absolute. It is determined by the opposition, the enemy, the struggle in which it must engage.

One aspect of this struggle, one of the acts of this freedom, concerns the social side of life. We are not reviving here the old liberal conflict between the individual and society nor adopting Rousseau's dream of primitive freedom. All the same, we have to see that we all live with a ready-made stock of ideas which, as precisely formulated, go back at least to Taine, and which have become our common legacy. For Taine, history shows that man, who is animal and savage, can acquire reason and justice only by the organization of society, institutions, and finally the state, i.e., by losing his liberty. It is by alienation that man achieves civilization and becomes himself, becoming at the same time useful to society. This presentation, which takes the actual situation into account fairly well, which seems to rest on the evidence, is also the basis of all egalitarianism, and, for example, Communism.

Now we have to make a decision at this point. What is supposed to make man real man is in effect the sum of the forces of alienation. We must be careful here. I am not saying that society is alienation. What I am saying is that the modern state is the focus of the cluster of alienations, and that social utility is the motive of all alienations. No conciliation is possible between the liberated man who knows his alienations and the social utility manipulated by the state. We shall have to return to this in the last part of the present study.

In fact the technological society is seeking to develop man's total adherence. In the western world, then, freedom risks being acquiescence in remaining aloof, resisting progress, not promoting happiness, and incurring social disapproval and failure. The free man is useless and is judged negatively, for his recognition of the determinations brings out the conventional, arbitrary, and artificial character of the mechanisms which produce alienation, powerful and constricting though they be.

It will be seen, then, that the act of recognition is no childish game which consists in saluting impossible freedom from afar. It is the act by which one may initiate the incarnation of the freedom won in Christ and received in faith. But it is also an act which scrutinizes the concrete world in which we live and calls it in question, just as the same world questions us and destroys us even while permitting us to live.

I realize that this world with its society, state, institutions, economy, culture, ideology, and religion which alienate us does permit us to live and make us what we are. Hence we can never make a simple distinction between the individual and society. Nor can we say: The individual in and by society. This would amount to saying: Society in the individual, excluding him while also including him. It is here that the freedom gained in Christ, which permits me to live out this situation, fuses with the recognition which permits me to know this situation. It is here also that we find the supreme vocation of man, which is to bring freedom into this twofold conditioning.

# Chapter 2

# Avoidance of Bondage

Freedom in Christ is not an inalienable gift, a non-defaceable form, an acquisition, a possession. It is not a quality which becomes a natural attribute. It is not incorporated into our being, changing this in such a way that it cannot be changed again. This intervention may be lost. We can become slaves again. We can destroy freedom by not living it out. Thus in Paul's day a liberated prisoner could become the slave of the patron who paid his ransom. The manumitted slave could become a slave again if he proved patently ungrateful to his former owner or acted in an ignominious way unworthy of a free man. In such a case he did not again become the slave of his former owner. He achieved a new status—a status of infamy which was worse than that of his previous slavery.

This is the danger which faces us. Paul gives a double warning: "All things are lawful for me, but I will not be brought under the power of any" (1 Corinthians 6:12), and: "Ye are bought with a price; be not ye the servants of men" (7:23). It is just because we have become free that these sayings make sense. I am now responsible for not falling into possible bondage.[1]

According to the two sayings of Paul bondage may come from external aggression, from forces which seek to enslave me, which come towards me and into me to take control of me, or it may come from my attitude to myself, which decides to become or lets me become the slave of men by my own abandonment of freedom. It is just because freedom exists that I can abandon it and make myself a slave, and it is just because it exists that the world tries to take it from me.

The temptation is to think as follows. (1) I know the "normal situation"; why then cling to freedom? I realize that I am caught in a web of necessities; is it not an illusion to think that I am free? I should abandon the dream and accept my bondage. Or (2) I am very busy. I have more important things to do than to save or safeguard my freedom. Or (3)

---

1  It is incredibly easy to lose freedom. F. Bovon in his notable article "Vivre dans la liberté" (*Centre prot. d'études de Genève*, 1971) shows how Jewish people changed the earlier tradition (proclamation of freedom, liberation by God) into a theology of free choice and free will: "Freedom becomes the human fruit of obedience and not the divine source of submission." Much of medieval theology offers a similar example of this way of losing freedom.

humility suggests that my person is not of such value that I should pay too much attention to it. Or (4) the world cries out for political justice; why should I waste all this time on freedom?

Now undoubtedly in Paul's day similar arguments were used wittingly or unwittingly by Christians. This was why Paul had to insist on the point. But Paul shifts the emphasis. It is not myself that is important; it is my freedom. If I must not lose this freedom, this is not because of me or for my own profit or for the sake of the great things I might make of it. I have no freedom of judgment or appreciation in relation to my freedom, for I myself have not acquired or won or elaborated it. It does not belong to me nor is it at my disposal. I cannot decide to lose it. Its end is not myself but the glory of God and love.

This leaves me with no choice regarding freedom. If it has supreme importance and I have no right to abandon it or to despise it, this is not because of me but because of Christ: "Ye are bought with a price; be not ye the servants of men." This freedom is given to us because the freedom of Jesus led him to death in order that each of us might be free. The price is God's self-despoliation. It is the rending of Father and Son. It is the Father's suffering as he gives up the Son to the cross. It is the suffering of the Son as he comes to know the totality of human suffering. This is an incalculable and inestimable price. It is equal to God himself. If we have caught even a glimpse of the price, we can no longer accept any loss of this freedom. If we have experienced even a little of the love with which we must have been loved for this price to be paid, if we have lived out even to a small degree the fulness of the grace which this gift represents, the thought of any such loss is impossible. We can no longer take our freedom lightly as though it were one possibility among many others. We can no longer act daintily, saying that we might have preferred this or that, advancing our independence and deciding, the moment that this freedom is given, that in our human dignity we would have liked to win it rather than being subjected to this kind of paternalism. Such ideas are a mere excuse for not risking the great venture of freedom. They are the reaction of the man who is self-confident but who in fact cannot bear to live as a free man since this involves risk, responsibility, conflict, and finally defeat, for, no matter how we live out this freedom, fatality will ultimately overtake us even if only on our death-bed.

If, however, we have understood what is the price of love that has been paid, or what this freedom means, or what is its content and meaning, we can no longer refuse it nor dodge and try not to live as free men. We can no longer acquiesce in new bondage. This would be radically to despise God's work. Indeed, to the degree that as Christians we try to live in faith, to be good, to serve, and to promote justice, we are still throwing contempt on the sacrifice of Christ, no matter how good our intentions may be, if freedom is not there first. In the sections which follow we shall give some illustrations of the varied and continuous temptation to lose our freedom.

## §1. Morality and Immorality

We have said already—and need not develop the point—that morality is not Christian. We have said already that it is not the commandment. We may simply recall at this juncture that morality is a form of new servitude after liberation. It is a constant temptation.

Morality has many attractions. The fact cannot be hidden that freedom is an exhausting business. Constantly to ask whether a decision or undertaking is to God's glory, whether it will edify the church or one's neighbors, is very tiring. It demands great force and intelligence, and delays action. Surely we need to be economical with our strength and time and hence to find a simpler way. Those who are not intellectuals, and who wrongly think that such questions are purely intellectual, may well argue that they are incapable of answering them. Activists will say that they have better things to do than to engage in paralyzing discussions; their freedom will naturally come to expression in and by action itself. Men of morality will claim that duty has a clear and precise content and so there is no point in incessant questioning. Intellectuals will deny that these questions are important and say that happily freedom has another basis and content; they will thus engage either in political discourse or metaphysics. All agree that the question which is put by God in terms of freedom is badly put. All are in effect trying to find a set and simple explanatory guide for life, thought, and action. The most zealous proponents of freedom are the very ones who formulate the most rules, precepts, imperatives, and limits.

Morality is incompatible with freedom. It is new bondage to the law. When Paul says: "If ye be dead with Christ from the rudiments of the world, why, as though living in the world, are ye subject to ordinances, (Touch not, taste not, handle not)" (Colossians 2:20), he indubitably has in view the Jewish law which there was a tendency to reaffirm as a necessary condition of salvation. But it seems to me that he also has the whole of morality in view as well, for he adds: "After the commandments and doctrines of men. Which things have indeed a shew of wisdom in that they indicate a voluntary cult, humility, and disdain for the body." This might equally well apply to Stoicism. In any case, when Paul speaks of the law as we find it in the Old Testament, he never says that it is a doctrine of men. Even when he attacks the law, it is still the revealed law of God. What we have now is something very different. It is the rabbinic morality constructed out of the law. This resembles every morality set up by men. Hence Paul is probably referring to all morality when he says that it is enslaving and that it is contrary to freedom.

The remarkable thing is that Paul recognizes the objective value of this kind of ethics. Humility and mastery of the body are things on which Christians and non-Christians may well agree, at least in some ages if not our own. But it is precisely this morality whose content might seem to be good to us that Paul rejects, not because of its content, but because of the loss of freedom that it entails. The very same text shows us how much we are in fact attracted to morality: "If ye be dead with Christ from the rudiments of the world. . . ." How difficult and intolerable this is—being dead with Christ. Having no further part in the fasts, pleasures, powers, libertinage, independence, and exaltation of the world, being dead to all that—how can we put up with it? If the death were a physiological one there would be no problem, for there would be no more participation. If the death were a spiritual one, there would be no problem, only confusion. But being dead with Christ from the essences, rudiments, and foundations of the world still leaves us alive in the world, participating, co-existing, the same even while we are different. The impossible thing is living out this death. It is so impossible that soon many Christians saw only one solution—the monastery. Living out this death is the very thing that man tries to avoid by creating a morality in order that he may live, whether it be according to fellowship with Christ, inspiration, principles, and so forth, but in any case not as one who has gone through death.

Morality is the means whereby the Christian dodges death in Christ and fashions a living way of his own. As such it is the worst of all illusions. For under the pretext of letting us live as good Christians it is negative towards freedom, i.e, life itself. In spite of Kant it contradicts freedom because, no matter what may be its basis, intention, or structure, it relates always to what has been gained. It rests always on a natural attribute, a scientific affirmation, or a collection of judgments *a priori.* It is incompatible with novelty, freshness, or invention. It is never more than a mechanism of application, a principle, an imperative, a system of values. It is never discovered. There is nothing new, spontaneous, or vital about it, in spite of Bergson. It is there prior to our existence, in spite of Sartre and S. de Beauvoir. It is a given factor which we cannot challenge, since even if we contest it we are still determined by it. All morality, Christian or not, is destructive of freedom.

We have to take seriously the morals of our century. In so doing, of course, we alienate freedom. To take current morals seriously may well be the price we have to pay if the society in which we find ourselves is to continue. All the same, we have to see clearly at this point, for the alienation entailed may well be the most serious act to which we can assent, and there is no place for frivolity here. If it is not absolutely necessary to obey these morals for the sake of love, or witness, or the support of the weak, then we should stand aloof and not only dispute them but actually act outside the body of this established morality.

It must be realized, of course, that the established morality is not just that of the dominant class or of tradition. It may be the anti-moral morality of the emerging class or of a specific social group to which we belong. Thus the morality of the leftist or the intellectual is also an established morality.

At this point we are led directly to an identical path, although it stands under a different sign, along which we can easily crush freedom. We refer to the pretext of freedom: "Use not liberty for an occasion to the flesh" (Galatians 5:13). This is the most gross and obvious and yet also the inevitable pitfall—the one against which the church very early set up the strong fences of Christian morality, the ecclesiastical institution, and canon law.

If all things are lawful, the argument runs, then I can give free rein to my instincts, passions, and fantasies. If every act is singular and unique, being done by a person who cannot be judged, since he has been assigned an incomparable destiny in Christ, then I can do anything at all. Again, if I am convinced that the Holy Spirit dwells in me and inspires me, and that my acts are the fruits of the transformation of the root of my being, then I may decide that theft and adultery, while they may be wrong and sinful for others and bring down eternal judgment on them, are for me only the manifestation of the freedom that I have won.

It is all too easy to think that I have an exceptional destiny, that the banal rules of middle-class morality are not made for me, that, on the contrary, I can transgress them in order to express my freedom. In this way freedom becomes a pretext and a lie. It is an opening and permission for the passions of the flesh. And in this area there has been no change. What Paul and John describe as being the passions of the flesh is still the same. Man may differ according to different cultures. Ethnologists can show us men in whom there is no tendency to murder, or in whom there are no complexes, or problems of adultery. It has never been said that every man or group follows all the passions of the flesh listed by Paul. But modern ethnologists hardly accept the myth of the noble savage. In tribes with no sexual taboos alcohol has caused havoc. In tribes where murder is unknown, avarice is common. Paul tells us that the flesh is "adultery, fornication, uncleanness, lasciviousness, idolatry, witchcraft, hatred, variance, emulations, wrath, strife, seditions, heresies, envyings, murders," etc. (Galatians 5:19f.). We do not know at what point giving oneself up to these things is testimony to a free spirit and to a life which has been freed from mediocre regulations that psychoanalysis has exploded and that have no serious reference. In effect, Paul's judgment is perfectly sound. This supposed freedom, which includes the supposed coming of age of modern man who wants to be responsible for his own acts, is in the last analysis simply a pretext for following the easiest path.

We have also a tendency to regard personal continuity as a limit of our freedom. This becomes a pretext to make us independent. In the name of freedom we join the movement started by Sartre's existentialism to suppress the element of engagement in relations in favor of constantly new decisions. Marital fidelity is thus viewed as a restriction of freedom; there have to be new commitments each moment. Anything in the way of faithfulness, promise, or plighted word is intolerable. It is an odd situation when people accept massive sociological determinations but are very sensitive to humble moral limitations. Perhaps the explanation is that impotence to break free from real conditioning finds compensation in victories over the virtues, which can be destroyed easily.

But this freedom means an incoherence of personality. True freedom is never linked with liquidation of what can build up personality and assure it continuity. It implies, presupposes, and demands durability of the person. Fidelity in love (even in marital love in spite of pseudo-scientific attacks on it) belongs to love constitutively, for it demands that the other be taken seriously. It also belongs constitutively to personality, preventing its dissipation. One might prefer a fluid, weak, and inconsistent personality. One might prefer irresponsible roaming to committed and ongoing coexistence. But this does not mean freedom. A fluid personality is subject to every influence and suggestion and is mediocre, being impoverished by the experience of discontinuity, the changing of marriage partners, and the seeking of refuge in drugs and so forth.

This is all explicable and understandable in non-Christians, but when Christians fall for such fables and live in such incoherence it becomes falsehood, hypocrisy, and treason against the Lord. God's constancy in Christ toward us, which is no cultural invention, is for us a sign of the faithfulness and validity of the future promise which we ought to live out as Christians. The constancy of the Lord is precisely a sign of freedom. It is so for us. Freedom is incarnated in personal continuity and fidelity to others. It is not a yielding to momentary circumstances and impulses. If we think it is, we make of Christian freedom a pretext for living as the rest do, giving way to all that is mediocre and banal in us.

For this path slopes easily and is one of pleasant mediocrity. It never gets above the level of what is agreeable. Among our petty immoralists there is none that evokes respect because his abominations are on so grand a scale. They simply talk and dream of incredible exploits—this is why Sade, the braggart, is their hero. But in fact their immorality is supremely middle-class. Paul is right; the line of least resistance is followed, and this has nothing to do with freedom. Freedom is advanced as a pretext for rejecting the current rules of social morality.

Now if the freedom alleged is only a natural freedom, it is simply a carnival mask worn on the face, and we can hardly be angry with those who parade in this appearance of freedom. If, however, the reference is to Christian freedom the matter is far more serious. In other words, to make freedom a pretext is stupid in the non-Christian. For the Christian, however, it is an attack on Christ. The Christian alone, then, can be regarded as responsible. For the freedom that he makes into a pretext is true freedom.

The Christian uses this authentically given freedom to do what is contrary to the will of Christ. In so doing he makes himself a new slave. To the degree that grace has not been withdrawn from him he still preserves this freedom. Nevertheless, he derides and ridicules it. He shows to what extent it is empty, since it serves only to satiate the passions. He uses it apart from its true meaning and merely in his own interests. He is undoubtedly free—free to dope himself or to kill himself. The atrocious thing, however, is that this freedom, which has been bought at the cost of the life of Christ, can serve only that which brought Christ to the cross—there is no getting off cheaply here.

Everywhere in this passage in Galatians Paul draws attention to a specific aspect of this freedom which is a pretext. He says that we should not use liberty as an occasion for the flesh "but" that by love we should serve one another. The "but" shows precisely what Paul means when he talks of yielding to the passions of the flesh. He is not talking generally as we did above when referring to his list in Galatians. The "but" followed by a reference to becoming servants shows that the carnal passion in view here is domination, the lust for power, the crushing of the neighbor, acting as a superior. It is the attitude which consists in commanding, humiliating, dominating, and breaking the neighbor.

Now it is evident, not merely that the lust for power is a dominant passion of the flesh, as the Bible everywhere shows,[2] but also that the freedom which serves as a pretext is the freedom of the self, i.e., the possibility of self-affirmation without considering others or taking them into account. It is the freedom to deploy my powers and energies with all their positive and negative implications. It is the freedom to go as far as I can go, to harness both natural forces and human beings; in this regard it bears a resemblance to freedom in Christ, since this freedom, too, summons me to do all that my hand can do in self-realization. It is, then, the freedom of self-expansion. Every human being inclines to expand, as indeed does every living creature. To absorb what is around us in our own life-interests is natural for us. Yet this freedom which is a pretext is not just an individual matter. It is the basis of almost all our society.

This freedom, which springs from Christian civilization, has inspired economic liberalism. We have been slow to denounce this, but in effect it is the freedom of the strong to crush the weak. It is the unregulated and unrestricted rivalry of inimical powers—and this is what we have the effrontery to describe as freedom. Its only justification is the efficiency of the system; the stronger carries the day, namely, the one who can produce more and better marketed products. But efficiency is not an adequate ethical criterion in the modern age. Hence freedom, the fruit of Christianity, has been taken over as a pretext.

It has been similarly used in the interests of political liberalism. The point here is to justify the domination of one class and to give an institutional aspect to a system of oppression. Here too freedom is a pretext for organizing a more total, rigorous, detailed, and authoritarian state in relation to a society in which the affirmation of freedom has

---

2  A weakness in Harvey Cox is his failure to see this and his concentration on sloth or resignation.

succeeded in breaking all man's defenses against power in the form of intermediary bodies. Under the pretext of freedom the groups on which man could rely in opposition to the state have been destroyed. Society has been reduced to a collection of individuals. A society of "sand" has been established. There has been talk of freedom but man has been subjected to the absolute state, which has become the dispenser of a freedom which the state itself doles out, which it gives and takes away, which it delimits, and of which it is the only judge.

Finally, the freedom which is a pretext may be seen flourishing today in the explanations that philosophers and theologians give on the subject of technology. Christian freedom has indubitably desacralized nature and opened up for man the possibility of intervening freely in the natural order, so that man can again fulfil the divine command to dress the garden and to keep it (Genesis 2:15). An unfortunate result of this desacralization of nature, however, is that now that nature is no longer protected by sacred terrors and powerful gods and solemn curses, man has not used it in the freedom of service, respect, and restraint, but has made of his freedom a pretext for giving free rein to his lust for domination. He has exploited nature without brake or limit. He has ravaged the planet. His only thought has been to enhance his means of power. He has violated secrets which God may well have given him but on which he has set an impudent hand like Adam. He has exhausted the resources of nature and destroyed animal species with unrestricted technical savagery. The very thing which characterizes modern technology is the lust for power which Paul warned us to avoid. And philosophers and theologians until recently have calmly said that this is simply man's freedom, that he is a co-worker with God, that he is fulfilling a command to exploit creation. They have failed to see that in so saying they have made freedom a pretext in justification of technological expansion and subjection to carnal passions.

It will be seen, then, that the command not to use freedom as a pretext embraces far more than individual conduct and questions that are normally described as moral. Whatever relates to freedom covers every dimension of life, whether personal or collective, whether spiritual or practical. When freedom becomes a pretext, it is a pretext for surrender to the passions, which is in fact a negation of freedom.

We must now turn to a neighboring area, namely, that of justification. We refer to self-justification. This is an operation by which again we deny our freedom. Self-justification is man's greatest enterprise along with the lust for power, or rather after the manifestation of this lust. For when man has acted or lived according to this desire, he cannot be satisfied with having achieved power. He has to say that he is just and that his power is just. He cannot tolerate opposition.

Justification is a permanent attitude. Man is constantly justifying not only his acts but also his condition and situation in the universe. He cannot accept the life under question or the life of venture and novelty and recommencement which is true freedom. Justification means acquisition, installation, and certainty. It means getting on lines of which the first is known to have been good and this guarantees what follows.

Man can achieve justification only on two levels, the first being that of truth and the second that of the community. First, man cannot accept himself unless he is sure that he has the truth, that he possesses it. Now we have seen that in fact the free man advances by receiving a revelation of the truth of God's act, and we have also seen that he never owns this truth. Abraham, when he was called to leave Ur and to become the father of the chosen people, was the free man *par excellence,* but he never owned the truth. He was always seeking it. He never had it. All that he had was a son who was called in question by God, and then a burial cave. Man, however, is not Abraham. He cannot accept this permanent quest without installation. To live, he wants reasons for living. The reasons he advances, however trivial, will be his truth. Hence anything negative, any negation of man, will be changed into a positive, into a value. When man achieves material happiness, this is confused with truth. When he has no spiritual cares but sleeps comfortably, this is peace. When he has no courage to go on, but stops, he says that he has reached his goal. When he takes a mediocre path, he is a positive apostle of realization. When he takes up politics, he says that he is fighting for the liberation of the oppressed.

Once man has justified himself by the possession of a truth, every detail of life has to be a truth. Every detail has to be repeated and reconstructed as such. Man pictures his life as a justified life. This justified life is a continuous life which has the same meaning both at the beginning and at the end. It has an inclusive value which can never be challenged.

This justification is in effect a negation of freedom, for it is a refusal of the conflict of life. It is a refusal of encounter with the Spirit who accuses us before justifying us. It is a refusal of any new commencement.

The justification may take many forms. Most often it will use some kind of orthodoxy. Most of us are incapable of inventing our own system of self-justification, which would imply that at some point we were already free and had struggled to grasp this truth. This is uncommon. For almost all men self-justification is furnished by a ready-made system that is set before them—an explanation of history, the political doctrine of a given myth, Hitlerism or Communism, a philosophical synthesis, the absolute truth of science. The more grandiose the synthesis is, the more facts it embraces, and the more answers it gives, the more it justifies. In our own age the great systems of justification and hence the great negators of freedom are Communism,[3] Teilhardism, structuralism, and, of course, Christianity.

To accept such systems a certain commitment and intellectual ability is needed. This can be counterfieted to help ordinary people. Thus at the

---

3 Thus the element of justification in Communism may be seen in recurrent purges or in movements such as Maoism.

average level justifying systems can be provided either along the lines of moralism or of scientifico-religious mysticism, as in works like *Reader's Digest,* which convey the tranquillity of truth to contemporary man. Contemporary man need not search out anything for himself even though it is said that the totality of life ought to be devoted to research. He has only to accept what these pseudo-authorities prescribe.

This agrees, of course, with an important side of actual self-justification. Man sees that he lives in a universe of great conformity and order. An implacable rigor rests over his life. It will not be justified except as adventure and freedom. The common feature in the systems referred to above is that they try to show man how his life is in fact an adventure. Communism says that the historical mechanism is freedom. Teilhardism shows that the mechanisms of evolution lead to freedom. Popular works refer constantly to the human adventure. The fact that we come up against this agreement in affirmation, however, shows that the systems are doing their work. They are giving man precisely what he needs. Going to work, as Léo Ferré says, is portrayed as taking the bus of adventure. Popular magazines offer this description of the justification.

Man thus receives his justification from the society in which he finds himself, and at this level it is the intellectuals who have the job of providing the justification.

But there is also a second level of justification. This is the level of social approval. As we cannot live without possessing the truth which justifies us spiritually, so we cannot live without the approval of the group to which we belong. We have to appear right to those around us, to friends, family (where it does not work out too well—hence the bitter family quarrels), our professional or political group, and neighbors. If others regard us as just, this makes us just in our own eyes.

We are ready to make sacrifices for this, and the literature of propaganda shows how this need is both used and reinforced by the artificial mechanisms of psychological action. The essential sacrifice is that of adaptation. We must accept complete adaptation to our group. We must be like the rest of the crowd. We must be conformists. We must do the same things, react in the same way, and use the same jargon. The rebel who negates and despises the family and middle-class morality is no better in this regard.

This adaptation or integration into the group is in the strict sense a rejection of freedom, an abandoning of personal adventure, a refusal of singularity, and deafness to the appeal which is made for free individuality. As in the case of spiritual and intellectual justification, so in the case of justification by group integration, the need naturally appears in all cultures and civilizations and it applies to men in every age, even though each age will have its own particular types of justifying systems.

Each society responds with different means to the need of its members. In our own age it seems to me that the two main features are the use of voluntary and systematic methods of integration as concerns social justification and the making of a virtue (or of freedom) out of necessity as concerns spiritual and intellectual justification. Reality is itself presented as truth. Matter is accorded an intrinsic value. The true is made dependent on the development of the actual. The values of economic growth and the spirit of technical growth are the justifications of a technical age—which simply means that history and spirit are confounded. We are thus justified in being technologists, in putting mankind under the yoke of unlimited work, in making dictators in the name of freedom. The concentration camp is the most logical material expression of the mechanism of justification as it has been summarily described in this way.

One might say that from the very outset, and without even consulting the resultant alienation in a group or ideology, the process of justification is an enterprise which presupposes the jettisoning of freedom. The man who sets out, even unconsciously, to justify himself, eliminates at the same time two conditions of freedom, first, openness to criticism, to questioning, to conflict in which the whole being is risked for the sake of being, and second, the rejection of fixation. He who justifies himself fixes on a past position and cannot leave it. In terms of it he determines to justify himself. He cannot get outside the set situations and hence get back ultimately to freedom.

For Christians the common danger has a particular aspect. This is that Christianity itself is made into a system of self-justification. The justification which is gained in Jesus Christ, given to man from outside, and assigned by God, is seized and made in one way or another into a justification which I possess. This might be reflected in justification by works, but also in the conviction of sin as the way to a good conscience, or the spiritual conformity which becomes pure and simple conformity to something fixed and given. The affirmations of the so-called new theology are the clearest forms of this type of self-justification. The great temptation for the Christian, the most profound threat, is to give to what is fixed and given, whether it be social, political, or economic on the one hand, or psychological, intellectual, moral, and domestic on the other, the label, seal, and guarantee of authenticity by simply giving it a new injection of faith, which is precisely what theologians like Bultmann and Tillich have tried to do.

Now it is difficult to avoid this. Even as Christians we are continually trying to achieve truth and justification. We cannot bear it that this should come from outside. We affect our freedom hereby. For the moment we try to justify ourselves, we become slaves of the system that justifies us. We have a part, as hostages, in the party, technology, economy, or philosophy which we have authenticated and in which we have involved the truth that has been revealed to us. We are destroyed as persons by the morality, theology, and works which we have developed to express our faith. We thus become extraordinarily defensive in relation to what can confirm us in what we are or justify us in what we do. No matter where the guarantee may come from or what the truth may be, we have always to realize that if encounter with the truth does not challenge what I am and do, if it is not a burning coal which even the angel can pick up only with tongs, then it is *ipso facto* an alienating truth, a negation which is addressed to me for my own happiness, good conscience, and comfort, a negation of my freedom. We may thank God, however, that no matter how Christians may betray or exploit revealed truth, the uniqueness of Christian self-justification—and it is unique—is that it contains within itself the power that destroys it. The Christian who builds up his justification verse by verse will one day reach the line of breakage. He cannot but come up against the question: "And whom say ye that I am?" At this moment self-justification is shattered and freedom is given.

### § 2. The Converse

If we return to the two texts in which Paul exhorts us not to lose our freedom, we shall again, curiously enough, find the two basic aspects of freedom that we have just been discussing.

The first passage concerns relations with a prostitute. "I will not be brought under the power of any.... shall I then take the members of Christ, and make them the members of an harlot? God forbid. What? know ye not that he which is joined to an harlot is one body? for two, saith he, shall be one flesh.... Flee fornication. Every sin that a man doeth is without the body; but he that committeth fornication sinneth against his own body" (1 Corinthians 6:12ff.).

Several themes occur here. One is the peculiar gravity of sexual sin. Today it is often said that Paul is simply following here the ideas of his own age. He could speak thus because he was not acquainted with Freud. Happily we in our age have set aside such prejudices. This is highly debatable, but the present context is not the place to debate it.

A second theme may well be sacral prostitution. The scandal of being linked to a harlot is that of linking Christ himself (living or not) to a woman who is consecrated to false gods.

The third theme, however, is the one which I want to stress. There is a general problem of prostitution in the Bible. Why is it that prostitution is condemned throughout? Monogamy is not the reason, since polygamy obtained among the patriarchs. Nor is sacral prostitution the true reason. The point is that prostitution has one very important feature. In most cases, be it noted, it is the man who has been with a prostitute that is condemned (except when the prophets compare Israel to a prostitute who has left her true Lord, and even then the real problem is adultery). In general the prostitute herself is not condemned.

The prostitute is to be avoided, not because of a sexual taboo, nor because she is tainted, but for a deeper reason. The relation with a prostitute is a relation without love. It is a counterfeit of love. It contains one of love's aspects, the physical side, but in detachment from and to the destruction of the totality.

In the relation of prostitution there is no love in the full sense on the man's part. The prostitute cannot be regarded as a unique and perfect creature of God. She is approached as a substitute for love. A gesture of love is to be made without any of its commitment or truth. This is precisely why the prostitute is approached. Love is broken in pieces.

Furthermore, it is obvious that in Israel as everywhere else the prostitute is despised. The Gospels remind us of this. A sham of love is to be made with a creature who is despised, who is treated as an object, who is disparaged. Nor should we imagine that it is just the material fact of sexual union that degrades her, nor the fact of payment. The disparagement is due to inner scorn for her. In biblical terms, her degradation is based, not on her immorality, but on the attitude of the men who come to her and yet despise her.

What is condemned, then, is not the fact that this woman gives herself to a series of men (though this is not commended), but rather that the man treats this woman who is a creature of God without any respect or love, going through the motions of love but not having love itself.

We can thus see why Paul gives this example of not being "brought under the power of any." His reference is to freedom without love. If all things are lawful, I may enter into union with a prostitute. But this is an act of freedom without love. This freedom which centers on man's desire, on his lust for domination; this freedom which is practiced in disdain for a creature of God; this freedom which takes form in a counterfeit and derision of love, is neither more nor less than a new bondage. I think that I am displaying my extraordinary freedom by going to a prostitute, but in reality this exercise of freedom, not being determined by love, is simply a striking witness to my lack of freedom. (Sade is a good example.)

The reason for this is that we are freed only by love of God. If we place ourselves outside love, we place ourselves outside freedom. Freedom exists only in virtue of the new relation which God sets up between beings. In the old relation, which was secular and depended on force, violence, and oppression, there could be no freedom of any kind.

Freedom of choice, conduct, and meaning is set up according to the measure of the new relation. But this new relation is the relation of the love which teaches us to have a concern for the interests of others. This brings us to the true freedom which Jesus himself practices in relation to prostitutes. He talks to them and receives their hospitality, but instead of indulging in the "normal" (i.e., sexual) relation with them, instead of taking them and using them as prostitutes, he brings to them the fulness of God's love, shows them respect, and restores dignity to them by pardon. He enjoyed full freedom regarding society. He mixed with prostitutes, and when people do this publicly they are censured for it, even by those who use them. Social etiquette in relation to these women did not limit his freedom. This was true freedom, for it was oriented to the authenticity of love. Jesus lifted contempt from them. He lifted moral judgment from them. He tore down the barrier which hemmed in prostitutes and set them in a ghetto in which man wanted no part. He made them worthy again of the full love of God and man. He did this in a way which differs totally from that of modern authors who glorify pan-sexualism with the prostitute after the style of Henry Miller. In his freedom he expressed in effect the new relation which God creates by his grace.

In the second passage Paul says: "Be not ye the servants of men" (1 Corinthians 7:23). He has in view the social meaning of the term in the setting of the slave system. We shall have to consider elsewhere the advice which he gives on the subject of slaves; he shows that to achieve manumission they must seek this freedom. In the present context, however, his point is the opposite one. If we are socially free man we must guard our freedom and not become the slaves of men.

This is obviously to be taken in the wider sense. It does not refer only to the institution, which is not generally practiced today. On the other hand, it must be construed in terms of the more specific reference.

As we have seen, freedom in Christ is not just a spiritual freedom. It is a full freedom. Hence it has a material aspect. It is restricted and assaulted when man is not free materially, socially, and politically. Freedom in Christ means, then, that we are not to submit to a dictatorial or authoritarian political regime, no matter what may be its orientation, intention, or theoretical basis. From this standpoint it makes no difference whether the dictator is of the right or the left, whether he is trying to protect capitalism or to save the proletariat, whether he is defending colonialism or trying to destroy imperialism. A dictatorship is always a dictatorship and we become the slaves of men in submitting to it. We amputate thereby the freedom that is given in Christ. If it is Christians who try to set up such a dictatorship, they are using freedom in Christ to make men slaves, and in so doing they themselves destroy freedom.

This applies equally to the totality of the socio-economic structures that oppress men. Along these lines it seems to me that the "good" realities are more dangerous than the "bad." For enslaving men by violence, imprisonment, and torture is certainly a terrible thing, but it does at least provoke reaction against it. Enslaving men by gentle and laudable institutions and intentions is in the long run a far greater threat. I have in mind means of enslavement like work, occupation, specialization, family, country, justice, culture, progress, intelligence, or science. Each of these values is both an inevitable and indispensable element for man and also an occasion of enslavement. The two aspects cannot be separated.

Thus one cannot say that a happy family is merely a gift from heaven.

Necessarily, and no matter how good the members of the family may be, or how well they understand one another, it is also a servitude which is the more to be feared the better it is concealed and the less it is resented.

Again, it is impossible to distinguish between a good and a bad occupation or good and bad science. Each factor in concrete life is both an enslavement and a realization of life.

Thus when Paul tells us not to be the servants of men he does not mean that we have to destroy the things without which life is impossible. He means that we have to introduce freedom in Christ into them. We are to make of them an occasion of freedom rather than bondage. We shall study this matter in the final part of this ethics of freedom.

Naturally among enslaving institutions we are to number those that belong to religion and Christianity, i.e., ecclesiastical institutions, the cultus, and even piety and charity, which can all be forces that alienate man.

Finally I want to insist on an aspect to which I have devoted a good deal of study, namely, sociological bondage. I mean by this following the social current. The fact that man adopts without thinking the customs, images, prejudices, and habits of his group, that he talks and judges and acts like the rest of its members, is bondage. Acculturation is the term. Now obviously a man cannot live without this culture and adaptation to it. It has always been thus in all groups and in every age. But when the adaptation is total and complete integration is achieved, both inner and outer freedom disappears.

The most difficult confrontation takes place here, and this is why the act of recognition is essential. The danger is much greater in our own time, since acculturation is now accomplished by much more precise and rigorous means, by multiple techniques, by pedagogy, by public relations, by information, and by propaganda. All these are ways by which society enslaves man. Christian freedom has to defend itself against them, since they entail a basic attack on this freedom.

The problem, however, is now slightly different. Whereas the issue earlier was to make these institutions an occasion of freedom in Christ, we are here in the presence of enslaving forces which cannot be utilized on behalf of freedom. They have thus to be resisted. I do not say that they are to be suppressed. This would be a mere illusion. The need is to manifest their true alienating character behind the benevolent appearance of respect and service, as in the case of pedagogy and information.

Once again, however, we have to seek the fundamental reason for this attitude of resistance. If the enslaving of man has to be resisted in every dimension, if freedom is so decisively significant, this is not because man himself is of such supreme importance. It is because the enslavement expresses the fact that authority, signification, and ultimate value are attached to man and to his beliefs and institutions. It means exaltation of the nation or state (dictatorship), of money (capitalism), of technology (the crushing of man in the technological society), art, morality, the party, and so forth. The work of man is glorified and this always entails the sacrifice of the human.

Finally, man himself is exalted, and, paradoxical though it may seem to be, this means the crushing of man. Man's enslavement is the reverse side of the glory, value, and importance that are ascribed to him. The more a society magnifies human greatness, the more one will see men alienated, enslaved, imprisoned, and tortured in it. Humanism prepares the ground for the anti-human. We do not say that this is an intellectual paradox. All one need do is read history. Men have never been so oppressed as in societies which set man at the pinnacle of values and exalt his greatness or make him the measure of all things.[4] For in such societies freedom is detached from its purpose, which is, we affirm, the glory of God.

Another aspect of unfreedom is the bad conscience. Essentially this means entering on the way indicated by the gospel but with fear and uncertainty. The bad conscience is a very serious temptation for modern Christians. For there is today a cult of the bad conscience of which protestantism is the jealous guardian. As is well known, since Kierkegaard one cannot be a Christian at all without having a bad conscience.

Now we are not denying that there is something good and healthy and validly Christian in this disquietude. In opposition to a good con-science, the bad conscience is a protestation of the greatness of God. We know only too well the horror of a good social conscience in middle-class Christianity. The middle class assimilates society and the good to its own conduct. The middle class reconciles justice and the good with making money and ensuring its own control. The middle class is not content to exercise power; it also wants to be right, to be able to show that it is just in fulfilling its duties. It wants the legally good conscience which is given by the scrupulous observance of duties and functions, by keeping to the rules. It wants the good conscience of the realism which accepts the fact that the big swallow up the small and that one cannot make omelettes without breaking eggs—an easy way to excuse wars and economic conflicts, but one which evades the obvious fact that the omelette is the good of all. It wants the good conscience which embraces and absorbs Christian faith, the reassuring certainty of being on the right side, on the side of the elect who confess God and who also have spiritual and economic guarantees: "Why examine me? I have done my duty. Of what can I be accused? God saves me." Salvation by faith is a remarkable element in this good conscience, which is always ready to feed on what is gratuitously given. We are only too well aware today of the horror of the good conscience of the middle class a century ago.

It should be noted, however, that this good conscience was the

---

4 Thus the oppressions and massacres of the middle ages were mere child's play compared to those in the U.S.S.R. and slavery was a real tragedy only in Rome after the first century and in the west from the eighteenth century onwards.

product of a period of social tranquillity, economic expansion, and political solidity. In that period to proclaim that a bad conscience was a necessary fruit of the gospel could only be a revolutionary act. There was truth in this proclamation. The bad conscience is that of sinful man who can only humble himself before the God who is perfectly just and holy. It is awareness of the men we are, those who cannot love as God has loved, who are always torn between the love of God for them and their own love for the world, who are under the command to sell all that they have, who see with astonishment that God himself has really died for them on the cross, for them personally even before they were ever born. A bad conscience is thus a questioning of what I am by him who alone can say: "I am." It means that the revolutionary revelation of the gospel is taken seriously in a living and vital way.

All this is true. We have come to see it. We have come to see it in two ways. We have come to see that the gospel is true. We have also come to see that a bad conscience is necessary. When did this become an acknowledged truth? Between 1930 and 1940, i.e., when it was realized that the world that had been destroyed by the war of 1914 could not be reconstructed, when the crisis of 1929 had brought to light the weaknesses of capitalism, when the different forms of fascism had cast their triumphant shadow over our mediocre consciences. In this endangered world we came to understand that a bad conscience is normal, and as the middle class had a spiritual attitude conformable to the world of 1860, so the youth of 1936 had an attitude conformable to the world of 1936. Disquiet, anguish, and a bad conscience became spiritual virtues. And as the world became increasingly entangled in the drama which followed, we became set in a bad conscience and began to domesticate it. For it certainly could not be left on the spiritual plane.

For the present world, even though in turmoil, is still "social." Hence the bad Christian conscience has become social. Christians have seen that a bad conscience which remains individual and spiritual is unproductive and can easily become no more than a source of comfort. In a reversal of the parable of the Pharisee and the publican, it has been shown that the publican with his bad conscience can also be a hypocrite (I thank thee, God, that I am not like this wicked Pharisee who has such a good conscience). The spiritual progress has thus had to be translated into facts. During the last decades, then, there has been a remarkable growth of the bad conscience. The virus has spread rapidly in the favorable environment of our shattered occidental world.

This bad conscience is not always voluntary nor is it always clearly understood. But it is basic if we are to explain the behavior of younger protestants during the years after 1946. Being middle class now gives a bad conscience. There is a desire not to have anything more to do with this class which is now seen to be so contemptible and unjust, the source of oppression, capitalism, colonialism, and every other abomination, the class that history itself has condemned. An attempt is thus made to break solidarity with this class for what are, of course, spiritual reasons and reasons of justice—these alone being conscious, and any others hidden. In the main it has been middle-class protestants—middle class both in manner of life and ways of thought—that have expressed most ardently their hatred and scorn for this class. They have made of their renunciation of it an expression of Christian virtue. We can only conjecture what part is also played here by shame at the fact that with all the fibers of their being they belong to a family, tradition, and class that society in general has now come to reject.

Being intellectual can also be the cause of a bad conscience. For in this period the intellectual, too, has not been viewed too favorably as compared with the technologist or the man of action. The intellectual cuts a sorry figure. He is supported neither by the powerful forces of technology and science, which justify all that they touch, nor by the forces of political and social action, which are the passion of the men of our age. He is an unproductive and useless man of leisure. If he wants to be taken seriously, he must dabble in politics. Signing manifestos and taking part in meetings replaces the intellectual function, and all that the intellectual needs to be is a representative public figure. Apart from this he may work in solitude to the general relief, for he has no very obvious function. The best thing, of course, is to be able to say that one is not an intellectual. We read this in article after article, and protestants in particular flood us with such disclaimers.

These two aspects lead us to a third, namely, bad conscience at being a pastor. The title itself is still retained. But how many pastors now say that it is a hindrance, a barrier between themselves and other men (which is not always true), a thing that sets them apart! And how many other pastors are timid in face of the men of the age, those who have a job and have mixed in the rough and tumble of social life! How many have been conscious of their unworthiness before God (and rightly so) and before men (but wrongly so)! How many dare not stand up against the preemptory positions of pagans! How many would like to be and to act like other men, having a secular job and taking part in politics!

The situation is surely an absurd one when the servant of God is paralyzed because the world says to him: "Justice, truth, and salvation lie with us," and the pastor, sensing the force of this, and always ready to accuse himself of what he has not done and to accuse the church of all sins, is prepared to give in and to acknowledge with the world that justice, truth, and salvation are to be found everywhere except in the church. How strange is this bad conscience, not before God, but before the audacity, pride, and lies of the world, whether it be middle class or communist, technological or political!

As is only natural, this bad conscience of the pastor spreads to many members of the church. As I see it, this comes to expression in two ways.

First, there is an extraordinary desire to be exactly like other men. We want no distinguishing marks. The Christian life is a good thing inwardly. Outwardly, however, we do as others do. We follow the dominant thrust of the age. We share the preoccupations, attitudes, and occupations of all the rest. The concerns and fads and allegiances and shifts of all are ours also. We do not speak boldly of a specific Christian morality or attitude. This would be to risk differentiation.

At the extreme limit even the inner Christian life can be eliminated. Being a Christian is simply being with others and like others. This is neo-Christianity. In my view, to reject what is specific in Christianity is the greatest delusion in our own generation.

Be that as it may, to separate between the inner Christian life and the life outside is simply to reproduce the hypocrisy of the middle class when it distinguished between the life within and the practical life of action. If the middle class did this with a good conscience and we do it with a bad conscience, the result is still the same. We refuse to incarnate our faith in thoughts and attitudes and acts which no one can have or do except Christians.

The second facet of the bad conscience is the refusal to aim at conversions. There has been much talk recently of protestant proselytism. Our predecessors wanted to convert men. How terrible! We are well rid of such desires. We no longer entertain such wicked notions. We want to be present everywhere, to have a part in all human activities, to be business-men with businessmen, royalists with royalists, intellectuals with intellec-tuals, trade union men with trade union men. That is all. We no longer talk of conversion. This would shock people. It would make us suspect. It would hamper our contacts. It would prevent us from being like others. They have to have confidence—full confidence—in us. To think of convert-ing them is to betray them, is it not?

But here again our bad conscience leads us into hypocrisy. For what is the point of being present as Christians if it is not for the conversion of men? What is the unique aim of Christian action if it is not to lead men to acknowledge finally that Jesus Christ is their Saviour and Lord? Why is it that we join parties or unions or associations? Is it simply that we may have a part in movements that we regard as right in themselves? And are we to be bashful about telling others that we are acting as Christians? If we want to make Jesus Christ known, what does this mean? It cannot mean only imparting a vague and general knowledge, a kind of insubstantial presence. The aim must be that men confess Jesus Christ in heart and mouth. Anything else is an illusion. For Jesus Christ has not come to establish social justice any more than he has come to establish the power of the state or the reign of money or art. Jesus Christ has come to save men, and all that matters is that men may come to know him.

We are very adept at finding reasons—good theological, political, or practical reasons—for camouflaging this. But the real reason is that we let ourselves be impressed and dominated by the forces of the world, by the press, by public opinion, by the political game, by appeals to justice, liberty, peace, the poverty of the third world, and the Christian civilization of the west, all of which play on our inclinations and weaknesses. Modern protestants are in the main prepared to be all things to all men, like St. Paul, but unfortunately this is not in order that they may save some but in order that they may be like all men.

This bad conscience negates freedom, not merely because it leads us to try to be like others, but also because it does not let us accept ourselves as we are or be what we are. For Christian freedom demands precisely that we be bold in the midst of a hostile world, of pressure groups, of strangers. Because we are free, we must be able quietly to affirm that we are different and to accept without a bad conscience the judgment of men and our eventual rejection by them. Men cannot tolerate freedom. But we alienate the freedom that Christ has given if we accept their judgment and, while still retaining the name of Christian, alter and soften revelation, adopting the conduct of others, attempting syncretism, seeking an exegesis which will satisfy modern man, and doing all this in order that men who have now come of age, and before whom we have a bad conscience, may ultimately lend an ear—however careless—to what we are saying. It is my belief, for example, that the audacious exegesis of Bultmann is the fruit of this bad conscience and that it is thus an alienation of Christian freedom even though the claim is often made that it is an expression of freedom in relation to classical dogmas.

The rejection of a bad conscience in the name of freedom has, however, another side. There is, we might say, no freedom where there is no criticism of this freedom. Spontaneous or natural freedom is simply an advance in any direction, even though choice is involved. But with freedom in Christ, which begins with Christ and has the two axes of love and God's glory, freedom entails reflection and self-criticism. This criticism is one of the surest signs of freedom. As it develops, freedom in Christ has to turn back on itself and consider what must be done from the standpoint of freedom.

Determination does not come into play before the act. There need be no tormenting search by all possible means, spiritual or magical, for God's will here and now, so that it may be done. This means a false obedience that negates freedom. But there is criticism after the fact in the concern and hope that what has been chosen is obedience to God. When we see the act and its results we can decide as to its validity or invalidity. Did it express freedom? Only the outcome can finally show.

Are we advocating the examination of conscience? Yes and no. For in the traditional sense this is a very different thing. It involves the questions of good and evil, obedience and disobedience, sin. Its aim is to present oneself to God for grace or pardon. It is individualistic. But criticism of freedom has the different objective of finding out whether what is done expresses the freedom given in Christ or determinism. It relates to objective acts and their results. It has a plural dimension. It is not an examination of conscience in the sense of self-criticism.

Without this critical turning back there is no lived out freedom, only an alienated freedom. One of the strongest signs of freedom in Christ is being able to put to the test what we think expresses our freedom and ruthlessly to expose the freedom as an alienated freedom. Freedom comes as I show that, believing I was acting as a free man, I acted once again as an alienated man. The absence of this criticism of freedom bears witness that there is no freedom. This is hard to grasp. But rapid and victorious advance in freedom is itself an advance into alienation without this looking back and exposing and expelling of alienation. There is, of course, no magical efficacy in our acts. Criticism of freedom does not automatically mean freedom. Only as it expresses our attitude before God does it have meaning and force.

This criticism has to take place humbly before God and according to the divinely given criteria of freedom, love, and the glory of God. The presence of God makes it an expression of our critical freedom. This presence has to mean intervention. God himself acts. He mediates between my enacted freedom and my critical freedom. This makes the latter real freedom and gives freedom back to the act of enacted freedom. But all this obviously cannot be taken for granted.

To be able to criticize enacted freedom there is needed another standpoint which is provided by love and the glory of God. These enable us to say whether our enacted freedom is authentic or not. Critical freedom consists, then, in examining whether the act which we believe expresses freedom conforms to the love of neighbor and the glory of God. We intend it to, but this is not enough. Only after, not before, can we see. It is in its outcome that we may consider whether freedom is expressed by it.

Critical freedom negates, denounces, and pillories lived out freedom if some other goal has been behind the act. One must ask whether the act of freedom has been done out of love of neighbor or, with very different motivations, out of love of man, out of solidarity of interests, or love of country, class, race, nation, or state. Does the act reveal a little of God's presence or has it been done simply to the glory of the state or a doctrine or society or some other power? Has it finally manifested the power of money or work or science?

No comfort may be found in the thought that God's glory shines through all these things. The choice is strict. God's glory does not shine through money or political action or science unless in my act these are vanquished forces, unless they have lost their power, unless nothing is expected from them.

If the true motivations of the act thought to be free are brought to light, it is also brought to light that God does in fact give me freedom. If, however, I cease using this freedom to criticize freedom, if I find freedom in and of myself, if I live as a free man without any scrutiny or feed-back, what I regard as freedom is a veritable bondage and alienation. How can this be if we are truly free as we say? How can the mere absence of freedom of criticism bring alienation? The problem is that freedom can so easily be an illusion. Man always has the spontaneous conviction that he is free.

This may be seen at all levels from complex metaphysics to the simple reaction of people when we show that they bear the burden of determinations. Even those who are aware of this burden still come back to a belief in the freedom of man. Even those who speak of historical necessity still say that man makes history. Innumerable works of sociology are based on the uncritical and undemonstrated and irrational assumption of human freedom. This incurable tendency should warn us that of all the factors in human life freedom needs the most cautious handling and is the most illusory.

This is the more true because, as we have seen, man does not want to live as free man. He fears freedom but wants to say that he is free. Freedom in Christ comes under this rule too. Since the illusion of freedom constantly recurs, Christians as men continually interpret the feeblest conformity as Christian freedom, but are unable to see it in and of themselves. Indeed they are the first to fall victim to the illusion just because they know that there is a liberating love of God.

When the non-Christian accepts the illusion of being free he has no firm basis for this and so his belief is fragile and can easily be overturned. But Christians have the assurance that where the Spirit of the Lord is, there is liberty. Obeying human nature they quickly change this solid reference into intolerable vanity. Their fall is even greater. Since freedom leads them to this illusion shared by all, they are more effectively alienated than before they knew they were freed, for their alienation rests now on the conviction that they are free in Christ and it is thus a perversion of freedom. The thinking of Teilhard de Chardin offers an illustration of this. They are also doubly alienated, falling back under the common determinations and yet imagining that they are free in Christ. Confusion of the freedom given by God with a freedom native to man; confusion of the act of grace with nature, brings them under the bondage of an illusion of freedom.

Thus Christian freedom becomes a source of alienation. This may be seen in the attitude of many Christians, who, persuaded that what they do expresses this freedom, regard every decision as an exercise in it as though it were a kind of state. But as we have seen, the Christian is still in society. Hence he cannot be totally different from others. His freedom is not a possession and he can fall back constantly into the fear of real freedom and the illusion and pretension of freedom without ever assuming it. More than anyone else he risks living in an alienating illusion when he engages in an uncriticized assumption of freedom.

What applies to the individual applies equally to the church as a whole. For many today freedom consists in joining a union or playing politics. Hence there is need of a careful examination of the sociological determinations which are at work in a society like our own (cf. my *Fausse Présence*). Let us be more precise. I am not saying that if honest and serious criticism shows that we are actually obeying human and sociological motivations all action and involvement should stop. Not at all! We may still take the course chosen. But we should be clear that it is not an expression of our freedom in Christ nor are we bearing witness to love of neighbor nor glorifying our Lord. We are simply acting like others, which is neither prohibited nor condemned. It is far more dangerous to act thus and to pretend that we are doing so as Christians. This is when we fall into condemnation, for it entails an abuse of freedom and the illusion that we are free when we are in fact acting like slaves. The illusion of freedom is the source of condemnation as well as alienation.

Thus critical freedom looking back on enacted freedom can become freedom's most decisive aspects. For at a moment of extreme sociological determination it can be the only part of authentic freedom that we can assume. This part, however, we can always assume. It is always freedom; no confusion is possible in relation to it. It is the distance that God himself sets up between me and the exact moment when God instals his own freedom in me. In other words, it is the only inner source of an assurance of freedom that we can have.

### § *3. Happiness and Conquest*

We now take up a third aspect of the loss of freedom. I believe that biblically there is a constant contradiction between the pursuit of happiness and obedience to the will of God. I add at once that this does not mean that happiness is forbidden the Christian. As Jesus puts it, happiness is given as an extra. It is given and not won nor passionately sought. It is an extra and hence it is not the essential and decisive thing but a secondary supplement. What I have in view in this context, then, is not actual happiness but the pursuit of it, the claiming of it, the passion for it, and the value attributed to it. It is the fact of finding the whole meaning of life in it, of sacrificing everything for it, and of justifying everything by it.

We shall not try to reflect on happiness here, to examine all its aspects, nor to elaborate a philosophy of happiness. We shall simply attempt to establish the biblical perspective on the relation between freedom as the Bible sees it and happiness as the Bible sees it. We are not concerned to justify this relation philosophically or psychologically nor are we interested in its general implications. The only point is that we are here confronted by a divine decision.

Now it may be true from one angle that it is a cultural matter that the authors of the Bible speak of happiness as a gift of God. Other religions, too, assign to their gods the function of giving happiness to their devotees. It seems to me, however, that at two points we have more than a matter of culture here. First, the happiness which the Lord gives is free; it is not bought. The God of Abraham does not grant happiness in exchange for certain sacrifices or offerings. Furthermore, there is no necessary link between happiness and goodness. The wicked and dishonest can be happy. They can be more happy than the righteous. This is what Job is all about. Job is not offended merely because he is unhappy (as in Gilgamesh). He is offended because the wicked and rebellious are happy. Many psalms speak to the same point (cf. Ps. 73:3). It is not a cultural matter that there is this break between happiness and righteousness, even though the Old Testament does in fact affirm that God is the one who gives happiness.

Secondly, happiness is not here the goal of life. For Israel it is accessory. Faithfulness to God, the covenant, wisdom, and the love of God come first and then we find happiness as a second and secondary benefit, as a kind of accessory consequence. It is by no means negligible. But it is neither the motive for what we do in relation to God (love of God should be completely disinterested), nor is it an ineluctable and logical consequence, nor is it a primary concern.

Sometimes a practical and almost materialistic wisdom associates it with material things and sets it firmly in its true place. "Whoso findeth a wife findeth happiness" (Prov. 18:22)—although it is added that a wife is a gift from God and hence that authentic marriage, the true union of man and woman, is grace. Again, "man's only happiness is to eat and drink and make his soul enjoy good in his labour" (Ecclesiastes 2:24)—this is a good summary of the view of the average man in modern society, although this text, too, adds that such happiness is from the hand of God. Again, "I see that there is no happiness for men but for them to rejoice and to do good in their lives" (Ecclesiastes 3:12). Again, "there is more happiness in a handful with quietness than both the hands full with travail" (Ecclesiastes 4:6).

Happiness means having a good wife, riches, good food and drink, comfort, and leisure. This agreement between Ecclesiastes and modern thinking is for me very striking. It puts happiness in its place, strips it of its prestige as a reward, and empties it of spiritual value and meaning. But it seems to differ sharply from Egyptian and Semitic thinking. (I am aware that Greek influences are often seen in Ecclesiastes, but this is not very convincing.) In effect, I believe that we have here an original view of happiness. Certainly its secondary character is maintained. Happiness is not invoked as either the goal of life or the supreme value.

In contrast, one need hardly recall the spiritual importance which is accorded to trial, misery, poverty, and suffering, since this is merely the other side of refusing to make happiness a value. The "blessed" or "happy" of the Beatitudes confirms this. The happy man is not he who has happiness according to human standards, who heaps up goods and profits by things; it is he who lacks all the sources of human happiness. The message of the Beatitudes may be found already in the Old Testament. In the Psalms especially this is the consistent view. On the one hand we have happiness according to man with human means and the importance which man attributes to it, while on the other hand we have what God says about the man who has not sought happiness or wealth nor bought up the earth, namely, that this man is happy.

If God says that he *is* happy and not just that he will enjoy eternal bliss, this does not mean that there is any opposition between happiness on earth and eternal happiness. We have here an actual reality, but one of a different order, which does not rest on feeling or the fulfilment of desires and needs, but on the declaration of God and the truth of the word of God. In other words, this man is happy even though he does not experience or feel it.

This affirmation has three implications. The first is that asceticism is not demanded. There is no need for the voluntary privation which might have a value of its own. The only point at issue is independence in relation to what men regard as the cause or source of their happiness.

The second implication brings us back to the realism of Ecclesiastes. When men speak of happiness, they think of winning the earth, of getting power over others, of not being persecuted, of avoiding troubles, of avoiding hunger and thirst, of being rich in intelligence, spirit, etc.

The third implication is that the validity of happiness, including that which might come from the fulfilment of needs and passions or the use of earthly things, rests solely on the recognition that it comes from God and is given by God. All happiness in which man does not recognize that it is God's work and stands in relation to him is rejected and is under condemnation.

The secondary, dependent, and accessory character of happiness is to be seen everywhere in the Old Testament, and it introduces us directly to the question of freedom. When happiness is self-reliant and is not referred to God, it comes under the parable of Jesus when he speaks of the rich farmer who has amassed great crops and says: "Soul . . . take thine ease, eat, drink, and be merry," but God replies: "Thou fool, this night thy soul shall be required of thee." The wisdom of the world, which bases happiness on the accumulation of goods and productivity, is mere folly before God.

It is against this background of the biblical view of happiness that we are to view the link between happiness and freedom. In this light happiness seems to be a force that is destructive of freedom.[5] In effect we have here two contradictory types of life. We are not saying that to want to be happy without God is bad or impossible, nor that to use this or that thing to create happiness is bad. This would make no moral sense. At a far more

---

5 No one has been more forthright on this than Kierkegaard, who points out that all men seek independence but few see that it comes by way of suffering. Happiness, or the refusal to suffer, rules out not only freedom but even the independence sought by men. The way of independence is the way of suffering.

essential level we are rather in the presence of two life-styles. For happiness is in itself a style of life.

I am not saying merely that happiness conditions or provokes, but rather that it is itself a global conception of life and hence a full type or style of life. As the Bible puts it, happiness seems to be man's greatest end. He rates it above all else. He is ready to sacrifice anything for it. It is the object of his preoccupation. It is thus a value that gives meaning to life. It is not just the fulfilment of needs. At this level, the satisfaction of having a full stomach is not wrong. But it does not give man real satisfaction. In reality, in biblical realism, happiness is only this elemental satisfaction, but man, since he also has religious and spiritual "needs," tries to give to this material fulfilment a value which will at the same time fulfil ultimate needs.

In other words, man is satisfied both materially and spiritually herewith, and he is satisfied spiritually because materially. This is the movement which is unacceptable to God. For man is now finding the meaning of life in the satisfaction of ordinary needs. He does not think life worth living if he does not have food to eat and does not heap up property.

When I say this I am not thinking only of the modern era, for the Bible is quite clear on the point. I am not thinking only of a particular economic system (capitalism) nor of a human category (wealth). This happiness is sought always by all men in this way. Precisely to the degree that man makes the gaining of happiness the meaning of life he cannot attribute it to any other or refer it to God. For it is just because he has staked everything on this value, and done all he can to reach this end, that he does in fact reach it. How then can he say that it comes from God and is his gift? He knows what this happiness has cost him in terms of work and hardship. He knows that he has devoted his whole life to achieving it, and that he has achieved it only by being pitiless to others.

To the degree that happiness has been his central preoccupation he is unable to escape its grasp. He cannot live as a free man, since he is tied to the fulfilment of these needs which are constantly self-renewing. No aloofness, respite, or disengagement is possible. Precisely to the degree that happiness is monopolistic, it cannot be an expression of freedom. But it has to be monopolistic. In effect, if the aim is the gratification of needs above all else, including emotional and spiritual needs, then happiness implies a seizure of the world (not necessarily along capitalist lines) and also a seizure of God, i.e., by the transformation of revelation into religion to satisfy religious needs.

To the degree that happiness entails a desire for security, it cannot be freedom. Happiness has to involve security, for this is another aspect of gratification. We may take our ease, for security is given by riches, or the city, or the state, or, for Israel, a king, who will deliver it from the insecurity of unpredictable and impetuous direction by the Lord. Thus happiness, which provides life with both motivation and meaning, is a complete life-style.

Now freedom, as we have already pointed out, is also a life-style. It is the specifically Christian life-style. Scripture tells us that it stands in direct contradiction to the life-style of happiness. The judgments of happiness and freedom are contradictory. To judge happiness in terms of freedom in Christ leads to the opposite of judging freedom in terms of happiness. An example of the first type of judgment is to be found in the Beatitudes. We need not go into these here except to stress that only the freedom of Jesus permits him to put out this collection of evident "contra-realities." It is because he is sovereignly free, and on the basis of this freedom, that he can reverse so radically human ideas of happiness. Freedom is what enables him to say that happiness lies here, i.e., in precisely what men regard as its opposite. The distinction between God's "happy" or "blessed" and what man calls happiness is the judgment of God on the life-style of happiness as man understands it.

The converse is also true. On the basis of happiness as a life-style man judges freedom and ultimately does not want it. He, too, sees that the two styles are contradictory. We will pick only one of many possible biblical examples to illustrate this. We refer to the children of Israel in the wilderness. They have been liberated. They have been chosen. They have witnessed miracles of freedom. They have seen God meeting their needs, e.g., at the waters of Marah. But they find this freedom bitter because they do not have enough to eat: "Would to God we had died by the hand of the Lord in the land of Egypt, when we sat by the flesh pots, and when we did eat bread to the full; for ye have brought us forth into this wilderness, to kill this whole assembly with hunger" (Exodus 16:3). This refusal is a constant one that we find in every age. The true cry of man is: "A full belly or death." Again, "wherefore is it that thou hast brought us up out of Egypt, to kill us and our children and our cattle with thirst?" (Exodus 17:2). We find the same complaint some years later enriched by recollections of the happiness that they had enjoyed in Egypt. "Who shall give us flesh to eat? We remember the fish, which we did eat in Egypt freely; the cucumbers, and the melons, and the leeks, and the onions, and the garlick; but now our soul is dried away; there is nothing at all" (Numbers 11:4ff.). Nothing at all—for freedom is nothing in the eyes of happiness, and the grace of God is also nothing.

After forty years in the desert, we are not to believe that Israel has learned the meaning of freedom or chosen it in preference to its imagined happiness in Egypt. When it comes near to Canaan, it learns that the inhabitants of the land are very strong and now it begins to regret not only the food it had in Egypt but also the security. "And the people wept that night . . . would God that we had died in the land of Egypt! or would God we had died in the wilderness. And wherefore hath the Lord brought us unto this land . . . were it not better for us to return into Egypt? . . . Let us make us a captain, and let us return into Egypt?" (Numbers 14:2ff.). They preferred the security of bondage, which they regarded as happiness, to the risks of freedom. So grave was this choice that it was frequently recalled, and centuries later the Levites, at the command of Nehemiah, would humiliate themselves because their forefathers had "appointed a captain to return to their bondage" (Nehemiah 9:17).

We may note the psychological realism of what the texts tell us. The men of Israel would rather die than take risks. They would rather die than not have their needs met. They would rather choose what is absurd if they cannot have happiness. The contradiction between freedom and happiness is so great when one is judged in the light of the other that no choice is in fact possible between them. If the choice is posed, a third possibility is brought in, namely, that of death. Man must have happiness or life is not worth living. In the long run, God accepts this logic, but the third term which he introduces is the death of Jesus Christ, i.e., the freedom of man by the death of Jesus Christ.

Freedom undoubtedly implies the non-satisfaction of needs that man regards as natural or essential, a non-satisfaction of passions, an insecurity, a risk, that man regards as incompatible with his happiness. We may again refer to the story of Israel. Israel has to face risks in order to bear witness to God's freedom and to advance man along the path of freedom. The story now is that of the crossing of the Jordan and the siege of Jericho. God orders the priests to take the ark on their shoulders and to move on into the river without halting. He has given no promises (Joshua 3). They must simply advance, obeying the Lord because he is the Liberator and because he liberates. When the priests enter the Jordan they run the risk of drowning, but the waters retreat before them as they advance, and when they reach the middle they stop in order that the rest of the people may pass over dry-shod.

We have here a good example of the affirmation of freedom even in relation to matter; the basis is God's freedom of order respecting his creation. But this freedom implies the acceptance of risk. It is not a situation that man would call happiness. It is the direct opposite of what we find in Israel's history in the days of the monarchy, when the great pursuit is that of security.

Under the monarchy the people wanted a king like other nations. Here we have another aspect of what man calls happiness, that of being like others, of being organized and governed like other peoples, of not being different. In its desire for a king Israel wants tranquillity and sameness rather than power. It does not want to stand out. To be happy, it wants to live like everyone else. This is obvious in the text. We also find the same stupidity as earlier in this matter of happiness. The people is prepared to let this king act like a tyrant so long as he gives it sameness and peace, and guarantees against the unpredictable.

The search for security will dictate the policies of the kings of both Judah and Israel after the rupture. The Second Book of Kings illustrates the same mechanism again and again. The kings play politics like everyone else.

They want to ensure the security and tranquillity of the people by alliances and organizations, by strengthening the power of the state, by clever shifts and maneuvers. An alliance is now made with Egypt, now with Syria, and now even with the Chaldeans, and each time to provide protection, security, and happiness, or the guarantee of happiness. The story is endlessly repeated. The alliance leads to disaster, whether by default on the part of the protecting power, or by involvement of the alliance in an unsuccessful war, or by the reduction of Israel to slavery by the ally itself. Israel, being God's people, belonging to him alone, ought in fact to live and act as a free people. It ought to accept the insecurity of freedom in God. It ought not to try to find human means of security, which may be happiness in men's eyes but which is also a negation of freedom. This is what Isaiah, Jeremiah, and Ezekiel are constantly saying in their prophecies. They show the rigorous mechanism of freedom-insecurity and security-bondage. This is why they recall what has been called the myth or ideology of the wilderness. In the desert the people was faithful and free. It obeyed God alone. It did not seek security. It did not play politics. In fact, as we have seen, the people in the wilderness was ready to give up freedom for happiness. But the prophets were not completely mistaken, for the desert was a situation of insecurity corresponding to freedom and even if the people wanted tranquillity there it could not have it. It was forced to wander, and this is a sign of freedom, since the prophets condemn settling down or taking possession as a basis of happiness. There is in fact a contradiction between the life-styles of the man who has no roots and the man who had settled down. In Palestine Israel became a settled people which was concerned only about happiness and had lost all concern for freedom.

God realized that this would happen. This is why he set at the very heart of the people a thorn of freedom in the person of the Levites. By law the Levites were not allowed any property in the promised land. They did not settle anywhere. They had to wander among the tribes. They were without homes or resources or personal income. They had to live by what was given them. God alone was their portion (Deuteronomy 10:12). They had both to be his witnesses and to live by his freedom and bounty. Every Levite had to move about and "come with all the desire of his mind unto the place which the Lord shall choose" (Deuteronomy 18:6).[6] One might say with full assurance, then, that as the Levites represent freedom in the midst of Israel, they do not take part in the happiness of Israel, i.e., in the human happiness which is modelled on that of all other men and which has as its content that which we read about in Ecclesiastes.

Finally, in relation to the contradiction between the two life-styles the Bible stresses the fact that achieved happiness destroys freedom. The Song of Moses vigorously reminds us how unfaithful happiness is: "Thou

6 The Levite, being without roots *for God*, is not like the rootless people of today's society.

art waxen fat, thou art grown thick, thou art covered with fatness; then he forsook God" (Deuteronomy 32:15). Having become fat, Israel on the one hand abandons its Liberator and on the other hand falls victim to strange gods, to idols that are not God. For the free and liberated people, who ought to be a witness to the freedom of God, happiness is thus the occasion of its losing this freedom. For always at issue here is the pursuit of happiness, not just by the natural man, but by the man who is liberated by God. Happiness is an alienation of freedom into the hands of the powers of the world, whether they be kings or idols, which in effect control what man calls happiness.

At the beginning of these deliberations on the destruction of freedom by happiness we said that the decisive thing is the pursuit and claiming and achievement of happiness at all costs. It seems to me, however, that we have now reached a point that demands independent consideration. The very grasping and achieving of happiness is itself destructive of freedom.

The only relation which God accepts is that of the man who freely acknowledges himself to be God's creature and who therefore expects and asks from God that which is good for him, i.e., his true happiness. What saves his freedom is this hand stretched out to God. Prayer is the sign of freedom.

It is this in two ways. On the one hand God gives us freedom to talk to him, to call upon him. This is an inconceivable privilege when we think about it. Indeed, God grants us the freedom to call him Father and to talk to him like a friend face to face. For in Jesus Christ a breach has been made in the impenetrability of God. We do not speak into a void which only the sound of our own voices fills.

On the other hand we acknowledge by prayer the origin and meaning of our freedom. We refer it to God (which establishes it securely) and we express the fact that freedom has no continuity except in the gift which God makes us. Hence our freedom lives in the relation of love. The moment we want to go it alone, to cease praying to God and recognizing his sovereignty, to seize and conquer, we destroy freedom.

It must not be forgotten that this is what Adam did. He disregarded God. He wanted to direct his own life. He wanted autonomy. He wanted the fruit of the tree. This attitude thrust him into the circle of determinations and included him inevitably in necessity.

It is useless to return to the fact that our freedom is an expression of God's freedom, that it is linked to him, that it is his reflection, once the link with God has been broken by our own desire for conquest and once our freedom has vanished. It should perhaps be shown, however, how this relates equally to all that we have said previously.

When man has a desire for conquest, there is a necessary incompatibility with love. For every conquest is at someone's expense. The conquest may be military, economic, or scientific. It may be the conquest of land or social success. It may be the conquest of money or cosmos. It may be the conquest of a woman or glory, of the state or freedom. The aims may differ. The conquest may be on behalf of the nation, one's own comfort, mankind, or the proletariat. The essential thing is the fact itself, the attitude of conquest, the desire to grasp and keep. But this cannot be done without scorning and crushing someone else who is an obstacle to our ambition.

All conquests are achieved along with others, i.e., members of our family, clan, nation, class, party, or church. But they are also and necessarily achieved in opposition to others, i.e., members of other families, clans, nations, classes, parties, or churches. In the former case we do not have an expression of love but of a sociological solidarity of interests. In the latter case we have division and conflict. All conquest entails a basic elimination of love.

To the extent that I destroy the freedom of others, however, I also destroy my own freedom. To use the vocabulary of Buber, to the extent that I make the other an object, so that he is no longer a Thou, I myself am not an I. Destruction of the other plunges me into fatality even though I get the impression of affirming and establishing myself by my own victory and superiority. My freedom was freedom to destroy my neighbor, just as that of Adam was the freedom to eat the fruit. But once I have destroyed him, like Adam I am under the ineluctable necessity of having to repeat the same act in order to try to regain the freedom which I am not aware of having experienced. Only one way, however, is open to me. This is the way of fresh conquest, of more destruction, of eliminating other obstacles, of following, like Adam, a way that is determined with increasing narrowness.

The moment that freedom is based on the desire for conquest, and prayer, asking, and waiting seem to be servile attitudes, at that moment freedom is the same delusion as the choice of good or evil by fallen Adam. As we noted in the Introduction, once Adam is separated from God even his determination of good is evil. In the same way, the freedom which man has achieved by conquest is intrinsically bondage.

We are not talking lightly here. We are not playing with words. We are not engaging in philosophical discussion. Revelation shows it to us and history confirms it. In human history there has never been a conquest of freedom without destruction, blood, and the enslaving of others. Always, too, the result has immediately been bondage for those who thought they were achieving liberty. The adventure of modern technology teaches the same lesson. This is the judgment on both politics and technology.

The bondage does not come merely from disregard for the others who are obstacles to our desire for conquest. It comes also from determination by the object. We have attributed a decisive, major, and incomparable importance to a certain object. Since we have a desire for conquest, what we want to conquer is, and can only be, an object. If it were a true person, it could not be, in our hearts, that on which we wish to set our hands. According to older usage, even women could be seen as "conquests." They were objects to be possessed and no shadow of the truth of humanity could find its way into the relation.

In effect, however, this attitude gives the object priority in my own conscience and existence. The trigger of my desire for conquest, the object itself, becomes the meaning of my life, the catalyst of my intelligence, the nerve of my energies, the pole of my orientation. In other words, I cease to have any other life-possibilities.

The desire for conquest puts me on a strict course that I no longer have the power to abandon. It steers me towards the object. It takes the fun out of my life and crushes me with implacable seriousness. Napoleon was totally determined by his conquests. He could not stop even though he might have wanted to do so. No one was less free than Napoleon. The same might be said of a Hitler or a Lenin. This is how it is with the desire for conquest. By riveting the object to its condition as such, we ourselves become objects. We are determined by what we desired to conquer in the foolish belief that this was an affirmation of our freedom.

We must now consider another aspect of the desire for conquest. A great number of means have to be used in its execution. One might say that the very essence of the desire for conquest is the multiplication of means. Now in our view the Bible teaches that the increase of means is destructive of freedom.[7]

This is partly because the relation increasingly becomes a mediated one. We have stressed already that love cannot be a relation of this kind. No doubt the man who justifies himself endlessly can persuade himself that the mediated relation he has with others is love. But the Bible shows us strongly the immediacy of love. Love cannot be lived out except in a direct personal relation. It is hypocrisy to think that love can be lived out through other persons or things.

We do not live out love when we preside over a committee which runs a clinic in which a great deal of good is done and the sick are helped. We do not live out love when we work hard to make social changes which will solve the problems of little children.

The more means we have, the more, then, the simplicity of the

---

7 I realize that many theologians believe that the act of freedom increases man's power and that we have no right as Christians to reject or even to be on guard against the technical means that science has put at our disposal. The time has passed, they say, when it could be thought that the increase of man's powers is an attack on God, for science has now completely displaced God. Louis Fèvre, whose *Liberté des chrétiens* is full of current platitudes, offers a good exposition of this view. Unfortunately, however, he begins by contrasting the Prometheus myth (which is hostile to progress) with the Christian conception (which is favorable to progress). As is so typical of theologians, however, he falsifies the texts here. He says that Prometheus was condemned for augmenting the power of men. This is quite wrong. Prometheus was in fact punished for invading the domain of the gods and stealing a divine power. This falsification of the Greek myth is comparable to the way in which current thought handles the biblical stories.

I-Thou relation is effaced, the more love vanishes, and the less indispensable it is as the one power that I have. Means such as money, technology, and politics give me many other powers. I can quickly help my neighbor by giving him a check or enlisting him in my party or church or finding him a place by a single telephone call. These things, however, relieve me of the commitment of love. I do not have to act as a free man in relation to another free man. "You want money from me," says Peter to the lame man. "I have no money. But what I have I give you: In the name of Jesus Christ, rise up and walk." This is the immediacy of love. It is total commitment on the part of Peter, who has only one thing and no means, who has only the love of Jesus Christ. What Peter does is a real act of liberation. He delivers the lame man from his lameness. He makes it possible for him to go where he wants. Now it might be argued that the modern surgeon does the same thing. But precisely because he uses means, there is not the same personal engagement. Hence the man might be made independent; he is not made free.

But we have dealt with this already. I now wish to emphasize another aspect. The dimension of means employed to express man negates freedom because it negates God's freedom. We have always to remember that in both the Old Testament and the New God manifests the fact that he is God by divesting the man who serves him of human means. Thus he takes the soldiers of Gideon away from him. He does not let the boy David use arms or armor. The disciples are told by Jesus not to take money or two coats. God's action always finds expression in the willed and accepted absence of human means. This is why what is done reflects God's glory. It is done by God's will through men but without means. This is why it reflects the freedom of God. God chooses the most feeble, ill-equipped, and humble man and makes him an instrument of his own work. This is why it also reflects the freedom of this man who suddenly, because he has no means, is capable of great things, of fulfilling the promises of God himself. The choice of the disciples of Jesus is a good example. Here are men without means, whether intellectual, political, social, or financial. This election is in line with the election of Israel, which was chosen because it was the smallest and weakest of all peoples.

Paul sums up this whole historical experience in the well-known passage in 1 Corinthians: "For ye see your calling, brethren, how that not many wise men after the flesh, not many mighty, not many noble, are called. . . . God hath chosen the weak things of the world to confound the things which are mighty . . . that no flesh should glory in his presence" (1:26ff.).

The problem is that the accumulation of means and the increase of technology can only serve, as we now see, to glorify man before God. It cannot be argued that this is not necessary, that things might be different. It is in fact absolutely and unavoidably necessary and obligatory. I do not base this conclusion on experience or philosophy. I base it on the totality of God's word.

Every glorification of man is a rejection of God. By the accumulation of means the freedom of God is negated. This negation, however, also suppresses our own freedom.

This strange spiritual logic, which overthrows human logic, alone explains what it happening to us today. Our world is driven by the spirit of conquest. This is its only spirit. In consequence it has heaped up means in the form of technology. A simplistic view lets us think that the more man acquires knowledge, power, dominion, and consumer goods, the more free he will be. The more he *has,* the more he will *be.* The more means he has at his disposal, the greater will be his freedom. Our present society, however, is in the process of learning the direct opposite. The more the means of action increase, the more man's inner and outer freedom diminishes. As technology becomes more rigorous, freedom is increasingly buried under the accumulation of means.

This experience, which is a living illustration of what is said in God's word, shows how vain and foolish is the attitude of the intellectual Christian who is dedicated to the political struggle for the liberation of the poor but who thinks that the development of more powerful organizations and the finding of more effective means is the only way to do it. Unwittingly he is simply repeating the classical middle-class attitude: "We have our assurance in God, but to put this into effect let us form an assurance company." Christians who are committed to the third world or the working class are doing precisely the same thing and in so doing they are at once destroying all possibility of real action and liberation.

Here, then, is the implacable spiritual law which, revealed in scripture, offers the key to the incomprehensible developments of our own time. In relation to what is done by natural man it is normal enough. But when it is done by men who are freed by Christ and who are called upon to take up their freedom, when such men engage in an accumulation of means, we have a new alienation. They makes themselves the slaves of men and powers afresh.

In opposition to secular logic, which thinks that freedom increases with the augmentation of means, but in conformity with real life, as a sociological analysis of technology shows, scripture makes it plain that the growth of means is always and intrinsically, not just accidentally, a suppression of freedom.

# Chapter 3

# The Historical
# Responsibility of Christians[1]

All that I have said thus far about the need to take up the freedom that Christ has won for us seems to have an individual aspect. When we talked about recognition and justification, we were obviously dealing with individual phenomena. Freedom is indeed an individual act and life-style. There is no collective freedom and Christ has not liberated man or mankind in general. Yet it would be a serious mistake to think that we have here only an individual matter which concerns and interests the individual alone. It would be a grave error to think that we are independent of others, that we are free to take up this freedom or not, and that we alone have to suffer the consequences. What I want to show now is that, while the act of the Christian who takes up his freedom does not have to have collective consequences, the decision of the Christian (even if it be only by default) not to take up his freedom does have collective consequences and that historically these have been very tragic.

Taking up freedom is indeed a personal act. No one can do it for his neighbor. But the man who is called by Christ is called upon to love. To love means not to be able to think of oneself in isolation but only in relation to others. Because all Christians are called upon to love, there is (or should be) between them a unique reciprocity and rapport with which no other in the whole world can be compared, namely, that of love. And because they stand in this relation, because there is this unlimited mutual love of which the only other instance is the love of Jesus Christ, there thus exists a common reality which is the church. But this reality also has a collective human dimension. It is a human grouping. This means that every decision of a Christian also engages the whole body and has repercussions on all society.

For the church is an element in every society. It is good that this should be so, i.e., that the church should not have a disincarnate life. The church is a social body which has to be marked by a unique sign. Hence every Christian decision is necessarily individual in origin and execution but also necessarily collective in its reference and consequences. There is no escaping this. The consequence of my Christian life is not my salvation but

---

1 In this chapter I am much indebted to the great work of B. Charbonneau, *Le mensonge de la liberté.*

the orientation of all the groups within which I live, of the society in which I find myself, and in some sense of the world as a whole.

## §1. Positive Responsibility

We may be very brief on this subject, for essentially it is the theme that we shall have to develop in Part IV of this ethics of freedom. We shall thus confine ourselves to a more precise definition of some preliminary matters.

We recall first that our free action does not leave the natural man or the world indifferent. We continually find in Christians a false humility, or hypocrisy, that what they do is of no interest to men. Paul, however, tells us that the eyes of men are in fact on us.

Even in a non-Christian society we may be sure that every act on the part of Christians is observed, evaluated, and analyzed. Probably because the word is so lofty and the witness so striking, the eyes of others are necessarily fixed on men who speak these things and claim to live thus even in an ancient Christian civilization, while the same is true in a secularized society because men are impatiently awaiting this declaration of pardon, of the meaning of life, and of the possibility of the Wholly Other. We must not deceive ourselves; the eyes of *all* men are fixed on us.

Non-Christians are often such because they are able to say: "Look, their lives and acts are just like our own. They do not correspond in the least to what they are saying." Our own way of life is itself, then, a counterwitness.

It might be said, of course, that this is a mere excuse for not following the Christian way. I grant this. Nevertheless, it is a real excuse that we ourselves provide for them.

Now if we understand that freedom is the life-style of the Christian life as such, then it is on Christian freedom first that the eyes of men will be fixed. Paul speaks of men who spy out the liberty that we have in Christ (Galatians 2:4). I believe that it is with this intensity that the conflict arises. We are being spied upon.

Paul also says, of course, that the aim of this spying is to bring us back into bondage, i.e., to bring accusations against those who practice freedom and to bring them back under servitude to the law. Nevertheless, spying may also be for the purpose of finding out whether we are genuinely free or not. This is a matter of supreme importance. Whatever may be a man's theories and conditions of life, whatever may be his ignorance of God or disobedience or estrangement or distance from God, he may fear freedom and even deny it, but he cannot do without it. Freedom is an unfathomable necessity. Man aspires to it, or claims to aspire to it, with all his being.

We have said already that at the most humble and most direct level man cannot stand having a master. He cannot stand being a slave or prisoner. He demands independence. He has to break his chains and flee. In these terms the word freedom evokes many associations and leaves no man indifferent. If it has no specific content, it has emotional power. It can stir into action. Man can always be roused in the name of liberty. He believes that he cannot be anything but free.

At the same time we have said that man cannot stand freedom. He hates it. There is no contradiction here. For he wants neither the condition of freedom (recognizing necessity and constant questioning) nor its consequences (risk, reduced happiness). When the implications of true freedom are seen, man flees and hides. For man is an alienated slave, far from God. When Adam, who had become the slave of his own knowledge of good and evil, heard freedom coming from God, he hid. The deep mark of his alienation is this inner division. He has an invincible attraction to freedom but he has a sacred dread of living in freedom. He resolves the contradiction by finding substitutes, e.g., political independence, immorality, disdain for others, economic freedom, or free thought. He has to have and hold and possess freedom; he will not be possessed by it or accept the responsibility it imposes. He wants a span of freedom even though freedom cannot perpetuate itself. He wants a situation or nature when freedom is in fact neither the one nor the other and cannot be worked out as either. Freedom is not a gift of the environment.

Man cannot tolerate true freedom. He knows only its impossibility. This is the reason why he notes and watches the one who talks about freedom. Because Christ has brought freedom into the world, those who profess him and live by his freedom have to be bearers of freedom into the world. They are for other men not just models but also witnesses to the fact that this freedom which man claims that he wants does actually exist and has become possible. They must also be those who undermine the pseudo-freedom of the structures and institutions of the world.

With all humility and prudence we have to say that Christians are the *only* bearers of freedom. It must be stressed again that this implies neither privilege nor superiority. It does not rest on their own person. The freedom in question is that of Jesus Christ. The individual Christian is of no account in and for himself. He is chosen, however, to show that this freedom is not just an inner spiritual matter. It is a general and universal matter. It is destined to overthrow society through the conduct of freed individuals.

When we say that Christians are the *only* bearers of freedom, this means that what others call freedom is never more than a substitute and fabrication.

An important decision has to be made here. Between the world and the kingdom of God, is there continuity or discontinuity? Between Christ as God and Jesus as the incarnation of Christ, is there continuity or discontinuity? Between the cross and the resurrection, is there continuity or discontinuity? Between Eden, where Adam was created, and the world in which we now live, is there continuity or discontinuity?

In the former case, all men's works as such, even though man does not know it, prepare the way for God's kingdom. They are as such prophecies of what God has in mind. *Eros* is a sign or prophecy of *agape.* What man calls justice, goodness, and freedom is a sign or prophecy of what God reveals as his own justice, will, and freedom. Man's religion is a sign and prophecy of revelation in Christ.

We own belief, however, as I have already stated, is that there is discontinuity. What man manufactures in these areas is illusion and self-justification, a means of escaping judgment and grace. As I see it, then, what man calls freedom is not a small part of the way to true freedom in Christ. It is not a beginning, a preparation, an intimation, or a reflection of authentic freedom. It is the very opposite.

To say this, however, is not to say that we simply have good on the one side and bad on the other. Such a division would imply that Christians have effectively taken up their freedom and that man has refused the freedom which is now visible to him. We are not saying that the ways of freedom that man has outlined for himself are to be shunned, for the Christian, like Christ himself, has to accompany man on the paths that he has chosen. We are not saying that the illusory effort that man calls freedom is to be regarded as nugatory. It is not nugatory, for it is illusory and a power of evil. It is not nugatory, for it too is set under the grace of God, and ultimately, when God has destroyed the world in judgment, he will take all that man has attempted by way of freedom, and receive, transform, and remodel it. The corruptible flesh will put on incorruptibility.

Nevertheless, on earth Christians *alone* can live out and bear witness to authentic freedom. If and when they do not, men have a right to call whatever they like freedom. There is no freedom on earth. When, however, Christians take this path they are not to expect miracles. Freedom will not be clear and evident and incontestable on earth because they assume it.

At this point we come up in an especially forceful way against one of the characteristics of Christian ethics. If Christians do not live out what Christ has given them to live out, we do not merely have their own disobedience but also an absence, void, or lack which affects all men. If, however, they do live it out, the results are not very imposing. Life is not changed in any very evident way. What Christians can express seems negligible to men.

When Christians take up their freedom, this does not have the clarity of a thousand suns. On the contrary, no matter what precautions are taken or what audacity is shown, we always have a confused and ambiguous situation. There are no obvious consequences that all can see and none can dispute. For the freedom is lived out in a world of necessity and alienation. It does not speak directly to man, for man does not know in truth what freedom is. As we have said, he is afraid of it. That sacred dread prevents him from receiving the witness to freedom. He thus finds refuge in ambivalence.

It is always possible to attribute to human acts various meanings and motivations. So as not to see freedom, man fastens on explanations of this type. This mechanism, which is a system of self-justification for not accepting the witness, can work in different ways. Some might think that Christians in their freedom are a little mad. Intellectuals will want to psychoanalyze them and discover their "motivations." Without judging whether or not Kierkegaard was a Christian living in the freedom of Christ, for Christians are not to judge one another, we may recall the enormous amount of interpretative material that clusters around his life and work. Some have tried to explain his acts in terms of a traumatic childhood. Others have tried to explain his work apart from the reference to Christ which he himself made so clearly in his own self-explanation. When Christian freedom is lived out, then, it is not received as such by men.

This means that we are not to expect collective consequences from the living out of Christian freedom. If the absence of this freedom does have collective consequences both social and political, the presence of this freedom does not appear to change anything in society. The work, if there is a work, is done underground in the collective sub-consciousness. It does not manifest itself in such a way that one can say: Look at Christian freedom in action. As is the normal lot of Christians in all aspects of their lives as such, we are thus faced with an austere work which carries no visible recompense and offers no palpable satisfaction on earth. The entire work of freedom can only dash itself against the wall of incomprehension, refusal, and judgment.

### §2. Negative Responsibility[2]

We now enter a sphere which arouses some apprehension since it contains an implicit philosophy of history and seems to indict Christians— the Christians we are trying to be—in a far more basic way than all individual confessions of sin or all proclamations of collective responsibility in relation to war and so forth.

The first truth that one has to accept—and it was felt very strongly by the first generation of Christians, much less so today—is that the incarnation of Christ, his coming to earth, has effectively changed human history. It is not just a spiritual event. It has effectively changed human history. Nor has it done this merely by introducing a new ideology, nor setting in motion a new religious trend, nor instituting a historically determined religious society (the church), nor giving the west a particular conception of society. These things are obvious but they are also very superficial. What I have in view is that Jesus Christ has set up a new relation between man and

---

2 Apart from Charbonneau, Käsemann is, I think, the only one who has shown that in effect freedom comes from Jesus Christ and later generations have not taken up this freedom.

society and also between man and nature, which has been implanted in the world and cannot be taken out of it, since he was the Son of God.[3]

In other words Christians have not themselves invented and progressively imposed this. We do not have here a mere movement of ideas. What has caused the mutation is the momentous event of God on earth. It is not the disciple who makes Christ what he is. It is not the faith of the disciple which sets the historical movement going. Behind it is the historical fact of the breaking of the barrier between God and man. A bridge has been built between the absolute and the relative, the eternal and the temporal (inadequate as these terms are). God in his totality has localized himself in flesh—an incredible mystery in spite of all the efforts of the new theology to explain that the problem has been badly put. This fact alone, as a fact and not just a belief, has cut history in two, launched man on an endless venture, and definitively exposed his situation.[4]

The incarnation has shone a ruthless light on the artificial unity that man has established, or tried to establish, in compensation for his break with God. The fall brought man into the universe of necessity, where he has formed a system which is both necessary and unitary. The city, which is its symbol, is a world of men enclosed in walls wherein the population is necessarily grouped and has an automatic solidarity. Man also has a unity with nature. He is in nature and belongs to it. He has links with the animals. Similarly he is included in his society. He cannot be distinguished from it. He *is* the social group. What binds him to other men is much more than a contingent relation of distinct beings integrated into the same group. It is no mere question of love or freedom.

Naturally I am not saying that men and women do not love. I am not saying that there is no personalism or impulsion towards freedom. Even among the Greeks, however, everything is included in the primary virtue of the city, in the relation with a system of satisfying and balanced institutions in which each man has his own place. There is a basic accord between the individual and the group. Conflict between them is unthinkable, for

---

3 Freedom has come into the world in Jesus Christ. But the foundations were already laid in Israel. For the God of Israel was the Liberator. Furthermore, as von Rad has clearly shown, the individual for the first time took a central place in Israel, a place which prior to the prophets had been unknown in the ancient orient and even in Israel itself. In immediate encounter with God and his plans for history, the normal conscience could develop to a point of intensity never attained in daily life. The discovery of the individual is the condition of freedom. Man finds himself as an individual in encounter with God. In Christ this encounter becomes a possibility for all—a possibility which is constantly acquired, constantly renewed, and eternally decided.

4 Auerbach has shown that freedom in Christ rules out tragedy. All tragedy was contained in the tragedy of Christ. Apart from this, there is no more tragedy, for it is by the tragedy of Christ that man can enter into freedom. All human tragedy was simply the logic or reflection of a single complex of events towards which it necessarily moved. This is what gives man the widest possible freedom.

each takes meaning from the other, and in the equilibrium there is uncontested blossoming. There is continuity between nature, society, and man.

Now what is declared in the Old Testament is precisely a negation of this continuity. The world in which man has set himself is destined to break up because it is not the world to which God has called man. One may no doubt speak of the innocence of pagans. The pagan has no consciousness of sin. He does not feel good or bad. He attributes evil to superior powers that are evil. He is in harmony with his own life. What the Old Testament announces is a break within man, disruption of the harmony, disturbance of the good conscience, the existence of the bad in him. It does not proclaim happiness. Possibly the pagan has a greater aptitude for happiness. What the Old Testament declares is that equilibrium, continuity, unity, and happiness are an expression of man's basic slavery and profound and hopeless alienation.

Now what the Old Testament declares has been accomplished, actualized, and lived out once and for all by Christ. Christ is the sign of contradiction which provokes divisions. The unity which man has created in society is broken because it has been re-established by God. The continuity between man and nature is shattered because man regains this unique position as the creature ordained to direct creation, which is put in his hands as an object. Suffering and death are no longer denied or mythicized. They are squarely faced. They are assumed by God himself. They are accepted as grace and promise.

Christ carries freedom to its limit by affirming in the world, among men and for men, the radical transcendence of truth, carried to its limit by Jesus, and also a perfectly clear and realistic recognition, with no false appearances, of the human reality called sin, poverty, and suffering, carried to its limit by Christ.

The misery of man is now taken up into God. The movement thus initiated seems to be the very opposite of anything that man might imagine. With the resurrection of Christ, we see life issuing from death. This is true at every level. Faith issues from doubt, knowledge from mystery, eternity from time, and freedom from bondage, not automatically, but by the sovereignly free intervention of grace and love. For, in order to manifest that man's existence is not absurd, God takes charge of evil and death.

If, however, love unites, this is because it distinguishes. In spite of all the debates about the Trinity, it is a basic truth that if God is love in himself he is self-distinguished. One loves what is distinct or differentiated from oneself. If, then, the law of love is totally formulated by Christ, this is because his presence brings divisions.

At the biblical level, to take a very simple example, Jesus says that if a man will not leave his father, his mother, etc. he is not worthy to be a disciple (the movement of division), but also that the man who will do this will receive fathers, mothers, etc. a hundredfold (the movement of love). We must be on guard lest love simply adds an innocuous good to a world which is a little bad but which we have to humanize and make a better place to live in. Christ is in reality the terrible presence of God of whom it is said that if he puts his foot on the earth the mountains will tremble, the rivers will dry up, the hills will be shattered, and the ground will open up. There is truth to these metaphors. The presence of Christ among men has literally shaken institutions, states, groups, and human relations. All that man has civilized, normalized, and unified (in separation from God) is called in question. What was thought to be order is now seen as bondage, what was called peace is now seen as constraint, what was called right is now seen as injustice, what was called religion is now seen as falsehood, what was called nature is now seen as artifice, what were called gods are now seen as illusion.

Thus the presence of Christ makes life completely unlivable, radically vitiates civilization, and renders society wholly untenable.

One thing alone remains. This is love. The relation of love now replaces all others, i.e., those of flesh and blood. It replaces all man's other possibilities of living and communicating.

We have to realize that the situation is not under our own control. One might gain the impression from the Gospels that everything depends on the decision man takes, and that this is an individual matter, as though there were a solid and stable order which remains intact, and man can leave this order, accepting other values and living according to another order. Some parables seem to support this, e.g., that of the treasure hid in a field, or the grain of mustard seed sown in the earth. The field or earth remains, i.e., the world, but within it there is now something extra which is hidden and secret.

Now it is true that the world as world remains intact even in its separation from God, even in its revolt and refusal. Man as the creature who has broken with God remains the same. Furthermore, this man's recognition of God's love and salvation is indeed an individual matter. Nevertheless, something changes. This is the totality of collective securities that man has set up in his separation from God.

The whole balanced system of powers, cultures, religions, magic, production, cities and commerce, all this, without God, was an order that man had set up in many different forms, in the Chinese and Aztec empires, in Greek cities and stone-age villages. It was a livable order for man. It was an order in which he could be comfortable. But the incarnation, objectively, destroys it.

From now on man can no longer be comfortable in these forms, for no less than God himself has come. The walls of his cities are all as open now as those of Babel. Man no longer has any cover. His right has become manifestly unjust, since it is an affront to absolute righteousness. The whole reality is called in question, since in Christ the real has been put in contact with the truth in such a way that the real and the true are no longer intact. Man can no longer reconstruct an order which will be satisfying to him. There will always be uneasiness and failure. We shall not see again the fine structures of the Egyptians and the Cretans, the Greeks and the Hindus. We shall not see again a perfectly integrated human order in which man finds himself in an order cut exactly to suit himself. The complex and integrative society of an earlier age has been shattered. Harmony and equilibrium can no longer exist.

Similarly, a kind of malaise has come into human relations, for since the incarnation man is no longer just a man. Between two men there is always now a third presence. There is always dislocation and misunderstanding. Communications which since Babel man has patiently restored and reorganized are no longer in tune or meaningful. They have been devalued by the presence of another sign, a new meaning which cannot be inserted into any human system of communication.

If everything has been changed in this way since the time of primitive societies and ancient empires,[5] the change has not come about naturally and spontaneously with the passage of time. It is not purely historical. Nor is it due to technological progress. A far more profound and instantaneous break has taken place. It took place on the day of the incarnation. This has to be taken seriously. If it is true that God himself has come, does this not mean necessarily that everything has changed?

By way of objection reference might be made to the divine secret and incognito. Now if there had been no secret and incognito the world would have come to an end. But in the secret and incognito the presence was strong enough to break all the old wineskins. They did in fact break. The veil of the temple was torn. This is an indication that one of the most essential foundations of ancient civilization, the rigorous separation of the secular and the sacred, had been ended.

Through the incarnation, then, the world and human society became chaotic. They were genuinely plunged into chaos. For the old relations, foundations, and habits, however, Christ substitutes new ones, those of love and freedom. In this chaotic society everything becomes livable and possible if man will act as a completely free man who takes up his freedom, if he will act towards others exclusively according to love.

The new order, that of the Beatitudes, makes society perfectly livable and possible. It is not even necessary (for there is no idealism in the teaching of Jesus) that all men without exception should live according to love and freedom. But this freedom has to be present and incarnate. This love has to be the bond of all things and a lived out ministry. When this is so, everything is possible again. The ancient order is not restored, but we have a society of a new kind. Love replaces the former order, justice, and communication. There is no love, however, without freedom. Freedom

---

5 Naturally I am not glorifying the past here. This is not the point. I am well aware of the famines, massacres, and general misery of past societies. But there was still an incontestable harmony between the individual and the group. There was still a human order which ethnology constantly echoes.

alone makes the new society livable. Only the free man can continue to live in a world in which there is no longer a distinction between the secular and the sacred. I do not say, of course, that the abolition of this classification makes man free. What I am saying is that man has to take up his freedom if he is to maintain himself in a world which is no longer oriented to this classification.

Again, the free man can continue to live in a world whose ethics and values have been so radically called in question as to be almost unworkable, or at least relativized in such a manner that man can no longer build his life on them. Here again I do not say that the destruction of morality in Christ makes man free. What I am saying is that once the destruction has taken place only the man who takes up freedom can live.

Again, only the free man can survive in a world which runs the risk at any time of returning to disorder, to chaos. This implies control, the possibility of choice and relative reorganization as this society deteriorates, a capacity for improvisation and restoration. Man is no longer living in a finished and given society. He is living in a society in the making which has continually to be started again.

Again and finally, for I could multiply examples, only the man who takes up his freedom can live in a society in which the integration of man has been broken. Only he can both live in this society and cause it to live too. For when society is no longer integrated, when the former relation between man and the group no longer obtains, relations necessarily have to be improvised relations. They have to be new relations between free men who act towards one another as such. In other words, the old system which men invented in order to survive (as they did) has to be replaced by a new system which God inaugurates in Christ and all whose structures and elements rest on the love and freedom lived out by man.

There is no middle ground. There is no mixture. There are no loose ends. The old system has in fact been destroyed and devalued. We can no more return to it than we can return to Eden. To do so would be to bypass the incarnation, to act as though it had never taken place. The break at this point is a thousand times more radical than that of the technical and industrial revolution of the modern age. The platitude that eighteenth-century man still lived like man in the B.C. era, and that the real break came through industry, may be true enough at the purely material level. But the incarnation changed life much more radically. Living within the structures of antiquity became impossible. Only the new way opened up by Christ is possible for man if society is to be livable and man is to be able to live in it.

But supposing this is impossible? For society there are then two possibilities between which the world has constantly vacillated since Jesus Christ. The first is in an incoherent and anarchical individualism, a mortal struggle between individuals and groups, the elimination of the weak, the disorder which is confused with liberty. The second is totalitarianism, calculated and deliberate external constraint, which crushes the individual, not achieving support but proceeding by violence and manipulation, so that the individual is artificially integrated into a collective. These are the two alternatives for society after the incarnation if man refuses the newly opened way of love and freedom which allows both society and man to exist.

Man is thus summoned to live in some sort as a free man. He is thus caught in a profound dilemma. He cannot ignore this freedom. He cannot refuse it. It is freedom that keeps him standing. It is implicitly because he wants to be a free man that he can say: "I am . . ." He cannot evade wanting to be free even though he does not know precisely what this entails. He is scandalized when science tells him that he is not free. He revolts when the police prevent him from being free. Nevertheless, he also runs up against the impossibility of accepting a freedom which is too much for him and is a burden to him. He cannot stand a life of permanent risk and responsibility. Even though he wants to be free, he cannot stand too full a recognition of his determinations. He cannot stand the contradiction, which is of the very essence of freedom, between too lofty, pure, and demanding an imperative and too clearly perceived and experienced a burden. This freedom, which is the only authentic freedom, is just as intolerable for him as its absence.

Man is thus faced with a dilemma of far more serious difficulty than any that existentialism has ever been able to describe. Because he does not choose the risk of freedom, he involves the society in which he lives in an incoherent and meaningless history. For in spite of Marx and others, history itself, the real history of historians and not the abstract, theoretical, and imaginary history of Hegel and the philosophers, has no meaning.

It is here that after a long detour we come up against the specific and decisive responsibility of Christians. We have just said that for society to be livable and to have a real history it is not necessary that all men without exception should live in love and take up freedom. All that is needed is that this should be done at all. As faith need be only like a grain of mustard seed, so love and freedom need be only like a grain of mustard seed for society to be already transformed.

Now we can understand why the man who has not met Christ should flee in horror from this freedom which is too much for him when he finds out what it really is, when he unveils the face of truth and abandons his imaginary dream of freedom. But what about the Christian? The Christian *is* freed or liberated. He does not have to take the impossible first step of advance into freedom. He has not created his own freedom by self-emancipation, which is, as we have seen, impossible.

Furthermore, the freedom which he has to live out is not a blank. It is not uncertain. The difficulty of being in freedom is in large measure spared him because he is not launched into a kind of vacuum. On the road of freedom he is accompanied by Jesus Christ. He knows that it is possible to live as a free man. This has been given to him and it has also been demonstrated by Jesus Christ. In this life he also has the support and inspiration of the Holy Spirit. All the resources of the Spirit are available for Christians as they launch into this venture—resources which are not available for others.

Finally the thing is not only possible; it is also necessary. The Christian is set in a position of responsibility before men as well as God, for it is Jesus Christ himself who in his incarnation has put the world in the situation of destruction to which we have referred, and who thus forces man up against the wall: Either you live by love and freedom, which will make the life of society possible and establish a new civilization, or finally there will be no livable human society or culture.

Jesus Christ has put men in this dilemma, and as the Christian professes Jesus Christ and becomes a member of Christ's body it is he who is responsible before men for the impasse and he who for and with all must live out freedom in order that society may be livable and civilization may be possible.

The Christian has to accept the consequences of his profession of Christian faith. It is not enough for him to say: "Since I have faith, I am saved and I now have to live out the Christian virtues." He has to be ready to say: "Since I have faith, I am also responsible for the presence of the Spirit among men. I am responsible for making possible the human city which according to the will of Jesus Christ will be a city of love and freedom, and which is not possible in any other way."

There can certainly be no question here of trying to set up a Christian organization nor of helping forward the constructive efforts of other men by adding a grain of Christian salt. The mistake is to think that men can build their own world, that this is good before God, and that Christians have simply to add love and freedom. In reality this is an idle dream and involves a new attempt at civilization which will fail like others.

We must now take a further step. Paul tells us that the knowledge of revelation is a "sweet savor of Christ, in them that are saved, and in them that perish: to the one the savor of death unto death, and to other the savor of life unto life" (2 Corinthians 2:14-16). This is a text that is not greatly liked. It reminds us that nothing here is neutral. The positive force of the gospel is a negative force as well when it is refused. To refuse the gospel is not just to make a dead letter of it. The man who refuses it does not remain unaffected. He does not just turn aside, leaving revelation where he has dropped it. Revelation is a power, and if it is not received and incarnated it is a power of destruction. We have to accept this truth of the totality of the content of the gospel, especially of its freedom.

This brings us to the crucial point in our responsibility. If the freedom which is brought to earth by Christ is taken up by Christians, it becomes a positive force for all men. But if it is not incarnated, lived out, and taken up, it becomes a terrible force of destruction. Again, one cannot say quite simply and calmly: "Ah well, if Christians do not live by freedom, so much the worse for them. There is no freedom, that is all."

Unfortunately, there is freedom. The work that Jesus Christ has accomplished on earth *has been* accomplished. The cross of Jesus *has been* planted on the earth and nothing can change this, even if it is not believed. Freedom is there, but if it is not received by men, if it is not incarnated, it becomes a devastating force. We can illustrate this from history.

The fact of the freedom that Christ has brought to earth has made possible the totality of what men call progress. Christ has desacralized nature and shown how men can effectively use a creation that is still in their hands. He has put man back in a world which was handed over to him.[6]

Christ himself is the new Adam who governs nature and whom things obey. His desacralizing has given man the courage to tackle nature, to wrest its secrets from it, and to turn it fully to his own use and profit, so that science and technology have developed.

Naturally, the movement did not take place all at once. In particular the great desacralization of the reformation had to come before the possibility opened up by Christ could be effectively grasped by man.

If, however, Christ destroyed false sacralizing powers, this was not in order to make his Father's creation an indifferent object that man can use in any way he likes. It presupposed the coherent and harmonious transformation of man himself.

In the mind of Christ the new relation could not be one of force or exploitation as concerns nature. It could be only a relation of freedom. That is to say, nature ceased to be hostile to man. It was no longer closed and wild. It was no longer peopled with spirits and fairies. It was no longer a prohibited area. For a man who took up freedom and lived it out as we have described, i.e., in orientation to love and God's glory, there could now be respect for nature and a humble recognition of the freedom of this creation.

This presupposes, however, that man takes up his freedom. In fact he has not done so. From this time on, then, nature has been a mere object commanding neither respect nor love. From this time on the great venture of science and technology has been possible: the separation of the world from the love of God, the penetrating of its secrets by methods of unheard of violence, pure and simple rape, limitless exploitation for the sake of money or power and to satisfy man's most brutal and ridiculous passions, regulated depletion to the point of exhaustion, and the extinction of entire animal species and every kind of natural wealth.

Freedom has been unleashed then, but negatively. It has become the

---

6 This is not in contradiction with what I said earlier, namely, that Christ's work has not changed the situation of man in nature and that this work is lived out only by the man who believes. What follows will resolve the apparent contradiction.

savor of death, for Christians have shown neither the will, the knowledge, nor the courage to take up their freedom, and they have thus permitted by default all the consequences of technology and all the results of a freedom in which they have no part.

An extraordinary inversion is to be noted here. Science is the product of freedom. It is free. It declares its autonomy. In so doing it is simply being true to its origin in Christ. But what it discovers can be summed up essentially as determinisms or laws. It is a tragedy to find that the world and man are subject to determinisms, to see that everything has to be, and that only scientific research itself is free!

If man had lived out the freedom of Christ, he would have been effectively liberated from the determinisms that science has discovered. This is one of the liberations of which we have spoken. But man did not take up this freedom. If he had done so, he could have faced squarely the determinisms, causalities, and necessities that science has discovered, and there would have been a precise equilibrium between free man and the world of necessity in which he lives. But once man fails to take up and live out the freedom of Christ, he sees only these "fatalities."

This is intolerable, however, for, as we have said, man can think of himself only as a free being. He wants to be free. He thus projects on science that which he does not live out for himself, namely, his freedom. In hypocritical self-justification, he claims that science frees him (when in fact it does the very opposite) and that it can discover not only reality but also truth. This leads to incredible confusion between science and spirit, between the works of science and the work of freedom. In this flight man turns his back deliberately both on the freedom of Christ and on the reality unveiled by science. He thus shuts himself up in his own cell. By describing as freedom what is only fatality he loses himself in a labyrinth of bondage.

The same thing happens in relation to the state. The work of Christ has desacralized society and power as well as nature. Christ demonstrates his sovereign independence of authority in the story of the coin and the tax. To be sure, the tax should be paid with a coin taken from the jaws of a fish. There is a grim humor in the story so far as the significance and seriousness of authorities are concerned. The freedom of Christ puts the powers in their place as mere administrators of earthly things which are legitimate but no more.

Hence the importance of society and the value of power undergo a radical reduction. Jesus lived in a world in which cities and empires were the things that counted. They had to be given a religious meaning, basis, and value. The gates of the city were consecrated and the king was a god. But Jesus smashes all that. Society is not sacred for him. It is not impregnated with religion. This is perhaps a point of conflict with the Jews too, for the temple and the Jewish authorities are also desacralized. For Jesus power is nothing in itself. Pilate is accorded no power in himself.

Serious confusion has arisen about the saying to Pilate: "Thou couldest have no power at all against me, except it were given thee from above" (John 19:11). This does not mean that Pilate *has* the power. It is *given* to him. It comes from another and belongs to another. The power does not reside in Pilate. He does not possess it or control it. Jesus, affirming the rigorous transcendence of God, breaks the integration between religion and politics. The fact that all power comes from God does not mean that the powers have a religious character or that power has a divine character or basis. Quite the contrary! The powers are not God nor is God in the powers. The fact that power "comes from above" implies distance and difference. This means that power as such is secular and in every sense human, relative, and secondary.

What we have here, then, is the opposite of the other saying of Jesus: "My kingdom is not of this world" (John 18:36). This is undoubtedly the most stupendous negation of all that pre-Christian societies were trying to do. It is an expression of freedom in politics. Man can be free because politics is not divine. Man cannot regard politics as essential even though he is subject to it and recognizes that it "comes from" God.

Society is likewise desacralized. As Jesus sees it, the social structure has no sacred character. There is no sacred order comparable to the taboos and sacral structures of primitive societies. The social hierarchy is not sacred. Prostitutes do not come under sacral laws nor do priests enjoy sacral respect. Hence man is in a society that he can manipulate, utilize, and alter.

In exactly the same way he is face to face with a political power which is only human. This power is uncertain and subject to variation. It can be criticized and changed. Man must obey it, but this duty comes from God. He must also pray for it, not because the power is divine, but precisely because it is so human and therefore stands in need of prayer. Kings and magistrates are not God. They are not divine. They are not even representatives of God. They are God's servants, but only as all men are called upon to be. We thus have a kind of secularization of the state.

This is livable and possible, however, only if man takes up his freedom in Christ. This is true in three ways. First it is only as he takes up this freedom that he can regard power as useful secondary organization, but no more, since he needs no divine guide to dictate and orient his conduct; his freedom in Christ teaches him what to do in the social body. But secondly this freedom is the limit which is imposed on the state, which desacralizes it, which brings it about, and does so continually, that power is not religious. Finally, this freedom establishes the state, for, as in all relations between superior and inferior, in God's mind, as we have already noted, everything depends on the obedience of the inferior and not on the authority of the superior. For God, then, it is freedom which leads me to obey the state. This is the only motive. My freedom corresponds to an obedience, as we have seen in the case of Jesus. This obedience of supreme freedom is thus the basis of the state.

But what if Christians do not take up their freedom? There then takes place what we have seen. The desacralized, "dereligionized" state becomes autonomous, rational, and totalitarian. Being no longer subject to the divine order which was integrated into it, it obeys its own law and intention and has in itself the principle and meaning of its own will. No longer having any secret, it obeys only the rationality of power, growth, external order, and excess. Being no longer tied to a divine element that conducts, measures, orders, and limits it, it becomes totalitarian.

I am aware that the objection will be made that all ancient societies were totalitarian. What could be worse than the Pharaohs' Egypt, or Assyria, or the kingdom of the Incas? There is truth here, but it should be remembered that the totalitarian element in these states is the divine order, or the integration of politics into the divine. The absolute element is the god who is in the king. Politics as such is not totalitarian because it has no real existence as such. The desacralization and secularization of power have not yet taken place. Since religion is totalitarian, political power does not have to be.

Once the break comes about, however, power becomes the abstract, authoritarian, and absolute state unless it comes up against the free man. The state absorbs religion. It reduces it to subjection. It commandeers and uses it. And by the same inversion as we have seen in the case of science, man calls the state itself his freedom.

For now that Christ has come man can no longer ignore his freedom. It has become for him an ideal and a reason for living. But if, even as a Christian, he does not take it up, he invests that which enslaves him with the very name of that which is necessary to him. This autonomous and absolute power will be the guarantee of his freedom, or the organizer of his liberties, or by way of intermediary individuals that which wins freedom for him. As Tito has put it so well: "The socialist state is the only protector of liberties, so that the more authoritarian it is, the more freedom there is." In fact, since man assimilates science and the state to freedom along these lines, it is science and the state which most surely destroy freedom.

We may now take a third example. This is respect for human personality. Here again it is Christ who has established respect for man on earth at the same time as he has given him freedom. We have to consider how these two things are related. It is because man is free that he has to respect others. His freedom permits him to ignore all differences, all social barriers, and all the divisions of race and opinion. Freedom in Christ permits him to take the other in his truth before God.

This freedom, as we have seen, is on behalf of others. It is oriented to and by love. It can be lived out only in love. Freedom in Christ is never a chance to crush others. On the contrary, it is the soil on which there may blossom a reciprocity of truth and not of mere appearance, exculpation, and falsehood.

In this freedom you have thus to respect the other. You cannot oppress him or neglect him. Since you are yourself free with this freedom, you can only live out this freedom in relation to the other. For him, you can only be a true Thou. You can only accept being the neighbor to whom he comes and whom he helps, and whom he thus respects in return.

Since Christ has come what there is to respect in man is not that he is the creature of God. It is not that he has a native dignity which belongs to him. It is not even that Christ dwells in him, as some Christians say. This is no doubt true. It is indeed completely true, but the basic problem still remains: How does this work out concretely? Well, the outworking in conduct and ethics must be that of freedom. It is service, and, as we have already seen, service implies the freedom of him who serves, or else it is servitude.

Freedom has to be recognized in and for the other. He has to be given an area of freedom. This is what it means to respect Christ in him. But what happens if the Christian does not take up his freedom? It has still been planted in the heart of man as a need that cannot be suppressed. So, then, man will try to secure it in his own way. He will pretend that he does not have to receive it from God or live it out in Christ, since Christians are not doing this. He will try to grasp it, to seize it, to win it. The first act in this conquest will be revolution.

For generations, then, men have been trying to gain freedom. But in these circumstances freedom means power. Freedom in revolution consists through the centuries of killing those who are blamed for impeding it and who are set in a bad light, of establishing personal power, and of crushing all inferiors. We do not have here the ruthless mechanism of class conflict nor the problem of opposition between the forces and relations of production. We have instead the expression of intolerable oppression for those who can think of freedom only in terms of becoming oppressors.

Men have, of course, attempted moderate courses to ensure respect and freedom for all. This is why we have democracy and liberalism.[7] I am not going to argue, as many do, that this amounts to no more than sham democracy, that there is a great gulf between liberalism and liberty, and that there is a total lack of respect in economic liberalism and a total lack of true freedom in democracy. Instead, I want to emphasize a point which is often forgotten, namely, that it is democracy which has given us total war. It is because the whole people has become political, because it incarnates liberty in its entirety, because the nation has the value of a democracy, that defense cannot be left to a few and all men must rally to protect democracy and freedom. Pseudo-liberty has engendered total war.

The current fashion today, then, is to claim that in these inexpiable wars the freedom, dignity, and respect of man are at stake. This was so in the colonial wars. We often forget today that the ideological pretext for

---

7 It is astonishing to find theologians (cf. the WCC) defending institutional freedom in terms of the responsible society. Wendland in his *L'éthique du NT* is completely ignorant of political and sociological realities in his unruffled acceptance of nineteenth-century ideals and the platitudes of American sociology around 1950.

*The Assumption of Freedom*

colonial wars was that freedom should be brought to poor black and yellow slaves, that democracy should be spread among them, that tyrannical rulers should be overthrown, and that respect for man should be taught. We now know the result. But the people of the day believed this. At the same time, I cannot help noting that the value of human dignity is now attributed to decolonization, that there is pompous talk about reaching adulthood, entering history, liberating the peoples, the rights of self-determination, setting up democratic socialism, and therefore that an identical or parallel parade of ideology covers up exactly the same procedure of exploitation, enslavement, and shame by which others alone profit. No matter what it may be, men will call it freedom.

Because they have not received the true witness to freedom from Christians, men have fallen prey to the demon Freedom. This demon is a bloody one who in the name of respect for the human person winds up destroying more men than simple conquerors and ridiculous autocrats.

The mechanism of freedom has been planted among men but, being rejected by those who ought to live it out, it has become a devouring force which unleashes human action instead of controlling it and produces the very opposite of what it is supposed to accomplish. What we have said might equally well be illustrated from the fields of art or finance.[8] The examples given, however, are enough to explain the movement that has characterized history for the last two thousand years. We can only conclude that it is Christians who must bear ultimate responsibility for the horrors and problems of this period.

Nor is this merely a magnanimous acceptance of responsibility on their part. For Christ's sake Christians are no doubt willing to bear responsibility for everything. What we have here, however, is a precise responsibility which can be calculated historically. Christians are responsible because they have not taken up the freedom which Christ gave them to live out. This is what has finally brought with it the sufferings of the working-class, the evils of colonialism, the scandals of dictatorship, totalitarianism, and concentration camps, and the triggering of technology.

We said earlier that if Christians do not challenge authority, conformity, and complacency, nothing else can, for everything else will simply bring with it new authority, conformity, and complacency. In other words, if Christians do not play their part they actually open the door to these other forces. The true drama is that behind all this there lurk the forces of enslavement which are hostile to Christ. We find veiled allusion to this in

---

8 Cf. Auerbach's *Mimesis*. By an analysis of literary style Auerbach shows how Christianity has brought sovereignty over the real in its concrete multiplicity. It has done this thanks to the freedom that it brings but by integrating the real into a figurative unity. From the renaissance, however, the change has not been a victory for freedom but a loss of the order in which the real was integrated and hence a loss of meaning and an involuntary weakening of realism at the intermediary and non-problematical stylistic level.

the mysterious verse in Revelation which speaks of the releasing of Satan after the thousand years, and this is perhaps an echo of Christ's own saying that he saw Satan fall to the earth like lightning.

The powers have been defeated and repulsed and deflected. But by the same token they have also been unleashed. They, too, have been liberated from the order that man had been able to impose on earth. They are on the earth with all the forces of powers which know that they have been outclassed and superseded and broken, but which for this very reason do not need to observe any rules or limits and can cause every kind of upheaval in expression of their final revolt.

The harmony and equilibrium which man had established, e.g., by magic, and thanks to which man belonged to the domain of the powers but the powers also respected the order of man, have now been shattered. Man has been wrested from the domination of the powers and they themselves have been freed from all rules. Any blow is permitted. The powers have in effect been vanquished by the freedom of Christ, but from this point on the only thing that can continue to vanquish them is following up this victory. This does not mean piety, or invocation in the name of Christ, or canticles, or even, as we are so often told today, service. It means freedom. For if these other things, and especially service, are necessary, they have to be by and in freedom. The service of the slave is of no worth and it certainly cannot combat the powers, which have always received service from man. What has worth and force is the service of the free man who serves voluntarily. If, however, the Christian does not take up his freedom, the victory of Christ is not followed up, and the powers can explode victoriously in the world.

One might say indeed that our western society with its insanity and increasingly complex and frightening problems is the product of the act of Christ that Christians have not followed up and made their own. In this context man cannot live without freedom, or some freedom. He seeks it desperately, and shams are offered him. The only freedom he knows is the alleged and comical freedom which is held out to him, cleverly but without the least shred of reality, by the majority of philosophers, and Sartre in particular. The only freedom he knows is the encapsuled and institutionalized freedom of political or economic liberalism. The only freedom he knows is the freedom of revolt, negation, nihilism, and despair. None of all this is real freedom.

Now a very significant and illuminating point is that movements of freedom are always aimed against Christianity and Christians. There is good reason for this. It is a kind of subconscious recognition that Christians ought to have engaged in this venture and brought freedom. Christians and the church are accused of not having done this. The arguments which oppose the teaching and attitude of Christ himself to those of the church may be clumsy, but basically they are correct. To say that movements of freedom among anarchists, philosophers, and others are all anti-Christian means also that they would never have arisen if Christians had taken up their freedom. They demonstrate that the part of freedom really belongs to Christians.

We have only ourselves to blame for the present situation. The secular world is by no means a world come of age. It is in fact the most infantile of all worlds. But it is so because Christians have not come of age, because they do not live as free men, and because they do not show the world what freedom is. Because they have not done this they have condemned themselves to be rejected by men and they have condemned men to pursue indefinitely a figment of freedom.[9]

For ultimately it has to be acknowledged that Christians have not taken up the freedom of Christ. Individual Christians through the centuries have been free men, but not the church. Throughout its history the church has studiously avoided the question of freedom. It has put it in parentheses. It has concealed and resisted it.

There have been various ways of doing this. One is morality. In the first part we dealt with the fatal manner in which the refabrication of morality eliminates freedom. We need not return to the point here.

Another way is organization, including canon law. Now there is always a particle of truth in everything the church undertakes. God is a God of order. The church has to have institutions. It cannot be an amorphous body or a loose amalgamation of individuals. But the application of this truth serves only to obliterate freedom.

In the middle ages, for example, the church had such an excessive concern for justice, order, harmony, and sanctity that it heaped up and endlessly refined institutions, examining things and providing for them with a seriousness which is alien to modern Christians and with a fulness of which we are no longer capable. One might say that all the economic, political, and social problems which agitate the church today were studied and investigated with almost inconceivable care by the theologians, canonists, and decretalists of the period from the eleventh century to the fourteenth century. Every step meant a refinement of analysis and an increase of regulations to give better answers to the questions and to get more authentically to the heart of the concern for justice and charity in each institution. But each time this also meant a little more exclusion of freedom, a refusal to engage in the venture or risk of life and faith.

The concern, of course, was not merely for Christians and the church. It was also for the world. It is easy to speak today about the stupidity of Christians who attempted to impose Christianity and a Constantinian order, although, as we shall see later, this is the unrecognized basic preoccupation of modern theologians too. We should also bear in mind, however, their seriousness, their authentic Christian concern, and the remarkable success they enjoyed.

---

9  Cf. B. Charbonneau, *op. cit.*

We are wrong to speak only of the ambition and pride of popes and prelates, of their ardent self-interest in trying to control temporal matters. There was here a genuine concern for the world. There was a conviction that they had the key to wisdom and justice for it. They thought that they could give the world just and good institutions in which men could live both as Christians and as true men. In this regard the medieval church mounted a positive operation except for one thing: it demanded the suppression of freedom.

Everything else was catered for. Everything was foreseen and calculated in advance for better truth and fuller justice. But the manifestation of freedom was out of the question. This is the one dimension that has been missing in the church from the very first. But this is the decisive dimension without which the Christian life is without significance for the world. In the absence of freedom the forms of the church's action have all become legalistic. Here is the real betrayal.

The church and Christians, in their defiance of freedom and their refusal to assume it, have also found other ways of evading or eliminating the question. Mysticism might be mentioned in this connection. We have in view the reduction of Christianity to the suprahuman or inner dimension in its various forms. Thus transcendence might be exalted at the expense of the incarnation. Scripture might be seen as a collection of myths and symbols requiring demythologization. We might have the individualistic focus on personal faith, or pietism, or symbolo-fideism. The common denominator here is avoidance of the translation of faith into a freedom which changes collective behavior.

Freedom is not now shut up in law. It is left on one side. The question is avoided by an escape into the spiritual sphere which upholds concrete conformity.

Freedom is certainly spoken of in these various movements. But it is always spiritual, metaphysical, or inner freedom. There is effected a great scorn for what is external and vilely material. As one Christian put it: "I felt just as free in a concentration camp as anywhere else."

Now again there is a particle of truth in this. Freedom in Christ does not depend on outward circumstances. It should also be realized, however, that what we have here can be a means of refusing to incarnate freedom.

This is why we may say again that, while Christians have often been free men individually, they have never been able to make the church a witness to freedom, nor have they taken up their freedom as the body of Christ.

Finally, we see in the actual situation in the church today another way of not taking up freedom. This error is the very opposite of the one that precedes it. The incarnation is broken, but this time by insistence on the fleshly or human aspect. The Christian realism of today which admires the world (naturally because God loves it) and which is prepared to question certain elements in revelation on the basis of science; the church of aggiornamento,[10] the church which accepts the works of the world as the works of the Saviour, the church which justifies the world in its course and tries to put itself at the head of sociological movements that can get along very well without it—in all this we have another way of enslavement.

In the preceding form the spirit is too pure to incarnate itself in reality. Hence reality is ignored or there is a pretense of ignoring it. This extreme purity leads to an ethereal freedom which is of no value to man. In the present form, however, there is no more spirit to incarnate. There is no freedom of any kind. A great deal is said to justify things as they are. Meaningless action is taken in a reality which is still ignored because in this situation the Christian is completely incapable of seeing the reality which he so greatly extols. I have adequately dealt with this particular betrayal, with this implicit refusal to take up Christian freedom today, in my work *The Presence of the Kingdom.*

In reality Christians are just as much conformists as any others. The freedom given them in Christ recoils on them if they do not live it out. It subjects them to determinations, conformisms, and ideologies. Not being a model of freedom, they are a model of mediocre bondage. If many intellectual Christians today refer to the determinative role of culture and setting in relation to scripture, it is because they themselves are sub-products of culture and setting. Determinism expresses itself in a remarkable way in intellectual Christians. They are at the mercy of every fad (ideology of science or history, existentialism, Freudianism, Marxism, Maoism, leftism, technology, structuralism, amoralism, anticolonialism, antiracism, etc.) but as Christians pretending to be free and knowing that where the Spirit of the Lord is, there is liberty, they combine the two things and show their freedom by being the most leftist of the leftists, etc., just as German Christians were more fervent Nazis than non-Christians. These Christians are at the head of all sociological trends, pushing the movement to an extreme, either to gain acceptance from others even though they are Christians, or for lack of historical knowledge. And they describe this hyperconformism as prophetic.[11]

Christians are in fact pushed from behind by the movement they think they are propelling. Their freedom is merely that of carrying to extremes the common determination and adding the spice of Christian ideology, thus prostituting freedom to it. They are more moralistic than the most middle-class of moralists when this is the fashion, and more amoral

---

10 This slogan permits a play on words which to my surprise no one seems to have noticed, for while it means "bringing up to date" on the one side, it also means "adjournment" on the other, and what happens is precisely that there is adjournment of being the church even as the church is brought up to date, i.e., brought into line with the actualities of today.

11 Cf. M. R. A. de Sousa, *Le Monde,* Oct. 1965, for a fine criticism of *l'aggiornamento* from the standpoint of an unbeliever. His demand that Christians renounce Christ as the truth for the sake of free dialogue gets to the heart of the matter.

than the most advanced amoralists when the vogue swings this way. The new movements among Roman Catholics and the striking statements of Protestant theologians (or laity, e.g., M. Mead on marriage in January 1970, a notable instance of hypersociologism) are the barometer of this prostitution of freedom to cultural determination. Christians do not know what they are doing. The combination of sociological conditioning and the prophetic spirit obscures their reasoning faculties. But what they are in fact doing is following the great perversion of the world in the sense that while, as Christians, they *are* the bearers of freedom in Christ, they reject this freedom, do not take up their vocation, and subject themselves to the world.

These, then, are the various ways in which the church during its history has avoided incarnating the freedom of Christ. For the most part we may see in all this the familiar swing of the pendulum. Institutionalism yields to the spirit, the spirit to the validation of the world, and so forth. But never is incarnation achieved. We may thus say that in every age, the modern age more than ever, the church has betrayed its mission on earth.

This does not affect the salvation of men. Salvation is truly by grace. All errors are covered by pardon. But it does have serious effects on the history of men and the misery of society. For the fire of freedom which Christ has come to light on earth, instead of being the fire of the Holy Spirit, has become through the church's delinquency a fire of hell.

# Part IV

# Implicated Freedom

# Chapter 1

# Strangers and Pilgrims

We have said repeatedly that there is no pure freedom. There is no freedom comparable to that of God. Freedom can be for us only a reflection, a composite of various tendencies and determinations, among which freedom enjoys some play. Similarly, there is no absolute freedom. There is no intrinsic freedom. We are freed always in relation to our precise, concrete, lived out situation in the world. When freed, we remain in the world, and it is in the world, not in the sky or the future or anywhere else, that we have to live out our freedom.

It may also be recalled that we do not accept any radical distinction between the spiritual and the temporal or spirit and matter. We do not deny, of course, that both exist and that there is a difference between them. What we deny is that there is antithesis. We do not agree that the spiritual element in man is free while the temporal element is alienated. The freedom in question cannot be a purely spiritual freedom. It is not freedom if it is thought to be only spiritual.

These presuppositions lead to the conclusion that we are wholly in the world whether we like it or not. We are implicated in it. The freedom that we are given does not take us out of the world. Nor does one part of us (the spiritual part) escape from it. When I say this I have specifically in mind the man whose faith links him to Christ and who might think that he escapes from the world thereby. This involves a complete misunderstanding of freedom.

It does not depend on us that we are in the world. We are so, and we cannot help it. This is why I prefer to use the term "implicated" rather than "committed." The latter word suggests a voluntary decision. Our implication is simply our situation.[1]

As Bultmann would put it, our liberation is from "in-sistence" to "ec-sistence," although I fail to see how Heideggerian vocabulary and thought add anything to the perfectly clear explanation which the Bible itself gives us. We are certainly to reject the view of Malet[2] when he says that Paul, like the Stoics, views freedom in an inner and spiritual sense

---

1 We need to make it clear that we are not dealing here with social ethics insofar as this concerns the ethics of the Christian in the society in which he lives rather than just a general social ethics.

2 Malet, *La théologie de Bultmann*, p. 267.

rather than an outer and sociological sense. He has in mind freedom in relation to the judgment of the world, the appreciation of man, the flesh, and all that is alien to the true ego. I believe that I can show precisely that there is no distinction between inner freedom and sociological freedom, and that if freedom in Christ is merely the achievement of the true ego then it is nothing. As for the difference that Malet does see between Paul and Stoicism, namely, that the latter makes freedom a personal acquisition whereas the Christian receives it from God, this is true, but in my view it is not enough to support the consequences that one might draw from it concretely.

If, then, we are implicated in the world, no matter what may be our moral estimation of this, I think that we must face up to it squarely. The reference, of course, is only to the Christian, i.e., to the man who has been liberated by Christ, to the free man.[3]

Now if this free man claims not to be implicated in the world, this means that he is denying the reality of his freedom, since he is pretending

---

3 We come up against a fundamental difficulty here. I am now describing the possibility of a freedom which is the fact and experience of an individual (in the etymological sense). Now in this time of collectivities, groups, associations, and communities, I realize that to proceed from the individual to the group is regarded as both mistaken and bad. The group is now the starting-point, as in group therapy, public relations, group dynamics, etc. But, as I have often said, I myself reject this. I do not believe that to give primacy to the group is the proper procedure in Christian theology. God always deals with men. He elects and calls men. He makes the covenant with the chosen people through solitary men like Abraham and Moses. It is as men withdrawn from the group (saints) that those to whom God speaks then act within the group. It would be grotesque, of course, to attribute the biblical data to an individualistic spirit here. Neither the people ⌐f Israel nor the populations of Hellenistic cities were individualists. On the contrary, the fact that God takes a man out of the group and calls him by name is abnormal and surprising and is not too well received; this is why God acts as he does. My own position is determined by the divine testimony. We undoubtedly live at a time when the group is growing in importance, but there is nothing which requires us as Christians to conform to this trend.

If in the nineteenth century it was necessary to oppose a false individualism which claimed to express the truth of man, today we face an absorption, assimilation, adaptation, reduction, and conforming of man into various groups, so that the collective becomes the substitute for truth. Over against this we need to affirm the exclusive value of the individual. The group exists only if and to the extent that it is composed of individuals who are strictly differentiated by their mutual relations.

The only thing is that we cannot stop at the individual. The particularity of the individual makes no sense and has no value unless it finds expression in a community, a collective, a group, a common venture. I stress the individual here only because the sociological trend today is to give primacy to the group with no safeguards for the force or validity of the individual, and modern Christianity tends to mythologize, glorify, exalt, and present as a sacred duty what is only a sociological phenomenon. My revolt is against the myth of the group or collectivity or universal humanity.

to have a pure and absolute freedom, which is impossible. He can live out his freedom only at the real level where he is. This means that he must accept his implication in the world and that he must live out his freedom as an implicated freedom. What is more, he must want to do so. This is the point of freedom.

We have said that man is implicated whether he likes it or not. But if he does not know or like it, this means that he is not clear about himself and that he is definitely absorbed by events, social structures, and ideologies, without being able to do anything about it.

If, however, he knows that he is necessarily implicated, but also knows that he is free in Christ, then living out this freedom as an implicated freedom means that he has considerable choice at the point where he meets the world, choice as to approach and choice of determinations. Instead of being carried along and claiming divine freedom, he is called upon to decide for this or that implication and to contest another, escaping the latter by accepting the former.

We must not think, of course, that this will be easy. It is not like a game of billiards or a balancing trick or the attaining of freedom by a system of checks and balances in group memberships. The freedom at issue is freedom in Christ, not the freedom of a force intrinsic to the world. This is the freedom that we have to live out.

This brings us up against what is often called the theology of the laity.[4] The layman[5] in this sector is the man on the frontier, as it is often put today. He stands on the border between the church and the world, although this distinction is increasingly contested, and rightly so if the distinction is thought of as sharp and clear-cut. I myself prefer to think in terms of the meeting-point of two elements rather than a frontier, which suggests that the church is a different place. It is in the layman primarily that the powers, preoccupations, interests, and activities of the world meet the power of the Holy Spirit. It is in him that the determinations of the world meet freedom in Christ.

The layman has to live out this freedom because he is the man who is concretely at grips with these problems. It is he who has the task of bringing freedom into the world. It is he who carries freedom into society because he meets the two forces within himself. He is not an external liberator who falls down from heaven. He is a liberator precisely because he himself has been liberated, i.e., liberated from these forces which constantly exist for him. He is a liberator because he is a participant. If he did not participate he would be a kind of angel. This applies, of course, to the

---

4  H. Kraemer, *Théologie du laïcat* (1965).

5  I realize, of course, that this is a bad term. It contradicts both the priesthood of all believers and the unity of God's people. Nevertheless, it corresponds to a valid reality. Whereas some people devote their whole time to the church's life others do not, and hence a difference arises respecting the relations of the two groups to both the church and the world.

priest or pastor too, but it applies especially to the layman (and for us there is a theological and not a sociological difference at this point).

Only the layman is fully subject to the forces of the world, e.g., earning his living and the pressure of his job with all its technical implications. The pastor can work as he chooses. He is under no constraint. He has, of course, his own determinations. He belongs to a background and is affected by ideologies. But he does not have to render account for his interests. If he shares the political conditioning of his intellectual group, he is also independent. It is the layman, therefore, who has to practice freedom in society.

Some misunderstandings should be cleared away at this point. If we recall the classical view that it is impossible to divide life into two parts, the one professional, scientific, or political and the other Christian,[6] this is not in order to indicate one of many possibilities of the Christian life, but in order to draw attention to the one and only possibility. Nevertheless, there can never be any question of, as it were, "infusing" clergy into the secular world, for it is not because there are worker priests that Christian freedom is lived out in the world. One might almost say, to the horror of some, that this takes place when workers are converted. Again, we are not thinking of mass action by which militant Christian groups enrol non-Christians into a party or union. Nor is it a question of the institutional transformation of society. Nor do we have in mind the diffusion, dispersion, fusion, or effusion of the church in the world. All these have been temptations during the last hundred years or so, and the last is our great temptation today.

What we have to maintain is that the church, too, exists at the organizational and social level. It is not just a gathering of believers around the Lord's table. If it is in symbiosis with the world, this is not because it merges into it. It is because laymen, living in the world and experiencing within themselves the tension of twofold allegiance, come out of the world into the church and then go back to the world. To achieve merger the church does not have to wither away. It has to exist in every possible visible dimension in order to make sure that it embraces every possible layman and is not just a bloodless fellowship.

This is an indispensable condition for the layman if he is to carry the freedom which is given him and inscribe the incarnate presence of the Lord in decisions which do not conform to the schemata of society. It is on the basis of a church which is a strong body and community that this is possible for the layman.

At this point another misunderstanding must be cleared up. How many times we hear Christians who are anxious to serve and are excited about secular causes argue that Christians are there to help the world forward. Christian freedom—although they seldom speak of this—has the

---

6 On this question cf. the many writings of the APP from 1944 to 1948.

job of helping the world to progress and assisting it to gain its own freedom. It seems to me that all this is sadly mistaken.

Love and the glory of God do not have the task of helping the world to go its own way. The aim of Christian freedom is not that society should be better or should function better.[7] This may well come about. It may be expected or hoped for. But it is simply an added gift when there are Christians who are living a genuinely free life. Again, this freedom is not established in order to help men find an illusory replica of freedom or in order to lead them to think or say that they are free outside Christ and apart from him. This would be an abominable deception under the cover of love, understanding, and service.

As Walz has well put it, freedom lived out in the world has a threefold orientation. First, it has an evangelistic role. Only the free Christian engaged in the world can evangelize. This does not mean bringing non-Christians into the church but carrying the church to them. Hence the life of the church has to be decentralized, although decentralization is not, of course, the same thing as dissolution. In reality, to want to bring people into the church, as has been done for centuries, means either rejecting pagans or making the church even more pagan than it already is. The church cannot continue to be a self-enclosed and self-incurved entity more or less tied up with sociological and class structures. On the other hand, taking the church to the world, which can be done only by laymen, has as its purpose the conversion to Jesus Christ of people who are reached in this way.

The second orientation is missionary. This is not quite the same thing as the evangelistic orientation. The objective here is presence rather than conversion. Jesus Christ is to be present among all creatures through his witnesses. There have to be Christians who take part in all activities and enterprises, who do not refuse to take part in this or that venture or commitment for moral or other reasons. Similarly there have to be Christians present in every setting and in every ideological option. They are to take part, not out of interest, but because they are the salt of the earth. They are to assure men at all points of the divine covenant.

The third orientation is mediation. This follows from the second. Christians must stop judging or moralizing on activities and institutions so that they can be agents of their sanctification by the sacrifice of Jesus Christ. As we said earlier, however, this can come about only by the way of

---

7 Cf. M. Dibelius, *Botschaft und Geschichte*, I (1953), pp. 178ff.: "The gospel is not a social message but it functions as a social demand. . . . The vision of the coming of God's kingdom shapes this demand . . . what we have here is not a programme for reorganizing the world but marching orders for every age. These marching orders are no more than one and the same eschatological summons to repentance. They are meant to lead the hearer to an understanding of his true position before God."

sacrifice or oblation. The reconciliation is both horizontal (among men) and vertical (of men to God), but either way it takes place only by sacrifice.

These three Christian functions are all the product and result of Christian freedom (which is only another way of referring to its two axes, namely, love of neighbor and the glory of God). They are possible only thanks to freedom and by freedom. This is why it is a mistake to present the demands of the Christian life on any other ground than that of freedom. Without freedom they are radically impossible.

What we have just said shows that in all circumstances one way is closed to an ethics of implicated freedom. This is the way of simple solutions. We constantly hear people asking today: "What must we do to be present to the world?" Or else—and this is even worse—we hear others stating: "To be present to the world we must join a union or party, or engage in scientific research, or vote in this way." These simplistic questions and answers are like the hints given for living the individual Christian life in the nineteenth century; the fact that these specific moral injunctions are now collective or social changes nothing.

We can never say: "This has to be done." For the hard-pressed layman who wants specific instructions there is no "Do this or that." There are no clear, simple, universal, Christian solutions to all the problems which arise. We can only put the problems as clearly as possible and then, having given the believer all the weapons that theology and piety can offer, say to him: "Now it is up to you to go and find the answer, not intellectually, but by living out your faith in this situation." There is no prefabricated solution nor universally applicable model of Christian life. Freedom itself causes the difficulty. If we give orders, we deny freedom. If we deny freedom, it is of little value that Christians are present at a given place and act in a specific way, for they do indeed manifest themselves, but not as true Christians. Freedom implies that each Christian discovers for himself the style and form of his action.

In this chapter, as we come up against the practical question, we can do only two things in writing an ethics of freedom. On the one hand we can show that freedom implies a certain relation to society, men, and things, that it gives rise to a certain type of relation which can in effect be described and even universalized, and that it expresses itself in a certain use of the things of society, institutions, groups, and so forth. This is the intermediary stage between the existence of freedom and the concrete situation in detail. Finding the proper attitude in a specific case is to be deduced from this.

On the other hand we can raise problems. We cannot do more. This would cut off freedom at the root. Hence there is no hope that the zealous reader will find a precise course of action set forth here. There is no hope that the hard-pressed man who has no time to spare will be given a formula for living out his freedom. It might indeed be added that freedom can manifest itself only when one is not hard-pressed.

## § 1. Pilgrimage

We have tried to analyze the relation between hope and freedom. We have said incidentally that hope, by linking us to what is permanent, evokes freedom in relation to circumstances, social structures, ideological movements, and everything that might be called history. We shall now examine some of the biblical orientations which give precision to this freedom, but we shall always remember that what we are about to describe here is the necessary condition of concrete engagement in the world and not an acquired and stabilized condition, which would be the very reverse of freedom.

"These all died in faith, not having received the promises, but having seen them afar off, and were persuaded of them, and embraced them, and confessed that they were strangers and pilgrims on the earth. For they that say such things declare plainly that they seek a country. And truly, if they had been mindful of that country from whence they came out, they might have had opportunity to have returned. But now they desire a better country, that is, an heavenly. Wherefore God is not ashamed to be called their God, for he hath prepared for them a city" (Hebrews 11:13-16).

The men of the Old Testament recognized, then, that they were strangers and pilgrims. This experience can be that of all men. It is not just the experience of those to whom God reveals himself. Whether we like it or not, we are, of course, strangers to what is around us. This is a commonplace experience, especially in these days of acute difficulty (almost to the point of impossibility) in communication, comprehension, and the attaining of what is dearest to us. Pilgrimage is a theme in philosophy too. We cannot keep anything. We cannot stay fixed on anything.

The situation of Israel in the wilderness may be recalled again. It is both an illustration and a lesson (Exodus 14:10-14). The choice is a radical one between a life of bondage which is nevertheless peaceful, secure, and comfortable, and liberation in the desert, for no other place is so appropriate for freedom. We ought to take this fact with the utmost seriousness when we speak about freedom. Freedom belongs to the place where all guarantees, assurances, protections, and orders are set aside. Freedom thrusts us into a wilderness which we have to inhabit, domesticate, humanize, and fill with our presence. To be called to be free means a break with all that we have hitherto taken for granted. To accept this call means to accept life in the desert in which all the securities of society are renounced. It is not possible to think oneself free in Christ within the framework of assurances, previsions, reciprocities, affluence, the desire for affluence, the attainment of it, the longing for comfort and happiness. There is here an incompatibility which is not just relative and accessory but radical and final. What prevents us from believing this and leads us to attempt conciliation is our weakness of character and generalized lukewarmness.

The desert situation is no doubt a despairing and desperate one for man. He finds it unacceptable. By every possible means he tries to escape it, to uproot himself from it. In the presence of this despair the job of the Christian, it might seem, is to give man a fixed reference point for orientation and rootage.

We spontaneously try to escape this situation. We try not to be strangers and pilgrims. We want to keep something. Our natural instinct, then, is to understand and accept this tendency, to help it to survive by giving it means by which to take root.

Christians, however, have to adopt a different attitude. They have not only seen that their natural condition is this. They have also willed it. They have chosen to be uprooted. They have been called by God and this has brought about a break with all else, a parting from it. On this basis they have seen and hailed the promises from afar. They have perceived the love of God at work in Jesus Christ. They have discerned the plan of God in history. They have seen the grace which was granted to them and which awaited them. They have realized that God is the one who comes. It is on this ground, and because they have believed these things, that they have *become* strangers.

They have become strangers to a degree that they were not strangers by nature and could never know from experience. They have become strangers to the world in which they live. They have measured this world. They have seen to what extent it is not their place even though they cannot avoid living in it. They have willed to be strangers in it instead of wanting to recover it.

They have become pilgrims, not in the sense that everything escapes them and they are looking behind in an attempt to recapture it, but rather in the sense that Paul gives, namely, that they reject and forget all that is behind and press on to what is ahead. They are not wanderers in the desperate situation of Cain but pilgrims in the situation of those who know where they are going and know that this goal is positive and authentic. We thus have a complete reversal of the wandering of Cain.

Cain was detached from men, but tried to attach himself by founding a city. He had no aim but continually tried to set his own aim. His wandering and uprootage were the very opposite of freedom.

All this is changed, however, for the pilgrim. As he advances he leaves a history behind him. In his forward march he knows where he is going and he waits for it. This kind of uprootage is not only the one condition of the Christian life; it is also a supreme expression of freedom.

The uprootage is total. It is a break with everything that seems "normal" in the life of man. Jesus himself constantly teaches it: Sell all that thou hast and come and follow me. Whoso sets his hand to the plow and looks back. . . . He that leaves father, mother, and brethren for my sake. . . . Let the dead bury their dead. If thine eye is an occasion of covetousness (of the desire to possess, to be integrated in worldly things), pluck it out. Here we have a break with all that is normal and legitimately dear.

How much more is a break entailed with country, nation, political party, social class, profession, union, economic structure, and economic conflict. These things are no longer our business. Or rather they can become our business only if we are radically uprooted in respect of them. They can be our business only if, instead of rooting ourselves in them, we summon this whole world to join our pilgrim march, only if we carry this world along with us, with uprootage as a condition. This is what Abraham and Isaac did, and yet they carried the destiny of their own authentic origin with them.

If, however, we grant any significance to this whole world, we are rooted in it. Our condition then, even if we confess Jesus Christ, is the same as that of Cain. We can thus be of no use to the world in which we are stuck. We can be only like the blind leading the blind, i.e., other men and society, into the ditch. We are like the blind, for we have our gaze fixed on these things instead of fixing it on the promises. We thus lead men into the ditch, i.e., into a final affirmation of fatality, for the only service that we can render to men is that of freedom. If we ourselves are not free, if we are rooted in society, we simply strengthen the determinisms by giving them the allegiance of the only ones who could be freed from them.

We are uprooted and can march forward, but toward what? Hebrews says: Toward our true country, the house of the fathers, the place where they are at home and are no longer strangers and pilgrims. This country of ours is the presence of God. For he is our Father. We find our country in encounter with him. The rest of God, that of the seventh day, is the end of the journey or wandering. It is the criterion of this country which shatters all engagement in the things of the world and society. As the text says: "They confessed that they were strangers and pilgrims. For they that say such things declare plainly that they seek a country." It is by seeking the true country without any reservations that we recognize that we are strangers and pilgrims, and wish to be so.

The standard of the promises that we have seen and towards which we march devalues everything else. I am aware that some will say: "This is the well-known mystical function, that of monasticism, that which led medieval man not to be interested in society." The first question, however, is not whether it is reactionary or anti-social but whether it is biblical. Do we not find this teaching throughout the Bible?

As I see it, the novelty is that of realizing that this attitude is not negative or aloof in our society but that it contributes to our society the thing it needs above all else. It must be emphasized once again that in being pilgrims we are not rejecting this society. We are not dissociating ourselves from it. We are still members of it. What we can give it is meaning. We can give it an understanding of its wandering and its blind history. We can try to transform the absurd succession of events into a real history. We can do this, however, only if we begin by fixing our gaze on the things that we see and by marching towards them.

Now at every step in this march, in this pilgrimage, in this uprootage, we can turn back. If we find the goal too uncertain, God does not compel us to go forward. "They might have had opportunity to have returned." They could look back at what they had left. They could think again (as we all can) of the happiness that may be enjoyed in a highly developed consumer society. They could come back to serious things like jobs, comfort, politics, money, progress, revolution, or society. This is always a possibility. At every moment we have to make a choice. As we have said so often, the wonderful thing about the freedom which God gives is that on the one side our salvation is achieved once and for all, and nothing can take it from us, but on the other side the decisions we take in life are never definitive. God always leaves open the risk of changing them.

The temptation to do this is great. For we hail the reality of the country of God only from afar. The men to whom the passage in Hebrews refers did not have or experience the things promised. They died without obtaining them, Abraham as well as Moses. They had no lasting or permanent gift. They had no evident, definitive, and irrevocable revelation. This is exactly how it stands with Christians.

We Christians, too, are on a path on which we shall not obtain what is promised in this life. We have to uproot ourselves on a simple promise. We have to leave the substance for a shadow. This is faith. It is in illustration of faith that Hebrews recalls the situation. It presents the uprootage as the only possible and reasonable expression of faith. The sayings that we quoted from Jesus to the same effect stand also in relation to faith. When the substance has been left for the shadow, the only actual reality which we are given by which to live is that "God is not ashamed to be called their God." To speak of God being ashamed is a striking anthropomorphism. But it is a good one. God is ashamed of what man does. He is ashamed of what has become of his creation. But when men confess that they are strangers and pilgrims, when they are no longer concerned to exploit the wealth of creation for their own satisfaction, God is no longer ashamed; he is ready to be called their God.[8] He accepts the fact that they call upon him, that they pray to him, that they call him Father as Jesus has given us the power to do. He accepts the fact that these men reveal him to others. Those whom God allows to call him their God are his witnesses, and this is true only of the uprooted who confess themselves to be strangers and pilgrims in society, for it is to the extent that they are this that they can bear witness.

---

8 Adherents of the metaphysical notion that God is dead—we can hardly call it a theology—ought to ask themselves sometimes whether they are not just expressing the fact that God does not accept their ideology.

When the question is raised by night: "Who is God?" God accepts it that these should be the men who reply. They have to do so, and their reply is true because God accepts them as his witnesses.

We know, of course, that the word for witness is "martyr." Yet we associate the word with the Roman arena or with missionaries who have been killed. In reality the man who gives up his desire for his social country is already a martyr. He bears witness by hazarding his life for the promises which he sees from afar. He wagers that the promises of God are more valuable than the important things acquired in our society. It is in virtue of this choice that God is not ashamed of him. It is in virtue of this choice that he is a witness. Freedom in respect of politics, society, worldly enterprises, interests, and money is the condition of the possibility of witness.

It is astonishing that we have to repeat something which is so obvious if we remember the instructions that Jesus gave to the seventy disciples when he sent them out to the townships of Israel. But unfortunately we have to repeat them, since we constantly hear the opposite today. In order to witness, we are told, we have to use the same language as others. We have to adopt their interests and style of life. We have to act with them and in the same sense. We have to have the same commitments and passions. We have to join parties and unions.

From the biblical standpoint, however, this is a monstrous misunderstanding. This is what prevents us from being witnesses. This is why God is ashamed to be called our God. If our word has no force it is not because we are not enough in the world. It is because we are far too much in it. As Christians we do not belong at all in this world of work, politics, economics, and ideology. Using this completely vain and empty language renders the language of the word ineffectual. This is where all hermeneutical reflection on the biblical text, or structural analysis of it, ought to begin.

If we are to be witnesses through whom the word is heard we have to become strangers and pilgrims in relation to material things. Our witness has no validity if we are conformed to the world. We have to ask ourselves with anguish, not merely what is the content of the witness, nor what demythicizing or remythicizing we have to engage in, but above all what is the quality of the witness. When God makes us witnesses, when he is not ashamed to be called our God, witness exists. But this comes about when we ourselves take up the freedom which God gives us by recognizing that on the earth, in the social milieu in which we are, we are there as strangers and pilgrims. All active participation in the works of the world undoubtedly ensures a presence but it also sterilizes witness.

Uprooting in respect of all normal or social relations is thus an expression of God's intervention in a life. Christian freedom brings about uprootage. The illustration which is constantly cited here is that of Abraham. One cannot be free for God unless one is uprooted from all that constitutes the world. This is just another way of saying that we have to be pilgrims and strangers.

One might refer again to the desert at this point. The Levites too, as we have already seen, are living witnesses to the uprootage which is the mark of freedom.

If a man is rooted, he cannot claim to be free according to the freedom of Christ. We must consider this rootage for a moment. Why is it so often condemned in scripture? What is condemned is not just attachment to a place, family, or things. Nor is uprootage merely a test, as is so often argued. The situation of rootage is much more than being in a place or using certain goods. In relation to the traditional question of being and having, rootage is a modification of being by having. It is the fact that possessing goods transforms what we are. If we are able to remain ourselves (questionable though the phrase may be), there is no rootage. This is why scripture attacks rootage rather than possession.

Rootage also involves justification of the situation in which we find ourselves. A mark of the transformation of being by having is that being goes on to justify being what it is and having what it has. We shall not insist on this, for we shall be returning to the point later.

An introductory question, however, merits consideration. It is often said that our mass urban and industrial society is a society in which man is uprooted anyway. He has lost his country and groups. He is the plaything of social forces. He is exposed to the chances of employment. He has to be mobile. If, then, we regard uprootage as an expression of freedom in Christ, we ought to rejoice in this social uprootage.

This is what Harvey Cox does in his *Secular City*. He tries to show that this evolution of society expresses a profound spiritual truth and is thus in accordance with the will of God.

I think that there is terrible confusion here. Scripture never says that the uprootage of Abraham or Elijah meant a better, a more livable, and a more agreeable situation. The man who is freed in Christ has a hard enough time of it. But what about those who are uprooted when they do not even know the grace and love of God for them?

The condition of such men is completely intolerable, inhuman, and tragic. Uprooting is a social ailment and it produces psychological sickness. We should not disguise this. Even when grace plunges us into freedom, we must recognize that in thus uprooting us it sets us in a situation of disequilibrium, in a situation which is abnormal and unnatural. For man it is natural that he should have a place or group in which to put down his roots. Freedom is in every way unnatural for man.

We are called upon to endure this situation by the love of God. We must throw ourselves into this venture because there is hope in Christ. Without this, even theologically, uprootage is a curse. It is the situation of Cain.

A comparison of the two types of uprooted men, Cain and Abraham, makes clear the impossibility of the thesis of Cox. Uprooting for sociological reasons does not fulfil the loving will of God for man. It corresponds to the curse laid on Cain. Even though man no longer knows the spiritual basis, he sees it as a curse.

This means that we have to adopt a contradictory attitude towards uprooting—and this is a sign of our freedom in Christ. At the social level, at the human, political, and psychological level, we have a duty as Christians to fight all forms of uprooting. It is required that man should be able to live. He has to have a healthy and just place or environment to do this. He has to have a framework and a suitable group.

In providing this, we certainly have to ask ourselves whether we are not acting contrary to the will of God, which is that Cain should be a wanderer. Yet as Christians we are never charged to carry out the condemnations and maledictions of God. Man himself in his sin imposes on himself the conditions of malediction and by his own acts executes the divine condemnations. Man himself, being a sinner, brings about his own uprooting, which revelation shows to be a curse. We must never reverse this and try to execute the curse because we know it is there. On the contrary, only the love which is in Christ should inspire our acts, whether this be on the plane of witness or on that of conservation.

Man has to be able to live in order that he may eventually glorify God by his life. He has to be able to live his own life in order that he may eventually love God. Hence we ought to struggle to make this life livable. We ought to reconstruct for man a place or group. We ought to help him in his uprootage. We ought to try to cure both the social ailment and the psychological sickness.

At the level of the proclamation of the gospel, however, it is incumbent on us that we have a very different attitude. It is incumbent on us that we summon the rooted to uprooting by grace. Naturally, the summons is not to go out to those who are uprooted and who wander about like sheep having no shepherd. How can these men see in their sociological plight a sign of the grace of the God of love?

It may be that after they have found out that God is love, and seen his grace, the sociologically uprooted may later perceive in the uprooting an act of God in their lives. It may be that they will come to regard it as an expression of the freedom to which God calls them. But they cannot do this in advance. Sociological uprooting is never freedom. It may be independence. Thus a man brought up in the country and moving to the city may find liberation there from the scrutiny and the sociological pressure of a small village. But this is rapidly replaced by a hundred new forms of bondage. Uprooting brings bondage with it. It has been constantly pointed out that Hitler's clientele was made up of all the uprooted.

For those who are rooted in sin, family, money, work, or property, the summons to uprooting by grace is indeed a summons to freedom. Liberation entails the breaking of all these bonds, of all these justifications of a man who is corrupted by having them. But for the sociologically uprooted the first step in the ultimate march to freedom has to be that of being rooted in a life that is humanly livable, unless conversion to Christ suddenly helps them to understand the true meaning of uprooting and they can thus skip the intermediary steps. As Christians, we cannot assume that this will always happen and hence we have to adopt two different courses, summoning the rooted to uprooting as the choice of obedience, as going into the wilderness, as a divine venture, but also showing that God's grace counterbalances the abnormality of the created situation, so that it is no longer so crushing and traumatic.

The two different orientations correspond to two levels. Obviously the summons to uprooting, like the summons to conversion, can be addressed only to individuals. It is at the individual level alone that grace can take this form of freedom. On the other hand, to work in the name of freedom to restore to man a stable environment which will help him simply to lead a balanced life—this can be done only on the collective level, i.e., the level of structures and sociology.

The latter is not by any means the summit of Christian action. It involves what we may call "good works" which are now grossly overestimated in the name of politics but which were for many years no less grossly underestimated in the name of the spiritual. In any case, we have to recognize that we do not have here the thing which is specifically Christian. To want to restore this rooting, this livable society, cannot be regarded as the essential thing in the work of faith except on the medieval view which seeks the creation of Christendom—a serious confusion. What we have here is no more than a work to be done. That man should be enabled to live is undoubtedly important but it is only the first word and not the last, nor is it in any regard specifically Christian. Christians are simply led by love to engage in this task alongside others. They are simply led by the hope of freedom to regard this rooting as essential for the possibility of freedom, but for this alone. The truly important and decisive thing which we cannot evade is that men should have an actual (and not just a potential) experience of freedom in uprootage.

Let us be more precise. "The time is short: it remaineth, that both they that have wives be as though they had none; and they that weep, as though they wept not; and they that rejoice, as though they rejoiced not; and they that buy, as though they possessed not; and they that use this world, as though they used it not, for the fashion of this world passeth away. But I would have you without carefulness" (1 Corinthians 7:29-32).

This passage undoubtedly does not prohibit marriage or starting a family. It does not prohibit weeping, i.e., regretting persons or things that we have lost. It does not prohibit life or attachment in the world. There is no advocacy here of a morality of renunciation. There is no advocacy of Stoicism. The passage does not prohibit buying, i.e., taking part in economic life. It does not prohibit a general use of the world. The only thing is that in these acts and situations Christians cannot possibly be like others.

When asked about what we should do, Paul answers by saying what we should be. The married man is not to leave his wife—and he is certainly not to follow the modern vogue of seeking sexual experiences elsewhere—but he is also not to be bound to the things of the world because of his wife (v. 34), nor is he to bank on his marriage as something achieved and complete. The man who weeps or laughs is to be as though he does not. That is, suffering and joy are not to affect the being that has been saved by Christ. Tears are not to lead to despair and nothingness, nor laughter to diversion and nothingness.

The man who buys is to be as though he does not own. For the man who owns is the one who claims to be a master before God. He confuses what he is with what he has. He thus links his own destiny to what he has. This is the problem of "where your treasure is, there will your heart be also." To have a sense of ownership is to be an owner, to "be" in what one "has." Desire of things is a dispossession of the self. This is a radical judgment on the total enterprise of modern civilization, which is totally oriented to achieving possession of the world. The more man does this, the more alienated he is. The experience of a century and a half strictly confirms the proclamation of the gospel in this regard.

Once again, God does not tell us this in order to prevent us from enjoying things. He does so in order that man may simply be. Now as those who are freed by Christ we can be only as those who do not possess.[9]

Using the world is perfectly acceptable. All the things in our own society may be employed. But the very word "use" implies detachment from the world[10] on the part of the one who makes this use. With no attachment, mythification, or magnification, things are used, and they are viewed simply as things without any importance being assigned to them,

---

9 The transition from a society of owning to one of consuming makes no essential difference. The reification by property of which Marx complains has simply been replaced by reification by consumption. The fact that we are no longer conserving or treasuring goods does not in itself mean "as though they possessed not." We are just as much enslaved in the need for ceaseless renewal or the creation of immoderate appetites for more and more consumption. Freedom is never brought by institutional or structural change.

It is significant that precisely in a consumer society both sociologists and novelists are constantly stressing that both ownership and consumption of more and more goods set man in a process of reification. Man himself has become an object in our society. As the person withers, objects become more and more autonomous and mutually strengthen one another. The person is replaced by a reified universe of objects of which the person itself is one. This is the concrete situation of man in a highly developed consumer society.

10 The word "world," at the end of a series including marriage, weeping, and buying, confirms once again our partial assimilation of the world and society.

whether in terms of party, technology, or art. Normally, of course, the use of social or economic things always has in view a specific result (often ideologized) or profit. This twofold orientation is rejected by the "as though not using them." This means that the use is not to lead to the normal result of such use. We are not to adopt the objectives that all men pursue in their use. We are not to seek any specific result or profit. We are simply to use.

Here again the command is that we should remain ourselves, the people we are as Jesus Christ frees us. We can use all things so long as this use does not corrupt what we are now in the process of becoming through Jesus Christ, so long as we are not changed or preverted by this use. The use, manipulation, and approval of the things of this world is no less dangerous than owning them. In our civilization, if possession of the world is the collective danger of society, using goods is the individual danger (assuming the diminishing role of individual ownership or property). The true problem is not that of corruption by individual property but that of corruption by increasing consumption. To be trapped in consumption and use is to be condemned to the fate of things which are essentially transitory (Matthew 6:21).

This is what seems to happen in, e.g., technology. The saying of Paul naturally permits the use of the technological methods of modern society. But it is impossible to stop either at the first part of the statement: You may use all things, or at the second: As though you do not use them. Two remarks seem to be called for in relation to technology. The first is that the attitude of using as though not using, while it provides us with a line of conduct with regard to technical goods, does not resolve at all the problem of technology in society as it now is. A first reason why this is so is that technology is not a collection of technical goods which may be freely used, but a total ideological and pragmatic system which imposes structures, institutions, and modes of behavior on all members of society. Hence the universal problem of technology cannot be solved merely by some people adopting a different attitude. A second reason is that the question, as I have often shown, is not just one of using a neutral object either well or badly.[11] Technology is not a neutral object or set of objects. It has its own orientation and we are not free to use it for good or evil according to our own choice. Within this limitation the injunction to use as though not using is still a most valuable one regarding the use of technical goods.

Our second remark relates to the meaning of the actual use of these goods. All technical means are means of power, seizure, domination, organization, and utilization. Technology always involves this even if the claim is made that the goods are being used for the benefit of mankind.

---

11 I am glad to note that G. Friedmann, who at one time argued that technology is a neutral object, has now changed his mind on this matter in his *Sept études sur l'homme et la technique* (1967).

Now the whole passage is put there to warn us against yielding to the mad desire to own, utilize, and dominate. It is put there to commit us to substituting a relation of love for one of possession. In so doing, however, it calls in question all utilization of technical means. These cannot be the agents or signs of love nor can they allow of a use governed and directed by it. I am well aware that a philosopher or a theologian might not think that there is any impossibility here. But this simply reveals his ignorance of the reality of the technological phenomenon. A car can be used to carry a person in need. Drugs can be used to help the sick. Love can be expressed over the telephone. But this tells us nothing at all about a technological civilization whose orientation is radically different.

One type of conduct (that of love) has to be substituted for another type of conduct (that of technology), since neither can be superimposed upon nor reconciled with the other. Does this mean that everything technological has to be rejected? That would be silly. It would be tantamount to thinking that we can already live in heaven. Naturally, we have to use technology. But we have to realize that in so doing we become involved in a type of universal behavior which is the complete opposite of that of freedom, so that we have constantly to call it in question by proposing and sometimes practicing the opposite behavior, which is that of freedom, and which in no way negates the concrete validity of the other.

Can that which we have been rapidly sketching be reduced to a matter of intention? Naturally, the basis of the attitude is an intention. The same acts are done but the motive is different (this is the root of the new tree). The acts have a different content and end. This is not immediately discernible. Thus one might take part in politics, not because of a belief in the value of politics nor in the objectives to be attained (although these might be relatively better than others), but purely because of the opportunity to meet men and to be present among them. This presupposes inner detachment, and it will of course come to some external expression in the mood with which we approach the matters that excite and concern men. For even though we take part in an action we will systematically refuse to grant it the significance that others do. For example,[12] we will not regard productivity as so highly important as all that. We will refuse to venerate the work of our hands, whether it be moon-landing, the nation, values, or something else. As we act, we will not expect the results or the logical reward that others expect. In politics, for example, we will not be interested in the triumph of a political idea. In our work we will not be interested in advancement or some other gain.

Now in all this we must be careful that the intention which remains an inner one does not become, as it very quickly can, a simple pretext and justification. It has to find expression in a quality in the action which

---

12 I deliberately use examples already given in order to show how the aspects of freedom continually overlap one another.

transforms it. The freedom to be turns against itself if it is not lived out in a freedom to do. This is already brought out by the term "to use."

If the action of Christians is identical with that of non-Christians there is no use which is non-use. The difficulty is that there is no prior criterion or determination of the action. If it is a direct expression of being free, no rules can be given. The expression has to be in the immediate circumstances and not in a systematic theory. Being controls having in the course of action.

A final step has to be taken. Is the text ultimately negative? Is it simply saying: Do not use? Is it also individualistic? Does it merely indicate a personal position?

What it really means is that the normal relation of ownership or use is to be replaced by one of love. If we must act thus because the fashion of this world passes away, this does not imply at all that we are to despise the men and things around us. It is not a warning to have nothing whatever to do with them. The point is that just because they are transitory, we are not to treat them as unimportant or in a purely utilitarian and egotistic way. Just because they are transitory, our relation must cease to be one of ownership, domination, or preoccupation. We have to place them under the cross. We have to set them in the light of the coming kingdom.

The attitude of extreme freedom defined by the "as though . . ." is in relation to what is around us an attitude of respect.[13] Respect here is not respect for men and things that deserve respect. It is not fear of powerful authorities. It is not interest in money because money is a pleasant and useful thing to have. This respect for men and things is respect, not because these men and things have value, but precisely because they do not. For we have always to bear in mind that the act of Jesus Christ which frees us (and frees us *from* things) puts everything in its proper place again. Such things as property, goods, family, and politics have in the strict sense no more importance than that which Jesus ascribes to them when he announces his kingdom. This is the importance of being able finally to be used in and for this kingdom. The radical devaluation of everything in society is accompanied by the revaluation (the only one) that everything, by the grace of God, may be able to serve the kingdom.

It may be that all these things—work, cinema, television, or city—are called upon to enter the New Jerusalem. I am not so sure that I ought to add prostitution, colonization, war, or the police—this would stir up some reactions. All the same, it is not we who are to judge what will finally serve

---

13 Kierkegaard tells us from another angle that the problem changes in accordance with the one who solves it. . . . Courage increases the danger and surmounts it. Generosity leaves injustice to its filth and regards it from above. Patience makes the burden heavier and carries it, while gentleness makes it lighter and bears it lightly. The free man changes the situation itself, although we so often think that it is man who changes at the whim of circumstances.

and enter into the work of God. The things have thus to be there. We have to do them, to take part in *this* way in the work of men.

The using, however, is not just a relation to things; it is also a relation to men. It thus corresponds to being all things to all men. The point is the same. Love is to replace the thirst to gain power over others. Being without law among those who have no law, and under the law among those who are under it, is to be free in relation to others and yet to act as though not free because of their weakness. Morality is not to be forced on those who do not believe in it. Acts which might cause offense are not to be done in relation to those who do. Giving offense to the weak is always condemned, for it is contrary to love. It causes the weak to fall into a snare—and the weak here are not the poor, workers, women, or colonial peoples. The weak are those who claim that they have no morality. They are also the moralists.

The freedom of the Christian leads him to take the point of view of others instead of imposing his own on them. In doing this, says the apostle, our aim must be to win these others. Conversion to Jesus Christ is the only goal. The Christian is not simply to undergo a mysterious change by which he is hidden in the world, never showing himself to be a Christian and relying on his presence alone to bring about a transformation. No, he is there to win men. This has the same meaning for men as earlier for things. They are to be brought into the service of the New Jerusalem. They are to be led into it. Nevertheless, they are to be won in such a way that the testimony is never constraint or propaganda, but only attestation of the love of Jesus Christ.

We are to be with men as Christians who know that they are saved but who are not superior to others, and do not crush them, because of this knowledge of salvation, since they have to remember that that salvation is the same for all in the relation of love. The relation of love which is to be set up expresses then a twofold freedom. There is first the freedom of using without owning, claiming, or dominating (even for the sake of evangelism). There is secondly the freedom of using without being owned by anything, whether things (money, work, etc.) or neighbors (which would be an absurd sacrifice). This is freedom truly to be while still participating in the life of the world.

Thus the relation of love properly expresses free being by a radical rejection of having. Love never finds expression in ownership, only in reciprocity. This love in effect gives content to free being, which has no significance when it stands apart but which receives it in (continually renewed) event, i.e., the event of freedom carried into a relation to the things and men of society.

"Let every man abide in the same state wherein he was called. Art thou called being a slave? care not for it; but if thou mayest be made free, use it rather. For he that is called in the Lord, being a slave, is the Lord's freeman" (1 Corinthians 7:20f.).

It is a well-known fact that neither the Lord nor the first generation of Christians adopted a general, doctrinal, and collective position in respect of slavery. This passage is not directed to slaves in general. It cannot serve as a justification for slavery. Nor is it advice to all slaves. It concerns only those who have been called. The problem is exclusively that of the Christian slave.

This has the strict application that a specific line of conduct is laid down. Each is to stay in the state in which he was. This means on the one side that becoming a Christian does not have to show itself in a change of state. One does not have to cease being a banker or soldier or husband or landowner when one becomes a Christian. Similarly, being clothed with the dignity of being a Christian does not mean that one must stop being a worker, slave, or beggar.

Nevertheless, the situation is not simply stabilized. Two limits are imposed. First, the existing state is not to be exalted as such. Belonging to it is not to be the theme of an ideology or belief. None but Jesus Christ should be the object of veneration. This is the point of the preceding "as though. . . ."

Secondly, if there is a chance to change, it should be used. It is not a duty to stay in the state in which one is called. It can certainly be changed. The possibility of staying in it is not stressed. The state in which we are is not enhanced by our becoming Christians. There is nothing intrinsically imposing about being a Christian teacher rather than simply a teacher. What the text is really doing is devaluating the problem. After all, since you have been called to belong to Christ, it is not so important whether you are slave or free, rich or poor, teacher or pupil.

What is attacked is escalation of the problem by making it an emotional issue. What is condemned is the idea that since I am freed by Christ it is scandalous and intolerable that I should be socially a slave. Conversion to Christ ought to carry with it a certain indifference to the self and its social condition or financial worth. These are outmoded and secondary matters. It is not worth devoting energy to them. We must cease to be preoccupied with problems of this kind. We must simply accept positive or negative changes. From this time on claims are no longer possible.

It should not be argued that, while the biblical teaching was valid at a time when such matters were not important, we have now come of age and our action today must be primarily in the economic and social field. Clearly it was just as important for a first-century slave to become free as it might be today. There were just as many social conflicts then as now, and each pursued his individual or collective interests in that age as we all do today[14] —we shall come back to this later.

---

14 Bonhoeffer's interpretation of the passage in *The Cost of Discipleship* is exactly the same.

H. Roux puts the matter well: "When the slave becomes a Christian, he does not escape his servile state. . . . His freedom in Christ, which has its root in grace received and brings forth fruit in faith and in the hope of total redemption, does not in itself constitute a natural right in virtue of which he might claim physical or legal manumission. The Christian slave is thus called upon in the first instance to live his life as a free man in Christ in and not outside his condition as a slave and under the yoke of servitude." I must repeat, however, that the decision is purely individual. It is a matter for the man who has understood what freedom in Christ means, who learns to put his preoccupations in second place, and who is prepared to stay in the state in which he is.[15]

It cannot be imposed as a law on others. A subordinate cannot be told that since he is a Christian he has to stay in his subordinate position. The injunction cannot be transformed into a principle of general organization, a system for the stabilization of society, or an instrument of social conformity. The level here is exclusively that of the use of freedom in Christ by the one who is freed.

Furthermore, in this freedom the state in which we are has a certain importance. The first task to which we are called, then, is not to leave it for a better one but to transform it inwardly by living in freedom within it from this time forward. This is what Paul is insisting on when he shows what the attitude of the slave should be.

Now there is obviously a great contradiction between the situation of the slave and that of the free man in Christ. Nevertheless, the slave has to live out his condition of servitude as a free man. He has to transform it hereby. We again quote H. Roux:[16] "It is not that a factual situation has to

15 I realize that the argument will be presented that this teaching opens the door to exploitation. Yes, it does. Christian faith cannot incarnate itself in personal claims and social pressures. It implies that the problem of social status take second place. Submission to a superior, even if he is unjust, facilitates exploitation by him. But this corresponds to giving cloak as well as coat. To adopt any other view is to yield to the modern ideology of claim and egalitarianism which is quite incompatible with Christianity. Yet two points should be made here which I have stressed already. The teaching of submission is given by scripture; it can never be given by the superior. This would be a detestable falsehood. Secondly, if the superior uses voluntary submission as a basis of exploitation, he heaps coals of fire on his head. The most serious possible condemnation awaits him. It might also be recalled that the decision here is one's own, not a decision for others.

16 In his fine analysis of the Épitres pastorales (1959) Roux stresses that the freedom received in Christ does not become a kind of natural right in virtue of which one can claim legal freedom. Freedom in Christ consists primarily (although not exclusively) in assuming one's human condition. This is not subjection. It is not respect for the establishment. It is not a justification of slavery. Instead, it is a new way of living. It is a living out of the relation with others (with masters) which also abolishes the dialectic of, e.g., slaves and masters. The transformation by grace of human relations leads to a transformation of the legal and social framework. This attitude implies the eschatological tension which prevents respect for the master from being confused with respect for the establishment.

be admitted and accepted. What is needed is the adoption of a positive attitude by authentic inner consent. . . . Such an attitude is not based on what is called respect for the established order, which might be only passive resignation in face of the world's disorder. . . . What changes is the heart of man, his new way of looking at himself and others under the lordship of Christ. This is the new and powerful force which interjects itself into human relations and sooner or later finishes up by calling in question and either modifying or shattering the institutions which govern them. The existence in the world of Christian slaves who have regard to their masters and set themselves in their service, not through force or resignation nor in a state of inner revolt, but through respect for their dignity as persons (even though they are unworthy of it)—this is an authentic sign of the kingdom of Christ and the redemption of the world which is far more revolutionary and effective than any legal or social claim. It is the way in which the slave confesses the name of Jesus Christ and lives as a free man by having regard to the personal dignity of his master as one to whom the liberation that Christ confers is promised also."

In fact, then, the social condition is very important, not because it is to be changed socially and externally, but because it is to be transformed from within and given a new meaning and content. This means that we should stay in the existing state. Indifference to social, economic, and political conditions as an expression of freedom is again affirmed by Paul (with respect to himself) in Philippians 4:11-14: "I have learned, in whatsoever state I am, therewith to be content. I know both how to be abased, [17] and I know how to abound; everywhere and in all things I am instructed both to be full and to be hungry, both to abound and to suffer need. I can do all things through Christ which strengtheneth me. Notwithstanding, ye have done well that ye did communicate with my affliction."

There are four essential points here. First, Paul has learned. This is not a faculty or disposition. It does not conform to man's spontaneous nature. Apprenticeship is required to be able to live in this freedom regarding honor or humiliation, riches or poverty. This is one of the apprenticeships of freedom.

Secondly, Paul does not say that he has experienced these different

---

17 On the identity of humility and humiliation cf. the author's *Man and Money*. Can one say that this attitude of Paul is one of resignation? Like many others I have often stated that resignation is not a Christian virtue since it implies passivity and acceptance of what comes, whereas freedom summons us to act and not to be resigned. But we have to know what action to take. Not to have confidence in social or political action is not on that account to be resigned. When Paul tells us about his work and his conflict with adversaries of every kind (including the powers of Ephesians 6), he shows no trace of resignation, but the object of his conflict is more important than a social object. Spiritual combat is just as brutal as human warfare, said Rimbaud. Paul's "I have learned" is the very reverse of resignation.

conditions, that he has been rich and poor, etc. He says that he has learned to be content. He has learned how to live. We have here a transformation of the concrete situation by the freedom of the man who can now be content with all events both positive and negative, who is satisfied with the situation in which he finds himself without devoting his energies and emotions to changing it. This is not worth doing if one is content. Yet we do not have here Stoicism or passivity. The point is that there are better things to do. There are more important things to do. One does not ask the President to clean his shoes or make his bed; he has other things on which to spend his energies. We thus have a relativization of social and political action.

Paul is not just content. He knows how to live. It is a big thing to know how to live in all circumstances, knowing that the modification of situations or contingencies does not modify the reality of life. This is possible only if the life in question is not narrowly determined by circumstances.

If we believe that living means being comfortable, having a good job, knowing how to enjoy ourselves, increasing our income, raising our standard of living, having good relations, going on foreign tours, and acquiring culture from television, then obviously prosperity and poverty can change the whole of life. We know, however, that in Christ living is something very different. This kind of living is possible in either prosperity or poverty. It is not intrinsically modified either by joy or sorrow, by possession or non-possession, by honor or humiliation.

The difficulty is to go into joy or sorrow, riches or poverty, honor or humiliation, in the life in Christ. The difficulty is that of not changing the life in Christ into a refuge where we are remote from human conditions. We have to live out these conditions. We have to assume them. We have to bear them with their light or heavy burden. We are not to refuse to live. We must not evade life in a virtuous and mortal abstinence.

It may be noted that Paul puts prosperity and poverty on the same level. He thinks it is just as hard to live in the former as it is in the latter. In practical terms this is not the common view. When the reference is to life in Christ, however, the whole Bible bears witness that this is more seriously threatened by riches than anything else. It is much more difficult to be free when rich. Personally I find it hard to think it is even possible to live out freedom in riches, but a miracle of grace is always possible. Similarly it is much harder to remain a free man in the midst of honors.

In any case, thirdly, this apprenticeship of freedom, this knowing how to live which Paul has learned, is not a situation or a definitive acquisition. It is never possible except through the strength of Christ. It seems to me that we have here rather more than the general theological truth that Christ does everything in us. What Paul is saying here, in my view, is that learning how to live in all conditions without wanting to change them but in effect transfiguring them from within is one of the hardest things a Christian can be called upon to do, and that it is literally an impossibility apart from the strength of Christ.

Hence we do not have here the line of least resistance. It is a modern idea that it is easier to accept a condition than to try to change it. For Paul—and the Old Testament witness is to the same effect—the opposite is true.[18] It is much easier to get alarmed, to begin making alliances, to engage in strategic planning, to group men for action, to set up claims, to unleash revolutions, than it is to live as free men in these conditions.

But may not this living as a free man be a mere illusion? Cannot any wealthy person living with his money and his luxury claim to be a free man? He certainly can. But I would point out that the illusion of politico-social action can be just as strong, and that thinking we can change man's condition by institutional change in the economic or political sphere is the worst of all modern illusions. This freedom cannot be possessed or retained in any way.

A fourth and final point in the passage shows how it relates to the teaching given to slaves. I can live in want, says Paul, but I am glad that you have helped me in my distress. In other words, I am quite prepared for poverty, but if someone comes to my aid and I get out of it, this is good. The idea here is the same as the advice to take the chance of freedom if it arises. The important thing is not to become obsessed with the problem of one's condition either positively or negatively.

We thus come back to relative indifference regarding the social, material, economic, and political condition. This attitude of indifference, or content, is an expression of freedom to the degree that a fourfold liberation is implied.

First, there is implied a domination of one's condition or situation. Instead of being crushed and enslaved by the worries of work, salary, the future, and so forth, through mastery of these things we are enabled to be true men.

There is then implied a certain ability to accept different situations

---

18 We may again refer to Kierkegaard's protest against the consuming and sterile passion for action and his advocacy of the efficacy of suffering. As he sees it, the example of the apostles shows that courage, when it suffers, does wonders it is incapable of when it tries to take action. The apostles did not merely suffer, for the man of action may do the same. Their whole conduct and attitude was one of suffering and submission. They did not preach revolt against authority. They recognized its power. In suffering they obeyed God rather than men. They did not ask not to be punished. They did not object to suffering punishment. But having been punished they continued to preach Christ. They did not try to constrain anyone, but being under constraint themselves they triumphed thereby. Apart from this, mere courage cannot work wonders. The wonder is that when the situation seems to be for everyone else a situation of defeat, for the apostles it is one of victory. When courage is not so strong, it wants to act, to reason, to enjoy recognition from men. It is neither able nor willing to submit to the folly in which what the world sees as a defeat, and in so doing contributes thereto, is for the secret of faith glory with God.

and variations, to make new beginnings. Freedom means that one is able to exist in the discontinuity of circumstances, in the refusal to become enclosed in continuity. This may seem to contradict the advice to stay in the same state in which you are called, but in effect it does not, for the advice presupposes a downgrading of the state and hence a readiness for any changes which may come.

More attention will have to be given to the third and fourth implications. The third is an attitude of indifference to the objectives which the social milieu advances as desirable. I believe that this is completely decisive in relation to our situation in society. For the slave the objective which society regards as desirable is obviously manumission. Paul demands that the Christian slave be free in relation to this objective. We have here a general principle. Freedom means not accepting what the group, the milieu, or society presents as an essential objective of action, as something which is worth living for. All such things must be submitted to the test of our freedom and to judgment before God. This does not mean that we must reject them. They may finally be accepted, but no more. All such aims as productivity, raising the standard of living, computerization, democratization, and so forth have to be seen in their true proportions and their relativity even if they are not on this account rejected.

The fourth implication of freedom is refusal of the central modern thesis that material change will bring about a change of life, being, and reality. The movement depicted here is the exact opposite. The slave has become a free man in Christ; this is what counts. His state has thus been transformed, and he himself has to transform it from within. Contingently his material condition may also change, but this is secondary. We have to realize that no economic or political transformation will bring about any fundamental change at all. What will happen is simply that one problem will give way to another and one injustice to another. Variations of degree are possible for a time, but nothing decisive is accomplished. It is from within and by the mighty act of Jesus Christ that situations change. While it may not be the normal view, I would argue that the contrary belief is mythological and that this attitude alone is realistic and consonant with freedom.

### § 2. Dialogue and Encounter

The freedom which is expressed in hope, and the combination of hope and freedom, enable us to live out dialogue and encounter. This is the point at which to discuss these commonplaces of contemporary ethics and theology.

We must being by asking whether encounter is an absolute point of departure, whether it is a reality in itself and as such. Without caricaturing the position of some thinkers we may go so far as to say that for them encounter exists at point zero, that on the one side I do not exist except in and by encounter (without which I am nothing), and that on the other side only encounter with the neighbor fulfils the will of God, so that all ethics is ultimately an ethics of encounter; indeed, God himself is not found except through the neighbor, so that it is encounter with him which makes possible the knowledge of revelation.

This is all bound up with the "theology" of Christian atheism, i.e., with the exclusive affirmation of the horizontal dimension and the elimination of any vertical relation between God and man.

Now undoubtedly encounter plays a decisive role in the biblical revelation. Love and the neighbor are what it is all about. The question is, however, whether the Bible presents things in this way. Can this particular theology be drawn from the text? Encounter and dialogue are ethical attitudes, but in relation to the modern problem a short digression must be made.

We should note first that this theology strikes out the first commandment, which Jesus himself also recognized to be the first. My own emphasis, however, will be on the great passage which is the basis of the modern presentation, namely, the judgment of the nations in Matthew 25. This passage, it is said, shows that the man who does not know God and is outside the church but who disinterestedly and with no ulterior motive does good to others (materially) in his encounter with them is in conformity with the will of God and has encountered Christ. The passage confirms, then, what is taught in the parable of the Good Samaritan who became a neighbor to the man who fell among thieves by simply meeting him and ministering to him. Christians, it is said, are simply to do the same. They are not to go up to others because they see Christ in them, nor for any other reason, but with the sole intention of serving them, and in this way they will encounter Christ without realizing it.

In my view the deductions drawn from this exposition are harmful. The parable of the judgment relates to judgment of the nations. The meaning of this is clear, for in a Hebraic context the nations are Gentiles, those who do not belong to the Jewish people. The point of the parable is thus clear. Jesus is answering the question as to the fate of those who do not have faith. The question obviously arises out of the repeated affirmation that faith in Jesus can alone bring to salvation. Jesus is telling us that those who do not have faith can still be saved, for he, Christ, has decided to be with the most miserable, and whenever a man comes to help a sufferer he is coming to Christ without being aware of it.

Such a passage, however, does not eliminate or contradict the totality of other passages in which we see that everything is decided by faith. Encounter does not replace faith. Again, such a passage does not offer a privileged way of encountering Christ. The great error is that of wanting to generalize the passage, of making it a résumé of the law and the prophets, and of building a theology thereon.

In fact we are told about two encounters with Christ. In the first

Jesus says: "I, Jesus, am the Christ," and this implies response, i.e., faith, on our part. Everything begins here. This concrete faith leads us to encounter with the neighbor because Jesus says so. We find Christ in the neighbor because we have received him through the word of God. The second encounter is by way of the neighbor. This applies to the one who has never heard about Jesus, who has received no witness or preaching, who has no knowledge. This encounter, then, is mysterious and secret. The man does not know it, but Christ is there.[19]

For this encounter, however, the state of happy ignorance is necessary. The man who enjoys it must never have read the gospel, or heard of Christ. For the Christian this is no longer possible. What is expressly demanded of him is not that he should go and help his neighbor but that he should confess the faith of Peter. A simple reading of Matthew 25 forbids us to draw from it the conclusions that are drawn by modern theology. It is no longer possible for us to say: "I never knew. . . . " We know in advance that when we go to help our neighbor we go to help Christ. We cannot play a game, acting as if we had no knowledge, and pretending that all our encounter with God is through Christ (there is after all an Old Testament) and that all our encounter with Christ is through our neighbor. Revelation restrains us. Through it we know that there is a very different encounter with Christ in the Word, and that this can stand alone. All that Matthew 25 says is that this is not the only possibility, that salvation is not our exclusive privilege, and that in any case the choice of the means of encounter is not in our hands.

In other words, scripture again distinguishes strictly between the situation of those who have received testimony about who the Christ is, the transmission of biblical knowledge, and the situation of those who have not received this testimony. The familiar dilemma—Is it through Jesus Christ that we encounter our neighbor, or is it through our neighbor that we encounter Jesus Christ?—is no dilemma at all. Both theses are true. But they do not refer to the same people.

For those who have never heard of Christ, it is through the neighbor that they encounter him by adopting an attitude of service. For those who do know about Christ, true encounter is possible only through him. They can no longer see their neighbor except through Christ, and if they do not see Christ in him there is no encounter. They realize that nothing in their lives takes place outside Christ. They cannot forget this or act as if they had forgotten it. This is precisely the thing they cannot do.

They can have no immediate encounter except with the Lord. All other encounters will be mediate. Glory has to be given to the Lord that in his grace he permits these other human encounters which normally could not be encounters with him at all.

19 It might be noted in passing that the "new" theology was a commonplace in the middle ages. We find it in many legends of the saints. Indeed, most of the Christmas stories of the nineteenth century are illustrations of this second encounter.

Now to say that the passage in Matthew 25 refers to the nations, and that it offers us consolation regarding all men, does not mean that we may twist it around and say that in consequence it need not concern us. As I have often said, the law becomes active when I look at myself as though I were not a Christian, which happens all the time. I have to fulfil the law when faith does not lead me beyond it, when it does not cause me to act beyond the demands of the law. The same applies here too. When I am incapable of encountering my neighbor in Christ, when my faith is extremely feeble, but when my compassion leads me to perform some simple service without seeing anything great or saving in it, then by grace it is the Lord whom I have again encountered. But this takes place on this side of the demand that I should live as a Christian, for I am not demanded to live in forgetfulness of the fact that Christ is my primary relation and my first love. I am not demanded to choose this mode of encounter, for he has chosen the other way.

Christ loved me and encountered me first. He came to serve me, and it is in the service that he renders me that I first meet him before I can meet and serve others. It is because revelation has been granted me, because he has served and loved me first, that I am now committed to loving my neighbor and serving him.

Under the pretext of humility, of setting aside Christian superiority, and of service of others, the current interpretation of Matthew 25 is yet another instance of the intolerable pride of man. It is because I first refuse to let myself be loved and saved that I decide that it is by serving my neighbor that I encounter Christ. It is because I refuse to recognize that the choice of mode of encounter belongs to God alone in every respect that I decide to choose on my own what the mode of this encounter will be. This is the tragic crux of the antithesis.

After this digression we may now return to the ethical question. It is true that when we speak of committed freedom, the commitment is in the first instance to others. The first act of our freedom is to go and meet others. All the rest follows from this first step and can be seen, thought about, and lived out only by way of this first act of freedom.

Nevertheless, it is an act of *freedom*. It is an act which neither demonstrates nor, of course, denies freedom, but presupposes it. We thus have to raise the question whether any encounter or dialogue of any kind is the encounter of which the gospel speaks, i.e., becoming a neighbor, or whether the dialogue is authentic dialogue. Can we go along with theologians who in a legitimate concern to avoid casuistry refuse to distinguish between eros and agape? Now eros exists and so does agape. Neither is a part or possibility or sign of the other. There is antithesis both of sign and significance. In the same way, one cannot agree that every encounter is a true one.

The element of truth in the contention that we cannot distinguish between true and false encounter (or dialogue)—and a point that we should never forget—is that encounter and dialogue must never be selective. That is to say, it is not for me to say whom I will encounter or with whom I will engage in dialogue. It is not for me to say that encounter and dialogue will be fruitful and meaningful with this person but not with that. For a long time Christians have in fact believed that it is particularly worth while encountering other Christians or people with spiritual interests or those who might be evangelized and converted. Now this selectivity in encounter is natural enough. It is based on the human sense of fellowship or a concern to pass on the good news. But preconceived choice of the subjects of encounter or dialogue implies an absence of freedom on the part of Christians who are guilty of it.

Today, of course, we are more familiar with selectivity in reverse. The value of encounter with other Christians is contested. Such encounter is regarded as banal and meaningless. It is supposedly the expression of a ghetto mentality. Dialogue and friendship within the church are viewed as false and absurd. I have even heard it said that neighbors may be encountered everywhere except in the church. More fruitful dialogue can be enjoyed with left-wingers. Once again there are good reasons for this selectivity, but it can hardly claim any greater legitimacy than the first form.

My own belief is that all encounter is to be taken seriously. No choice should be made. No preconception should be entertained. No prejudgment should be obeyed in dialogue. Only one form of encounter or dialogue seems to me to be completely inauthentic. This is the planned and organized encounter between specialists in dialogue in which we leave altogether the sphere of gift and grace and put ourselves afresh in a total determinism, not an ecclesiastical determinism, but that of the society in which we live. In sum, any encounter except encounter for its own sake seems to me to hold out possibilities.

In the first instance, of course, true encounter is of no apparent significance. It has no given content. It also has no intrinsic value. The fact of encounter is not the fruitful thing. It simply opens up a possibility. It has the potentiality of becoming authentic.

To do this it has to take place. I have to see someone and clasp his hand. Dialogue has to begin. I have to speak and an answer has to be given. The preliminary remarks may be very trivial, e.g., about the weather. The encounter and dialogue may never get beyond this. They may remain trivial and inauthentic. For example, they may be predetermined by social conventions, by prejudices, by the roles we play (out of habit and so forth). They may have a false intention, as when I want to convince the other. They may be the occasion of mutual concealment, as when through fear or caution there is no willingness on the part of the two to open themselves to one another. It all depends on the partners whether there is real encounter or not. On the partners? On both? As a Christian I cannot say this. The encounter between Christ and me does not depend on both of us but solely on Jesus Christ.

All encounter is in the first instance meaningless. But all encounter may take on meaning. This is why we vigorously reject any prior selectivity. No one is an apt subject for encounter. But no one is not an apt subject. Each may become an apt subject or the opposite. This is why it is ridiculous to exclude or to single out encounter either within the church or with radicals, etc. All relations, whether in the church, family, business, party, or union, may be true ones. It is the Christian who has the task, function, and mission of giving the dialogue or encounter both meaning and authenticity.

This will happen when I put myself in the service of the other. I become his neighbor by ministering to him, by rendering him the service which he really needs, by putting myself in his service. There is no other way.

In effect the encounter will be authentic only if it carries the sign of Christ. It can do this only if the other can see a reflection of grace. He can finally do this only if the act that I perform in relation to him, and for him, is of the same nature as the act that God has done for me in Jesus Christ—a pure gift and absolute service. Similarly I can give meaning to the dialogue, not by overwhelming the other with pious speeches (although this does not mean that we are to avoid speaking about Jesus Christ), but by self-engagement with the other.[20] The dialogue has to stop being a mere exchange of words and become the engagement of the one in the life of the other and with the other. This engagement in the same venture as the other is what gives the words we exchange irreplaceable value.[21] The exchange of

---

20 This engagement underlies the distinction between witness and propaganda; cf. J. Ellul, "Christianisme et Propagande," *Revue de L'Evangélisation.*

21 I will not insist on the word "dialogue," for it is now bandied about everywhere and has become for some a universal panacea. As J. Lecroix finely puts it, "dialogue has become the answer to all difficulties. To make problems go away we have only to enter into dialogue. Religious differences, class divisions, diversities of interest, and psycho-sociological contradictions are all magically dispelled by the one force of dialogue. This is not only false; it is dangerous. There is nothing worse than verbalizing a man's humanity when the situation renders it impossible. Better sometimes naked violence than a pseudo-dialogue which is merely a hypocritical mask." This is why I never present dialogue as a way of resolving conflicts. I simply present an attitude of freedom which allows conflicting situations and tendencies to meet in truth, and thus opens the way for love to heal the breach. But this does not lead to a smoothing over or a solution. On these problems cf. especially Kohler *et al., Le Dialogue* (1967), which discusses the problems and specific cases of dialogue, and M. de Goedt, *Foi au Christ et dialogues de chrétien* (1967), which is an excellent discussion, first of the concept, field, demands, and implications of dialogue, and the bad faith which is always possible in pseudo-dialogue, and then of the possibility of dialogue that is opened up by faith: "It is in avowal of its impotence that dialogue must find its power." "The role of faith is to open up an absolute future for the words that men exchange." My only reservation in

words between Jesus and his disciples is engagement of this kind. All that we are told shows indeed that there is in each case engagement between Jesus and those who accompany him. Jesus does not expect reciprocity. He might hope for it, and he can thus make its absence a matter of reproach in the blind, in lepers, in Simon, and in the disciples in Gethsemane. But in dialogue only Jesus himself is engaged. Then in the dialogues in Acts we find that there is engagement only on the part of the disciples. The others do not share this engagement and yet authentic dialogue takes place. The point, then, is that the genuineness of encounter and the value of dialogue depend on every Christian. It is the Christian's engagement which transforms a conversation and makes trivial contact into a decisive force.

This brings us, however, into the sphere of freedom. Service is preceded by freedom. This is a reality which is constantly forgotten in the modern view. I cannot serve my neighbor unless I am free. I cannot put myself in his service unless I am not in servitude to someone else, unless I am freed from such servitude. Freedom, then, is the first step which makes encounter and dialogue possible. Everything that I serve—money, self, state, party, family, class, profession, or church (attention today is devoted to this alone)—is a power which, when I encounter others, finally seeks only to bring them to servitude as it has already brought me. A prior work of God has first to be received and lived out in me. This work is a miracle. Hence it is not in encounter alone that I find Jesus Christ. Jesus Christ has already been the Liberator in my own life. If not, encounter is meaningless.

If we gather up the various elements analyzed above, we perceive that freedom plays a constant part and is the condition of this whole enterprise. There is, however, no reference to it today. It seems to be taken for granted as an implicit condition. In fact, of course, we have seen that there can be nothing implicit about it. We have seen that it is a genuine miracle. It is my belief that theologians of encounter have simply forgotten about it.

Everything, however, depends upon freedom. Initiative does so first. Encounter cannot take place in the daily topsy-turvy of city life. We have said, of course, that every contact can be the occasion of encounter. But encounter has to be willed. The freedom of encounter can be born only in freedom.

The one who takes the initiative in encountering others, who seeks out others, who wants to be a neighbor to them, can do this only if he himself is free, only if he is disengaged enough from what weighs on him and conditions him, only if he can unite himself with others authentically.

relation to the subject of this book is that, while the possibility of dialogue is here located in the reconciliation of men with one another by God (which is true enough), it is not set in the framework of freedom, which seems to me to be the only possibility from the ethical standpoint. For the link with the modern trend toward a theology of revolution cf. Jules Girardi, *Dialogue et Révolution* (1969), who still believes in the direct possibility of dialogue and entertains the pious notion that it is itself a cultural revolution.

The presence of God is already manifested in this initiative, and this obliges us to accept the fact that it is through Christ and the freedom which he gives that I am enabled to encounter others.

The same applies no less to non-selectivity. Everything constrains us to have chosen and particular encounters. Our background, convictions, and situation fashion our contacts with others. This is why we meet some people and not others. We always meet those who resemble us. But the commandment to become a neighbor, which is the same as the commandment to love even enemies, deconditions us. If we become capable of encountering and receiving all sorts and conditions of men, if we become capable of taking the initiative with all sorts and conditions of men, this can happen only if we are free enough not to select whom we will meet, not to pass a prior judgment on whom we can meet, and not to decide in advance whom we cannot meet.

We now take a further step. Normally, it has been seen, everything is falsified in our contacts and approaches. Everything is made meaningless and inauthentic. But this means once more that freedom is a condition. Only in my freedom in Christ can I escape the imposed dialogue of the social world and reject the prejudices which in my eyes render all attempts at dialogue futile. Only in this freedom can I step out of the normal role that society makes me play.

Great importance is assigned to role playing by modern sociologists and psychologists. Man can even be regarded as intrinsically no more than a succession of roles. If this is so, then necessarily authentic encounter is quite impossible. But a miracle is also needed to make man something else. The butterfly becomes free when it emerges from the chrysalis. In the same way I am summoned to be free for encounter by emerging from the role that I have to play as a member of society.

Similarly, to engage in dialogue I have to have self-detachment. To have this presupposes the supreme freedom that Christ himself had. None of the falsifications of dialogue or encounter can be avoided unless I am free.

We now come to the most important thing of all, i.e., freedom from superiority. If I approach others aware only that since it is I who search for authenticity in the encounter I am superior to them, aware only that as a Christian I have to give them something (which is true enough, since I am Christ's witness), aware only that I have to contribute to their well-being and salvation (which is again true, for through witness they may be saved by grace, and this must be part of the dialogue), aware only of the dogmatic armor which will be my safeguard and offer me protection against anything that might happen in the encounter (and I do have such armor, and it is good that I should be aware of the fact), aware only of a certain superiority over others that I enjoy as a result of faith—then all is lost. I shall not be a neighbor to others, nor a witness of Christ to them, nor a disciple. I shall not be able to be these things precisely because of my awareness of being them.

This awareness of a true reality becomes a false and falsifying awareness because it prevents us from loving our neighbors with agape (not eros, if I may be allowed the distinction). If we do not love our neighbors in freedom from this awareness, encounter without love falsifies what we have to bring them. It makes it impossible for us to declare God's grace to them or to formulate the truth for them. Our awareness destroys what God has given us by making us feel superior to those whom God has given us to love. For if love is impossible a tragic chain reaction follows which destroys everything else.

But how are we to avoid awareness of what is a genuine reality? If we try to peel off this awareness, to be simple, to divest ourselves of Christian superiority, this attempt also makes the dialogue strained and false, for it can never be more than a mask.

The answer is that all this presupposes freedom. I have to be freed also from that awareness. This is what happens naturally when the grace that is granted me disengages me from myself and centers me on God. If christocentricity is a doctrine, a theological type, a key to the interpretation of scripture, all this may be very interesting, but in the long run it does not amount to much. The epistles bring before us a different kind of christocentricity, i.e., that which in the life of the man who is called by God causes Christ to occupy the whole stage. At the very center of the ego the world and the flesh are replaced by him. When this happens, I am stripped of the hampering awareness of being saved and of having received the truth. I still know these things, but my knowledge is no longer a screen between me and my neighbor. The freedom which God gives me sees to this.

Receiving this freedom, as I have often said, is not a magical operation. I am not transported like a thing into the condition of a free man. I am not fashioned as such without having any part in it. When I am given freedom I am also given thereby and therewith the freedom to grasp it, to assume it, and to live it out. If I do not do this, if I do not take this first step of freedom and take up myself the freedom in which I am made anew, then everything is frozen. Thus if I do not approach the other in this climate of freedom, in this glad stripping away of superiority, my own freedom is made sterile.

On the other hand, we must not think that an attempt at humility, a forced desire not to be superior, and (what is even worse) the disdain that some feel today for biblical knowledge and anything specifically Christian— we must not think that this intentionally willed attitude has the slightest value or will in any way promote encounter. What we have here is the other inauthenticity, which is simply a refusal to be what one is. Dialogue is completely falsified when it is said that the Christian knows nothing of truth, that the Christian is no different in virtue of grace received and known, that the Christian is a sorry kind of person of no particular quality. This is scorn for the great work of God in us. It is a lack of freedom. It is a work of man which falls under the judgment of the familiar text which speaks of works that have a show of wisdom but in the event simply feed human pride. Our own acts have neither meaning nor value unless they are based on the freedom that is given and received in Christ prior to any intention which we ourselves might have.

This brings us to the very heart of the relation between freedom and encounter or dialogue.

It is a commonplace to say with Buber that I am not myself, an I, unless I am this for someone, i.e., unless I am a Thou for another person. On this view there seems to be a reciprocal creation. Each becomes an I because each is called Thou by the other. It seems to me that this circular relation is not an accurate depiction of the situation.

All that we have said thus far about the indispensability of freedom for the possibility of encounter, about initiative, non-selectivity, and the shedding of superiority, presupposes that the Christian who engages in dialogue is already an I. The very fact of freedom clearly intimates this. In fact I cannot encounter the other unless I myself have become an I. It is not the other who makes me this.

If I become a neighbor for another man, it is not the other who makes me a neighbor. The man wounded by the wayside is not the one who makes a neighbor out of the Samaritan. God himself has already been at work. God himself makes an I out of the It. He does this by having already engaged in dialogue with the man. It is because God first talks to me, because he summons me, because he calls me by name, because he reveals his name to me, that I myself, being called a Thou by God, beco   an I, that I can then in turn encounter the other authentically and be a Thou for him, and that since he is at the same time a Thou for me, I make him authentic and he in turn becomes an I. None of this is true except on the basis of the act which constitutes me an I, i.e., the act of God, the act of freedom which liberates me so that I can be a neighbor to the other and the other can be made a man for God. Any other analysis is simply an attempt to escape the free initiative of God. It is a reawakening of the pride of man which results only in solitude and inauthenticity.

It must be understood, of course, that this encounter can take place only if I am also free in relation to the other. What has to be said here will inevitably cause offense. We have spoken of liberation from self and the powers. Necessarily there is also liberation from the other. We have referred repeatedly to the demand of Jesus that family and so forth must be forsaken if we are to follow him. Liberation in Christ has an effect on all natural bonds and hence on those which tie us to other men. In some sense I become strange and a stranger to them. If love is the point of freedom, this cannot in any way be assimilated to obedience to sociological relations with others. Others cannot be a law for me in Christian freedom.

Free in Christ, I have to be different. I have to reject all solidarities, whether mechanical or organic. Freedom in Christ carries with it this breaking of spontaneous solidarities. The other who constantly invades me in the enormous crowds of contemporary society, the other who drowns me out with noise, movement, and smells, the other who participates with me in the vast creative work of this society—this other is one from whom I must free myself, since it impossible to follow Christ and also to follow the crowd. It is impossible to accept the law of freedom and also to accept the law of others.

I am aware that readers will seize on passages in the Sermon on the Mount. If anyone wants our coat, we are to give our cloak too (Matthew 6:40). This is surely acceptance of the law of others, of their demands. It is our submission to them. Surely our relation with others is essential and paramount. Our answer is that this is a false conclusion, for the reference here is to love, not to the other. Love, however, implies freedom if it is to exist. It implies freedom in relation to the other. If there is to be encounter and dialogue, I and Thou, there has to be separation, rupture, difference, and distance. I have to be free in relation to the other to be able to love him freely, to be able to encounter him as he is and for what he really is. To love one's neighbor is not to be under submission to a common sociological bond. Two oxen yoked together are not in a relation of encounter. To go two miles with someone who forces me to go one is the act of a free man who willingly submits to the demand of the other. The text itself speaks of being forced to give one's coat or go a mile—a situation of unfreedom. But giving one's cloak and going an extra mile restore the situation of freedom. They are a recapturing of distance, initiative, and the possibility of loving the other.

The point here, however, is not that a bond of sociological servitude is transformed into a bond of love. It is not true that through freedom and love in Christ I am united with my parents and children unless I have first been freed and separated from them. It is not true that in freedom I am united with members of my profession, class, race, party, or ideology (even if Christian) unless there has first been a radical break which makes me free in relation to them, yes, free with all that this means in terms of distance, aloofness, and even indifference, criticism, and non-communication. Only in this freedom of separation can I rediscover truth in the other and love him freely because, behind every false front, he has now become what he is in reality, i.e., a stranger and an enemy.

This situation is studiously hidden by sociological solidarities. To think that we can transpose economic, political, and technological solidarities into the key of love is to enter into the game of social hypocrisy.

The break with the other is not, of course, the same thing as an objectifying of the other or as the existentialism of Sartre, for liberation in respect of the other, the refusal which becomes a law for me, is not the result of my act, conscience, will, or insight; it is the result of Christ's laying his hand on me: "Come thou and follow me." The other is dead; leave him then to his fate. Let the dead fulfil their sociological rites, their elections, their production and consumption. It is because there is this act of the Liberator on me that I can say that I am liberated from others and that I can live as one who is liberated from others.

Apart from this, i.e., if the movement came from me, it would be intolerable pride. But when this break has taken place, we also recognize the point of it. If there is liberation from others, it is in order to make true encounter possible. If there is a break, it is in discipleship of this Jesus and with a view to finding the other in a love which overwhelms him. There is, however, no transition from the relation of sociological encounter and solidarity to freedom and love. There is only a break.

To say that by grace I have the task of instituting the other in turn as an I is to interpose the dimension of hope. We have a circle here. Encounter is not possible unless there is freedom. But it also makes no sense unless there is hope. Once again this hope is a hoping against hope. We know very well the human condition. We know that men pass each other by, that they misunderstand one another, that they live behind closed doors, that they do not help one another, that words wither and die once they pass our lips. All this is true. We know it, and hence there is no possibility that encounter will take place or that dialogue can be achieved.

But now freedom is given to us to take the initiative. This freedom is also release from the ineluctability and implacability of the human situation. This freedom introduces an I into this world. In consequence it introduces a hope. I cannot take the initiative unless I see hope.

The hope is that the initiative in encounter will not be frustrated, that a true dialogue will be entered into, that a word will be heard and received, that there will thus be a genesis, a beginning, and that each encounter will be a beginning, since freedom sets us each time in a beginning.

This means that I can never be blasé. I can never be guided by experience when I approach a new encounter. Experience of frustrated encounters and of dialogues that lead only to misunderstanding might well cause me to be sceptical. It is good indeed that I should be sceptical and critical. But all this is transcended by the new beginning which brings me before a new face with the ingenuousness of youth, and which causes me to fumble my way across the obscure language of the other.

If experience makes me alert, hope rejuvenates me. Hope does not, of course, make me a fool. It does not annul the disappointments of the past. It does not make me naive like a child or a choirboy. It lays a strong hand on my experience, my knowledge of men, my disappointments, my errors in encounter, and instead of letting me be dominated by these it turns the sceptic into a man who is alert to new possibilities. Hope shows me to my astonishment that encounter is still possible. This astonishment comes only on the basis of the gloom occasioned by past encounters. It is the silver lining of the dark cloud.

Hope makes my criticism a self-criticism, i.e., a criticism of my lack of freedom and my wrong methods. Hope holds up the mirror to all my unsuccessful encounters in order to show me that hope itself is true because Christ is there. It becomes the vital force which enables me to make the difficult new approach to my neighbor.

Hope also puts a new complexion on the totality of dialogue. If the dialogue in which I engage is without hope, of what use is it? If its only point is to convey to others my pain, my despair, my dejection, the lack of any meaning or goal, then why speak to them? Similarly, if it is only to share with them their own despair, anger, or view of the world, so that the way is itself the goal, what good is it? They have no need of me in this regard. Dialogue makes no sense unless there is hope, unless I share their bread of tears because I have to give them the cup of joy.

My presence and approach have value for others only if they are a sign of hope for them, only if they open up for them a way of total hope, i.e., of hope which, if it is not just spiritual, is also not just material, like the shrunken hope of so many modern Christians who make of it no more than a political or economic matter. This is all the hope that is held out by Christians who participate in political and revolutionary movements, and it falls far short of the required totality.

I cannot engage in dialogue unless I finally have the hope that the gospel will reach the other, so that I will be for him a true neighbor. I must repeat this. Nothing makes sense, whether it be encounter or service, if the other does not encounter Jesus Christ in the knowledge who he is and not just in the silence of service rendered or in ignorance. For no service is worth anything if it does not culminate in the joy of making the Saviour known to those for whom Jesus died. No service is worth anything unless it culminates in conversion—we have to use this word which is so much detested today.

Certainly we do not have in mind a conversion which is designed to show what a fine evangelist I am nor to increase the number of members in my church nor to subject the poor man whom I take under my care to pious moralizing. The conversion in view is recognition that I have been loved from the foundation of the world, that I have been chosen, that I am genuinely delivered from my terrors and from the evil that I know so well. The other has to know this, and if I do not have the hope to pass on to him this precious treasure, nothing is worth while.

If I am convinced that my word will not get past my books, that the service I render will never mean anything except in the horizontal relation between men and men, that this encounter will fail like all the others, all is in vain. There has to be the hope that this time something extraordinary will happen. For the freedom for encounter is given us in fulness.

## § 3. Realism and Transgression

It might seem strange that realism is here regarded as an expression of the Christian life and that it is linked to freedom. Yet as I see it this is essential. But first a definition must be given of what is meant by realism.

At the simplest level[22] realism is the consideration of facts and situations as we actually know them, i.e., in which we are implicated. It is taking these facts and situations as they are. To a certain extent, then, we have to trust our senses and our reason. To refuse to accord reality to what we experience is to put reason and folly on the same level, to despise common sense, and to affirm incommunicability. I am well acquainted with these teachings; they are all a flight from uncomfortable reality, which it is much easier to deny by heady thinking.

Naturally realism teaches me to apprehend things, to fight against prejudices, to contest interpretative systems. To have this apprehension, then, I have to criticize my means of apprehension. Nevertheless, realism is also the (relative) ability to set facts and experiences in a hierarchy and it leads me in consequence to act according to my comprehension of the real.

This is not, of course, an intellectual attitude. It is an attitude which is humbly everyday. But perhaps only intellectually trained men can adopt it consciously, because this attitude entails a break with modern society, which is increasingly leading us into irrealism.

Realism, then, presupposes the rejection of all idealism, spiritualizing, conceptualizing, or verbalizing. It repudiates such notions as the intrinsic power of truth to conquer, the permanence of man, the superiority of the soul over the body or of idea over matter, and the primacy of the spiritual which leads to neglect of the real. Clearly there is also implied a rejection of the contemporary attitude which confuses what is with what is hoped or

---

22 Naturally I do not have in view realistic philosophical systems. Nor am I thinking of the reality which many philosophers and theologians speak of when, e.g., they say that God is a reality or that he is the ultimate reality (I obviously agree with this). The reality to which I am alluding here is a much more direct one. I am referring to everyday experience, to the people around me, to the environment in which I live, to the situations in which I find myself; cf. P. Laberthonniere, *Le réalisme chrétien* (1966). It is fundamental that stress should be laid on realism to the extent that we are now seeing the recrudescence of a disturbing idealism, e.g., Bultmannian idealism, or the sociological idealism of the World Council. The latter finds expression, among other things, in the talk about "responsible society," a notion invented by American sociology in 1935 and adopted as a Christian idea by the World Council. In fact, of course, the proposals for a responsible society are valueless if there is no correspondence between these proposals and the actual state of affairs. The four volumes of *Church and Society* are stultified by this idealism. Socio-political idealism is both useless and harmful. It is useless because the ignorance of reality which it displays renders quite futile the ideas which are expressed and which simply manifest once again the muddle-headed good will of Christians. It is harmful because it prevents Christian thinking from moving in other directions, because it falsifies the situation, and because it leads Christians into wrong actions and commitments, as we have seen especially since 1967.

believed. Modern man lives in total confusion because, in the system of information which now prevails, he can no longer distinguish fact from the ideological interpretation which society systematically imposes on fact. This means that pure hypotheses (e.g., mass culture or a civilization of leisure) are taken as facts.

More subtle procedures may also be seen. Thus spirit can be integrated into the real as though it were a natural dimension of it. This is a temptation for both Christians and non-Christians. Again, spirit can be utilized as though it had the task of offering solutions to the problems and difficulties caused by encounter with the real. Or it is argued that, since we can grasp the real only through our own experiences and images and mental universe, the real has no reality. Distinction between subject and object may thus be obliterated in the sense that the object is only part of the subject and not in the true sense that the object exists only in relation to the subject and *vice versa*. Finally, Christians theorize that the form according to which everything can have a concrete material aspect in the Bible is a deformation of truth, for it gives expression to our illegitimate attachment to material signs such as the miracles or the bodily resurrection of Jesus: a full-blooded spiritualizing!

Now the accusation might be made that I am dismissing these views too summarily. Complex and powerful thoughts are being summarized incorrectly. There is truth in this. I am listing the trends that I oppose only to call them to mind, not to discuss them. It is my belief that all these intellectual attitudes, which are always presupposed and never proved, prevent us from taking seriously the actual situation of man in his conflict and ambiguity.

Realism implies a rejection of every systematic explanation of the world, whether doctrinal or general. A global system, whether it be Christian, idealistic, or materialistic, necessarily leads at some point to the denial of reality. No system can embrace the totality of known facts, whether in Aristotle's time or our own. This is shown, e.g., by the extremely limited character of Aristotle's experience in the sphere of politics. Similarly a system of global explanation like that of Marx is erroneous precisely because it tries to be global. The criticisms of Bernstein and Sorel are worth noting in this regard, since they are offered from a Marxist standpoint.

Realistic systems, however, are equally mistaken. One might refer, for example, to those which think they can present an accurate view of the world by the application of an exclusively quantitative or statistical method. But spiritual and qualitative elements are also facts, and these cannot be reduced to statistical form.

When all that surrounds us is taken into account, no logical and coherent system of explanation is possible. Only partial systems of relations and contradictions exist. The only thing is that man has to have a system of interpretation, for he needs to give coherence to the world.

Finally, the realism that I have in mind is a repudiation of the contemporary realism of the politician and the business man. The realism of supposedly realistic politics and business is scepticism. It is a consecration of fact as value. It rejects all truth and advocates the primacy of economic utilitarianism. It applies the criteria of success, usefulness, and interest. This kind of realism is a definitive absence of reality, for it sees only what is immediate, and it sees this only in an extremely limited sector (what is before one's nose).

When this realism gains ground, its meaning for the business man is that he should make as much money as possible without regard to the reality of those around him, nor to the consequences of his attitude, nor to his own reality. This is why the capitalist is so stupid.

What, then, does it mean for the politician? It means that he must stay in power and that he thus regards political maneuvers and combinations as the essential thing to the neglect of the general context. This realism is a complete failure to understand political reality in the full sense.

Having made these negative delimitations, we must now ask what a realistic attitude means from the positive standpoint. It contains three elements.

First, it means considering the facts and accepting them as they are in spite of ideologists who say that we can never grasp a fact because there is no such thing as a fact (the whole of science rises up against this philosophical illusion), or who argue that facts exist only within a system. It means accepting the facts for what they are in all their dimensions and in their global totality without denying (either through forgetfulness or for convenience) any of their forms or perspectives, for each fact opens up several possibilities, and this future dimension has also to be taken into account.

Do we have a similarity here to the scientific method? Assuredly, but with the difference that the scientific observer tries to stay out of the game. He tries to get the most precise and the purest possible data. But in ethics, since we deal with the political, sociological, and economic facts about man, and the personal, domestic, and professional facts, it is not our concern to observe facts in a disinterested and artificially isolated way. In this sphere reality is not truly known unless one is a participant in it. One cannot try to stay outside. One has to try things out with all one's being, with mind, emotions, and "flesh." This is what yields a true relation to reality.

Without this involvement there is no knowledge. When reality is made abstract or is merely "considered," it is not taken seriously. What we are defining here is an attitude of life. Realism as I understand it is not a game or a luxury; it is a necessity. I have in mind the traditional attitude of the peasant to nature. He is defeated if he does not participate in the rhythm of nature or accept the reality of nature as it presents itself to him.

The second essential aspect of realism is that, accepting reality for what it is, we do not view it as more than it is. When we take reality seriously and participate in it, we tend to merge into it, to overestimate it, to champion reality alone (as in theories of involvement or historical necessity), and to make fact or the real into a value or criterion. Taking reality as it is means refusing to let it be a value or criterion.

Reality is not a value which allows us to judge action (this is one of the errors of Marxism), before which we have to bow, and to which we must submit. Fact, as we have often said, is not a criterion of truth. To think that it is, is one of the most serious intellectual mistakes of our time. Fact and truth belong to two different orders. On the other hand, they are not strangers to one another. They unite, or can do so, in man.

Hence realism does not presuppose a primacy of matter or efficacy. To believe this is a renunciation of man himself, who on this view obeys what is not a decision for his life. Furthermore, through this confusion of fact and truth, through the transformation of fact into a value, we are finally led in most cases to a negation of fact as such, since fact, when concretely present, cannot have in effect the appearance of a good or a value.

Marxism again offers a good example. The desire to observe facts leads to a system which veils all reality. To make fact a criterion means its denial as fact.

For me simple, everyday reality is a given factor, a presence that precedes my own, a nexus of situations in relation to which, as men, we have to take a stance, to act, and to decide. Hence reality is always a resistance, opposition, and contradiction. It is resolved neither by denial (idealism) nor by submission.

Recognition of this reality in and for itself is an act without which there can be no human life. For here is the measure of our freedom. Freedom takes place only if there is a weight which prevents us from being free and only if we know the size of this weight. If we do not, freedom is a mere dream. Reality gives meaning, vigor, and content to our freedom. If we fail to see it, we also deny ourselves. This happens to those who surrender to a pseudo-reality, e.g., those who confuse reality with what they read, hear, or see in the media.

Realism has also a third element. It presupposes morality in the broader sense (and not just as Christian ethics). It implies an ethical attitude. For recognition of reality is possible only on the basis of an ethical decision. Only on this basis can we test it, i.e., experience, and prove it.

Naturally ethics means taking doctrinal positions, but these will be set in relation to the facts and hence called in question. If an ethical attitude is not adopted, reality is no longer a valid given. The one exists only in relation to the other. The man without an ethical attitude renounces existence within and in relation to reality. He is simply absorbed in the real. He can neither master it nor can he adopt a position regarding it. On the other hand, if ethics becomes a closed system, reality is denied. The bond between the two, their relation, is obviously action (I am close to Marxist practice here), but it is action which is strictly measured by the demands of both and which has no intrinsic value, but only the value of a bond or relation.

This action has to be tested if ethics is to be called in question. Only in relation to an accurately known reality can this calling in question be valid. This is what prevents ethics from developing into a closed system. Thus the man who tries to live according to some ethics (especially here Christian ethics) should continually submit this ethics to the test of reality. The real, however, must not be a false, illusory, and inconsistent world. Nor must it be a system of combined values. The real must be known for what it is according to the two preceding orientations.

Realism, then, has the virtue of calling ourselves in question in terms of our ethical decisions and attitudes. It is the direct opposite of all justifications. Realism should lead us to shut the door against all evasions so that we can measure ourselves as we are (with no illusions) by the reality that we have perceived. In the first instance, then, realism is a training in honesty.

To the extent that it strips away our justifications, establishes our limits and possibilities, and shows that there is no good or progress without the opposite, realism leads us to acknowledge that there is no solution to some situations and it also forces us to accept contradictions as such without claiming that they can be artificially dealt with, e.g., by dialectic. Realism, then, demands great strength if we are not to despair and great honesty if we are not to give ourselves a false picture of what takes place. This means that we must adopt some very precise attitudes, of which I will give three examples.

The first attitude relates to proposed solutions in a political drama, an economic development, or indeed a personal problem. Such solutions have to be weighed with the greatest strictness, with readiness to consider every new solution that might be suggested, and with a radical refusal to accept closed eyes in the name of belief. There has to be intellectual judgment or experimentation (so long as this preserves the same lucidity towards the facts and does not come to focus on the act itself). If no solution is perceived, there has to be the courage to say so. False and illusory solutions must be rejected as forcefully as possible, for these hamper man's self-realization. To say that there is a solution when there is not can bring comfort and pleasure, and it may achieve its end, but it is hypocritical and dishonest.

Realism should be merciless towards chimerical solutions such as those we so often hear today, e.g., mass culture, a civilization of leisure, the entry of the third world into history, etc. It should also be merciless to doctrinal solutions which are solutions only because the doctrine or system veils the facts, as is typically done by the systematic structuralism of our own age. Man does not like looking at reality. He tries to circumvent it, since it is not in itself agreeable or consoling. If the difficulty cannot be set aside, another possibility is that of painting reality in such absolutely dark colors that it obviously cannot be true. This is what Sartre and Beckett and their like do. They do not show us the real at all. We have in them a supreme irrealism as in de Ségur. It is not true that everything is absurd, tragic, mediocre, hopeless, and petty. But this is the way chosen by some intellectuals in their escape from reality to a nightmare world which emphasizes absurdity.

If realism does not accept simplistic solutions, if it is prepared to go through the crucible of criticism and rigorous experience, it also refuses to accept a position in which the whole situation is portrayed as hopeless. It is always open to other aspects which have not yet been seen, to other possibilities which have not yet been explored, to new facts which can overturn conclusions that have thus far been regarded as true. Rejection of doctrinal solutions means also the rejection of systematic pessimism.

As concerns Christians, a particular point is that Christianity should not be regarded as a solution nor should it be thought that Christianity imports a solution into reality. It should be accepted, however, that faith in Jesus Christ can be a reference in the real and can be a motive for mastering it. Hence this faith leads us to accept situations of conflict and tension as they are with no need for further inquiry.

The second attitude which I offer as an example is that of not attaching ourselves in a narrow, obsessional, and final way to a particular form of action or thought. This is very difficult. When a "problem" has been seen, a "solution" analyzed, and a "work" undertaken, there is in us a persistence which does not let us change our course easily or admit that we are mistaken. There is a tendency to continue basing our intellectual, moral, domestic, spiritual, or professional life on a set of images acquired at the age of twenty or so, so that, as reality changes, life is passed on the margin of the real.

Thus the revolutionary thought of 1900 begins to get through in 1950 and a gain is seen for revolution. But this is a tragic error. The word has itself changed. The revolutionary thought of 1900 is mere conformism in 1950. Marxism is an example.

When a form of action is found, we have to realize that it is relative to a given situation and does not have the same validity in a different situation. This is why it is so childish to try to import Maoism into the west. Realism forces us continually to revise our style of life and choice of action. It demands self-renewal. This is not just opportunism, for we have shown already that what is presupposed is ethical choice, an attitude which relates us to the facts but in which we are also liberated from the facts.

The third attitude which might serve as an example relates to a very serious difficulty in which realism places us. Jean Rostand has said that inertia rather than life is the dominant force in the universe; dying is passing over to the stronger side. There is truth in this, sociologically and politically as well as biologically. Living means being on the weaker side. [23] Realism is seeing and accepting this.

It thus sets us at the point where we must decide—and we recall once again that this is an ethical decision—between, on the one side, all the reality that inclines us to join the strong, to yield to the facts, to adjust to what comes, and, on the other side, everything that leads us to want to be alive. We have to realize, of course, that logically, and also in the physical, physiological, and sociological structure of the world, the side of life is the weaker one.

When we meditate on what it means to be human we must not forget the essential aspect that being human means going against the normal law of reality. We can take a further step at this point. Realism helps us to see clearly what determines us, what logically awaits us, what puts us already on the side of death even before we are dead. Realism is the attitude of facing this reality and measuring our strength to persist in it. For I cannot possibly separate myself from this reality. Realism is a scrutiny both of the real and of myself as part of it. It tells me ultimately that if I choose reality, if I go with the facts, if I accept the system of determination as it is, I have in the last resort opted already for death.

For many years it has been thought that Christians are completely unable to grasp reality, to be scientific or realistic. They supposedly live in a dream. They share an illusion. They are enclosed in a system of ready-made truths.

This idea is not based on the Christian revelation as made in Christ and known through scripture. It derives from two complementary factors, namely, Christendom and the confusion between revelation and rationality, i.e., the wrong idea that philosophers have had of theology.

My own claim is that (apart from a miracle) only the Christian can in fact practice an authentic realism. This statement might seem to be astounding and it seems to be given the lie by the dogmatism and irrealism of the past. Yet I stand by it. The Christian is more able to be realistic than other men for the following reasons.

First, in order to see reality we have to participate in it without being swallowed up, buried, and determined by it. But this is the condition of the Christian (if at least he is ready to live out the condition that God has fashioned for him—we shall have to make this proviso at every point in the present ethics). It all amounts to being in the world but not of the world. The Christian has a part in all reality because he is sent by Christ, but he does not belong to it. He is a stranger and pilgrim. He is not integrated into reality. He is on a different wavelength. His interests are not those of the world. They are not, nor should they be, bound up with this world. He can

---

23 Defining "weaker" raises problems. Politically, for example, it is hardly true that the working-class, especially when backed by the U.S.S.R., is the "weaker" class.

be independent, although this does not happen necessarily or auto-matically. The trouble is that the Christian generally does not know how to live in this condition which is fashioned for him. He does not know what to make of it. For its orientation is to realism, about which he never thinks.

The second reason why the Christian can most easily be a realist is that he is able to accept the real as it is, no matter how black. He can look at hopeless reality, for he has an unheard of opportunity before him, that of hope in Jesus Christ. At this point we touch on one of the most powerful forces that usually restrain man from looking at reality. This is the unbearable character of reality which causes man to start back and say: It cannot really be as bad as that. He thus invents false answers. He seeks a way of escape at all costs. He adopts an illusion and rejects the real. For man cannot live with his back to the wall, as Camus has shown. He is incapable of viewing reality. He has to superimpose his own images and his hopes for improvement in a possible and even a foreseeable future. The inclusion of this false hope already distorts and obliterates the real. With unprecedented grandeur and exactness this is just what happened to Marx. It is the weakness of sociologists and economists that they seek refuge in scientific facts, and thus reject one part of the real, because they cannot tolerate the real in the true sense.

The case of the Christian, however, is very different. There ought not to be anything to prevent him seeing this reality clearly in all its dimen-sions, for he realizes that there can be no answer in the real and that no solution will spring forth from it. He does not have to seek false comfort. He does not need to try to find a way out when the situation, realistically, has no way out (I am not saying that this is true of all situations). He realizes that in this realistically impossible moment everything is in the Lord's hands, so that there is in fact an answer. On the realistic level, of course, this answer is inadequate. We do not deny this. Faith in the risen Christ allows us to consider the real exactly as it is without any shift or evasion.

A misunderstanding needs to be corrected here. Often after studying a situation, I have made an affirmation of faith in Christ. Often, too, Christians have protested that my invocation of Christ is an imposture. I am supposedly bringing Christ in as the solution to a situation which I have described as having no solution. This, it is said, is also bad apologetics. Man is shut up in despair in order finally to bring him hope. That is, he is led to believe that if he becomes a Christian every problem will be solved.

Now these two objections are fallacious. They rest on a hasty and tendentious reading. It is not a matter of saying that Jesus Christ or faith is a solution. Not at all! It is simply a matter of affirming theologically that the political or economic situation described lies within the lordship of Jesus Christ and therefore that humanly speaking there is no reason to yield to despair even if every solution is barred from the human standpoint.

In any case the reference to the lordship of Jesus Christ does not offer even the beginning of a reply. This is not where we begin intellectually in trying to work out a solution or find a way. But it gives us the strength to continue in a hopeless situation. This is its significance.

The difference lies, then, in the human ability which faith gives to face the seriousness of the situation realistically without giving way to madness or despair. It does not lie in the ability to furnish solutions where others cannot find any.

In relation to others this attitude is not one of superiority. It is an example of lucidity and strength based on something other than human qualities.

Nevertheless, if faith allows us to see reality no matter how dark or difficult it may be, it also prevents us from painting it darker than it is, from regarding all issues as hopeless, from playing down all efforts if their validity does not stand up to rigorous criticism. We are not allowed to press realism to the point of absurdity, nonsense, and despair. We must reject all philosophies of hopelessness and all catastrophic readings of the political and economic situation.[24]

We have always to bear in mind that this world which we have to view realistically is the world into which God has come and which he has chosen to love. We cannot blacken it. Neither Sartre, Godard, Antonioni, nor Genet gives a true picture. These are false prophets who on the pretext of realism offer a blackened interpretation. Because God has chosen to love the world in which we live we must be open to any hope or solution. We must be on the watch for any invention or discovery that might produce positive change. We cannot take up dogmatic positions. Among human efforts there might be one which solves an issue or answers a problem.

Yet here again we have to be realistic. We are not to believe that chalk is cheese in order to maintain Christian hope at all costs. Militant Christians who, limited like all militants, think that anti-colonialism is the answer to colonialism, or that black independence is the solution to the oppression of black peoples, show precisely to what extent Christians are too immature to live out freedom in realism.

We must be open, of course, to all the good that can come from politics, economics, art, and social reality. We are not to deny this. It is frightening to read from the pens of Christians that occidental marriage is the source of neurosis and hypocrisy and is breaking up. This is just not true. Even if it were true 80 percent of the time today, we could not generalize from this, nor project it into the past or future, nor erect a value judgment on it. Observation of reality would allow us to say just as well (and just as falsely) that rejection of occidental marriage is the source of neurosis and hypocrisy. All positive things which can be conserved should be conserved and adopted as a sign of the divine patience.

---

24 Rather oddly the very people who reject a catastrophic Christian apocalyptic and the authenticity of the last judgment are those who accept the idea of political catastrophe and favor revolution and Communism.

Thirdly, the Christian can be realistic because he is not out to justify himself. One of the important mechanisms which prevents the achievement and exercise of true realism is the concern to have justifications, to find them in a given setting or reality or in the pure and simple adoption of an approach. Each of us wants to transform reality into a plea for himself. Scientists, technologists, and economists cannot help but view the object of their work as a justification. Man always acts thus in relation to the real, whether justification be sought in social relations, political action, work, morality, or knowledge. But such self-justification prevents accurate identification with the real.

Only the Christian, I think, can (or might) accept the real without seeking justification in it. For the Christian is freed from this urge by the justification which he receives in Jesus Christ. He is not justified by his own acts, nor by reality. Hence he can have a correct appreciation of these acts and this reality. He does not have to seek a fresh justification in them. He can thus go ahead even as one who is accused in history.

For ultimately, on a realistic view, the history in which we take part in some way or other brings an accusation against each of us. The tendency is thus to seek in our acts or in reality a place to hide from this accusation. But the Christian, being justified in Christ (alone), can (or might) accept the accusation, see what it implies, and in the light of what is deduced from it make a fresh start. To engage in action of a kind which can come under accusation—which is tolerable only if one is justified, which is ventured in a hopeless situation, and which is tolerable only if one knows that the whole situation is in the Lord's hands—is the only sane attitude that makes possible action which can truly change the human condition.

The mystery of satanic power over Christians, the abomination of desolation, is that this has never been lived out by Christians and that they have thus betrayed man and the opportunities of history.

The realistic attitude which we have just been describing rules out the construction of a Christian system of economics, politics, society, or philosophy in any form. It also rules out the spiritual retreat which consists in taking part in an evil society, in the ongoing decay of its institutions, and in the withdrawal of the individual into his private life. It finally rules out the integration of the church into society as though this spiritual addition would change social reality. We have incidentally touched on these three points before and we shall not develop them here.

In speaking of this realism we have often alluded to general social and political problems. We must also show, however, that there is a similar application to individual situations. Searching of conscience as practiced elsewhere should not lead to a frenzy of accusations but should simply teach us to see ourselves as we are in our reality and to see the reality of our children and family and professional activity from the twofold angle of participation and detachment, or love and objectivity, which constitutes realism. We have thus to practice it at every level of life.

I am well aware that the objection might be brought that all this is in the clouds, since no man can see himself as he really is, or his children as they really are, or the government as it really is, etc. I have three points to make in reply.

First, an attempt to achieve this knowledge is better than stagnant ignorance or blind involvement. The fact that I cannot prove that the earth goes around the sun does not mean that I should say that it follows the moon. We have to achieve the closest possible approximation.

Secondly, all situations are relational and therefore reality "as it is" is not the same as reality "in itself." I am not to see myself as I am absolutely but as I am in given circumstances in which I manifest myself in some way, i.e., in an area which can be known and appraised.

Thirdly, this realism is not the fruit of exceptional intelligence but of the freedom which is given to us in Jesus Christ. The existence of this freedom sets the problem in a new light and blunts the objection, which can see only the situation of human subjection to fatalities.

Freedom is what authorizes us to take this position of realism. For it is this that detaches us from ourselves and our milieu in such a way that we can stand at a distance and consider the situation. Freedom enables us to achieve the distance of which we hear so much today.

Without distance, or transition to another dimension, realism is impossible. For if we are not free we are necessarily identified with environment, work, condition, and so forth. Man is the product of his condition if he is not free. It is freedom that makes us subjects in a world of objects—I am here interrelating rather than opposing the two terms. In relation to these determining factors I cannot have an attitude of apprehension, knowledge, or evaluation unless I am free even as I am defined by them. This is my subject situation which implies realism and without which I am in the condition of a mere object.

The freedom, however, which is a condition of realism and of which realism is an expression cannot be created by me myself. My own will or intellect cannot make me free. Nothing in the environment in which I am set can permit me to achieve freedom. Either I am free by liberation or I am never free. If I am part of this world and rely on the natural situation, I have to accept this dilemma. This is why we always find a common need to declare that man is intrinsically free as a metaphysical situation prior to all analysis. Existentialism has changed nothing here. The only trouble is, as we have seen, that this runs contrary to the conclusions of various sciences.

If man is determined, however, nothing can let him become what he is not. Neither knowledge of the situation nor action regarding it can make him free. This is the main weakness in the thought of Marx. To say that man by acting on his environment creates himself is both true and false. It is true at the modest level of self-modification by modification of the conditions of life. It is false if what is meant is transition from a man who is determined to one who is free. No altering of the environment by me, my work, etc., can bring it about that I am free. I remain an object. I am still part of a universe of which only the determinations change. Freedom has to come from outside this situation. He who is outside the system of determinations has to come to set me free. This transition can be achieved, not by a modification within the system, but by an intervention from outside the system.

By means of this I can become what I was not and begin to live in a universe which continually produces its determinations but which I can continually escape again. In the distance achieved in this way I can learn to describe and know my environment in a new way.

But why should I grasp the real which I thus learn to know? Of what use is it to practice the realism which is the fruit of freedom? For if realism is the first step which in freedom is the condition of all other acts of freedom, I do not practice it for the pleasure of more specific knowledge nor as the precondition of a more exact science.

The point is that I must live as a Christian. There are, briefly, two sides to this. On the one side it is in the real as thus known and lived out that the witness borne to Jesus Christ should and can be given authentically. This witness must be the fruit of faith. It must engage the whole being. It must set the witness in a personal relation of love with the neighbor to whom he transmits the deepest thing he has. It must be witness about known truth given both very seriously and very humbly. But beyond all this it must be given in real life.

A score of misunderstandings can arise about this witness when it is "cast before swine," i.e., when no account is taken of those to whom it is addressed, nor of the environment in which it is given, nor of socio-political or cultural conditions.

When I speak of socio-political or cultural conditions it might be argued that this implies a need for preliminary sociological or psychological studies. The objection might then be made that Paul and Francis of Assisi did not engage in any such studies. This is quite true. But we have to remember that their society was much less difficult and complex than ours is. All the same they display a very strict realism in relation to the environment, as do also Augustine, Luther, and Loyola. They have an accurate and penetrating grasp of the world to which the word must be preached. This realism suffices.

When I referred to psychological conditions, I did not have in mind a scientific analysis but the realism of a clear apprehension and objective participation. This is no simple matter in our day, for we clothe reality with lies, ideologies, images, doctrines, and information. Reality for us is that of the daily paper. It is a nonentity. Addressed to this reality, our witness is addressed to nothing and nobody. We are no longer in direct touch with the real. We have to will it and create it to make witness possible. It has to be given to us in the act of freedom.

The truth which is given by the revelation of the Holy Spirit, and my word which becomes God's Word by the work of the Holy Spirit, are not enough. The apprehension of the real by my freedom must also be the product of the Holy Spirit acting in such a way that I may see to whom it is that this word is in reality addressed.

But this realism contains a second possibility, or rather it is the condition of another expression of freedom, namely, transgression.

Transgression is the extreme act of freedom. One might almost say that freedom is achieved in transgression.[25] This is partially true. I thus espouse the most extensive freedom. There is never freedom without transgression. This means danger, but it also shows how serious freedom is. Knowledge of the real fixes our limits. This is the first thing that realism imposes on us. Our reality lies at the point where I am limited in this way. These are not just the limits of my particular being, my finitude or fragility, although this is fundamental, and without recognition of these limits I am introduced to a false freedom, which is the worst of illusions. Limits are also imposed, however, by circumstances. I have to examine these and orient myself to them to know where my limits are. It is in the interplay of my own strength and circumstances that I fix more or less experimentally the moving line which will be the limit of my potentiality, action, and intelligence.

---

25 The concept of transgression is in fashion today. Mauss has shown its importance in primitive societies and he has been regarded as the father of its conceptualization. But it is with G. Bataille that transgression has attained the place of honor in contemporary ethical thinking, and structuralism takes it over in turn with Lacan (*L'Inconscient*, No. 1, March, 1967). Perhaps one might recall that transgression both as a reality and as a fully developed concept is found already in the Bible, especially in the Old Testament. Modern thinkers would do better to reflect first on this source. I should like to mention also two remarkable studies by Vidil (*Le Semeur*, 1964, No. 1 and No. 3). I do not accept all his basic affirmations, but they refer to other limits than those which I have in view here. A good survey of transgression in Jesus (with regard to the law and taboos) and in Paul (with regard to circumcision) may be found in Bovon, "Vivre dans la liberté." Finally reference should be made to an excellent study by B. Morel (*Cybernetique et Transcendance*, 1964), which shows how transgression becomes the central and specific Christian act in a world subjected to cybernetics. I think Morel is the first to bring to light what specific form Christian action should take in the technological society. Since prohibitions protect the cybernetic scheme and the world looks to technology for salvation, the expression of Christian truth by faith can no longer be anything but transgression. God once evoked the idea of a sovereign law but he is now synonymous with transcendent freedom. All Christian symbolism, biblical, liturgical, and theological, must be reinterpreted, stripped of its character of moral or intellectual obligation, and become the sum of the conventional myths of a sacred transgression. I am in full accord with this orientation and project. But transgression must imply a clear conscience with regard to what is done. God-given freedom does not exist if man does not know why he is transgressing the commandment. I recall the verse in Luke 6:5 D: "Seeing on the same day someone who was working on the sabbath, Jesus said to him, Man, if thou knowest what thou doest, blessed art thou, but if thou dost not, cursed art thou and disobedient to the law." Transgression is a fulfilment of the law when it expresses the freedom that God gives to man, he being aware of what he is doing. If he is not, it is a curse. The freedom of transgression implies that man knows what he is doing, e.g., why he is free in

Some of these limits are set by natural endowment and some by society. One is not to be stressed at the expense of the other. I cannot say that only the limits set by society count. I have to see that I am limited by the frontier of my body, and it is not just an insignificant matter of humility to know this. Nevertheless it is true that as a provocation to faith the limits set by society are more direct and threatening.[26]

While not forgetting these first forms, which realism teaches us to know or recognize just as a prisoner in a dark cell learns to know its boundaries by following the walls and counting his steps, we accept what Vidil says when, even though he rejects the first limits, he claims that the limit is the sacred. But the sacred is nothing in itself. Always something has to be sacred. An existing limit in society or man is proclaimed to be sacred. We are not dealing with an empty word.[27] The limit exists in the real world which I follow or which is around me, but it is strengthened by the intervention of an unexpected factor, namely, the sacred. The real limit is this combination of what is actually impassable and the inviolably sacred.[28]

This is the limit which my freedom opposes. Now when we tried to show what is the freedom which we acquire in Christ, and from what it is

---

relation to the sabbath, why the sabbath was given as a sign of freedom, why it was made for man, who thus transgresses the law that man makes of it. But if man does not know this, if he has neither knowledge nor conscience, this act is transgression not only of the law but also of the will of God. It is a sign of disobedience and not of freedom, of indifference to the will of God and not of entry into the kingdom. This is why realism and transgression are so basically linked.

26  An interesting study by Morel ("L'avenir du Ministère de l'Église dans un monde en voie de sécularisation," *Bulletin Centre Protestante d'Études de Genève*, XIV, 1962) has shown clearly that modern society has seen a reversal in respect of the interdicting of transgression. In traditional society up to the nineteenth century, prohibition belonged to the sacral and religious sphere, and what constituted transgression was the act of the non-religious infringing the rules and crossing the boundaries. Under the old regime the church was the guardian of laws and prohibitions. The secular attacked the sacred. Today, however, the world which was once profane tends to become sacred. It sets up prohibitions of increasing severity and invests them with religious meaning. Prohibitions come from politics, science, and technology. These prohibitions have to be viewed in the same way as the earlier ones. They are a collection of rules which are not just useful and relative but which tend to be made absolute. Hence it is now the church which in the name of freedom must engage in transgression. Christians must do this as the carriers of freedom. It is not so much a matter of fighting the limits imposed on man's autonomy as of shattering their sacral character, their ideological exaltation, their institution as new and secular religions. When this is done the freedom given by God finds its proper function again, namely, the destruction of idols.

27  This is why I cannot accept the fashionable linguistic preoccupation of Vidil according to which language is only language and does not presuppose any content or reality. This seems to me to be a mere playing with words and an evasion which allows us to avoid the real difficulty by posing a succession of intellectual difficulties evoked by mirrors. It seems to me that Vidil is too ardent a follower of Foucault.

28  J. Ellul, "Le Sacré Aujourd'hui," *Le Semeur* (1963).

that we are freed, we said that we are freed from conditioning forces, including the law, morality, religion, and so forth. But we might have given the impression that there is a kind of break between past and present. In fact the liberation is actualized only in the act of freedom. Being freed, we have to be free. This means, however, that the forces from which we are freed are still encountered as limits in our lives as free men. The act of the free man, i.e., of the man who is freed from these forces, is thus to transgress the limit which they impose. For if they no longer exist as a determination, they still do so as a limit. Hence the only attestation or witness we can give is that of transgression.

Etymologically transgression means passing beyond. On this side of the frontier a life is possible. The life of the free man may even take the by no means negligible forms of obedience and convention. As we have seen, in some cases it may not be able to be any other than a life under the law. Freedom, however, will never be visible or instantaneously explosive except in the act of transgression, of passing beyond. The rest can be only the (free) situation of waiting for transgression, of preparation, of the maturation of this privileged, unexpected, and uncontrived moment. There is no ethics of transgression, since there is nothing to say about it. There is no ethics of lightning. On the other hand, there is no ethics of freedom unless it is affirmed that transgression is the core, meaning, and synthesis of all that can be said about freedom. When Vidil says that man is born in transgression, he is right so long as we are speaking about free man and so long as the act is not his own or determined by himself but is a sword used by another and piercing the screen which is around us.

This realism is indispensable to show me my limits and as a preliminary condition of transgression. Realism in itself, the exercise of freedom, does not lead anywhere and is not an expression of freedom. But this realism has value because it brings me up against my limits. It forces me to see them. It forces me to touch what is not my freedom. It teaches me my true limits in this time and place.[29] It prevents me from viewing myself as a free man by alerting me to eveything that is not my freedom. It does not let me play the comic role of a free man.

Nevertheless, I know that in Christ I am a free man. I am thus forced to decide. Either I can remain within these limits and continue to live like an honest Christian, in which case I cannot be sure that I am not re-establishing constraints, mechanisms, and organizations, and that I am not playing the

---

29 It is a strange weakness of Michael Foucault (*Préface a la transgression, critique*, p. 195) that he can say that the only transgression today is in the sexual sphere, which he views as the last refuge of the sacred. This is doubly false. The sexual sphere is not absolutely sacred in our society. It does not matter who gives himself to what in this area. In fact no sphere is more profaned, desacralized, and demythicized than this one, whether it be by current practice, the cinema, science, or "thought." Many other sacred areas are far more important, e.g., money, the state, etc. Cf. J. Ellul, "Le Sacré Aujourd'hui," *Le Semeur* (1963).

game of the secular power with my "as if." Or else, when I come up against the limits with the double movement of "You are free" but "Here are your limits" (as the realism of freedom brings them to light), I can transgress them and pass into a beyond of uncertainty. And after all, is not the "as if," the knowing how to live, itself a transgression of what constrains us, since we cannot adhere to "using as though not using" if we transform it into a situation instead of living it out as the constant risk of transgression? Transgression of the social order by the action of the Good Samaritan, transgression of the religious law by healing on the sabbath day, transgression of the idea of justice by the equal pay given to the laborers in the vineyard—it is worth noting that Matthew's Gospel not only shows how Jesus fulfils the law but also speaks most clearly about transgression (Vidil)—transgression of the powers of the state in the incident of the two coins, transgression of the sanctity of the temple in its cleansing and in the prophecy concerning it, transgression of scripture by Jesus' application of Isaiah to himself—the whole of Jesus' life as well as his teaching is from one standpoint transgression.

The life of Jesus, however, is also relative to that of the chosen people. It is not separate from it. Now in the history of the chosen people we find that transgression has the same decisive importance. When Terah leaves Ur with Abraham they cross the Euphrates and this gives their descendants the name "Hebrews" or "Ivrium," i.e., those who have crossed over.

Abraham is one who crossed over the limit. He did so by divine impulsion. He came to birth in this transgression. Because of it he was given the promise that a great people would be born of him. He entered the waste of the desert, but this waste was inhabited by the promise.

The second great traversal was the pesah or passover. There are many aspects to this passing over. The angel who spares and gives life passes over, and in this terrible transgression which is characterized by the slaying of all the firstborn of Egypt, there is life for Israel. Passover means grace, as we read in Exodus 12:27. Passover grace is victorious.

We are reminded also of the Red Sea passage. Here is another trans-gression or crossing which gives birth to Israel. The features are all exactly the same as in the case of Abraham's crossing. Transgression, then, is a constant element not merely in the teaching of the Bible but in the history of the man or people that belongs to God. On each occasion there is the same entry into life and freedom.

From another standpoint, this means that freedom is not discovered or enacted except through the existence of limits. A man who is not constrained nor subject to determinations can never be free because there is no transgression to effect nor obstacle to overcome. He can never know the only true freedom which is liberation and conflict. He will be a shadow in the realm of shadows.

When young people want freedom, their parents must not let go and give it to them. This will result only in incoherence, dissatisfaction, uncertainty, and disillusionment for the young, as is plain to see in our own time. The young can find freedom only as they confront the authority of their parents, progressively break down the resistance, transgress, and overcome. If this freedom is not effectively won, it is nothing. On the other hand, it is plain that parents ought not to take advantage of their position of strength and authority to crush their children. The pedagogy of freedom, as this is illustrated for us by God in the Old Testament, implies on the parents' part an exact knowledge of the measure of the obstacles, prohibitions, and sanctions which they lay down, so that the force of freedom may be exercised, but not exhausted in a mortal conflict that leads to hatred. The law of the parents should be rigid from the standpoint of the children who contest it, but not too lofty for them. It should be elastic from the standpoint of the parents who are leading their children to freedom. This is the meaning of the limit. This is why it is necessary for transgression.

The importance of limits and the need for them are to be seen everywhere, but we must be clear that these are not limits of freedom within which freedom is situated. They are tests and proofs of freedom which provoke or evoke the freedom that is exercised only in confrontation with an obstacle. Limits are not bad, then, because they present a test for freedom; they are rather the condition of freedom. This is why the law is not an evil imperative but a schoolmaster of freedom. From this standpoint it is the limit which God has established in order that we may exercise before him the freedom which he gives us.

This law is in fact always at the level of our possibilities. It is not in itself *the* will of God. It cannot be assimilated to this. It is not an irreversible absolute. If it were it would be completely outside the range of our human possibilities and even our understanding. It is within our range, not in order that we should fulfil it line by line, but in order that we may surpass it as freedom enables us to do so.

It is the border on which our freedom is situated. If we transgress it in disobedience, we give evidence of a greater bondage, namely, to evil, sin, and fatality. But if we transgress it by the Spirit, going beyond its demands, there is freedom. The law has taught us precisely where our act might be directed to express this freedom.

The law becomes dead when it is taken literally. We thus deny our freedom when we force ourselves into conformity with it. The man who is freed in Christ denies himself when he observes the will of God as a total and absolute law. Hence freedom in transgression is just the same as freedom in (true and not legalistic) obedience.

Abraham when set in his limited situation is not more free than Moses. Not at all! It is when we put the two together that the reality of freedom in God comes to expression. This freedom is an active and lived out relation. It is a tension between obedience and transgression, between the imperative and the present, between duty and the challenge to it. The obstacle has to exist in order that there may be freedom. One can neither reject the law nor repudiate freedom.

Within the church we may say exactly the same thing in relation to the confession of faith. In fact many theologians today reject the very possibility of a confession on the ground that revelation is always questioning and never constitutive and also on the ground that it is our task to give fresh life to scripture, the actualized word, and not to congeal the word in new written forms. This argument, however, fails to see that the word cannot be revitalized if it is not congealed, or that the final question cannot be received when the answer has not already been received.

The confession, as a law, is also indispensable to our freedom. Only on the basis of its assurance are attempts at freedom possible without fear or remorse. Only in the full, proclaimed assurance of pardon, salvation, life, and love can we move out into deep water without being too much afraid of what might happen. Only as the word becomes concrete, only as it is engraved in rock (as Job puts it), only as it acquires fixity and permanence, only then can we take it up and bring it into action because we are free. It is a living word only in confrontation with scripture, which we have to go beyond. Apart from this, having no limit, it is transitory, evanescent, inconsistent, and pure fantasy, which is the very opposite of freedom.

To think that the freedom of the word entails the impossibility of a confession of faith is to have a metaphysical view of freedom which is finally possessive and static. It is to believe again in an attributed freedom which we possess and demonstrate. It is to believe in the freedom of the liberal ideology of the nineteenth century. In Christ freedom is an exercise. But it is a solidly based exercise which stands in relation to constraints and norms.

The same might be said with reference to institutions in general, particularly institutions in the church. The law, the confession, and institutions find their true value and meaning only when freedom contests, challenges, and transgresses them in the Spirit of the Lord. If freedom ceases to play a part, if man renounces his freedom, then the law becomes legalistic, the confession becomes dogmatic, settling what is orthodox and heretical and giving a full and permanent account of the whole of revelation, and the institution becomes juridical. When this happens, when there is no more freedom, when there is no longer an Abraham or Paul to transgress the law, a Luther to challenge the confession, or a Calvin to shake up the institution, then, since there are no free Christians by the Spirit of God, the law, confession, and institution lose their point and no longer have any content. For these essential realities find their meaning only in their relation to freedom.

Freedom is both confirmation and transgression. Its aim is not to destroy or erase these realities but to force them to be what they are meant to be in the order of God. In other words, freedom is not expressed by closed, delimited, and clearly decided doctrine or practice. Only with reference to a limit, in a given situation, can doctrine be an expression of freedom, when it transgresses and guarantees in the same moment, preventing solidification or sacralization. As Ricoeur finely puts it, I cannot actualize the word without transgressing at once that which is in process of becoming sacred. This is freedom.

Nevertheless, there can be no actualization of the word unless something is in process of becoming sacred. In a situation, then, when all limits, rules, and principles have been broken down, the work of freedom is first to reconstruct these structures without which freedom is incoherent, frivolous, and captious. In the modern church those who take freedom seriously should first restore to scripture its position as integral and undivided revelation (without fear of being charged with fundamentalism), then try to frame a possible confession for the church, and finally draw up a Christian ethics, so that in relation to these freedom can assert itself again in virile and coherent fashion, having found in them its meaning and determination.

This forces us to accept the fact that the Christian life is not just a life at the border or on the border. We have said already that it is possible to live on this side of the limit. This does not simply mean, however, under the shelter of religion, morality, something sacred, a social or family situation, a relation to work, money, or political or economic activism. All this would be a pure negation of life in Christ.

In this situation it is not enough to go up to the limit. We continually do this in the Christian life. We see that staying on this side of it offers us security. It enables us to live, for this is what limits are for. At the same time, however, it seals our true death. To set up a law is to give ourselves a rule which allows us to condense the will of God and hence to live tranquilly in the world. Nevertheless, all the teaching of Jesus shows us that this law is death. Paul explained this long ago.

What we have here are arrangements which permit us, as men of this world and this society, to stay alive, to have relations, and so forth. But we cannot avoid transforming all this into something sacred and religious, into a good. Hence it is the very thing which certifies that we are dead before God. "Whosoever will save his life shall lose it" (Mark 8:35).

In contrast, to transgress the limit is to enter into a sphere of radical insecurity, into a place with no orientation. It is to offend dangerously against the sacred, against which Moses protected the people by the veil on his face. It is to risk irreparably all that has been gained. It is to take the final venture. But all this is precisely what is meant by life in Christ.

The supreme transgression in the Bible is miracle. Miracle is the transgressing of all limits, whether those set by nature, society, or God himself, no matter whether we regard sickness and death as the consequences of sin or as a divinely willed order.

In this transgression man does in fact risk everything. First and foremost he risks his own faith which he has received from God. For a miracle does not have to take place. It is not magic. It is not the product of an intrinsic force. It is a pure decision of the grace of God. The man who asks for a miracle, who demands it from God, hazards on this request the totality of what constitutes his life. If the miracle does not happen, he is faced with a negation of his freedom and of grace. This is why we do not like praying for miracles today. But this is also why Bultmann's analysis of miracles cannot be accepted. It offers a superior spiritualizing which enables us to avoid being backed up against the wall or facing the seriousness of our situation. For this spiritualizing there is obviously no limit and therefore no transgression. But there is also no seriousness any more.

In attributing this importance to transgression, I am not suggesting that the limit is evil and transgression good. We are not operating in these categories. The two are correlative. The limit cannot be a source of death unless it is not transgressed. It is indispensable if social, biological, intellectual, and even spiritual life is to be possible. But it is also a constant danger.

On the other hand transgression has no meaning unless the limit really exists as a danger: a threat if we remain within it, but also a demarcation of the no-man's-land beyond it. If there is no border, transgression is a mere banality, as we have seen in relation to the so-called sacred sphere of sex and what is called sexual transgression in our own society. In this domain of the erotic, etc., we find only pseudo-transgression. A gratuitous thrill is found when the spice of imaginary danger is added to routine conduct. This is the very opposite of transgression. It is the confirmation of new limits. This type of conduct is itself sacralized. Transgression can take place only when there is a set and recognized border. Freedom comes into operation only in relation to its limit. Let there be no mistake, an appeal to freedom is itself a limit which needs to be transgressed.

We must try to see what this transgression expresses and what is its result. For it is not a pure act. To think this is an illusion. For Vidil, transgression is necessarily self-renunciation and self-discovery. Is it possible to turn with lucidity to this "nothing" which every frontier hides and to find there a place, time, and sphere in which to live? Is it possible even to use the vocabulary of limits without self-renunciation? The frontier may impose itself on me. I may know that it will also be my death, that nothing will finally be left for me, that I shall have nothing in my hands, even though at this moment to transgress is for me to live. I believe that in fact transgression is both an absolute risk (before both God and man) and a mark of life. It is self-renunciation, for everything on this side of the border which is crossed forms the nexus of my prior personality and its culture and human context. It must be noted that transgression is not possible unless it is juxtaposed with all this. Transgression is at the same time both abandonment and more. It has no meaning or bearing if it is not this kind of passing beyond. But transgression is also self-affirmation.[30] In the men to whom we have referred one of the achievements is the radical act in which man rises up as a being that even dares to confront God, since it is in relation to the law that transgression is to be effected.

But at this point the question of obedience also arises. Vidil finds a radical antithesis here. Speaking of Jesus he says that, when he refuses the way of transgression which would be for him the way of life, his only remaining option is the way of obedience which is the way of rejection, defeat, and death. Jesus submits to the law. A passage of this kind brings to light the ambivalence in this matter. Would transgression really be for Jesus the way of life? A usurped life no doubt. Is obedience really the way of death? Undoubtedly obedience to the will of the Father, which is transgression of the law of the world, implies defeat in the world which necessarily condemns Jesus to death.

In what he says here Vidil is reproducing the temptation of Jesus. For Jesus does not *submit* to the law. He *fulfils* it—a very different thing. He does so in freedom. This means that he transgresses what men have made into law but accomplishes the will of God revealed as law.

There is thus no true antithesis between transgression and obedience. It is simply a matter of knowing what we are transgressing. Obedience to God implies within itself all transgressions. It is better to obey God than man. This is said in the context of what is from the human and religious standpoint a very serious transgression.

Conversely transgression is nothing other than obedience here and now to the law of liberty, the commandment to be man, in an irreversibly radical decision. This is why we cannot accept Vidil's antithesis, namely, that the only way to live everyday life is as obedience (considered as a defeat), and that obedience and the death which is its necessary consequence must be accepted as the first condition of transgression, so that the non-value of obedience has to be recognized. But there is no such thing as abstract or intrinsic obedience. In our view it is not true that obedience is purely negative and leads only to death. We have seen earlier that obedience is directly and indissolubly linked to freedom. What Vidil says

---

30 Tillich attributes this to every moral act, which introduces confusion between the results of force and the moral act of a man. Yet he is well aware of the importance of transgression. In his *Theology of Culture* he says that since ethical authorities are not absolute, every moral act involves a risk. If man wants to achieve humanity he must transgress his state of innocence. When he has done so, however, he finds himself in self-contradiction. Man must always transgress the security zones marked off by moral authorities. He must penetrate the domain of insecurity and uncertainty. True morality is a morality of risk. It is based on the courage to be, on man's dynamic self-affirmation as man, which must accept the threat of non-being, death, culpability, and nonsense. Although this is all admirable if it is describing the moral situation in the freedom gained in Christ, it cannot be sustained theologically by Tillich's idealistic description of man or by his belief that in effect man becomes capable of true morality in virtue of his separation from God.

can be right only if we grant his premise that law, any law and any aspect of law, is always the law of God. But to admit that we must first admit that God is only a religious concept created by man and that this concept is in effect the cause of laws, including the laws of economics, sociology, and so forth.

The Father of Jesus Christ, however, is not a religious concept, nor is the God of Abraham, Isaac, and Jacob. If we accept the witness of scripture that God is, and that his will is not ours, that his perfect and holy will has nothing to do with what we establish as laws or as the religious and sacred, that these are a lie and a counterfeit, then obedience to the will of God is life and not death, except insofar as it is death to the world.

It is true enough that obedience has no intrinsic value. As we have seen, it confers no salvation. Nevertheless, there is no meaning or freedom without it. Nor is there any transgression. We are not even to contrast it with transgression in terms of plan or system. Planned and calculated obedience may well be negative and destructive. But the same applies to transgression. As Vidil justly observes, to plan to transgress is to condemn oneself like Sade perpetually to cross the same border, or like Hitler to create an organization. All calculated transgression is from the very outset religious and false.

This is correct. Transgression cannot be a principle of life. It cannot be a system. There can be no casuistry of transgression. We cannot say that this is to be attacked or that these limits are to be crossed or observed. We are not even to be on the watch for chances to transgress. To the degree that we have here a full expression of freedom, the act that is sovereignly free *is* transgression even though we do not see clearly what border is crossed or what sacred thing is violated. Intention, e.g., the intention of scandalizing, overturning, provoking reaction, or attacking God, spoils the act. Jacob had no intention when, attacked by the angel, he wrestled with him. Job had no intention when he bitterly protested against the injustice of God.

We are not to say that transgression is good or that it is life any more than we are to say that submission, staying on this side of the limits, is bad and is death. Such categories are unacceptable when we are talking about what ought to be decision, spontaneity, upsurging, and event. All that is needed is that this possibility should always be open and present. It should always be a question.

Even when transgression is not achieved and does not take place it should be unceasingly present in the Christian life. Its very absence should call this life in question. This openness to radical change should make it impossible to put down roots. Thus the order issued to the rich young ruler that he should sell all, give to the poor, and come and follow Jesus, is not a commandment to be carried out to the letter but a thorn in the flesh which cannot be taken away (for servile obedience means nothing) and which prevents us from profiting by our goods, which prevents us from finding a solution or making a compromise, since it is the presence of something which may supervene at any moment. The bolt may fall. At any moment it may no longer be possible not to do it. The social, moral, and economic order will then be transgressed.

What then? After transgression, says Vidil, comes the void. The essential thing about transgression is the void which follows it and the giddiness which this causes. The salvation which Jesus brings to men rests uniquely on itself in the void of transgression. This is all true, as is also the claim that man cannot tolerate this, that he organizes and fills up the void, that finally this transgression is recouped by society, and that the individual act of this freedom is transformed socially into revolution.

D. Joubert is right, then, when he contrasts revolution and transgression as follows.[31] A revolutionary ethics thinks that the limits are illegitimate as they are, so that we must cross them in order to find a better world on the other side. Transgression, however, finds nothing beyond the limits. Revolution presupposes a possibility beyond reality. Transgression is never on the side of negativity. Even the void of transgression might be viewed simply as the vertigo of destruction. Transgression does not negate anything (which can hardly be true). It does not oppose anything. Revolution is always a betrayal of transgression.

This shows clearly that transgression can only be the free act of a single man. It can have no social or political intention. But if it is effective it cannot help changing relations, affecting a given historical context, and thus becoming for men at its maximum the opening up of a beyond which they will regard as revolutionary and at its minimum a sign which they will have to interpret.

For a true transgression can never be kept secret. If it transports the transgressor into the void, or, to put it religiously, causes him humbly to commit himself into the hands of God, for spectators—and there are bound to be such—it will always seem to be a revolutionary act.

Two inferences may be drawn. First, as far as the transgressor is concerned we are not to constrast the void of transgression with a fulness, e.g., the experience of the fulness of the Holy Spirit. To be sure, this void is not a new fulness. Yet to the extent that this transgression stands in direct relation to Jesus Christ, in whom trust is placed, there is a fulness which surpasses all experience. The void is not that of an absence. It is the void in which the only presence is found. If it is not, there is no true transgression. There is only a pushing back of limits, or a substitute, or an illusory transgression produced by belief in it.

Secondly, to the degree that the act is fleeting and is necessarily recovered by society, the church, or the transgressor himself organizing his situation as such, we have to remember that transgression is never completed, or rather that it was fully completed only by Jesus Christ when he

---

31   D. Joubert, "Un nouveau Kierkegaard," *Le Semeur* (1964).

cried: "My God, my God, why hast thou forsaken me?" This completion, however, coincides precisely with Jesus' fulfilment of the law.

But what about us? Well, we have to realize that each of our transgressions—if we ever achieve any, which is not easy—will finally be a scandal, a futile laceration, and a defeat which will lead to recoupment. In other words, our transgression, indispensable though it may be, needs to be pardoned by the Lord—this is the void into which I fall—and the question is then posed afresh, and new transgression is demanded, since the act of freedom does not set me in a settled state. New acts of freedom are incessantly required. There is no such thing as a state or an acquisition in this matter. Reality encircles me. The sacred hems me in. I have to respond afresh to the summons of the thunder.

### §4. Risk and Contradiction

(1) Risk.[32]    The free man is a man who takes risks. He goes forward without securities or guarantees. He is always in a new situation. He always comes up against his adversary at point zero. He dispenses with the armor of tradition, of the past, of the institution. He takes risks. He risks the social structure and may involve others in the risks he takes.

This is a contemporary view of freedom in general. But it applies also to the Christian who is freed by Christ. Often a different opinion is advanced. Faith is seen as the supreme security. The Christian lives in comfort, tranquillity, and assurance because he is confident of his salvation and of eternal life. This is the current view. A reference to God simplifies everything.

In reality the freedom which we are given by God plunges us into a risk which the non-Christian cannot even imagine. This risk is in the strict sense the culminating expression of freedom in Christ.

Naturally risks arise in relation to that from which we are freed in Christ. Risks are also taken because of God and on God's behalf. To be prepared for these risks is a proof of freedom. On this side it may be always very doubtful.

---

32 For the most part France Quéré's work *Dénuement de l'espérance* (1972) is banal and unconvincing in its portrayal of the decline of faith as the area of faith is restricted and assailed by scientific and technological progress. Yet it deserves notice for its rediscovery of risk, of the battle for meaning, of engagement in a wager, not that of Pascal but that of the victory of love. Similarly Bultmann has well brought out—although he is not the first to do so—the antithesis between freedom and security. In his *Glauben und Verstehen*, II, 281-286, he points out that true freedom is not a freedom of security but a freedom which must conquer in the responsibility of decision, which is always an event. It is freedom in insecurity. Bultmann can thus criticize liberal subjectivism, which out of a need for security emphasizes the institution as the guarantee of freedom. He can also criticize the flight to authority in which the men of our age engage as they try at all costs to find someone who will organize their lives for them.

When the Hebrews come into the wilderness they are given manna as food. They are not to seek or demand anything else, e.g., quails. They are not to try to keep any manna for the next day; it goes bad. They receive exactly the amount needed from the hand of God, neither more nor less. Jesus' teaching in the Sermon on the Mount is along the same lines. We are not to be concerned about food or clothing. Sufficient to the day is the evil thereof. A duty of improvidence is imposed.

We have here a very exact description of freedom in relation to worldly systems and the security the world sets up. We have to note that if such security is not condemned as such in respect of social organization and other people, and if the Christian is even permitted to provide for his own security and to economize, this is at least a testimony to his lack of freedom. It is terrible hypocrisy to provide for the future, to heap up reserves, and to pretend at the same time to be free in repect of such things. If we are indeed free in this area, we must act accordingly, e.g., by not economizing. This improvidence is the very opposite of the modern outlook in which an attempt is made to foresee and calculate everything, to enter already into that which is still ahead. It should also be noted, however, that the improvidence which is an authentic expression of freedom in Christ should not be imposed on a global society or on good Christians who have no reason to take the risk. We may raise the problem of provision or improvidence only in the church or for an assembly of brethren.

A second group of texts refers to risks at the command of God. The widow of Zarephath risks giving her last remaining food to the prophet. Abraham risks sacrificing Isaac. The disciples risk leaving their homes and families to follow Jesus. When the Word of God comes into a life it divides as with a razor the new venture with God from the normal context of life. What matters now is in truth God and God alone. It is this or nothing. The risk consists in practicing freedom to determine one's love. For the definitive question is: Whom do you love? Since a choice is demanded, the love you avow eliminates others, and this elimination can take place only if you are free in relation to what comes second. The choice of freedom consists in loving him who frees you more than that from which you are freed.

We do not refer, then, to any risk, venture, or hazard. This freedom in risk, too, must be oriented to love and the glory of God. The reference, then, is simply to the risk posed by the Word of God, the risk of freedom which is obedient because it is begotten of the Word. We cannot believe that any risk expresses freedom and constitutes the Christian life. Many other forms of risk are to be set aside. The risk to be taken is projected by the Word. It is enough. There is enough risk in this alone.

For this risk affects almost every human situation. I have only to follow the commandment of God precisely, and the order which he has set for the freedom of my life, to see a whole swarm of risks. But finally they all boil down to only one. I wager on the faithfulness of God. I advance into the wilderness on the sole guarantee that God has promised he will be faithful to me.

Freedom is at issue here, for this detaches me from all that made up my former life, plunges me into radical uncertainty, and yet demands that I make my human decisions with full seriousness, since I cannot wait for God to do something. We are thus set in the movement from obedience to freedom and from freedom to obedience. This is where the risk lies.

The one risk is that of God's faithfulness. Will he be unfaithful to his promise? Will I be such a person that he can no longer keep it? Will he grant the promise in such a way that I am totally deceived at the human level? These are valid questions. But freedom consists precisely in wagering on the faithfulness of God, in accepting the risk that he might deceive us rather than reshuffling the promise, changing his plain orders, and hobbling our feet by trying to follow two different paths.

The moment I reject the risk, or at least its possibility, I cease to be truly free, for I put something else above love for the one who has freed me, and then he no longer frees me. The stake in banking on the faithfulness of God is the attestation of love (Simon, lovest thou me? with the prediction of the risk involved when he says he does) and the glory that is given to God. When the risk is accepted other men can have a slightly less mediocre testimony to God, for they see that those who believe in him are free and that they hazard their lives on his faithfulness. In this way God is glorified.

All this enables us to cast a negative glance on the other risks taken by man. Risks should only be taken for oneself on the basis of faith. There can never be any question of involving others in risks. The Christian cannot express his freedom by leading others to take risks. I have in mind youth workers who put young people in situations of great spiritual and moral risk on the ground that this is the Christian life. To go on the path of risk with mature Christians, who can feed on more than the milk to which Paul refers, is right enough. But to subject the young (in age or faith) to shock treatment, whether it be in the form of political involvement or sexual freedom, is to scorn them and to tempt God. It is the very opposite of love. Each must take the risk of his own freedom and not set traps for others. To push infants in the faith into random involvements and risks is not to manifest one's own faith or freedom. It is to manifest the human stupidity which does not know the real world or have the realism that results from freedom. It is to manifest childish trust in a mechanical God, which is the very opposite of faith. Or it is to disdain the the other who is exposed in this way without the assurance of a direct expression of the will of God such as Abraham had.

Other forms of risk should also be eliminated. We cannot endorse gratuitous risks, mere gestures, surrealistic and absurd acts which are performed because life is absurd and the world is absurd, and the risk gives flavor and adventure to existence, temporarily endowing what I do with a certain significance. Risk for risk's sake is to be completely ruled out. If our life and powers are claimed for the service of God or the expression of freedom, then we must deploy our powers where God expects and control our life in such a way that it will be exposed for God's glory and otherwise conserved. Risk is valid only as an expression of freedom and not of other things such as my spirit of adventure or my boredom. Non-Christians may take risks of this kind. We do not speak of them. But Christians should not drive at 125 miles per hour or attempt dangerous climbs merely for the fun of it.

Again, risks should not be taken outside dialogue with God, i.e., from a desire to win autonomy. We have referred to this already and may simply add here that if the acceptance of a risk is that of freedom it does not bear witness to what is now called the maturity of the Christian adult. It is indeed stupid to think that a Christian can finally come of age in this life. The whole witness of the Bible is against such a notion. The risk which is based on confidence in the faithfulness of God is in contrast a witness to sonship.

A choice has in effect to be made. On the one hand I may choose my risk or venture and claim that it is my own affair. If I do, I have to realize that in so doing I am not acting as a liberated Christian. I am acting simply as a man who is ready to risk his skin for a thousand valid motives. I am signing up as a mercenary or an astronaut. On the other hand I do not choose my risk but accept that which God asks me to choose as an expression of my freedom in respect of the things and fashions of the world. This is a risk which is accepted for God, because of him, and in attestation of his glory.

We have seen that the risk lies precisely in the relation to God. We are banking on his faithfulness. In the relation to him we thus put ourselves in the situation of creaturehood and the relation of faithfulness. In the relation of faithfulness the son trusts the Father. He is convinced that the Father will not deceive him. This is the only Christian risk. Freedom lies here and here alone. Once the risk becomes an expression of my maturity (or autonomy), freedom is no longer at issue. I am always conformed to the powers of the world. This leads us on to another series of risks that have to be rejected and set aside no matter how tempting they may be.

There is the extreme risk of martyrdom. We all know the exaggerated tendency to regard martyrdom as the only mark of authentic Christianity. Concretely it no longer concerns us much in many of our churches, although it is always a theoretical possibility. The desire for martyrdom, however, has never been an expression of pure freedom. In this regard we need only say that it is not necessary to be aggressive or provocative to unleash persecution or martyrdom. If we are strictly faithful to God's decision in, e.g., refusing to worship Caesar or mammon with all that this involves, if our obedience is intransigent enough, we can rest assured that persecution and martyrdom will soon come. But this is not to be confused with somewhat random commitment to political causes that we think are good.

Calculated risks are also to be rejected, namely, the readiness to risk oneself so far but no further. Deciding the limit in advance is a refusal of the risk into which God leads us. Here, then, we are not in the sphere of a freedom which involves the whole life but in the sphere of a partial and negotiated service which a worker renders to his employer. There is here no wagering on the faithfulness of God. There is no freedom of venture, only the mediocre bargaining which is—we have to say it—the very warp and woof of Christian life today. Our rejection of calculated risks is by no means contrary to wisdom. On the contrary it is wisdom which finally expresses itself in the absolute risk which is taken in proper understanding. I am not saying that this implies unlimited risk. I am simply saying that it is God who sets the limits and not we ourselves.

I must now refer to a final form of unacceptable risk, i.e., the risk of losing ourselves.[33] In our choices—and I am not speaking of the risk of obedience or of trust in the fatherhood of God, for God will never ask us to risk losing ourselves—in the human choices which also express, as we have seen, our freedom in Christ, we have no right to enter into situations or actions in which, even as we accept solidarity with others, we risk losing ourselves. If there is a decisive, exclusive, total limit which we cannot transgress, before which our freedom has to halt, transgression of which brings only bondage, and which constitutes a solid wall against our savage desire for autonomy, this limit is the salvation which is given to us in Christ. As we said before, the apparent audacity which tries to leap over this barrier seems to carry with it a love for others that is ready even to go to perdition with them. But this is only an apparent love, for if we go to perdition with others we become no more than the blind leading the blind. This is not love, for real love means, not losing one's salvation, but having a part in the salvation of others. Anything else is mere chatter.

Losing God's love is no manifestation of love for others. It is indeed a very grave matter, for it is a despising of the love of God and of the acts of incarnation and crucifixion which God performed to save us. It is no less than this. Hence we must now go on to say that salvation is a limit of freedom too. It is not at our disposal. To lose one's salvation, and even to accept its ultimate loss, is to become a slave.

The history of Israel makes this plain to us on the temporal level. This people becomes free by the act of God. It is called upon to live as a free people for God. But it agrees to enter into the play of worldly cultures, politics, and economic forms. It does so in spite of the warnings of the prophets and at the risk of losing the freedom which God has won for it. After playing the game for some time, it falls back into slavery. Nor does it

---

33 I am taking up again here a theme in my book *The Presence of the Kingdom* (1967).

ever emerge from this. The Babylonians are followed by the Persians, the Persians by the Greeks, and the Greeks by the Romans. Its desire to enter into the game played by others entails its loss of freedom.

This is, however, only a figure. The decision to engage in the risk of losing oneself is a thousand times more serious. And how can it fail to involve the loss of freedom too?

The risk which is willed by God, and which expresses both the freedom that he gives and also obedience, is the situation which sets a definitive limit to freedom. It is the extreme point to which God leads us—thus far and no further—as the place where freedom is attested and proved. Are we truly freed from the world and its powers? Are we truly freed for God? Only lived out risk can teach us this.

This risk, however, has to be a risk which is received from God and which is also appropriate. We obviously cannot duplicate the risks described in scripture. We cannot go into the desert and wait for an angel to bring us a cake. We are not to set off on foot on the highways without a change of clothes. The risk has to be an appropriate one which we ourselves can discern—a risk in our social, domestic, professional, or political setting which is appropriate to our situation, condition, abilities, and the measure of our faith. But it will also be a risk which always has the features that we have tried to set forth above. No matter what form it takes, it will always come after our liberation, after we know we have been freed, after we have concretely received in our lives the witness of freedom.

There can never be a risk before this, a risk in order to become free, or a risk which we take so as to know whether we are free. The tamer who enters the lion's cage takes this risk because he is a tamer with increasing skills. If a young man were to do this in order to find out whether he is a tamer or not he would be mad. This is why we are engaging ·· this meditation on freedom and risk. The temptation is to begin with risk: "Risk it, throw yourself in the water and find out, trust in God." The risk of crossing the Red Sea and living in the wilderness with its uncertain future was presented to the people (the people did not choose it) when it had already received a guide, the word of divine liberation, attestation of the saving and judging power of God, a sacrament, in a word, all the elements of freedom. Then, but not before, freedom is to be lived out in act or risk.

There is no test or proof of freedom before freedom itself is given, strengthened, and assured by God. Risk proposed apart from this can never be more than rejection in favor of security. It can be only a demonstration of non-freedom, as in the case of the rich young ruler, for whom risk brings only refusal in the bondage of wealth. In this case, of course, we have a saying on the part of the Saviour who loves him, but the saying, prior to liberation, simply brings out, with its proposal of a risk, the real if invisible bondage. How much more does this apply if we ourselves choose the risk we are going to take! We cannot by ourselves set ourselves in the borderline situation. God liberates us and thereby puts us very quickly in this situation and hence in that of risk. This is bound to come, and that should suffice.

With risk we show in fact where we have started. For the risk of freedom is no more and no less than encounter on our scale, in our measure, and in our own setting, with the three temptations which Jesus Christ encountered and by which he showed that he was free by accepting the totality of risk that he might have escaped so easily. If he had, of course, he would have been neither Son of God nor Son of Man. He would have escaped his freedom.

(2) Contradiction and synthesis. One of the most profound aspects of risk is contradiction. We live in a world of contradictions. We have already spoken about this feature of the world—the only one of which we are certain that it represents the difference with reference to creation. Instead of living in a world which is harmonious in its communion with God, we live in a broken world in which everything is contradiction.

This is not merely true at the intellectual level or at the level of different orders, e.g., scientific and religious. Everything is contradictory also in our lives and in our political and economic systems. The experience of contradiction is the easiest of all to have. We may think, for example, of the contradiction between the Soviet constitution of 1936 and actual political practice, or of the contradiction between the liberalism of America and its imperialism.

It is impossible to make a list of all the contradictions. We need only affirm that they are there: contradictions between level and level, system and system, system and practice, the whole and the part, or contradictions within the same system, thought, and both individual and collective practice, or contradictions within the same life. We need only note that, while contradictions are no doubt very scandalous for logical thinking or a moral system, they are perfectly normal. This is how it is.

At the ethical level we already came into contact with contradiction in an earlier volume when we tried to show what is the place of non-Christian ethics. We said, it may be recalled, that ethical systems are essential to man, so that from the Christian standpoint there can be no question of condemning or rejecting them, no matter what they may be. We cannot judge the conduct or ethics of others in terms of Christian faith and the Christian commandments. We have to accept them as they are, since they are useful to men.

On the other hand we pointed out that these systems cannot be regarded as implicit Christianity nor can we see in them a universal Christian basis and consensus, e.g., the decalogue. The decalogue is not general or universal morality. There is no such thing as general or universal morality. There are actual moral systems and there is a morality which derives from revelation. To admit this is to admit a major contradiction on the ethical plane.

We have seen in effect that these two co-existent moralities may finally come together. For the most part, however, they simply give evidence of contradictions, so that, as Christians, we are set in a situation of conflict. We are not to try to resolve this; it is a vital feature of risk. Our freedom may be seen in the personal decision we take in the presence of these two moral imperatives.

We can see the issue. On the one hand is the weight of conformism, determinations, and sanctions, On the other is the Lord's summons to act as responsible men and to choose our line of conduct when there is conflict between the two ethics, each of which is valid in its own way. We are to know what we are doing and not to try arbitrarily to reconcile the two imperatives.

We have to realize, however, that from the Christian standpoint the contradiction is even more fundamental. Christ incarnate in the man Jesus is the sign of the contradiction. This is the contradiction between the Lord and his now autonomous creation. It is the contradiction between the God who accepts the way of humility, abasement, obedience, and suffering, and the man who continually chooses the way of conquest, power, rigor, and system. It is the contradiction between the one mediator and the innumerable multiplicity of means put to work by work itself. It is the contradiction between the wisdom of God and the intelligence, philosophy, and science of man.

We recall the many radical sayings to this effect. "My ways are not your ways" (Isaiah 55:8). "These things have not entered into the heart of man" (1 Corinthians 2:9). "God hath chosen the foolish and weak things, and things that are not . . . " (1 Corinthians 1:27ff.). The wisdom of the world cannot know the wisdom of God (1 Corinthians 2:6ff.).

What a contradiction it is to be told that there is only one strait gate, one narrow way, and one salvation among a hundred human means of salvation and realization! There is a contradiction within being. There is a contradiction between the way which God has chosen and followed, which leads from God to man and which thus "descends" according to the traditional image, and the way which allegedly goes from man to God, which mounts up, and in relation to which Paul says that he regards all things as loss (Philippians 3:8), good, beautiful, legitimate, and useful things, which he does not simply set aside as indifferent but regards as loss. There is contradiction between the justice of the world and the justice of God, which does not correspond to any philosophical or legal rule of man, as may be seen from the payment made to the workers in the vineyard.

Contradiction is swiftly manifested in the concrete setting of life when we give our allegiance to God. We see it in this normal and yet contradictory co-existence of two ethics. Texts may be recalled in this connection too. The man who wants to be a disciple must hate his father, mother, brethren, and friends (Luke 14:26). The man who puts his hand to the plough and looks back is not fit to be a disciple (Luke 9:62). The dead must be left to bury their dead (Luke 9:60). Better is a morsel and peace than a full house and trouble (Proverbs 17:1). We are not to take thought for the morrow; sufficient to the day is its own evil (Matthew 6:34). One might continue to give texts indefinitely.

Jesus Christ is the sign of contradiction. We do not mean only that his cross has split the world in two and split history in two. The most radical contradictions have established themselves around him, and continue to do so. He is not the sign of union. He has certainly come to call all men to himself, but this alone provokes division. He certainly recapitulates all history, creation, and men, but only at the end of time. For the time being he stirs up division. He has brought a sword rather than peace. He sets the father at odds with the son and the mother with the daughter. A man's enemies are those of his own house (Luke 12:51ff.). It is hardly possible to go further than this in causing division.

We should not forget, however, that he is the sign of division rather than the one who provokes it. A sign implies that division already exists. It is permanent and fundamental. It precedes the birth of Jesus. It is the same contradiction as that to which we have just referred. It simply comes out with all its force at the incarnation. At this moment the contradiction between the choice of God and the work of abasement on the one side, and the choice of men (already in Adam) and the work of conquest and seizure and uplifted arm on the other, is brought to light in a decisive and definitive way.

The contradiction does not cease with the incarnation and redemption. On the contrary, it becomes all the more lively and radical. In a strange and contradictory way, the union of God with man in Jesus, Emmanuel, does not mean the end of contradictions, as generations of theologians have tried to show with much intellectual skill. Unity is not regained herewith. On the contrary, this unity simply manifests and brings to the point of ultimate exasperation all the conflicts, tensions, and contradictions with which humanity is afflicted.

The lordship of Jesus Christ does not usher us into a united world but into one which is much more dangerously divided. The Lord reigns over a seething world. It is in this situation that we have to live out our freedom. We have to accept the risk of contradiction.[34]

Now it is painful to live in contradiction. It is painful to engage in thought in which the elements are opposed to one another, or to live a

---

34 I want to make a summary reply here to the charge that I am a Manichean. The only possible Manicheeism in my thought is that I recognize the difference between life and death or God and man. It is easy to make this kind of charge. I might retort by charging my opponents with monism, which is no better from a Christian standpoint. Positively, however, I uphold the irreducible character of the situation of God and man and the contradictory character of the world in which we are. This has nothing whatever to do with Manicheeism in any precise or accurate sense. The fact that I do not set the terms in opposition but show that they are decisively linked rules out Manicheeism, which is characterized by a passivity of the good that I have never espoused.

divided life. "O wretched man that I am, who shall deliver me from the body of this death?" (Romans 7:24). We feel a great need to escape this situation and to find refuge in a recessive unity, which will link us again with the earth, by means of a womb fantasy. To achieve this reintegration we are ready to try all the means known to modern psychiatry. Or it may be that refuge is sought in a progressive unity. We project ourselves into the kingdom of God before the time. This is a more political or ideological form of the same temptation. Either way, the point is to flee the contradiction, to avoid the risk, and hence not to take up our freedom.

In this way what is normal and natural for the non-Christian, whom we need to understand in his recessive or progressive movement, in his flight from contradiction, in his blind desire for unity, becomes a serious fault in Christians, who ought to take up their freedom, the only freedom there is, precisely in this situation of risk and conflict.

Now among the means of negating contradiction, i.e., the real situation in which we are, the one most commonly used by Christians is ideology, philosophy, or theology. Innumerable Christian systems of philosophy or theology have tried, or are still trying, to achieve a unifying synthesis and to demonstrate the absence of contradiction or the presence of unity and harmony between all parts of the world and society or between a global philosophical system and Christian thought. This culminates either in syntheses or in the elaboration of a unitary theological system which explains everything, the world, society, politics, man, and so forth, in a single totality.

My own belief is that strivings of this kind are strictly the inverse side of a Christian thinking which cannot take the risk of contradiction and find there and there alone the path of freedom. Need it be recalled that this has been the great temptation of Thomism? Need it be recalled that in the philosophical sphere it is the temptation of Hegel? Hegel's system would be of no interest to me were it not that in his universal understanding he tries to do justice to Christian thought, which even in a sense was its transposed inspiration. In our own time Teilhard de Chardin obviously represents the same basic error as he tries to reduce science and theology, faith and scientific research, socialism and Christianity, technology and God's work, etc., to a single movement.

This kind of synthesis is as such a negation of revelation. The point to grasp is that when harmony is achieved the totality of the truth revealed in Jesus Christ is eliminated. All that remains is a little bit of Christianity mixed with other things. Nothing of the living work of Christ in us is left. Nothing of the incarnation, crucifixion, and resurrection is left.

I have less objection to Ricoeur. Ricoeur uses philosophical insights and methods the better to know and examine the revealed text. This is perfectly valid. The only problem is that he tends to slip over from the use of the instrument to its validation and then to its integration into christiano-philosophical thinking. This is very evident in *Finitude et Culpabilité* and then in his contribution to *Demythisation et Morale* (1965).[35] In this work Ricoeur uses the thought of Freud to "demystify accusation." He also gives precedence to this thought over what the Old Testament has to say on the subject. He thinks that Freud's reading of the Old Testament is true. This seems very dubious. Why should we not criticize Freud in terms of the Old Testament idea that the father figure derives from God's work rather than *vice versa*? But having swallowed this he arrives at the kerygmatic core of ethics and concludes by stating that for the philosopher Christ is the schema of hope. For what philosopher? I can hardly believe that his demonstration is convincing for a non-Christian or that a Christian has need of any such demonstration.

This demonstration is possible only as the thought of Freud, which allows us to eliminate everything in the Bible which is contradictory to the desire for no accusation (and this is the first movement in the rejection of the "sacralization of interdiction"), is combined in a system with what is retained of the revelation in Christ, namely, the single element of promise and revelation which corresponds to the natural desire to be and offers a schema of totality. In this way reconciliation is effected.

What happens is that strictly non-Christian thought is integrated into the total movement of a type of Christian thought with elements of the kerygma, but at the price of a dubious interpretation of one part of what the Bible offers and a radical sacrifice of the other part.

Man certainly has a desire for unity and a wish to escape contradiction. But is he sure that this attitude is an authentic one and one that is right before God? Is he not wanting purely and simply to regain paradise by crossing the boundary that God has set? Is he not trying to set up the heavenly Jerusalem before the time? I for my part am convinced of this, and these attempts at unity and reconciliation seem to me to be the main danger, since they are a rejection of the possibility of living out freedom.

Now we have seen that if freedom is not lived out, there is not even the slightest possibility of the Christian life or the slightest reality of revelation. Hence in this brief reflection on intellectual, philosophical, or theological attempts at synthesis and the resolving of contradictions, we are operating on the ethical rather than the theological plane. This is true in two ways.

First, our reference is to the ethical behavior of the intellectual who either tries to move on to synthesis or accepts the fact that his thinking is contradictory and broken and involves confrontations and divided allegiances—a choice that he constantly has to make afresh.

Secondly, our reference is to the ethical behavior of the man who is seduced or not by unitary systems and who either renounces his freedom in

---

35 In the same collection we find another type of reconciliation when Fessard tries to show that Levi-Strauss refers without knowing it to the God of Jesus Christ. Adopted for sympathetic non-Christians, this strategy is clearly unacceptable.

order to enter into the system or attempts with his feeble resources to find his way in a world of contradictions.

The spirit of synthesis is in Christianity the truly Machiavellian temptation of the serpent.

If there is an ethics of freedom, we have said, the Christian has to have the possibility of his own creation and action. He must not act as a simple replica of God or automaton of the Holy Spirit who merely obeys scrupulously the letter of the law. God institutes us in this freedom. But it is freedom in the world of contradiction. Indeed, the fact of instituting us in this freedom provokes contradiction, since what is at issue is always freedom lived out in a world of necessity and determination. The simple fact of liberation provokes contradiction in the group in which we are. Even those of our own house are against us.

But the contradiction is an inward one too, for the freedom that is given by God comes to a man who is looking for independence and autonomy. This brings us to the deepest level of contradiction. Far from acceding to the natural thrust of man toward liberty, his instinct, his eagerness to break his chains, God liberates him, but not as the individual hopes. Man does not want a master but he finds himself in service. He wants to choose good and evil himself, to become autonomous, but he finds a formal judgment concerning good and evil. He wants to change his social and political condition, to be independent, but he finds that he is to stay in the state in which he is. On the other hand, he does not want the unheard of venture of entering salvation history and taking up the radical freedom of the Lord. This neither interests nor concerns him. This is what he fears. But this is precisely what he is given to live out.

His desire for independence, however, is not dead. He finds in himself the contradiction between the freedom that God gives him and the freedom he wants. He is torn by this conflict. He is constantly confusing the one freedom with the other. Above all he is always ready to despise the freedom that God gives.

What we have to realize is that it is on the basis of this situation that we have to live out freedom. It is on the basis of the existence of contradiction that lived out freedom is possible. It is in the conflict at the heart of these contradictions that man learns what the freedom which is given to him really is.

There are two aspects to this. The first finds expression in the observation of Gurvitch that it is only when there are contradictory groups and forces in society that men can achieve freedom by playing off some against others and participating in both. The existence of opposing forces is what allows a man to choose his own path. This is true in the present field too.

Contradiction limits the integrative power of systems as well as groups. It is thus a condition of the Christian's possibility of living out freedom, at least so long as the second aspect, which we have yet to study, is met. If this is to be so, however, the two factors in contradiction have both to be admitted and considered. Contradiction must not play off a positive factor (good) against a negative factor (evil). If the Christian chooses good and takes no account of evil he will destroy the contradiction to the profit of legalism. But the grace of God covers the work of man and hence does not annihilate what man does (the first term in the contradiction). The love of God transforms the negative factor, i.e., all that deserves condemnation, the expression of hatred and revolt against God, all abuses, power and conquest, into a factor which, if not legitimate or holy, is positive. God turns demonic work into positive work.

To be sure, this work is still contrary to his good will. It does not cease to be revolt, hatred, and domination. But even as such it is positive. This is the condition if contradiction is to be maintained. Without it we should be in a Manichean universe which is not that of revelation.

The situation created by man becomes positive in spite of his opposition to the good will of God. For it is produced in a reconciled world, even though the reconciliation is not yet visible. Man's break with God is the source of positive values because God reconciles himself with man even though man neither knows this nor wants it. If things were different, there could be no Christian freedom, for all that the Christian could do or would have to do would be to advance in exclusive obedience to God, without choice, invention, or creation, without participation in the life of the world, as a mere automaton.

If Christian freedom is to come into play, then, there has to be contradiction, but between two positive situations, even though one of them is contrary to God's love. The Christian, therefore, must be on guard lest he fall into one or the other of two errors.

First, he knows that God is reconciled to man. He knows what this means. He knows that the acts of men, for all that they are fundamentally bad, become positive before God. But knowing this, he must not see in it the possibility of doing whatever he likes in the history of society. He must not use reconciliation speculatively. To do this is the same temptation at the historical level as we find at the personal level when sin is committed because, where sin abounds, grace superabounds. Judgment falls on this type of speculation, since it is engaged in by someone who knows what he is doing.

Again, the man who knows reconciliation must not think that he can accomplish reconciliation. He must not think that he can bring it about here and now in an impressive way by accepting, as God does, the sinful work of man. This is the temptation to achieve a synthesis such as we were just discussing. It is also the suppression of freedom.

Here, then, is the first aspect of the relation between contradiction and lived out freedom. From this angle freedom follows its course thanks to contradictions. It does its own work by utilizing the contradictory factors with which God and society present it.

The second aspect seems to be inseparable from the first, of which it is also a condition. It is that freedom in Christ consists in learning to live in contradiction. This freedom means that we do not wish to achieve a synthesis. We do not wish to achieve a united world, a unitary society, or a system. We are ready to live in a relative, temporary, and broken world. We are ready to accept the fact that relations between men are contradictory, that things are at odds, that there is friction in social and political mechanisms.

Freedom in Christ means living in the real world and not a utopian world. It means living in these contradictions. This is not easy when one is impelled by the absolute of faith and revelation. It is difficult to accept rifts within oneself, or with others, or in society. This acceptance is not, of course, resignation or passivity, for I make it a condition of the work of freedom. But it is a recognition of weakness, of the insignificance of our history which allows freedom to go ahead and do within the work of societies the work that God expects.

# Chapter 2

# Concrete Implications

## § 1. Christian Freedom in Politics[1]

Our concern here is not with a theology of the state. I do not deny that our attitude to the state may depend on teaching derived from the Bible. But I am not giving this here. It is well enough known even if not altogether certain. I also want to make it clear that instead of following the usual course and discussing the Christian and the state, money, and so forth, I shall begin at each point with the ethical situation, e.g., the Christian as a free man in politics, the Christian as a saint in politics, the Christian as an agent of love in politics. For we must not forget that the state is one thing and political life another. Politics and the political are not the same thing.[2]

Only too often the practice in this matter is to sketch a doctrine of

---

1 Cf. on this subject H. Gollwitzer, *Forderungen der Freiheit* (1964), which is lively and profound, but which seems to me to have a very idealistic view of politics under the guise of a para-Marxist pseudo-realism. I thus part company more or less completely with the author's analyses. The theological reasons which are given for Christian participation in politics are all very odd to me. I agree with some of the negative conclusions, e.g., that there is no such thing as Christian politics and that the Christian should not try to introduce into politics Christian principles that are supposedly taken from the New Testament. But I must also point out that Gollwitzer himself offends in this regard (*Église et Société*, II, 31) and that he does so as an evident consequence of his other principles: "Jesus Christ, in sending out Christians into the world and giving them the commandment of love, imposes on them the duty of taking part in politics." A closer reading of the Gospels would show that the very opposite is true. This is a gratuitous proposition. To say that the Christian must take part in politics to save the world seems to me theologically untrue. What is at issue is the freedom which serves God in the world. Service of the world, even of the world which God has so much loved, is never enjoined in the Bible. To say that the establishment of terrestrial justice is a concrete way of expressing love and that power is a way to achieve it seems to me historically and politically untrue. Some fine approximations to terrestrial justice may be found which are the opposite of love, e.g., the admirable Roman system. No one has ever gone further than the Romans in the concrete search for justice, and this not merely at the legal level, since they inscribed in their system the criticism *summum jus, summum injuria*. Communists are a long way from achieving anything as good. It is true, of course, that a superficial view of Rome records only conquest and slavery and ignores the rest.

2 J. Ellul, *The Political Illusion* (1967), c. 1; "La problématique théologique de l'État," *Les Chrétiens et l'État* (1968).

the state and then to try to show that politics corresponds to this when a specific Christian attitude to the state is deduced from theology. Thus we are to pray for the state, to render obedience, and so forth. In most imstances no actual consideration is given to political action or participation. Even Karl Barth is guilty of confusion here when he lumps together obedience to the state, service of the state, and participation in political life.[3] This is what leads him to make the strange statement that Christians cannot have a hostile attitude to the state. They must give it their loyal, active, and total approval. This does not seem at all obvious so far as political activity is concerned.

We shall begin by eliminating what seem to be two incorrect relations between freedom in Christ and politics. The first concerns liberalism. For some time it has been thought that Christian freedom implies political freedom—a question to which we shall return—and that this finds expression in liberalism. This idea arose in the eighteenth century and came to full flower in the nineteenth century. It argued that political liberty is embodied in formal democracy, bourgeois parliamentarianism, and economic liberalism.

This political liberalism was trying to answer the following very precise question. Man is free. But he lives in society. In these conditions how is he to institutionalize freedom? This is the only serious political question. The not very adequate answer was a purely formal system which does not express the freedom of man, a materialistic system which allows both the domination of the strong and the suppression of other possible liberties.

This whole construction became an obvious deception when the state became stronger than ever and this made it the giver and guarantor of freedom. Freedom could then be given in such a way that on this understanding it became an abstract freedom considered in isolation from the reality of man, whether as an objective freedom, a freedom inscribed in the nature of things, a principle, or an organization. This freedom was safeguarded by a legislative mechanism, by a constitution, which is poles apart from lived out reality.

The final mistake of liberalism was to regard the collectivity or the masses as free without any necessity for commitment. Simply being left alone was enough to constitute freedom.

Obviously we cannot describe here all the forms of this liberalism or the progressive development of institutions corresponding to this ideal.[4] For all its faults it was a great human achievement and we are not to dismiss it contemptuously by calling it middle class or class politics. It showed extraordinary inventive force and created a new political world. In its own way it was a Promethean effort, and we have to realize that if it had

---

3 *Church Dogmatics*, II, 2, pp. 721ff.
4 For a detailed study cf. J. Ellul, *Histoire des Institutions*, Vol. V.

not been invented economic progress would not have taken place and socialism would have been nipped in the bud.

The mistake, however, was when Christians of this age saw in it an incarnation of Christian freedom. Confused here were a freedom contained in nature and the freedom given in Christ by his death and resurrection. A stable organization which guarantees freedom was confused with the act by which man expresses his freedom. Christians at that time were not realists. Nor did they think of freedom as transgression.

There were, of course, two trends among them. The majority accepted the ideology of the epoch. They regarded man as good. This was why he could be allowed to be free. He would obviously make the best possible use of his freedom. In contrast the orthodox viewed man as corrupt. But they arrived at the same result as regards liberalism. For, they said, those who exercise power are men like the rest. They, too, are bad. It is thus better that rulers should have as little power as possible. For the citizen, left to himself, will in any case do less evil than a prime minister, king, or president. This is a problem that we shall have to take up again in another context.

Either way, however, the main error, i.e., that of confusing political liberalism and Christian liberty, is no longer of primary importance today. We may simply note it without discussing it at length, for the pendulum of history has now swung to the other extreme. The present-day conviction in many circles is that socialism best expresses Christian truth. There is also far greater insistence today on justice, encounter, and solidarity (charity) than there is on freedom.

The second error in my view is the temptation to shun politics. I want to point out at the very outset that this attitude rests on some very weak arguments, e.g., that Christianity is concerned with spiritual things, the inner life, etc., but that it also rests on an exact and valid analysis of scripture. I may recall this briefly.

The texts of the New Testament show that neither Jesus nor later his disciples ever engaged in or showed any interest in politics.[5] What we are told about the state is theological. What we are told about conduct in relation to it is not at all political. We are to obey, to show honor and respect, and to offer prayers.

Now the argument often used in explanation of all this is that in those days people did not engage in politics as they do now. But this is incorrect. If what Cullmann says about the relation of Jesus to militant Zealots, and the recruitment of his disciples from among the Zealots, is right, as I believe it is,[6] then it is the more significant that Jesus refuses to engage in any political action. It seems that he accepted and adopted their "zeal" but stripped it of its political orientation and content.

---

5  Cf. F. Biot, *Théologie du politique* (1972); J. H. Yoder, *The Politics of Jesus* (1973).
6  O. Cullmann, *Dieu et César*.

It is not just that Jesus rejects violence. We all know this. What is called in question is the importance of the political itself. He launches the same accusation against both Sadducees and Pharisees, who were political adversaries, the latter hostile to the Romans and trying to promote a politics of resistance, the former compliant. He recruits among the Zealots but at the same time appeals to publicans like Matthew and remains in contact with them.

All this shows that the great problem of the time in Judaea, the problem of being for or against the Romans, which agitated Jewish opinion and divided it as the attitude to the Germans agitated and divided France in 1940–44, or the attitude to the Vietnam war agitated and divided America more recently, this problem is one which he simply sets aside.

Jesus refuses to be the liberator of Israel. He refuses to answer the question whether he is for or against Caesar or whether taxes should be paid or not. Indeed, his rejection of the central problem that divided the Jews is not even grave and serious. He devalues it by subjecting politics to a kind of ridicule.

We have noted already—and in my view it is essential—what attitude he takes to paying taxes (Matthew 17:24–27). This is an important matter. Jesus begins by showing that normally one should not pay. Imposition of the tax is illegitimate in his eyes. But we will pay so as not to give offense.

We have here an act which specifically expresses freedom. Paying or not is unimportant. I am free to do it or not to do it. Doctrinally I should not, but out of love I will. But to devalue even further the content and importance of this political act, Jesus connects with it a somewhat magical and absurd miracle: "Take up the fish that first cometh up, and when thou hast opened his mouth, thou shalt find a piece of money. . . ." This is derision. It shows that the political attitude is not important for Jesus. In relation to it we are to practice complete freedom and a certain demystification.

As regards the apostolic writings there is a strong argument which I have never seen presented. All recent historical investigations of institutions show that, contrary to the hasty conclusions of many previous historians, an intense political life existed in the countries conquered by the Romans. The Romans were not colonizers who stamped out autonomous life. On the contrary, they allowed the subjugated peoples their rights, institutions, and political systems, organizing links with Rome in a very elastic way. In particular, throughout the Orient and Greece, a strong political life obtained with elections, parties, magistrates, and so forth. But where do we find the epistles recommending voting at elections or joining parties, as Christians might have done in Ephesus or Corinth? Again, in Rome after Augustus there was a concerted effort to interest the people in political assemblies and the election of magistrates. But does Paul allude to this in his epistle to the Romans? From all this one might infer a supreme indifference towards politics.

Rather oddly, since it is not his usual practice, Bonhoeffer has to admit that this is so, and that the Gospels are not riddled with political allusions as J. M. Paupert avers. He says in his *Ethics*[7] that Jesus was not concerned about solving temporal problems. When asked to do so he took odd evasive action (Matthew 22:15; Luke 12:13). He never gave a direct answer but always moved on to another plane. His Word does not answer human questions but gives divine answers to the divine questions addressed to man. In its essential determination it moves from above down rather than from below up. It is not solution but deliverance. It does not proceed from division, as in the case of man when he puts the question of good and evil, but from the total communion of the Son with the will of the Father. It is situated on the far side of all human problems. Who tells us any way that all human problems should or can be solved? Perhaps unsolved problems are more important for God than solutions are, says Bonhoeffer, since they remind us of man's sin and the divine redemption. Perhaps man's problems are so complicated and so badly put that they are in fact insoluble. The problem of wealth and poverty will never be solved except as it remains unsolved. The organized battle of the church against temporal evils like slavery, intemperance, and national division runs into the same difficulties as the Crusades. Its experience gives us good reason to ask to what extent it is the church's mission to solve these temporal problems. I have cited the views of Bonhoeffer at length—and I fully agree with them—in order to let this theologian, who is usually regarded as progressive, bear the responsibility for statements which in our sophisticated modern jargon would be styled reactionary.

Now in spite of modern beliefs to the contrary we often find exactly the same orientation in the prophets. It is a mistake to think that all the prophets are dominated by the problem of social and political justice.[8] On the contrary, they oppose the current idea that political revolution will emancipate man from servitude and that moral freedom and political freedom go together. The nabi bears daily witness to the ineluctable imperfection of human liberty. Each day he sets before the people the great part played by necessity in the life of man. The presence of the prophet is evidence that freedom remains a problem. The prophet is the precise opposite of the demagogue, according to Neher's strict and rigorous analysis. The demagogue preaches independence whereas the prophet opposes the desire for it, rejects utopian political schemes, and offers no political opinion nor party program, never engaging in politics at all. Amos unceasingly denounces the desire for political independence. Wherever man tries to construct his own world, Amos intervenes and issues the constant reminder that man is already committed to a covenant. For the prophet it is blasphemy to kick against the divine order and to think that one can

---

7  D. Bonhoeffer, *Ethics*.
8  Cf. Neher, *Amos*, p. 159.

achieve hereby the good (or freedom) of society, the nation, or the individual. This is far more central than any political or social preoccupation. As distinct from Greek thinkers, the prophets are not really interested in the state or politics. To find such an interest in them, to think that the political debate is central in their message, is simply to conform to the platitudes of our own society. This hardly qualifies us to make any serious assessment of the content of revelation.

Does this mean, however, that we are to stay out of this area altogether? In fact no directly biblical or theological argument seems to support participation. It is a matter of regret to me that Barth's presentation[9] tends to show that, since we are told to pray for the powers that be, this implies that we have also to take part in politics. This argument does not seem to me to be a sound one any more than the further argument that an a-political attitude is ruled out by the fact that for Christians the state is a dispensation of God, so that the Christian should play a part in its provisional order. We find here the same confusion between recognition of the value of the state, participating in upholding it by prayer, which is a specifically Christian attitude that we shall be looking into later, and political commitment through propaganda, voting, militantism, and so forth, which is of a very different order. There is a world of difference between praying that God will give rulers a spirit of wisdom and justice and joining a political party which is designed to support or to attack the government. In my view political participation cannot be based on this type of argument.

On the other hand, an a-political attitude is in no sense a mark of freedom. This is what I want to stress. As I have often said, freedom consists in doing something with and in freedom. It rarely takes the form of abstention. The freedom to be uninterested, to turn aside, or to sleep is not Christian freedom. An a-political attitude in modern society is not an expression of Christian freedom but of fear and weakness. I need not press this, for the general tendency of Christians today is similar to the general tendency of the population at large, namely, to be very much oriented to politics and to want to play a part in them.[10] This leads us to a consideration of Christian freedom and political participation.

Let us be honest and realistic. If Christians have to take part in political life today, it is not for reasons of faith and theology, but for reasons of fact and circumstance. All life today is in fact oriented to politics. If it is incorrect to say that everything is political, it is true that, rightly or wrongly, politics has gradually invaded everything. There are various reasons for this that I have analyzed elsewhere. The political question imposes itself on everything, and voluntarily or involuntarily all our judgments are political.

It is a wrong question, then, to ask whether the Christian should take

---

9  *Church Dogmatics*, II, 2, pp. 721ff.
10  Cf. *The Political Illusion*, Introduction.

part in politics. He is fully doing so already. This is not a duty of conscience. It is an order of necessity. The only question is to know how to participate in such a way as to bring a certain freedom into this order of necessity, or to manifest Christian freedom within it.

The Christian certainly needs to be aware of his political orientation and he needs to make his decisions in terms of his situation and his freedom. It is pure delusion to think that we can lead the Christian life today outside this reality.

This does not weaken what I have just said about the indifference of the New Testament to politics. In New Testament days there was a lively political life but it did not touch everything. Far from it! Most of life then was non-political. Hence one need not be interested in politics.

Today, however, the activity of the state has wound up by making everything political. We can no longer pretend that we are not involved in politics. Even without our consent we are involved. Hence we have to ask what is implied by the exercise of Christian freedom in political participation.

We may dismiss at once some traditional issues, which are mentioned only to refresh our memories. Participation does not mean that we have to work out a Christian doctrine of the form of government or the economy. Scripture has nothing decisive to say on such matters. Many political systems can be justified from it. Thus Calvin argues for aristocracy, Barth for democracy, Bousset for monarchy, etc. No precise guidance is to be sought. Another way that is closed is that of wanting to christianize society or the state. The state is not meant to be Christian. It is meant to be secular.[11] A necessary duality has to be upheld between church and society, between political will and proclamation of the gospel. If, as we noted earlier, there is no Christian liberalism, there is also no Christian socialism. Or both may be Christian to a degree. As one might put it, here and now, in a fragmentary and temporary way, there might be coincidence between a certain teaching and an aspect of the Christian faith. We shall return to these questions in another context.

What, then, are the signs of freedom in Christ in this field? In my view there are two. The first is the exercise of political choice and the presence of Christians in politics. The second is the relativization of politics.

(1) The exercise of choice and the presence of Christians in politics. If we live in politics, this implies the exercise of a certain choice. The choice is not simply between Christian teaching and teaching that is not Christian. It is a choice that is made between political parties, ideas, and actions, i.e., parties, ideas, and actions which relate to, express, and issue from society.

Now the choice cannot be made for Christian reasons. Among the

---

11 I am not insisting on this. What I said in 1946 in "L'état chrétien, état laïque," *Cahiers des APP*, was new enough at the time but since its popularization by Cox, Schaull, Wendland, and others it is no longer of great interest.

parties and teachings of the world there is not one that is more Christian than others. I have found no Christian reasons, based on revelation, why I should be more right than left or *vice versa*, to take a modern example. Leftist convictions about progress, reason, productivity, and happiness are no more authentic or Christian than rightist ideas of country, hierarchy, honor, and order. Nor are they less so. Socialism's trust in the state does not seem to me to be more valid from a Christian standpoint than liberalism's distrust of the state. Nor is it less so. The optimism of the left regarding man is neither more nor less legitimate than the pessimism of the right. Equally respectable values are found on both sides. No choice on Christian grounds can be made between justice, equality, and revolution on the left and liberty, tradition, and responsibility on the right.

The worst thing a Christian can do is to try to find theological arguments in justification of the position chosen. Thus some Christians in 1942–1958 elaborated a theology of Israel first to explain their choice against Hitler and then to show how completely different Stalin's dictatorship was from that of Hitler, the latter being anti-semitic and the former not (?), so that Hitler's dictatorship was diabolical before God whereas Stalin's was acceptable. After 1965, when politically-minded Christians in France became such strong supporters of Algeria, a number of Christians, often the same ones, changed their theology completely and worked out a different theology of Israel in order to show that the new state of Israel should be opposed. As circumstances changed, the theology changed too. This proves that it was a mere matter of self-vindication. The Word of God was utilized to provide reasons for emotional choices already made.

Nevertheless, we should consider an argument which carries a good deal of weight today and is decisive for many Christians. It is profoundly true that the Christian ought always to be on the side of the weak, the minority, those who are humiliated and oppressed. Therefore, it is inferred, one should be on the left, as the poor are; the left is the party of the poor. It seems to me that there are two errors here.

The first is that it is a hundred years behind the times. Thus in 1848 the French left represented the most miserable of the population and it was itself poor, embattled, and oppressed. The men of the left were victims, and victims were defended by them. Today, however, most of the poor seem to belong to the right. As a society becomes more affluent, it adopts the ideas of the left. This is at least true in the west. The conscience of the working class becomes stronger with the rise of the standard of living. It is no longer a fact that the poorest workers are on the left. It is a mistake to equate the working class with the poor. It may be granted, of course, that an ideological mutation is now taking place. Today the left is putting the third world in the place previously occupied by the proletariat. This is not to be denied. Not by a long way, however, does the left either represent or help the peoples of the third world in any effective way. The aid given by the U.S.A. is a hundred times greater than that given by the U.S.S.R.

The second error in the idea that the left is the party of the poor is as follows. Is it a matter of being always with the poor and abased or is it a matter of being with a very strong power which claims to represent the poor and abased? Do we have to recall that in 1931–35 the very poor and humble in Germany, the true workers, were in the Nazi party? Was this a good enough reason for collaboration with this party? Today we see the same problem in relation to Communism. Is it that the U.S.S.R. is a nation of the proletariat? Or does a party qualify as the party of the poor because it has strong weapons, is financially sound, and has enormous resources? It is often said that the Communists still in fact defend the poor and seek a better future for them. To this I reply that the Communist party is a machine for propaganda and conflict which uses the poor as much as it serves them and that the real objective is not the rehabilitation or happiness of the poor but the victory of Communist countries. It may be noted that Marx showed no compassion for the most disinherited (the "proletariat scum"). He had absolutely no interest in them. For they did not constitute a revolutionary force. It may also be noted that Lenin distinguished between the proletariat masses which had to be led and the political proletariat which was the active minority and which was not recruited from among the poor. It may be noted further that the result of the Communist revolution has not been to wipe out misery but to plunge a whole new class, the older middle class, into misery. If a Christian can say, as the Communist does, that this class deserves it as an exploiting class, then he no doubt belongs to the party, but I cannot believe that there is anything Christian about accepting the enormous sufferings that have been inflicted on the world by Communism, equal at least to those inflicted by Hitlerism, capitalism, or colonialism.

Unfortunately there is no real party of the poor. The humiliated and oppressed have no true political defenders. Even the so-called revolutionary governments of the peoples of the third world do not really work on behalf of the weak. Hence the choice between political options definitely cannot be made on Christian grounds.

It is no use pretending that our orientation is decided by faith or the Bible. We must accept the fact that it is a matter of free choice. It is not guided. Each of us makes it on his own responsibility. There is no Christian cover or guarantee. It is a matter of environment, education, temperament, political knowledge, prejudice, and interests. This is the level on which we and all other men choose. But this means that as Christians we already have to relativize to a high degree the importance of this choice.

I thus agree with Bartsch[12] when he argues that what we have to look for in this commitment as in all political social ethics is not the material content of instruction but the structure. Where is it that we find the command to obey those who rule over us? To what does the Christian

---

12 *Église et société*, I, 48.

action relate that is evoked by this imperative? What is the aim of the proposed political action? These are the real questions which must be asked.

Bartsch reminds us that, when we consider politics, our basis must certainly be the concept of the neighbor but that an essential part of political participation is rejection of the institutionalizing of this neighbor and constant and concrete recollection that we become the neighbors of others by the fact that an action or demand creates a relation.

From this one may deduce two essential consequences which seem to me to be the primary characteristic of the presence of Christians on the political scene. The first is that if we have to take part in politics, to join parties, unions, clubs, etc., this is not because of the ideas espoused in them. It is not because of the justness or justice of the cause. It is not in the name of ideology. We are not to fight for the triumph of a political idea or the application of a program. No doubt we should do all this as well, secondarily, since it is part of the game. But we have to realize that it is not all that important. We have to remember always that our choice has been made for purely human and relative reasons. The determinative factors are not, e.g., justice and freedom but our own temporary emotions and opinions.

The important thing is the presence of Christians among other men. The important thing is that witness should be borne to Jesus Christ on the political scene. What is needed is express, total, and hence verbal testimony which is designed to carry the good news to men in this area and which is therefore designed to teach them that Jesus Christ is their Saviour, to lead them to faith, to evangelize or convert them, as we used to say. The latter terms are anathema to many today. They are condemned from a Christian standpoint. It is my conviction, however, that this reaction against open and verbal proclamation, and against the desire to convert our neighbors to Christ, is in fact an expression of timidity, of the fear of being different from others, of being a late representative of outdated ideas. It is because society as a whole is against Christian thought that we are ready to compromise, settling for service instead of proclaiming in words the salvation which is in Christ. In our age it is much easier to serve, to work with others, to engage in activities that are secular, than it is to proclaim the good news. Let there be no mistake, however! It is only by verbal proclamation that Jesus Christ is known. It is not by works, service, or incognito presence. All this is useful but it can be no more than a preparation, foundation, and preliminary for explicit proclamation.[13]

I believe, then, that in the Christian life the first valid reason for

---

13 The strange fact may be noted that once theology thinks it can explain everything in the Gospels in terms of proclamation or kerygma, the very Christians who do this abandon oral proclamation and take refuge in the incognito of service. This phenomenon would make an interesting psycho-sociological study.

taking part in political life is that we should be present among men, not primarily to cooperate with them but explicitly to declare the gospel to them. To avoid misunderstanding, I may add that when I say "not primarily to cooperate with them," I am not suggesting that we should not cooperate with them. In our jobs and all our social life we have to cooperate with men. The same holds good in politics. But at this level it does not matter whether what has to be done is done by a Christian or not. Again, I am far from suggesting that this is without value or interest. Naturally it is better to run a city well than badly. If a Christian has a hand in this and is a good administrator, that is all to the good. But any man can be a good administrator. Being a Christian is no absolute guarantee that one will be a better politician or administrator. Seeking the good of a city is not a specifically Christian thing. Obviously we will participate in this to the best of our ability. But if we are to give a manifestation of Christian freedom we shall view this as secondary and relative, transforming it into an occasion or possibility for witness to Jesus Christ. This is what I have in mind when I say that the only specifically Christian point of entering politics is to bear witness and to try to convert men, not in the sense of proselytizing, but because we know that their peace and joy and fulfilment can be granted to them only by their conversion to Christ. It is for their sakes and not for the sake of ourselves or the church that we have to announce the gospel to them.

If Christians are to be in political life to bear witness, if this is in truth their only motive, then Christians are needed in all parties and movements. All opinions should have Christian representatives. Only in this way can the scandal of the political divisions of Christians be avoided. If some Christians are socialists or Communists while others are monarchists or constitutionalists, if some belong to the right and others to the left, and they are convinced that theirs is the Christian position and find a theology on which to base it, then scandal arises. What is seen is the inconsistency of Christian thought, its inability to formulate specific politics (as though this were its task). Furthermore, discord and division are caused in the church in the name of politics. If, however, Christians take up differing positions knowing that these are only human, and having it as their primary goal to bear witness to Jesus Christ wherever they are, their splitting up into various movements, far from manifesting the incompetence of Christian thought or the inconsistency of faith, will be a striking expression of Christian freedom.

For in effect—and this is the link to the second reason for Christian participation in political life—the result is that Christians join different parties with the same motive, namely, that of proclaiming Jesus Christ explicitly to their neighbors. Hence they are more united among themselves by their faith than they are with their political associates. This is what really counts. If within the different groups they see that their political position comes second and their confession of Christ comes first, then in effect they are closer to their brothers in Christ in the opposing party than they are to non-Christians who share the same political view.

We thus see what Christian freedom means. It means that political adversaries can be fully united in Christ. If militants can put their political opinion behind their faith, this is freedom in relation to the world. Others will then look with astonishment at these odd people who instead of doing like others, i.e., hating one another for political reasons, are full of love for one another beyond these secondary barriers.

"See how they love one another" means something if this is how it is. Loving within established social categories has no value as witness. The important thing is that political opponents should love one another because they are Christians and not reject one another because they are political opponents. A good deal is said today about the scandal of the divided church, but it is an even greater scandal, not that Christians belong to different political parties, but that they should hate and excommunicate one another for differing political choices. If, however, they know how to love one another on the far side of these choices, then they can play effectively their role as the salt of the earth, the witnesses and guarantors of the covenant.

For if Christians, belonging to different parties, are basically and totally united among themselves, if they can pass beyond the political barrier, then they build a bridge between the different groups and opposing factions. By their work as intermediaries they promote better understanding among men. They serve as interpreters and stand surety for members of each group to the other. They lessen the hostility. Furthermore—and I think this is a crucial thing—they help men to see themselves from different standpoints. They help them to stop being enemies. As reconcilers, are they not witnesses to the covenant?

This obviously means that they will work to reduce class conflict. Thus they will try to change the attitude of the upper classes with a view to eliminating the power of exploitation. But on the other side they cannot be in full solidarity with the opposite party or the unions. A choice of loyalty has to be made. Loyalty to fellowship in Christ is not compatible with unconditional party loyalty. This is the same choice as the choice between God and Mammon.

We cannot serve two masters. He who thinks that his primary obligation is class solidarity or political allegiance disrupts fellowship in Christ. He has chosen the other master. He who desires above all things fellowship in Christ has to retreat or default a little in relation to his party or union. He will be very like the unjust steward of the parable. Other men will pass an unfavorable moral judgment on him. He will manifest the same dishonesty as the steward, using worldly goods, not in the service of Mammon to whom they belong, but in the service of God. Yet even at this distance Christian freedom will be vividly displayed—the freedom without which political involvement is bondage, and for whose loss a high price has to be paid.

In this attitude, which naturally should be perfectly clear, frank, and open, and about which there should be no misunderstanding or concealment within the party or union, there lies the question which is put to people around us and which is perhaps the question that they put to us and that leads us to witness to Jesus Christ. This is the question of our freedom and the question of our faith.

What a miracle of freedom is needed, however, if Christians are to adopt this attitude, if they are to remain in fellowship with one another, if they are to be able to stand at a distance from their parties or unions without detaching themselves from them! I have still to see it happen, and yet if it does not the participation of Christians in political life is worthless. It is the absurd prattling that we actually see in practice.

(2) The relativization of politics. This is the normal consequence of what we have described as the first effect of the introduction of freedom into political participation. What has finally to be brought into politics is a sense of the relative, not in order to devalue politics, but, as we shall see, in order to restore it to health and to make it possible. I can hardly do better than quote here the excellent definition of P. Prini: "Christian freedom ought to be a continuously fresh and implacable contesting of the false myths of human sufficiency."[14]

It is essential that we consider to what extent the existence of an absolutization of political questions unleashes passions which in turn cause a great deal of anguish. We are put in a position of all or nothing. This is the worst possible situation in which to practice or to take part in politics. As Bataille rightly puts it, "solving political problems is very hard for those who let emotion alone pose them. It is necessary that emotion should pose them. But their solution demands the elimination of this emotion at some point."[15] In my view the precise role of Christians in politics is that their freedom should permit the elimination of emotion or anguish. This can be done, however, only by the introduction of another hope which finds necessary manifestation in the relativization of politics.

I thus agree with Gollwitzer[16] when he stresses that the Christian has the task of mediation and reconciliation, that he must reject the methods of hatred or the exclusion of minorities, that he should not sacrifice those close at hand to the advantage of those who are at a distance, that he cannot accept bonds of subordination as temporary relations imposed by circumstances, that he should work to set limits to political power, that he can neither submit passively to the *status quo* nor regard political action as

---

14  P. Prini, *Herméneutique de la liberté religieuse.*
15  G. Bataille, *La Part Maudite* (1969), p. 18.
16  *Église et société*, II, 31ff.

a way of salvation which will bring about the kingdom of God, and that the criteria of politics can be neither the greatness of an empire nor the principles of a doctrine, but service with a view to the good of men. All this is excellent and corresponds to the features that I have tried to sketch here.

We must now examine the aspects of this relativization. The first is that as we engage with others in the political venture we have goals and objectives which, if they are not unimportant, are still relative.[17] We must never forget that politics works in the sphere of the provisional and penultimate, so that the ultimate, which in my view is the life and death of men and not just theological truth, must not be subjected to it. But what seems to be obvious is not. To say that politics works in the sphere of the provisional implies a refusal to absolutize it by history. If the truism itself is readily accepted, however, the relative unimportance of politics is usually avoided by a magnifying of history. Politics makes history. But history, it is held, is more than the mediocre paths that man opens up as he is able. This history of little events is transmuted by the magic of Hegelian and Marxist philosophy into the great goddess History which is decked out with all the attributes of God. If, however, our banal history is in truth the History which carries the future, then politics in turn becomes a major and almost transcendent activity. This was Hegel's view. But this is precisely what the Christian has to reject radically.

Our freedom leads us resolutely to adopt the relativity of politics. Only on this understanding can it express itself non-mythologically. This relativization implies the de-ideologization of politics as well. We have to work hard to get it admitted, by ourselves first of all, that politics is an honest concrete exercise in administration or management but that it has no spiritual, ideological, or doctrinal content. Supposed content of this kind is a harmful superstructure by means of which man tries both to make himself more important and to conceal from himself the reality of his action. Here again Christian freedom should make use of realism.

Realism, by helping us to see politics in its actuality, demystifies it. When it is simply a matter of handling our common patrimony well, there is no need for passionate debate. I realize that in middle-class families arguments about the patrimony and its distribution or administration are still embittered by emotional interests and can even lead to mortal hatred. I cannot help comparing these struggles, which used to be concealed under such great words as tradition, family honor, or morality but are now known for what they are, with the influence which in modern society we give to politics, which is of exactly the same order. We should speak of management and equitable distribution and stop exploiting superior interests such as justice, the sense of history, or progress.

---

17  It seems to me that among many others Kierkegaard is the one who best represents the relativization of politics, e.g., when he says in his *Journal* that "from a Christian standpoint what is new comes from God, but from a political standpoint what is new comes from the street" (p. 156).

Christian freedom ought to lead us to treat seriously these very relative problems (which we recognize to be relative), to tackle technical questions as technical questions, to refuse sharply to go further, and to view grandiose proclamations and doctrines with humor. We know that the results will be half good and half bad. No revolution will bring about the change desired. All the same, even if their results can be only provisional, these little works of politics should be well done.

Much humility and soberness is needed rather than passion, for the exercise of power is always dangerous. Coolness is essential if verbal or ideological transports are to be avoided. When politics is properly seen at its concrete and relative level, a different political attitude may be adopted in the relation to others. We need no longer treat opponents as enemies. There is in fact no political (or class) enemy. It is ideology that transforms a conflict of interests or techniques into war and thus transforms the opponent into an enemy.

To relativize and to take away passion in this way makes honest competition possible. It makes possible a politics in which we do not render evil for evil but can envisage a common good.

Naturally this will not be achieved on a general scale. Freedom in Christ is needed to be able to live out this kind of politics. But one of the most important functions of Christians is to be a cooling and peace-making factor among other men. Christians should be those who do not render evil for evil nor fight and conquer enemies, i.e., the men who will not accept their offer of peace. As Barth puts it, Christians should never be the enemies of their opponents, not even in the sphere of the state and the necessary political fight against disorder. This is what they should also tell their associates in the struggle.

Unfortunately I have to confess that Christians who have plunged into politics have in fact heightened passions and intensified the volume of ideological conflict. Indeed, they have more often been instigators than the reverse, probably because they are incapable of action and have found a substitute in their skill in exercising influence through words.

If, however, we try to reduce passion and to relativize, is there not a risk that we will also de-politicize? We must be clear about this. To the extent that we make politics into a battle of ideas, philosophies, or doctrines of man and God, we undoubtedly de-politicize. On the other hand, there is great gain when we banish false conflicts. Nevertheless, if politics is reduced to no more than the best possible management of the common patrimony, will not people lose interest and turn aside? I believe that in this regard, too, Christians have to set an example. They have to show that these technical (and not ideological) tasks must be taken seriously and that these wholly relative ends must be pursued seriously.

Making men interested in these relative and disinterested questions is an admirable goal, for it sets matters on their most realistic level and leads to the greatest possible honesty. If to reduce the flow of words is to de-politicize, then de-politicizing is an excellent thing. If it is said that without propaganda and emotion men will not be interested in politics, then all the worse for politics! Men do not have to be stirred emotionally at all costs. What matters is to conduct politics with more truth and a deeper realism than we see today.

To be sure, this involves a measure of what might be called de-politicizing. De-politicizing, however, is not a rejection of politics. It is a rejection of illusion and ideology. This does not mean, of course, that an a-political stance is better. I have tried to show that this idea is hypocritical and false. Nor am I advocating passive submission. De-politicization implies a true interest in political questions. It implies involvement. What is superfluous will be stripped away, but politics itself will be taken seriously. There is thus a vigilant struggle for freedom.

De-politicizing comes after engagement and not before. It is the attitude of those who are already committed to politics and not of those who regard such commitment as absurd and useless. It is thus an attitude which is not only sane but also fruitful for politics itself. We do not say that it leaves us free personally either for involvement or withdrawal. On the contrary, this attitude means deflating and rejecting the politician who is puffed up with words and trying to achieve competence in dealing concretely with the real questions of politics.

I say that this attitude is fruitful because it makes a true democracy possible. Democracy implies in effect the triumph of the relative and the reasonable. It means that questions will be discussed rationally and not emotionally. General desires, which are usually inadequate, will not be interjected. Opponents and the minority will be regarded as eminently respectable. Means of incitement, which lead to frenzy and hatred, etc., will be renounced. Democracy presupposes a clear recognition that political conflict is not ultimate in nature and that each of us must take part, contributing, not a massive and exclusive doctrinal movement, but a little stone of truth. The first step in democracy is a recognition that opponents may have something in their favor, and that whatever is good in their program should be adopted.

All this, however, presupposes the presence among others of men who are aware of these rudimentary elements of democracy. Christians, since they are oriented to ultimate truth and are called upon to live out their freedom in Christ, seem to me to be the ones who should fulfil this role.

Are we then choosing a form of government? it will be asked. Do we think that this form of government is better and more Christian than others? Not at all. It seems to me, however, that if democracy is this recognition of the relativism of politics, the validity of opponents, the limitation of political means, the worth of minorities, the legitimate difference of opinions, the general distribution of competence and truth, and the reduction of power, then precisely by reason of its modesty this form of government offers a better chance than any other for Christians to take part as free men in Christ. Hence Christian freedom should strive to make true politics possible in a true democracy. This means in the first instance trying to find, not a Christian political doctrine, but a Christian life-style in politics.

## §2. Dialogue with the Sovereign

Taking part in politics obviously means being in contact with power, the state, or, as I prefer to put it, sovereignty of whatever kind. How is this contact to be made from the standpoint of Christian freedom?

The state as a political power is not Christian,[18] nor does it have to be. It does not have to apply the law of Christ. It does not by nature have to observe a moral code. I do not believe that there is any such thing as a natural political morality.[19]

The state is there to exert force. It does not have by nature the ability to discern what is right. Nevertheless, its role is a useful one. It has to see what means serve the common interest of the community which it governs, and to the degree that it ensures the greatest common good one might if one wishes speak of justice. For it is a kind of justice to allot to each his own, as the classical definition has it, although in effect this is really a matter of the common good. It is also a kind of justice to administer the common patrimony as usefully as possible. This evaluation in terms of usefulness is perfectly consistent with man's rational capacity without any appeal to the good or other values. But it is a limited evaluation and one which can also be upset.

What is needed is that power should be confronted by someone else who uses other means, who says other things, and who even says them to the true sovereign beyond the state. This other is the Christian, or the church. It is essential for the political health of the nation that power should not merely be in encounter with itself.

We need to be careful here. A political opponent can never shatter the

---

18  I agree wholeheartedly with the Wuppertal theses (recalled by Bartsch) when they state that the problem of the Christian ethical attitude in politics cannot be based on a theology of the state. It is a mistake to think that individual duties to the state (obedience, etc.) can be deduced from the theology of the nature and objectives of the state. Obedience cannot be viewed as resting on a specific quality inherent in earthly power but only as an expression of the faith which confesses Jesus Christ as Lord and which thus sees in him the master of the relation between the individual and the state. As for Romans 13, Bartsch rightly points out that we have here a doctrine neither of the state nor of submission to it at all costs but a duty of cooperating with the state here and now in a loyalty which is determined and limited by love of God and waiting for his kingdom. Passages that teach obedience to the state do not enjoin unconditional obedience, for the Christian stands over against the state rather than in it, since he is free in his relation to neighbors, including the authorities. Cf. Bartsch, *Église et société*, I, 4ff.

19  J. Ellul, *The Political Illusion*, c. 1.

solitude of power. For the opponent of an existing government is himself in a sense part of the system. His only desire is to replace the government. He does not represent something else. Even if, like the Marxist or Maoist, he wants to shift the basis of power, he is still operating within the political system as I have just defined it. If the state is given a new foundation in the working class, this will not seriously alter the essence of the state—it will still be a class state—nor will it alter the exercise of power. Only anarchists offer serious opposition to the political organism, but the state cannot accept this challenge since it involves its own destruction.

If, then, the solitude of power is to be shattered in order that political balance may be preserved, the challenger must not come from the political sphere and his opposition must respect the existence of the state in order to be accepted. The Christian seems to be the only one who meets these two conditions. He recognizes that power is from God, so that there can be no question of suppressing it. But he is within another sphere of reference and it is from within this sphere that he can engage in dialogue.

On the one side he does not contest the fact that the state lies in the sphere of utility and should take its decisions accordingly. He does not pretend to be christianizing the state. On the other side he presents a series of demands based on another view of reality (ultimate reality). He does not try to get these accepted by compromises, nor does he try to show that what is at issue in them is nature, morality, and so forth. He has to affirm them, however, as an element of the real which is imperceptible to the state.

This is why Christian freedom is so important. Only on the basis of freedom is this confrontation possible.

Tillich shows remarkable insight when he says that the state itself can enter into the I-Thou relation. If this is not attempted, he claims, then the state, or political power, is almost entirely delivered up to demons, to an absolutized I-It relation. There is no justification for this. The state, too, is potentially open to the I-Thou relation. It can be regarded as one of the spiritual forms which for Buber arise out of the third type of I-Thou relation. There is no reason why this should not be so, since everything that has been created is included in the divine sphere and is capable of consecration (*Theology of Culture*, p. 163).

It is true that this relation should be attempted. Yet as usual there is confusion here. If dialogue is possible with the sovereign, it is not possible with the state. Obviously Tillich does not know what the state is. He shows this when he says that it is part of what God has created. Clearly his experience of National Socialism has not caused him to reflect on the reality of the modern state. On the other hand, his recognition that if we cannot enter into dialogue, into a personalized relation, with the sovereign, we are plunged into the demonic I-It relation, is indeed worth noting.

If there is to be dialogue, there naturally have to be two different speakers. This implies certain conditions. On the side of power the first requirement is that the state should see that it is different from the church, that it must have no religious pretensions, that it must not build itself up into a church, that it must not try to seduce or to make itself loved. The second requirement is that it should support and tolerate somebody or something other alongside itself which says something completely different.

It may be stressed once again that two opponents who simply hold different views in the same political sphere are not different in the sense required. They do not provide the other over against power. For a time Marxism aroused fear. It was such a monstrosity that it seemed to be an authentic other. But now that we perceive that it gives birth to a state like any other system, that the differences are merely in organization and vocabulary, that nothing essential is at stake, Marxism has ceased to cause fear in the political order.

It is by no means easy for political power to accept dialogue with something that is radically other, with someone whose starting-point is authentically different. This is why Christians may have to force the gate even in the interests of the state that has need of dialogue. Two speakers are necessary for dialogue.

We find conditions on the side of Christians and the church as well. The most essential condition is that the church should have something to say. If we cling to evaluations based on abstract values, if we simply adhere to theological or theoretical positions, if, for example, we tell a military power which is engaged in revolutionary conflict that torture is a wicked thing, then power will turn its back on us on the ground that we do not know the reality about which we speak, and that our eternal judgments are superfluous. On the other hand, if we think that we can give the state technical advice, proposing a different political or economic order, etc., we are undoubtedly at the level of that reality and what we say may be very useful, but I am not so sure that the church has real competence in this area[20] and the state for its part may legitimately reject encroachment on its own specific domain. Finally if the church limits itself to saying the same thing as power does—and I understand by this the opposition party as well as the existing government—then its blessing of this or that opinion is worthless. The church is no longer the other.

The church has to have its own distinctive word which is not identical with that of power but which is not without some relation to it. If the church has nothing of this sort to say, there is no dialogue but for the state there is also no truth. In order to show more precisely what the role of the church is, some familiar biblical passages may be recalled.

(1) Ezekiel speaks about the watchman (33:1-20; cf. Jonah 4; Luke 13:1-5). Christians and the church are charged to warn the people. It is their responsibility to give this warning. They will be under condemnation

---

20 We can see this from the debates and reports of the World Council of Churches on political and economic problems.

if they do not. But does this passage have merely a spiritual or moral application? Is the reference merely to bad moral action? Or is the warning given only to individuals? It seems to me that this is not so.

The warning is addressed to the whole people, which is a people that belongs to God but is not ready to acknowledge him. Now what was then the particular situation of Israel has become today, from the time of Jesus Christ, the situation of every people and nation. The fact that the warning is given to the people is especially important in our own time when we remember that the people is now the true political sovereign. It is to the sovereign that we must speak. In relation to this people the task of the watchman is to remind it that it belongs to God.

But this is not just a spiritual message. It is set in a specific historical context. Hence, like every prophetic message, it has a political reference. It states that every political act carries its spiritual significance and judgment.

Now when the prophet, the church, or the Christian speaks, what is said is heard from God. More than a human opinion is offered. (Here, then, we have the opposite and complement of what we described earlier as the choice of a political position.) Furthermore, the prophet does not just speak in regard to a single event or in an occasional manner under the pressure of a crisis or a war. The church, unfortunately, is often disturbed only in a crisis or a war when everyone else is disturbed, and it regains its ease when "order" is restored and everyone else is at ease. This ought to arouse our suspicions. For it suggests that in fact the church has not heard something from God but that Christians are seized with panic when everyone else is. Obviously, then, it is simply saying what the world is saying except that it often pushes it to extremes.

Now this is not its vocation. God summons it to take the initiative in what it says. It must speak in season and out of season in the name of truth. When the Word of God is truly heard it teaches Christians to see signs where other men see only events. The Christian learns the meaning of these signs. He sees what they signify. This meaning may just as well be spiritual as political. He is thus called upon to read history in the making, but in a very different way from Marxists or nationalists, since his reading will be point by point rather than continuous. It will be the reading, not of political choice, but of spiritual judgment and warning. It should be stressed, too, that the Christian and the church are not free either to do this or not. If they do not, they bear responsibility for what happens. Their freedom lies, not in a choice, but in their ability to stand at a distance from the event, to plumb its depths, and to take the initiative of movement.

(2) In I Kings 18:16-40 we have the well-known story of Elijah and the prophets of Baal. In this context we merely want to bring out its exemplary character in the political domain. Here again we have address to the true sovereign, the people (vv. 17, 20, 30). The relation is not in the first instance a relation between the prophet and the king. The people is at

the same time the point of departure, the stake, and in a certain sense the true bearer of sovereignty and choice.

In this story the warning of the watchman becomes a direct attack on the actual holder of power, i.e., on the state which has set up a state religion. We shall not discuss here the problem of idolatry, reserving that for a later stage. We shall simply point out that established power is attacked when it has become in some manner a church.

Emphasis must be laid on another point of comparison with the previous passage. This is the initiative of the prophet (Christian or church) under the impulsion of the Word of God. This is what provokes the struggle. The king or state does not in the main seek the conflict. There are troubles enough without it. Peace is desired with the church so long as it will stay in its proper place. In effect the church can be tranquil or not according to its own choice.

For the most part persecution occurs only when the church attacks at a sufficiently sensitive and profound point, a point of truth. If it simply adopts the position of opponents of the government in power, the situation is simple for this government. If it is leftist the church is a reactionary force, while if it is rightist the church is a revolutionary force. This does not matter much. What matters is when the church dislocates the problem and puts everything out of joint by speaking the Word of God instead of adopting one or the other of the current political options.

Wherever we find the worship of power—and this is a common phenomenon today—the church should be ready to attack.

The final lesson to be learned from this passage is that when the church makes this decision and has real confidence in the Word which is disruptive because it is creative, then, its act being the occasion, it brings miracle into history. The introducing of this unpredictable event is what really makes history.[21]

The intervention of the church in this dialogue with the sovereign is then much more decisive and results from authentic hearing of the Word and not from an arbitrary or casual opinion such as that which leads Christians to take part in specific movements. This shows us that the dialogue can start on the level of contradiction (although not necessarily), conflict, and tension.[22]

Certain inferences must now be drawn. If we have a dialogue with the two aspects mentioned, then we have a movement. We are not confined to the traditional framework in which there is reference to the relations of church and state and the analysis views these as two institutions. Through the centuries theologians and political thinkers have examined the relations

---

21  J. Ellul, *The Politics of God and the Politics of Man*, c. 5, pp. 133ff.
22  For the political necessity of tension cf. J. Ellul, *The Political Illusion*, c. 5 and *Problématique de l'État*.

from this static standpoint. Attempts have thus been made to balance the two forces, to give them their own spheres of competence, and to delimit their interconnections legally, as if we had two powers which had to be organized and a satisfactory system had to be thought out. In reality, however, no system could be devised, and for good reason, for while the state is a power to be organized, and an organizing power, if the church sets itself on the same plane it ceases to be authentically the church.

Now as the Lord never leaves his church even when it is guilty of betrayal, he steadily dismantles the organisms which are carefully set up in the politico-juridical, sociological, or administrative sphere. This means that a system of church and state can never succeed. The relation has thus to be thought of dynamically as the encounter between an organized, institutional, and organizing power with a power of a very different order which has no pretensions to the exercise of political power or the division of human powers but which unceasingly represents another thing or rather another person—one that is fundamentally other and that belongs to a different sphere.

We have to realize that if we do not intervene in the name of the Wholly Other, i.e., the God who is radically different, who is transcendent, then all that we have is Christians playing politics, and, since they do not even confess that they are Christians, it makes little difference what they do; this is the price of death of God theology. If, however, we claim to be intervening in the name of the living God, then the relation is one of movement and of life, and it can be fruitful in the socio-political realm.

This means, however, that the dialogue with the sovereign amounts to a good deal more than passing political resolutions or presenting pleas to the government. This dialogue is conducted at every level of power by the voice and presence of each believer or group of believers so long as they are true ambassadors of the Wholly Other and not just participants in the power of the sovereign.

The movement implies, then, that the church is genuinely an external power which comes from outside to the political power just as our Lord is the one who comes, i.e., who is not included in either human nature or the social body. If he is in these it is because he comes into them from what is not human nature nor the social body. Hence the church should not let itself be absorbed or politicized. It has its own function, which is an indispensable one if sane politics are to be possible. I have tried to show what this function is in relation to democracy, and elsewhere I have done the same at a sociological level.[23] No one else can fulfil this function. It is the function of weighing events by the Word of God and of explaining the meaning of the political path or of decision. It is the function of showing the significance of the human venture.

---

23  On the tendency of the social body to become closed, and the mission of Christians to open it up, cf. J. Ellul, *The Presence of the Kingdom* (1967).

This dialogue, which is not to be a dialogue between the deaf, brings us face to face with different expressions. On the one side the state *acts* with *force*, whereas on the other the church *speaks* about *justice and love*. This introduces a tension which can be fruitful for political action since there can be no true politics outside this tension between him who acts and him who speaks (i.e., speaks a true word), between him who has force and him who represents justice and love.[24]

We must now take a further step. This introduces us to the problematical nature of power. We have here a much neglected aspect of the theology of the state. The Christian is not called upon to contest the validity of the state. Nevertheless, by his participation in political life as we have sketched it above, and also by way of the dialogue between the church and the sovereign, a number of values, judgments, and attitudes surge up in politics which thrust power into a movement of necessary uncertainty, this being a witness to the introduction of freedom into the political domain.

In other words, as Christians we must bring into the sphere of authority a fundamental ambiguity in which it emerges that there is for it no basis either divine or human. It exists, but this is all that we can concede to it as Christians. We do not have to find a theological basis for it. If we do, we betray revelation, which calls power into question rather than setting it on a throne.[25]

The bringing to light of this problematical aspect is what distinguishes a biblical and Christian view of the state from all others. It can be expressed only in practice and not in doctrine. This is why a theology of the state is very useful but also most inadequate. It has no meaning unless it is

---

24 As regards the latter the church has to speak even though it is aware that the word is despised and contested in the modern world. It must now try to do more. Its ultimate action can be only an expression of this word and a form of the word, for its only ministry or service is that of the word. As it speaks, however, it should state calmly and with no false shame that it alone has been given the task of carrying truth, love, and justice for the world, all the rest being a sham, and that it alone knows the source of light, all the rest being darkness. Christians today in their false and fearful humility are not ready to accept this. We should not have a bad conscience when we speak to men about God. Such humility merely causes Christians and the church to lose their true role, so that they become useless and do not render any service at all.

25 Cf. the fine passage of Tillich (*The New Being*, p. 170). He argues that no ultimate answer can be given to the question of authority. Why not? Because—even though it may seem blasphemous to say this—God himself can give no answer to this question. For the decisive act of God is the cross of Jesus Christ. The authority of Jesus Christ is not that of a dictator. It is the authority of a man who is without any authority. It is the authority of the man on the cross. It is one and the same thing to say that God is Spirit and that he is manifested on the cross. Those who fight for or against the authorities should listen to the story which tells us that Jesus fought against the authorities and established an authority which cannot be established. The answer is that no answer can be given but this one. Beyond all authority we must be open to the power of him who is both the ground and the negation of all that has authority in heaven or earth.

associated with a practice which effectively introduces power into this situation in which it spontaneously denies itself. The problematical aspect arises from the different elements analyzed above and from the setting of limits in relation to the state, especially the limit of its secularity.[26]

The problematical nature of power is not brought to light, however, merely by proclamation of the Christian message and the resultant attitude. This attitude should also include a reference to the understanding or program which the state cannot help setting up and proclaiming.[27] Now we may agree with many of the affirmations of the state and we can choose, as we have seen, between many political options. But we must say to the state: "You choose justice. Very good! We agree. But now we must be serious. We must seriously seek justice. We must be radically committed to it." Along these lines the Christian or the church will become the watchdog in relation to the state's affirmations.

The first step in dialogue, and also in challenge, consists in taking seriously the words which authority pronounces, in transforming them into an authentic word, and in demanding that authority acts as it speaks. It seems to me that this is a human and concrete expression of what I called above the word of truth, love, and justice. "I take your human word seriously but let us remember that we shall be judged by our words. Since I, the church, accept your declaration of intent, on the basis of what you, the state, have chosen, I can proceed to a criticism of what you are doing. I do not ask transcendent things from you. I ask only simple respect for the word which you have spoken from the heart."

Thus the church should accept the serious element as well as the relative element. This is what prevents authority from being a unilinear power with a tranquil heart. This is what brings its problematical nature to light. If, however, we fail to do this, if we do not remind the state of its own words, its limits, and its gesturing, if we do not engage it in rigorous dialogue and give it a prophetic warning, then the state is bound to increase and its power will become totalitarian and dictatorial. It may be a truism to say that dictatorship is the fruit of acquiescence. Nevertheless, the truism is true.

I am certainly not forgetting that the sociological or economic context might be favorable to dictatorship. It is still a fact that the state will grab as much power as it is allowed to grab. If there are no free men, there is no political freedom. As Marx rightly says, the power of the state is

---

26  For an analysis of the main views and for the ambiguity cf. J. Ellul, "Rappel de quelques doctrines sur l'État," *Les Chrétiens et la Politique* (1966). For the biblical basis of the problematical nature of power cf. J. Ellul, "Le pouvoir royal en Israël," *Mélanges en l'Honneur de Brelles de le Gressaye* (1966).

27  I am again in accord with Bartsch (*Église et société*, I, 48) when he says that the concept of the neighbor in the heart of the Christian enables him to control the limits of the duty of obedience by whether the action of the state serves this neighbor or harms him.

precisely that which we attribute to it. Or, as Calvin says, the people has the government it deserves. It falls victim to tyranny if it gives up the struggle.

All the same, a more powerful force is needed if freedom is to be imposed on the state. As may be seen throughout history, freedom which is based on man himself or on institutions does not cast any ambiguity on the state. To think that it does was the monumental mistake of Montesquieu. As I see it, only Christian freedom lived out in this relation with power can truly achieve the desired end of a decisive questioning of power without being a negation of power. In this relation, which is constituted by the successive decisions of Christians and the church in expression of their freedom, the state can be a valid state and liberties become possible.

It should always be remembered, however, that the state, holding power, can refuse the dialogue and questioning in which it finds itself engaged. It can seek to be univocal and totalitarian. It can seek to destroy that which confronts it. This is the way of direct opposition and open conflict. In this situation it will be by martyrdom that the Christian will not only bear witness to his faith but will reintroduce, whether the state like it or not, a political challenge. If, as we have said, taking the words of the government seriously is the first form of this challenge, martyrdom is the last. What we have to realize is that, if the church is faithful and is prepared to go to the limit, the state cannot by merely breaking off dialogue, and thus shuffling off this embarrassment, reaffirm its power.

Need it be recalled that the great witnesses of the faith have always regarded martyrdom as the supreme act of freedom of conscience and religious liberty, and that the way of martyrdom rules out the way of revolution, since he who is ready to lose his life does not fight others but refuses to kill them? For the enemy is the neighbor whom he must love even though he be unjust towards others. To accept martyrdom is certainly not passivity or resignation. On the contrary it is a royal affirmation of the sovereignty of our Lord. As Tertullian strikingly puts it, "I am not a Christian except as I will to be so. Hence you cannot condemn me unless I will to be condemned. Since, then, you cannot do what you can do against me unless I wish it, what you can do depends on my will and not on your power" (*Apology* 49, 5).

Today, however, Christians do not like to talk much about martyrdom. It is not their style. They prefer violence. They justify their hatred of oppressors by their love for the oppressed, with all the nuances that this involves in concrete cases. It is not on this basis, however, that dialogue can be set up with the sovereign.

The persecution and stifling of the church calls power in question no less surely, if more concretely, than open dialogue. Once the church is planted, even though it seems to be impotent and uprooted, power becomes problematical and this leads to its uncertainty and limitation. The only change that can alter this is when the church becomes unfaithful and ceases to listen to the Word of the Lord, trying instead to find a basis in the world and by reason of its treachery becoming a part of the world. This is always possible when the church stops taking up its freedom and lets itself be enslaved. This is the one possibility in the modern world which seems to me to be truly disquieting.

We must finally say a word or two about the problem of the whole or an elite. We have said a great deal about dialogue. But who is to conduct it? We have referred in a general way to the Christian, Christians, or the church. And in fact it may be any of these. None is excluded.

The easy solution is to put things in the hands of the ecclesiastical organism. The institutional church will speak with the institutional state. I have already pointed out why I am not too happy about this. In any case, it is hardly adequate or satisfying. For even a general synod is not the church, nor is a message from such a synod necessarily the voice of the church.

In contrast, many Protestants are tempted to exalt the individual prophet, i.e., a Christian who stands up and speaks the Word of God. This is valid too, but it is no more satisfying. To be sure, the Holy Spirit can inspire either a synod or an individual. We are not denying this. But we are here in presence of that new reality which is the church. And it is as this, i.e., as the body of Christ incarnated in a sociological reality, that we must be engaged in dialogue.

Normally dialogue is the function of the whole church both as a totality and as individuals. It is a relation with power at every level. It may be a personal relation to some holder of power. Or it may be a group relation in which a political authority is addressed. But, since we are dealing with the sovereign, i.e., the people, the relation may also be with a civic corporation, a club, or a union. The official level, both ecclesiastical and political, is included, and so too is that of the individual addressing other individuals or the whole. Christian political movements also have their place.

The important thing is that no one form excludes the others. The various forms are complementary. Again, no Christian or group of Christians should consider themselves outside this matter or count on others. In other words, we have here a task for the whole church and all its members.

In fact this is hard to conceive of concretely. Only militants, it seems, can address other militants. We cannot imagine reaching the people, since the people does not exist as an entity and in any case vast numbers of them are not interested at all in what Christians have to say. Again, we find it hard to think of plunging all believers into dialogue when neither theologically nor politically are they prepared for the confrontation. Only groups specially oriented to the various problems can speak. But this raises another difficulty. Do such groups speak authentically for the church any more than individuals? Above all, do they not have this vocation because they are composed of men who are very politically minded, who are much agitated by problems of this kind, and who will often speak much more because they are politically minded than because they are Christians? In any case, will they not speak much more in terms of their political opinions than in terms of their faith and their hearing of the Word of God? This is how we see it in practice.

If, however, the situation is that only groups of militants can engage in dialogue, they ought to be militants who are as free as possible from political emotions and as solid as possible theologically. We certainly need Christians who are strong in faith and who work at political questions, and enter into relation with political groups, with no great zeal for this kind of thing, with no craze for politics, with the detachment which alone makes possible true Christian involvement. Above all, such men are not to become delegated specialists. Nothing is more distressing than to find in, e.g., so-called dialogues between Marxists and Christians, the same two or three Christian spokesmen engaging in perpetual monologues alongside the same three or four Marxist spokesmen, all of them knowing exactly what the others are going to say, and coming not so much as experts in the subject but rather as specialists in dialogue. This is the very thing we ought to avoid. For we have here neither a true representation of the church nor prophetic inspiration, but an ossified ecclesiasticism.

In any form, dialogue with the sovereign implies an awakening of interest and vocation among as many Christians as possible and the preparing of Christians for the task. Apart from such preparation—let there be no mistake at this point—there is no political relation between power and the church and hence an aspect of Christian freedom will be missing, as the world will also be deprived of an indispensable challenge to the state.

But can we stop here? Having said earlier that no political position can be justified from a Christian standpoint, and that any Christian can engage in a political orientation for personal reasons, have I nothing to say for myself? Do I not have to say what I regard as the most serious commitment of all? Do I not have to give some human reasons for this view?

Assuredly I do. And what I have to say is that for most men today the involvement which is most useful, and which best expresses Christian freedom, is involvement in anarchy. I am well aware of all the arguments that can be brought against this. I know that Calvin viewed it as the one orientation which cannot be accepted. I realize that there are texts in the Bible which tell us that authority comes from God. Nevertheless, in my opinion Calvin's judgment relates to the circumstances of his own time and the passages in the Bible are not contrary to my thinking, paradoxical though this may seem to be.

What reasons drive me to this view? I certainly do not say that it seems to me to be a direct expression of Christian freedom. What leads me in this direction is the constitution and development of the modern state. All specialists agree that we now have to speak of the nation state, i.e., the state which absorbs into itself the entire life of the nation. They also agree that the state is bureaucratic, i.e., abstract and anonymous. It is authoritarian, even when democratic. It is arbitrary, for no state observes rules and constitutions. It is universal. It wants adoration; no state can really govern today without obtaining the adherence of the heart and the emotional support of the masses. It knows neither limit nor humanity.

These characteristics, which have often been analyzed, mean that in certain circumstances—and again I am not trying to lay down what should be an intrinsic or permanent Christian attitude—the state in any country, no matter what may be its form, whether democratic or dictatorial, new or popular, is in fact the chief danger known to man, whether from the material standpoint or from the spiritual standpoint.

The danger is not the absence of authority or even the misuse of authority. Calvin could see it thus because in his place and time, both in France and in Germany, the danger was indeed anarchy, the weakness of authority, and the unleashing of the passions of the mob. In our day the exact opposite is the case. For when the mob gets out of hand and revolts today the final result is always the creation of an even more powerful state.

In this area the only danger known to man in our age is the tendency of the state to become absolute in every field. This is aggravated by the fact that this power which tends to become absolute is set in a technological society, i.e., in a society which provides the state with a fantastic number of means. The state is totalitarian, not because of totalitarian doctrines, but because of the vast array of means, e.g., in planning, economic and administrative management, forecasting, investigation, control, research, inquiry, and psychological action.

Every modern state is totalitarian. It recognizes no limit either factual or legal. This is why I maintain that no state in the modern world is legitimate. No present-day authority can claim to be instituted by God, for all authority is set in the framework of a totalitarian state. This is why I decide for anarchy.[28]

We must be more precise, however, in two respects. The first has to do with the common accusation brought against anarchy. This is that it is too utopian and idealistic. No society can last in conditions of anarchy. This is self-evident, and I am in full agreement. But my aim is not the establishment of an anarchist society or the total destruction of the state. Here I differ from anarchists. I do not believe that it is possible to destroy the modern state. It is pure imagination to think that some day this power will be overthrown. From a pragmatic standpoint there is no chance of success.

Furthermore, I do not believe that anarchist doctrine is the solution to the problem of organization in society and government. I do not think

---

28 This evaluation of the state is naturally a résumé of several important studies; cf. Charbonneau, L'État; Aron, Démocratie et totalitarisme; also Doctrine des libertés, and my own The Technological Society (1964) and The Political Illusion (1967).

that if anarchism were to succeed we should have a better or more livable society. Hence I am not fighting for the triumph of this doctrine.

On the other hand, it seems to me that an anarchist attitude is the only one that is sufficiently radical in face of a general statist system. For there can be no question of being able to overcome the system by changing it from within. The failure of Lenin, Castro, and others is all too evident. The system absorbs those who think they can utilize it. Nor can there be any question of finding a *modus vivendi* or achieving attenuations. It has been demonstrated how a liberal state becomes an authoritarian state. The course is set and no accommodation will be either lasting or sufficient.

In face of this absolute power, only an absolutely negative position is viable. What we have in mind is the attitude that conscientious objectors take on a specific point, and not without good reason. In the present set-up the anarchist attitude of a total refusal of validity or legitimacy to any authority of any kind seems to me to be the only valid and viable one. The point is not to enforce a particular view of society but to establish a counterbalance, a protest, and a sign of cleavage. In face of an absolute power only a total confrontation has any meaning.

When we speak of dialogue with the sovereign, it seems to me that this can be definitively initiated only on the basis of the greatest possible intransigence, for power today is completely alien to any real discussion. It is true that discussion is allowed within the system. But the quarrels between right and left seem to me completely futile, for in every possible way they simply lead to an enhancement of the power of the state.

Democracy is a mere trap with the party system as it is and a bureaucracy that cannot be altered. Discussion may go on about taxes and the improvement of social services. But power is totally deaf to the individual, indifferent to the interests of freedom, and ignorant of the true concerns of the nation. Only a radical opposition, i.e., an attack on the root of the situation, can engage it in authentic dialogue.

The second point that I wish to clarify has to do with concrete organization. What we have in mind is a radically negative attitude to the validity of any undertaking of the modern state. This means on the one side that it is possible but by no means necessary to associate with an anarchist group. This is good if Christians can bring new blood, and useful and serious contacts are possible. On the other hand, it is clear from our first point that the Christian will always be in an ambiguous position in any such group.

It must also be stressed that this is not the only possibility of anarchist action. Links can also be forged with situationist and pacifist groups. The actions entered into can also be of very different kinds, e.g., ideological action, propaganda, direct action, refusal to vote in elections, conscientious objection, refusal to pay taxes, and so forth. This is where each individual must decide for himself. The essential thing is the decision to challenge the modern state, which without this small group of protesters will be checked by neither brake, value, nor reason.

### §3. Christian Freedom and the Fight for Freedom

It seems to me that the free man, i.e., the man freed in Christ, ought to take part in all movements that aim at human freedom.[29] He obviously ought to oppose all dictatorship and oppression and all the fatalities which crush man. The Christian cannot bear it that others should be slaves. His great passion in the world ought to be a passion for the liberation of men.

He should thus take his place alongside the humiliated and offended, not out of charity, but because he is with men who must be freed in the same way he has been freed, and because every moment he must stretch out his hand to the Lord to receive freedom from him. He takes his place alongside the despairing because in himself he too is a slave, whether of a master, a political power, economic conditions, or more subtle psychological and sociological forces. He is thus in a situation where nothing is expected from man.

The Christian, however, brings into this situation the fact that nothing is expected from man because everything is expected from God.

Two preliminary difficulties obviously seem to arise here. Have we not said that each should abide in the state in which he was? Can we then, as Christians, take part in the movement of revolt by which men want to change their state? It must be remembered that this saying is addressed specifically to Christians and not to others. Knowing the extraordinary joy of freedom, however, the Christian is under constraint to help others to aspire to this blessing.

Nevertheless—and this is the second apparent difficulty—the Christian has perceived and experienced the fact that all his attempts to free himself were futile, that he always came into fresh entanglement, and that the struggle was in vain. He is aware that he has been liberated by the one who as the Lord of all things is able to liberate, and to do so uniquely in this way. In other words, only freedom in Christ and by Christ is freedom. The rest is an illusion, a sham, new bondage. Man can expect no freedom from any human movement. Man has not been freed, nor will he be freed, by a republican or democratic movement, nor by free thought, nor by collectivization, nor by the establishment of Communism, nor by the achievement of national independence, nor by technological progress, nor by the mas-

---

29 We may recall a passage of Barth here. He argues that ultimately all men have need of the freedom of the Spirit. The Christian community cannot give them this. It can only bear witness to it in the hope that this witness will not be in vain, that God will use it, that he will manifest what it attests. The community can do this work of witness, however, only to the degree that it loves men and that it does so in deed, first accepting as a basic concern the freedom of creatures who suffer the lack of it (*Church Dogmatics*, III, 4, p.503).

tering of the laws of economics or matter. None of these things can free man.

Are we to conclude, then, that all these things are futile, that we should have no part in them, that we should perhaps even discourage those who are zealous for them? Should we say that, since Christ alone delivers, the only movement of freedom is preaching, the declaring of the Word of God? Since faith in Christ is the only thing that enables us to take up freedom in Christ, must we infer that the only decision that we should try to bring men to is that of conversion?

Although it runs contrary to the views of modern Christians, this is certainly the logic of truth. But this logic leads us to only one of the aspects of this truth, and hence it can finally lead us to error. For scripture tells us in many places that as Christians we are bearers of Christ. Our bodies are temples of the Holy Spirit. But "where the Spirit of the Lord is, there is liberty" (2 Corinthians 3:17). This means that in the social or political setting in which we are called upon to live, we are directly the *bearers* of freedom. We are not just examples or signs. We are in effect the bearers of true freedom, with all the terrible responsibility that this involves, as we must always remember.

This freedom, as we have said often enough, cannot remain inward and spiritual. It has to find incarnation as it affirms itself in a political, economic, or social setting. Hence it is not possible to stop at preaching alone or attempts at conversion. It must also be demonstrated what this means.

Thus we must take our place at the side of the poor and humiliated in order that they might cease to be poor and humiliated. We realize that the human struggle will not bring fundamental liberation. But we also realize that to declare to them freedom in Christ without having a share in their struggle can be hypocrisy and cowardice (I do not say that it always is or is so necessarily). In their battle for freedom men should always find Christians at their side to give their efforts a meaning, fulness, and dimension that they do not have in themselves. At the side of those who fight for freedom, Christians have a kind of sacerdotal function. The movement is not complete in itself. The presence of Christians imparts to it something of the freedom which is in Christ.

What is needed is both that the Christian should truly take up his own freedom and that he should take part in the various movements of men towards freedom. Dependent on this is whether these efforts lead to an authentic liberation—authentic even though provisional, local, and incomplete—or whether they are meaningless. We have to work at this freedom in order that it may be real freedom instead of judging the men who engage in the attempt, despising their efforts and discouraging them. As Barth says, when the freedom of the Lord manifests itself, it is objectively impossible that those who are placed together under the judgment of the Lord should begin to judge one another. On the contrary, the objective possibility and even the necessity is that they will free themselves mutually for the Lord and live alongside one another and for one another in a free association. [30] This is the aim and the final reality of this association for freedom.

We may thus take a further step. Christian freedom does not merely open up the possibility of political action as we have just examined it. It also carries with it the necessity that Christians should take part in the movements for freedom which men initiate, whether the freedom be political, economic, intellectual, moral, or religious. They will not attach the slightest value to these freedoms as such. But they will regard them as concrete possibilities of life and in this sense they will see in the human attempt a relative attempt at liberation. In other words they do not have to subscribe to a doctrine of freedom or to what is said about it. They have to give themselves to the actual tasks of freedom. This is the principle.

To say this, however, is not to solve anything. Only now do we come up against the serious difficultites. Of these there are three that call for particular attention.

For if the political struggle is necessary, it is wholly inadequate and inapplicable to freedom. I cannot do better here than refer to the warning of Kierkegaard, who in his *Gospel of Suffering* (p. 184) says that to the degree that superficial culture expands, the diversity of human studies increases, and unceasingly jealous, fearful, and shabby comparison spreads its contagion, to that degree one may say that everything conspires to stifle the frank courage of man. As men fight to topple thrones and kingdoms, they seem to be working with might and main to develop a more dangerous bondage, namely, pusillanimous fear of their peers. A tyrant, if he really is one, and if an ancient fable is not being exploited to arouse opposition against him, can be overthrown, or at least he can be more or less clearly envisaged. Today, however, fear of potentates should be regarded as ancient history. Many fight in this field against a danger that is no longer of any great seriousness. The inexperienced reason as follows. This must be a serious danger, since so many are opposing it. The more experienced, however, rightly conclude that this danger which so many oppose is of minor importance, for there are so many defenders, and we never see many defenders when the peril is great. But this poor spirit, this pusillanimous fear of equals and their tyranny, this poor spirit which we ourselves evoke and which without dwelling in any one person in particular insinuates itself secretly, gliding into human relations, this poor spirit which has as its task the destruction of the individual relation to God, is extremely difficult to extirpate. We are hardly even aware that it is bringing us into bondage. In face of it we forget the zeal which is deployed in freeing men by overthrowing kingdoms. The very fact of bondage is doubted. How can one be the slave of equals? We have been rightly taught that man is the slave of

30 *Church Dogmatics*, II, 2, p.717.

that which he serves and on which he depends, but our age, so enamored of freedom, thinks differently. It believes that when we do not depend on a sovereign, when we are no longer slaves, when we do away with tyrants, we abolish slavery. It is not suspected that bondage is still promoted, and this is what makes it so hard to throw it off. For this subjection does not mean that one man wants to oppress many others—this would be easy to spot. It means that individuals, forgetting their relation to God, are afraid of one another. The individual is afraid of some or all who, driven by the same feeling, forget God and form the crowd which renounces the nobility of eternity in which it is given to each to be an individual. We are thus reminded by Kierkegaard that, while politics is of the order of necessity, it is not of the order of freedom.

The first difficulty, then, is as follows. As Christians, i.e., as those who bring to a human movement the dimension of the presence of Christian freedom, can we cooperate in any or every human movement which professes and declares that it is working for freedom? Can we lend our aid unconditionally? Is a declaration or program enough to command our support?

An obvious limitation springs to mind at once. We certainly cannot associate with a movement whose aim is to destroy the Christian influence of the church, to liberate man from Christianity. In *Fausse Présence* I attacked Christians who applaud movements that are directed against the church and theology and who accept all the criticisms made of them. Nevertheless, this does not mean that there may not be a legitimate cooperation even with such movements. To the extent that they are challenging a degeneration of Christianity into religion and morality, or rejecting a Christian social system (Christendom), or fighting against oppression by Christian forces, e.g., the church, or an alliance of church and state, it seems to me perfectly valid, and even sane and holy, that Christians should side with them.

For one thing this forces Christians to take revealed truth seriously and to strip it of meretricious adornment. For another the presence of Christians among these non-Christians can help the latter attain to a deeper view of what the truth of revelation is as compared with the intellectual, political, and social betrayals of those who represent it.

We must exercise discernment, however, and not engage blindly in all kinds of ventures so long as these ventures involve attacks on what we regard as the errors of Christianity in the past. This cooperation must not rest on a misunderstanding. Thus it seems a serious matter that in the dialogue of Christians with Marxists the latter appear to be much more lucid than the former. When we read of an actual arrangement between them, it is on the basis of the leftism of Christians who plead for a community of interest on the part of the victims of capitalism in spite of differences of ideology, and because violently anti-capitalist Christians think that Communists are the best defenders of popular demands in face of the essential evils of the capitalist system.[31] This is true enough. But if it is legitimate for Christians to act thus, they must do so in the hope of giving the movement the stamp of Christian freedom. If they participate only as leftists and not as free Christians, there is little point in their action.

Clarity is needed. We have to test ourselves by two criticisms. First, does the movement in which we want to cooperate manifest a genuine concern for the freedom of man? Secondly, what means does it employ? The first criticism has to do with real objectives. Does the movement use freedom as a screen or propaganda tool, pretending to seek freedom but in reality espousing a doctrine which is just as totalitarian, oppressive, and anti-liberal? Is it a rigid military organization which negates human freedom? Is it leading to the establishment of a social, economic, and political system which is in fact dictatorial?

We cannot evade this test by arguing that the dictatorship is good, or that it is a dictatorship of the people, or that true freedom is possible only as one lives in a stricter organization. These are the excuses and new hypocrisies of the day. When regimentation, administration, and planning increase, it is not true that freedom is gained. The well-known arguments to this effect are sophisms.

Even if, however, we are not too sure of the ultimate objective, why should we not approach a movement which says it wants freedom and join it in seeking at least a provisional goal? This theory of the provisional goal has enjoyed a vogue for some years now. It is argued that at some points Christian ideas and the ideas of this or that party converge. It is thus possible to cooperate in limited spheres. The same detailed aims can be pursued. Differences and even basic antitheses can be put, as it were, in parentheses.

I should like to say three things about this theory. First, it is not necessary to appeal to it to take part in political action according to the conditions already described and as an expression of freedom in Christ. But we have to be on guard lest this cooperation signify that Christians become pledges or hostages or even decoys or propaganda objects to lure people of good faith and commit them beyond this limited action. We must also be sure what is the place and meaning of the limited action in which we can cooperate within a more general strategy and among other objectives. Obviously if we work for a specific end which is acceptable but this is only part·of a larger plan which is abhorrent, we can hardly agree to the provisional goal. Thus the Nazi Party wanted to deal with poverty and unemployment in Germany in 1932, and this was a laudable effort in which any Christian might well participate. But when set within the total policy and strategy of the Nazi Party, this kind ofcooperation can hardly be regarded as still permissible.

---

31  A. Casanova, *France Nouvelle,* June, 1966.

The Christian, because he ought to engage in real action, must not become blind or stupid. He has to realize that in the political, economic, or social sphere there are in fact no limited sectors or specific works or provisional goals. There is a commitment which necessarily becomes general even though it be meant to be particular.

My second observation is that in experience one provisional goal is always succeeded by another.

Finally, on the theory of the provisional goal there can never be any question of giving the stamp of Christian freedom to any kind of work. Since I cannot engage in this work with the whole of my faith, I am obliged to have mental reservations. I know that finally it is not freedom in Christ that triumphs, but just the opposite.

In my view, therefore, the idea of a provisional goal is both dangerous and illusory. We have to consider a movement in its totality. We have to put to it the question whether it is in the last analysis fighting for freedom.

At this point I must refer briefly to an issue of some urgency. I do so in the form of a quotation from Bataille:[32] "The movement which demands the raising of the standard of living is a protest against the luxury of excessive wealth. It is thus attempted in the name of justice. While no objection can be made to justice, it might be noted that the word is a cover-up for the profound truth of its opposite, which is freedom. Under the mask of justice it is a fact that general freedom takes on the tame and neutral appearance of an existence subjected to necessity. We have a reduction of its limits to the most just. It is not the dangerous unleashing which the word might otherwise signify. It is a guarantee against the risk of bondage, not a desire to take up the risk without which there is no freedom." Bataille is entering here into the conflict between liberty and equality, which might be summed up schematically as follows: Either we leave men free and soon there will be no equality, since the stronger will carry the day, or we may insist on equality and are thus forced to interfere with liberty. Later explanations that liberty is representative or collective, or that it comes through planning and administration, are feeble illusions designed to stop us facing the true facts.

Bataille is right when he says that what we now call the fight for social justice is strictly a fight against freedom. This is unavoidable. No reconciliation is possible. The imposing of social justice is the establishing of a life subject to necessities. The only contact with freedom is that social justice is a guarantee against the risk of bondage. This does not mean, however, the presence of freedom. As we have already pointed out in an earlier section, there is an indissoluble relation between freedom and risk.

We thus accept the antagonism and incompatibility of justice and freedom. This does not have to imply that we must choose freedom. It does imply, however, that there has to be a choice if we are honest. Those who

---

32  *La Part Maudite*, p. 49.

think that they can effect a reconciliation are either theorists who do not know modern socio-economic life or Machiavellians whose stock in trade is double talk and illusion. A choice has to be made.

Now Christian freedom may, of course, choose justice and decide for participation in a movement to raise the standard of living. If so, however, the same Christian freedom demands that the lies of its friends should be unmasked and that men should be shown clearly that this will not bring freedom. In all freedom I can certainly join the fight for justice, but in so doing I have to realize and say that I am necessarily fighting against all forms of freedom. If there is one thing that Christian freedom does not allow me to do, it is to deceive those whom I address, to make them the victims of illusions, to give them hope that freedom is the goal of a struggle for consumer growth and equality of income, to make them believe that they will find the dignity of free men along these lines.

This deception, and not my involvement in a movement for social equality, is the thing which decisively destroys my own freedom. I have in fact seen many Christians who, involved in such a movement, have fallen into the trap of this illusion. From that time on they have tragically ceased to talk and act as men who are freed in Christ. They have become no more than partisans.

Even if, however, we can meet the first criticism satisfactorily, this is not the end of the matter. We have to consider a second criticism, namely, that of the means employed. Our starting-point here must be an idea which I have developed several times. This is that not only does the end not justify the means but the means transform the end. End and means have to be carefully dissociated. Only in Christ do they meet.[33]

From this unity the Christian learns two things. In relation to his own life he learns first that if it is lived in Christ he lives out this unity. That is, the means which he employs are the whole. They are the end and the fulness. This is why proselytizing in the bad sense cannot be evangelizing. In each of our acts the whole of the life in Christ is committed. Secondly, and reciprocally, the ends which we may pursue are not set at the conclusion of a long work or way or construction. They are present every moment that we are engaged in seeking them. Thus the kingdom is already present in the discovery by man of a treasure hidden in a field which he does not yet possess.

We are thus led to a concentration on the question of means. This is in accord with the situation in which we now find ourselves in this world, which is above all a world of means. It is required that we be very scrupulous and circumspect in the use of means.

When, for example, we join a movement for freedom, we have to engage in a constant criticism of its means.[34] For in the transition from

---

33  J. Ellul, *Présence au monde moderne*, c. 3.
34  In this regard too Kierkegaard shows almost prophetic insight, putting the problem

means to end there is no break, i.e., no leap from the quantitative to the qualitative. Means not only have expected effects. Much more often they have invisible and unforeseeable effects which in the long run turn out to be hostile to the objective sought, so that often no trace of the end remains.[35] Thus, if men use cruel or treacherous means to achieve a good and generous end, they necessarily give rise to ways of thinking and acting which in the long run will gain the mastery over what was originally undertaken, so that they will not just make it impossible to achieve the desired goal but will often increase the distance from it.

Hence a special examination of means is needed. They must be justified not just by their efficacy or end but by themselves and in themselves. Each means is a distinctive action with its own value and meaning. This is the level at which we have to investigate rigorously the means employed by a party or on behalf of a cause which arouses our spontaneous sympathy.

Thus means which negate freedom can never lead to freedom. It is falsehood, deception, and hypocrisy to think or say that a people can be led to freedom through dictatorship. No dictatorship or authoritarian means can steer itself or a people or state towards greater freedom. The familiar example of liberalization in the Soviet Union is not an accurate one. For it is to the degree that the people has already been psychologically conditioned and moulded by propaganda into what it was meant to be that the state can now begin to relax external constraints. Internal unfreedom has replaced external unfreedom, and even the latter has far from disappeared.[36]

It is untrue that growth in the power of the state guarantees in the long run greater freedom for individuals—the theory of Tito. If we want to work for freedom, we must use the means of freedom. We must show direct respect to individuals and especially to adversaries. We must reject the well-known formula: "No liberty for the foes of liberty." The means of freedom are means that rule out violence, hatred, and lying.[37]

---

of means as no one ever did before him. He notes that means are not only identical with the end but they are more decisive, for the end is at the end and the goal is rarely attained, whereas the means are there at the very beginning and then at every stage. Kierkegaard then shows in an extraordinary way that the assessment of end and means is very different in the world on the one side and faith on the other. In a temporal sense the end is more important than the means, but in the eternal view the relation between the two is reversed, for man bears absolute responsibility for the means he uses. This is a remarkable insight in an age when means were not yet exercising their blinding force.

35 Cf. Fourastié, *Idées Majeures* (1966). I am pleased to note that in this work the author adopts the thesis that I have been espousing for many years.

36 These lines were written at a time when there was general rejoicing at the increasing liberalism of the U.S.S.R; subsequent events have shown that this rejoicing was premature.

37 On violence cf. my book *Violence* (1969). I may refer also to P. Blanquart, *À la recherche d'une théologie de la violence* (1968), a confrontation between theologians

Whenever we find ourselves in the presence of an appeal to hatred, of a movement which exists thanks to the hatred it spreads and whose chief means of recruitment is hatred, we may rest assured that it will not lead to any kind of freedom. Christians certainly cannot join in, e.g., demonstrations for peace which carry placards expressing hatred for others, no matter how legitimate the aim of the demonstrations may be.[38] For one thing it is scandalous to talk of peace and at the same time to pillory opponents. For another it is not by diffusing hatred that one can hope to achieve any kind of liberation.

Thus militant demonstrations against the Vietnam war could only indicate support for the Vietcong and North Vietnam and a desire, not for peace and liberation, but for the subjugation of South Vietnam to communist dictatorship.

If hatred is manifested in a means, this means must not be used. Not only does the law of love tell us this. Christian realism does so too. We have to realize that the employment of means of hatred and violence brings a like result. It is perfectly clear that only a greater violence will be engendered and a dictatorship of one kind or another established. In other words, the use of means of violence is just as disastrous on the realistic plane as it is on that of human relations.

Naturally I have nothing more to say if Christians believe, as some do, that the only thing that counts is the triumph of their cause by any means. I can only warn them that what will come will inevitably be a regime in the style of Stalin or Hitler, even though it may be excellently camouflaged as in many modern instances on both right and left. Apart from the inspiration of the Holy Spirit, the use of violence is always and *a priori* contrary to the will of God.

Obviously it is understandable that non-Christians who are the victims of injustice, oppression, or violence, and who have no other way of defending or expressing themselves, may well take this path. But it is impossible for Christians to justify this or to join them. I will not discuss again the violence which supposedly liberates. It is not worth our while to

---

and non-Christians which puts certain problems very lucidly but offers little new apart from a reduction of Christian distinctiveness and the acceptance of Freudian-Marxist discourse; J. M. Muller, *L'évangile de la non violence* (1969), which unfortunately I did not know when writing my own work; and J. Girardi, *Amour chrétien et violence révolutionnaire* (1970), which contains all the current platitudes: institutionalized violence, the need to change the world in order to make heaven less incredible, participation in the class struggle as an expression of love (naturally a struggle without hatred), but which is a good warning against the danger that violence will lead to dictatorship and block the development of conscience.

38 As Kierkegaard says, the very people who as isolated individuals may truly want the good are corrupted when they unite. Hence the man who seeks the good must beware of relying on a crowd to disperse a crowd or of having a crowd behind him when he goes forward to disperse a crowd ahead of him. This is an excellent way of putting the problem of means and of revolutionary action.

waste time on so empty a concept. I will simply recall that violence is always of the order of necessity. It may be obedience to bondage to the passions or to bondage to a society of violence. It may be thought of as a necessary response to violence done to us. No matter what its origin may be, however, it belongs always to the domain of necessity, i.e., the opposite of freedom.

The justification which is regularly advanced is in effect that violence is no more than counterviolence. All that this signifies, however, is that its necessity is accepted. But necessity never gives birth to freedom. Violence arises in the absence of freedom. Its use is antifreedom. Its result is the perpetuation of this. Insofar as it is adjudged necessary, it expresses a necessity and destroys freedom. All this may be normal for man but it is unacceptable for the Christian.

Even when we recognize a cause to be just, then, we must refuse to be associated with the injustice of its means. It makes no difference that these might seem to ensure its victory. The victory of violence will inevitably recoil on those who have won it. Hence we must not join it but stay on the other side, not in order to betray or sabotage, or to give in, but because it is the side of power, and the task of Christians who are persuaded of the justice of a cause is to work at showing those in power that right is on the side of the rebels, that their violence should not be met by violence, and that the way of justice, pacification, and pardon should be taken. It is by working in this way in the camp which he views as unjust that the Christian can truly manifest his freedom and at the same time cooperate more effectively in the cause of the poor and oppressed than by fighting in the streets or supplying justifications.

Another means that must be considered is the appeal to public opinion. I regard this just as negatively as violence. The Christian must not manipulate public opinion as a political means. Placards, petitions, proclamations, and meetings may be effective but they also corrupt the man or cause that is defended. Any appeal to public opinion today carries with it an element of deception and falsehood to the degree that it does not offer complex, detailed, and rational information. The appeal to public opinion plays on the emotions and glorifies a party position. It also tends to unleash a blind mob and to set up enemies who must be demolished.

In virtue of these inherent and inalienable elements the appeal to public opinion involves a clear negation of freedom. It merges individuals into an emotional, irrational, and explosive mass. It denies even the freedom of public opinion itself as well as the freedom of those whom one wishes to move by launching public opinion against them. From the standpoint of freedom, then, it is impossible for the Christian to have a hand in the use of propaganda that is designed to stir up opinion.

I realize that this attitude will entail a certain ineffectiveness. But we must not set too much store by the effectiveness of passion and excitement. We must also ask what true effectiveness is in the long run.

Naturally I need not spend too much time on the problem of torture. Torture is always to be condemned. There is no possible justification for its use. It is intrinsically evil no matter what useful results it may bring from the standpoint of effectiveness.

This discussion of means, however, must not be merely negative. We have to do more than reject certain means. There is also the option to choose others.

Now the deliberate and consequently free choice of other means, which may be ineffective at a first glance, in the short term, and in the view of political realism, is the most fundamentally revolutionary act that can be performed in our society. To choose the least return in the work of agitation, the least expenditure of time, the least rigidity in the use of time, reverie rather than calculation, poetry rather than conquest, political reflection rather than stirring up of the masses, detachment and comprehension, minimum speed for one's car, less information so long as it is judicious and profound, less overall organization, an interlacing of work and leisure in such a way as not to have slices of vacation and slices of toil—these are all means of modifying profoundly a social context and hence they are means of action. It is on this kind of level that the churches and Christians should act together to affect their society and to give concrete expression to their freedom. What does not have this orientation is a product of the sociological mechanism, of necessity, and of the exclusive determinations of all freedom.

The means of freedom are the means of a liberal organization which does not create in its members a spirit of orthodoxy,[39] nor demand of them a total commitment, but trains them in the practice of concrete freedom and criticism, acting by means of this freedom and not by means of a systematization of action and thought. The means of freedom are the means of rigorous honesty which offers the best possible information, which describes its party exactly as it is, which does not hide its designs, objectives, or means, which tells where its money comes from, which does not bluff its opponents, which does not confuse people with doctrines so complex that no one can understand them, which shuns tactics, and which openly announces its strategy, if it has one, and explains why its various decisions are made.

These, then, are examples of the means that should be employed. They rule out collaboration in the pursuit of freedom with any party that wants to set up a temporary dictatorship in order to create the conditions of freedom. For if we engage in such collaboration we are creating a dictatorship which will never be anything but a dictatorship and will never lead to freedom. We are thus radically renouncing Christian freedom. This is one of the many acts by which Christians can lose their freedom and

---

39 Cf. Jean Grenier, *L'esprit d'orthodoxie.*

cease to take up the freedom which is won for them in Christ.[40] If there are still those who mock at freedom, who argue that violence must be met with violence, and who want to set up a dictatorship of the proletariat, so be it, but people who take this line are ceasing to refer at all or in any sense to Christianity.

Independence and freedom—we live in a world which totally confuses the two. Caution is needed here. We have seen that when Adam achieved independence from God, he entered the circle of necessities and determinations. Freedom in Christ is not independence in relation to God. It is the restoration of a situation of free dependence. Nevertheless, there seems to be a curious confidence that the quest for independence will lead to freedom.[41]

This leads us to the reflection that Christian freedom as we receive and understand it by revelation limits and judges other freedoms and what man calls freedom in the absence of Christian freedom. Christian freedom must serve as a critical instrument in relation to every movement of freedom.

This must not be taken to mean that I am adopting a position of total negation or even reserve in relation to such movements. I have said it before, and will say it again, that movements for human freedom are needed in the world and that Christians should join them. The only point is that we must not be blind or act in the dark here. Today, in the present situation, my stress must be on the critical side. On the one hand, to see that one should take part in such movements is for me very simple and relatively easy. On the other hand, with the swing of the pendulum which characterizes the church, the general tendency among modern Christians is

---

40 Cf. V. Eller, *The Promise: Ethics in the Kingdom of God*, where it is shown clearly that freedom necessarily leads to an ethics of non-resistance and that means are defined by the kingdom itself.

41 We may refer here to Neher's *Amos*, which offers a fine analysis of the contradiction between political freedom and prophetic freedom. The prophet bears ongoing witness to the imperfection of the idea of political freedom. The demagogue (politician) preaches independence, constructs ideas, and affirms liberty. The prophet attacks the longing for independence and rejects all utopian constructions. Reference may be made to the many passages in which Amos denounces the desire for emancipation. At all points where man tries to fashion his own world Amos intervenes with the reminder that man is already committed to the *berith* and that there is no escape clause. Even if movements of liberation are meant to lead to social reforms, they are still opposed by the prophet. Neher shows how mistaken is the interpretation which makes Amos a prophet of revolution. This is to confuse prophetic thinking with Greek thinking. It is the same confusion that makes of Amos a spokesman for the poor of the people in the political sense. Amos never represents the "people of the land." On the contrary, the people is his fiercest enemy. Prophetic freedom challenges fundamentally the attainment of what is thought to be political freedom. It reminds us unceasingly of the imperfection of all man's independence. It presents freedom as at best a problem according to Neher's remarkable analysis.

towards total involvement and blind participation in anything that says it is fighting for independence and autonomy. My insistence on the negative aspect is related to this situation and this difficulty. Critical participation is in effect much harder than blind involvement.

Christian freedom is the limit of other freedoms. This does not mean that it hampers them. What is meant is that it is the ultimate point on which tendencies towards freedom converge. There can be no freedom beyond this freedom in Christ. Any freedom that claims to be this can be only a relapse into greater and more complete bondage than before in the sense that its intention and claim is simply a repetition of the sin of Adam.

There is a thrust, then, towards freedom on this side of freedom in Christ which can be a reflection of this freedom and a summons and aspiration towards it. On this movement of effort freedom in Christ casts a kind of light and benediction and approval.

There is also a thrust, however, towards freedom on the far side of freedom in Christ. This has no validity and is by nature a reversion to even worse bondage.

Christian freedom, then, is a criticism of movements of freedom, for it is their critical point. We cannot accept all aspirations to freedom. On the individual level, for example, we cannot endorse the human pretension which seeks (or more often merely declares) independence in relation to other men, conditions of life, or environment. For such an attempt or declaration is not true. It is mere pride translated into an illusion. To think that we can be independent of our family, education, or background is a mistake. The first step of freedom is recognition of this dependence. It must be accepted. Its validity must be perceived. We must learn to know its limits in relation to our own powers. At the very most we can do no more than set ourselves in conditions in which we can act as independent beings, and then help others to achieve a similar result.

Even here we cannot agree that this type of sociological independence should be viewed in the same way as independence in relation to one's neighbor. If moral freedom leads us to treat our neighbor as an object or thing, or if our egoism entails rejection of a relation of mutuality, we cannot as Christians support this claim to freedom. For in the former case the affirmation of freedom presupposes the enslaving of others. This is the problem of capitalism on the economic plane and of sadism on the aesthetic plane.[42] The two orientations are one and the same.

Always at issue are the exploitation of others and the founding of independence on their servitude. Now it is our contention that the analysis of Hegel, Marx, and others is wholly correct and that this attitude towards others destroys our own freedom. The Christian has to reject this autonomy in all its forms. He cannot help the man who acts thus. Or rather he

---

42  Cf. Klossowski's introduction to the reading of de Sade.

410

*Implicated Freedom*

can help him only by teaching him to criticize his own orientation and to discover that liberation is inseparable from love.

For the same reason we cannot endorse the attitude which consists in wanting freedom in isolation, all the bonds that bind us to others being severed. This attitude differs from the preceding one in the sense that no attempt is made to exploit others but they are regarded as an obstacle to personal freedom, as in fact they always are, and hence there is a break with them and withdrawal from them. This is the attitude of a superb romantic individualism, and it is no less fatal than the first one. We cannot support the man who affirms his freedom by scorning the vulgar herd.

This desire to maintain freedom by separation from others can, of course, have two aspects. In effect the man who tries in this way to cut his determination by others may do it only to achieve the distance which enables him to practice love and to live by it. After all, Jesus tells us to sever the human ties which bind us to others, e.g., parents, or children, and the Good Samaritan breaks the bonds which tie him to his environment and interests in order that he may live in love. This implies in effect an element of distance from others. In this case we have a freedom which is oriented to love and which has been forcefully illumined by Christ. We may thus support the man who seeks freedom in this way, aid him without taking him under our tutelage, and follow him along his path without leading him to ours, realizing that our companionship in his effort is precisely the secret stamp of the freedom of Christ on his enterprise, and that this will finally be approved by Christ himself.

An action of pure independence, however, does not have the same features. In this case we may have the claim of a man or group to be living on the margin without taking part in the activities of society or of other men, etc. This break is illusory and cannot be approved because of the implied contempt for those who live as others do. How many little movements, especially those which are opposed to technical progress and the march of civilization, finally share this attitude, which can yield only paltry results in view of the belief that freedom rests on a break and inversion that are not truly oriented to a love which wins others, this solitude being ultimately sterile.

The independence sought by women or children is of the same order. Woman is here regarded as "the last colony," to use the phrase of G. Tillon. We thus have the strong movement so familiar to us today, i.e., the fight against the subjection of woman to man and the assertion of a wife's independence of her husband. Similarly children are struggling to establish their independence of parents or even their superiority over them. In order that they may develop their personalities, it is claimed, they must be granted liberty, autonomy, and freedom from all guidance or constraint.

It may be noted that these movements adorn with concepts and ideology some simple and well-known realities, i.e., the working woman, the husband without personal authority, the family unity that has lost any meaning, place, or function in the modern socio-cultural system, parents who are so harassed with work that they no longer have any effective time for their children, interests which give each member of the family a life of his own, individual means of transport that separate them, and the fusion of each into some other sociological grouping. These and other facts explain the movements for the liberation of women and children. The ideological pronouncements count for little, although it is on them that interest usually focuses.

The main point here, however, is to ascertain whether the attainment of independence will lead women or children to true freedom. There are two possibilities for women. They may go out to work or they may remain unemployed. A career for women is often extolled as a way of permitting self-fulfilment. In reality we have here another fictional notion advanced in justification of a fact. In by far the majority of cases women have boring and meaningless jobs which demand no rich qualifications and contribute nothing to the development of personality. Work is an absurd constraint and obligation. Women find no more fulfilment in it than at home.

There are, of course, two definite advantages. The first is that they come into contact with more people and the second that they have their own money. As regards the first, however, there are already plenty of neighborhood contacts, while as regards the second a new dependence is substituted for the old one, since the employer now supplies money instead of the husband. But the relation to the employer is hardly a liberating, stabilizing, or joyous one. In reality all that women do here is to come under the bondage which afflicts all workers, namely, bondage to a universal social and economic system and to employers. We have a change of dependence but not an attainment of freedom.

If women remain unemployed, we now know that an equally serious problem is posed. Women are independent of their husbands because they have managed to gain ascendancy over them. They receive money with no corresponding duties. They are emancipated from household tasks by labor-saving devices but a void is left. This is filled in any way possible, e.g., drink, play, drugs, or unregulated passion for the children which produces possessive or unsuitable mothers. Out of all this, serious neuroses gradually develop. Now it might be argued that what we have here is a misuse of freedom rather than another instance of bondage. This may well be true. Nevertheless, it raises the question whether freedom is a state into which we may easily install ourselves. Finally, the things that women go after in order to relieve their boredom become another nexus of constraints. They acquire habits and vices which enslave them far more surely than any external authority.

The situation is much the same with children. These break free from family constraint or paternal dictatorship. But we find among them the same twofold situation as in the case of women. The child is now included in a social system of work which exerts real authority over him. The work is educational. The modern child works as no children have ever worked before, for we have to remember that child labor in nineteenth-century factories affected only a minority and work in the fields, e.g., herding or harvesting, is normally not all that arduous except at special periods. The educational system puts children under a much greater constraint with long hours of work—as much as forty hours a week from a relatively early stage. An apparatus of anonymous authority is also imposed. In reality the child who is liberated from his family is now placed in subjection to an administration.

On the other hand, children too in their leisure hours face a void. They experience boredom. But they are also confronted with the full force of modern society. Previously children in the family unit knew social, political, and economic phenomena only through a screen or filter or softener. The walls of the family protected them from all but a minimum of social information and the related shocks and tensions. Today, however, the destruction of this cocoon exposes the young to immediate contact with every global phenomenon. The experience is profoundly traumatic. They come under severe pressures and impulsions. They face enormous temptations. The world is difficult enough for adults. It is shattering for the young with their more acute sensitivity, their lack of structures, and their pliability. They naturally revolt against this absurd, wicked, and scandalous society, and hippies and their ilk are the result.

Here again we confront the twofold problem of a change of bondage and the placing of the individual in a situation of catastrophic freedom. This example seems to be teaching us two things (which are by no means new). The first is that there is freedom only where there is authority. Freedom goes to work in face and in terms of authority. But this authority needs to be near, accessible, visible, and commensurate with the powers of the one who is demanding his freedom. The authority of the father which wife or child might be contesting is no doubt constrictive and hard to bear. But it can be contested. It is close at hand. It is a concrete obstacle against which one may fight for freedom. In contrast, the abstract authority of a social system, an administration, or an economic or educational mechanism is beyond the resources of man. In face of it he cannot achieve freedom, for he is dashing himself against a system of authority which is too strong, remote, and intangible. If he wants to fight, he must join larger groups and engage in actions which are not in keeping with his individual situation. He will be fighting for a theoretical freedom in a distant future. He will be doing things which are no doubt very concrete and forceful but which are finally abstract in relation to the immediate bondage which he feels and experiences but does not discern or understand. One might even say that the actions are in fact little more than symbolical.

An abstract global constraint is thus substituted for a direct and personal constraint. Freedom itself is not advanced in any way.

The second point is that freedom is not a state or situation which is assigned to us like a slice of cheese. Freedom cannot be lived out except by a free man. To set anyone else in a situation of freedom is to hand him a poisoned gift. For an individual who does not have a sufficiently strong and developed personality, a true autonomy, an ability to lead his own life, an energy and equilibrium to survive tests and tensions, the situation of freedom is simply a void or desert in which he will wander without a compass, an intolerable tedium, a vacuum which must be filled with anything that is to hand, so that there is immediate relapse into mediocre pursuits and welcome but for that reason all the more destructive constraints.

This is why we cannot engage without hesitation in these modern movements. In view of the forms they are taking, Christians can hardly support them. What is at issue today is not the liberation of women or children. This has already been achieved. It has led to a worse situation in which there is no Christian freedom nor any possibility of it. This independence is no longer a goal which one might wish to achieve in spite of all that has been said. The resort to platitudes in this domain proves that the thing has been achieved and also that it has failed. Hence Christians do not have to engage in this battle and give it the stamp of authenticity by their own freedom in Christ if in fact they have assumed this freedom and are living it out in their lives.

Another common theme of freedom today, which is based on the same confusion of independence and freedom, is the theme of happiness. It is quite legitimate for a man to want happiness. We shall not deal with the question of the validity of a society which is built solely with a view to happiness, or the relation between this and Christianity. What interests us is simply the relation between happiness and freedom.

One of the most commonly accepted ideas today is that man can know no freedom in poverty and that it is only with happiness (normally reduced to a high standard of living and consumer growth) that he begins to live in freedom.

In our view both these ideas are erroneous and the truth lies in de la Fontaine's fable of the wolf and the dog, simplistic though it may be. There is in fact an antinomy between happiness and freedom.

We have to agree that freedom is hard and costly. It presupposes will, renunciation, and self-mastery. Happiness, on the other hand, presupposes many constraints, at least in the form in which it is sought in present-day society. These constraints lie in work on the one side and consumption on the other. Happiness may be summed up in a high consumer rate, which implies work and its elements of degradation, and the possibility of leisure pursuits that are essentially empty and whose meaninglessness has already been perceived.[43]

---

43 On the contradiction between leisure and freedom cf. Charbonneau, *Dimanche et Lundi*.

When happiness is spoken of today, what is in view is obviously not hedonism or epicureanism but this modern understanding. But this has nothing whatever to do with freedom.

In the direct and immediate sense, in real life, happiness is more often achieved by the man who wrestles with nature and has the ability to use his powers and win autonomy for himself. The myths of the medieval navigator (whom solo sailors today are trying to emulate), the western cowboy, and so forth offer us true images of what man regards as his freedom. The images are all the more living, rich, and meaningful because they relate to a freedom which has been lost and is now inaccessible.

Now in modern society man may well want to raise his standard of living but he feels that he is under increasing constraint to do so. Of what freedom, then, can we speak in relation to him? Freedom from power? Not in the least! Freedom, then, from sickness or hunger? Yes, but these freedoms are achieved only if his fate is put in the hands of authorities over which he has little or no control. Indeed, freedom from famine has to face the fact that there is no guarantee (not even in the U.S.S.R.) against eventual unemployment. The individual may have the impression that he can fight against nature and wrest nourishment from it. But he also has the impression that in our society his destiny is decided by others, which is worse. Thus, to the extent that we cannot give a clear, objective, and measurable definition of freedom but are forced to make do with a subjective image or feeling or impression, we must accept the image which modern man has of himself as happy no doubt but in no sense free.

At this level there can be no discussion of the reality of freedom, especially as that which is advanced to prove it usually relates to a completely abstract freedom. The sense of diminished freedom goes far to explain the reactions of modern man—reactions which are not justified if we assimilate freedom to a rising standard of living, but which have as their unfortunate result the loss of a taste or desire for freedom.

In fact we have to realize that happiness is not related to freedom. The two contradict one another. A rise in the standard of living does not strengthen the infrastructure of freedom. Through it man is no more the master of his fate, no less alienated, no more able to choose, no more independent of socio-political influences. This is why we may well try as Christians to increase the happiness of man but in so doing we shall see and say that this has no evident connection with his liberation. In other words, we cannot join movements which hope to achieve the freedom of man by promoting his material happiness. The important thing is to dissociate freedom and happiness and to show that, while both may be legitimate objectives, they are not compatible. In Christian freedom we must have the honesty to testify to this if we do have a part in any such movements.

We now come up against a new problem regarding independence and freedom and the participation of Christians in man's desire for independence. This is the political problem of revolution. Is Christianity itself revolutionary?

I have tried to show elsewhere[44] that it has to be. A Christianity which is not revolutionary is nothing. Faith is not lived out if it is not revolutionary, i.e., if it does not constantly challenge the existing situation, if it is not continually at work as a ferment. When faith settles down in a society, when it does not seek to overthrow both the social set-up and the individual set-up, revelation is betrayed.

In saying this, however, I have in mind what ought to be the specific decision of the Christian, i.e., the fact that the Christian must take the initiative in true and permanent revolution, in a revolution in depth which attacks the essential elements in a society or culture.

This is a very different thing from participation in a revolutionary movement which finds its origin and inspiration in a thought or myth or experience that has nothing in common with revelation in Jesus Christ.

What man is always seeking in such a movement is his own autonomy. As we live out our freedom in Christ, ought we to join a revolutionary movement of this kind?

We first have to ask a question already hinted at above. Is this a serious revolution? Is there a chance of attaining freedom for man? Or can we expect only a little more independence? If it is only the latter, is it worth while? As exact an evaluation as possible is thus demanded.

In effect the experience of history is not encouraging. We believe that in fact revolution has very seldom led man to freedom. Successful revolutions known to us have all brought a strengthening of authority, an increase of power, and a reduction of freedom. This is true of the revolutions of Cleon and the Gracchi, Marius and Augustus. It is also true of the revolution of Cromwell, the French Revolution in 1789, the revolutions of 1848, 1917, 1933, and 1961 (Castro). The final result is in every case dictatorship.[45]

Only revolutions that failed can still be regarded as potential freedom movements. The rebellion of Spartacus, the medieval Jacqueries, the first revolution of 1848, the commune, and the Hungarian revolt of 1956 are acts which, it seems, might have resulted in freedom. But all of them were unsuccessful.

This brief survey of familiar historical data has something important to teach us. This is that if a revolution is pressed to its conclusion we cannot take it for granted that it will be in favor of freedom.[46]

---

44  J. Ellul, *Présence au monde moderne*, c. 5.
45  J. Ellul, *Autopsie de la révolution* (1969).
46  Freedom should make the Christian aware of the mistake in objective of those who seek revolutions. Note should again be taken of Kierkegaard's observation that in our time fear of potentates and the great should be regarded as ancient history. Many are fighting the danger but it is not very acute and men of experience will conclude that there is no need to fight since there is a crowd of defenders and the crowd is the last thing one sees when there is real peril. This criterion applies today to socialism, the third world, etc. A radical distinction must be made between revolution, which is so

Three questions must be asked before we decide whether or not to take part. What are the real aims of the revolutionary movement? What is it attacking? Is its objective a false one, e.g., a reality which is already outdated? Thus many attacks today are aimed against the structure of private property, religion, morality, or the ruling class, or else revolution is used to try to set up a socialist form of economy, or to bring to power subject classes or races. But movements of this kind leave on one side the real problems of our society. They focus attention on structures and movements which already belong to the past. This is not to mount a revolution. We may be sure that movements which set themselves objectives of this kind will quickly be diverted into an enhanced conformity and will only confirm the basic situations preceding them. It is not worth while engaging in this type of revolution. It does not bring any freedom to man.

The problem of the declared objective and the secret objective of a revolution is the crucial one. We are not to participate blindly on the assumption that if it is a revolution it must be good. We must know what we are doing. Behind the blind movement of manipulated crowds there is a desire to mould history, to shape destiny. What we have here, then, is the promethean or Babel enterprise of man, who is not willing to receive his future from God. In the situation of pride this seems to be legitimate.

The other side of it, however, is the praiseworthy desire of man not to yield to historical determinisms. This is the fundamental ambiguity.

The Christian should certainly help in the task of lifting all the fatalities of history, although today, unfortunately, I should have to reckon socialism among these fatalities. He must play a critical role in this fight, opposing those who start revolutions only to set up their own power. In this regard the struggle of Makhno against Lenin is an example of no less total support for revolution than that of Lenin but accompanied by a rejection of the mechanism set up by Lenin.[47]

---

completely misunderstood in our age, and revolts, which are a spontaneous expression of human suffering but from which both perspicacity and freedom are absent.

47 The generalizations of M. Berque in *Dépossession du Monde* are astonishing in this regard. How can we conclude from Algerian pride in independence, or Egyptian pride in the seizure of the Suez canal, that there is irreversible movement or radical newness in history? It may also be noted that there is no reference to the enthusiasm of the people of the Congo or Cuba at their liberation. But these events do not fit into his pattern. Perhaps those in Algeria did, but this hardly permits us to see here an expression of the general feeling when possession yields to dispossession, domination to emancipation, and imperialism to decolonization. It is surely a gross generalization to say that we have here an absolute tendency of human nature to confer dignity on all things human. To declare that this accession to freedom is a new phenomenon in view of the fact that it applies to the third world which has neither technology, economy, nor system, and that we are in the presence of the rights of the poor and ignorant triumphing over those of the strong, is to obey an idealism which is no doubt very laudable but which has not a great deal to do with reality. Unfortunately these good people who have been liberated are not very good at reuniting nature and culture. They soon begin to attack their neighbors as in the case of Egypt and Israel or China and Tibet or India. They set up as

To take another example, we are now in the presence of revolutions on behalf of justice, which consist of the destruction of the haves, the equalizing of incomes, or participation in economic management. Now, while not ceasing to be alert, we may join in this struggle, even though the true revolution is that on behalf of freedom, which is an entirely different thing. In this conflict, however, the Christian should be the element of reconciliation. He should be the bearer of the reconciliation effected in Christ. There is no justice without reconciliation—this is the revolutionary message of the Christian within the revolutionary movement.

To take part in this way, however, is to risk being treated as a counterrevolutionary. For reconciliation has to be with enemies such as colonialists or the middle class. If he is not prepared for this, the Christian may well take part in any revolution, but in so doing he radically ceases to be a Christian, betrays his Lord, and becomes no more than a revolutionary conformist.

If a revolutionary movement is found which attacks fundamentally a given structure of society, as the situationist movement actually does, the second thing to do is to examine the means which it employs. We shall not go into the problem of means again, but we may recall that if the revolution uses authoritarian means, it is not going to lead to freedom.[48] I realize, of course, that a revolution will entail blood and violence. This is not what I am condemning here. My attack is on the establishment of an authoritarian, statist, and centralized regime. We can see the transition to this in France in 1793, Russia in 1919, and Cuba shortly after the triumph of Castro. Revolutionary means of this sort can lead only to the destruction of freedom.

The third question relates to the heads of the revolutionary movement. On their personalities depends in part the movement toward freedom or the reverse. At a time of revolution the element of personality is in effect much greater, since the objective situation is more fluid. When a global challenge is issued, the individual will more easily show what he

---

quickly as possible military dictatorships such as we find in the African states. They exploit the world by technology and become enslaved to other powers and mechanisms. All that we can say—and it runs contrary to the rather romantic and not in the least sociological thinking of Berque—is that we have here a critical transition from a pretechnological situation characterized by the direct rule of man over man to a technological situation in which objective mechanisms of domination are established. If these peoples have been liberated, it is to enter a new stage. The enthusiasm of the crowds in Algiers or Cairo is simply the prelude to integration into a technical system in which freedom will be much less than under the colonial system. Berque has failed to see the problem and has simply given up the struggle, as one may see from his own enthusiasm and friendship for the Algerian people.

48 Kierkegaard has many discussions of the problem of means. He points out that justice can never be obtained by injustice, that the search for good is corrupted when the mob is brought in, and that the man of action cannot attain a desired good by the use of any means he chooses.

really is, whether it be a dictator or a representative of the people. Great attention must be paid to the quality of leaders.[49] Once a taste for personal power appears, it must be realized that this will entail the loss of freedom.

We have to recognize that if a revolution refuses to employ authoritarian means, and develops under the direction of a non-dictatorial leader, there is every likelihood that it will fail. In the reverse case it may well succeed but in so doing will set up a new situation of oppression, bondage, and unfreedom. All that will then take place, as in the instances adduced above, will be the substitution of one alienation for another.

We recall what was said above about the difference between transgression and revolution. A revolution, if it succeeds, will necessarily result in new power and a new society. Even an anarchist revolution cannot lead to a blank. But this will mean the reconstitution of certain alienations. These will become the more serious to the degree that the new power is a revolutionary one. In face of a traditional state, there may always be recourse to the revolutionary opposition, but once the state and the established order are themselves revolutionary, since they have been set up by the revolutionary movement, all is lost. For all opposition will now be described as counterrevolutionary or reactionary and man will find himself subject to authority with no way out.

This is the movement by which a successful revolution ineluctably entails an even greater bondage. For this reason it is at first glance difficult to associate Christian freedom with any such venture, quite apart from the special problem of the bloody character of most revolutions.

But we cannot stop here. Other aspects of the question must be considered. We have noted that in an objectively revolutionary situation the effect of revolution is to create a social structure which is temporarily more fluid. This in turn may give concrete support to the revolutionary belief in, and desire for, the malleability of history. In face of the "laws" of history and the sociological pressure of real or apparent economic mechanisms, man seeks an affirmation of himself which will set him above these forces or even enable him to say that he is their master. This is both normal and perfectly legitimate. It is the conflict between man and his destiny. When in the course of a revolution man is able to relieve these pressures even a little, when he puts himself in a universe which, in reality or illusion, is under his own control, he is simply seeking self-fulfilment. This is just as true of such primary and spontaneous revolts as that of Spartacus or the Jacqueries as it is of the revolt which is transformed into a conscious and planned revolution, as in anarchism, syndicalism, or Marxism. Too much should not be made of the difference between revolt and revolution or spontaneity and calculation.

---

49 It is obvious that for the most part the leaders in the 1968 riots in France were little people whose main concern was personal success.

The point is that the revolutionary act in any form, whether it be that of the individual, group, or class, of Blanqui or Lenin, is the closest to an act of Christian freedom, for, at the moment of its occurrence, it offers a reflection of true freedom. I realize, of course, that from the standpoint adopted here this act can be only a false replica, and yet in spite of everything, at the level of aspiration if not of realization, it is true and consequently free.

At the moment of the revolutionary act, in the brief interval between the overthrow of one order and the establishment of another, when the unleashing evokes forces which normally remain hidden, when the expression coincides exactly with straining for something beyond, when we find neither dialectic nor limit nor contradiction between the contrived and the real, this act is very close to transgression.

To be sure it is transgression by revolt (against God) and negation. Hence it is the exact opposite of the transgression of Christian freedom. Nevertheless, the image in a mirror, even if it is not the original, is still an image.

I know that it might be said that the angel of light imitates God best, that Satan can give us the reverse image, that in doing this he is a deceiver, and that revolution is thus a satanic image of Christian freedom. There is a good deal of truth in this. But I must put myself on the level of those who experience this adventure and who know nothing at all about that satanic power. As they simply live out their aspiration for freedom, how can we fail to be their companions? As they express their rejection of alienation in a privileged instant, how can we fail to try, precisely in the more fluid situation which is now created, to communicate to them what freedom in Christ can be?

For this is the moment when the demonic act shows that the intervention of the Holy Spirit is far more glorious. I would say, then, that in spite of all our strictures on revolution Christians should be present in it, since they ought to have a hand in the one desperate attempt of man at freedom. Just because the attempt is so desperate we ought to bring the prop of our hope. Just because man is groping after freedom, we ought to attest to him the authentic freedom of which his own can be only a false replica.

## Appended Note

Theologians today are just discovering revolution. I might point out that in the *Bulletin des Liaison des Groupes Esprit* as early as 1936 I wrote an essay on Christianity and revolution in which I drew attention to the revolutionary character of Christianity. Then in 1946 I attended a conference on the theology of revolution at the Ecumenical Institute at Bossey, and in 1947 in my *Présence au Monde Moderne* I had a chapter on revolutionary Christianity. In all candor I am forced to say that the studies of the question by Lehmann, Schaull, and Wendland between 1962 and 1966 are far less advanced than my earlier works and are hardly more than preliminary stutterings. Schaull's "Point de vue théologique sur la révolution" in *Église et Société* (1966), I, 12ff. is particularly open to criticism.

This essay is full of serious mistakes in its understanding of the sociology of modern society (p. 13), and the author obviously takes no account at all of sociology or of even a superficial history of revolutions. He continually confuses revolution with technical and industrial evolution. He also uses a very inexact vocabulary in this area. He heaps up commonplaces, arguing, for example, that the church and theology have always been conformist and have always supported the establishment. If he would only read the five volumes of Lagarde's *Naissance de l'esprit laïque au Moyen Age* he would come across theologians far more revolutionary than he is. But he shows no knowledge at all of medieval theology.

I agree with Schaull on the need for a theological consideration of revolution, on the ambiguous character of revolution, on the rejection of natural law (cf. my *Fondement théologique du droit* in 1946, E.T. *The Theological Foundation of Law* [1960]), on the fact that the penultimate must be seen in the light of the ultimate (an essential principle which unfortunately Schaull does not apply in his study), and on the fact that technology at one and the same time brings both the amelioration of conditions and the dehumanization of man.

Apart from this, however, there is not much to this examination of the theology of revolution. The platitude of an ongoing humanization of history and society is repeated and revolution is regarded as a factor in this process. This is pure idealism and is not in the least Christian in spite of Lehmann's unillustrated statements about God's humanizing work in history.

Revolution is defined first as a desire to have a share in economic and political control, which is very vague, since the aim is often to wrest control from others. It is then further defined as a reasonable freedom to discover new structures of society, or as a search for justice.

In the light of these uncertainties and superficialities Schaull's theology seems to me to amount to no more than a statement to the effect that God does everything in history. It is God who knocks down ancient structures in order to create the conditions for a fuller development of human life. This is about the only theological idea in the whole study.

The creative power of human sin is ignored. So, too, is the very effective action of Satan, who has fallen down to earth and become the ruler of the kingdoms. But probably Schaull does not accept the existence of Satan.

Once Schaull descries the work of God through revolutions he calls on Christians to join them without further ado. There is, he says, no revolutionary attitude outside this struggle, no matter what may be the outcome. The Christian is obviously called upon to engage fully in the development of the revolution. Any revolution? Would Schaull really have had us engage thus in Hitler's revolution?—for this was a revolution no less than the communist revolution or the upheavals in Latin America. Would he have had Christians take part in the military coups in these countries, or the Makhno revolution of 1919, or the national revolution in France in 1940?

Schaull's work gives us no help at all in seeing what a revolution is. His view of revolution is wholly conformist. What are the objectives of revolution apart from the very hazy idea of humanization? Schaull offers us three: to have a hand in economic planning, to work with competent technicians, and to ensure the well-being of man. It is all very brief and platitudinous.

To be sure he recalls what are for the Christian the decisive elements of pardon, justice, and reconciliation, but he does not draw from them any concrete ethical inferences.

In contrast, I agree with the way in which Rich, in his *Glaube in politischer Entscheidung* (1962ff.), presents the need for a critical and revolutionary element in Christian ethics. He bases revolutionary Christian thinking on eschatology. This is in effect the only factor which can validate and which indeed necessitates a constant revolutionary attitude in the Christian, as I showed long ago in my *Présence au Monde Moderne*. But if this is the basis of the revolutionary attitude, it also signifies the main difference from all other sources and causes of revolution.

Hence there can be no simple identification with nor inclusion in a human revolutionary project, as ultimately both Schaull and Wendland suggest. The eschatological dimension is a critical dimension even within the revolutionary process—this is what they fail to see. Hence the eschatological motivation involves both association with a suitable revolutionary action and distance from it.

The attempt of Cardonnel to prove that it is the revolutionary act which, as an act of freedom, is a demonstration and attestation of the resurrection, and that the movement should be from the (political) emancipation of man to the resurrection, which has no other reality, rests only on a flow of words and a heaping up of formulae but offers no real evidence and amounts to no more than the opinion of the author. It is poetically persuasive and politically useful, but finds no place for Christian distinctiveness, rationality, nor reality.

A bibliography of the theology of revolution may be found in my work *Autopsie de la révolution*. To it we may add the important work of Comblin, *Théologie de la révolution* (1970), which is a fine synthesis and offers a judicious historical survey, but has the fault of believing that after a long antirevolutionary period the church is finally giving up such attitudes. This is incorrect historically and may be traced to the absence of an operational concept of revolution. Little is added in respect of the theological foundations of revolution, and the treatment of the relation between revolution and Christianity is much too hackneyed, especially with regard to the ideology of class conflict.

Much to the same effect is what is said by Iwand, *Von Ordnung und Revolution*, and Lochman, "Oekumenische Theologie der Revolution," *Evangelische Theologie* (1967). For these authors Christian theology since the early nineteenth century has focused on the principle of order and has been led to regard revolution as anti-Christian. This follows a theological tendency since the middle ages to treat theology as a function of institutions and ethics as an ethics of institutions. The plea of these writers is that we must work out a theology of revolution and an ethics of transformation. This is interesting, but we need to ask if it is the function of theology and ethics always to follow the trend. It might be objected against nineteenth-century theology that it provided justification for the prevailing middle-class establishment. But if there was great insistence on order and institution in the middle ages and at the time of the Reformation, this was not because order prevailed but because it did not. In the middle of incredible disorder, civil war, insecurity, and constant revolution, the church's main job was not to come up with a theology of revolution. Instead, it had to make an appeal for order and conciliation. Since the world was flouting institutions, it had to stand up for institutions. Today the situation is more rigorous, fixed, and complex. We have reached a sociological level of totalitarian order, i.e., that of technology, the state, and profound and immovable structures. We have also reached a sociological level of fluidity, mobility, and uncertainty, i.e., in politics and psychological reactions. A theology of revolution and ethics of change is demanded on the first level, but on the second we need to recall the importance of respect, harmony, order, and the relief of anguish. The call, then, is for the very opposite of what is the fashion among authors of the theology of revolution, among whom we find always the schematic attitude that since there is agitation and revolution throughout the world, we must fashion a theology of revolution. This seems to me to be the reverse of intellectual renewal.

Other works that should be consulted are A. Dumas in *À la recherche d'une théologie de la violence* (1968), Le Guillou Clement and Bosc, *Évangile et révolution au coeur de notre crise spirituelle* (1968), and especially Jager, *Ethik und Eschatologie bei Leonhard Ragaz* (1971), who gives us a useful reminder that the idea of a theology of revolution and of Christian participation in revolutionary movements is by no means new. This is finely demonstrated in W. Daim, *Le feu sur la terre (christianisme et révolution)* (1967), which unfortunately I had not yet come across when writing my own works and which is a notable study of the revolutionary implications of Christianity in history. This book is the only one I know which poses the real problem and sets forth the true relation between Christian freedom and revolution. It is a superb work.

In contrast we must beware of works like those of Maray (*L'église contestée*) and Serrou (*Dieu n'est pas conservateur*, 1968), which are only of fleeting interest and try to set up a theology on what is merely accidental and superficial. More serious account should be taken of Henry Mottu (*Vers une théologie de la libération*, 1972) and of James Cone (*Black Theology and Black Power*, 1969) and R. Alves (*A Theology of Human Hope*, 1969), whose works I know only from Mottu. I agree profoundly with Cone that Christian theology is to be defined as a theology of liberation, but it does not seem to me to be possible to define the black people as the people of Jesus Christ simply because it is oppressed. The equation of chosen people and oppressed people, or of the work of salvation and the fight of the oppressed for liberation, is surely a false one. Israel's election rests on God's decision and not on the fact that it is oppressed. A hundred peoples were oppressed at that period; only one was chosen. Is there an identical election of the American blacks? If so, Jesus Christ is not the liberator. It is also a little simplistic to equate Moses and Malcolm X.

To be sure, a good and even classical analysis is given of oppression and of the relation between oppressed and oppressor, but if the history of Israel is the action of the Liberator, it is a mistake to think that the history of salvation is no more than the history of human liberation—for it is not man who brings this about; this is the point. It is also impossible to agree that there is opposition between the God who is Father and Lord and the Liberator God. As for the interpretation of Jesus Christ as the leader of rebellious slaves, as a hounded slave, as an assassinated agitator, with the stress on assassination rather than death, we can only say that this involves spiritual and theological regression. The whole world, and the disciples especially, knew already what Cone and Alves say they have discovered. Jesus was the head of a band and he was treated like a criminal being harried to his death. But the truth of revelation consists in not insisting on this aspect, in not stopping here even though we do not forget it, but in passing beyond it to the recognition that this criminal is the Son of God, that this condemned man is the Saviour, that this assassinated one is the Lord.

This is no ordinary slave. He cannot be put on the same level as Spartacus. What counts is not the incidental aspect but the relation between this aspect and God's revelation about Jesus. We have no right at all to transfer this relation to anyone else.

Seen as a whole, the theology of Cone and Alves seems to be a strong regression to political infantilism in the inexplicable guise of theology. They follow a direction which is the exact opposite of that of the early church under the guidance of the apostles and Paul. The procedure is the same in their treatment of the Old Testament.

Along with this main criticism there are many lesser ones. A new predestination is introduced, the poor being righteous and saved, whereas the politically and economically powerful are damned. The crassest ideology of revolutionary practice is followed, with no serious consideration of what revolution really is. Christ is not identified with man or men, only with the oppressed.

We also find errors in detail. The publicans are placed among the poor and oppressed. Moses is said to have been a slave. Jesus did not choose to die; death was heteronomous and was not mastered, contrary to the biblical testimony. The command that we should destroy our being in the world as whites in order to reveal our being with God as blacks replaces the scriptural affirmation that there is neither Jew nor Greek, etc. Many others could be cited.

The books are undoubtedly full of noble sentiments, eloquent words, moving appeals, sincere piety, genuine enthusiasm, authentic witness on behalf of the poor and oppressed, and exalted hope. They are the works of zealots. They would have been admirable a century ago. Today, however, they express Marxist conformism and alignment with the thinking of the world, for we must not forget that if structures are still oppressive and capitalistic, ideologies become increasingly favorable to rebels and revolution, and hence revolution is now a commonplace.

We now come up against the hardest question. I have said that the Christian may participate in the political, social, and economic liberation of man so long as he realizes to what extent all this is relative, contradictory, hopeless, and even illusory. But the further question at once arises: If the movement of liberation succeeds, who will finally be liberated? The answer is that it will be the man who, as we well know, both is and will also remain basically alienated, the man who is a sinner, who commands destructive forces, who has a fatal death wish, who lusts for power, who puts his resources to evil use, who wanted to be free from God, and who in virtue of this does nothing but evil. For, as Genesis tells us, his very first act after securing liberation from God is murder. Yet Cain was a religious man. He made offerings to God. In spite of his religion, however, he was close to death and to death-dealing because he was free from God. It is by him that death, intimated in the saying which God pronounced over Adam, came among men and offered the first example of man's use of freedom—freedom and death.

This warning must be taken very seriously. Only too often the problems of society are reduced to whether or not a good use is made of things. No more is needed than that man should make a good use of freedom, of technology, and so forth. Now it is true that man can find a good use. We see it all the time. There is no point in denying it. Man has preserved an excellent sense of what is useful. He can see what is useful in himself, his group, family, or nation. He can invent useful techniques, useful law, useful morality, as I tried to show in the first volume of the Introduction. Hence he can also conserve. He participates positively in the conservation that God has willed. But from the time of his break with God, he is inhabited by a death wish too. He is irresistibly attracted to the void, chaos, destruction, and madness. Whenever he introduces order, he plunges afresh into disorder. His technological progress is ambivalent, and this is no mere matter of good or bad use. His construction of a framework of life entails the destruction of freedom. His affirmation of independence carries with it the destruction of a legitimate framework of life. The seduction of death works invincibly on man. He wants to die. He constantly puts himself in a position of dying. His supreme celebration is war. Every massive holocaust finds an innumerable host of participants. Are they deceived? Are they led astray by bad leaders? Not at all, but by themselves! All that man finds useful he can at once turn towards death. It is this passion for the void rather than original sin or a basic evil which is the fundamental characteristic of man once he has broken with the source of life, with him who brought his creation out of chaos. This is inevitable. It is why I have to say that man is a dangerous criminal, offensive though the phrase may be. Man is undoubtedly more than this, yet he is this too in the sense just indicated. While this does not characterize a nature, it characterizes his being in its lived out expression, even though only on a single occasion.

This is where the whole difficulty arises for a Christian. How can man make a good use of things when, separated from God, he is plunged into radical chaos, when he is indwelt by powers which psychoanalysis is bringing to light, when he is oriented to destruction. Freud's analysis does not contradict this exposure of man by revelation. But what bearing does all this have on the liberation of man? It means that a dangerous animal is being set loose. This is why the traditional Christian doctrine of political power insists on its character as a limit or restraint. Political power is given by God to avoid the ultimate consequences of the evil unleashed by man. It is a servant of God because it prevents man from being a murderer, thief, or adulterer, which he would be all the time but for this barrier.

Calvin tells us that power exists because men are like wild beasts towards one another. This obviously means that power has to be authoritarian. Only the state can prevent the situation from degenerating into a disaster. It alone can dispense justice among men. Men apart are capable only of injustice. If there were no state men would plunge society into chaos and would destroy the world. This is why Calvin says that he would rather have a tyrannical and despotic state than anarchy, in which the maximum evil would be done.

A remarkable thing is that Barth, whose theory of the state rests on a different basis, comes finally to exactly the same conclusion. God is dealing with the man who has illusions of grandeur and whose pernicious lust for power characterizes the present century. He weighs the danger which is presented by an intelligence that has been renewed and that leads man to regard himself as wise. He does not want men to devour themselves, as would happen, men being what they are. According to Romans 1:24, 28 he has not abandoned man to his covetousness. He has prevented the total ruin to which his passions would lead. God is patient. He wants to given fallen man a chance to know his grace. He wants to give the community time to proclaim this grace. This explains political authority. It is the order of the sword. It is an order safeguarded by fear and force. This is due to the end which God has assigned it where his grace is not yet known and extolled, where it has not yet found obedience. Here the sword, fear, and force must reign.[50]

In this noteworthy passage we thus find exactly the same orientation. Fear and force prevent man from going to the extreme of evil and therefore of destruction, as he would do if left to himself. I recognize, of course, the Christian authenticity of this analysis. But I cannot help thinking that it is still not a good thing for man to be reduced to slavery, to be alienated, to be subjected to the authority of this type of state. In such an analysis it is all too easy to forget that the power of the state is not an abstract or theoretical power. It is not the power of a juridical construct. It is the very concrete and practical power of some men over others. And why should I have any particular confidence in the excellence of these political men?

Nevertheless the problem remains, and I am in full agreement that the growth of independence is for man the growth of freedom for the evil that is in him. Some modern examples may be given.

In most countries it has been thought necessary to control the private possession of guns and poisons. To let these be distributed indiscriminately is regarded as an invitation to murder. This is true. Contrary to the well-known theory that if there were no police there would be no criminals, today there are in a city like Paris, proportionate to the population, only about 3 percent of the murders there were at the end of the seventeenth century. All the same, to take guns and poisons away from individuals is a reduction of freedom. An Arab deprived of his dagger is deprived of his honor and virility. Many Americans feel the same way about their guns.

The question is, however: What concrete use is made of this freedom? Motorists often argue that imposing speed limits is a restriction of the freedom of the driver. This is undeniable. Yet high speed contributes to fatal accidents. The use of the freedom of speed by the motorist constitutes a serious danger. This is the problem in gun control. To take another example, recent statistics in France show that the system of self-service has greatly increased the number of thefts. The freedom given to the shopper to serve himself is indissolubly connected with the growth in felonies. Experience in other countries bears this out.

The constant question is: Who is going to use this freedom? If we think that man is good, reasonable, self-controlled, responsible, and mature, he may well be given freedom, total freedom. If, however, we believe that sin is not just a spiritual matter but finds expression in conduct, if we believe that grace gives man the promise of salvation but only faith in him by whom grace is given can carry with it the fruit of changed behavior, then

---

50 *Church Dogmatics*, II, 2, pp.721f.

to increase freedom outside faith is simply to increase the possibility of doing evil.

This assessment is not altered if we follow the analysis of Freud or even Marx, e.g., in his criticism of Feuerbach. To increase freedom is like putting a tommy-gun in the hands of a six-year-old child. For this freedom is ultimately an increase in power. This is the true problem of modern society. Technology supplies an indefinite augmentation of means, i.e., means of external action. The freedom we claim operates on the level of these means. But the means of action which express freedom for modern man are put in the hands of a man who intrinsically is not free, whether from passions, instincts, environment, or appetites. He is given control, but the power is exercised by one who is not free in himself. He is like the slave in early Rome who one day in the year was granted absolute powers and could ask anything he wanted, but was still a slave.

It is generally thought today that freedom consists in giving man control over himself, i.e., the right to do what he wants with his mind and body, as in contraception, or control over things, e.g., in technology and planning, or even control over others, as in human technology, which is, of course, in contradiction with the first form of control. Now it is very interesting that we catch in this modern tendency a pure and simple echo of traditional liberalism. When we are told that women have the right to choose when to have children, that it is their own responsibility, that this is part of their freedom, we recall that the liberal economists of the previous century said exactly the same thing about the freedom and responsibility of industrialists. This led to capitalism. Nor do I think that we can ever expect better results from freedoms that are asserted and claimed in this way. For in antithesis to freedom in Christ they are always the freedom to exercise power.

This brings us face to face with a problem which in the last analysis is the only true ethical problem of our age and which might be formulated thus. The growth of scientific knowledge and technical means leads to a situation which is new from two angles. On the one hand man achieves increasing awareness. Phenomena which were once mysterious have now been explained. Adjustments which used to be made spontaneously by progressive adaptation and instinct are now achieved deliberately by knowledge and systematic intervention. What was once the domain of instinct has ceased to be instinctive and has become voluntary and calculated. We now have awareness of many previously unconscious situations, of questions that were once lived out but not thought out. Marriage, suicide, obedience, maternity, and social taboos, which hitherto belonged to the arena of primitive thought, have now become problems.

A good illustration is offered by drugs and especially by L.S.D., which has the effect of unleashing the potentialities of the individual and taking the brakes off the personality. It is thus fundamentally dangerous and destructive, and neither brings liberation nor opens the way towards superhumanity.

Borg, who is an expert on the problem, tells us in his *Le voyage de la drogue* (1970) that the person who has not been able to find in daily reality any happiness, meaning, or strength will not find these in an L.S.D. trip. The drug will launch the weak and neurotic into a wasteland of absurdity and incomprehension, into the sharp glare of their mediocrity, and into the quadrature of their vicious circle, while it will bring failures face to face with the intolerable edifice of their conflicts.

But who is going to admit his neuroses, his mediocrity, or the absurd nature of his conflicts? Who can bear seeing how pitiful he is, or even face up to himself in his true reality?

Those who say that they are ready to undertake one of the most daring of human ventures can hardly face up to the ordinary difficulties and strains and stresses of life. Who can claim, without feeling slightly ridiculous, that he is prepared to see himself brutally—naked, scorched, and withered—in the intolerable light of unsuspected reality? Who can stand up to six hours of errant surgings which would otherwise be slowly distilled over five years of psychoanalysis?

In Christian terms, we may say that giving more power and freedom to the man who is indwelt by sin is a danger and disaster for himself and for others.

Man has to try to find an answer. The increase in his knowledge and awareness leads to increasing difficulties, even if we can also say that it is ineluctable and that man is honored to be engaged in it.

The second aspect is as follows. Technology has increased our power indefinitely. We can do almost anything. But this unlimited power is destructive of limits. If we have characterized freedom in terms of limits, the basic thing, it seems to me, is that man by his means of power—and not by an act of freedom or by transgression—removes the limits without this bearing any relation to a moral choice or ethical decision.

The growth of power also has the result of suppressing values, for there are no values except in a situation of limited means. When a state achieves omnipotence, there is no distinction between good and bad, or just and unjust, in politics. Values have meaning and weight only in relativity. When power passes a certain point, values are banished and we have only the void of an unlimited increase of power.

Here again, however, we have a path on which there can be no going back. If, as I have said, we come up here against the main ethical problem, it is because the individual unceasingly has to make a twofold choice and arrive at a twofold judgment. Now that he has achieved awareness, he has to face the fact that an action which is profitable in the short term will be a disaster in the long term of foreseen evolution. He has thus to choose not to use all the means that are now at his disposal.

The growth of freedom would give man total responsibility in this situation. But he is manifestly incapable even to the slightest degree of playing the part which he is given. If the problem is central, man has achieved no strength to follow this part or to make the right response in this predicament. Hence to increase the freedom of man is on the one hand to increase his autonomy in evil while on the other hand it is to burden him with sole responsibility in the extraordinary difficulty of the ethical problem of our age, which is the only true ethical problem today. Only with great difficulty can a Christian know how to proceed at this point.

### Conclusion

We have now tried to analyze the very serious reasons why we should not join individual or collective movements towards a freedom which in reality is only independence and autonomy and which can lead only to the catastrophes of a new bondage worse than the old, a use of independence for the power of evil, or Babel confusion in consequence of the loss of limits and values. The rational conclusion is that ethics should lead Christians, not to resist independence movements, which would in my view be an impossible course, since it would range them on the side of oppressive forces and they would be upholding a present evil for fear of a future one, but at least to stay clear of all such movements.

Nevertheless, faith, the guidance of the Spirit, and revelation in Jesus Christ are not rational phenomena and they do not lead us to purely rational behavior. I said earlier that freedom in Christ needs to be oriented to love. Now this is not a simple and direct sentimentalism. Man has to be taken seriously as he is. We have seen that what finally keeps man alive is his bent for freedom—not being free but wanting to be free. This is true even though each time he brushes against freedom or risks being truly free he starts back in terror from such a venture or such a responsibility. It has been noted that this is what happens in the case of Christians. Nevertheless, although man rejects true freedom, he still wants to be free and likes to think that he is free.

Modern findings on this should be consulted. Thus we may refer to what Pavlov calls the reflex of aim and of freedom. When an animal does not have this reflex it dies. Suicide in man, according to Pavlov, simply relates to the disappearance of this reflex of aim and of freedom. Marx says much the same when he tells us that man makes himself as he makes his history by acting on the conditions of life. This is his freedom, and if in practice he loses this possibility of action neither his life nor history is of the slightest significance.

The same point is made when phenomenologists and existentialists speak about the dimension of project. Here again it is said in a very concrete and not at all metaphysical way that all man's life resides in the possibility of living in a project. This project may be grandiose or mediocre, but no life is possible without it, for then man ceases to be man. What is this project, however, but the belief that freedom is being brought into a situation which is otherwise closed and hopeless? The project is the opposite of the locked door.

Finally, a recent study of the problem[51] has claimed that the desire to plan is a temporal dimension of man which distinguishes him from the rest of nature. Man has to dispel the halo of indetermination which surrounds him. He has to establish calculated control. Planning enlarges the freedom of action of the human species. This analysis, which I am summarizing very briefly and fragmentarily, shows, as I indicated above, that power and freedom are very closely linked. Man can win freedom only by power. Power over the world can be the instrument of his pretended freedom. It is this array of means and objectives which characterizes man and distinguishes him from the rest of creation. This is his distinctive feature.[52]

If, then, the desire for freedom is from any angle that which characterizes man, if it is an essential and existential condition of his being, then we are bound to have it as Christians too. This is true even though originally and basically it is a desire to rebel which is obscurely directed against God. We are not exempted from it by the love with which Jesus Christ has loved all men, and with which he commands us to love one another in the church and also to love our neighbors, who are obstacles and enemies. We cannot be mere spectators while man is making frantic attempts to win freedom.

As I write this I have in mind what I said about human moral systems in the first book of the introduction to this ethics. These systems are the fruit of disobedience. They are constructed in virtue of man's separation from God. They never express the good. Nevertheless, they are not futile. We must not reduce them to a blank. We have as Christians to accept and follow them so long as they are not directly opposed to the will of God.

The same applies here. In spite of the wrong reasons behind this desire for freedom, in spite of the poor results that may be noted, in spite of the lies and illusions which accompany it, man believes and judges that the whole of his life is at issue and our very freedom thus obliges us to go with him on this path. "To them that are without law, I am as without law, being not without law" (1 Corinthians 9:21). As Christians we have to take part, in our freedom, in man's efforts on behalf of freedom.

This participation, as I have already said, is not unconditional. There are three reservations which involve difficulties and unusual features.

Thus (1) I may recall very generally what has been said about means in relation to political movements. No matter what the effort on behalf of

---

51  Junk and Mundt, *Modelle für eine neue Welt: Der Griff nach der Zukunft—Plannen und Freiheit* (1965).

52  The study adds that planning can also be destructive of freedom when man and society themselves become its object. We then have the movement described earlier. When the thrust towards freedom finally touches reality it produces new alienation.

freedom may be, we have to examine the means very closely and refuse absolutely to be associated with means which are deceitful, unjust, and cruel, and in which human perversity comes to expression. Such means do not manifest freedom nor even true independence, nor can they lead to these.

Then (2) the Christian participant, in his role as watchman, has to estimate what will be the significance of the movement over the long haul. I believe that this is an essential function of the Christian. It is the main value of his participation in a movement for freedom. His role is to predict the long-range results. At this point I may recall the noteworthy (if limited) definition of the moral life given by Fourastié:[53] "It is a difficult and precarious attempt to see and control short-term thrusts which may lead to long-term mistakes."

Now any independence movement involves short-term issues and actions even though we try to forestall them. We shall find a mass of fleeting opinions, emotions, gut reactions, mass feelings, and collective enthusiasms. A revolutionary movement consists of these. We have to realize, however, that what may seem legitimate in the short term in the midst of all this tumult can ultimately be disastrous in the long term. If it is argued that this is not easy, who said that the Christian life was ever easy? And how can we serve other men if we are not prepared to fulfil a task of this order which is extremely difficult but also absolutely indispensable, and which presupposes a combination of technical competence and great spiritual audacity?

The service that we can render our fellows in a freedom movement is that of showing them what is most likely to be the final outcome. What use is it participating if we are just going to howl with the pack, becoming tame little members of the movement like all the rest? If we do this we just become an extra voice or vote no different from a million others. We might just as well stay out. Our only serious role is seriously to examine the long-range effect of what we are taking part in.

Finally (3)—and this is what will probably give the most serious offense—we must not give up our striving for freedom when the movement in which we have a part succeeds. In effect, as I said earlier, sociologically and historically all man's efforts at freedom can lead only to a situation which at best has changed but is no more free, and which at worst may bring an increase in slavery, although perhaps for different people. The question thus arises whether we have really acted in love. Have we really been bearing witness to freedom in Christ and not to an absurd political passion or an infantile conviction that a step will be taken towards freedom if only this government or class replaces that government or class? If we have acted in love and given witness to Christian freedom, then eventually

---

53  *Idées Majeures*, p. 190.

we shall have to turn against our former friends whose success we have helped to achieve. This is the point of offense.

We are faced with a dictatorship. We take part in a movement of liberation seeing that man's desire not to be subject to dictatorship is a valid one. If the movement succeeds, we see the pursuit, execution, and liquidation of those who have been ejected from power. But as Christians, even though we recognize the faults of these men, we must at once side with the defeated. We must try to protect and save them in the name of the same love and pardon which originally ranged us on the side of the oppressed.

Independence movements in the third world, especially in Cuba, have shown us indeed that once dictatorship is toppled and colonialism ended, a new dictatorship can arise which is worse than the one that preceded because it is more highly systematized and rationalized, or a new colonialism can move in, e.g., the economic colonialism of China or America instead of the political colonialism of France or Britain. The moment this happens, we Christians have to enter a new conflict and continue the march of man which must not be halted even though we know that what is finally sought is not freedom itself but what is only thought to be freedom.

Naturally we are not to fight to try to restore the former government to power. We are once again to come to the defense of the oppressed and to advance to a new hope. This can never be a backward movement.

All the same, we shall be charged with treason and disloyalty. We shall be a scandal to the world. If we are loyal to Jesus Christ and meddle in this kind of matter, we have to understand that this is bound to be so. In our various alliances, however, this freedom is the decisive condition of our participation. If we are not capable of these breaks and changes, if we cannot take our place genuinely with the weak at any given time, even though these might be the Soviet koulaks of 1921 or the middle class in Hungary, Roumania, and Czechoslovakia after 1948, we are in no sense witnesses to freedom in Christ, nor are we free ourselves. We simply express our sociological conditioning. We show that our faith is not primarily that of Christ but belief in a political and social objective which we are pursuing and to which we are so committed that we close our eyes to any possible consequences. Now we may, of course, do this. We may go on with the task. But if we do, we should stop mumbling pious phrases or saying that we are Christians. We should be consistent. We should not claim to be fighting for the independence of man in the name of freedom in Christ. A reversal of the kind indicated and for the reasons advanced above is the most authentic sign of freedom in Christ that we can possibly give in the world. Before undertaking it, however, we must examine ourselves to see if we are humanly able, when the moment comes, to stand the test to which the Holy Spirit will in due time lead us.

Thus even as Christians join human movements for freedom they must be constantly relativizing these movements, remembering that, while they are very important, they are not all-important. They must try to see such movements in proper proportion and never proceed to absolutize them, as Christians are always tempted to do as they seek a will of God which will confirm the will of man and hence confer absoluteness on it. They must warn their friends that the result will certainly be a modest one and may well be deceptive, and that there will probably be a thrust towards the creation of new bondage, since every revolution produces dictatorship. They must demythologize liberation movements, including those of women, children, and homosexuals as well as political movements, rejecting the ideology of human freedom, socialism, eroticism, and a better future. Finally they must issue a constant reminder that freedom does not exist in a vacuum but only in relation to obstacles, so that to remove the obstacles is automatically to suppress freedom.

It might be objected that all this will rob our associates of their courage, deprive what they are doing of its point, and undermine their will. To say such things is surely to argue that the supposed liberation movement is in reality a movement to enslave others and ourselves. It is an illusion based on bad arguments and misleading good intentions. It falls into the same category as crusades or wars for justice and the right. If a liberation movement cannot stand up to this contact with demythologization, we must reject it altogether. On the other hand, the Christian cannot bear this witness unless he himself is totally involved and is offering an example of serious action, authentic solidarity, and unlimited commitment.

Necessarily, then, we must join such movements, although with the function of being at the same time both a No and a Yes, just as God himself pronounces both No and Yes on the activity of every man, society, church, and Christian. For if in the drive for freedom man has to win an autonomy which is sheer power, it has to be realized that this power will be used to oppress others and to destroy the self, as the tragic experience of many of the new independent nations of Africa demonstrates. As Christians we cannot favor the acquisition of such power. Safeguards must be multiplied, and while we are not to fight against the movement we must try to introduce a deviation in it, to set going a discussion which will reduce the possibilities of this power.

On the other hand, insofar as the aim of a drive for freedom is to free man from the outer and inner enslavements which oppress him and crush him and put him at the mercy of other men or social structures, as he earlier was of nature, we have naturally to help man and sustain him and encourage him and join him.

In practice, of course, the matter is never plain or clear. We do not have a simple conquest or a simple attempt at dignity. The two are inevitably intertwined and sometimes confused. The most that we can expect is that one or the other aspect will be predominant.

This is why I say that the presence of the Christian must be a subtle

*Implicated Freedom*

interplay of No and Yes, of approval and rejection, of caution and support, of impulsion and restraint. This demands great perspicacity, full commitment, strong consecration and dedication, wholehearted service, and total good faith. In fact, only the Christian who obeys his Lord can give himself in this way with no hope of recognition by the men with whom he will be and whom he will help to live and perhaps to die.

## §4. Religious Freedom

When man is not free he necessarily takes away the freedom of others. He cannot bear that they should be free. He can only try to break their freedom to his own advantage. The man who is not free seeks to free himself, and there are few who, like Bakunin, do not think they are free if others around them are still slaves.

The familiar struggles for freedom are all struggles for personal freedom even when it is alleged that the freedom of others is sought. What we see everywhere without exception is the ferocity of individual conquest which establishes my freedom (individual or collective) at the expense of the bondage of others or another group.

Christian freedom, however, leads to a very different attitude. The Christian has not to fight for his own freedom, for, having been freed in Christ, he is already free and external conditions are no longer so important.

The Christian also perceives that the freedom from political or economic powers which man demands is simply independence. While this is not negligible, it is also illusory. To the degree that this independence is a result of man's first break with God, there is no need to fight for assurance of it.

We have seen that from the New Testament standpoint the converted slave need not seek to cease to be a slave. Freed in Christ, the Christian does not have to fight for political, economic, or domestic freedom. Such freedom is not a direct or necessary consequence of his Christian freedom.

This is why I have refrained from rushing into a problem that commands such universal attention, namely, the problem of religious freedom. It is odd that religious freedom has often been advanced as a definition of good government, even in Calvin and Barth, as though the freedom which the state gives to Christians were so supremely important.

As we have seen, what matters is that the state should be truly secular and that it should not impose any obligatory intellectual, religious, doctrinal, or metaphysical truth. None at all, not even though it be Christian! Apart from this, we are not to demand any special recognition of Christianity nor any freedom for our religion, since this is securely given by the freedom granted in Christ. The most that we can ask is that no obstacles should be put in our way by the state.

After all, why should the state see any exceptional or pre-eminent value in the Christian confession? It has no competence to do this. The state is not a theologian. It is not the judge of truth. If we are authorized to believe in Christ and to practice our religion, this should be only the result of a general order, a common situation, a collective civil liberty, political tranquillity, and public order. As Christians we have to share the common lot. Christian freedom must never take the form of a privilege which is conferred by the state or some other social force. When Christians demand religious freedom, they enter the fatal circle of misunderstanding and compromise.

For what can the state grant when it is a matter of religious freedom? Can it recognize the truth, Jesus Christ? Can it recognize the authenticity of revelation? All that it can recognize and allow is what Christianity has in common with all religions. Hence, if Christians ask for religious freedom, they are asking the state to recognize revelation as a religion. If this freedom is accorded to everybody, this is normal and no danger arises. From a rational, political, and humanist standpoint, it is just and legitimate that Christianity should be viewed as a religion.

On the other hand, when Christians think that this freedom should be given to them as a privilege, serious consequences follow. Christianity now becomes *the* religion. Necessarily, then, it is paganized. This is an ineluctable effect of the sanctioning of Christianity by the authorities and of its official recognition. The normal thing, of course, is that faith in Christ should necessarily be misunderstood and that the truth which is in Jesus Christ should be rejected, denied, and persecuted. Only in virtue of a common order can faith be tolerated and the worship of God permitted. Hence the Christian, because he is free, must not fight for his freedom, not even his religious freedom, since this will simply be the source of errors. On the political and social plane, he has strictly no demands of his own to present.

In contrast, he must not fail to take part in the fight for the freedom of others. He is well aware that this is not authentic freedom. It never can be. It can never be more than pseudo-freedom or independence. Nevertheless, the fight for it is a decisive one.

We can see from the Bible that whenever man puts himself in an impossible situation by his disobedience to God or by his rejection of God, God does not wipe out the new situation (except at the flood) but tries to make it livable for man and to set up in it a way by which he can get to man afresh. Christians are not to be more jealous than God. They must adopt his politics and not their own. They must take up his strategy, which in any case is always carried out and accomplished by human hands.

The problem is that man, by his break with God, and in the desire to be free, has made himself the slave of far worse powers than the heavenly Father. In the midst of the resultant mire, smog, and illusion he fights incessantly to achieve and confirm his freedom. We know that he can never win it. Temporary independence and autonomy is all that he can achieve. This is the condition into which he has brought himself.

Now we must accept this even though it is radically evil when measured by God's revelation and totally false when measured by historical reality. Since man puts his whole passion in the struggle to be free, the Christian must join others in this attempt at liberation. For now it is no longer an attack on God, for the break has already been risked and made. In the situation in which man has set himself, we have to realize that what oppresses him is always the satanic imitation of God. God was regarded by man as the oppressor when Satan accused God and "opened" man's eyes. From that moment on man broke with God, and God showed himself not to be the oppressor, since he allowed the break to take place. Man, then, is constantly in the presence of powers which ape God and restrict the freedom of man by the mechanism which Satan described as that set up by God, although in fact it has been established by Satan himself.

In the battle for the freedom of man which the Christian is called upon to join two aspects may be discerned.

The first is that of the simple hope that tomorrow we will finally be autonomous. Here the Christian can see that it is all an illusion. All the same, it is not completely futile to replace a bloody dictatorship with a more liberal and weaker regime.

The other aspects is that of the fight against the satanic imitation of God, i.e., against the one who usurps God's place and instigates oppression. The oppressor is in effect the one who turns dialogue into constraint, commandment into dead law, the state into a dictatorship, ideas into ideologies, beliefs into dogmas, and economic organizations into mechanisms of exploitation. All this is the fruit of the interference of the oppressor who imitates God but turns his work upside down.

This is why the main fight that man now has to wage is for his independence. This may be false and foolish but it is indispensable. Freedom will never be gained in this way. The outcome of the fight will always be the creation of fresh dictatorship and oppression. Nevertheless, in the situation which man has made for himself, nothing is possible or livable without this passionate quest.

How, then, can the Christian stay out of this project which is essential to man? This is the first reason why he has to seek the independence of beliefs. Even though he knows that what men believe is wrong, he must demand for them the right to err. How else will they some day, through love and the Word, receive the witness to the truth?

Battle is joined. Christians must unceasingly call others to have a part in it. They realize that the outcome is failure. What is sought is never won or established. Freedom is never given. It is never institutionalized. Yet the moment of combat is the one when man comes closest to freedom, midway between hated oppression and illusory independence, between misunderstood independence and oppression which there is refusal to believe. The moment of combat is an ongoing reflection of the encounter between Jacob and the angel, the unknown wrestler who was God.

Let there be no mistake! This independence never gives rise to freedom in Christ. The latter, with the dimension already noted, contains within itself all other freedoms at all levels. No line runs, however, from human freedoms to freedom in Christ. Human freedoms, e.g., political and social freedom, are not the foundation nor are they are the necessary condition of Christian freedom. They are not its sign or *res significans*. Hence the presence of Christians at the side of others in the fight for the independence of all is completely disinterested. For we have to realize that this freedom, while it is indispensable to man, is illusory. It is not authentic freedom. It has neither future nor hope.

Nevertheless, how can a Christian help loving the one who is a slave? At the spiritual level, then, participation in man's struggle for independence means fighting the powers, while at the human level it is an expression of love for our companions. Realism, however, should keep us from falling into the illusion of a triumphant march of humanity towards increasing liberty in respect of destiny, matter, state, or class.

It is in this struggle that we come up against many theological works on the theme of religious freedom.

Religious freedom[54] is usually construed as freedom of belief (cf. Coste and Cren)[55] and then as political freedom to practice the religion of one's choice in a given society without fear of molestation.[56] More than freedom of opinion is at issue. The reference is also to freedom publicly to confess the religion preferred. Religion is thus, as Ricoeur says, a cultural magnitude, a recognized public force. The freedom claimed is more legitimate inasmuch as religion is not the exclusive beneficiary. Freedom of religion is not just claimed for oneself as the practice of religion. It is claimed for all as the right to any ideology desired.

From the standpoint of Christian freedom, then, religious freedom is not primarily the freedom we may claim to be Christians in a chosen

---

54 Works on the subject may be grouped in two categories. First there are those which study the philosophical dimension of religious freedom; cf. esp. *L'herméneutique de la liberté religieuse* (1968), which contains the discussion at Rome presided over by M. E. Castelli, and in which special attention should be paid to Castelli's own article and to that by Ricoeur on freedom according to hope. Then there are those works which discuss the political problem; cf. the Reports of A. F. Carillo de Albornoz to the Ecumenical Council (1963f.) and the same author's own works: *Le catholicisme et la liberté religieuse* (1961) and *Le fondement de la liberté religieuse* (1961). The central work, of course, is that of R. Coste, *Théologie de la liberté religieuse* (1969), which discusses with great lucidity the problems involved.

55 Cren, "Liberté de l'acte de foi," *Lumière et Vie* (1964).

56 For these questions cf. esp. the review *Conscience et Liberté* (from 1971), which has studies of the basis and also of the actual situation in different countries, e.g., in socialist countries (No. 2) and Roman Catholic countries (No. 3).

denomination. Essentially it is freedom for others. Every man ought to be able to be free to profess the ideology, religion, philosophy, or lack of religion he chooses. This freedom for others is much more important than the former freedom. As regards their own religious freedom Christians should always remember that the essential thing is Christian freedom and that the absence of religious freedom does not prevent them from being free.

Certainly Christians must never claim a privileged position in society. Their own religious freedom must always be an expression, consequence, and particular instance of religious freedom for all. Hence it is for this freedom for all that they must fight, hoping only to be put on the same level as others, and not making the claim simply in their own interest.

A further point is that Christians should never forget the sayings of Christ to the effect that the Christian faith will normally be subject to persecution. Both in the Sermon on the Mount in Matthew and the Parting Discourses in John Jesus tells us that if the Christian is truly faithful, society normally finds his witness intolerable and will react by persecuting him. Hence even where religious freedom obtains, as it did to a large extent in the Roman Empire, it is by no means certain and cannot be taken for granted that Christians will profit by it.

It may thus be seen how far we are from common ideas about religious freedom as it concerns Christians. Up to quite recently many theologians defined religious freedom in relation to the state as freedom to worship, to teach, and to evangelize.[57] If a state grants this, there is little more that one may ask. But this seems to be out of the question.

No less unacceptable is the traditional claim of the church that Christianity should be the only religion, that it should be recognized by the state, and that the church should be a privileged body. It is hard to understand how such an inversion of the thought of Christ and such a perversion of love should have come about, or how proclamation of the love of God could change into monopoly, inquisition, and denial of the freedom of others.[58]

---

57 How much deeper is the analysis of Castelli (*L'herméneutique de la liberté religieuse*) who discerns the following aspects: (1) freedom of belief and the implied toleration of the beliefs of others; (2) freedom of interpretation of the unchanging kerygma, e.g., in asking who the neighbor is whom we are to love; (3) freedom of choice among the many implications of scientific research for the concept of nature; and (4) freedom of judgment regarding the concept of tradition as unchanging tradition freely translated into the modern idiom.

58 In this regard we have to take very seriously the formulation of the problem in James M. Robinson's article on "L'herméneutique du Kerygma" in *L'herméneutique de la liberté religieuse*. Robinson argues that the absurdity of the church's position is that on the one hand it offers liberation and a truly free humanity but on the other hand it has to recognize that the way of offering this is in contradiction with religious freedom and human dignity. He also claims that the movement for religious freedom developed outside the church and Christianity and was designed to achieve liberation from the

We are familiar with the arguments. When we know the truth and it is one and irreplaceable, how can we allow persistence in error? When we know salvation, and there is only one way of salvation for all men, how can we allow men to be lost because they adopt other religions or philosophies?

It will thus be seen that the call for religious freedom offers a challenge to many things regarded as essential. For (1) a specific conception of truth is implied. Truth is not possessed by man. It cannot be transmitted by direct means. It is never so well known that we can separate those who know it from those who do not. It is always subject to a new interpretation of the one complete revelation.

(2) A specific view of the church is also implied. The church never has the whole truth. It is called upon to suffer for its witness. It must not seek secular advantage nor use the weapons of power and authority. It must never equate truth with definitive dogma.

(3) A specific view of salvation is implied too. Salvation will be universal. Three positions are possible. We may accept the perdition of the majority of men, whether by reprobation or by the passing over of the non-elect. We may accept the fact that some men choose perdition. Since voluntary adherence and individual conversion cannot be counted on, pressure may be brought to force men to believe and be saved (compel them to come in, Augustine), or magical means, as, e.g., in sacramentalism, may be used to achieve this result. Finally, we may accept a universal salvation which is given by the God of love whether men believe or not. This seems to be the view of salvation which religious freedom implies.

(4) A specific conception of faith is also implied by the proclamation of religious freedom. Faith is no longer a necessary condition of salvation. It is a commitment to responsibility, witness, and service. It can never be brought into being by force. It must be the free response of man's love to God's love when man sees this love and is convinced of it.

(5) Finally, a specific conception of the state is implied by religious freedom. This can act only as a secular state. It cannot proclaim any truth of any kind. The state is the executive of the community. If it has not to defend Christianity, neither has it to support a political or ideological truth that might be in necessary opposition to religious freedom.

It may thus be seen that the understanding of religious freedom draws us into many theological problems and entails a stand at many levels.

We have to ask, however, whether this appearance of the demand for religious freedom among Christians during the modern period is not the simple result of a crisis. The discovery of religious freedom as an expression of Christian freedom seems to coincide with the break-up of Christendom

---

dogma of the established church even though this was offering salvation, human freedom, and the authentic freedom which the Christian religion gives. My only two reservations are (1) that this is not the situation today and (2) that if the church has denied religious freedom it is because the church has not itself assumed its freedom.

or Constantinianism, the loss of power by the churches, and the secularization of the state. This is clear enough.

All the same, it is an excellent thing that this break-up should have led Christians and the churches to salutary reflection and to a fresh understanding of the essential elements of revelation. It seems to me that when theologians think out this problem which is put to them by sociological evolution, when they rediscover the fact that revealed truth is the truth of the love of God, and that this truth entails respect for the convictions of others, they are doing much more than justifying a situation which is imposed on them, as I must often accuse them of doing. They are led by circumstances to a better understanding of revelation.

This is more than making the best of a bad job. It is being converted to the humility of Jesus Christ and accepting his judgment on the powerful. At this point, then, the historical process leads to an authentic spiritual conversion.

It might be asked, however, whether acceptance of religious freedom is not a mere expression of indifference or scepticism regarding the truth—there is truth everywhere—and hence of a cooling off of faith.

The question undoubtedly has to be put and the church must examine its conscience, as follows. Are we sure that if we Christians were again in a position of strength we should continue to espouse freedom of conscience and religious freedom? Is this proclamation of religious freedom linked, for us, with the acceptance and practice of full and complete Christian freedom? Are we working for evangelization in all possible ways? Do we ardently desire the conversion to Christ of those around us? Do we think that there is one unique truth revealed in Jesus Christ and that even if we do not know this in its fulness there is still no other truth? Do we believe that divine grace is really adequate for every need and offers an answer to material and psychological as well as religious problems? Are we bearing daily and unremitting witness to the return of Jesus Christ?

If we can answer all these questions in the affirmative, then our proclamation of religious freedom is authentic and is not just a result of our situation or our indifference. But without examining our consciences in this way we have no right to talk about religious freedom, for it will simply be an expression of political liberalism.[59]

Authentic religious freedom rests on a number of theological founda-

---

59 Significant in this regard is the book by J. Roche, *Église et liberté religieuse* (1967), which gives a good survey of the Roman Catholic Church and its elasticity, but which also contains some striking ideas, e.g., the distinction between freedom of conscience, which is inadmissible because it would be man's absolute independence in relation to God, and freedom of conscience, the distinction between thesis (no freedom) and hypothesis (concrete freedom), the distinction between the internal domain of the church in which it must be totalitarian and its external domain in which it must risk making mistakes. All this is honest but it shows that religious freedom can be a last resort.

tions which have been clarified recently, especially by Roman Catholics writing after Vatican II. Thus it rests primarily on the transcendence and sovereignty of God, for if God is truly transcendent man cannot claim to know his ways or means of action. Religious intolerance implies a claim to absolute justice. The transcendent God is hidden and this means humility on the part of those who know him. He alone is absolute and therefore I cannot say for certain that my understanding is good. This is not relativism. It is a referring of the absolute to him who alone is transcendent. The use of creeds or dogmas to justify religious oppression definitely constitutes a form of idolatry.

Respect for the divine sovereignty demands that we do not limit in any way God's communication to man through man. The freedom of God to act and to work in any person, through any person, and in any circumstances should not be counteracted by efforts to silence men of other confessions. Religious freedom concerns not only man's freedom but supremely God's freedom to speak to all and by all. . . . Religious freedom is not an act of charity towards equals but a mark of respect for the absolute sovereignty of God.[60]

This coincides with respect for the judgment of God. We ourselves are never qualified to judge the faith, belief, seriousness, or authenticity of others. To refuse them religious freedom is to assert a power to judge them. But he who makes this kind of judgment is himself subject to the judgment of absolute truth. This means that he is disqualified from judging.

Here we have the first basis of the Christian demand for religious freedom.

The second basis is obviously respect for the consciences of others. [61] What is at issue is respect for man in his integrity as the image of God which was fulfilled in Christ and which each of us is called upon to be. Each of us is called upon to judge himself according to his own conscience and this debate has to be left open. Reference should be made here to the theology of conscience in Paul.

Does this mean, or can it be rendered as, the "rights of conscience," or, in the current phrase, the "dignity of the human person"? Considerable confusion arises at this point. Is there an intrinsic dignity that we have to respect? This is what is asserted when a rational basis is sought for religious freedom or when there is belief in natural freedom.

Now we are not denying that man has personal dignity or that biblical support could be found for this. We do say, however, that this is not an absolute datum of the conscience and that it is not evident for those who are without faith in God. It might just as well be argued on the rational and natural level that man is a simple animal with no particular dignity.

---

60  See B. B. Beach, "Le fondement de la liberté religieuse," *Conscience et liberté*, 1 and 2 (1971).
61  Cf. especially chapters 2 and 3 of R. Coste's work.

The same problem arises with all other natural and objective foundations of freedom. The quest for truth is an example. Thus Vatican II claimed that in virtue of their dignity men are constrained by their very nature to search for truth. Obviously if this is true we have in it a strong basis of religious freedom. Unfortunately if we consider the facts and not an imaginary essence of man we find that he has a passionate desire, not to seek the truth, but to flee it, to denaturalize it, to conceal it, and to dissipate it. Theologians must not indulge in illusions in this regard.

Even with reference to the good and natural character of the religious quest, and the right and duty of following one's own conscience above all else, it is evident that this whole idea is a result of the Christian revelation. It is neither universal nor natural.

In other words, these different foundations,[62] and others that might easily be found, do not seem to be natural ones but they are actually based on divine revelation even if this is secularized. Hence they are obviously valuable and serious for the Christian, for the Jew, or for those who, even if they are not believers, are still steeped in Christian ideology. Outside this sphere I cannot find any universal obligation of religious freedom. This freedom may be declared and proclaimed, and so may its opposite. This is what I want to underline. I do not say that it is impossible or inconceivable to formulate a principle of religious freedom outside the Christian faith. Instances can be found in Buddhism, the Greek world, and the Roman Empire. What I do say is that the opposite would be just as logical and self-evident. Nothing binds religious freedom necessarily to Greek thought or Roman ideology. Constraint and religious obligation are just as legitimate in these spheres.

In contrast Christianity carries with it the proclamation of religious freedom. It gives this freedom its basis in the content of revelation. We are not free to choose whether or not to proclaim religious freedom. If we do not, we deny the very essence of revelation, we reject God's action in history, and we make light of his revelation in Jesus Christ.

I do not say, of course, that Christians are in fact, or that the church has been in fact, the supreme promoter and defender of religious freedom. We know very well that the very opposite has often been true. We are well aware of the extreme dictatorship, the attempt at unification, and the elimination of nonconformity that the church has undertaken in its days of power. (In many cases this is all that is remembered and the many occasions when the church and Christians upheld religious freedom prior to the twentieth century are forgotten.)

What I do maintain is that when the church and Christians reject religious freedom they deny themselves. They do not speak the word they are charged to speak. They ruin their message and Christ's own

---

62  Cf. the fine analysis in R. Coste.

work. When the church denies this freedom, it destroys its own freedom. This is the point.

The situation is very different from that of Stoicism, for example, in the Greek and Roman world. For Christians religious freedom is a matter of being or non-being. It is not one possibility among others. If this freedom is not proclaimed, supported, and defended, proclamation of the love of God is no longer possible. Hence no form or species of Christianity is left. What is presented and supported is an ideological system which claims to have the truth but which in reality stands in no relation to it, since revealed truth is the love of God for man and it can be received only in the freedom of the Holy Spirit.

Let me not be misunderstood! The thesis that there is an indissoluble relation between religious freedom and the announcing of revelation does not mean validation for all forms of religion (nor indeed for one!). No declaration is made that there is good in all religions nor that ultimately they all converge in that of Christ. In general this thesis coincides with the affirmation that, apart from a small element of truth in them, the religions will have to be replaced by Christianity.

Proclamation of religious freedom does not rest on a recognition that all religions are true or that the religious phenomenon is valid. It rests on attestation of the fact that the love of God has come for rebels and sinners and those who are in error, and that only love, only free conversion, only encounter with God, only the authentic freedom which is in Christ, can lead the believer in a false religion to the truth of Christ.

It is thus essential to evangelism that there should be religious freedom, or, from the standpoint of Christian truth, the freedom to err. It is in this situation and not in rigid orthodoxy that the love of God reaches man.

Naturally this means that, when we proclaim religious freedom, we also proclaim, not that the religions are good, but that the revelation which is in Christ is not a religion, and that, so long as it remains what scripture shows it to be, it cannot be transformed into a religion. It is when Christians transform this truth into a religion, setting it in rivalry with other religions, that they begin to be intolerant and authoritarian and proclaim the supremacy and finally the exclusiveness of the Christian religion.

Hence we are not to contend for the freedom of religions, among which stands the Christian religion. We are rather to support religious freedom as an expression of the love of God, who upholds the independence of the rebellious creature, and coerces it only by grace, i.e., by gift, love, and freedom.

Religions have always been an inevitable factor in the structure of human groups. They have been a means of human survival. They have been an instrument of the will of man to surmount obstacles and dangers. They have thus been a necessary structure in human life. Yet we should not forget that they have also been an important factor in human alienation. I need not develop this theme here, for it is still fresh in our memories.

To proclaim religious freedom is thus to proclaim man's freedom to choose that which will estrange him, reduce him to bondage in his inner forum, and falsify his conscience. Yet what can we do if this is what man wants? Religion is characterized by the same ambiguity as every other human enterprise. Man has also invented arms to fight wild beasts and get food. These arms are an essential condition of his survival. Yet they can also be the means to slay his brethren and reduce them to slavery. The same applies to religion.

Hence when we have to proclaim religious freedom, we need to know what we are doing and what the issue is, namely, independence and not freedom, an independence which is hazardous and ruinous for man. At the same time, then, we are obliged to fight against enslaving idols and to proclaim the falsity and danger of the religions for whose freedom we contend.[63]

Opinions, political doctrines, and religions should not be allowed freedom because they are good and true. Nor is this the reason why men should be free to choose between them. Such freedom is enjoined because there is no way to proclaim the love of God for man without defending man's independence and without respecting the will of this rebellious man as God himself does.

Religions are false and dangerous. Heresies within Christianity, which are a condition of its development, are tragic and fatal. Nevertheless man has to explore every religious possibility. There must needs be heresies. Again, however, this does not mean that we are to look on them with an indulgent and comprehensive eye. We have to fight for the freedom of man and we have to do so in order that he may receive the true love of Christ and enter into freedom in him. For there is no other freedom.

Man is not brought to freedom, however, by coercion or the destruction of that which permits him to live until he encounters the word of life. Hence the battle that we have to fight for religious freedom is not just an

---

63 This is why on the matter of religious freedom I have stayed on the two classical levels and refrained from taking up the problem raised by Ricoeur, namely, that of showing that religious freedom signifies the quality of freedom which strictly belongs to the religious phenomenon as such. Ricoeur, of course, equates the religious phenomenon with the basic word or proclamation of the kerygma. In fact I find in his study a fine understanding of freedom in hope and a sharp analysis of freedom in the Christian faith, but I fail to find any reference at all to religion. What he says at the philosophical level, on the basis of Kant, seems to me to concern only the Christian religion and it is hard to relate it to religion in general or to religions as they are known in history, ethnology, psychology, and sociology. Ricoeur's excellent and astute analysis seems to me to lie within Christological thinking and not to embrace the broader manifestations of the religious phenomenon.

expression of revealed truth as the cause. It is also the possibility of witness.

Man has to have the chance to hear this word among all the words that he himself invents. How can he do this if every mouth is stopped except that of abstract authority? The fight for man's opportunity of freedom in Christ cannot be dissociated from the fight for his independence, i.e., for his supreme disobedience, which is constantly forging new chains and new errors but which is also the very essence of his life and the energy which holds him up.

It is certainly not the job of Christians to knock him down. We have to point him to the one truth, and in so doing we have naturally to denounce the falsehood which enslaves him. We have to bear witness to God's love for him, and in so doing we have to show him the non-love of all that he believes to be the gods.

In this process religious freedom has a part to play. This independence leads man to want to cast off the chains which he himself has forged. He makes a religion in which he thinks he finds an expression of freedom. In reality, however, it simply expresses his independence of the Father. He soon finds out that he is simply making himself a slave and he joins in the fight against this religion.

An obvious condition, however, is that religious freedom should reign, and this includes the freedom to criticize religion. When this criticism turns against the religion that man has made out of Christianity, the criticism is still true, for it destroys the religious aspect of Christianity. It thus obliges us afresh to be what we are called upon to be by Christ.

This criticism is what makes an authentic Christianity possible. Religious freedom, therefore, is not just the possibility of inventing new religions and, at an elementary and simplistic level, choosing the one that suits us best. Nor is it just the possibility of criticizing all religions. It is also the possibility of criticizing the religious form of Christianity, i.e., the alienation to which Christians subject revelation. There is thus a kind of critical exchange in religious freedom. Christians criticize the religions, but exclusively, we repeat, by the proclamation of love. Their argument is that the religions alienate the very possibility of being man. On the other hand non-Christians criticize the Christian religion—even though they really do not know what they are doing—as an alienation of revelation.

Christians have to accept this criticism as ancillary to their own activity. It obliges them to come back again and again to the starting-point which is also the starting-point of the proclamation of religious freedom.

This freedom, within the Christian faith, cannot be regarded merely as the freedom of the act of faith, nor of the possibility of professing any religion one fancies, but rather as the freedom to interpret revelation.

Revelation is what it is only if it is accepted as a kerygma. On this basis, however, one cannot evade the attempt to understand it and hence to construct a doctrine. Doctrine is the doctrine of the divine kerygma which the church repeats and re-presents. The kerygma is not free. Doctrine is to the extent that it is constructed by human reason and is as such verifiable. But it is not insofar as a specific formulation is proper to it at the level of a linguistic system of expression. It is what it is. The act of faith, which implies grace, is free. Hence one has the freedom of the act of faith in doctrine (Castelli).

This is how it stands with the problem of religious freedom within the church. This "within," however, is never sealed off. It is necessarily defined by its movement "without" to fight for religious freedom and its reception of what comes from "without" to challenge free doctrine, which is not free inasmuch as it has a constant tendency to harden into an exclusive system.

## §5. Freedom in the Family, Work, Sex, and Money

It may be noted once again that my theme is not an ethics of the family, work, and so forth, but the ethics of freedom. At a later point we shall have to come back to the same questions from the standpoint of holiness and then of love.

Traditionally when an attempt is made to construct an ethics of work, family, sex (and marriage), the first step is to advance a theory of the primary orders willed by God, i.e., the order of preservation, and of the conditions (including finitude) which the Creator made for the creature and which embrace the marriage of Adam with Eve and the work done by Adam in the garden of Eden.

In my view this is a poor way of putting the problem. It necessarily presupposes that there has been no break and that man continues to live as though he were in Eden. It is maintained that man is free, that he is made for marriage, and so forth, and direct inferences are drawn from this.

In effect no middle ground is possible here. Either this is all true, although incompatible with scriptural teaching, or there has been a radical break, as we asserted in the Introduction, and ethics cannot be built on this foundation.

Mediating solutions have been adopted since the fourth century. These accept an element of modification or transformation, although theologians vary widely in their assessment of the profundity of sin. Casuistry is the result. What has been overthrown and what has been preserved? No definitive answer can be given.

This is not the only reason, however, why I think this is a mistaken approach. In the Introduction I also tried to show that for Christians all ethics must be eschatological. The starting-point must be the end, the last things (whose globality I accept as they are described in what is often disdainfully called the "little apocalypse" of Matthew), the final recapitulation, and the ultimate creation.

It is in terms of this point of arrival that we are to think out our ethics, for this point which, in relation to the development of time, is regarded as that of arrival, is in fact the point of departure. That is to say, it is the point of departure for the kingdom which comes to us. The movement of the return of Christ is the movement which gives point to our history and which already presses with all its weight on time as it now is.

We have to understand this fact as the constitutive basis of ethics because here alone do we learn how God views our activity, how he judges it, and how finally he assumes it. We do not begin at a fixed introductory point. We begin with the movement of the Lord's coming to what we have undertaken and can regard as our own action.

If we adopt a point of departure, if we adopt "what was in the beginning" as the rule of ethics, then we are obliged to view ethics as conformity to a prior given. We have to build a static edifice. We have to enumerate duties and think in terms of structures. Our ethics will necessarily be permanent. In any case, even if this attitude were legitimate, we could not in the strict sense envisage an ethics of freedom in terms of this prior given, for, if the situation of Adam allowed this initial freedom, this situation can no longer be reproduced as it was.

An ethics of freedom can exist and can be envisaged only if we start with the final event. The Lord who comes has respect to the ways that we take in the course of our history. This history is not the repetition of a first law. It is the successive invention of our own forms of life and action. These are what the Lord sees and accepts or rejects. Either way, he commits us to taking this risk. This is his general will, and not that we should endlessly repeat the same motion or develop possibilities within what is created. Only as we start from the end does an ethics of freedom make sense.

Now we have tried to show that for Christians ethics can only be an ethics of freedom. Hence it has to be thought out in terms of the end. In the spheres which now concern us, however, it does not seem that the end provides us with many clear indications. Work, indeed, seems to have no place there at all. Does this mean that the initial law has changed and that there will be no more work for those who live in the new Jerusalem? Will life there be a life of leisure? Shall we enter into the rest of God which is finally achieved?

Similarly we receive little guidance on the subject of marriage. Jesus himself deals with the problem in such a way that we do not know for certain whether the purely temporal duration of marriage is implied or its eternal and monogamous character.

Then as regards the family nothing is said about the ties of parenthood nor is it clear whether those of sonship remain either. The demand that we must leave parents or children to follow Jesus seems to indicate that these ties have only reduced value, that they are purely secondary, and that they do not enjoy eternity, since the Christian is promised new and innumerable fathers, mothers, brothers, and sisters, and this is what finally counts.[64] Here again a term seems to be set for the structure. It is not negated but it is brutally relativized and it seems to have no future from the standpoint of the kingdom.

As regards money or wealth, absolute ambiguity marks its future. In Revelation we see both its destruction and its assumption. It is destroyed with Babylon, which is characterized by great riches, the accumulation of consumer goods, and, as we should say nowadays, a rising standard of living. All this is destroyed because of the prostitution which marks this desire for power and wealth.

On the other hand, we are also told in Revelation that the nations will bring all their treasures into the heavenly Jerusalem. They will present the totality of their works, and this will include their riches. Everything will enter into this Jerusalem and everything will in a certain sense be received and accepted by God. Everything will not be destroyed; on the contrary, everything will be or may be accepted, yet so as by fire.

As regards the sex life, we are told nothing except that there will be final judgment on the unchaste and impure. The reference here is obviously to those who give themselves without check to sex and make a god out of it. We should remember that in the days when John wrote Revelation, as also when the prophets attacked the cult of the bull and when Paul insisted so strongly on the importance of sex, a very realistic deification of sex was a permanent factor. The phallus cult in different forms, with different hopes, and on different foundations, was always present. This cult implies an unregulated sex life. In my view it is at this level that we should understand the judgments pronounced in scripture. It is more a matter of rivalry with God than of morality.

Furthermore, it should be noted that when we read of the sexual taboos of primitive civilizations, these again are related to a sex cult. The taboos exist precisely because of the idolatry. Hence they do not imply a normalized, balanced, and controlled sex life. On the contrary, they imply a fixation on the inordinate value of the sex act.

Is the situation really so different today? Many centuries of Christianity and middle-class respectability have given rise to the mistake that this is all a matter of morality, that the sin is that of transgressing sexual morality, and that this is sin *par excellence*. We need not pursue this, for today this attitude and morality have been everywhere abandoned. Various forces—a more or less badly misunderstood Freud, the biology which reduces sex to a purely physiological function, psychology which integrates the sex experience into a normal psychology without any sense of right or

---

64 See Tillich's fine study of the non-conformity of the Christian in relation to the family in *The Eternal Now* (1963). As he sees it, an indispensable requirement is the wisdom whereby both parents and children recognize the limits of their authority and independence.

wrong or culpability—have all combined to transform the sex life into a very simple matter which is just as ordinary as eating or breathing. Sex on this view is simply one function among others and there is no point in making so much out of it.

Nevertheless, something very strange has happened. For out of this animal naturalism, which seems to be pushed to an extreme in Sweden, there has arisen a kind of exaltation of sex. We see this in literature, where Henry Miller is the prototype of an exaggeration of sex, and Lawrence had already tended to deify it. We see it in psychology, where a kind of pansexualism comes into being with Reich. We see it in philosophy and theology, where the idea persists that sex is the great taboo that must be shattered—this shows both ignorance of the actual situation today and perhaps also the fact that the taboo still exists for the authors themselves. We see it in art and the cinema, the great audacity on the screen being to portray the sex act itself. What all this proves is, not that a taboo persists in the average man, but that among the elite there is a (religious) exaltation of sex.

The average man today has one or several mistresses. He visits prostitutes. He may be a homosexual—the modern legalization of homosexuality between consenting adults in some countries is significant in this regard. Strip tease has become an acceptable performance. Abortion is so common as to pass unnoticed and has also been legalized in some lands. The great aim is to make a pluralist sex life as little inconvenient as possible. This explains the stress on contraceptives. Social pressure is so strong on this point that even the Roman Catholic Church is not far from yielding. It is generally agreed that pre-marital sex for both boys and girls is natural—just as natural as it is for animals which have practiced sex pluralism for a long time. The term sometimes used in connection with such relations—the "partner"—seems an indication of the dissolving of the special and serious character of sexual behavior.

All this is attested by investigations, polls, and statistics of every kind as well as by daily experience. What it implies is that in real life today man is acting without any great complexes in this naturalized domain. I prefer not to speak of the "demoralization" of the young in this regard. The process applies to a whole century and not just to the new generation. Furthermore it is not in this particular area that one should speak of "demoralization" if this is in fact taking place. What interests me is, first, that the general naturalism leads to the creation of a new cult of sex and, second, that sexual freedom becomes the absolute criterion of freedom.

Thus the negation of marriage and fidelity is made part of a transcendent ethics. Homosexuality becomes the symbol of revolution (cf. Jean Genêt). The sexual explosion is accompanied by a new desacralizing fervor which, being fervor, is at the same time also sacralizing. Eroticism is said to be the only possible result of the technologizing of society. In other words, we can see the emergence of a new cult of sex.

If the analysis that I made in an earlier work is accepted,[65] modern man in modern technological society stands in just the same relation to his new technological environment as did primitive man to his natural environment, and he reacts in the same way by deifying and sacralizing certain factors on the basis of natural behavior. Now it seems to me that today sex is one of the specific points in this new deification. It is all the more important because it is the most anti-technological factor, the one which thrusts man most powerfully into the sphere of the natural, the one which finally ensures the continuity of man in a technological setting.

The sex explosion and sexual freedom are points of conflict for those who do not want to yield to technological confinement. For this reason they are extolled almost to the point of deification. A universal and controlling liberative function is ascribed to them. But they had exactly the same function in primitive times. Hence the biblical judgment passed on the sex life and its implications is still valid, although the reference is not just to morality nor is the struggle merely against sensualism.

If we were to try to sum up the general bearing of eschatology, we should have to say that essentially it gives us a perspective of freedom. Work ceases; it is replaced by rest. Ties of parenthood lose their distinctive character and become universal, i.e., they are no longer coercive. Money is both destroyed in Babylon and offered to God, so that it no longer has any constraining power over man. Sex is robbed of its significance by the rejection of unchastity. The result is liberation.

This must be the starting-point for our deliberations, for if we look at the concrete situation, we are forced to say that these elements of human and social life, even though we call them divine orders or orders of creation or nature, have in fact *become*—I am not speaking of what they originally *were*—powers of human alienation, oppression, and exclusion.

Thus when I look at the family or the state as it really is, and not abstractly, I have to admit that I am in the presence of alienation. I can no longer accept the classical analysis of the state, namely, that it is willed by God, that it is the minister of God for good, that it is normally just even though it may become oppressive, evil, and unjust, that it is indwelt by angelic powers which were good in origin, which became evil, but which were defeated and subjected to the lordship of Jesus Christ, although they may still be rebellious. I recognize that all this has, no doubt, some theological validity, but I do not find it very satisfying.

Again, when we look at the concrete reality of political power, work, money, or the family, we see that these are all factors that are useful to man and offer him some satisfaction, but also that they are factors of constraint, oppression, and human alienation. In all history there is no society in which political power has been the power of liberation, balance,

65    J. Ellul, *La technique ou l'enjeu du siècle* (1952).

and pure justice, or in which the family has been an ideal setting for the unfolding of individual personality and happiness, or in which money has been a means of justice or true communication, or in which work has been a way of expressing an integrated personality, a kind of game, a participation in creative activity. To take the opposite view is to refuse to look at reality and fall victim to a simple idealism of words.

Nor should we imagine that, if work today is crushing and the state is totalitarian, things were much better in some previous age. The only difference is that oppression took a different form, and what concerns us today is its present form. We have to accept the fact, then, that no matter what the original intention of God may have been, all institutions have become forces of alienation and enslavement.

When we look at the end, however, we have the promise that we will in fact be liberated. For those who have the assurance of the actual reality of the freedom gained in Christ, the ethical problem is then that of knowing how to express concretely this freedom which has already been won. To give signs of the final freedom which is promised—this is the problem.

A first and common solution seems to me completely fallacious. We are often told that the freedom of the Christian comes to expression in obedience. Indeed, in the preceding chapter we ourselves have shown that in effect obedience cannot exist except on the basis of freedom. But what does this imply?

The question which can dispel confusion here is as follows: Obedience to whom and in what regard? The obedience which scripture tells us about is either obedience to God and his commandment or obedience to neighbors.

If we turn to the latter obedience, we know that the act by which we obey the orders, authority, requests, or needs of others is what makes us their neighbors. When a child cheerfully and thankfully obeys his father, he becomes the neighbor of his father and by this act his father becomes his neighbor too.

In the sphere of what we might call voluntary social relations, relations are always man to man. Scripture teaches us very firmly to deinstitutionalize structures. This applies especially to the state. We are to have in view only the men who hold authority. We are thus in the presence of the one we must obey, whether the relation be that of wife and husband, child and parent, employee and employer. The only obedience at issue is man to man.

We thus have a relation in which, as we have often said and must say again and again, the (Christian) superior cannot demand, impose, or crush. He is entirely dependent on the free and voluntary obedience of the subordinate, who obeys because he has established a new relation with his superior. In these conditions obedience is included in love. It is free.

The only problem—and this is what complicates matters—is that we cannot separate this obedience of a personal relation from the sociological reality in which it lies. The superior may not be a Christian, and even if he is, the superior-inferior relation which we have been describing is embodied in a social system which is not and cannot possibly be Christian. The fallacy is that of failing to see that it is quite impossible to speak of the personal relation as though it were not enclosed in an institution but could be isolated and considered in insolation.

Everything lies in a given social system or institutional form. The family is obedient to a family institution, work to a specific organization of labor. In terms of the institution, each person adopts a certain role in the psycho-sociological sense. Each is invested with a specific function which may be quite different even though the same word is used. Thus the modern father does not have the same function or play the same social part as the dynastic head of the thirteenth century or the *pater familias* of the third century B.C. The father-son relation persists, but it is lived out in different social models with widely different implications.

One might say that the more important the social role of the function is, the less easy it is for the personal relation and the less possibility will there be of a transformation into the relation of neighbor. The more the social group which encloses the relation is enlarged, structured, and institutionalized, and the more distant and abstract the relation becomes, the less possibility is there of this transformation.

The fact is, then, that within the same institution, e.g., the family, there will be at different periods greater or lesser chances of living out obedience as a neighborly relation and hence of expressing freedom by and in this obedience. Furthermore, even in the same period and within the same society, the structures of different relations will vary, so that it will not be possible at every point to express freedom by and in obedience.

It is in fact much easier to express freedom thus in the modern family than in some other types of family. In the modern western world the family no longer has such great weight nor such a strongly developed institutional structure. The same applies to marriage and the sex relation. Everything now depends on the free consent of those concerned, whether it be the obedience of the child or wife, or respect for the sex life. Now that sociological independence has been achieved in this sphere, Christians have a wonderful chance to express freedom in this mutual obedience, in the choice of fidelity by husband and wife, in the choice of respect for their children by parents and of obedience to parents by children, and in the choice not to yield to sexual drives.

It is undoubtedly true that when structures are broken up in this way Christians have an excellent opportunity to manifest their freedom by nonconformity of choice, by still ascribing value to that which no longer has any social value. This is often argued in relation to the church. When the church has lost any sociological value, when it no longer has power, structure, class support, nor money, then being a Christian, being an active member of the church, will be an act of freedom and a genuine attestation of faith. Nevertheless, true though all this may be, it is not a good reason for wanting the church to be persecuted.

It is also true that when the pill grants all girls sexual freedom without risk, the Christian girl will prize her virginity and the Christian boy will realize and live out the fact that authentic love does not accept this laxity and may indeed find in it a serious obstacle. An act and attitude of freedom is thus achieved. Nevertheless, Christians will also see that the freedom which this situation gives them, unless, of course, they are mere conformists, is purchased at the cost of terrible problems and losses for non-Christians. Hence it is not something to be earnestly desired.

Unfortunately some Christians seem to think it is. A whole theological school today welcomes social disintegration. Indeed, it goes further and claims that love should express itself in a plurality of partners, that the obedience of wife or child is a purely sociological concept deriving from patriarchal ideas of the family, that the notion of a single married couple is not Christian, and so forth. Obedience, fidelity, and so on are thus identified with a transitory institution. In other words, this theology of the "generalized neighbor" is an urge to swim with the modern sociological current. It expresses no freedom. It is a mere justification.

In contrast the relation of work or money has become in our society much more coercive, institutional, and abstract. In this context the neighborly relation is hard to imagine or depict. What does it mean to obey an employer whom one never sees or meets? What does it mean to obey an anonymous society? It is absurd to suppose that we have here ultimate neighborly relations because we have ultimate mutual services. How can this obedience express any real degree of freedom when no choice is possible, when the choice is made by the institution irrespective of my own will, e.g., by collective bargaining or contracts, when there is not the slightest possibility of transforming the relation of obedience in work into a relation of love? No freedom is or can be manifested in obedience to the man who commands me in a strictly anonymous way within a strictly institutional system.

For what, after all, is a modern army or industrial concern or commercial enterprise or administration? We well know that in reality it is a bureaucracy and no human power can change its ultimate character. The most vigorous and characteristic undertaking along these lines is that of "human relations," which is in reality a complete mystification,[66] a false front of humanization which in effect leaves the true anonymity and abstraction of the situation intact. Thus our obedience is in no position so to transform the relation of work or money that freedom can play a part in it. This obedience is not obedience to a man but to an abstraction, and within a system of abstraction freedom cannot be expressed in this way.

---

66  J. Ellul, "Les relations publiques et humaines," *L'année sociologique* (1964).

We have also said, however, that freedom can be expressed in obedience to God. Hence the following argument might be advanced. A specific will of God stands behind the orders of marriage, family, work, or money. God has instituted these things. It is he who has set up the orders. In obeying these, then, we obey the will of God himself. Even in the areas examined we thus come back to the truth that obedience is an expression of freedom.

My own belief is that this interpretation is radically false. It is so for two reasons.

The first mistake, in my view, is as follows. When we obey the state or an employer, our obedience towards God is only vicarious. It is not direct obedience to the will of God. For the effective object of obedience is still the state or employer. Only as it were by ricochet can one speak of obeying God.

We cannot make the simple equation: To obey one's parent is to obey God. To obey one's parent is to obey the one who has been invested with a certain authority by God. It is to obey an order set up by God and only secondarily to obey God.

Recognized here is the necessary formal independence of the orders. If there were direct obedience, this would imply that the powers are God's powers and then their form and expression would obviously be always the same in relation to society. In fact, these forms vary enormously. This shows that the orders stand at some remove from God.

Nor can we argue that there is on the one side a basis or dimension or core which is the authority willed by God and on the other side a contingent form. This is a feeble evasion. For in fact the form is the totality in all institutions. Nothing in common can be found between the authority of a thirteenth-century worker over his fellows and that of the president of a corporation like General Motors. Everything lies in the form which the institution takes. It cannot be said that obedience to any institution, to any kind of labor organization or money relation, to any structure of sex relationship, is intrinsically obedience to God. Nor can this be said of obedience to any political set-up. Not by a long way can such obedience transform these structures. Hence it is not a form of freedom in them.

The second mistake has been well brought out by Bartsch in relation to the state,[67] but it can be seen in relation to other areas too. For a long period institutions were thought to have intrinsic value because they are willed and ordained by God. The basis of institutions was thus regarded as a ground of obedience on our part. If this is so, however, we have to see that this obedience is in no sense an expression of freedom.

In fact, however, as Bartsch rightly stresses, the will of God prescribes a certain attitude and line of conduct in relation to this or that institution,

---

67 "Nouvelle manière d'aborder l'éthique sociale chrétienne," *Éthique sociale chrétienne dans un monde en transformation* (1966).

organization, or power. The commandment of God is what entails obedience, and hence our obedience is what finally gives the institution its authority. The only thing at issue, then, is a relation of God to me which is translated into a specific attitude to work, parents, and so forth. To the degree that obedience to God alone is the point, this can express my freedom. But this confirms what we said a moment ago about the forms adopted by the organization of work, family, etc.

All this leads us to the consideration that if concrete situations are studied, and not just ideas about work or family, obedience will certainly not be the way of freedom in these spheres. Once again we have to face the reality. This, as I see it, is the greatest difficulty for theologians, who tend to talk abstractly about work or money.

Now we have often made the point that freedom in Christ is nothing if it is not translated into real life. But this cannot be done unless it is expressed in an actual situation which can be known and experienced, not just in terms of an idea on the subject.[68]

Another erroneous view is that in this social context freedom will be expressed by the individual decision. Each must find his own form of freedom in work, family, or sex. As in the preceding case there is a grain of truth here. But there is also a great deal of error. This individual solution can be seen in two ways. Let us begin with the more superficial. One might describe it as a matter of disentanglement.

I am called to be free. I have to express this freedom by my own methods. I have to choose and decide. I am in a society which organizes work in a coercive and totalitarian way, in a system of professions which is absurd or unjust, in atomized work, in an economic order which I cannot accept. I live to work, and the more society organizes itself, the more it thrusts the totality of my life in this work, so that I have to try as   ch as I can to keep the main thread of life clear of entanglement.

Is there really any job that is more independent than others? To become a workman is to bind oneself hand and foot. To be an executive in a big corporation is certainly to make a lot of money but it involves a personal bondage that can be worse than that of the ordinary employee. Finding a job which will give the maximum of free time and personal initiative and the minimum of external control is by no means easy. Such jobs still exist, but their number diminishes from year to year.

Things are less difficult in the family. Here I affirm my selfhood in relation to the others. I am independent in relation to my parent or spouse. I am myself. Even if my father tries to exert authority, I am increasingly able to handle it. I constantly increase the sphere of my independence until

---

68 This is why I am forced to say that Karl Barth's discussions of work, the death penalty, war, and so forth in *Church Dogmatics*, III, 4 are misleading. He never refers to the practical situation but always speaks in the abstract. We shall return to this later.

I am able to master that authority. If necessary I can leave the family. Sociological pressures all force me in this direction.

As regards money, considerable freedom exists. I can try to make a lot, I can restrain my desire for it, I can give it away, or I can remain in honest mediocrity. The individual element is by no means negligible here. We are not confronted by a social current or a common decision. These seem to be truly significant acts. They seem to be authentic acts of freedom. We shall have to return to this. All the same, they are purely personal acts. They are a private solution as in the preceding cases.

I may also claim to be establishing my freedom individually in the sphere of sex by breaking taboos, by following my instincts, by seeking pleasure, by removing all the barriers I might find to sleeping with any woman I choose, or in the case of the woman by freely practicing contraception so as to sleep with any man. Here, however, as in the case of the family, my alleged freedom amounts to little more than obedience to the sociological current.

It is indeed extremely important to dispel the illusion that we have a purely individual operation in any of these areas. Individual choice seems to be the most important thing. I can spend my money as I like. I can choose my own profession; it is the place of my own decision. Now that family planning is available I can have what children I want: what better sphere of freedom can there be than this? This impression is false.

It is remarkable that Barth develops his thinking along such lines as these.[69] At some length he describes the choice of vocation as a free choice. He has many fine things to say in this regard on the basis of the idea that there is real freedom to choose one's job. But all this applies to a liberal and individualistic world, to nineteenth-century society, and it pains me to have to say that Barth's deliberations here are no more than academic hypotheses. They completely ignore the internal and external transformations of this "choice."

In particular they ignore what might well be the most important factor in modern society, namely, inner conditioning by means of psychological pressure. We think we can spend money as we like. But in fact advertising makes us spend it in a way which is good and useful for a society of mass production. One of the great economic illusions is that the consumer rules the economy. In reality the producer does. The consumer is brought into line with production by advertising. It might be argued that we are free to resist this. I reply that the cleverness of modern advertising techniques makes such resistance very difficult. When one adds the force of the worldwide social current it is well-nigh impossible.

There is a universal demand for winter sports. There is a universal demand for boats. There is a universal interest in hobbies. There is a

---

69 *Church Dogmatics*, III, 4, pp. 595ff.

universal demand for gadgets. There is a universal clamor for plastic objects. In no sense do we really spend our money as we choose. For why do we buy one thing and not another? Basically they are equivalents and are equally interesting. Again, if we want to be economical, an appeal is made to our noblest sentiments. It is a national duty to spend. We shall ruin the economy if we do not.

As for vocational choice, it is increasingly restricted. Quite apart from environmental pressures, we find that the actual choice is greatly restricted by external constraints, e.g., diplomas, competition, and labor legislation, as well as by psychological constraints, e.g., professional orientation and propaganda. Among rural and urban workers choice is restricted by environment and social or racial barriers even though financial help may be available. In middle-class circles choice is increasingly limited by haphazard and implacable administrative selection. The many ramifications of the modern educational system mean that "choices" which are hard to change are often made at a very early stage. What do "choices" really amount to in this case? The pressures of the labor market send people from one job to another, and in a society in which unemployment is always present, can one really speak of choice? In a socialist society, with authoritarian professional direction, there is even less possibility of choice, and when qualifications have been won assignments are made from above and choice of profession is thus ruled out. Furthermore, even socialist societies are now threatened with unemployment, so that yet another pressure is added to that of centralized control.

If we still believe that the choice of profession is free in spite of the force of propaganda, we shall find it hard to maintain this. When around 1958 great stress was laid on the need for science, and the future possibilities of a scientific career were extolled, the number of students in this area increased rapidly. Later when it seemed that the field was becoming too crowded, the number leveled off.

If one adds to all this the increasing need for retraining and readaptation even in limited fields and the revision of priorities according to global economic decisions, it will be seen how illusory is the idea that professions can still be chosen. Naturally, what Barth says about the divine determination in this regard is still true and incontestable. But what he says about the free responsibility of man is completely anachronistic.

The point is that it is very hard to modify the way in which we interpret the reality in which we live. It is very hard to see it as it actually is. But we have to do this if we are to give an adequate ethical answer. If we reflect on a situation which is no longer our own, the ethical answer given will still have value as a reminder of theological truth, as in Barth's case, but it will have no relevance to existing reality. This is why we have to reject the possibility of an individual decision in the present situation, although we shall have to come back to it later from a very different angle and much more positively.

Finally, the least satisfactory attitude in these areas is that which is formulated at the level of motivation. It is often said that the distinctiveness of Christianity lies in the sphere of motives.[70] In other words, we do the same things as other people. We do not try to develop a specifically Christian answer or attitude. But in doing the same things, whether it be making war, voting for the right or the left, marrying, or doing our job, we have different motives from others. This is to be completely rejected, in my view, for motives which do not find expression in a particular attitude or new behavior are false motives. There is no purely inward freedom at the level of motivation. All that we have are good intentions, with which hell is paved according to medieval wisdom.

If, however, we must reject this final case, which is one of extreme individualism even though it might lead to social commitment, we must reject the other attitudes too, since they all ignore the dimension of love for one's neighbor.

To find a personal solution by disengagement, to express freedom in this manner, is to practice freedom without taking into account two indispensable orientations, namely, that of God's glory on the one side and that of love on the other.

If freedom leads to withdrawal into a purely personal enterprise, it is not to God's glory, for it does not bear witness to anything. The theory of motivation is ultimately a case in point. It bears no witness because it is an inner affair. But without the glorifying of God there is no freedom. Furthermore, the freedom which we are given has to be lived out with others. It must be the Christian's opening up of himself to others.

This brings us back at a more serious level to the doctrine of work in Barth. If we leave on one side his general overestimation of work, in at least two ways the problem of an individual solution is posed. Barth tells us that we should work in order to promote, facilitate, illumine, and embellish human existence. Work should be in the service of mankind.[71] Now no one can quarrel with this criterion. But one can see in it only a pious wish, for it is hard to find any way in which, concretely, this result can be achieved. When Barth goes into details, he tells us that we should reject any work which preys on human folly, vanity, lack of taste, errors, or vices. We cannot take up jobs simply because there are always people who want to ruin themselves physically or morally. Again we agree, but let it be applied and we shall see whole sectors of the economy collapse, not just those which are genuinely harmful like the manufacturing and sale of drink or dope, but those that cater to leisure, e.g., juke boxes or television, for these undoubtedly play on cowardice and weakness by offering reassurance, or on vanity by providing aesthetic surgery, and to these sectors we might add

---

70 Cf. R. Mehl, "Fondement de l'éthique sociale chrétienne," *Éthique sociale chrétienne dans un monde en transformation* (1966).
71 *Church Dogmatics*, III, 4, pp. 529ff.

that of advertising and most of the world of bureaucracy. We are thus brought face to face with a serious issue, but what actual steps to recommend it is difficult to say.

With reference to unworthy or oppressive work, Barth also calls upon employers and those who direct labor to ask themselves whether they could not offer some better work which is more respectful of human dignity. We agree once more with the intention but the lack of realism in this whole approach is surely apparent by now. To address such a request to a non-Christian would make no sense at all, for with rare exceptions a non-Christian employer cares not a whit for human dignity. We are not thinking merely of terrible capitalists here. I cannot help remembering with some depth of feeling a medical convention at which an eminent physician, to unanimous applause, said that the problem is not that of knowing whether there is good to be done, but whether it will pay well enough. Even if we turn to a Christian employer and put the same question to him, however, what are we really asking in specific terms? Are we asking him to switch his production to a new line? Or are we asking him to grant conditions of work which will satisfy his employees? Either of these could be costly, and in the competitive system of free enterprise changes or improvements of this kind might well drive him out of business. Perhaps the Christian employer ought to be prepared for this, but if it happened he would simply be contributing in the last analysis to a rise in unemployment.

It must also be asked what the question raised by Barth could mean in a socialist or semi-socialist state. When salaries, working conditions, and standards are regulated and fixed, what can the employer or manager do but apply the vast collection of rules? Another passage shows how far Barth is from reality here. He tells us that the organization and division of work rest on the initiative of some on whom others depend. A contract is thus needed to fix the nature of work, working conditions, and pay. Where is this still true today? Possibly in Switzerland, but it is no longer true in the United States, where such matters are arranged at a collective level and trade unions play a leading role.

The initiative and independence of individuals are infinitely reduced, whether in bettering the lot of employees, or in making it harder. Wages, for example, are not a matter of individual negotiation. Barth has in mind a labor situation which has been out of date for something like half a century, and was already out of date when he wrote this chapter on ethics shortly after the Second World War.

Furthermore, it has to be recognized that even if an employer may still enjoy a relative measure of initiative or independence, an essential fact is that one undertaking depends on a hundred others, and that within the same process jobs vary enormously and workers have to put up with different working conditions at different stages of production. Is production of an admittedly useful object to be stopped because one of the stages in the process involves unsatisfactory conditions? Should we halt the process because an essential material has been produced under unsatisfactory conditions? Once one examines the implications more closely, it is obvious that these proposals are inoperable and do not measure up to the realities of the situation. An individual solution, which is to be rejected already because it entails disengagement, is shown to be an illusion in face of the real questions raised by Barth. Man is hardly able to express his freedom in respect of work along lines such as these.

In practice the same problem confronts us in the other questions at issue. The only difference is that it may now be less complex to the extent that the involvement in collective organizations is less rigorous.

The first positive act which signals Christian freedom in these matters of work, marriage, and family is the act that consists in a restoring of meaning. At this point we enter a domain which is dear to Ricoeur. We also come up against one of the important discoveries of the present age, for we have here both the response to an urgent need and an expression of freedom.

Our age is characterized by non-meaning. All psycho-sociologists agree ultimately that the work we do is marked by this fault. It makes no sense. It has no obvious value of its own. We have on the one side the dividing up of tasks, monotony, and the production of articles of no evident utility, while on the other side we find a break with matter, then with the machine, then a break between the function of thought and that of execution, the growth of an enormous labor organization and bureaucracy, a mass of paper work, often with no recognizable content, for every conceivable function, and finally the wastage of giving complex and highly advanced training to men who are then entrusted with jobs far below their competence. These things, and many others, contribute to the fact that work has no meaning in modern society.

It is simply a way of making a living. Now we may allow that this is not bad in itself. Nevertheless, man needs some additional justification for something on which he spends most of his time and his creative powers. Hence he suffers from this lack of meaning. He feels that he has become a machine which performs meaningless acts whose relation to other acts and to the rest of life is not perceived.

One of the tragic questions which parents with children in their upper teens confront today is the question: "Why do we have to work? What is the point of it?" Unless one is prepared to exalt work as such, it is hard to give any reasonable answer to this question in the actual situation of work today. No explanation is adequate. None can satisfy a critical mind.

The same loss of meaning may be seen in relation to the family, money, and sex. Because the family no longer has a clear function in society, and conditions of work and residence make a true community life difficult, it seems that this grouping is anachronistic. There is no evident reason why members of the family should live together. Children see no point in staying at home and submitting to parental discipline, just as spouses see no point or sense in continuing their marriage. So long as there was a need to bring up children, and this could not be avoided, the plea "for the sake of the children" made sense, but today children can be put in the care of society and in any case one can easily avoid having them in the first place. We are thus confronted with a loss of evident, felt, and experienced meaning in relation to this social group.

The group can be kept in being only if we want it. We can want it, however, only if it has meaning for us. Without this, what is the point of husband and wife forcing themselves to stay together, when the first flame of passion has gone, merely to bring up children? The basic question of the transmission of life also confronts us, as we have seen above. What was previously a matter of instinct has now come into the sphere of intention in a technological society. As we see it, the philosophy of the absurd has found a monstrous echo in our western world. The consequence usually drawn from it is a refusal to transmit life.

The logic is hard to resist. If life has no meaning, as literature and the cinema are constantly telling us, why should we not commit suicide? And why should we transmit this life to a poor wretch who will have to carry the same burden? If life is so bad, and if it is so cheap, as the experience of wars and concentration camps shows so clearly, why should we bring babies into the world? Here again I suspect that many modern parents have had to listen to the harsh complaint of their children: "I did not ask to be born."

This explains the widespread use of contraceptive devices, whose usefulness is plain, as well as the rapid rise of abortions. But what can we say in reply? Is not this the only consistent attitude in confrontation with an absence of meaning?

Man feels a need for meaning precisely because the role of instinct has diminished. He is no longer satisfied with "joy that a man is born into the world" (John 16:21). He is no longer satisfied with the wonder of this new presence and solemn glance. He wants to know why, and he can find no answer. Abortion is thus preferred.

As regards money, the situation seems at first glance to be very different. Money and its possession and use always have meaning. Is not this self-evident? Yet it is not as certain as all that. Economists and sociologists have noted a change in the attitude to money. People recognize that there is now no point in being economical, in building up capital, in looking ahead. Economizing? What sense does this make when prices keep going up and the value of money constantly falls? Capital? What is the point of going without things to build up a reserve when there is an increasing socialist trend, when more and more funds are held collectively, when capital is increasingly social and individual capital is threatened and might in the long run be confiscated? Money is simply a thing in transit.

This does not mean, of course, that the power of money has decreased. Not at all! But it no longer has any meaning in itself. It is becoming either an instrument of social power and prestige (if one has enough of it) or a means of consumption. It is linked to consumer growth.

Psychologists and sociologists, however, tell us that this is not enough to satisfy modern man. Modern man finds no happiness in high consumption. Affluence grants him a moment of pleasure but over a long period it satiates him. The pleasure it gives is fleeting. Consuming does not fill his life. He wants something else.

Here then, in brief survey, is the situation of meaninglessness which characterizes the whole structure of modern life. We have to realize that it is all quite normal. Neither work, family, marriage, sex, nor money has any intrinsic, ontological, or natural meaning. It is not just that these things have lost their meaning in our own age. A study of the extraordinary diversity of situations and considerations in relation to these elements in human society at different times and in different places[72] shows how false is the idea that they have ever had any meaning in themselves.

When it is said that work is a normal means of human self-expression, this is only a recent idea of western civilization—no more. When it is argued that marriage and the family are constant factors in society, it is easy to see that a thousand different things are covered here by the same words. In reality these activities or institutions have an attributed meaning which comes on them from outside, whether from a religious outlook, an ideology, or the structure of society itself. The evidence is overwhelming that the social structure is what gives meaning to the transmission of life, or value to work, and so forth.

To take an extreme case, we may refer to the situation in Barjavel's novel *Ravages*. Here an isolated human group in an emergency situation has to rely on itself and its cultivation of the soil for survival. In this setting the need for rules of marriage, procreation, and work is clearly seen. The question of meaning is not posed as it is in modern society.

This question arises only when three factors combine: (1) a high abstractness of social relation; (2) a breaking of the causal nexus in regard to the acts we do and the results which are essential to life; and (3) a multiplicity of interpretations of social conduct. When even one of these factors is missing, there again exists the possibility of finding a sufficiently strong and universally recognizable meaning in such things as family, marriage, or sex to give them adequate value and undergirding.

Today, however, all three factors are present. Meaning is not unavoidable. It is not attributed *ipso facto* to what we experience and do. We live indeed in an absurd society. Life itself is not absurd, but life in this absurd society. We do many things that have no value in our eyes. Hence we can either plunge more deeply into absurdity, whether it be in dreams, comics, or surrealism, or whether it be in activities that express the absurd, such as the revolts of hooligans or hippies, or else we can try to recapture meaning.

---

72  Cf. Stoetzel, *Traité de psychologie sociale* (1964).

Since it does not appear that life can be lived at all on the hippie level, even though we have to take this very seriously, and since we surely want to go beyond the stage of adolescent revolt, which cannot last, it is essential that meaning be recovered.

Now as Christians we know perfectly well that all these things do in fact have a meaning which is very different from that which society imparts. The difficulty is, however, that even as Christians we have grown used to the fact that meaning is provided for us by others. We have become accustomed to getting the meaning of marriage from the blessing, or the meaning of work from the idea of vocation, or the meaning of sex from middle-class morality. But these things will no longer do.

Today, therefore, we have to face up to the question of meaning individually. We have to make our own reply. We have to find in these things a meaning which is not furnished in advance. We have to find it in a way which will have more than individual cogency. This is not enough, seeing that the activities themselves are all collective. We have to do it in such a way that the meaning which I discover and attribute can be valid for my neighbor too.

The unheard of difference here in comparison with earlier societies is that previously there was no need to look for meaning. It was lived out without being understood or intellectually apprehended. It lay at the level of the instinctive.

Today, however, we are forced to find volitionally and intellectually a meaning in whatever life brings us. This is the result of the immense technical mutation which we are experiencing.

When we use the word "intellectually" this might suggest that we have here a purely formal and external matter. A meaning is to be affixed to the activity but will remain outside it. This is the great difficulty. Meaning has to be an integral part of the operation. I have not found meaning if I have not impregnated the whole with a sure and incontestable value which is now conscious and reasonable. The fact of the technologizing of society means that we now have to be aware of what we are doing and of what we are. This is neither progress nor disaster. It is as it is. Hence its meaning has to be clear. But it is not.

As we have seen, trying to find an intrinsic meaning will not do. There is no such meaning. This is what has brought defeat and disillusionment to all the advocates of natural law. Meaning has to be invented, and it has to be such that all will accept it.

Now I can certainly see the meaning of many of my own acts and decisions both for myself and my neighbors. I can give meaning to my own moral conduct and my own marriage. I can undoubtedly do this. Perhaps this is the place to begin.

It must be realized, however, what this will mean. I shall be exactly like a rock surrounded by the sea and battered and often submerged by the waves. For, with the meaning that I personally attribute to my life, I am encircled by a swelling ocean of non-meaning, and I cannot act as though this did not exist. I am incessantly attacked by this non-meaning, which makes it clear that the meaning which I have attributed on my own account is no true meaning at all. I may resist heroically but I have to admit that my attitude is ridiculous and that the meaning which I have given to what I see merely augments the absurdity of life as this is demonstrated to me by society as a whole. I may resist heroically but I have always to remember that in this struggle between the sea and the rock the sea always wins.

Thus the meaning which I have given to my individual adventure is not one that I can pass on to my children. Authentic meaning has always to be lived out in concert or else it is nothing more than a terrible enterprise of superhuman virtue. I cannot be content, then, merely to discern meaning in, and grant it to, the affairs of my own life, e.g., my work, marriage, and family. I have also to be able to pass it on and share it. Others must find meaning too, and the meaning that they see must coincide with mine.

In these circumstances, the matter must be, as I have said, a matter of awareness and intellect. Meaning will never be brought to light by the transmission of a doctrine or by explanation. If I can find meaning for work or marriage in faith and in biblical thinking, this is certainly good and valuable. But as a Christian I cannot regard this as sufficient. For I cannot transmit this meaning directly to others. These others have to go through conversion. They have to acknowledge Jesus Christ as Saviour and Lord. Then they, too, can find meaning in the unique opportunity which they are offered in life.

We have said, however, that outside faith meaning is a collective affair. As a Christian, I cannot expect that all men will be converted and will thus find the ultimate meaning of life. Nor can I believe that there is a natural meaning that any man might find. Nor can I bear it that the men with whom I come into contact, and the society in which I live, should be plunged purely and simply and permanently into absurdity and meaninglessness. Ricoeur is right when he claims that one of the essential tasks of the Christian in society is to be a creature of meaning.

What is needed is a meaning which will be acceptable to all, whether Christians or non-Christians, as the ultimate meaning supplied by faith can never be. What is needed is a meaning which will not just be a continuation of that which used to exist but which will relate to modern conditions of work and family life. What is needed is an explicit meaning even though it is realized that understanding and doctrine will not suffice.

Now meaning embraces two things: direction and significance. With Christians exercising the function of leaven, salt, ferment, initiative, and will, we have to find these two things together. What is the orientation of the work I do? What is the direction of this marriage or family group of which I am a part? What is the value for myself, for others, and for the society in which I find myself, of this use of money, and why this use instead of some other use? What is the significance of this type of sexual behavior?

Now in my view, if the Christian will put himself on the level of others even while strongly living out his faith, if he is ready to feel and experience meaninglessness in solidarity with others, not judging them but referring all things to Christ, then he can serve as a fixed point in the charting of meaning. What goes for the Christian goes for the church too. The church cannot drift with the current. It cannot accept the irrational and absurd. It has to be a haven of reason. Above all, it has to be the center of fairly stable and possibly common values.

What man needs is not that the church should deliver itself up to meaninglessness. What he needs is not the *aggiornamento* of the church. The ambiguity of such an affair should be noted. It is legitimate insofar as dead traditions and outmoded cultural features are set aside and the church is modernized. But insofar as the church adopts the main fashions of the world, giving its allegiance to technology, socialism, movements of liberation, and the fight against hunger, it may well be guilty of egoism, plunging into these things because it is afraid of being forgotten on the highroad of history and trying to give itself a historical chance. It may well be treading in the footsteps of others because it is frightened of being left out in the cold.

If this is so, the church has no concern for the real need of man in spite of its imposing statements about oppressed peoples, hunger, and so forth. For if it were truly in touch with modern man and truly concerned about him (and not just its own possibilities of making contact with him), it would recognize the fact that he needs more than bread and productivity. He needs benchmarks. He needs meaning. He needs to find himself in the shifting world of information, historical acceleration, intellectual delirium, atomic uncertainty, and cultural clamor. He needs a compass which will point him firmly to the north. He needs lights which will show him his position. We face rocks, but on a good chart rocks can become points of reference.

If Christians have a true concern for man, they will try to find fixed points which are valid for all instead of doing what they have been doing the past twenty years, namely, stirring up passions and joining in every new social, political, and intellectual movement. Fixed points, however, are useful only if they are indicated on a good map. Hence they presuppose a global meaning or a vision of the world. Each element—money, sex, etc.—is called upon to acquire a meaning, just as each Christian life can be exemplary. But these specific elements can exist only if they are part of a larger meaning, a global significance, which we have to create.

Two observations may be made in this regard. First—and I am now developing what was said earlier—this common and universally valid meaning will not be found by yielding to the delirium and disarray of the men of this day and age or by regarding their folly as wisdom. It will not be found by adoption of the philosophy of the moment or by turning to Communism, eroticism, and so forth. We shall not serve the men of our generation by letting go what is specifically Christian. We do not promote the true interests of others by preaching Christian atheism or proclaiming that God is dead. We do not do anything for our traveling companions by giving way to the common despair under an empty heaven. We do not give them any consolation by saying: "Look, I am just like you." A rich man who becomes ashamed of his wealth might burn all his titles and certificates and join the indigents on skid row, but while this might be very edifying, the latter would not thank him for coming to share their meager supplies of food and wine; he would just be another mouth to feed. This is what is implied by the proclamation of Christian atheism, which rests on an infantile logic akin to that of the most superficial scholasticism of the middle ages. If God does not exist, neither does Christ, and Jesus, the model of humanity, is a childish fantasy.

The freedom which leads us to invent meaning and to ascribe meaning is precisely the freedom not to be carried along by secular currents and not to be like those whom scripture calls fools, i.e., men deprived of sense or meaning.

If, however, we differentiate ourselves in this way, it is not in order to occupy a place of privilege and bring pressure to bear: "We Christians 'have' the meaning of the human venture"—this is not true, for we do not possess it—"and you others who are disoriented must accept it or you will have nothing."

It seems to me that two different levels have to be distinguished here. Faith in Christ does indeed give us meaning, direction, and significance. This must be the object of preaching and witness. But men today—if I might put it thus—are "more" lost—not from the eternal but the historical standpoint—than those of other ages. We live in a period of human disarray not unlike that of the twelfth to tenth century B.C. or especially the fifth to tenth century A.D.

Now in this latter period the monasteries tried to save culture and technology, to restore the possibility of economic life, and to defend morality, i.e., not just Christian morality but common morality in a pagan setting. In other words, they tried to create possibilities of life for man.

There are epochs, then, when the church has a double task. On the one hand it must give a loud and clear affirmation of the gospel of salvation. On the other hand it must join in the work of conservation. The two things are not the same and we must be on guard against confusing them.

A line of defense does in fact need to be set up which will enable man to live a human life. To do this, however, is not to bear witness to the gospel. Again, this man who is defended in his quality as such needs to become a Christian. But merely preaching the gospel to broken, assaulted, bewildered, and lonely man may well be to betray the gospel. To be sure, Moses remains alone in prayer while the people fights. The point is, however, that there is a people of God which fights. Hence we should not ignore either the one thing or the other.

It is in the area of the conflict for man that we need to consider what it is that man really needs. The first thing to realize here is that nearly all the reports on church and society presented at Geneva or Uppsala are pointless because they do no more than repeat what is to be found in the secular press. A common meaning which is valid for all men will not be found in this way. I must insist that man in our age needs more than the approval and blessing and support of the church for what is going on in modern society. What good will it do for Christians to say that they are in favor of economic planning? This is not what will give meaning either to the life men lead or to productivity. A global response has to be found for the question "Why?" which man is asking today. This response has to be generally acceptable. It has thus to open up a future for man. Within this global response the particular meaning of family, money, job, and sex will come to light so long as we have also done some work on this matter of specific meanings.

In any case giving meaning entails an act of will and a choice between a falsified sense (which yields nonsense) and a possible attributed sense. In these circumstances we might possibly reach the following conclusions.

As regards work, we must reject such meanings as self-realization, self-enhancement, or vocation, and accept the fact that in our life with its obstacles and limitations, limit itself has meaning. At issue, then, is a positive confrontation.

As regards marriage, we must reject such meanings as romantic love and the middle-class establishment and accept the venture of encounter, of the breaking of solitude, of knowledge of the other with acceptance of the fact that one cannot be oneself except in relation to this chosen other who remains unique and is for me a final earthly witness to humanity.

As regards money, we must reject such meanings as commercial operation or accumulation for security in old age and accept the fact that it should be lived out for spending and given a place in the aesthetic understanding of life.

As regards sex, we must reject such meanings as need and pleasure and accept the meaning of the power of constantly renewed questioning, of a disquietude in which the biological finally corresponds exactly to questioning by the Word of God. (This is precisely the reason why sex cannot be naturalized or made into a simple biological process like digestion.)

As regards children, we must reject such meanings as the transmission of life or self-prolongation and find meaning again in the direct, elemental, and least intellectualized joy "that a man is born into the world" (John 16:22).

In other words, in all these areas we must strip off the false meanings which are attributed by our society, by ideologies, or by the past, for it is the false meaning which stirs up such a terrible feeling of meaninglessness in our society. The new meaning can come, however, only through a choice, through decision at the level of the possible, and on the condition that it is lived out.

For it is precisely here that freedom comes to expression. We are thus led to two final reflections on meaning.

First, it is self-evident that, in the last resort, if, as we have said, this is not a dogmatic and intellectual matter, it is a matter of life. As we live out circumstances in a particular way, meaning appears. As we become wholly authentic we can show that the life of man has meaning in these circumstances.

But this way of living, this attributing of meaning by life, implies freedom. It is as we are free in relation to meaninglessness, to the destiny which oppresses man, and to given social and economic factors, that we can restore meaning to what is lived out and even to these social and economic factors themselves. This is why the role of Christians is necessarily so essential here. Christians must grasp the freedom that they are given. They must be able to apply it, as, unfortunately, they seldom succeed in doing.

Our second concluding remark embodies an appeal to wisdom. We must not try to import meaning into anything and everything. All the things in modern society today, and in the elements which make up our life, are not called upon to have meaning. If it is good to look for meaning, to live it out as indicated, I am not sure that Christians are summoned to attribute meaning to economic growth, technology, war, or racial conflict. It is perhaps as well that these things should plunge into meaninglessness and remain there. The search for meaning should not become an obsession. All things do not have to be given meaning by Christians. The things to which we do not have to give meaning are the very ones (and almost the only ones) which evidently have meaning in the eyes of modern man.

In essence meaning must be refused to that which is in some way destructive of man, whether blatantly as in the case of war, or subtly as in the case of technology, psychological action, and ideology. To want to give meaning to absolutely everything in the life of modern man, to his total environment, is to fall into a new automatism and consequently, under the guise of extreme freedom, into a new bondage.

As we attribute meaning, however, we must be vigilant lest the meaning we attribute is a false one. Nothing is easier than to pass over from meaning to false meaning. We must be ceaselessly critical in relation to meaning, especially in respect of such reference points as ideology, religion, and illusion.

The meaning that we give might in effect be nothing more than an ideological product of the situation, Again, it might be no more than the creation of a religious belief in respect of the phenomenon to which we are trying to impart meaning. In other words, I impart meaning, but if I reach the public, it is accepted by them as a religious value. We must always be on guard here, since the public in a secularized society is only too ready to fall headlong into religious emotions. Finally, the meaning might be a mere illusion which by psychological methods succeeds in getting itself accepted as a reality. The whole apparatus of public and human relations is a method which western society uses to give an appearance of meaning to the experiences of life.

It is necessary, then, that the search for authentic meaning should be accompanied by vigilant and constant criticism of the false meanings which, whether we like it or not, are continually growing up around us.

Attribution of meaning to what we are called upon to live out in common is thus an essential work in the Christian life and an expression of Christian freedom. It seems to me, however, that this is not wholly adequate and that a further step is demanded.

We have seen that concretely, in our society, money, work, family, and sex have become factors of alienation for modern man. To destroy this alienation it is not enough merely to give meaning to these things.

Again, we have reached the by no means negligible conclusion that life is becoming unlivable for man. But this can be very dangerous, for man may accept the life he lives as entirely bearable and acceptable because of the meaning we discover even though he remains in a situation of alienation. After all, this is precisely what the techniques of human relations are designed to achieve.

The supreme task and venture is to try to transform these factors of alienation into signs of the liberation of man in Christ. To bring this about there is needed not only the lived out reality of my Christian freedom but also contact between the sociological dimension and the dimension in Christ.

Now, while every Christian must try to achieve this transformation, it is quickly evident that many ways to this goal will prove to be dead ends. This is true, for instance, of the institutional way.

Without going into details, let us examine the various levels. It is obviously impossible to achieve a non-alienated condition of life for man by institutional transformation. We are confronted here by the constant illusion of jurists and revolutionaries. The error is brought to light by a hundred and more experiences in the west and more recently by modern decolonization. But Christians continue to fall into it.

I will not investigate the illusion in detail, for my only purpose in this context is to underline the simple fact that we cannot possibly proceed by the institutional route. The churches today have become minorities in consequence of the process of secularization. They have less and less opportunity of achieving anything by institutional transformation. At this simple level of possibility the way ahead is closed.

For example, we shall not see again the great campaigns which the Roman Catholic Church mounted against divorce. This is because we do not have to try to set up a Christian society. We do not have to try to give an institutional form to money, job, or family which will transform these into means of human liberation.

In any case it is an illusion to think that this would happen. It is never by way of the institution that man achieves a measure of independence in spite of the persistent belief that the institution guarantees human freedom. There is no point, then, in attempting to form a society on the Christian pattern or inventing Christian forms of such things as marriage, etc.

Even if institutions achieve general validity, man himself has to be free before these institutions can be for him a framework of freedom, and we have already had occasion to note how illusory this freedom is and how independence and freedom are so easily confused. It is not at this level, therefore, that we must try to act.

Shall we make our effort, then, within the church? This too, as I see it, is a dead end. For the church does not have to be a complete and closed society of its own within secular society. It does not have to duplicate the institutions of society in its own institutions. Its task is not to organize a society of the saved in opposition to a society of sinners. It does not have to create new institutions in respect of family, marriage, property, money, and work—institutions which will serve the freedom of these liberated men who are Christians. Indeed, in a society which is so strongly integrated and totalitarian as our own it is an illusion to think that we can or should live out our Christian freedom or run the church in this way.

It is not, then, by the institutional path, whether in society or in the church, that we can transform those alienating factors into signs of freedom in Christ.

Nevertheless, one line of action is possible at the institutional level. This is an attempt at de-institutionalization. I do not mean, of course, that we should seek to overturn law, which fulfils a necessary function. But alongside the juridical institution there is an equally strong and even more menacing sociological institution. Now the spheres of money, work, and marriage are very highly institutionalized. This is one of the aspects of their alienating power. Man is trapped in a set of tight frames which are either formulated legally or put together sociologically, and one of the very first acts of freedom in Christ is to repudiate the institution.[73]

This de-institutionalization or destructuralization is of inestimable importance in modern society. As Lefebvre has well seen, it is the true work of revolution and liberation. Anything else is mere façade. What must be contested is the ideology of structuralization according to which a society does not exist unless it embodies a principle of cohesion or coherence, a latent or manifested structure. This is completely false. But we

---

73 At this point I am in full agreement with Lochman when in "Ekumenische Theologie der Revolution," *Evangelische Theologie* (1967), he argues that we need to pass on from an ethics of institution to an ethics of movement.

live in a world that is haunted by the obsession of structure. Structure is always a negation of freedom.

This is true not merely at the economic or collective level but also in the intellectual and spiritual sphere. We may say with Lefebvre[74] that any transition from the spontaneous to the conscious is necessarily accompanied by subjection to authority. At the level of private life the same factor occurs. Lefebvre shows that everyday life itself becomes an institution. The work of Christian freedom today should focus primarily on destructuralization at every level.

Nevertheless, two limits must not be forgotten. The first is the limit of the possible. We must not be under any illusion. We shall not get very far. Organizations in our society are large and powerful. Only with great difficulty can we make any impression, loosen the rules a little, and remove the heavy yoke. All the same, we must make the attempt.

The second limit is that of the desirable. Even if it were possible to destroy the institution altogether, we should not do it, for the institution has a part to play. Freedom, as we have said already, can be expressed only in terms of it, in relation to it, and to a certain extent under its protection. Hence we have to fight the institution, not in order to destroy it, but in order to secure some play for freedom and to achieve the salutary effect of inserting tension into the institution itself.

The attack should be directed against two specific aspects of the institution, namely, abstraction and bureaucratization or convention—the two terms relate to the same reality in different contexts. The institution is always a power of abstraction. It replaces regard for the object with regard for the rules which are imposed on it.

It is easy to see what this means for the questions at issue. Work is subjected to regulation, the education of children to pedagogy, and sex or marriage to a system of schemas (even if they are revolutionary!). The first act of freedom is to set aside the rules and retrieve the object itself, i.e., that which truly concerns us in the relation.

Thus we must stop disregarding money itself and focusing on the rules of its management, employment, and use. We must turn our eyes off the rules and practices relating to money in our society and in the first instance come face to face with the reality of the monster itself.

Again we must stop thinking of children in terms of pedagogy or of women in terms of rites. It is essential that Christian freedom should lead us—this is another aspect of realism—to set to work restoring to these beings or objects their lived out reality face to face with us and alongside us. The institutional system which makes them abstract must be broken. By this already we are brought into an uncomfortable situation. But freedom is never comfortable.

In the same movement we are also led into a struggle against all

---

74 *Position contre les technocrates*, 1967-1970, pp. 167ff.

bureaucratization (in relation to sex, marriage, and the family). If there is any freedom in Christ, then we must always live out these situations as new ones. We must always be rediscovering the element which transforms the real instead of letting it be prevented from coming to manifestation by the force of bureaucracy or convention.

In other words, the first step which I indicated above must lead on to a second step. The object which is rediscovered in and for itself must retain its possibility of intrinsic evolution and not be sterilized.

We have only to try to introduce this new attitude into these areas and we shall soon see how difficult and explosive it is. If an employer stops looking at his employees in terms of rules and institutions and sees them in their concrete reality, or if an employee stops looking at what he does in terms of norms and organization and sees it in its meaning or lack of meaning, and if there is in this way a return to the real, the institution will certainly not be changed but there will be brought into it an element of uncertainty and room for maneuver. For no institution is so well adjusted that this possibility does not remain where there is energetic action. The starting-point for such action, however, is this way of looking at the situation or at reality and the rejection of the institutional image.[75]

This presupposes authentic freedom on my part. It also poses a challenge as I stand in confrontation with these institutions. In extreme cases, if it is truly impossible to fight against this abstraction and bureaucratization, then sabotage should be considered. If the institution has become so hard, sacred, and rigid that there is no possibility of loosening it, only an aberrant action can give life and movement to that which is stifled.

When we mention sabotage, we are not thinking merely of an employee and his work. We have in mind all the spheres under discussion: sabotage of the rules of money, the rules of allowable sexuality, the rules governing relations between parents and children, the rules of compulsory education and examinations. This is the way that many young people are going today, but they are clumsily expressing revolt against what is unacceptable rather than true freedom. If they are acting, however, it is because Christians are not.

Sometimes we find a higher level of understanding and sabotage, and this is an example of what Christian freedom ought to make possible. The norms of the social system should be broadened, not by absurd negation, juvenile reaction, or simple destruction, but by sabotage in the sense of considered action at the weakest and most sensitive point with a view to restoring authenticity of life where now there is only repetition and bureaucratic vacuity.[76]

---

75 The most notable instance of this attitude that I know is given by R. Mothé, *Militant chez Renault*.

76 I wrote this passage prior to the student revolts but decided to let it stand. I will only add that leftist agitation in the colleges does not correspond at all to what I had in mind. There are two reasons for this. First, it does not attack what is most rigorous and

We are already in the presence of a summons to consider our liberated human condition within the structures of society. It is within them that we have to live, not outside them, or in what is thought to be outside, nor with the obsession that we must change the institution. The only thing is that within these forms and this framework we must substitute movement for sterility and tension for equilibrium.

This is not incompatible with what we said earlier about providing landmarks. The church and the Christian ought to express their freedom by furnishing these points of reference for man, while in relation to institutions, since Christians are willy-nilly implicated in society, they should express their freedom by constantly introducing pressure and movement into that which seizes and hardens, as every institution tends to do.

If it is unrealistic and utopian to consider action outside the concrete institution of the family, work, and money, it is by no means unrealistic or utopian to try to live out the realities found behind and within the institution in a way which is dynamic and not static. This is a second aspect of freedom in this area and a first fact in the transformation of the powers of alienation into a means of freedom.

It is no use pretending, however, that this desire to introduce movement into an ossified institution can have as its goal the perfecting, improving, or streamlining of the institution. The more one tries to humanize an institution, the more one gives it ossifying force and the power to swallow up man. The more one humanizes it, the stronger it is. An administration which is elastic, agreeable, and comprehensive, and which does not bury itself in paper work, is much more dangerous, for it is not resented so much, nor does it arouse the same opposition, even though it does the same job and pursues the same aims.

A free Christian cannot do anything in this sphere except try to show how stupid the machine is. To the degree that the modern politico-administrative institution, whether in capitalist or socialist countries, is in fact ridiculous to man, it can be for the man who is liberated in Christ no more than the object of a sabotage which is designed to make this absurdity increasingly clear and obvious.

For example, during the past decades attempts have been made to find a grading system in schools and colleges which is adequate and reasonable. But all the time this system has been becoming more complex and impossible until we have reached the point of madness. The only

---

totalitarian in our society but what is most fragile, liberal, and tolerable, namely, the university. In so doing it offers a poor illustration of Lenin's rule that we should attack at the weakest point, for it is not perceived that destruction of the university fails to attack the system as a whole, which can reconstruct and strengthen the university, making it into a functional organization. Secondly, instead of opening the door to freedom, leftists (apart from anarchists) act in the name of a doctrinaire theory which will lead to the establishment of a worse dictatorship and a new orthodoxy.

sensible thing is not to attempt reforms, which have already failed, but to sabotage the present order by suspension. Since grading stands in so slight a relation to anything real or humanly reasonable, sabotage is the only serious starting-point, since it will make the construction of a sane institution necessary. To this end, however, we need professors who do not believe in their sacerdotal character as examiners, nor in the value of the diplomas which are their justification, but who are free men.

If it is true, however, that there can be no question of an institutional transformation which can give true freedom and not merely a little more justice, if there are factual as well as spiritual reasons for this, if the transition from the institution (a factor in alienation) to freedom cannot be brought about by institutional change, then this transition can be effected only by a series of individual acts on the part of free men. We say individual and not individualistic, presupposing that each individual will be moved by the same concern for the same obedience to the same Lord.

This is what we are told in scripture. In this regard we may refer again to the well-known problem of slavery in the Gospels and Epistles. Everyone knows that neither Jesus nor the apostles thought they could solve the problem of slavery as a social problem. They did not revolt against the practice. They did not contend for the dignity of the human person. In other words, they did not attempt institutional transformation. The first Christians were content to adopt an individual relation to slaves which changed the situation from within. This is what finally brought about, after many centuries, the abolition of slavery.[77]

Now the clear directions given in the biblical texts were once taken to mean—rightly in my view—that Christians should not get mixed up in institutional reforms. What should be revolutionary, and what should bring about a change in institutions, is the individual behavior of Christians within them. Under the pressure of social Christianity, however, it has increasingly become the fashion to accord far greater importance to the global changing of institutions. This culminates in the modern attitude of churches, especially in the Ecumenical Movement.

To blunt the force of the embarrassing biblical references to slavery, it is argued that they must be put in their proper setting. The age when Paul and others were writing was not concerned at all about social change. The abolition of slavery could not be envisaged. No one even thought of it. Slavery was regarded as an institution backed by natural law. Even modifying this type of institution was never considered. Thus the apostles were content to follow the collective current and adopt the common ideas of the

---

77 I still accept this interpretation in spite of the thesis of Marxist historians that slavery disappeared for economic reasons. In fact this economic explanation is pure imagination. The imperial legislation which successively abolished slavery was wholly a product of the influence of the church, and economic development did not contribute at all to the change.

age. There is nothing distinctively Christian in the passages at issue. They simply present average views about the institution. In terms of the dignity which they perceived in man, however, they tried to show both masters and slaves how they ought to act individually within the institution. By way of appendix it is also noted that the number of Christians was so small at this time that it would have been ridiculous to propose institutional reform to a vast organism like the Roman Empire. This would have been sheer arrogance. If, however, the apostles had lived in our own time they would have seen matters differently. Hence their directions are not normative.

These arguments, which are generally accepted today, are totally unconvincing in my view. Like similar arguments about the state and political participation, they rest on a misreading of history. It is not at all true that slavery did not pose a social, philosophical, and legal problem in the apostolic age. The question had been raised much earlier in philosophy. We are all familiar with the weak arguments that Aristotle finally used to justify the institution. We are also familiar with the Stoic position and with the way in which Cicero in Rome echoed Stoic teaching in the legal sphere. Slaves had attempted revolts. There was a tendency to recognize both the human and the legal personality of the slave. If natural law was invoked to support the institution of slavery, this was precisely because there were so many criticisms of slavery and so many challenges both to the trade in men and to the status of the slave. Indeed, the age of the apostles was the very time when the legal status of slaves was beginning to be modified and increasingly liberal legislation was beginning to grant them more extensive rights. A movement towards abolition had started even though it was not clear how this would be attained. The issue was a live one. But still the early Christians stayed out of the matter.

The generalization that the spirit of the age was against reform on a global scale takes no account at all of the movements of global social reform which had been agitating Rome for the past two centuries. In the areas of property, the distribution of wealth, the social hierarchy, and the family, there had been widespread debate (if not the desired political conflict) which culminated in the legislative achievements of Augustus, under whom the socio-economic structures of Rome were profoundly modified.

Since the whole empire was informed about this, and the provinces, especially in the east, played an active part on the one side or the other, it is completely impossible that the apostles should have remained in total ignorance of what was going on. On the contrary, the attitude they adopt is in my view highly significant. They are seeking to tell us that true change will not come about through legal, institutional, and global transformation. They do not take sides because they are not persuaded that this is the right course. They tackle the immediate, concrete problem, i.e., that of the actual relation between master and slave in the situation in which they are.

This is where the profound change which is the product of faith should manifest and express itself in direct fashion.[78]

The argument that Christians were at first so weak numerically that it would have been ridiculous for them to try to promote radical institutional reform has in it an element of truth. The apostles limited themselves to what was possible. Three points may be made in this regard. First, the question of the possible should always be raised in matters of this kind. Secondly, numerical weakness would not have mattered politically if it was simply a matter of supporting the position already taken by a political leader and strengthening his party. Thirdly, the secularization of society tends slowly to put us in a situation comparable to that of the primitive Christians; we are becoming a small and disregarded minority which is arrogant to think that it can be an autonomous pressure group in this secularized society.

Thus the teaching of the epistles is far more applicable to us than it was at the time when the church was a politico-social force in Christendom. This teaching ascribes two characteristics to Christian behavior when it is confronted with a social institution of global dimensions like slavery.

First, Christian behavior in this situation is individual. The problem is tackled on the level of reality, not ideology. No transformation of the social structures is expected but the transformation of man himself. The importance of the social problem is played down, not to diminish the Christian's responsibility, but to enhance it. This is essential, In reality man is much less committed personally when he subscribes to a party and works for the general transformation of society over one or two centuries than he is when he gets to grips personally and directly with the difficulties of social problems that he personally has to resolve.

When the texts tell us that there is neither slave nor free, this is not a way of getting slaves to accept their situation nor a way of justifying that

---

78 Although the (classical) inferences that I draw from the Epistle to Philemon are obviously not to the taste of L. Simon, I am obliged to state that they find indirect confirmation in Simon's admirable commentary on this epistle (*Semeur*, 1965). I refer to the way in which he brings out the individual relations between Paul, Onesimus, and Philemon—relations in which the true community of the church is instituted by the miracle of the Spirit. In this community, although institutionally Philemon is still master and Onesimus slave, Simon shows how the roles are reversed. If Onesimus is a debtor, Paul stands security for him and ultimately Philemon is Paul's debtor. If Onesimus is a slave, Paul calls Philemon his servant and he himself is the slave of Christ. Thus Paul is a slave and Philemon is the servant of a slave. If Paul is an apostle, Onesimus is the one who now becomes the apostle. This is how the communion of faith is set up. Each is "fellow-man" (Simon) to the other. Each assumes the past of the other and is set up as the hope and promise of the other. Our only regret is that this fine exposition is spoiled at the very outset by historical mistakes about runaway slaves. But this only shows to what extent theologians disregard the reality of the historical, social, and legal setting in which the works of the Bible were written.

of their masters. If it were, how could faith in Christ have grown precisely among slaves? The point is that the distinction must be transcended and outmoded by communion in Christ. The one important thing is that Christ is all in all. Everything else is secondary.

On this basis there can indeed be a social transformation. It will not come about, however, by a collective movement or a politico-juridical decision. It will come from below by the accumulation of a vast number of individual decisions. For it is at this level alone that one sees "Christ in us" at work. A genuine transformation of the human condition is not to be expected from government action.

What we have always to remember is that according to the gospel movement among men is from below upward and never from above downward. The weakest is the one who testifies, the servant is the one who obeys. The wise man is not chosen as a witness nor is it the master who affirms his authority. Similarly, social transformation comes from the bottom, not the top.

Furthermore, it seems to me that what is possible and specific is action in the spiritual and intellectual sphere. The constant mistake of Christians is that of trying to express their freedom in material and even institutional action. The revolution which they have in view is structural. They thus render themselves ineffectual. They get caught in the socio-historical mechanism of all institutional transformation. They point evolution or revolution in the worst possible direction, that of hopeless but violent coercion and conflict.

What is possible, and what I would describe as the singular task of Christians, is the attempt to transform the ideological and intellectual milieu, for this later permits institutional action and makes it effective. If there is not this prior conversion—I say prior, not concomitant, nor, as certain leftists would have it, subsequent; after all, did not Marx himself begin with ideological action!—then no change in structure, however revolutionary, can bring about any serious modification. Exploitation will still be exploitation unless there is a change of spirit; it will simply be something that other people do! Similarly, dictatorship will remain dictatorship. The fight against imperialist structures is meaningless if it is not a fight against the spirit of imperialism, which implies indictment not merely of American imperialism, but of every other kind—Russian, Chinese, Israelite, or North Vietnamese. As regards this task of bringing about intellectual and ideological change, Christians are in an excellent position, but unfortunately they prefer to "act," i.e., to do nothing effective at all.

Secondly, the behavior demanded will be profoundly revolutionary. It will lie outside the norms accepted by society and the establishment. Because Christian conduct is revolutionary in this way, something has already changed.

We have tried to analyze above the way in which this conduct is different both in basis and expression. We are still referring to problems like money, family, and property. In this type of conduct, and this type alone, there is freedom.

To make the family serve the freedom of each of its members, the relations prescribed by society need to be reversed. The father should live out patience, service, hope, and intimacy, while the child should live out authority, initiative, aloofness, and scrutiny.

To make money serve freedom, normal social relations must be similarly reversed. The wealthy person should not economize, should not be niggardly, should not be worried about the future, but should spend lavishly, while the poor person should not focus his life on acquiring money. How hard it is to reduce the importance of money in all situations, but if success is achieved at the individual level, what enormous social implications it has!

An objection arises here. We began by rejecting individual choice and decision, i.e., an individualistic affirmation of freedom. But have we not come back precisely to this orientation? Now undoubtedly in this civilization and epoch we do have to reaffirm the primacy of the individual vocation and say again that nothing can be done without the prior attestation of freedom by the individual. What we were rejecting earlier was the individual decision which is regarded as a direct expression of freedom, emanating from it, representing it, and formulating itself in terms of it. What we were rejecting was the individual decision which is no more than this, which is satisfied with the discovery of an individual means of being free, which does not go beyond this, which does not throw down any challenge to structures and institutions. What we were rejecting was finally the individual decision which proclaims its possibility as an affirmation of freedom.

This possibility we cannot accept. When the individual choice which presents itself as free is proclaimed to be possible we are in the presence of falsehood. Only when we have recognized the fundamental impossibility of this freedom, of being an individual, of making an autonomous choice, are we given the chance to offer an attestation of freedom if, in spite of everything, we take the risk of fighting the establishment. This comes, however, only in confrontation with the full power of institutional necessity.

We cannot deny institutions or think we can destroy them. This is an illusion if they are strong, like those of society, and it is vain if they are weak. What we have to do is to come to a meaningful and significant decision, within the social context, to engage effectively in de-institutionalizing and to oppose the endless growth of institutions. In other words, an attempt must be made to reorganize the group in which we find ourselves so that it is no longer controlled by the necessity of growth. Direct opposition to institutions is both impossible and useless. The base of the movement must be attacked, i.e., the meaninglessness which is inherent in its structures.

In reality, as institutions in our society become stricter and tighter, they also become weaker at the psychological level. They can function only if they have the allegiance of the heart of man. This is why the true issue in contemporary society is the attempt to achieve intellectual integration, or to win the allegiance of the heart, by psychological means, e.g., propaganda, publicity, television, entertainment, human and public relations, ideology, management participation, recycling, modern pedagogy, systematic acculturation, and the like. This is where the true battle of social freedom is being fought. Revolutions, acts of decolonization, and racial explosions are side issues compared to this.

The decisive question is whether society will succeed, and man will be definitively alienated, no matter under what form of government, for the greater the psychological integration the more socialist and liberal a regime will be, or whether man will retain his intellectual autonomy, so that there comes about an institutional regression, an imbalance, and a lessening of efficiency.[79]

Now Christians seem to be in a very favorable position in relation to this issue. On the one side they can resist psychological integration because their "psyche" belongs to another Lord. Hence they have to be aware of the problem and on the watch at this point. On the other side they also have the means to resist integration on behalf of others. For this fight does not demand such extraordinary means as power and money. A few can do it, and all they need is the word. Hence Christians should not let themselves be diverted into the more spectacular political operations (e.g., concerning race or the economic system) which our society is able to use as traps to head off more serious attacks.

The problem of alienation needs to be tackled at the point where it arises today. Thus far we have always spoken of the alienation caused by these institutions. Now if we take the commandment of God seriously, we have to recognize their validity. If, however, we look at the modern situation, we see that they are called in question in such a way that practically nothing is left. How, then, is freedom to find expression?

In the area of the family, it will not come to expression in the desire to achieve independence from a despotic father. On the contrary, it will be expressed in a desire to uphold the family as the authentic center of education and the raising of children, an authentic setting for personal relations, and an authentic background for the positive meeting of two or three ages and generations. Freedom today is wanting the family.

Similarly, freedom is wanting to achieve a sex life which is designed for joy but which will shun exaltation and deification no less than naturalization and biologization. It is a recovery of the mystery of sex, which ought to be a sign and reflection of the creative work of God and the union between God and man, as scripture shows us in many places.

---

79 For details cf. my work *L'illusion politique* (*The Political Illusion*).

Similarly, freedom is so acting in the sphere of work that this becomes a setting for human encounter. It is not dedication to work, not making it an end in itself. Nor is it rejection of work nor doing it grudgingly. It is not the division of life into two spheres, the sphere which is sacrificed to work and the sphere of leisure in which a man can finally be himself. No, work is the place of meeting, even though it can no longer be the place of that which is done in common. I can always make it this place of meeting. Here again ideologies are to be shunned on the one side and futile revolts on the other.

At this level, then, we can see that living out freedom in these situations always consists in rejecting the false independence that society gives us in these fields and that we all want to profit by, whether it be in leisure, extravagance, demythicized sex, or the broken family. This independence typifies the absence of freedom today.

This does not mean, of course, that we are tied to the past. If private property is really being squeezed out, we need not mourn except that it represents a means of independence and protection for those who had it, and from the personal point of view we have to admit that Proudhon was nearer the truth on this issue than Marx. Nevertheless, let private property go so long as something equally good will ensure the protection and living-space of the individual with the same firmness and at the same personal level. So far I cannot see what this might be. Laws are little help and social security seems to be no more than the means of new bondage.

Again, it is easy to attack the family. But quite apart from its status as a divine ordinance, psychologists, psychiatrists, and psychoanalysts are now telling us increasingly that it is an irreplaceable setting for the child. Modern psychiatrists of all schools argue that the child has a basic need for an identity image which has to be close at hand and desirable, and which only the father can provide. Again, the child has no less vital need of the love and presence of its mother. Recent studies tend to show that the best material care is inadequate and that manifestations of love by a third person, an attendant or nurse, cannot play the same role. Parents are irreplaceable. It is hard to explain this, but the fact remains. Much juvenile delinquency today undoubtedly is the fault of the parents—this is a truism—but not just in the generally understood sense. What is to blame is not a weakness of the parents, nor a poor method of upbringing, but quite simply the mediocrity of the personality of the father and the failure of the mother to be present with the young child. Now I repeat that these are not the findings of "reactionary" psychiatrists alone, but of a large consensus. We need the courage to question the wisdom of mothers going out to work and of fathers working too long hours. A choice seems to be demanded between too much work on the the one side and the upbringing of the child on the other. Combining the two seems to be impossible.

Obviously what we have said thus far applies equally and with no distinction to both man and woman. Both are summoned to this freedom in Christ which is to be lived out in similar fashion. "There is neither male nor female" (Galatians 3:28). In this way, and in this way alone, does equality between the two exist. There is equality because both are equally liberated by Christ. This liberation is what gives an equality which naturally is not to be translated into an identity of functions.

As we noted earlier, it is childish to think that woman is equal to man only if she has total sexual freedom and a job which enables her to earn her own living. Only a futile psycho-sociological analysis can achieve this result, the more so as its credibility is contradicted by other psycho-sociological analyses which are no less serious. The diversity of social roles and functions, e.g., the fact that the wife has a larger responsibility for the upbringing of children, can be a ground of inequality only on the basis of certain ideologies and beliefs, e.g., those which regard productive economic work as the only type that counts, which attribute mental problems to sexual repression, or which think that sexual anonymity is an aid to personality development. These erroneous ideas, which are often found in the thinking of Christians, are the only basis of the claim for equality when this is viewed as an equality of functions. Apart from this type of equality, there is also the equality of dignity and worth which should undoubtedly be upheld and defended by Christians but which finds its true meaning, basis, and fulness only in freedom in Christ.

Perhaps after all the family is not an outdated structure belonging only to the medieval period and the age of the middle class. What I have been trying to show by this and other examples is that freedom certainly presupposes voluntary use, yet that it is not necessarily the destruction of limits but may be the constitution of a setting, and finally that it operates at two levels, namely, that of the object under consideration, e.g., marriage or money, and then that of global society, i.e., the place which society assigns to this particular object. We have to relate to the object from the standpoint of its upholding, its limitation, and its transformation in terms of what global society makes of it, but always in such a way that we approximate the use for which it is divinely appointed in the heavenly Jerusalem, and also in such a way that we all find herein the means of living out the commandment of God in a human setting.

We have thus tried to pose afresh certain classical questions and to find out on what basis and in what way freedom can find expression in this world of money, work, and the family. We must now take up the problem from another angle and attempt to single out pseudo-factors of liberation and erroneous theological constructions. We shall take only two examples.

## § 6. Freedom, the Pill and Sex[80]

Invention of the pill has provoked innumerable discussions, and I shall not examine here the question whether or not, in using it, a woman

---

80  For literature cf. the bibliography in *Amour et sexualité* (1968), and especially Dr.

disobeys the commandment about procreation. I will simply deal with the problem of freedom in this area, for this, after all, is the central issue here.

Our first point is that the argument from nature cannot be used successfully against the pill. To condemn the pill because it means circumvention of the natural connection between procreation and sex is to repudiate all that man has been doing from his early origins, for man has been engaged in a constant struggle for independence from nature. It is in fact to deny the distinctiveness of man. Man is not an animal precisely because he does not accept the natural conditions in which he is set. He has mastered nature and by this very fact disobeyed it. This involves dangers. We see all around us the incredible perils in which we are placed by technological advance. But dangers or not, this is man's history. There are no natural limits to his activity. He has constantly transcended the limits.

Hence we have either to reject all that man has done from his first beginnings or we have to accept the pill, which is simply another step on the same path. The only problem is whether this step is a step of freedom.

The arguments of those who think that the pill brings freedom are as follows. It frees woman from bondage to repeated pregnancies. It also establishes equality in sex life between the man, for whom sex carries no serious consequences, and the woman. Again, a married couple can now choose whether or not to have children. Procreation is no longer an accident but a choice. Hence it is an expression of freedom. The children born are also wanted children and therefore loved children. They are not unplanned children who are rejected from the very outset and regarded as a burden. They are children of love and desire in the positive sense, not desire as sheer lust or love as illicit love. They are loved from the outset. They have been chosen to express the culmination of love between the man and the woman. Finally, thanks to dissociation of the sex act and procreation, the sex life on both sides can be fully developed, freely chosen, and organized without constraint, so that there can be a full flowering of the personality too.

This is the paradisal account of the pill which many Christians present. It would be accurate if only we were still in Eden and if only we were still free, genuinely free, and could use the instruments we have with justice, truth, and love. But dreaming is futile.

It is true, no doubt, that for a good, sane, and right-minded couple the pill offers the possibility of having children who are chosen and loved, although one might well ask whether such a couple would not be capable of loving children who are not desired or planned. The problem is: How many couples of this kind are there?

We know very well that for many couples today any child is a hindrance since it forces duties and responsibilities on them. It is not the number of children that matters. Even one child is one too many. Not to

Lagroua-Weill-Hallé, *La contraception et les français* (1967) and *Contraception orale ou locale* (1962), and Lucien Neuwirth, *Le dossier de la pilule* (1967).

have children at all is the only guarantee against restriction. What the pill brings to expression is egoism pure and simple—self-centeredness. In far too many cases the pill does not grant couples the choice of freedom to act. It puts them in a situation in which they can finally cast off that which would hamper, not their freedom, but their selfishness. The pill is not a triumph of freedom. It is a triumph of egoism.

If only this were a noble egoism! What triumphs in the systematic refusal to have children, however, is an extremely narrow and mediocre view of life.

The position is much the same in relation to the sex life. If the pill were an instrument used by a wise and free man to establish a balanced and harmonious sex life, this would be excellent. But where is this wise and free man? In reality the only thing that counts for many people is that sex can be indulged in without risk. What is called a fully developed sex life is an excessive, obsessional, and frantic sex life. This has nothing whatever to do with freedom. The girl risks nothing and the man has no moral responsibility. Naturally, I am not saying that pregnancy was a sanction. But it was at least an obstacle in the way of a devastating instinct.

The only positive gain here is that of equality. The woman can now give rein to her sexuality with the same grossness and banality as man has traditionally done.

Nevertheless, it is argued, she can choose to have children or not. She can choose when she wants them. She can plan them. This being so, we are told, the couple is placed in an ethical situation. Moral responsibility is increased by this situation of pure choice. The act carries no necessary consequences and therefore we have a higher situation of pure freedom. The freedom of man is enhanced.

Now it seems to me that there are two errors in this analysis. First, man's responsibility is not increased in the slightest. He can merely act without his acts having any consequences, without having anything to fear. If the police and the law-courts were abolished, do we really think that this would increase the responsibility of someone who is planning an assassination? Nor is freedom hereby enhanced. The only thing is that man is given greater autonomy.

I will restrict my analysis to these arguments, for I can accept much that is said from a sociological standpoint. The number of abortions can be reduced in this way. Above all, there is a relaxation of morality, an exaltation of sex. As society becomes increasingly narrow, rigorous, and regulated, man needs an outlet, and he finds it in a wild sex life, real or imaginary. Everyone is sleeping with everyone else. If in some places the divorce rate is decreasing, this is simply because adultery is now a way of life for many couples, and sexual ambivalence tends to be admitted more and more.

We cannot say, however, that this is an augmentation of freedom. We simply have here compensatory phenomena which are easily explained from a psycho-sociological standpoint. These attitudes are fully and totally controlled by circumstances.

If in these circumstances, in order to make pansexualism easier, contraceptives and the pill are used, this is normal enough. But the thinking which produces it is based only on a desire to enjoy every possible sex experience without risk. The other motives adduced by doctors and theologians count for little beside the circumstances, the sociological trend, and the sexual appetite. In the vast array of arguments advanced, scientific and theological arguments are only the icing on the cake, although there are few who have to courage to admit that what we have here is 99 percent sexual desire and social conformity.

I am prepared to accept the element of social conformity. If it is said that in the actual state of modern society we are forced to authorize contraceptives, there is no disputing this. I also accept the sociological argument that we must try to check the inordinate growth of population, especially in the third world. This, too, is a real factor in the situation.

What I cannot accept is that this should be called freedom. What I cannot accept is that it should be called an increase in responsibility. What I cannot accept is that it should be grounded in the will of God, i.e., his will that man should be master of himself. What I cannot accept is that morality and religion should be dragged in.

Here again philosophers, theologians, and Christians are guilty of falsehood. Their arguments rest on the tacit presupposition that man is still as he was when he came from the hands of God, intrinsically free and good and able to use his autonomy aright. To want to be autonomous, however, is precisely the sin which Adam committed.

An appeal might be made to a deeper spiritual motivation which gives man an attitude of responsibility and thus permits him to use contraceptives in true responsibility and freedom. My reply is that to achieve birth control and good spacing for the mother and family there is no need for contraceptives in the case of those who are well developed spiritually. There is still continence. Those who are not capable of this genuinely free and responsible attitude will obey their instincts and drives, whether it be in the form of a woman having a child every year or in that of young people engaging in collective sex. In such cases the use of contraceptives will not make them responsible. It will simply compress them within obedience to the sexual instinct, absence of self-control, and the sociological trend. This is all.

It is a mistake to think that a device can augment the possibilities of choice. If there is no self-control to begin with, it will not come through possession of a device. Nor can world control be established in this way. What determines an authentic situation of choice is the way one comports oneself and not the date or number of births. From an ethical standpoint contraceptives evade true decision and responsibility, i.e., the decision and responsibility which relate to the control of instincts, passions, and impulses. Contraceptives substitute sociological determinism for biological determinism. In the strict sense they bring neither responsibility nor freedom.

That Christians, being free, can use them aright I do not dispute. But they should realize that in so doing they are falling behind rather than making headway in personal freedom and fulfilment.

I realize that to talk of continence and chastity today sounds childish and old-fashioned. It is as though we had never heard of Freud. The first objection is based on contemporary values and is of no importance. The second seems to me to leave out an important aspect which comes from Freud too, namely, that of sublimation.

Up to our own time man had to exert some control over his own instinct if he really loved his wife, if he loved her enough not to impose successive pregnancies on her, if he was ready to make some sacrifices because of this total love which he had for his wife as a person. Similarly the wife had to make herself loved as a person if she was to avoid the burden of constant childbearing, just as the man had to restrict his impulses because of this love. Without this his relation was simply to an object who counted for little more than a prostitute. It was a relation of purely sensual pleasure.

The pill has given new impetus to this relation. The woman can be a mere object of pleasure and the man no longer needs to love her in the true sense, since he no longer needs to exercise self-control. Necessarily, then, sex relations between husband and wife take on the same character as those with a prostitute. Ironically, however, the unlimited and uncontrolled multiplying of the sex act is in many circles confused with a full development of the sex life.

In other words, arguments to the effect that the pill is a contribution to freedom rest on the presupposition that the natural man is truly free. They confuse freedom with autonomy and independence. These, we know, are related to the thirst for power and domination, to the desire for aggrandizement, to incoherence of personality. They are the very reverse of freedom.

We thus need to turn the question around and ask if the pill does not in fact lead to situations of enslavement.[81] This will mean considering as far as possible all the complex implications and not just the liberation of women from constant childbearing. Thus it had been hoped that thanks to

---

81 I readily endorse the judicious remarks of my friend Maillot ("La déesse pilule," *Réforme*, August, 1968), especially when he stresses two important aspects of the problem. The first is the growing obsession with the pill. The insomniac, he says, is less tied to his barbiturate, or the diabetic to his insulin, than the couple to the pill. The former are sick. Are not the latter sick too? Does not the pill produce in them a psychology of sickness? Does it not end up by treating the normal woman as sick? The second point he emphasizes is that it is a mistake to think that a pill can make us mature and responsible. To rely on a pill for achieving responsibility is an illusion. The new

the pill men might find full sexual satisfaction with their wives or mistresses and that this would diminish prostitution. It has not worked out this way. The number of professional prostitutes, so far as this can be ascertained, has remained stable. Moreover, thanks to the pill, occasional prostitution has increased. Much younger girls, often from affluent homes, so that they do not know the miseries of prostitution but simply want easy pocket money or luxury articles, are now engaged in it. Can we really say that this is an increase in freedom or even independence? In fact girls are entering on a path of enslavement much more than when they were restrained by fear of pregnancy.

Naturally we run up against the argument: Well, if that is what they want. . . . But the problem is always the same. The moment quickly comes when it is no longer what they want, and yet they cannot escape from it. "What they want" is in fact the worst possible expression of liberalism; it allows the strong to oppress the weak.

Another point is that the pill makes possible a multiplication of sexual relations with different partners. Now this diversity of partners, hand in hand with the theory of eroticism and a distinction between total love and sexuality, rapidly produces on the one side lassitude and indifference, so that the sex act becomes no more than the satisfaction of a biological need like going to the toilet, while on the other side all sense of the profound relation of love is lost. This is the unhappy experience of young girls who take the path of prostitution. Very quickly sex comes to have no true meaning any more.

Now we have observed earlier the indissoluble relation between love

---

maternity is just as irresponsible as the old. This is why it feels a need to drag in a fine word like responsibility in self-justification.

The great merit of Maillot is that he has shown us to what extent the pill neither expresses freedom nor engenders it.

In contrast I find no cogency at all in the arguments of Dumas and de Pury. When they say that biologically a woman can have fifteen children over thirty years of fecundity, and that we cannot possibly allow this, I agree. When they argue that there has always been some form of birth control, I agree again. When they go on to say that the absolute principle of *laissez-faire* cannot be asserted here, whether we are leaving it to God or to nature, this is self-evident. All that I ask is that propositions from Christian ethics and theology should not be dragged in. Let us simply recognize that in this area Christians are obeying necessity like everyone else. There is no need for the terrible claptrap about women becoming real persons because they have fewer children. This is in such total contradiction with all that traditional civilization has taught us about women that only the profoundest historical ignorance or the most dogmatic party spirit can believe that up to now woman has never been anything more than an object.

I am not arguing for woman in the home or woman as the mother of a large family. My only desire is that honest arguments should be used. Thus it is said that to ask for continence is to demand the kind of heroism that the Christian life does not exhibit. It is heroism, of course, if the abstinence is forced and strained and legalistic. But it is freedom if it is an attitude deriving from faith and obedience. In default of this freedom in relation to sex, I have no objection at all to the use of contraceptives. But we need to realize that this is a striking sign of our lack of freedom.

and freedom. If there is no bond of love with a person, it is a serious error to think that one is free. Freedom is not the equivalent of drifting or of following one's instincts. But the constant changing of partners is nothing more than drifting. The only level of freedom here is that of a young child wanting to touch everything. Modern theories of eroticism remind me irresistibly of a relapse into infancy. There is no freedom in this explosion of sexual activity. There is only waste and dispersion in an indifference made up of satiety, meaninglessness, and glorification. The situation of indifference, however, is not that of freedom.

Finally, among the secondary effects of the pill which work against true freedom we may mention the increase in venereal disease. Some twenty years ago there were hopes that this scourge was being brought under control. Today there has been a frightening upsurge of venereal disease and its forms seem to be much more serious, while the remedies are progressively losing their effectiveness. Furthermore, the disease is most rampant among the young and is rapidly spreading to all spheres of life, being no longer restricted to those who make use of prostitutes. Another significant fact is that the increase has been most pronounced in places where the "freedom" of sexual morals is greatest. By far the biggest increase has taken place in Scandinavia and the United States. Thus between 1950 and 1970 we find a 35 percent growth of gonorrhea in Sweden and Norway, 100 percent in Denmark, and 50 percent in the United States. Naturally I am not saying that the pill causes genital weakness in women and thus predisposes them to venereal disease. This is suggested by some scientists but opposed by others. What I am saying is that the growth is connected with the multiplication of sex relations with different partners and with no restraint. The pill is what makes this sexual "freedom" possible. We are not speaking here in terms of principle; we are simply facing the facts.

Is it not obvious, however, that venereal disease, which is increasingly difficult to cure or check, entails a frightful loss of freedom? The lesson is that, if we want to evaluate the social effect of a phenomenon like the pill, an attempt must be made to cover all its aspects.

We now turn to another point. Is it true that unlimited and unmastered sex, which is not subject to any moral, personal, or volitional control, nor to any social control by ritualization and the weight of public opinion, is authentic freedom? We have just considered some consequences which bear witness to a deprivation of freedom But what about the heart and center of the thing? Basically, we have here a confusion between freedom and glandular secretion.

Can I say that I am free because chemical imbalance makes me feel hungry and I want to eat? This is no more than obedience to a physiological function. Freedom does not enter into it. I realize that the argument will be advanced that not satisfying glandular needs is repression. We are not free, it is said, if we can find no food or if we cannot have a sex relation when we feel like it. This is true in its own way. All that I am saying, however, is that strictly freedom is not the issue here. A choice has to be made between the social repression of instinct and brute obedience to physiological phenomena.[82] Nor does the intellectual embellishment of eroticism confer freedom in any form on this submission to chemistry; it is simply a decorative justification. In neither case is there any real freedom.

It might be said that thanks to the pill one may choose to follow sexual instincts or not. One is free to master them. One is truly free since there is no longer any fear of pregnancy. My reply is that there is equal freedom to apply social constraint to oneself so that repression comes from within. This is at least an equivalent freedom. Furthermore, we know only too well what man is. He never chooses pure control of himself or his acts or thoughts unless he runs up against some force or obstacle which helps him to solidify his will. Left alone with the choice of aberrant sex or self-control, he will always choose the former, since at the first stage it is the easier, the less demanding, and the more pleasant. To make the harder and stricter choice man needs to be led more or less by some constraint, or at least his will needs to be aided by something external.

But why in any case choose what is more difficult and demanding? Surely this corresponds to a dubious morality of will and effort. Two things may be said in answer. First, what has made man what he is from the very beginning is a refusal to let things be, to be an animal organism subject to the objective conditions of nature, to be the reflection of an ecological system. But this is what he would be doing if he accepted the easier and less demanding situation. One may say that the continuation of human history depends on the choice of what is more difficult. To reject this in favor of the line of least resistance is not freedom (over against repression) but the loss of what has hitherto constituted man.

Secondly, we may obviously refer to sublimation. This is an accepted and interiorized restraint which brings about an orientation of the person to a higher response to sexual need. I do not have to expand on this, for the theory of sublimation is well known. Without this sublimation, however, nothing that man has invented would exist at all. Now it is in sublimation that man reveals himself to be free, not in direct subjection to sexual need. Confusion in this sphere, as in all others,[83] is the way of enslavement and the point of man's greatest weakness and vulnerability.

We will not pursue this point here, however, but simply insist on the fact that when an easier way opens up for the non-Christian in a society which, like our own, is made for ease and comfort, then he will rush on to it with neither mastery nor control. I am not saying that difficulty as such is virtue. I am simply saying that virtue is not indulgence, flabbiness, and mediocrity.

---

82  Cf. the interesting study by the psychoanalyst André Stephane, "La liberté sexuelle pourquoi faire?" *Contrepoint* (1971).
83  Propaganda deliberately exploits this kind of confusion; cf. my *Propagandes*, c. III.

To carry the discussion of contraceptives further, some comparisons are necessary. For example, are stimulants legitimate and acceptable in sport? Christians should not say that the situation here is different. Basically it is the same. The only difference that can be observed is numerical. Contraceptives concern many Christians but few are athletes. Outside the church, however, there may be in many countries as many athletes as there are Christians, so that the matter is not without interest.

To allow stimulants is to regard records as ends in themselves. Ideological arguments can be found for this view. Man can achieve a higher degree of excellence and self-realization. He can enhance his resources. This is the same kind of false reasoning as we find in respect of freedom and contraceptives. For personal resources, or virtue, there is substituted a chemical or mechanical means which permits of a superior result without the least participation by man in the totality of his being. This is then called being more responsible, being freer, and developing human potential to a higher degree.

A Christian, however, should begin by conceding that the rule of winning at all costs, and the principle of the intrinsic value of records, cannot be accepted. He must protest that the sporting contest is a personal one. It is thus incompatible with the substitution of an external means for the person so that the latter is transformed into a mere muscular machine.

Drugs offer another example. Dr. M. Masure, quoting Dr. Blewitt, [84] tells us that the new drugs are the most powerful instruments ever dreamed up by man for his own amelioration. They enable us to solve many problems. They can change enemies into friends and make neurotics into normal functioning persons. They open up for man an exciting prospect. Even control of the atom is secondary compared to the discovery of scientific means to enable us to act on the tool on which all others depend, namely, the human brain. Thanks to these substances a state of beatitude can be attained which mystics knew only after lengthy meditation and strict asceticism. What sages aspired to is now reached quickly without any forfeiture of value. A few specialists support the use of these drugs on the ground that they make possible a transcendental experience, i.e., vision outside oneself.

According to Leary and Alpert what is at issue is the very principle of inner freedom. In this context, I shall not discuss the risk involved any more than I did in the case of the pill. This problem is no part of the argument from the standpoint of an ethics of freedom. On the basis stated, however, I am certain that we shall soon have a Christian movement for freedom in the use of drugs. I realize that for many Christians drugs are less important than contraceptives, first, because they do not have the same social aspect, then because mysticism is involved and this does not enjoy such a good press with Protestants. All the same, a drug which can do the

---

84   M. Masure in *L'Église Reformée vous parle* (February, 1967).

work of the Holy Spirit is by no means negligible. If one of its effects is to change enemies into friends, if it can bring in the reign of agape without effort, surely it cannot be ignored.

The same arguments recur. If drugs are used wisely, with moderation, and in clearly defined circumstances, then, it is said, they can be of remarkable value. They set man in a situation of choice or freedom, and this augments his inner liberty and extends his field of vision.

My reply is the same. The man who, in faith in Christ, is capable of prolonged asceticism may use a drug like L.S.D. if he pleases. But I doubt whether he will, since it will be for him a poor substitute, and he will realize that the beatitude which awaits us in the kingdom of heaven is not a goal to be attained by any or every means. It has no intrinsic value. What counts is Christ and communion with him, which no drug can ever give. As for non-Christians, drugs can only divert them from Christ. They are also an instrument of self-enslavement. Furthermore, they are an expression of their sense of the absurdity of life. Authorization will have to be sought for unbelievers, however, since the bondage into which they are plunged by drugs is all the more dangerous if it is illegal.

When Margaret Mead, an "expert" in ecumenical circles, offers us the usual platitudes about marriage and fidelity[85] under the cover of sociological necessity, we are given more or less exact notice of what is implied. The only thing at issue is obedience to necessity. A Christian cannot be asked to act any differently than anyone else. He has to be like other people. He has to come under the yoke of his culture. This is in every way, however, a formula for non-freedom. Obeying sex and deifying it are on the one hand man's absurd claim to be free and on the other hand the reality of his bondage.

In a society which is dominated by strict morality, by an authoritarian or religious class that lays down the moral rules, if one man takes the risk of affirming his sexual freedom, then, even though I cannot endorse his

---

85 In 1966, at the Conference on Church and Society, Mead, along with many others, proposed trial marriages so that couples might see if they were sexually compatible. She went much further in an interview in 1970, arguing that the biblical rules of fidelity and lasting marriages simply express the conditions of an age when people died young and marriages would last only a few years. When expectancy of life is seventy years, she said, it seems evident that husbands and wives cannot love one another that long and hence the duty of fidelity should not be imposed on them. Marriage should be for a short period, the average being five years, which is about as long as "love" lasts sociologically. Then separation should be normal. There ought not to be any crisis either for the spouses or for the children. The church should make a joyful ceremony of divorce so as to take away any guilt feelings from the couple. In all this Mead is simply following the sociological current. She shows a total lack of freedom and denies the possibility of a Christian life, since she does not accept the view that the intervention of Jesus Christ changes anything in sociological behavior. As to the role of the church in removing culpability, she is reducing it once again to the function of the opium of the people. Thus this "advanced" thought is in reality nothing of the kind. It is the very opposite of freedom and seems to give evidence only of an "advanced" state of putrefaction.

independence in relation to what is still the will of God until a proof to the contrary has been advanced, nevertheless he is making an authentic bid for freedom.

In a society like our own, however, the position is very different. Immorality now brings with it fame and money. Sexual freedom is complete. Art seems to rely on the deification of sex for self-expression. Eroticism is confused with thought. Those who protest against all this are ridiculed. Thus the proclamation of sexual freedom is now an expression of the strictest conformity. Man wants to affirm his freedom, but, in choosing this area for the purpose, he merely shows that he is a slave of his glands, whose effects he cannot control. He is a moralizing slave, since he seeks self-justification and wants the glory of art and freedom as well as satisfaction. He is a slave to the sociological current, which drags him into the practice of porno-eroticism by billboards, the theater, the cinema, and the whole background of life. This bondage does not differ in the least from bondage to the conventional morality of sex. This obedience is still passive obedience to the average behavior of the group. The liberated are still passively obedient.

In reality the sex explosion, and especially the deification of sex, are simply a compensatory mechanism for general powerlessness. Man thinks that he can free himself from this powerlessness by putting sex at the center of his personality and pretending to liberate his sex life. In so doing he unwittingly surrenders to what P. Chauchard has finely called the technocratic manipulations of sex, which are an important factor in its degradation. What he does not realize is that this technocratic manipulation provides the easiest way of handling man through propaganda. All propaganda (e.g., war propaganda) which has used the glorifying of sex as a point of contact has always been successful.

Chauchard recalls that what characterizes man is the mental control of sexual activity. This control can show itself in erotic invention. This is one of the themes in the publicizing of pornography; it will teach us to do what animals cannot do. In this area, however, one cannot speak of control in any authentic sense. We simply have the submission of intellectual curiosity to glandular impulsion and social mores. In other words, what ought to be the center of control becomes the servile instrument of uncontrolled impulse.

Hence it is not just at the level of Christian freedom that the so-called sex liberation shows itself to be simple bondage. At the level of the natural reality of man, too, erotic conduct denotes a degradation of what has hitherto constituted the distinctiveness of man. There is no greater denial of all freedom than the sex revolution and the exaltation and deification of sex.

Two general conclusions may be drawn. First, we are confronted once more by a common sociological phenomenon. Each time that man makes some gain in independence he brings about an inevitable compensatory enslavement. To see this, of course, we have to consider the global aspects of sociological phenomena and not just their individual or statistical manifestations. The meaning is not that every situation is the same but that there is no absolute progress. All progress is balanced by regress. In the area of independence we simply rob Peter to pay Paul.

This is not always evident or immediate. In revolutions, as we have seen, there is a point—that of the revolutionary explosion—when those who participate think that they have finally won freedom. Only later do the dictators come. Similarly, thanks to the pill, and at a very direct and elementary level, a girl who can now sleep with anyone she pleases without fear has an obvious sense of freedom. The repressions and losses come later. But the new bondage is not an exact reproduction of the old. The lack of freedom which follows the explosion of independence is not felt as such directly because it is not brought about by the same causes. A man needs time to see that he is not free. He has to make a fresh analysis of the situation.

The second general conclusion relates to the illusory character of the constantly recurring idea that man achieves freedom through material change. When a man is given an automobile he becomes free in respect of time and space. When a girl is given the pill she is freed from bondage to her femininity and sex partners become sexually free. The great dream is that by creating new material conditions man will finally be free without having to make any effort of will or pay any price, apart from the cost of the pills. Everything will come to him. He will finally be placed in conditions of freedom. Freedom will come from without.

The same idea is found again and again: Institutional change will bring human freedom. This was the liberal dream. It is the socialist dream. It is the basis of all the arguments in support of the pill.

We have to realize, however, that the institution never creates freedom. Economic, scientific, and material transformations do not confer it. Independence may certainly be achieved at individual points. But giving man independent choice in a given sphere through a change in organization has nothing whatever to do with genuine freedom. Freedom, as I have often said, arises only in a situation of compulsion and necessity. It is when there is necessity, and in opposition to it, that man finds freedom. To place man, through material change, in a situation of indifferent independence is in reality to increase his anguish, uncertainty, and sense of insignificance.

Thus we need to examine the relation between the sexual freedom which the pill has brought and the rate of suicide among adolescents. I am sure that a firm connection would be found. In other words, the pill alone does not create freedom. While giving a certain indifferent independence it creates new bondage. It does not set man in a situation in which he can genuinely choose and be free. By making sex so banal it leads to greater anguish and contributes to the collapse of personality.

Does this mean that we are against the pill? If we are, it is not on the grounds of traditional morality, nor in order to keep woman in subjection, nor because of an inviolable "nature." In my view the very question itself is now pointless. The pill is here whether we like it or not. If we lived in a society where there were a moral, spiritual, or even a political power so incontestable and uncontested that it could do away with anything regarded as bad, then the question whether we are for or against a thing might have some meaning. My arguments would then be aimed at persuading the authorities to do what I think to be right. But such a situation does not exist, even in the Soviet Union. The only possible example of it is China. Hence being for or against the pill makes no difference. Even if my arguments were absolutely superior and decisive, they would have no effect, for no power can challenge the dominion of fact, to which each of us must bow.

Since the pill is a fact, my answer must again rest on what is to almost everyone the scandalous distinction which I make between Christians and non-Christians. As regards the former I would say that if they know how to put on the freedom of Christ, if they know how to live out this freedom, if they can give proof of authentic freedom, then the pill is an excellent invention. For Christians of this kind it is a real call to responsibility. For they will now be faithful because they want to be. They will be good fathers and mothers because they want to be. They will maintain married unity in sexual harmony because they want to. They will strive for a new sublimation because they want to. They are no longer under a material constraint. The conditions are ideal for a full exercise of freedom. The possibility is provided for a new construction of personality, of life together, of recognition in the true sense. All that has been said about the positive aspects of the pill is true when those who are called upon to use it already have authentic freedom.

We have tried to show, however, that this freedom is achieved only in Christ, by the miraculous action of the cross and resurrection. We have also tried to show that it is conditional on the fact that those who are in Christ by faith want to live out this freedom—a condition which, as we have often noted, is seldom realized in fact.

For all those who do not have this freedom in Christ, or who do not live it out, the pill in real life, in terms of the brute fact of its spontaneous use, has effects which can be described only in negative terms. This means that education in its proper use is demanded. Simply to hand it over, even by medical prescription, for use as indicated on the label is in the main disastrous. Psychological and moral instructions are also needed. All young women need to be warned about the dangers which exist, not merely the possible biological dangers but more especially the psychological dangers, when they use the pill. Special education is required, which will, of course, be linked to sex education in general, but which will consist of much more than a physiological description of the mechanism. What is needed is true education in will and choice—advanced instruction which will ensure that the adolescent is not abandoned to the sway of impulse but can control and use correctly the technical instrument.

To use an automobile, we have to learn to drive it. To handle a racing car, we need advanced training. The pill is a far more formidable instrument than a car and one that is much more difficult to use except at the purely pharmaceutical level. A much more advanced course of instruction is imperative.

In other words, far stricter social acculturation and integration are required. No other conclusion is possible. Either the pill will lead to disasters or we must provide the type of education which will ensure that the pill is used properly. This means that we are entering the path of social conditioning, which will become more and more necessary as the technical instruments that are put at man's disposal in the supposed interests of freedom become increasingly powerful and entail increasingly radical consequences.

### §7. *Freedom and Vocation*

Even a cursory study of the Bible soon shows that it contains little that corresponds to our modern ideas of work and vocation. Terms are used which we have to translate by "vocation" or "the call of God," but the context makes it apparent that what is at issue is always a summons to the specific service of God. Thus a man is called to be a prophet or apostle. He is called to be a king, as David was. He is called to serve God by some exceptional act and without even realizing that he is doing it in God's service, e.g., the king of Syria, the king of Assyria, or Cyrus.

Work does not enter into the question apart from the work that Hiram contributed for the building of the temple. Work is a natural exercise of human activity which sets man in a relation to creation that is either positive, as in Eden, or negative, as after the break with God. In the latter case work is laborious and necessary to survival. Either way, however, it is not presented as the service of God. It has to be done, and the Bible is realistic enough not to overlay this necessity with superfluous spiritual ornamentation. Moreover, the Bible displays no essential interest in the situation of work. Work is the painful lot of all men but it is not particularly important.

It has often been pointed out that in the Old and New Testaments we are told very little about the way in which the judges, prophets, apostles, and disciples earned their living. Amos was a herdsman and Paul was a tentmaker, but these statements are exceptional and of no great significance in themselves. It might be argued that the reason for this is that culturally work had little place or importance in the Jewish and the Graeco-Roman world, though this is arguable, and that there was in any case little reference to it. Hence, it is claimed, work is not necessarily unimportant in the eyes of God. The indifference of the Bible in this regard is not, then, to be regarded as normative.

This argument lacks cogency. For if work were viewed as a divine vocation, the Bible would surely have accorded it an importance which it could not have culturally. Furthermore, one might ask why attempts have been made to find the idea of work as a vocation in the Bible now that work has taken on cultural importance.

We do in fact face an attempt to exalt work. This has become classical in Protestantism, if not from the sixteenth century as Weber thought, at least from the nineteenth century. A general ideology of work has been fashioned. Brunner contributes to this exaltation when he speaks of the cult of work as an agent of civilization.

What must be recalled is that work is a simple necessity. Those who are not prepared to work should not eat. It has no specific value. The Bible never speaks of it as a vocation. If not in the pure sense, at least in the form in which we know it, work is a result of the fall. It forms part of the divided, separated, and alienated condition of man. Work itself is an alienating factor, irrespective of social or economic conditions or of ideology.

In saying this, I am not saying that work is bad. What I am saying is that its value is purely utilitarian and that it is one of the necessities of life. We should simply accept it as such without exalting it and without confusing it with the call of God. How misleading it is to deduce from Genesis 1:28: "Replenish the earth, and subdue it," the idea that work is a divine vocation! We simply have to work—that is all.

Jesus never calls upon anyone to work. On the contrary, he constantly takes the men he calls away from their work, e.g., Peter, James, Levi, the man in the parable who wants to try out his oxen, and so forth. It is possible that Jesus himself worked, but this is by no means certain, and even if he did, it proves nothing. Like others he obeys the necessities of human life.

Finally it should be noted that the Old Testament makes a great deal of the sabbath. It is a sign of liberation. This shows that work is not after all so excellent or desirable a thing as people often tell us. Freedom has to have a place in the pure and simple necessity which is work, since work itself never expresses this freedom.

It seems that it was when Christianity began to become dominant in the Roman Empire, at the end of the third century, that some theologians began to attach value to work. This went hand in hand with what was happening politically. The empire had at this time an increasing need of workers and labor. But this is not the whole story. I do not accept in the least the Marxist view of things according to which Christianity is exploited here as it was, e.g., by the western middle class in the nineteenth century. Theologians did not simply develop an ideology of work as the service of

God in order to induce people to work conscientiously, seriously, and honestly. The idea that work is a vocation seems to me to derive from two ideas which emerge progressively in Christian theology during the period from the third century to the fifth.

The first originates in Greek philosophy. One might call it a passion for unity. The ideal is a single undivided life, just as a single organization is the ideal for the city. All philosophy is oriented to this desire for the one. The world is evil because it is broken, divided, and split up. The one is both a return to the original situation and a fulfilment of every convergence. Man should develop a single life and not a double life. He should not be divided. In these conditions it is evident to faith that since God is the one essential thing in life, unity should be constituted around and in terms of grace, the revealed word, and faith.

Man must be in God and for God with all that he does and with all his works. His life is not made up of successive and unrelated moments. It is one in the recapitulation of Christ. Similarly his different works are not haphazard. They form a unity in terms of grace given. Each work, then, is related to God. If one is a believer, it is also a result of the known, discerned, accepted, and loved will of God. Hence divine vocation embraces more than the service of God and proclamation of the gospel. It also embraces the states of life which we adopt, e.g., marriage or celibacy. It thus embraces work too, and even this specific work. This is a condition if our life is to be one in God.

A second idea goes hand in hand with this. We have just referred to the service of God. Now increasingly from the fourth century this service of God was no longer restricted to preaching, church work, the diaconate, and so forth. By way of the doctrine of providence it came to include service in the world. God wills that his creation go on. He wills to preserve it. He wills a specific secular order. Hence all that we do both to uphold creation (to keep it going by having children and working) and to maintain its order is service of God.

This is why military service can become a vocation in the fourth century. The same naturally applies to work. All this finds clear formulation in the fourth and fifth centuries. This theological understanding is lost again, however, during the unsettled period from the fifth century to the tenth.

During the middle ages, from the tenth century to the fourteenth, the situation is very confused. Two contradictory forces are at work in this period. On the one side work is regarded purely and simply as a curse. It is a mark of the condemnation of Adam. Hence it has no intrinsic value and cannot be an object of vocation. True vocation finds expression in, e.g., the acceptance of poverty. This is the position of the friars. Extremists could even say that this world is the place of evil governed by the prince of this world and that we should try to hasten its end. This is the point where catharism joins forces with a certain Christian outlook. We must do nothing to perpetuate the world. On the contrary, we should make every effort to bring in the kingdom of God. We should be working for the end of the world—this is why the *cathari* reject procreation.

On the other side, we find among theologians an ongoing ideology of work, an insistence on its sanctifying value and its integration into the unity of life, and consequently support for the idea that God calls us to specific jobs. Nevertheless, a distinction is still made between different forms of work. Agricultural work is sanctifying and can be the object of a divine vocation. It is the service of God in nature. Commerce and finance, however, cannot come within the scope of divine vocation. In general all the theologians who tried to construct a dogmatics came up against this problem of work in the middle ages, and they solved it forcefully by calling for a choice between work which is acceptable to God and work which stands under a curse. The unity of human life is still affirmed. The man who is totally subject to grace is called upon to bear witness to this grace by his works. Work is not excluded. It is thus an object of God's calling to man. In the main, however, this calling is global rather than individual.

A further development takes place in the fifteenth and sixteenth centuries. The great movement of secularization which begins in the fourteenth century, and the growth of economic activities, especially commerce, contribute to an enhancing of the value of work. As work becomes more essential than during the preceding period, it is also ennobled.

The idea of work as a curse fades increasingly into the background. From the fifteenth century one begins to find the argument which is often used during the Reformation age and then again in the eighteenth century, namely, that monks, and especially mendicants, are useless because they do not work and do not produce anything. Work begins to become something which it never was up to the thirteenth century—a value and a virtue.

It is against this cultural background, and in the midst of this psycho-economic change in relation to work, that Martin Luther bursts on the scene. He cannot put the clock back. The society to which he belongs is settling down to work as never before. The social group to which he primarily speaks is making of work the aim and meaning of life. The view is still held, however, that everything relates to God and comes from God. Hence work, too, stands in relationship to God. It has its own validity as such, but only because it proceeds from God and is part of the order of God for man.

Luther then, in his well-known statement about the cobbler, can say that by making shoes this man is serving God and following a vocation no less than the preacher of the word of God.

In the Reformation period we also find occasionally the idea that work is the service of God mediately through the service of men. By rendering service to other men, the workman obeys the commandment of God.

Another interpretation of vocation also calls for notice. Work can be very laborious, crushing, and mortifying. But this is God's will. The burden and condemnation of work have to be accepted because they come from God. This leads on rapidly to an idea which developed in the seventeenth and eighteenth centuries, namely, that work plays a redemptive role. Work, then, is obviously part of man's vocation, but an important change has taken place.

Luther insisted strongly on the individual character of grace and the singularity of each vocation. What was right in the spiritual sphere could hardly be wrong in the secular sphere if God was being served equally in both. The man who does a particular job does it because he has been effectively called by God to do this specific job and not another. Each man enters particularly into the design of God. There is no general vocation or call to work, but a specific call to each individual man to become a mason, a doctor, etc.

This means that it is now impossible to group trades into those that are acceptable to God and those that are under a curse. God calls each man to a particular job. It also means that each individual has to ask himself: What is the work that God wants me to do? This in turn introduces an uneasy conscience into Protestantism. For how can we be really sure that we are obeying a call if the call is not so dramatic as to remove all doubts?

On the other hand, strong professional conscientiousness is also developed. Obviously the man who acts under a sense of vocation will throw all his zeal and love and energy into this service of God.

This can have economic results in the rise of capitalism and the middle class. Another result is the further enhancement of the value of work. We see here a development by reciprocal interaction. The more the value of work is enhanced by the idea of vocation, the greater the increase in economic activity. But the greater the increase in economic activity, the higher the value placed on work.

This has two results in the ideological field. The first is that the middle class carries to an extreme the emphasis on the requirement and concrete value of work. Various truisms express this. Thus we are told that work is prayer—a direct consequence of the confusion between work and divine vocation. Again, work is said to be freedom. The redemptive value of work is also stressed.

At the same time the middle class exploits this supposed will of God in its dealings with the working class. In the nineteenth century religious ideas are used to keep employees in submission, which can now be presented as obedience to a divine order. At this point the vocation to work becomes collective once again, and it also becomes an instrument of social pressure. In the middle class itself, however, there remains a sense of individual vocation, i.e., the personal service of God in a profession. This implies the putting to work of exceptional qualities. Work has to be done with all the greater passion, taste, and care because it is work for God and by God's order.

We must now turn, however, to the second ideological aspect of work as vocation as we find this in Marx. Marx carries this ideology of work to its ultimate extreme. As he sees it, man is what he does (in his work). Work is that which marks man out in nature as a whole. Hence an exceptional place is given to work and it is viewed as an exceptional virtue.

Work is thus the supreme mediation. As Marx himself says, when others use my product, I have a direct sense of having met a human need, of having been an intermediary between them and the race, of having been recognized by them as complementary to their own being and as a necessary part of themselves, of having been confirmed in their thought as well as their love, of having created in the manifestation of my life a manifestation of theirs, of having confirmed and realized in my activity (or work) my human and social essence.

Now obviously if this is what work is (or ought to be), we are confronted by a contradiction when we look at the work done by the proletariat. This is one of the basic themes in the condemnation of capitalism by Marx. By exploitation, capitalism does not let work play its dominant and constructive role. This extravagant enhancing of the value of work by Marx, for which there is no precedent, results partly from the great growth of work in the west during the nineteenth century and partly from the secularization of the idea of the divine vocation of man in work.

Now it is obvious that with the evolution of our society it is impossible to cling to this kind of ideology of work. Philosophically, of course, we can say anything we like, but it is plain that nothing in any epoch justifies the idealism of work. Since the nineteenth century we can see its degradation in three successive stages.

It is now emphasized, of course, that there can be no question of glorifying one type of work, whether it be that of the artisan or the farmer, as easier, less tiring, etc., compared to the other. Formerly there was perhaps some possibility of confusing work in these categories with the order of God. Thus the artisan did more individualized work and this both left the impression of personal service and involved the type of work which expressed the personality of the one who did it. Success or failure could be seen, and the work had a certain completeness and followed the rhythm of the workman. On the other hand the farmer worked with nature, and inevitably we still have the medieval idea that nature, which is man's natural setting, is good, and that the man who works in it is closer to God, even if the work itself is not on this account any more attractive. These aspects of work obviously favor the confusion of work and vocation. Today, however, these aspects have gone and we have seen the breaking of the unity between the two.

The first thing to bring this about is capitalism. With salaries work becomes a commodity to be sold and bought. A man trades his working strength and the product of his work for payment which simply enables him to stay alive. This payment does not represent in any sense at all the true, higher, transcendent value of his work. On the contrary, it reduces work to the level of merchandise. The one whose work is sold in this way can have no initiative or joy in work. His work cannot be an expression of his personality, since its only aim is to produce objects which will enter into commercial circulation. In these circumstances it is difficult to maintain the idea of vocation.

The situation is aggravated with the development of mechanization. This problem has been thoroughly studied, as, e.g., in Friedmann's *Le travail en miettes* and *Où va le travail humain?* Work is separated from its product. It becomes a pure and simple obligation without meaning. It is broken up by parcelling out and specialization. The workman does not finally know what he is doing or what is the utility or value of his work. He does not even know what he is making but simply knows the machine on which he is working. The fragmentation and distribution of work on the production line exclude any understanding of the total process. Professional specialization confines the worker in a very narrow sphere of execution. Reflection on the purpose of work is ruled out. A rift develops between action and thought. Everything that is done by the man at the machine is calculated by a third person who is an expert at matching men and machines and at matching machines themselves so as to achieve a smooth flow of production. Thus a man's work is totally subordinated to the machine and to the need to organize the working of the machines. The problem is that of production rhythm. Man is completely dispossessed of his work. It cannot be anything but an alien activity which is imposed from without, corresponds to no inner reality, and in the strict sense no longer forms a true part of the life of man even though it takes up the major part of his time.[86]

In these conditions it is evident that work can no longer be a vocation. It might still be argued that God is able to transform even the worst situation and that he can restore a sense of vocation even in the case of the most absurd work. But this is little more than a convenient refusal to look at the true facts. This type of work can no longer be presented generally as vocation. The most we can say is that God in his grace may miraculously enable a man to live out this kind of work as a gift and calling

---

86 I cannot agree in the least with Barth when he says that the concrete sociological conditions of work do not constitute a determination (*Church Dogmatics*, III, 4, pp. 620f.). He argues that to take this view is to give way to a superstitious fatalism. Barth, however, is here confusing metaphysical fate and sociological determination. When he says that environment has an influence but is not determinative he is minimizing the true situation and offering an easy solution to the problem of the extent of influence without ever facing the problem itself. It is true that conditions vary, but, if so, it is also true that every gradation is possible. We can certainly say that the being who is loved by God and hidden with Christ in God can escape these determinations. But in concrete life we cannot get rid of the problem by saying that since this true being is not determined, therefore determination does not exist. On the contrary, determination by work seems to be crushing to most people. Far more realistic are the analyses in

of God. The theological link between vocation and work, however, is snapped.

The universal technologizing of society has further aggravated the situation. Technology has become a mediation in all actions and for all purposes. The technological path has to be taken to do anything at all in the world. Technology also has its own exclusive efficiency. This is what characterizes it. It thus cuts off all recourse to other types of efficiency. One can no longer say as Ambroise Paré did: "I bandaged him and God healed him." One cannot say: "I pressed down the accelerator and God accelerated the car." The regularity of effects, the exclusiveness of means, and generalized mediation leave no place at all for the concept of vocation.

On the contrary, the concept comes under criticism. When a good technician is needed the man who is full of his vocation or divine calling is of no use. Vocation is a poor substitute for competence. We all know of people who apply for posts as professors, educators, or psychologists because they are following a call from God when in fact they are very poorly qualified. Even in the case of a specialist, vocation may cause him to make foolish mistakes in the use of his skills. The nurse with a vocation can allow emotions to creep into her work when it should be governed by the most rigorous criteria of efficiency.

There is, of course, another side. We know only too well what happens in social, educational, or medical work when there is no sense of vocation. Technique is frigidly applied. Radical indifference prevails at the personal level. The right motions replace human relations. The subject is changed into a case or number. All this is the result of a generalizing of technical mediation which leaves no place at all for the idea of a vocation.

The prevailing position is that it can be said only abstractly and theoretically that vocation truly exists and that those who have it will become good technicians, or that vocation is a miraculous adjunct to the practice of perfect technique. This is no more than romantic idealism. The reality is that the very idea of perfect technique rules out the idea of vocation. The only thing we need bear in mind is that technical efficiency enables us to deal with far more "cases." The human resources of pity, sympathy, understanding, and love cannot be multiplied.

The more or less complete break between work and vocation under

---

Marx and more recently Bataille in his *La Part Maudite*. Bataille is worth quoting because he does not merely look at actual work as most writers do (e.g., Friedmann) but concentrates on the reality of work in itself (p. 74). As he sees it, the introduction of work into the world substitutes for the intimacy and depth of desire a rational nexus in which the truth of the present moment means nothing but only the final result of what is done. Work first creates the world of things and with this man himself becomes one of the things of this world, at least when he is working. This is the fall that man in every age has necessarily sought to escape. This is a realistic view, and it is by this view of work, of what work has always been, that we must take our bearings rather than by the romantic ideas of vocation and man's demiurgic being. Only with this kind of reference can Christian freedom play its proper part.

the pressure of capitalism, mechanization, and technologization is accompanied by a crisis of vocation among Christians themselves. As I see it, this crisis has three aspects.

First, in Europe at least, it has been much emphasized that the theory of vocation has been made an excuse for not paying the proper wage for services rendered. Just as the middle class secured the obedience of employees by showing them that their condition was a fruit of their divine calling, so in many branches of Christian or church work vocation is advanced as a reason for paying lower salaries (or none at all) to pastors, social workers, administrators, and nurses. The argument that since these people are following a vocation which comes from God, they will not want to press for remuneration for their obedience, has proved to be a very convenient one for those who are in charge of the church's enterprises. In fact, a normal reaction has taken place and those who do work of this kind are now asking for stipends such as are paid to those who do the same type of work without any vocation. But in addition the whole idea of vocation has been brought under suspicion. When a professor or teacher hears the word "vocation," for example, his reaction is that if an appeal is being made to his vocation he is not going to be paid properly. In consequence even serious Christians are hesitant about speaking of their vocation; they know it will be used as a means of bringing pressure to bear on them at the financial level.

From a different standpoint vocation is contested by Christians because those who bear responsibility in the church, e.g., pastors, feel that they are undervalued in a technological world in virtue of the fact that they themselves are not specialists and especially technicians. Obeying a vocation and therefore preaching, directing a congregation, and engaging in the cure of souls can seem to lack seriousness in a world of engineers and producers. The result is that these shamefaced pastors want to become technicians themselves. They take up psychoanalysis, group dynamics, social psychology, and communications. It is as psychoanalysts and so forth that they want to act in the Christian community and no longer because they are called by God to his service.

Here again it is an illusion to think that technology may be appended to a vocation or will serve it. In fact it becomes a substitute for it.

When these two questionings of vocation among Christians are combined, we very quickly arrive at a third one. This is a final refusal to acknowledge that any call by God is needed even to render service in the church. In other words, there is a fall into exactly the opposite error of that of relating work and vocation. There is now no call even to be a pastor or deacon. Being a minister is just another job like all the rest.

Some younger pastors, e.g., in France, carry this thought to the extreme of saying that they work in an organism which is the church, that they are paid in the ordinary way and thus constitute the proletariat, and that they are used by an employer (the church) which is no different from any other employer. They, too, employ techniques, for even biblical exegesis and preaching have been given the status of pure techniques. The question of vocation, of a choice that comes from God, does not enter into the picture.

This rejection of any possibility of vocation does not simply express the normal consequences of technologizing nor of the political orientation of many younger pastors. It is above all an indication of the fact, which is very strongly if unconsciously felt, that in our society vocation can no longer find any proper incarnation. If the call of God exists, a way has to be found to express it or incarnate it. This has now become impossible in practice. Vocation, then, remains something which is purely spiritual. In a faith which centers on the incarnation, however, we cannot accept this.

There is thus a complete divorce between what society, work, military service, and so forth constantly demand on the one side, and the will of God on the other. The service of God cannot be put in terms of a job. But what can it be put in terms of? In face of this unanswerable question the reaction is obvious. It is easier to eliminate the concept of vocation, the idea that God issues a call to us. Everything is simplified if, even in church work, we preserve only the technological and social aspect and scrap all the rest. Whereas we previously unified by absorbing jobs under vocation, we now unify by abandoning vocation, seeing it has become completely impossible. Our problem today, then, is that we are torn between meaningless work which offers no satisfaction and a vocation which it is no longer possible to incarnate.

In these circumstances we need to ask what responses are possible if we cannot accept the total elimination of vocation but continue to believe that God calls us to fulfil a specific service. One position which is frequently adopted is that basically there are still some professions which can be viewed and lived out as a divine vocation. Thus the physician brings healing and helps to save life. The advocate defends widows and orphans. The teacher contributes to the development of the personality. The psychologist and social worker might also be mentioned. Hence, it is argued, Christians ought to gravitate towards this type of work.

In my view this is no reply at all. For one thing these are middle-class professions and the implication is that Christians will become an elite. Again, it is a complete illusion to think that these professions are still vocations. They are now as technical as other jobs, and professional demands quickly efface the sense of calling. Finally, these professions can often be regarded as ways of shoring up our technological society. The idea of taking up law as a vocation may sound very good. It may be the expression of a generous and idealistic spirit. But to think this way is to be the victim of an illusion and to live in ignorance of modern realities. In our age there is no such thing as a professional vocation.

Another answer might then be attempted. This begins by admitting that work in our society is an evil. It is the part of life that lies under a curse. We have to take jobs which are worthless, meaningless, and uninteresting, which simply provide us with a livelihood, and which force us to find our real focus of interest elsewhere. This is the line of thought of sociologists and psycho-sociologists who believe that man today finds his authentic life in leisure. We do not really live at all in our work. We do this work in a kind of lethargy, in blindness, in unconscious sleep, with no sense of conscience at all. We wake up again, become ourselves, and come to life only in leisure.

This is where vocation comes in again. It is actualized in leisure, whether by studying the Christian life in our free time, or by following tradition and dividing the week into six days for the world and one day for God. This dichotomy makes everything much easier. For six (or five) days one may be an efficient and ruthless man of affairs and then on Sunday the whole of Christian vocation will find expression in worship, in church celebrations, and in church work.

Obviously this is not wholly satisfactory. There is no need to insist on this. Sunday Christians have often been lampooned. But we should not forget that it is more or less impossible today to permeate modern work with Christianity. The common attitude of the Roman Catholic Church certainly offers no solution. We can no longer bless work externally, i.e., christianize it by adding a little prayer or benediction to a professional activity. Work is not transformed by offering a brief prayer to God either before or after it. This may well be an additional hypocrisy. Obedience to the call of God that we should live as Christians needs to be given clear manifestation in the practice of the profession. It needs genuine incarnation and not just the addition of pious words. Unfortunately we are unable to achieve this incarnation. What more can we say then?

The first point that we must make from an ideological standpoint is that work belongs in every sense to the order of necessity. If God gave it to man as a means of survival, he also made it a condition of survival. This is what Paul has in mind when he says that if a man will not work, neither should he eat (2 Thessalonians 3:10). Work is no part of the order of grace, liberality, love, and freedom. Confusion must be avoided in this regard.

What I wrote about violence applies also to work. Like violence or political power, work is part of the order of necessity. There is no escaping it. It is man's condition after the break with God. It should not be forgotten that even subsequent to the incarnation and reconciliation we are still men. We have not become angels. We must still eat if we are to live. We are still under the necessity of aging. We are subject to the final necessity of dying.

In Christ the order of necessity is by no means abolished. There is victory over it. The risen Lord has triumphed over death. The crucified Lord has triumphed over the powers. Love has triumphed over evil. But death, evil, and the powers still exist. They constitute the order of necessity in which man is always set.

Work belongs to this order. From no angle can one ever say that biblically work is freedom. It is the exact opposite. Human experience agrees here with revelation, and revelation never fosters illusions. Hence we have to accept the situation. We must not pretend that things are different. Pascal warns us that to try to play the angel is to play the beast. We have to accept work as also a vocation, not a vocation to live as Christians, as those who are redeemed and free, but a vocation to recognize that before God we are creatures, finite, limited, and subject to necessity, and that we are also sinful creatures, bearing the consequences of our break with the Father.

Work has to be accepted in faith, then, as a sign of our creatureliness and our sinfulness. To this extent it is "normal" even though it is alienating, crushing, and meaningless. We have to accept its stupidity as a mark of the absurdity of our life. Work has no ultimate or transcendent value. Before God it is simply that which makes our survival possible and keeps us in being.

This realism coincides with our thesis and implies the destruction of every romanticizing or idealizing of work, whether bourgeois or Marxist.

On the other hand the recognition that we are in the order of necessity in no way implies contempt for work, rejection of it, or carping criticism. Work is simply part of the order to which we are subject—no more.

The one thing which we are forbidden to do is to confuse the order of necessity with freedom, i.e., with grace, i.e., with vocation.

A further point is that before God work is wholly relative. After the analysis of work in Ecclesiastes all sociological studies are futile. No illusions are left. Work leads nowhere. In particular, in spite of what Marx says, it does not constitute the being of man. It cannot give meaning to life. It cannot really show what man is. It cannot lead to any truth.

We need to admit that in our work we are totally in the sphere of the relative. This is the point of the dominical saying: "Sufficient unto the day is the evil thereof" (Matthew 6:34). Work is an everyday affair. It is banal. It is done without hope. It is neither a value nor is it creative.

When satisfaction is given, e.g., by a successful cure or the production of a work of art, we are not to say that this is the true measure of work by which all other tasks are to be measured, including the worker on the belt or the unfortunate unskilled laborer. No, it is from the latter jobs that we learn the true reality of work. When human work produces joy or what seems to be outside the everyday, we have to realize that this is an exceptional event, a grace, a gift of God for which we must give thanks.

To view work along these lines is to combine realism with biblical insight. It is also to clip the wings of an idealism which projects a marvelous future when everybody will be doing rich and meaningful work. On the other hand, relative work is not completely devoid of value or interest. For it offers the possibility of sustaining life, of upholding the world, and of a continuation of history.

At this point the interpretation of Marx is valid. Work is what makes history possible. And this is God's will. At this level then, if at this level alone, we have vocation. God calls us to work (of any kind) in order to keep going this world which he has not yet decided to stop and judge. The task may be wholly and utterly relative. But we have to perform it.

What I said above needs to be repeated. The fact that a thing is relative does not mean that we are to despise it. Christians hanker too much after the absolute. The relative does not interest them. This is what leads them to make so many mistakes, e.g., in politics. A shift is needed here. The relative is what concerns us; the absolute is the Lord's affair. It is in the relative that we have to engage ourselves precisely as Christians. We have to regard the relative as our proper habitat. Hence we have to take it with full seriousness. "Thou hast been faithful over a few things . . ." (Matthew 25:21). This rules out, however, the decisive importance of the choice of a job. It rules out the concept of vocation in the sense in which we were using it earlier.

If, then, we cannot unify our life or incarnate our Christian vocation in work, if we are brought by the technological society into the harsh condition of relative work that has neither value nor ultimate meaning, then we obviously have to discover a form of activity which will express our Christian vocation and thus be an incarnation of our faith. Since our responsibility is to the world, this cannot be a purely inward affair nor a good work in the ordinary meaning of the term, e.g., a work of charity. This vocation must find expression in an action: an action that will have a social and collective impact which in one way or another can change the form of the world in which we are; an action that has to be gratuitous even though it retains the features of seriousness, competence, continuity, and invention that we attribute to real work. It seems to me that only thus can this kind of activity express vocation. As vocation is free and an expression of grace, so this activity must be free in return.

On the one hand, then, it must enable the men around us, and society as a whole, to continue in being. It must be an equivalent of work. On the other hand it must be something more, something which has meaning. In illustration I will draw upon my own experience, while not in any sense holding up myself as an example. In response to my Christian vocation I have worked in an organization which is designed to meet the challenge and supply the needs of young people who might be called misfits, i.e., beatniks, drug addicts, rebels, delinquents, pre-delinquents, the maladjusted of every type, and especially those with suicidal tendencies.

Now the aim of this society is not to hedge these people in or to make them take medical treatment. They are simply offered an agreeable location to which they can come if it proves to be compatible. They will find there congenial activities and company. Again, we are not trying to make them "normal" young people. We do not ask that they conform to the social pattern or to ordinary kinds of work. We simply want to offer a means of changing their negative non-adjustment into a positive non-adjustment. We want to help them to build up their personalities in such a way that they will transform their negativity into inventiveness and their aggressiveness into controlled force, so that they themselves will be able to endure the difficulty of their life, integrate its tensions, and thereby render them fruitful.

This is accomplished in part by activities in which they learn control and cooperation and which are dangerous enough to offer a real challenge. In part it is accomplished by a free intrapersonal relation which one might, if one wishes, describe as a psychological cure, but which never has the character of a strict application of psychological techniques.

To direct an enterprise of this kind, which obviously needs a full-time salaried staff, is real work. Yet it forms no part of the necessary work provided by society. It also presupposes autonomy, inventiveness, and free choice. To this extent it seems to be in true relation to the personality of the man who takes part in it. Here is possible meaning. An obvious implication, however, is that each must seek and invent a parallel activity of his own and not just copy what is being done by others. Copying is the great problem of all Christian "works." If we have received a vocation to live in this world as witnesses, this means primarily the discovery of an incarnation that cannot be repeated.

In this situation, however, do we not run up against the same difficulty as we found above? Is not life divided into two parts, the one devoted to work without value, the other endowed with value by vocation? Is not this a counsel of despair? It may well be so if we adopt the idea of a unified Christian life which integrates all actions and feelings. But we have seen that this is not necessarily an authentic Christian conception of life. If we perceive the true place of work according to scripture, we need not be shattered by the fact that our Christian vocation does not come to fulfilment in work.

Even if this is so, however, it does not mean that work is the part of life which is under a curse, which has no interest, and to which we must submit while always looking ahead to the next holiday or vacation. In fact we must accept work positively, take to ourselves this mark of our separation from God, and live out this order of necessity to the full in order that the freedom which is granted to us by God and the vocation which is possible for us may achieve their true value. For it is only in terms of the work which is a burden rather than a vocation that the vocation incarnated in gratuitous action takes on any real meaning.

It would be disastrous indeed to suppose that I obey God only when I do my club work and that the rest of my activity is anonymous, boring, and meaningless. I need the assurance that even when I am doing work without meaning I am still within the plan of God for me.

The Christian life, then, presents itself as a dialectical movement, not of reasoning but of living. What is devoted to meaningless and unavoidable work is the negative side. It is the negative side of vocation. It is the direct opposite of vocation, an expression of the impossibility of living this out, of assuming it, or of incarnating it. This opposite image is needed, however, if we are to be driven to bring vocation itself to expression.

Vocation is a reality. If technological work in modern society makes us certain that this is not our Christian vocation, it does so, not to cause us to desist in discouragement, but on the contrary to force us to seek the incarnation and accomplishment which are possible on the basis of the negation.

Conversely, when we have discovered the form that our vocation might take, when we have found the mode of concrete witness, on this basis the work that we have to do for our living ought to be found to have a new wealth, value, and even to a certain extent meaning.

Here, then, we do not have two separate parts of life but two aspects of the one dialectical movement. For obviously we are not dealing here with a stable situation of possession. We are dealing with a relation which is constantly called in question. Progress is by the influence of the one aspect on the other. The negative part has a creative function because it is always questioning and requestioning, so that I have always to find a more satisfying way of incarnating my vocation.

All this presupposes, then, that there is a certain relation between the two sides. The choice, invention, and discovery of the form of vocation have to have something to do with the work done in necessity.

If I am a physician by necessity and I regard it as my vocation to build boats, there is obviously no relation between these two things. The second activity cannot give meaning to the first. It is a leisure-time hobby and not a vocation. It comes under the heading of specious sociological freedom and not of the true freedom which is grace and gratuitous.

If I understand correctly the example of my own organization, I should say that a professor who is under professional obligation to deal with students can express his vocation in a free relation with young people of a different kind and in a different context. In turn this work among maladjusted adolescents can help him to discover a wholly new aspect of his students which he could never see as a professor. He can thus enter into a new relation with them too. His work will still be done under coercion and necessity. He will come under the full weight of the institution with its absurd rules and meddling or unjust authorities. But the center will shift from his function as a professor to the global human relation, not through humanitarianism or liberalism, but through the effective discovery of the questions that young people are asking.

Reciprocally the negative side of being a professor teaches him what he must not be among the maladjusted young people. The negative side of university organization shows clearly what must be avoided in the running of the society.

Each, then, must choose his own way of incarnating his vocation in relation to his place in the order of necessity. This involves, however, a change on our part regarding the manner in which we regard our life and our relation to society.

To sum up, I do not think that the true issue is, as was thought for a long time, that of entering an order (of life and the world) which is willed by God as it is, and of staying within this order by vocation. The point is rather that we enter a disorder which, even though it seems to be ordered, has in fact been set up by man, so that the moment we try to express our vocation in it we upset things and call them in question.

### Conclusion

When all has been said, nothing has been done. Yet all has been done, for who can go beyond the Word? The only thing is that the Word must become flesh. It must be initiatory, evocative, and meaningful. Scripture is not statically the Word. It can become the Word. I have written a great deal about freedom. I have made a long journey through unknown territory which is almost like paradise lost. Man passionately desires it, but the gate and only entry to it he obstinately rejects, trying to force his way in by a way which merely exhausts him. I have tried to find out where freedom is and how to receive it. But now that I have finished I seem to have enclosed a cistern instead of opening a spring. I seem to have walled in hidden riches instead of distributing sparkling diamonds.

The Word is a diamond, but how can we express its brilliance? Fire cannot be put in words. Freedom is wind, fire, a living fountain, nothing else. Should we be silent then? In this time and place we have to evoke it, and it is the reader who must make the decision. To say too much about a thing is to testify to its absence. But this witness, if it is received, is finally the last overture. It is truly the last. I believe that freedom is always ready to extend itself. But we cannot know at once what this might mean even as an aspiration. Perhaps this whole book is simply a seal on its disappearance. It certainly will be unless it is taken up by him who alone was free and by the believer who may now begin to be so.

# Indexes

## Index of Persons

# Scripture Index